CONTENTS

INTRODUCTION

Please be aware that laws change from time to time. Consequently, the authors of this book have provided a free updates service, which is available at www.hoddersamplepages.co.uk, and provides the most recent information available at the time of writing and posting to the web page. After accessing the main page, click on the Law section under Hodder Gibson Resources for Scotland.

This book is intended as a general introduction to the laws of Scotland in business.

It has been written in simple and everyday language wherever possible and is particularly suitable for students who are new to legal studies and those who are studying Scottish Qualification Authority units in law and legal studies at National and Higher National Qualification levels. It will also be of use to students who are studying Scots law for the first time in university courses or professional level courses and also to those with a general interest in Scots law.

The authors are experienced educators with almost 20 years of teaching experience between them gained in the secondary, further and higher education sectors. They are graduates of both Scottish and English universities and have studied both Scots and English law.

Each chapter is structured in the same way for ease of use and comprises:

◆ Chapter introduction

◆ Main content
  ● Key points
  ● Highlighted cases
  ● Highlighted legislation

◆ Summary

◆ Revision questions comprising
  ● Short answer questions
  ● Case studies
  ● Essay-type questions

We hope that the reader will find the book both interesting and easy to use.

Alistair B Wylie
Seán J Crossan

May 2004

CHAPTER 1

SCOTTISH LEGAL FRAMEWORK AND SOURCES OF SCOTS LAW

Introduction

This Introductory chapter to the book looks at the framework of the Scottish legal system. The impact of the creation of a Scottish Parliament and continuing European legislation cannot be underestimated and this has an influence on the laws of Scotland and the UK as a whole. The sources of Scots law are also identified and considered along with a detailed look at the civil and criminal justice systems.

This chapter covers the following areas:

- The Scottish Parliament
- Sources of Scots law
- The legal profession in Scotland
- The civil justice system
- The criminal justice system
- The Judicial Committee of the Privy Council
- Alternative methods of resolving legal disputes
- The influence of European Courts

The Scottish Parliament

Devolution is the process by which a national body (the Westminster Parliament) delegates or distributes powers to a local or regional body (the Scottish Parliament). In theory, devolution should mean that laws and decisions are made at a level closer to the point at which they will have an impact. The devolution settlement means that Scotland has a Parliament with devolved powers within the United Kingdom. Any powers that remain with the UK Parliament are reserved.

Since the introduction of the Scotland Act 1998, Scotland now has two parliaments which make laws that have a direct impact on Scottish society. These two parliaments are the Westminster or United Kingdom Parliament and the Scottish or Holyrood Parliament.

Key point: There are now two Parliaments which make laws for Scotland – Westminster (London) and Holyrood (Edinburgh)

On 11 September 1997, the people of Scotland in a referendum voted overwhelmingly for the creation of a Scottish Parliament which would have tax varying powers. This would be the first time in almost 300 years that a Parliament making laws for Scotland would sit in Edinburgh. However, unlike the previous Scottish Parliament which was abolished by the Act of Union in 1707, the new Scottish Parliament is not a completely independent body. The Scottish Parliament is an inferior body in comparison to Westminster. True, Westminster has given many powers and responsibilities to the Scottish Parliament, but it is worth bearing in mind that a simple Act of the Westminster Parliament is all that would be required to abolish Scotland's new Parliament. Indeed, Westminster has already abolished a local assembly or parliament.

During the 1970s, Westminster abolished the Stormont Parliament or Assembly which made laws for Northern Ireland. Stormont had been in existence for approximately 50 years, but this did not prevent Westminster from reimposing direct rule on Northern Ireland from London. Admittedly, the abolition of Stormont was carried out against a background of increasing Irish Republican and Loyalist violence in Northern Ireland. However, the lesson to draw from Stormont is that Westminster will remain the supreme law making authority in the United Kingdom despite devolution.

The creation of the Scottish Parliament

On 6 May 1999, the Scottish electorate voted in the first election for the Scottish Parliament. No political party secured a majority and this situation led to the formation of a coalition government (the Scottish Executive) supported by the Scottish Labour Party and the Scottish Liberal Democrat Party. Labour's Donald Dewar would become Scotland's First Minister (Prime Minister in all but name). The first session of the Scottish Parliament would begin in July 1999. However, the first few months of the Parliament were seen as an introductory session with Members of the Scottish Parliament (MSPs) being given a chance to settle in to their new positions.

 Key point: The First Minister is effectively the Scottish Prime Minister in all but name.

The organisation of the Scottish Parliament

Currently, the Scottish Parliament has 129 members – 73 are directly elected from local areas corresponding to the 72 Westminster constituencies (the Westminster constituency of Orkney and Shetland has been split in two) and the other 56 members are elected using a system which achieves an element of proportional representation (the Additional Member System).

Drawn from these 129 Members of Parliament is the group of Ministers who will form the Scottish Executive or government of Scotland. The political party or parties with a majority of seats will usually form the Scottish Executive. The First Minister heads the Scottish Executive with the assistance of the Deputy First Minister. The First Minister is nominated by the parliament and his appointment is confirmed by the British Monarch. The First Minister will advise the Monarch when it comes to the appointment of other Scottish Executive Ministers, the appointment of the Lord Advocate and the Solicitor-General for Scotland and the judges of the Court of Session and the High Court of Justiciary. Legal advice is provided to the Scottish Executive by the Lord Advocate and the Solicitor-General for Scotland.

The Scottish Parliament elects one of its members to serve as the Presiding Officer (this individual would be referred to as the Speaker at Westminster) and two other members to serve as his deputies. The Presiding Officer and his deputies chair sessions of the parliament, convene and chair meetings of the Parliamentary Bureau, interpret the rules in relation to parliamentary procedure and, generally, represent the parliament at meetings with other parliamentary and government bodies.

 Key point: 129 Members of Parliament (MSPs) sit at Holyrood who elect a Presiding Officer (speaker) from their number to chair sessions of the parliament.

Devolved powers

Clearly, the Scottish people had expressed their desire for the creation of such a body in the referendum of September 1997. This was the easy part. It took specialist government lawyers a considerable amount of time and effort to draw up the detailed plans for the Scottish Parliament. Subsequently, these plans were introduced in the shape of the Scotland Bill in January 1998 to Westminster where they had to pass through both the House of Commons and the House of Lords before being given the Royal Assent. As a result of the Scotland Act 1998, the Scottish Parliament was given powers to make laws for Scotland.

Before the first session of the Scottish Parliament 1999–2003 (each Scottish Parliament sits for a four-year fixed period), all statute law for Scotland was dealt with by Westminster. Many Scots felt that Westminster's role in the law-making process for Scotland was unsatisfactory because it made laws for the United Kingdom as a whole and these laws were not always suited to Scottish local conditions.

 Key point: Devolution allows the Scottish Parliament to create its own laws in certain predetermined (devolved) areas of policy.

With devolution, the Scottish Parliament can now pass laws in the following areas:

- Agriculture, forestry and fishing
- Arts, culture and sport
- Education and training
- Environment
- Health
- Housing
- Local government
- Planning
- Scottish legal system (including criminal and civil justice)
- Social work
- Statistics, public registers and the Scottish records
- Tourism, economic development and financial assistance to industry

◆ Transport
◆ Police and Fire Services

By September 2003, the Scottish Parliament had already passed some 64 Acts as a result of its devolved powers since 1999. This quickly led to some major differences in the law between Scotland and the rest of the United Kingdom. Examples include the abolition of tuition fees for students courtesy of the Education (Graduate Endowment and Student Support) (Scotland) Act 2001 and the provision of free care for the elderly in the Community Care and Health (Scotland) Act 2002. The rest of the United Kingdom has not followed Scotland's lead in these areas.

Reserved matters

Despite the introduction of devolved government, Westminster will continue to make law for Scotland in many important areas. In fact, Acts of the Scottish Parliament are considered to have the status of secondary legislation which has an inferior status to primary legislation which Westminster deals with. The areas of policy that Westminster will continue to have responsibility for are known as reserved matters. These include:

◆ Abortion, human fertilisation, embryology, genetics, xeno-transplantation and vivisection
◆ Common markets
◆ Constitutional matters
◆ Data Protection
◆ Employment law
◆ Energy
◆ Equal opportunities
◆ Foreign policy, defence and national security matters
◆ Gambling and the National Lottery
◆ Immigration and nationality
◆ Social security
◆ Taxation, economic and monetary matters
◆ Trade and industry (including competition policy and consumer protection)
◆ Transport

 Key point: Acts of the Scottish Parliament are regarded as secondary legislation and therefore have a lower status than Acts of the Westminster Parliament.

If, for example, the Scottish Parliament wished to introduce a new law which had the effect of closing down the Faslane nuclear submarine base on the River Clyde, this would not be permissible. The Scottish Parliament has no right to legislate in defence matters. If the Scottish Parliament did go ahead and pass an Act which attempted to close down Faslane, this would be at best an example of gesture politics and, at worst, would leave the Parliament open to a serious legal challenge in the courts. Put simply, such an Act of the Scottish Parliament would have no legal effect.

The distinction between devolved and reserved matters is in theory a simple one, but practically speaking, there may be areas of policy where both parliaments could potentially legislate. In the future, this may lead to conflicts between Holyrood and Westminster. Immigration issues, for example, are a reserved matter, but as the row over the Dungavel Detention Centre during 2003 has shown, the division of responsibilities between Holyrood and Westminster is not always clear-cut. Controversy has arisen concerning the practice of forcing the children of detainees to be educated in Dungavel itself thus denying them the opportunity to be taught in local schools. At first glance, it would appear that the UK Home Secretary has responsibility for Dungavel, but the education of children is a matter for the Scottish Parliament.

 Key point: The Scottish Parliament cannot legislate in policy areas, for example, defence that are regarded as being reserved matters.

The Sewell Motion

There will be occasions when Westminster will introduce a law to Scotland which, strictly speaking, could have been dealt with by the Scottish Parliament. Under what is known as the Sewell Motion, the Scottish Executive can ask Westminster to pass laws for Scotland. In September 2003, the Scottish Executive passed the issue of same-sex relationships being given similar status to marriage to Westminster. This means that Westminster will introduce a Bill which covers the whole of the United Kingdom, not just for Scotland. The use of the Sewell Motion can save valuable Scottish parliamentary time. However, this procedure has been criticised because it gives the Scottish Executive an opportunity to avoid legislating on awkward social issues like same-sex marriage.

 Key point: The Sewell Motion allows the Scottish Executive to ask the Westminster Parliament to pass laws for Scotland.

How a Bill becomes law in Scotland

In common with Westminster, a draft law or Bill introduced in the Scottish Parliament must complete various procedures in order to become part of Scots law. The three main types of Bill are:

- Executive Bills
- Committee Bills
- Member's Bills

Executive Bills are promoted and supported by the Scottish Executive. If the Scottish Executive wishes to introduce a Bill it must also be accompanied by extensive notes detailing what impact the Bill will have on a range of issues such as, for example, human rights and equal opportunities.

 Key point: A Bill is a proposal which may or may not become law at a later date.

Committee Bills are introduced into parliament by one or more of the various parliamentary committees whose membership consists of different MSPs from the different political parties.

Member's Bills are the result of an individual MSP taking it upon himself or herself to introduce a Bill with or without the support of the Executive or a committee.

There are, however, a number of important differences between Westminster and the Scottish Parliament. It should be remembered that Westminster has two Houses of Parliament – the Commons and the Lords – with a Bill having to pass through each House in order to receive the Royal Assent. The Scottish Parliament by comparison has one chamber only through which a Bill must pass.

The committee system in the Scottish Parliament is much more powerful than its Westminster counterparts. Unlike the committees at Westminster, a Holyrood committee can take the initiative and introduce a new Bill to parliament. As there is only one chamber in the parliament, it was always intended that the committees would play a powerful role. A Scottish parliamentary committee is the place where MSPs can really scrutinise the contents of a Bill and propose all sorts of changes or amendments to it. Currently, there are 16 parliamentary committees operating, each one chaired by a Convener. In order to coordinate the work of the committees, the Conveners regularly meet with one another as the Conveners' Group.

Finally, individual MSPs have more of chance of introducing Bills to parliament and achieving success. Tommy Sheridan MSP was able to introduce a Bill to outlaw the practice of warrant sales which later became law as the Abolition of Poindings and Warrant Sales (Scotland) Act 2001. Considering the stranglehold that the British Government has over Westminster, it is very unlikely that an ordinary Member of Parliament could have achieved similar results as Tommy Sheridan. Perhaps emboldened by this success, Mr Sheridan has introduced a Bill in October 2003 which proposes to abolish the Council Tax and replace it with a local income tax. Who knows, he may well succeed.

 Key point: There are three types of Bills that may be introduced in the Scottish Parliament – Executive Bills, Members' Bills and Committee Bills.

When a Bill is introduced to the Scottish Parliament there are three stages which it must undergo:

Stage 1: a parliamentary committee (the 'lead committee') will be appointed to consider the general principles of the Bill. Having done this, the lead committee will then report back to parliament and if parliament is in agreement with the Bill's general principles, it will be referred back to the committee and Stage 2 of the process can begin. However, if the Bill failed to secure parliamentary support the Bill is effectively dead and it will progress no further.

Stage 2: here, the Bill will be heavily scrutinised and amendments (or changes) can be proposed by the lead committee, by a committee of the whole parliament, by another parliamentary committee or other committees – not just the lead committee, by a combination of the lead committee and by a committee of the whole parliament or by a parliamentary committee or committees other than the lead committee.

However, if the aim of the Bill is to change existing secondary or delegated legislation, it will have to go to the Subordinate Legislation Committee for examination and a detailed report will be produced by this Committee.

Stage 3: once the Bill has been scrutinised, it will return to parliament which will consider the amendments made to it and, finally, a vote will be taken on whether the Bill should become law. A quarter of all MSPs must register a vote in the final debate and vote otherwise parliament will lack the authority to use its law-making powers.

If parliament votes in favour of the Bill it will then be presented to the Monarch in order to receive the Royal Assent thus becoming an Act of the Scottish Parliament.

 Key point: A Bill undergoes three stages as it passes through the Scottish Parliament.

Overview

Although the Scotland Act 1998 gives extensive law-making powers to the Scottish Parliament which will have a direct impact on many areas of Scottish life, it should not be forgotten that the Westminster Parliament remains the supreme law-making authority in the United Kingdom. Unlike the old Scottish Parliament before 1707, Holyrood is not an independent body. It is an inferior and a subordinate body to Westminster and this will remain the case if and when the people of Scotland ever decide to vote for Scottish independence. Westminster has not given up its right to legislate for Scotland completely. Holyrood will have to be particularly careful that it passes laws in the areas of policy which have been devolved to it by Westminster. Failure to do so may incur Westminster's displeasure and, more seriously, a challenge before the courts.

Sources of Scots Law

The laws of Scotland simply do not appear out of thin air. When we talk about the sources of Scots law, we mean where does a law come from come from and how is it made? The Scottish legal system has developed over hundreds of years and has been influenced in all sorts of ways by Scotland's history and culture. The feudal system, for example, which was introduced into Scotland from England during the reign of King David I (1124–53), directly influenced how land was owned in Scotland for nearly a thousand years. The remains of this system of landownership are only now being phased out.

 Key point: The Scottish legal system has evolved and developed over hundreds of years.

Scots law is a mixed or hybrid system of law drawing upon many different influences, for example, Roman law and common law. Other hybrid systems of law include Quebec, Louisana and South Africa. England and other Commonwealth countries like English-speaking Canada, New Zealand and Australia are common law jurisdictions where judges have had a great deal of influence in the development of the law. The United States of America is also a common law jurisdiction.

The most important sources of Scots law today are Acts of Parliament, common law, delegated legislation and European Union law. Some sources of law such as feudal law and canon law are of historical interest only. Many of our laws in modern times are deliberately written down for the benefit of future generations. However, there are numerous legal rules that are unwritten which have been handed down to us as customs and practices. Furthermore, judges very often make laws when they sit in court and these judicial decisions are followed by other courts so that they in turn become binding legal rules.

Key point: The most important sources of modern Scots law are statute (parliamentary) law, common law and European law.

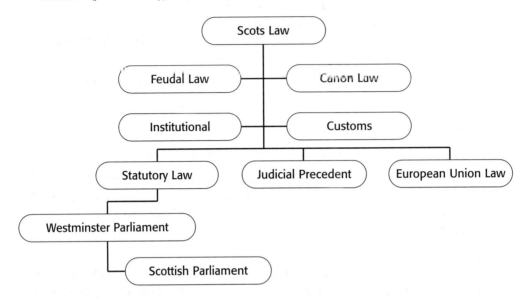

Acts of Parliament

Acts of Parliament are often referred to as legislation or statute law. Before the introduction of the Scotland Act 1998, the Westminster Parliament (the national parliament of the United Kingdom) alone made laws for Scotland. However, Westminster has given the Scottish Parliament authority in many different areas of policy to make law. This does not mean that Westminster has become irrelevant. Far from it. The Scottish Parliament is an inferior body to Westminster and all it would take is the passing of a simple Act by Westminster to abolish the Scottish Parliament. Westminster is still the supreme law-making body in the United Kingdom despite the introduction of devolution. When we talk about parliament we mean the Houses of Commons and the Lords and the Monarch. To become law, a Bill must pass through the House of Commons and the House of Lords before being sent to Her Majesty, the Queen who will sign the Bill into law.

 Key point: Acts of Parliament are often referred to as legislation or statute law.

Westminster is the supreme law-making institution and no other court or body can question the validity of an Act of Parliament. Courts must apply an Act of Parliament and cannot declare it illegal. Before Westminster can make a new law, certain procedures must be followed. Proposed laws are presented to parliament in the form of a Bill. The Bill does not simply become law there and then, it must be debated and eventually voted upon before it can be said to form part of the law of the land. A Bill may be introduced by either the House of Commons or the House of Lords.

Public and Private Bills

Most Bills will be public Bills in that they apply to society as a whole. Public Bills are sponsored by Government Ministers or individual members of the Commons or the

Lords. Private Bills, on the other hand, are usually very restrictive in that they apply to a very small group of people or a particular organisation or body. They do not apply to society or to the public across the board. Recent examples of private Bills which became Acts include the London Development Agency Act 2003 and the Nottingham City Council Act 2003. Clearly these Acts apply only to the London Development Agency and to Nottingham City Council.

 Key point: Public Bills are much more common than Private Bills and affect society as a whole.

Parliamentary Procedure

The way in which a Bill becomes law at Westminster is outlined below.

First Reading

The Bill is introduced to the House of Commons. A vote does not take place, but the Second Reading of the Bill is arranged. The contents of the Bill will then be published.

Second Reading

The Bill will face its first test in that it will have to face a vote. If the Bill is defeated in the vote, it can go no further. The Bill would have to be reintroduced in the next parliamentary year at the earliest. If the House approves the Bill then it can proceed to the next stage. The debate is not usually lengthy as most of the detailed work on the Bill is yet to come.

Committee Stage

A small group of members of the House of Commons from both the Government and the opposition will form a committee to discuss the Bill in detail. There is nothing to stop larger groups of MPs or even the whole House sitting as a committee. The Committee stage is where the Bill will be most likely to face major changes to its original content. The meaning of words and phrases will be picked over by the members and even entire sections of the Bill could be rewritten or taken out completely. The Bill may now be completely different from the version that was first introduced to the House. If the Bill relates to Scotland only, it will be referred to either the Scottish Standing Committee or the Scottish Grand Committee. In practice, referrals to these Scottish Committees will tend to be less common these days because the Scottish Parliament now deals with the bulk of new laws for Scotland.

Report Stage

The Committee will have to give a progress report about the Bill to the House of Commons. The Commons will want to know what changes have been made to the Bill and these will have to be considered in detail. The Report Stage is also an opportunity for more changes to be made to the Bill.

Third Reading

This will be the crunch time for the Bill. The House will debate the final version of the Bill and a vote will be taken. If the Bill is defeated, then it will have to be reintroduced during the next parliamentary year – provided of course that the Government has the stomach for a fight. If the Bill is supported by a majority of MPs, then it will go to the House of Lords.

Key point: Bills passing through the Westminster Parliament go through the following stages: First Reading, Second Reading, Committee Stage, Report Stage and Third Reading before they can become Acts of Parliament.

The House of Lords

The House of Lords has very similar procedures to the House of Commons, but there are some differences. The Chancellor of the Exchequer does not have to submit his Budget to the Lords (a Finance Bill) because since 1911 the Lords have had no right to deal with such a Bill. During the Committee Stage of a Bill, the entire House sits as a Committee in order to propose changes to the Bill's contents. Once the Bill has successfully passed through the Lords, it receives the Royal Assent and thus the Bill becomes an Act.

The new Act may now come into force immediately or there could be a delay. The Employment Act 2002 received the Royal Assent on 8 July 2002. However, important provisions of the Act were not made effective until 6 April 2003. In fact, implementation of some of the rules in this Act were delayed until October 2004. Copies of the new legislation will be made publicly available in print or on the Internet by Her Majesty's Stationery Office.

The powers of the House of Lords

It should be noted, however, that the Lords can only delay the passage of a Bill. Certainly, the Lords can make its own changes to a Bill, but these changes can ultimately be rejected by the Commons. If the Lords decides to block the passage of a Bill twice in one parliamentary session, the Commons can use its powers under the Parliament Acts of 1911 and 1949 to force the Bill through despite the Lords' hostility. The Bill would then go the Queen in any case and receive the Royal Assent. The Bill would, therefore, become law. It is worth pointing out that the days are long gone when a King or a Queen could refuse to give the Royal Assent. In modern times, this stage is purely a formality.

 Key point: The House of Lords is the weaker of the two Houses of Parliament because, unlike the Commons, it has no power to deal with Finance Bills and it only has the power to delay Bills.

Where do Bills come from?

The vast majority of new legal proposals will be introduced in the House of Commons. The Commons is the more important House of Parliament. The government of the day, headed by the Prime Minister, and its supporters sit in the House of Commons. When a general election is held for Westminster, the voters are being asked to vote for members of the House of the Commons who are called Members of Parliament (MPs). The political party that secures the largest number of seats in the House of Commons will usually form the next government. The purpose of a General Election is, therefore, to elect a parliament which, in turn, will make laws for the United Kingdom. The members of the House of Lords do not face the British voters and, therefore, they cannot be said to enjoy the same authority as MPs who regularly have to stand for re-election. In any case, in 1911 the Commons emerged as the winner in a power struggle with the Lords and since then the Lords have accepted that they are not as powerful as the Commons.

 Key point: The House of Commons as the democratically elected chamber will introduce many more Bills than the House of Lords.

It should be appreciated that a government will come to power with clear ideas about the kinds of laws that it wishes to see introduced. These ideas are contained in a manifesto which contains all sorts of proposals for running the country. In this way, a political party is advertising its policies and telling the voters what it would do if elected to form the next British government.

When the present Labour government was first elected in 1997, it had already made clear that it wished to introduce devolved parliaments or assemblies for Scotland, Northern Ireland and Wales. Legislation to set up these three bodies soon followed the Government's election victory. However, governments will often consider legislation to cope with particular problems that arise from time to time, for example, tougher laws to combat illegal immigrants or the introduction of identity cards to crack down on terrorism.

A government will often wish to see whether it has enough public support before introducing a Bill to parliament on a particular subject. A Green Paper will be published outlining the government's proposals. If public opinion is broadly favourable to the government's proposals, then a White Paper will be published which provides much more detail. When the government minister has prepared his Bill, he will approach the government's business manager in the Commons (the Leader of the House) and ask for parliamentary time to be allocated.

 Key point: Governments will often give advance warning of their legislative proposals by publishing a Green Paper. Once confident that support exists for its legislative proposals, the government will then publish a White Paper.

Getting a Bill through Parliament

In 1997, Donald Dewar, the then Scottish Secretary, had spent a considerable amount of time with his team of civil servants and other experts preparing the Scotland Bill. The Scotland Bill proposed to establish a Scottish Parliament. The Bill was given a slot in the parliamentary timetable in January 1998 and, after having passed through both Houses of Parliament, it was sent to the Queen in order to receive the Royal Assent in November 1998. Upon receiving the Royal Assent, the Bill became law as the Scotland Act 1998. From January to November may seem like a relatively short period, but it is worth pointing out that ten months of parliamentary time was required and this Bill was considered to be a priority.

It is perfectly possible for an ordinary Member of Parliament to introduce a Bill to Parliament. This is known as a Private Member's Bill. These types of Bills, however, do not have a very high success rate. The government controls the parliamentary timetable and naturally it will give priority to its own Bills. If there is not enough time for a Private Member's Bill to be debated and voted upon, then that is simply too bad. Admittedly, some significant changes to the law have been made as a result of Private Member's Bills. The Abortion Act 1967 was originally introduced as a Bill by David Steel, the Liberal MP. Steel's Bill later received support from the then Labour government and went on to become an Act. If the government had not supported Steel's Bill it would have probably failed.

Parliaments are elected for a maximum period of five years and the government will want to use as much of this time as possible to promote its own Bills. Theoretically, if the government controls a majority of seats in the House of Commons it should face few problems getting its Bills through. However, governments can upset their own supporters who may then choose to rebel by voting against their own government's proposals. Even if the government manages to get a Bill through the Commons, as we have seen, the House of Lords will still have the right to examine the Bill and make all sorts of changes to it.

 Key point: Most public Bills will be promoted by government ministers, but it is possible for ordinary MPs to introduce their own Bills (Private Member's Bills).

Secondary or delegated legislation

As we have seen, there are various parliamentary procedures which have to be followed before a Bill can become an Act. These procedures can be very time consuming and Bills can fall victim to all sorts of delays. There are ways in which laws can be introduced very quickly without having to introduce a Bill to parliament and get it through the legislative process.

Statutory Instruments

Very often, an Act of Parliament may contain powers which allow a government minister to make new laws without the minister having first to consult parliament. Such Acts are known as Parent Acts. The Scotland Act 1998 is one such example, where the appropriate Scottish Executive Minister can introduce regulations or statutory instruments (as they are often called) to deal with particular problems or issues, for example, Statutory Instrument No. 1017 of 1999 (Removal of Judges) Order gives the First Minister of Scotland powers to convene a Tribunal which can remove Scottish judges for misconduct.

In this way, time can be saved and all the First Minister will have to do is to provide the Scottish Parliament with a report (usually at a later stage) about the operation of the new rules. However, the First Minister must stay within the powers that the Parent Act gives him or the new rules could be subject to a legal challenge.

In an emergency situation, for example, during times of war, Orders in Council can be used by the British government to introduce new legislation. This type of legislation can be rushed through both Houses of Parliament very quickly

Acts of Sederunt

This allows the Court of Session to make laws which regulate the conduct of business in all the Scottish civil courts.

Acts of Adjournal

The High Court of Justiciary can introduce these Acts to organise the business and procedures of the High Court of Justiciary and the lower Scottish criminal courts.

By-laws

The Westminster or the Scottish Parliament will often use a Parent Act to give law making powers to an inferior body such as a local council. An example of this is the Licensing (Scotland) Act 1976 (soon to be amended) which deals with the licensing of public houses, bars, nightclubs and restaurants in Scotland. Under this Act, local councils have been given powers to make rules or by-laws which regulate the opening of such establishments. This is not a matter which should take up the Scottish Parliament's valuable time. Local councils are best placed to understand local conditions and what may be appropriate for the City of Edinburgh may not be right for a rural area like Argyll and Bute. It is vital, of course, that councils do not act beyond the powers granted to them otherwise there is every possibility of a legal challenge being mounted.

 Key point: Secondary legislation allows new laws to be brought in very speedily and effectively without the need to seek Parliamentary approval which can be very time consuming and which is not always granted.

The unwritten laws of Scotland

So far, we have examined written sources of Scots law, but not every legal rule in Scotland will be in written form. The unwritten laws of Scotland fall into two categories:

◆ Custom
◆ Judicial precedent or case law

 Key point: Unwritten laws arise from custom and judicial precedent (case law).

Custom

Customs are practices which have been handed down over many generations. In order to have the force of law, customs must be well established and they must continue to be in force. If a custom has fallen into disuse, it is highly unlikely that it will continue to be enforceable. Furthermore, customs can be overruled by superior forms of law such as Acts of Parliament or other legislation. It is worth pointing out that custom as a source of law is not as important as it once was.

 Key point: Customs develop over a period of time and are commonly accepted practices.

The use of customs in relation to landownership and use is particularly common. *Udal tenure* is one such example. This is a curious system of land tenure and is found only in Orkney and Shetland. *Udal tenure* was imposed on the islands by the Viking conquerors who originally came from Norway and is a type of freeholding. Unlike the feudal system, the Scottish (later the British) Crown was not acknowledged as superior – this is due to the Vikings' hearty dislike of authority and the fact that they did not acknowledge the Scottish Crown as the relevant authority. In fact, the Vikings were more likely to be loyal to the Norwegian Crown!

The Vikings took the land by force and, very often, held on to it by violent means. The Vikings regarded it almost as a sacred duty to fight off all comers who might have designs on their land. Under the Udal system, an individual's tenure of the land was, therefore, as strong as he was. The Udal system is not as common in the islands now and, in modern times, there has been an increasing trend towards the introduction of feudalism.

In certain trades or professions, customs or business practices were given explicit recognition by the courts. In international trade, strange initials or phrases such as FOB, CIF, ex-factory or ox-ship would often feature in contracts. To an outsider, these initials or phrases are completely baffling. However, to someone who works in a particular trade or business, the initials FOB would make perfect sense. In an FOB (free on board) contract, a buyer of goods will become responsible for any loss, damage or theft to the property when the goods have passed over the ship's rail. If the goods are damaged, lost or stolen before they pass over the ship's rail, then the seller would be responsible.

In criminal law, certain types of behaviour will be automatically regarded as reprehensible and as such will be regarded as threatening the security of society or the community as a whole. Those individuals who commit crimes will run the risk of being imprisoned or fined. Not every rule of criminal behaviour, however, will be contained in an Act of Parliament. Some crimes have always been forbidden by society. The crime of murder is one example. There is no written rule in Scots law which says that murder is a crime, but society has always regarded the taking of innocent, human life without justification as an evil or wicked act.

Judicial precedent (case law)

Legal rules are not always as clear as we would like them to be and this will mean that the courts have an opportunity to clarify the law. Test cases will often be brought before the courts which raise a very important point of law and judges will have to make a decision. When a judge makes a decision at the end of a court case, he is often not just making a decision which applies to the immediate facts of the case before him. The decision which the judge has made may actually become a legal rule in its own right which future judges and courts will be under a duty to follow if they encounter a similar legal problem. The practice of following previous judicial decisions is known as judicial precedent or *stare decisis* (standing by previous decisions).

 Key point: Judicial precedent develops from case law and the 'testing' of laws in court. The rulings of a higher court decision must be followed.

How do judges make rules of law?

Not every judge can make a new rule. The authority of the judge or the court will be a major factor to consider here. If the judge holds a relatively junior position, for example, a Sheriff or a Justice of the Peace, it is very unlikely that he will be able to create a new rule of law. If, on the other hand, the ruling came from superior courts, for example, the Court of Session or the House of Lords, this decision would have to be followed by the lower or inferior courts. Therefore, the position of the court is very important. As we shall see when we come to an examination of the legal system, the Scottish courts are ranked in order of importance from the highest in the land to the lowest. If a lawyer wishes to use a previous judicial decision in order to argue his case, the decision must be in point. When a lawyer talks about a previously decided case being in point, he means that the legal rule which it established is relevant to the case that the judges are currently considering. In order to follow a previously decided case, a court must be absolutely certain that the case presently before it raises exactly the same legal issues as an older decision. The facts of the older case and the facts of the current case do not have to be the same. Two recent criminal decisions of the Appeal Court of the High Court of Justiciary, which were decided on the same day, demonstrate the doctrine of judicial precedent in action:

 Procurator Fiscal, Dunoon *v* Dominick (22 July 2003) the accused had allegedly displayed material of a pornographic nature in a manner that two girls aged nine and ten-years old could not avoid seeing it. It was also alleged that the accused had conducted himself in a disorderly manner and that he had followed the two girls in an attempt to force them to view the pornographic material. This caused the girls to experience a state of fear and alarm. The accused was charged, amongst other things, with the common law crime of shameless indecency.

 MacLean *v* Procurator Fiscal, Inverness (22 July 2003) it was alleged that the accused, a female teacher, had conducted a relationship of a sexual nature with a 15-year-old boy while he was a pupil at the school at which she taught English. This alleged relationship continued after the boy was no longer a pupil. The accused also allegedly indulged in communications (telephone calls and letters) with the boy which were inappropriate and of an indecent nature. The accused was charged with the common law crime of shameless indecency.

The question before the judges in both cases was whether the charge of shameless indecency was unspecific and unclear and, therefore, a breach of the European Convention on Human Rights which demands that the accused must be charged with a crime that is reasonably clear and certain. The main criticism of the common law crime of shameless indecency that it is used to cover all sorts of behaviour. A problematic area was whether it covered indecent acts committed in public or whether an accused who committed similar acts in private could also be charged with shameless indecency. In **Procurator Fiscal, Dunoon *v* Dominick** it was held that the crime of shameless indecency as it now exists has no satisfactory basis in the law of Scotland and these types of behaviour should be treated as falling within the scope of the crime of public indecency. Whether a particular act is indecent will depend on the circumstances of the case judged by social standards that will change from age to age and these will be the standards that would be applied by the average citizen in contemporary society. Where indecent acts are committed in private, the option of charging the accused with lewd and libidinous behaviour is still very much open. The precedent laid down in **Dominick** was followed in the related case of **MacLean *v* Procurator Fiscal, Inverness**.

These two cases effectively reformed an area of Scottish criminal law without the consent and the participation of either the democratically elected Scottish and Westminster Parliaments. Unless the politicians decide to intervene and pass a law overruling the High Court of Justiciary, the lower Scottish criminal courts must follow these rulings in **Dominick** and **MacLean**. It is now no longer competent to charge an accused with the common law crime of shameless indecency.

 Key point: Somewhat controversially, senior judges can make a new rule of law without either the participation or prior approval of democratically elected politicians.

Persuasive precedents

Many previous court cases are merely regarded as persuasive in the sense that a lawyer could choose to use legal arguments from them, but it is by no means certain that a court will follow the decision. English cases, unless previously accepted by the Scottish courts, may raise some interesting issues but they will not be automatically accepted as authority in Scotland. Similarly, decisions of the lower Scottish courts such as the District Court, the Sheriff Court and the Outer House of the Court of Session may be regarded as persuasive, but not binding. A case will be regarded as having binding authority in Scotland if it is a decision of the High Court of Justiciary, the Inner House of the Court of Session, the Privy Council or the House of Lords (in a Scottish appeal). Generally speaking, judges or courts are bound to follow the decisions of superior courts.

 Key point: Some previous judicial decisions will merely be persuasive in that they are not regarded as binding precedents.

A previous judicial decision consists of two parts:

◆ The *ratio decidendi*
◆ *Obiter dicta*

The *ratio decidendi* or simply, the ratio, is the actual legal rule which is established by the court case. This rule can often be simply expressed in one or two sentences. However, the report of the actual judgement could run to many pages. It is very common for judges to go on at length when they deliver the judgement. Statements or examples which the judges provide when they make their decisions are of interest to academics and lawyers, but they do not actually form part of the judgement. Such statements or examples are known as *obiter dicta* (or things said by the way). It is very important to be able to distinguish between the *ratio decidendi* and *obiter dicta*.

Many important areas of Scots law are made up of rules which judges and not parliament have made. Contract law is only one example where many of the legal rules governing the creation of contracts and the rights of the parties are contained in previously decided court cases. Judges have to be careful that they are not seen to be overruling laws which either the Westminster or Scottish Parliament have made. Both parliaments are very jealous of their powers and will often express disapproval if they believe that judges have gone too far by making a new law. Judges, after all, exist to interpret and to give effect to the will of parliament as expressed in various Acts and secondary legislation.

Judicial approaches to statutory interpretation

When a Scottish judge attempts to interpret a statutory provision in an Act of Parliament or a piece of secondary legislation, he or she can apply one of three possible rules:

The literal rule – means that the words used in the legislation are given their everyday, ordinary or literal meaning. Such an approach will be taken by judges who are firmly of the opinion that they have been appointed merely to apply the law and it is not their place to become legislators or law-makers. The literal rule is obviously an example of judges erring on the side of caution, but it can lead to absurdities or injustices. This will be especially the case when Parliament has drafted legislation poorly. The application of the literal rule can be seen in an example involving the **Sex Discrimination Act 1975**. The Act makes it very clear that central to the success of any claim is the complainant's ability to compare his or her allegedly less favourable treatment to an actual or hypothetical male/female comparator. If he or she cannot do this, the claim will fail. A woman claiming that she has suffered discrimination on the grounds of her sex must be able to carry out a like with like comparison. The woman's circumstances and those of her male comparator must be the same (they should not be materially different) otherwise a meaningful comparison cannot be made. When the Act of 1975 was first introduced, cases involving alleged discrimination connected to a woman's pregnancy encountered an unexpected problem which the Parliamentary draftsmen had not taken into account: how you can compare a pregnant woman's situation with that of a man. This is not a valid comparison and, therefore, many of the earliest sex discrimination claims failed because some judges applied the literal approach to the Act even if this made the law something of an ass and, more seriously, led to a blatant injustice.

The golden rule – this an attempt by some judges to get round the problem caused by the application of the literal rule. The judge will apply the law literally, but he or she will do so in a way that avoids the creation of absurdities or injustices. This approach is sometimes referred to as the gloss on the literal rule.

The mischief rule – in this situation the judge will ignore the wording in the legislation and instead will examine what mischief the statute was supposed to cure. There are dangers here because the judge is obviously second guessing the will of Parliament and using his or her own interpretation in order to decide the legal issue at hand. This approach is often referred to as the purposive approach.

 Key point: A judicial precedent consists of two parts – the *ratio decidendi* and the *obiter dicta*.

The European Union or Community

The European Union is an organisation or a club of 25 member states. Like most organisations or clubs, the members have to obey the rules or laws in order to reap the benefits of membership. Britain has been a member of the European Union since 1 January 1973 as a result of the European Communities Act 1972.

The development of the European Union can be traced back to the Treaty of Paris 1951 when the original six member states – Belgium, France, Germany, Italy, Luxembourg and the Netherlands – established a single market in coal and steel by creating the European Coal and Steel Community. The Community was formed some six years after the end of the Second World War (1939–45) and was a deliberate attempt to heal the tremendous damage that had been inflicted on Europe as a result of that War. A Coal and Steel Community had tremendous symbolism, not just because former enemies made a commitment never to go war with one another again, but the fact that coal and steel were used to make weapons. In 1957, this cooperation between the six states was deepened with the signing of the Treaty of Rome and the Euratom Treaty. It was the Treaty of Rome that particularly captured the imagination with its dream of creating a single European market where the free movement of people, goods, services and capital could be promoted. It was hoped by promoting deeper economic cooperation between the member states, that the desire to go to war would be a thing of the past. The single market was eventually established on 1 January 1993.

Although the three Treaties laid down a blueprint for the single European market, it would take many years of planning and the introduction of a huge range of laws in each of the member states to make this dream a reality. In order to make the single market a reality, the member states would all have to introduce laws which brought their very different legal systems closer together. This process was known as harmonising the laws in the different member states. Regrettably, Britain chose not to be involved in the European project until much later and, arguably, missed its opportunity to be a major influence on the development of the European Union. By the time Britain became a member of the European Union in 1973, many of the key laws were already in place and Britain had to accept these as the price of membership.

 Key point: The European Union is an organisation or a club of 25 member states and, as with most organisations or clubs, the members have to obey the rules or laws in order to reap the benefits of membership.

Sources of European Law

The laws of the European Union can be used in any of the national courts by member states, by private individuals and by organisations. There are two sources of law:

- Primary legislation
- Secondary legislation

 Key point: Sources of European legislation can be found in primary and secondary legislation.

Primary legislation or law is contained in the original three Treaties – Paris 1951, Rome 1957 and Euratom 1957. These Treaties lay down broad goals which the member states will attempt to achieve. They can often be sketchy where details are concerned. However, it is possible to use Treaty Articles to enforce a variety of rights if the Article in question is sufficiently clear and precise. Other Treaties such as the Treaty on European Union 1992, the Treaty of Amsterdam 1997 and the Treaty of Nice 2000 have also added to the primary law of the European Union.

 Key point: Primary legislation or law is contained in the original three Treaties – Paris 1951, Rome 1957 and Euratom 1957 and any other subsequent Treaties, for example, Maastricht, Amsterdam and Nice.

Article 249 of the Treaty of Rome 1957 lists the five sources of European law which are known as secondary legislation. The Treaties list broad aims or objectives, but they often do not provide the details. Secondary legislation is, therefore, necessary to flesh out the Treaties of the European Union. Secondary legislation includes:

- Regulations
- Directives
- Decisions
- Recommendations
- Opinions

 Key point: Secondary legislation is made up of Regulations, Directives, Decisions, Recommendations and Opinions.

As soon as Regulations are published in the Official Journal of the European Union, they are legally binding. They do not need to be implemented by the Westminster Parliament or the Scottish Parliament. They can be enforced in all the national courts. In this way, Regulations are said to be directly applicable and have direct effect.

 Key point: Regulations are legally binding as soon as they are published in the Official Journal of the European Union.

In order to have legal force, the Westminster Parliament must pass legislation to make Directives effective. The Sale and Supply of Goods to Consumers Regulations 2002 began life as the European Directive 1999/44/EC on Certain Aspects of the Sale of Consumer Goods and Associated Guarantees. It was only when the Regulations were passed into law on 31 March 2003 that the Directive became effective. However, member states will have to obey a strict time period for implementing directives because failure to introduce legislation could result in legal action being taken against the British government.

Decisions include judgements of the European Court of Justice and the courts of the member states will have to obey these and follow them. The Council and the Commission can also issue decisions but these are usually addressed to particular member states, individuals or bodies who will have to abide by them.

Recommendations and opinions are generally held to have no binding force, but in **Grimaldi *v* Fonds des Maladies Professionelles (1990)** it was held that they may have some indirect legal effect. The European Court of Justice stated that domestic courts are bound to take recommendations into consideration in order to decide disputes submitted to them, in particular where they are capable of clarifying the interpretation of other provisions of national or Community law.

We also have what is known as 'soft law' i.e. resolutions, programmes, notices or guidelines. This is an imprecise term, but it can still be quite useful as a general category. Other sources of law include international treaties which the European Union has made, for example, the Lomé and Yaoundé Conventions giving trade rights to African, Caribbean and Pacific nations.

The institutions of the European Union

Article 7 of the Treaty of Rome 1957 (or EEC Treaty) lists five main institutions of the European Union:

- Parliament (Articles 189 to 201)
- Commission (Articles 211 to 219)

◆ European Court of Justice (Articles 220 to 245)
◆ Council (Articles 246 to 248)
◆ Court of Auditors

The European Council

The Council is by far and away the most powerful institution as it represents the interests of the member states directly. Representatives of the government, for example, the Foreign Minister or Finance Minister of each member state, sit on the Council. At the most important meetings of the Council (the European Council), the Heads of Government will take their places at the table to make the most important policy decisions.

The European Parliament

Parliament was first known as the Assembly, but since 1962, it has been referred to as the European Parliament. When the European Union consisted of 15 member states (until 30th April 2004), the Parliament had 626 members or MEPs. The 1997 Treaty of Amsterdam set a limit of 700 members. This limit was soon viewed as unrealistic given the fact that, on 1st May 2004, 10 new member states joined the European Union. From 2004–2007, the Parliament will have 732 members in total and, if Bulgaria and Romania become member states in 2007, the number of MEPs will increase to 786. The word 'Parliament' can be very misleading – it in no way resembles the Westminster Parliament and it is often restricted in all sorts of ways. Additionally, it cannot pass laws in its own right, but a failure to consult Parliament might lead to any subsequent legislation being cancelled. In **Roquette Frères v Council (1980)** rules for regulating the use of isuglucose were challenged and annulled because Parliament had not been given a reasonable opportunity to scrutinise the proposals. Parliament's role is now more than just an advisory one.

The Single European Act 1986 and the Treaty of European Union 1992 introduced a cooperation procedure and a co-decision procedure respectively in relation to parliament. These had the effect of giving Parliament much more power in the area of legislative proposals. In many situations, the Council will not be able to pass laws without the cooperation and consent of Parliament.

Over the years, the Parliament has acquired more powers and it was instrumental in getting rid of the European Commission led by its former President Jacques Santer in 1999 in the wake of serious allegations of corruption and maladministration.

The European Commission

The European Commission is effectively the civil service of the European Union. The Commission employs a staff of over 21,000. The Commission has no formal power to make laws. It can propose new laws, but the Council and Parliament may have other ideas. The Commission's main task is to ensure that member states, business organisations and individuals follow the laws of the European Union. The Commission will not be slow in taking parties to a court if it considers that laws have been broken or ignored.

The Commission will have a membership of 30 Commissioners from 1st May 2004 (this will include 10 new appointees from each one of the new member states). Each Commissioner will take responsibility for a particular area of policy, for example, the

Single Market or external relations with third countries. Presently, the "Big Five" member states: France, Germany, Italy, Spain and the United Kingdom each appoint two Commissioners, with the other 20 states appointing 1 Commissioner each. However, from 2005, the "Big Five" will lose one of their Commissioners meaning that the membership of the Commission will be reduced to 25. If Bulgaria and Romania join the European Union, as expected in 2007, both countries will have the right to appoint a Commissioner of their own bringing the total membership to 27. In theory, the first loyalty of each Commissioner is to the European Union rather than to the member state that appointed him or her.

The European Court of Justice

From 1st May 2004, the European Court of Justice (ECJ) consists of 25 judges (each appointed by a member state) who are assisted by eight Advocates-General (who will themselves have been lawyers or judges of extremely high standing). The Advocates-General are appointed by common agreement of the member states. A Grand Chamber of 11 judges can sit to hear cases from around the European Union. In practice, however, it is more likely for the ECJ to be split into a number of Chambers where 3-5 judges will sit to hear cases. The ECJ sits in Luxembourg and its aim is to ensure that the laws of the European Union are properly observed when the member states implement their Treaty obligations via their domestic legal systems. A President of the Court is elected for a renewable 3 year term from amongst the 25 judges.

The Single European Act 1986 also established a Court of First Instance in order to ease the pressure in relation to the European Court of Justice's workload. The Court of First Instance deals primarily with issues such as agriculture, state subsidies, competition, commercial policy, regional policy, trade-mark law, transport and disputes between the European Union and its staff. The Court of First Instance has a membership of 25 judges each appointed from one of the member states.

The Court of Auditors

This body is a relatively recent addition to the major institutions of the European Union, having only been established in 1977. It has primary responsibility for the scrutiny of the European Union's finances i.e. that the budget is being spent correctly. The Court will attempt to expose any financial irregularities in the European Union's budget and this is a very politically sensitive role given the huge amounts of money involved and the perception (rightly or wrongly) that the money is not being spent correctly. The Court will submit an annual report to the Council and the Parliament which contains detailed information about the European Union's finances for the previous financial year. This institution is becoming much more important as time passes and it played a major role in forcing the European Commission to resign en masse in 1999 after allegations of maladministration were widely exposed.

The Court has 25 full-time members appointed for a renewable term of six years from each one of the member states. These members will have been professional auditors or will have special experience as accountancy practitioners. In order to have more efficient procedures, the Court can organise its members into units called "chambers" who will be allocated particular areas of responsibility. A President of the Court is elected by the members to serve for a term of 3 years. The members of the Court are supported by a staff of approximately 550 – about half of whom are professional auditors. The Court can send these staff members out on inspections throughout the European Union to investigate the different ways in which money is being spent. As one would expect, the Court is a completely autonomous institution and its members enjoy complete independence. However, the Court of Auditors has no legal powers of its own, and when it uncovers fraud or improper practices, these should be reported to the appropriate European Union institution which must take the necessary action to rectify the situation.

 Key point: The five main institutions of the European Union are the Council, the Commission, the Parliament, the European Court of Justice and the Court of Auditors.

Why is European law so unique?

It cannot be altered unilaterally by the governments of the member states and all are collectively bound by it. Fundamentally more important, is the fact that European law confers rights on and duties without the further participation of the member states. Unlike other international treaties, the citizens of the member states can enforce Treaty provisions against one another, their governments and the European institutions. The view that the European Union is a different and autonomous (independent) legal order has been consistently promoted by the European Court of Justice.

 Key point: European law cannot be altered by any one state and all are bound by it.

In **Van Gend en Loos (1963)** the Court stated most clearly that the states have limited their sovereign rights. Again, in **Costa v ENEL (1964)**, the European Court of Justice stated that member states had experienced a 'permanent limitation of their sovereign rights' when they joined the European Community. European Community obligations would not be unconditional, merely contingent, if they could be called into question by the member states. In the view of the European Court of Justice, European law always prevails over national law. In **Internationale Handelsgesselschaft (1970)** the European Court of Justice stated that even constitutional provisions of the member states can be struck down. In **Simmenthal (1978)** it was stated that national courts must set aside national law which may conflict with European law, and it did not matter whether the national law had been passed before the state become a member of the European Union. In **Francovich and Bonifaci v Italy (1992)** it was held that an individual may sue a member state (the government) for damages for loss suffered as a result of a member state's failure to implement a European Union Directive.

However, the idea that European Union law is superior to the law of each member state has caused serious problems for Britain and this argument has not always been easily accepted. The British courts appear to have reached a compromise which amounts to the following: as long as Britain remains a member of the European Union, European law will be regarded as superior to British law. Should Britain choose to leave the European Union at any point in the future or if the Westminster Parliament passes an Act that expressly contradicts the idea of the supremacy of European law, then the position will most definitely change.

Key point: The British courts appear to have reached a compromise which amounts to the following – as long as Britain remains a member of the European Union, European law will be regarded as superior to British law.

The Human Rights Act 1998

This Act came into force on 2 October 2000 and it implements the European Convention on Human Rights directly into United Kingdom law. The European Convention aims to protect basic human and democratic rights. It was partly incorporated into Scots law a year before the rest of the United Kingdom by means of the Scotland Act 1998.

In 1950, the United Kingdom signed the European Convention on Human Rights and Fundamental Freedoms which was inspired by the Universal Declaration of Human Rights of the United Nations – a direct response to the horrors of the Second World War. These documents laid down minimum standards for the protection of human rights which signatory states aimed to respect. In 1951, the United Kingdom became one of the first states to ratify the Convention and, by 1953, a sufficient number of European states had ratified it to make it effective. The United Kingdom, however, chose not to incorporate the Convention directly into British law and this caused a number of problems. The main problem being that British citizens could not enforce the Convention in British courts.

 Key point: The European Convention on Human Rights aims to promote respect for basic human rights and democratic freedoms.

Since 1966, these positive human rights in the European Convention could be challenged in another forum – the European Court of Human Rights at Strasbourg. Under Articles 25 and 26 of the Convention, the United Kingdom accepted the compulsory jurisdiction of this court. As we shall see, however, this route has not been without its problems. The United Kingdom is, therefore, under a Treaty obligation to adhere to the principles of the Convention. Ironically, despite the fact that the United Kingdom was the first signatory of the Convention, there have been all sorts of problems relating to its incorporation into British law. As British citizens had no right to enforce the Convention in British courts, they were forced to turn to the European Court of Human Rights. On average, people who took the legal road to Strasbourg could expect to wait at least five years to have the case heard and decided. When the Labour Government of Tony Blair was elected in 1997 it decided to bring a halt to this and make the Convention directly enforceable in British courts. The introduction of the European Convention now means that British citizens should no longer have to wait five years for a decision.

It is also worth emphasising that the European Court of Human Rights is a completely separate body from the European Court of Justice (the court of the European Union) and the two courts should not be confused.

 Key point: Since 1966, the United Kingdom has accepted the compulsory jurisdiction of the European Court of Human Rights in Strasbourg.

The European Convention Articles now incorporated in United Kingdom law, and listed in Schedule 1 of the Human Rights and Scotland Acts, cover the following matters:

- The right to life (Article 2)
- Prohibition of torture and cruel and degrading treatment (Article 3)
- Prohibition of slavery and forced labour (Article 4)
- The right to liberty and security (Article 5)
- The right to a fair trial/hearing (Article 6)
- The general prohibition of the enactment of retrospective criminal offences (Article 7)
- The right to respect for private and family life (Article 8)
- Freedom of thought, conscience and religion (Article 9)
- Freedom of expression (Article 10)
- Freedom of assembly and association (Article 11)
- The right to marry (Article 12)
- Prohibition of discrimination (Article 14)
- No restrictions on the political activity of aliens (i.e. those are not British or European Union citizens) (Article 16)

It is important to note that the European Convention is only enforceable against the British state or institutions and organisations that carry out public functions, for example, universities, colleges, schools and local authorities. The European Convention is a very important source of new law, not only because it promotes the protection of human rights and democratic freedoms, but also for the fact that it cause profound changes to be made to the legal system. As a result of the Human Rights and Scotland Acts, all United Kingdom legislation – whether it was passed before or after the introduction of the European Convention – will have to be interpreted in order to protect human rights and democratic freedoms. This will be less of a problem for legislation which is introduced after the European Convention came into force and which will often have been drawn up with precisely these issues in mind. The more problematic area will be older legislation which does not protect human rights or democratic freedoms.

 Key point: The rights guaranteed to individuals under the European Convention are enforceable against the state or bodies that carry out functions of the state.

Primary legislation (i.e. Acts of the Westminster Parliament) which is not human rights friendly, can be challenged in the Scottish courts. If the judges find that the legislation does indeed breach the European Convention, they can issue what is known as a declaration of incompatibility. Only certain courts (the Court of Session, the High Court of Justiciary, the Privy Council and the House of Lords) can issue such a declaration. This signifies that the legislation in question breaches human rights in a particular way and it is now up to the Westminster Parliament to take the appropriate steps to bring the law into line with the European Convention. There is a fast-track procedure whereby a Minister of the Crown can change an incompatible piece of legislation by way of an Order-in-Council or a statutory instrument.

Furthermore, the previous case law of the European Court of Human Rights can now be pleaded before Scottish courts.

Significantly, the legislation of the Scottish Parliament is considered to be secondary legislation and this means that judges can strike down those parts which breach human rights or democratic freedoms. In practice, however, much of the legislation coming from the Scottish Parliament will be accompanied by a statement to the effect that it complies with the European Convention.

 Key point: Courts such as the High Court of Justiciary, the Court of Session, the Privy Council and the House of Lords can issue a declaration of incompatibility if legislation does not comply with the European Convention. However, the courts cannot strike down primary legislation which is not human rights compatible.

The rights which are introduced by the Human Rights and Scotland Acts do not all have equal weight and they are certainly not all absolute. Some are absolute and inalienable and cannot be interfered with by the state. Others are merely contingent and the British state can opt out of them in certain circumstances. By Article 15 of the Convention, states have a limited right to suspend certain rights 'in time of war or other emergency'. The United Kingdom has done exactly this in relation to extended periods of detention for those suspected of terrorist offences in Northern Ireland and the United Kingdom has been successful here (**Brogan v UK (1988)** and **Brannigan and McBride v UK (1994)**) in pleading that it should be allowed to suspend or derogate from the provisions of the Convention.

The effect of the European Convention in respect of Scots law

Some important cases have occurred as a result of the introduction of the European Convention into Scots law.

 Starrs v Ruxton (2000) the two accused were tried and convicted before a temporary Sheriff. The question arose as to whether or not this temporary judge was an 'independent and impartial tribunal' and, if not, did this represent a breach of Article 6 (the right to an impartial hearing) of the Convention on Human Rights? This case, in effect, challenged the right of the Lord Advocate (a politician and a member of the Scottish Cabinet *and* head of the Scottish system of public prosecution) to appoint temporary judges. The argument that the lawyers for the two accused used was that such judges, lacking job security, would not display sufficient independence when arriving at their decisions as such a course of action would threaten their continued employment. The High Court of Justiciary, in a landmark ruling, held that the widespread use of temporary Sheriffs did indeed breach the Convention. The accused had not been given a fair trial according to the provisions of the Convention because they could not be sure that a judge appointed by a politician would be sufficiently independent. The Convention states that judges, for the most part, must be independent of political control.

 Brown v Stott (2000) the owner of a vehicle was compelled under the Road Traffic Act 1988 to give information as to the identity of the driver at the time when the relevant offence was committed. The offence was one of drunk driving. The accused argued that the very fact that she had to admit to the police that she had driven the car in response to their questioning of her amounted to self-incrimination. Her response would, of course, be used against her at the trial and she claimed, therefore, that her right to a fair trial had been breached under Article 6 because she had self-incriminated herself. The accused was convicted in the Sheriff Court. The High Court of Justiciary held that the prosecution had no power to rely on evidence of the admission which the accused had been compelled to make under the 1988 Act. The appeal was allowed. However, the Privy Council later overruled the High Court and stated that the provision of the Road Traffic Act that had compelled the accused to reveal the identity of the driver at the time of the alleged offence was not a breach of Article 6 of the European Convention. This decision also allowed the police to continue to use speed cameras because it is the car not the driver who is caught on camera and the police will, therefore, have to ask the owner of the car to identify the person who was driving the vehicle when the speeding offence was committed.

 Clark *v* Kelly (2003) was an appeal by Hellen Clark, the procurator fiscal for Kirkcaldy which raised an important question in relation to the structure of and procedure in District Courts in Scotland. The case involved an alleged violation of Article 6 of the European Convention on Human Rights. The accused in this case, who had been charged with theft, claimed that he would be denied a fair and public hearing by an independent and impartial tribunal if his trial in the District Court was allowed to proceed. He claimed that the practice whereby the clerk of the court often gave legal advice to the judge was in breach of Article 6. The question was an important one, since most of the judges in District Courts in Scotland are lay Justices of the Peace. This particular case had consequences for England too as Magistrates' Courts in England and Wales are, in all essentials, similar. It has been calculated that 97 per cent of criminal cases begin and end in the Magistrates' Court in England and Wales.

Held: that the practice whereby the clerk of the court advised lay Justices of the Peace privately about matters of law and procedure was not a breach of the right of the accused to a fair trial under Article 6. The clerk of court was completely independent (usually a qualified lawyer i.e. a solicitor or an advocate) and who was on hand to provide impartial advice and who was trained to such a professional standard that he would be able to spot any potential conflicts of interest. The clerk would not, for instance, advise the judge when he was the father or some other close relation of the victim of the offence for which the accused is being tried. It would offend the clerk's professional code of conduct if it could be suggested that he took instructions or orders from a local authority or other external body regarding the advice provided to the judge.

 Key point: As a result of the introduction of the Scotland Act 1998 and the Human Rights Act 1998, the European Convention can now be directly enforced in the Scottish Courts without people having to lodge a case at the European Court of Human Rights.

Historical sources of law

These sources of law are now very much on the margins and play little importance in the development of Scots law. The historical sources of law include:

 ◆ The institutional writers
 ◆ Canon Law
 ◆ Feudal Law

 Key point: Historical source of law include the institutional writers, Canon Law and Feudal Law.

The institutional writers

In the past, various Scottish lawyers have contributed in an outstanding way to our understanding of the development of the Scots law. The ideas that these individuals promoted are still debated in Scottish universities to this day and may even be used in court cases to illustrate important legal points. These individuals include:

 ◆ Sir Thomas Craig who published *Jus Feudale* in 1655
 ◆ John Dalrymple, Viscount Stair, who published *Institutions of the Law of Scotland* in 1681
 ◆ Lord Bankton who published *An Institute of the Laws of Scotland* in 1751
 ◆ Professor John Erskine who published *Institute of the Law of Scotland* in 1772
 ◆ Baron Hume who published his *Lectures* between 1786 and 1822
 ◆ Professor George Bell who published *Commentaries on the Law of Scotland and the Principles of Mercantile Jurisprudence* in 1810, followed by the *Principles of the Law of Scotland* in 1829

As should be somewhat obvious, the institutional writers have not published anything since 1829!

In **McDyer *v* Celtic Football and Athletic Company Ltd and Others** (3 March 2000) the Court of Session heard arguments from both lawyers that drew heavily on the work of Bankton and Hume (see Chapter 3).

 Key point: The institutional writers are historical individuals who have recorded the development and contributed to our understanding of Scots law.

Canon Law

This is the law of the Christian Church which is based on the biblical books of the Old and New Testaments. It is worth remembering that this source played a very important role in the development of Scots law. When the Court of Session was created in 1532, the first Lord President was the Roman Catholic Abbot of Cambuskenneth. Furthermore, half the judges of the court were either Roman Catholic priests or monks who arrived at their decisions based on their training in Canon Law. After the period known as the Reformation from 1560 onwards, the influence of the Roman Catholic Church was swept away and the new Calvinist (Protestant) religion promoted by John Knox and the other Reformers held sway. However, Scotland remained a remarkably religious country until the 1960s.

Key point: Canon Law is the law of the Christian church.

Today, we obviously live in a less religious age, but the influences of Canon Law can still be felt. The Scots Law of Incest is based almost in its entirety on the Old Testament Book of Leviticus. The Book of Leviticus also forbids marriages between same sex partners and Scots law, despite recent proposals, has not yet recognised such unions. The fact that murder is also a crime could be said to be directly influenced by the Old Testament Book of Exodus which tells the story of the Jewish Prophet Moses who received the Ten Commandments directly from God. These Ten Commandments were a set of legal and moral rules for the Jewish people which were later adopted by Christians. Whether the vast majority of us like it or not, the influence of Canon Law is still felt in modern Scottish society.

Feudal Law

The feudal system is described as a multi-tiered system of land ownership and, consequently, it can be very complex. It was introduced to Scotland during the reign of King David I (1124–53). From the earliest days of the system, it operated, however, on very simple principles. The King (the Superior) would grant parcels of land to his supporters (vassals) who, in return, would administer the land (very often in the role of Sheriff – another English practice) and, more importantly, they would provide the King with soldiers in times of war or civil unrest.

In other words, the feudal system was all about maintaining royal power in Scotland (i.e. land for loyalty). The land was *never* granted absolutely – if a vassal (i.e. the person who held the land) failed to keep his side of the bargain, the King would remove all his rights to the land and appoint someone in his place. These supporters would in turn distribute parts of the land to their followers in order to retain their loyalty. Property is divided into two categories:

- Heritable property
- Moveable property

The fundamental principle of the feudal system always centred around tenure. This means that the land was granted according to certain conditions which the vassal had to carry out dutifully. It may be rather hard to believe, but the feudal system has survived into the twenty-first century. Nowadays, holders of land are not required to supply soldiers to the Crown, but they may be expected to pay for the privilege of owning the land to someone who holds the feudal superiority and landowners may even still be restricted from using their land in a particular way.

The feudal system is now set to be abolished in November 2004 when the provisions of the Abolition of Feudal Tenure etc. (Scotland) Act 2000 take effect.

 Key point: Feudal law is an ancient system of land ownership which is due to be abolished in November 2004.

The Legal Profession in Scotland

In Scotland, as in England, practising lawyers are divided into two groups:

- Solicitors and solicitor-advocates
- Advocates

Solicitors

This term has been in use in Scotland since 1922 and originated in England. Before 1922, solicitors in Scotland were referred to as notaries and writers.

Most practising Scottish lawyers will be solicitors. A solicitor can be hired directly by members of the public and solicitors' firms can be found in the high streets of most towns and cities in Scotland. Solicitors are trained to deal with all sorts of legal matters from the beginning of a case to its end. All solicitors must hold a current practising certificate and be members of the Law Society of Scotland. The Law Society is the recognised professional body which regulates solicitors and which disciplines those members who break the rules.

Solicitors will appear before both the criminal and the civil courts. Before the introduction of the Law Reform (Miscellaneous Provisions) Scotland Act 1990, solicitors were confined to the lower Scottish courts, namely, the District and Sheriff Courts. It is now possible for a solicitor to take further examinations in order to gain a qualification which makes it possible for him to appear before the higher Scottish courts such as the High Court of Justiciary, the Court of Session, the Privy Council and the House of Lords. This now means that a solicitor-advocate can appear before all the Scottish courts.

To become a solicitor, there are two possible paths:

By Law Society Examinations – a trainee must first register as a pre-diploma trainee with a firm of solicitors. The Law Society stipulates what exams the trainee must pass in order to complete this course. Trainees must become familiar with the three compulsory areas of conveyancing, court work and either trusts and executries or the work of a local authority. This initial training period will last for three years.

By university degree – a student will register for a Bachelor of Laws degree (LLB) in a Scots Law at one of the nine Scottish universities offering this course. It will take a student three years to gain a Pass degree and four years to gain an Honours degree. Many students will now complete an Honours degree owing to the very stiff competition for jobs with law firms.

Passing Law Society or university exams is only part of the training process. Budding solicitors will have to register for a Diploma in Legal Practice at one of the Scottish universities which provide this training. Entrance to the Diploma is by no means automatic and universities can afford to pick and choose the best students. Students are expected to attend the Diploma course for a period of 26 weeks. The Diploma course is highly practical in content and nature and students will often be taught by practising solicitors.

After completion of the Diploma in Legal Practice, the trainee will have to complete a period of further training of two years with a qualified solicitor. However, trainee solicitors can apply for a restricted practising certificate after one year which means that it is possible for them to appear in court as long they are supervised by a qualified solicitor. When trainees have finished their training, they can apply to the Law Society of Scotland for a full practising certificate. This will allow them to set up in business on their own, set up in partnership with other solicitors or become an employee of a firm, then an associate, then perhaps a partner.

Advocates

There are just under 500 practising advocates in Scotland today. These lawyers are specialists in pleadings in court. The pleading in court is concerned with the preparation and presentation of a case. Some Advocates have the reputation of being experts in a particular field of law and, as a result, they provide opinions on complex legal questions. They are a completely separate branch of the legal profession from solicitors. They are self-employed and do not form partnerships with other advocates. Advocates, unlike solicitors, are not members of a law firm. Advocates tend to be organised into units called stables with a clerk who will be responsible for administrative matters. Members of the profession will either be referred to as Junior Counsel or Senior Counsel. Senior Counsels are referred to as Queen's Counsels and have the initials QC after their names. Practising advocates of ten years' standing can apply to the Dean of the Faculty of Advocates to be admitted to the ranks of QCs.

As previously mentioned, the Law of Society of Scotland is the professional organisation which represents the interests of solicitors. The body which represents the interests of advocates is the Faculty of Advocates in Edinburgh. This a democratic organisation headed by a Dean who is elected by the membership. The Faculty of Advocates is self-regulating and it determines who can become an advocate.

In order to become an advocate, an individual will usually have gained at least a lower second class LLB Honours degree from one of the nine Scottish universities which offer this course or have passed the Law Society exams. There are other recognised degrees which would be acceptable to the Faculty of Advocates. Upon admission, the candidate (known as an Intrant) will have to pass Faculty exams and obtain a Diploma in Legal Practice from a Scottish university. The Intrant will have to complete a training period of 21 months with a qualified solicitor and serve an apprenticeship of nine months with a recognised advocate. The apprenticeship with an advocate is known as 'devilling'. Finally, the Intrant must pass the Faculty examination in Evidence, Practice and Procedure. An Intrant will then be admitted to membership of the Faculty of Advocates.

Advocates can appear in all the Scottish courts whether criminal or civil. Before the introduction of the Law Reform (Miscellaneous Provisions) Scotland Act 1990, only advocates could appear before the most senior Scottish courts – the High Court of Justiciary, the Court of Session, the Privy Council and the House of Lords. Solicitors were, therefore forced to instruct an advocate to appear on behalf of one of their clients before these courts. Now, of course, the small number of solicitor-advocates will be able to represent clients. However, ordinary solicitors will continue to instruct advocates or solicitor-advocates.

Advocates will be instructed by solicitors to appear in a case. They do not deal with members of the public directly. Advocates will attend consultations with a client, but this meeting will almost always take place in the presence of the client's solicitor. It should be appreciated that the solicitor will have done most of the work when it comes to preparing the case such as taking precognitions (witness statements) and keeping on top of the vast amounts of paperwork that the case will no doubt generate.

When appearing in court, a QC or Senior Counsel will be assisted by a Junior Counsel. Advocates have a distinctive appearance in that they wear a wig and a gown. This marks them out from a solicitor who will wear a simple black gown when appearing in court.

 Key points: In order to be regarded as a qualified lawyer in Scotland, an individual must either be a solicitor, a solicitor-advocate or an advocate.

Unqualified persons in the legal profession

For many years, clerks have been employed in law firms to undertake particular types of legal work in the areas of conveyancing, executries and trusts. An increasing number of law firms are also employing paralegals. Paralegals will often have a professional or vocational qualification, such as a Higher National Certificate or Diploma in Legal Services, often gained at a Further Education College. These types of employees, although not solicitors nor advocates, will have a background in the law and have a good working knowledge of legal procedures.

Law Reform (Miscellaneous Provisions) Scotland Act 1990

Under this Act, there exist provisions which would allow certain suitable persons to represent members of the public before the Scottish courts. These legal representatives would not need to be solicitors or advocates. Safeguards, however, would have to be in place to allow these individuals to practise law in Scotland. The people most likely to benefit from these provisions would be those individuals who possess a law degree, but who are not practising lawyers. The provisions in the Act of 1990 were never brought into force. In 2003, the Scottish Executive was considering proposals to open up the provision of legal services in Scotland in an attempt to increase competition by bringing the 1990 Act fully into force. This development is partly in response to events in England where it looks as if the Law Society and the Bar Council will lose their monopoly on legal services. Whether similar reforms will be introduced in Scotland remains to be seen.

 Key point: Many individuals who are not qualified lawyers also provide legal services, for example, paralegals and those individuals who hold a law degree.

The Law Officers of the Crown

Since the introduction of the Scotland Act in 1998, there are now three Scottish law officers. These individuals are:

- The Lord Advocate
- The Solicitor-General for Scotland
- The Advocate-General for Scotland

Before the creation of the Scottish Parliament, Scotland had just two law officers – the Lord Advocate and the Solicitor-General. The Lord Advocate and the Solicitor-General are members of the Scottish Executive in Edinburgh (the government of Scotland) whereas the Advocate-General is a member of the United Kingdom government in London.

These appointments are political in nature in the sense that the First Minister for Scotland will appoint the Lord Advocate and the Solicitor-General and the British Prime Minister will appoint the Advocate-General. Previous holders of the two most established law officer posts were often active politicians in either the Conservative or Labour Parties. Presently, however, only the Advocate-General is an elected politician who represents the Westminster constituency of Edinburgh Pentlands for the Labour Party. It will be appreciated that these individuals may have to leave their posts if there was a change of Scottish Executive or a change of British government.

Colin Boyd, the Lord Advocate is the most senior Scottish law officer. He is an advocate and holds the rank of Senior Counsel (Queen's Counsel). He has a number of important functions:

1 He is the principal state prosecutor with responsibility for the Scottish public prosecution system

2 He will appear as the prosecutor in major criminal trials, for example, the Lockerbie murder trial before the High Court of Justiciary

3 He is the head of the Crown Office and Procurator Fiscal Service, the Scottish Executive department with responsibility for all crimes in Scotland

4 He is the legal adviser to the Scottish Executive

5 He represents the Scottish Executive in the Scottish Courts, the European Court of Justice and the European Court of Human Rights

Elish Angiolini is the current Solicitor-General for Scotland. Mrs Angiolini is the first women and the first solicitor to hold this post. The Solicitor-General is the Lord Advocate's assistant. She is the first holder of the post not to be an advocate. However, the Solicitor-General can use the title Queen's Counsel and the initials QC will appear after her name despite the fact that she is a solicitor. Mrs Angiolini is entitled to use the initials QC because she acts as counsel to the Crown despite the fact that she is not and never has been a member of the Faculty of Advocates.

The Lord Advocate and the Solicitor-General are assisted in their duties by Advocate Deputes. Advocate Deputes are usually experienced, practising members of the Faculty of Advocates and they usually hold these positions for three years. Advocates Depute appear as prosecutors before the criminal courts in jury trials. The two law officers of the Crown Office and the Advocate Deputes are referred to as Crown Counsel.

The post of Advocate-General for Scotland was introduced as a result of the Scotland Act 1998. Dr Lynda Clark QC is the first holder of the post and she is an advocate. The Advocate-General is a member of the United Kingdom Government Department for Constitutional Affairs. The Advocate-General has a number of important functions:

1 She is a legal adviser to the British government on matters of Scots law.

2 She can represent the British government in legal proceedings before the Scottish courts and the Judicial Committee of the Privy Council where the case involves devolution or human rights issues.

3 She has the right to refer Scottish Parliament Bills to the Judicial Committee of the Privy Council in order to ensure that the Scottish Parliament is acting within its powers.

4 She serves on a number of British Cabinet committees.

The Advocate-General is also referred to as Crown Counsel.

Key point: There are three Scottish Law Officers who provide legal advice to the Crown on matters of Scots law – the Lord Advocate, the Solicitor-General and the Advocate-General.

Judicial appointments

All appointments of Judges and Sheriffs in Scotland are within the gift of the Queen acting on the recommendation of the First Minister for Scotland. The First Minister, in turn, seeks the advice of the independent Judicial Appointments Board which was established in 2002. The Board now advertises judicial posts, as and when appropriate, and will interview candidates and provide a shortlist of people suitable for appointment as judges. The Lord President of the Court of Session (Scotland's most senior Judge) is also consulted by the First Minister before recommendations are made. The Judicial Appointments Board has its own Secretariat but once they submit their reports, the Justice Department will have responsibility for implementing the Board's recommendations. The Board consists of ten individuals having an equal number of lay and legal members.

On 1 November 2002, the first judges and Sheriff Principal to be appointed under the new system were announced. Mr Philip Brodie QC and Mr Alistair Campbell QC have been appointed as Senators of the College of Justice. Lord Brodie replaced Lord Coulsfield and Lord Campbell replaced Lord Cameron of Lochbroom.

The Queen also approved the appointment of Sheriff Iain Macphail QC to be Sheriff Principal of Lothian and Borders who succeeded Sheriff Principal Gordon Nicholson QC. These judicial posts were advertised in the press.

In order to be appointed as a Sheriff, suitable candidates must have been practising lawyers, either as solicitors or advocates, for a period of at least ten years. As for appointment to the High Court or the Court of Session, Sheriffs or Sheriff Principals with five years or more experience can be appointed to the senior bench. It is possible for solicitors to be appointed directly to the High Court or the Court of Session. However, a solicitor must have had rights of audience before these courts and exercised these rights for a continuous period of five years.

 Key point: All appointments of Judges and Sheriffs in Scotland are within the gift of the Queen acting on the recommendation of the First Minister for Scotland. The First Minister, in turn, seeks the advice of the independent Judicial Appointments Board.

The appointment of judges to the House of Lords is not the responsibility of the Scottish Parliament. These judges will continue to be appointed by the Queen. The British Prime Minister and the Lord Chancellor will continue to advise the Queen in relation to these appointments. It is normal practice for the Prime Minister and the Lord Chancellor to consult with the Lord President of the Court of Session and the First Minister for Scotland concerning the appointment of Scottish Law Lords.

A Scottish Law Lord must have held a high judicial office for a period of not less than two years or have been, at or before that time, an advocate in Scotland, or a solicitor entitled to appear in the Court of Session and the High Court of Justiciary, for not less than 15 years.

Key point: Appointments of Scottish judges to the House of Lords are made by the Queen who acts on the advice of the British Prime Minister and the Lord Chancellor. The Lord President of the Court of Session and the First Minister for Scotland are usually consulted in relation to these appointments.

Sheriffs and judges of the Court of Session and the High Court of Justiciary are completely independent of the Scottish Executive. The Justice Department of the Scottish Executive can investigate complaints regarding the way in which a Sheriff handled a case, but the decision of a Sheriff can only be challenged by way of an appeal to a superior court. The appeal system is the way in which the decision of a judge can be questioned.

The First Minister, however, can when asked by the Lord President of the Court of Session or in such other circumstances as the First Minister thinks fit, form a tribunal to investigate and report on whether a judge of the Court of Session or the Chairman of the Scottish Land Court is unfit for office by reason of inability, neglect of duty or misbehaviour. If the tribunal decides that the person under investigation is not fit to hold judicial office, section 95 of the Scotland Act 1998 gives the First Minister the right to make a motion to the Scottish Parliament seeking a resolution that he should recommend to the Queen that the judge be removed from office.

The removal of Sheriffs is within the power of the Scottish Parliament in terms of the Sheriff Courts Act 1971. Such a drastic step would occur only if the Lord President and the Lord Justice-Clerk recommended such action. The grounds for removing a Sheriff are by reason of inability, neglect of duty or misbehaviour.

 Key point: Sheriffs and judges of the High Court and Court of Session are completely independent of the Scottish Executive and Scottish Parliament.

The Civil Justice System

The civil justice system, unlike criminal law, exists to resolve legal disputes between private individuals in areas as diverse as family law, company law, partnership law, banking and finance law, sale of goods and services, consumer law, personal injury claims, trusts, defamation actions, succession issues and divorce.

 Key point: The civil justice system exists to resolve legal disputes between private individuals.

In many situations, the main function of the civil justice system will be to compensate the victim who has suffered a loss as a result of someone's wrongful behaviour. Surprisingly, most legal disputes are firmly in the realm of the civil jurisdiction. However, amongst members of the Scottish public, there still remains a surprisingly high degree of ignorance about the importance of the civil justice system. Crime, of course, grabs the headlines and takes hold of the public's imagination in a way that civil law never could.

Criminal law, on the other hand, is an attempt by the state to maintain law and order by punishing certain individuals who indulge in behaviour which is regarded as criminal and anti-social. The state uses the criminal law, therefore, to punish criminals on behalf of the community or society.

 Key point: Criminal law is an attempt by the state to maintain law and order through the punishment of criminal and anti-social behaviour.

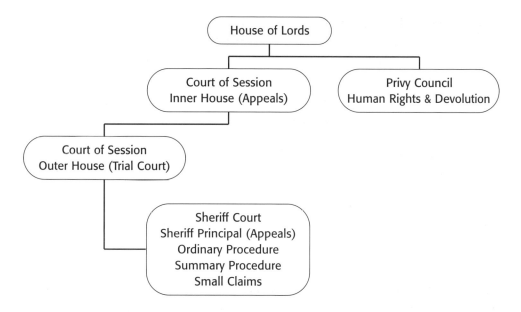

Unlike criminal law, the parties to a civil action are not required to demonstrate that their version of the story has been proved beyond a reasonable doubt. Civil trials have a much lower standard of proof or evidence. A judge in a civil action will decide the outcome of a case by weighing up the balance of probabilities. This means that a Sheriff, for example, will decide to favour one party over the other by favouring the version of the facts which he considers to be more accurate or more believable. Technically, it is possible for the Sheriff to decide the case on the testimony of one witness and that witness could be one of the parties. Corroboration or the ability to back up all the evidence is not strictly required as in criminal law. Obviously, the more reliable witnesses and evidence that a party in a civil action can rely upon will strengthen the case in their favour.

The parties to a civil action are referred to as *litigants*.

The *pursuer* is the person who brings the dispute to the attention of the court by lodging a legal action. The *defender* is the party against whom the legal action is being brought. At this point, it is important to stress that the civil courts are a facility or a resource which the state provides in order to resolve civil disputes in a peaceful fashion.

People cannot be forced to use the civil courts if they have no desire to do so. If, for example, someone owes you money for work that you have performed for them and you do not receive the money, it is entirely up to you whether you decide to pursue the matter before the courts if persuasion fails. A judge will not come to your door and issue you with a personal invitation to attend your local court and have your case heard. If you do nothing, you have no one to blame but yourself for your predicament. The state merely provides court facilities which the parties to a private or civil dispute are free to use if they wish.

 Key point: The pursuer and the defender are the parties to a civil action and together they are referred to as litigants.

The civil justice system in Scotland consists of three major courts:

◆ **The House of Lords**
◆ **The Court of Session**
◆ **The Sheriff Court**

The Sheriff Court and the Court of Session

The Sheriff Court and the Court of Session are both courts of trial and courts of appeal. The House of Lords, by comparison, hears Scottish civil appeals only.

Civil cases are allocated to the various courts for trial by reference to the value of the case. The Court of Session can hear cases which have a monetary value of more than £1500. If the case is valued at below £1500, it must be heard in the Sheriff Court – although the Sheriff Court can also deal with actions which have a value greater than £1500. It is possible, therefore, for a case which has a value greater than £1500 to be heard by either the Sheriff Court or the Court of Session. This is known as concurrent jurisdiction.

 Key point: The value of a case does not include any claim for expenses or interest. These matters are dealt with after the court has made its decision.

Where the pursuer has a choice of whether to raise a claim before the Sheriff Court or the Court of Session, he will often choose the Sheriff Court for very sensible reasons. The Sheriff Court is a local court and if the pursuer lives outside Edinburgh he may not want to go the bother of travelling to and from Edinburgh (not to mention the travelling costs). There are 49 Sheriff Courts located throughout Scotland, whereas there is only a single Court of Session with 32 judges. It is likely that the Sheriff Court will be able to deal with the case more quickly than the Court of Session. A pursuer attending the Sheriff Court will normally make use of the services of a single lawyer (his solicitor). If the action is before the Court of Session, the pursuer will have to hire a solicitor who will then have to instruct an advocate to appear before the Court of Session.

 Key point: the shared jurisdiction of the Sheriff Court and the Court of Session is known as concurrent jurisdiction and this applies to cases valued at £1500 or more.

A pursuer will only really prefer the Court of Session if the cases involves very large amounts of money or if it is likely that the defender will eventually appeal to the Court of Session if the pursuer wins the case. However, as already discussed, the Sheriff Court is not restricted in any way to the value of cases that it can deal with. The choice of court will often be dictated by the pursuer's particular needs and personal circumstances.

The Sheriff Court

The Sheriff Court is the lowest civil court in Scotland. However, it is also the busiest civil court in Scotland. The Sheriff Court is organised into geographical units called sheriffdoms. There are six sheriffdoms in Scotland:

◆ **Glasgow and Strathkelvin**
◆ **North Strathclyde**

- South Strathclyde, Dumfries and Galloway
- Tayside, Central and Fife
- Lothian and Borders
- Grampian, Highland and Islands

The six sheriffdoms are further divided into 49 Sheriff Court districts. These districts are, however, not divided equally between the sheriffdoms. The sheriffdoms which are located in the central belt of Scotland i.e. the geographical area roughly between the Rivers Clyde and Forth, has the largest concentration of Sheriff Courts. This arrangement clearly makes sense because most of the Scottish population lives in this area and there is a much higher demand for Sheriff Court services.

 Key point: There are six Sheriffdoms and 49 Sheriff Court Districts in Scotland.

In each Sheriff Court district, there will be one or more Sheriffs who will act as judges and administer justice in the various civil disputes that are brought before the court. Each sheriffdom has a senior Sheriff known as the Sheriff Principal whose responsibility it is to hear civil appeals from the Sheriff Court.

The jurisdiction or powers of the Sheriff Court in civil cases

The Sheriff Court can hear all sorts of civil disputes and it is most definitely not limited to dealing with cases which involve small amounts of money or are of little importance. There is nothing, in principle, to prevent the Sheriff Court from giving judgement in a multi-million pound legal action. The jurisdiction or powers of the Sheriff Court are very extensive as to the types of cases that it can hear. In fact, the Sheriff Court has privative or exclusive power to judge cases which are valued below the sum of £1500. This means that all cases valued below this figure must be dealt with by the Sheriff Court. As for cases which have a value exceeding £1500, the Sheriff Court shares jurisdiction with the Court of Session in Edinburgh. Unlike England, Scotland does not have an institution like the Coroner's Court which deals with fatal accidents and suspicious deaths. In Scotland, therefore, the Sheriff usually deals with fatal accident enquiries and suspicious deaths.

 Key point: Cases valued below the sum of £1500 must be dealt with by the Sheriff Court.

If a pursuer is determined to begin a legal action against a defender in the Sheriff Court, a key question must be asked:

'Which Sheriff Court has jurisdiction or the right to hear the case?'

It will be remembered that are six sheriffdoms and 49 Sheriff Court districts in Scotland. However, there are rules of jurisdiction which can help the pursuer to choose the correct Sheriff Court. The jurisdiction of the Sheriff Court is extremely broad and will be based on a number of factors. These grounds of jurisdiction can then be used to decide which Court will hear the case:

1   In which Sheriff Court district does the defender live?

This is usually the most common way in which a particular Sheriff Court can be said to have jurisdiction over the defender. The pursuer will quite simply find out where the defender lives. If the defender lived in Greenock, then the pursuer would lodge his claim at Greenock Sheriff Court.

2   Does the defender carry on a business within a particular Sheriff Court district?

This is particularly useful if the defender is a business or carries on a business. The pursuer would make enquiries as to where the defender has his physical place of business. If the defender carried on a business in Paisley, then the action could be commenced at Paisley Sheriff Court.

3   Does the legal action centre around the performance of a contract (a legally enforceable agreement) and, if so, in which Sheriff Court district was the contract to be performed or carried out?

What if the defender, a builder, had agreed to build a garden wall for a pursuer who lived in Aberdeen and, subsequently, the defender failed to carry out his side of the bargain? The pursuer could argue that as the contract was to be carried out or performed in Aberdeen, then Aberdeen Sheriff Court should have jurisdiction to hear the case.

4   Does the legal action involve heritable property (i.e. land, buildings and things which form part of the land) and, if so, in which Sheriff Court district is the heritable property physically situated or located?

What if, for example, a tenant wished to force a landlord to comply with his contractual duty under the terms of lease to carry out repairs to the leaking roof of a property? If the property was situated in Edinburgh, then Edinburgh Sheriff Court could have jurisdiction over the dispute.

5   Does the legal action relate to a delictual action (an action for damages for loss or injury wrongfully caused) and, if so, in which Sheriff Court district did the loss or injury occur?

What if the defender, as a result of his dangerous or careless driving, knocked down and seriously injured the pursuer? The question to ask here is where did the accident occur? If the answer is somewhere in Glasgow, then Glasgow Sheriff Court could have jurisdiction if the pursuer or his family decide to raise a personal injury claim against the defender.

 Key point: The Sheriff Court is said to have geographical jurisdiction, jurisdiction over certain people and jurisdiction over certain property.

Civil Procedures in the Sheriff Court

There are three civil procedures in the Sheriff Court:

◆ Small claims
◆ Summary procedure
◆ Ordinary procedure

Technically, small claims are part of the summary procedure, but it is often more sensible to separate small claims from summary procedure. We shall look at each procedure in turn.

An important feature of civil justice in the Sheriff Court is that the Sheriff sits alone to hear the case. There is no jury and it is very rare in Scotland for a jury to participate in a civil trial.

 Key point: For practical purposes, there are three procedures in the Sheriff Court: Small Claims, Summary Procedures and Ordinary Procedures.

Serving a summons in a Sheriff Court Action

A pursuer, who is an ordinary member of the public, cannot take it upon himself to issue a summons to the defender personally. There are certain procedures which must be followed. Before serving the summons, the pursuer or his representatives must secure the permission or authority of the Sheriff Court that will hear the case. It is also important to bear in mind that, in the interests of fairness, the defender must be given a reasonable opportunity to weigh up his options when he is served with a summons.

The court forms or summons will contain all the essential information of the case i.e. the names and addresses of the pursuer and the defender; what action the pursuer wishes the court to take; the amount claimed by the pursuer plus expenses and interest the name of the pursuer's solicitor or authorised lay representative; and the pursuer's statement of claim i.e. an account of why he is raising the claim in the first place.

The summons that the defender receives is similar to the pursuer's copy. However, there are important differences. The defender's copy will spell out the various options open to the defender. These options include admitting the claim and paying the pursuer. The defender may be able to make payment to the pursuer by instalments if he is not a business. The defender may choose to object to the claim and he can give the pursuer notice of his intention to defend the claim. Finally, the defender could choose to do nothing at all. This is not a very wise course of action because the pursuer could ultimately ask the court to award a court order or decree against the defender – even if the defender failed to turn up in court.

There are three possible ways in which a summons can be served on the defender:

- Service of the summons by the Sheriff Clerk (available to members of the public, but not companies and partnerships in small claims only).
- Postal service by a solicitor or a sheriff officer where Royal Mail recorded delivery will be used.
- Personal service by a sheriff officer accompanied by a witness where the summons will physically be handed to the defender or his representative. Failing this, the sheriff officer can pin a copy of the summons to the door of the defender's property and, as a back-up procedure, a copy of the summons will be sent to the defender by recorded delivery.

 Key point: There are three ways in which a summons can be served – service by the Sheriff Clerk, postal service and service by Sheriff Officers.

The pursuer must make sure that the defender is given a period of 21 days to respond to the summons. If the defender lives or carries on a business outside Europe, 42 days is the period of notice which must be given.

In small claims and summary actions, there are pre-printed forms which are available from the Sheriff Court. The pursuer or his solicitor will have to complete the various forms which make up the summons. In ordinary actions, however, the pursuer's solicitor will have to draft a summons as the Sheriff Court does not provide a form. This type of summons is referred to as an initial writ and they tend to follow a particular pattern.

Small claims procedure

The small claims procedure was introduced to the Sheriff Court on 30 November 1988 by the Law Reform (Miscellaneous Provisions) (Scotland) Act 1988. This new procedure was implemented as the result of the recommendations made by the Royal Commission on Legal Services in Scotland (The Hughes Commission).

The Commission's main recommendation was that:

There should be a small claims procedure within the Sheriff Court which is sufficiently simple, cheap, quick and informal to encourage individual litigants to use it themselves without legal representation. . . . Small claims justice should not be seen as second-hand justice.

It is arguable whether the aims of the Commission have been met. The small claims procedure in the Sheriff Court is now little better than a debt collection agency used mainly by banks, credit card companies and finance companies to pursue feckless debtors. In point of fact, the number of ordinary members of the public making use of the system has decreased dramatically over the last few years. The high expectations which greeted the introduction of the small claims procedure in 1988 have almost certainly not been realised.

A great deal has also been made about the simplicity of the system. However, ordinary members of the public who have attempted to take a case to the small claims court have often been baffled by the complexity of the procedure. This means that, at some point, legal advice will have to be sought in order for the claim to proceed – something that the architects of the system were keen to avoid.

 Key point: The small claims should be sufficiently simple, cheap, quick and informal in order to encourage individual litigants to use it themselves without legal representation.

A small claim will include actions that have a value of £750 or less. If your claim is valued at above £750, then you would not be able to commence a court action using the small claims procedure.

 Key point: Small claims actions can be raised where the value of the claim does not exceed £750.

There are three types of small claims action:

An action for payment of money

This is the most straightforward type of claim. Here, the pursuer will be raising a court action to recover a sum of money (which must not exceed £750) that he alleges is owed to him by the defender. This type of action usually involves the failure to repay private debts, business debts or loans from banks, building societies or finance companies. The small claims procedure can also deal with smaller types of personal injury claims.

An action for an implement of an obligation

The pursuer is asking the court to force the defender to carry out some duty which he has undertaken to complete usually under the terms of a contract. If, for example, the pursuer had entered into a contract with an antiques dealer (the defender) to buy a valuable painting and the dealer later refused to hand over the item, the pursuer could raise this type of action in order to get possession of the goods. The item which is the centre of the dispute must be valued at less than £750 because the pursuer must also state that he would be prepared to accept an alternative sum of money as compensation if the item was no longer in the hands of the defender.

An action for the recovery of moveable property

This type of action allows the pursuer to recover property which the defender is refusing to return to him. If you had put your television into a repair shop and the shop later refused to return your property to you, you could raise an action at the Sheriff Court to have the item returned to you. Again, you would have to state that you would be prepared to accept an alternative sum of money which must not exceed £750 if the defender could not return your property to you.

 Key point: There are three types of actions in small claims – payment of money, implement of an obligation and recovery of moveable property.

Starting a small claims action

The pursuer must first complete the appropriate pre-printed forms and return these to the correct Sheriff Court which has jurisdiction to hear the case.

Once authority has been granted from the Sheriff Court, the pursuer will have to serve a copy of the summons on the defender. The summons contains two important dates – the Return Date and the Calling Day. The Return Date is the date by which the defender must return his copy of the summons to the Sheriff Clerk's Department. The Return Date will normally be exactly one week before the case is first to be heard in court.

The second date on the summons is known as the Calling Day. The Calling Day is the date when the case will first be heard (or called) in court. Both parties and their solicitors (if any) must attend court on this date.

Both copies of the summons, must be returned to the Sheriff Court by the parties before the Return Date.

In a defended small claim, the parties will first meet formally on the Calling Day when a Hearing will take place. At the Hearing, the Sheriff will attempt to establish the broad facts of the case and to discover if there is any common ground between the parties. The parties will be asked if there is a possibility that the dispute could be resolved there and then. If this is not possible, the Sheriff will continue the Hearing to a later date when the parties will have to attend court in order for a trial to take place. At the trial, the parties will come to court with their respective witnesses and evidence. A trial or proof will usually take place some six weeks after the Calling Day.

Key point: In a defended small claim, the parties will first meet formally on the Calling Day when a Hearing will take place. The dispute could be settled at this Hearing but, if this is not possible, the Sheriff will continue the Hearing to another date.

The conduct of the Hearing in the small claims court is very informal. The Sheriff usually chooses not to wear his wig and gown in order to put the parties at ease. Furthermore, the Sheriff will often come down from the bench and conduct the Hearing by sitting with the parties at a table in the courtroom. The parties usually address the Sheriff simply as 'Sheriff' and not by the more formal title of 'my Lord' or 'my Lady'. The Sheriff will hear the parties, their witnesses and scrutinise the evidence presented. At the end of the Hearing, the Sheriff will make a decision or, failing this, a written decision will be issued within 28 days.

The parties in a small claims dispute are not required to hire the services of a solicitor. It is perfectly possible for a party to represent themselves from beginning to end. If, however, a party lacks the confidence to do this, they can appoint a suitable person to act for them. The Sheriff must give his approval before such a person can act for one of the parties. Suitable lay representatives might include Citizens Advice Bureaux Workers, Trading Standards Officers, community workers, individuals who hold a law degree but are not practising solicitors or any decent and articulate members of the community.

Very often, a party will be forced to represent themselves or ask a suitable person to conduct the case on their behalf because Legal Aid is not available to ordinary people to help them pay the costs of legal representation in the Sheriff Court under the small claims system. However, Legal Aid Advice and Assistance might be available to offset the costs of an interview with a solicitor when a party is first seeking advice in respect of the small claims system. The fact that a party does not need a solicitor to conduct the case for him has been hailed as an advantage of the system whereby ordinary people can take a case to court and do the whole thing themselves without running up huge legal bills. Cynics might see this as a distinct disadvantage as people might lack the necessary confidence to pursue or defend a claim without the help of a solicitor, especially if you happen to come from a poorer or less well-educated background.

 Key point: The procedure at the small claims Hearing is very informal and the parties need not be legally represented.

The amount of expenses claimable

Another advantage of the small claims procedure is the amount of expenses that can be awarded to any party. A maximum of £75 can be awarded and if the claim is less than £200 no expenses will be granted. This is regarded as a huge incentive for parties to use the system because a characteristic of the civil legal system is that the loser has to pay the winner's legal fees in addition to their own legal expenses. Restricting the amount of legal expenses payable to £75 should, in theory, encourage more people to use the procedure. However, £75 might be viewed as a large sum of money by an unemployed, single parent on state benefits.

 Key point: As regards expenses in Small Claims actions, a maximum of £75 can be awarded and if the claim is less than £200 no expenses will be granted.

Appeals

It is possible to appeal against the decision of the Sheriff, but the party wishing to do so must lodge an appeal on a point of law. Appeals are made to the Sheriff Principal, the senior Sheriff in each Sheriffdom. In practice, appeals from a small claims case tend to be rare.

Quite simply, the party making the appeal (the appellant) must demonstrate that the Sheriff got the law wrong. The person making an appeal cannot do so simply because they happen to dislike the Sheriff's decision. The appeal must raise an important point of law and, therefore, any doubt or confusion regarding the law can be removed.

In an appeal, the procedure is much more formal and the parties will have to hire solicitors to appear for them. The normal rules of expenses apply in an appeal and this is something the parties will have to bear in mind i.e. the loser will usually have to pay the costs of the winner which could amount to quite a substantial sum of money. However, Legal Aid is often granted to a party who cannot afford to pay the services of a solicitor from his own pocket.

 Key point: An appeal on a point of law regarding the decision of the Sheriff can be made to the Sheriff Principal.

Summary procedure

This procedure was first introduced to the Sheriff Court in 1976 and was supposedly aimed at making the Sheriff Court much more efficient and more accessible to members of the public.

Claims which are dealt with by summary procedure are valued at between £750 and £1500.

The Sheriff Court under summary procedure can deal with a variety of actions:

Payment

These types of action are similar to a small claims action. The main difference here is that such actions are for sums of money from £750 to £1500.

Specific implement

Again, as with small claims, the pursuer is asking the court to force the defender to carry out his contractual duties. If, as an alternative, the pursuer is seeking compensation, this sum of money must fall between £750 and £1500.

Recovery of heritage or moveables

This involves situations where the pursuer wants the court to order the defender to return the pursuer's property. Theoretically, the value of the property is not important, but if the pursuer wishes to claim a sum of money as an alternative to the property this amount must fall between £750 and £1500. Unlike small claims where the pursuer can only recover moveable property, this action allows the pursuer to recover heritable property (land and buildings) which the defender is preventing him from using, for example, where the defender refuses to leave a house that he is renting from the pursuer when the lease runs out.

Sequestration for rent

This allows a landlord to sue for outstanding rent from a tenant. It does not apply to any other debts that the tenant may owe to the landlord. With the authority of the court, the landlord can instruct sheriff officers to enter the premises used by the tenant for the purpose of making a list of the tenant's goods. This list (or inventory) will represent the value of the debt (between £750 and £1500) that the tenant owes to the landlord. Once the sheriff officers have completed their task, the tenant cannot sell or give away these goods until the debt is paid. If the tenant did this, he would be in contempt of court and he would face the possibility of prison or a fine.

Multiplepoinding

This is useful where two or more people claim ownership of the same property, for example, when a car has been stolen and the ownership of the item is in question, the court can decide who is the legal owner of the goods. Such an action is also useful where businesses come to an end and questions will arise concerning who owns certain property such as money in a partnership bank account or office equipment.

Furthcoming

The pursuer will always be concerned that the defender will empty bank accounts or get rid of assets before the court has made its decision in a payment action. Furthcoming allows the pursuer to apply to the court, pending its decision on the main action, for an order to freeze the defender's bank accounts or property which may be held by third parties for the defender. If the defender is prevented from getting access to his bank or property, he has real incentive for paying what he owes to the pursuer. It should be noted that furthcoming applies only to the defender's assets which are held by third parties and not to assets which the defender controls personally.

 Key point: Summary procedure in the Sheriff Court deals with a variety of actions valued over £750 but less than £1500.

Starting a Summary Procedure Action

As with a small claims action, the pursuer must first complete the appropriate pre-printed forms and return these to the correct Sheriff Court which has jurisdiction to hear the case. These pre-printed forms are very similar to the ones used in a small claims action.

The pursuer will have to have the court's authority before the summons can be served on the defender who, again, will have to be given the appropriate notice period. The summons will alert the defender to two dates, the Return Date and the Calling Date. The defender must return the summons to the court by the Return Date. If the parties are unwilling to settle the case on the Calling Date, the Sheriff will have to arrange a civil trial or a proof.

 Key point: The pursuer can commence a summary cause by filling in a pre-printed form which must be served on the defender using either postal or personal service.

In summary procedure, however, the parties should be legally represented by solicitors. The normal rules of expenses also apply to summary procedure in that the costs that the losing party may have to pay are not restricted to £75. It is highly likely that the loser will have to pay his opponent's legal fees (which could be substantial) as well as his own.

At the proof, the parties will come to court with witnesses and evidence. The parties' solicitors will lead their clients and their witnesses through the evidence. Both solicitors will have the right to cross-examine the other party and their witnesses. At the end of the Hearing, the Sheriff can make a decision or he can reserve judgement for 28 days and then issue a written decision.

 Key point: A summary cause Hearing is more formal than a small claims action and the parties need to be legally represented.

Appeals from a judgement of the Sheriff in a summary procedure action go to the Sheriff Principal and the appeal hearing is very similar to a small claims Hearing. Appeals must be made on a point of law i.e. one of the parties must claim that the Sheriff got the law wrong. There may even be the possibility of a further right of appeal from the Sheriff Principal to the Inner House of the Court of Session.

 Key point: Appeals on a point of law from the judgement of the Sheriff in summary causes go to the Sheriff Principal – there may even be a further appeal to the Court of Session.

Ordinary procedure

This type of action must be used by a pursuer where the sum claimed exceeds £1500 in value.

Ordinary procedure covers a wide range of cases:

- Payment actions (such as debt recovery)
- Delict (such as personal injury and property damage claims)
- Family law (such as divorce, custody, separation, paternity and adoption)
- Recovery of heritable and moveable property
- Specific implement
- Multiplepoinding
- Interdict (a decree preventing the defender from doing something or requiring the defender to do something)
- Furthcoming
- Declarator (a decree which sets out the rights of the parties to the dispute)

Many of these actions can be found in small claims and summary procedure. However, they will have to be dealt with under ordinary procedure because the value of the case is over £1500. The Sheriff can also chair fatal accident enquiries and hear applications from Social Work Authorities.

 Key point: Ordinary cause actions deal with a variety of cases that have a value of £1500 or more.

The ordinary procedure is the most complex type of case in the Sheriff Court and individual litigants would be very unwise to represent themselves. Generally speaking, a solicitor will represent a party in an ordinary procedure action, although it is perfectly possible that an advocate may appear for one of the litigants at the trial.

There is a great deal of preparation that will have to be carried out before a trial or a proof can be set. Once the parties have prepared their evidence and identified their witnesses, the Sheriff will set a date for the trial or proof.

As with the other Sheriff Court actions, the parties or their solicitors will be given every opportunity to cross-examine the other party and witnesses at the trial or proof. The Sheriff can usually decide the case after the Hearing has been completed. Sometimes, the Sheriff will delay judgement and issue a written decision at a later date, but there must be no unreasonable delays on the Sheriff's part.

 Key point: Ordinary cause actions are the most complex type of Sheriff court case and the parties will need to be legally represented at the Hearing.

Appeals in ordinary procedure are more complicated. A party has the choice of appealing to the Sheriff Principal or directly to the Inner House of the Court of Session. It may be cheaper and more practical in the long run to appeal to the Inner House because decisions of the Sheriff Principal can be challenged by an appeal to the Court of Session. There may even be a further appeal from the Court of Session to the House of Lords.

Appeals are, again, made on a point of law whereby one of the parties is claiming that the judge or judges got the law wrong.

 Key point: In Ordinary Causes, appeals can go the Sheriff Principal and then go further to the Inner House of the Court of Session. Alternatively, appeals could go to the Inner House directly, thus, cutting out the Sheriff Principal altogether. An appeal may even end up going to the House of Lords.

The Court of Session

The Court of Session is Scotland's supreme civil court and it has its permanent headquarters in Parliament House in Edinburgh. It is both a court of first instance (where cases will be heard for the first time) and a court of appeal. The court was founded in 1532 by the College of Justice Act. The first Lord President of the court was the Abbot of Cambuskenneth. The background to the creation of this court is an interesting one as Pope Clement VII provided the financial assistance which led to its establishment. This papal handout was granted on the condition that half the judges on the new court were clerics i.e. Roman Catholic priests or brothers with a strong background in Canon law. This arrangement remained in place until the Reformation, led by John Knox, established the Protestant faith as the new state religion of Scotland later in the sixteenth century.

The present membership of court numbers 32 judges who are given the formal title of 'Senators of the College of Justice'. Alternatively, they may be referred to as 'Lords of Council and Session'. The two most important members of the court are the Lord President (currently Lord Cullen) and his deputy the Lord Justice Clerk (currently Lord Gill). These two individuals, of course, also hold the most senior positions in the High Court of Justiciary.

 Key point: The Court of Session is Scotland's supreme civil court.

Unlike the Sheriff Court, which is restricted to hearing cases from a particular local area in Scotland (from the appropriate Sheriffdom or Sheriff Court District), the jurisdiction of the Court of Session covers the whole of Scotland. The Court of Session will only be excluded from hearing cases by an Act of Parliament or where the Sheriff Court has exclusive jurisdiction to hear a case i.e. summary actions with a monetary value of under £1500. In turn, the Court of Session has the sole right to hear the following types of cases:

- Declarator of marriage
- Reduction (cancellation) of a contract
- Tenor of a lost document where its authenticity has to be proved
- Actions of adjudication where rights of ownership of heritable property are granted to a pursuer
- Actions which involve the authenticity of lost documents
- Liquidation of limited companies where the share capital has a value of more than £120,000

 Key point: The jurisdiction of the Court of Session is the whole of Scotland.

However, it should be remembered that the Outer House of the Court of Session and the Sheriff Court will potentially share jurisdiction where the case is valued at £1500 or more. In such situations, it will be up to the litigants whether they decide to use the services of the Sheriff Court or the Court of Session. Obviously, matters of cost, time and convenience will play a large part in deciding which court is chosen to hear the case.

The court is organised into an Outer House and an Inner House. Cases in the Outer House are either commenced by way of an action or a petition. An action involves the pursuer serving a summons on the defender. A petition, on the other hand, seeks the assistance of the Court of Session in some matter and is a less formal procedure than a summons. The petitioner is asking the court to do something which is right and proper and which he has no authority to do himself.

The Outer House has a membership of 19 judges who are known as Lords Ordinary. The Lords Ordinary will usually sit alone to hear cases, although on extremely rare occasions a civil jury of 12 may be present. The services of a civil jury may be called upon in a defamation action or even certain personal injury claims. Jury trials also take place where the case involves essential error and allegations of force and fear in relation to contract (see Chapter 2). The Lords Ordinary will hear cases for the first time which involve delict, contract, commercial cases, trusts, succession, family actions and judicial review. Until the 1970s, the Court of Session was the only court in Scotland which had exclusive jurisdiction over divorce actions. The Sheriff Court can now hear divorce cases.

As can be seen, the Outer House of the Court of Session deals with a very broad range of legal work. Certain judges are regarded as experts in a particular field of law. Currently, Lords Clark, MacKay of Drumadoon and Drummond Young are regarded as the leading commercial judges in the Court of Session. Commercial actions cover cases involving sales of goods and services, banking and insurance transactions and issues relating to contracts generally.

 Key point: The Outer House is primarily a trial court.

It is rare for the Inner House to hear cases at first instance. To all intents and purposes, the Inner House is really an appeal court – although it does sometimes sit as a trial court. The Inner House is organised into two units known as the First and

Second Divisions. It is wrong to assume that the First Division is superior in any way to the Second Division as both have equal authority. The Lord President heads First Division and the Lord Justice Clerk is responsible for the work of the Second Division. It used to be the case that, until 1933, a litigant had a choice as to which Division heard a case, but this right was abolished and given the fact that a lot of emphasis is placed on the equality of both Divisions this would appear to have been a sensible reform.

Sometimes in a particularly difficult case, both Divisions will come together to form a court of seven judges as in the case of **Scottish Discount Company v Blin (1986)**. However, in **Wright v Bell (1905)**, the entire court of 13 judges heard the case. The members of both Divisions will be appointed by the First Minister of Scotland, on behalf of the Queen, after consultations have been held with the Lord President and Lord Justice Clerk.

Each Division has a membership of four Judges, but in order for the court to sit and make judgements, three judges must be present. In more recent times, the increasing numbers of cases being brought before the Inner House has meant that it will be common for an additional or Extra Division of three judges to be formed to hear cases. This arrangement is a convenient way in which pressure can be taken off the other two Divisions. The main task of the Divisions is to deal with cases on appeal from the Outer House, the Sheriff Court and certain tribunals and other bodies, for example, the Employment Appeal Tribunal and the Lands Tribunal for Scotland to name but two. Sometimes if a case is particularly important or it involves a particularly complex point of law, or if it is necessary to overrule a previous binding decision of the Court of Session, five or more Judges may sit together to hear the appeal.

 Key point: The Inner House is primarily an appeal court.

There is nothing to prevent people from representing themselves in the Court of Session. However, this is not recommended as procedures of the Court of Session can be very complex. More usually, a litigant will be represented by an advocate, who is also referred to as 'counsel'. Companies and partnerships must always be legally represented. Since the introduction of the Law Reform (Miscellanous Provisions) (Scotland) Act 1990, solicitor-advocates – solicitors who have completed additional, professional examinations – have the right to appear before the Court of Session and plead cases on behalf of their clients. Solicitor-advocates are members of the Law Society of Scotland while Advocates will be members of the Faculty of Advocates (in England such lawyers are known as barristers). Lawyers from one of the other 24 member states of the European Union also may have a right to appear on behalf of a client in the Court of Session.

 Key point: The parties to a case heard by the Court of Session will be legally represented by either a solicitor-advocate or an Advocate.

The House of Lords

This court sits in Westminster, London. Originally, the House of Lords was not to have any right to hear appeals from the Court of Session. In fact, the Treaty of Union of 1707, whereby Scotland and England became the United Kingdom, appeared to rule out any role for the House of Lords in the affairs of the Court of Session. The case of **Greenshields *v* Magistrates of Edinburgh** in 1711 shattered this belief and, since this date, it has been the practice of the House of Lords to hear Scottish civil appeals.

 Key point: The House of Lords has heard Scottish civil appeals since 1711.

Until 2003, the Lord Chancellor was the most senior judge in the House of Lords. However, the current Lord Chancellor, Lord Falconer of Thoroton has chosen not to exercise his right to sit as a judge in the House of Lords. Presently, the most senior judge in the Lords is, therefore, Lord Bingham of Cornhill.

The judges in the House of Lords are referred to as Lords of Appeal in Ordinary or Law Lords (who normally number between nine and twelve). Two Scottish Law Lords normally make up this number. The Queen appoints members of the Lords on the advice of the Prime Minister with an input from the Lord Chancellor. The judges of the House of Lords have usually practised law as a barrister or an advocate.

Currently, the House of Lords as a court of appeal is living on borrowed time. The present Labour Government indicated in 2003 that it intends to introduce legislation to replace the Lords with a Supreme or Constitutional Court for the whole of the United Kingdom. This development is viewed as necessary in terms of recent legislation which introduced devolved government throughout parts of the United Kingdom and the growing importance of human rights legislation.

 Key point: The House of Lords consists of the Lord Chancellor and between nine to twelve Lords of Appeal in Ordinary.

From which civil courts does the House of Lords hear appeals?

The House of Lords will hear criminal and civil appeals from the English Court of Appeal, the English High Court and the Divisional Courts of the English High Court. Additionally, the Lords will hear appeals from the Court of Session in Edinburgh and the Supreme Court of Northern Ireland in civil cases only. In Scottish appeals, one or two Scottish law lords will normally participate and, if the appeal comes from Northern Ireland, one Northern Irish law lord will usually be part of that court. However, there is nothing to prevent a Scottish appeal being heard by a court of English and Northern Irish judges. The procedure in the House of Lords is informal in the sense that judges do not sit in a courtroom to hear appeals. Appeals are usually heard in one of the committee rooms of the Houses of Parliament and the judges customarily wear business suits rather than the more formal dress of wigs and gowns. Appeals to the House of Lords must be heard by at least three Law Lords – although it is more likely for five or even seven judges to sit in order to hear a case.

 Key point: In relation to Scotland, the House of Lords has jurisdiction to hear civil appeals only.

The Criminal Justice System

There are three courts which make up the Scottish criminal justice system:

◆ The District Court
◆ The Sheriff Court
◆ The High Court of Justiciary

It should be noted that, since the introduction of the Scotland Act 1998, the Judicial Committee of the Privy Council can hear appeals from the High Court of Justiciary where devolution and human rights issues are raised (see, for example, **Brown v Stott (2000)**).

The criminal justice system exists to protect society or the community from those individuals who would carry out acts which are regarded as being so outrageous that they should be punished by a prison sentence or the imposition of a fine. Additionally, people who are convicted of a crime will go on to possess a criminal record. The aim of the criminal justice system is to punish those people who would undermine law and order and threaten the very security of society.

 Key point: The Scottish criminal justice system consists of the District Court, the Sheriff Court and the High Court of Justiciary. The Privy Council in London can hear appeals from the High Court that involve human rights or devolution issues.

Criminal law is a reflection of the important values of a society or a community at a particular time. Over time, certain behaviour may come to be regarded as not an issue to be dealt by the criminal law. In ten years' time, it may no longer be a crime to use or possess certain drugs like cannabis or marijuana. Who knows what the future holds? In the past, certain activities like being a member of an independent Trade Union would have been regarded as a crime under the Combination Acts. Those individuals brave enough to join such an organisation may have found themselves convicted of a crime and transported overseas to Australia which, in earlier days, was a very harsh penal colony. Obviously, values and attitudes have changed over the years. However, certain types of behaviour such as murder, theft, criminal damage, assault and sexual offences involving children remain very much forbidden by the criminal law.

There are three possible verdicts or decisions in a Scottish criminal court:

- ◆ Guilty
- ◆ Not guilty
- ◆ Not proven

The last two verdicts are acquittal verdicts where the accused (the person on trial) will walk free from the court. The not proven verdict is unique to Scotland and its continued use has been heavily criticised in that it tends to leave a stain on the reputation of the accused and fail to satisfy the expectations of the victim or the victim's family. A not proven verdict is an alternative to a not guilty verdict. However, critics might point out that it is a mechanism whereby a judge or a jury can make a statement that they are not completely satisfied about the accused person's innocence, but at the same it is condemnation of the prosecution's failure to present a sufficiently strong case that will secure a conviction.

The person on trial is always referred to as 'the accused' in Scotland. It is worth bearing in mind that it is a hugely important principle of criminal law that a person on trial is innocent until proven guilty. It is totally inappropriate to refer to the accused as the 'guilty person'. It is up to the state prosecutors to prove that the accused is guilty. Should the prosecutor fail to convince the court of the person's guilt, then the accused must be acquitted of the charge and be allowed to go free.

 Key point: The person trial in a criminal court is the accused and he will face three possible verdicts – guilty, not guilty and not proven.

In a criminal trial, the prosecutor must prove that the accused is guilty of a crime beyond a reasonable doubt. This is a very strict burden in that the prosecution must be able to corroborate its evidence against the accused. Corroboration means that the evidence must be proved by witness testimony and the use of expert and forsenic evidence. A reasonable doubt is a nagging doubt which would lead a reasonable person to the conclusion that it would be unsafe and unjust to find the accused guilty.

It is the British state which will determine whether a person faces trial in a criminal court. In Scotland, the prosecution of a crime and the whole system of public prosecution is the responsibility of the Lord Advocate (currently Colin Boyd QC). The Lord Advocate is, of course, the Crown's chief law officer in Scotland and the person who is in charge of the Crown Office (a Department of the Scottish Executive) in Edinburgh. The Procurator Fiscal is the Lord Advocate's representative at local level. Theoretically, the police follow the instructions of a fiscal when carrying out a criminal investigation but, practically speaking, the police will be left to conduct their enquiries. However, it is not the police who will determine whether a criminal trial will go ahead in Scotland. This is ultimately the decision of independent state prosecutors. However, once the procurator fiscal has decided that an individual will face trial for the most serious types of crime, the accused will have to undergo trial within 110 days. This time limit of 110 days will be extended as a result of new rules contained in the Criminal Procedure (Amendment) (Scotland) Bill which is set to become law in 2004. It is worth pointing out that individual members of the public do not have the right to insist that someone face a criminal trial in Scotland. Private prosecutions in Scotland are very rare and do not, on the whole, have a good track record. Furthermore, private individuals cannot insist that the criminal law be used in such a way to promote their own private interests in disputes involving other private citizens. It would be totally improper for someone to insist that the person against whom a personal injury claim was being raised should be imprisoned if compensation was not paid. Such actions are not the responsibility of the Scottish criminal courts.

 Key point: In Scotland, the prosecution of a crime and the whole system of public prosecution is the responsibility of the Lord Advocate. It is up to the prosecution to prove that the accused committed the crime for which he is on trial.

The District Court

The District Court is the most junior criminal court in Scotland. Its jurisdiction is purely local in that it will have responsibility for certain crimes which are committed in a local authority area, for example, if the accused commits a breach of the peace in Glasgow City centre on a Saturday night, it will be Glasgow District Court which hears the case.

The current use of District Courts to try criminal cases in Scotland was introduced as a result of the District Courts (Scotland) Act 1975. Unlike the Sheriff Court and High Court of Justiciary, local authorities run the District Court and not the Scottish Court Service.

The judges of the District Court mainly deal with less serious types of crime in comparison with the Sheriff Court and the High Court of Justiciary. The District Court will tend to deal with matters such as breach of the peace, assault, vandalism, theft (excluding housebreaking), speeding, vehicle excise, TV licensing, electricity fraud and various other road traffic offences. The District Court cannot deal with assaults where the victim suffers a wound, for example, where the skin is broken or where bones are broken.

 Key point: The District Court is the most junior of the Scottish criminal courts and it deals with relatively minor crimes.

All trials in the District Court are conducted under summary procedure meaning that the judges sit alone. In other words, there is no jury. The District Court judges are masters of the facts in that they alone will decide whether the accused is guilty or not. If the judges should find the accused guilty after the trial, then they will also impose the appropriate sentence.

There are two types of judge who sit in the District Court – a Justice of the Peace and a Stipendiary Magistrate.

Justices of the Peace

Justices of the Peace are most likely to be found in the District Court. Generally, these individuals are not legally qualified. Justices of the Peace have been in existence since 1609 and currently there are approximately 700 of them dispensing justice in Scotland. In other words, they are not qualified to act as solicitors or advocates. The District Court Association, a voluntary body representing all District

Courts in Scotland, does provide regular training programmes for Justices to ensure that minimum standards are maintained. Justices do not receive a salary for their services, but they may be reimbursed for travelling expenses. Many Justices will be recruited from the ranks of Scotland's councillors – although being a member of a local council is not an essential qualification to become one of these judges. The Scottish Executive will make appointments to the ranks of Justices of Peace as and when required.

 Key point: Two types of judge can sit in the District Court – a lay Justice of the Peace and a legally qualified Stipendiary Magistrate.

A legally qualified clerk of the court will be present to advise the Justices regarding matters of law and procedure. The clerk is often a solicitor who works for the local authority. The Justices merely rely upon the clerk's legal advice. The clerk does not have a say in the magistrates' actual verdict. It should be noted that Justices have complete independence when it comes to making a verdict. Justices can sit alone or a bench of three Justices can often sit.

A Justice of the Peace can impose a maximum prison sentence of 60 days and impose a maximum fine of £2500 (known as a level 4 fine).

Stipendiary Magistrates

A Stipendiary Magistrate, on the other hand, will be legally qualified. Such individuals will have been practising lawyers for at least five years i.e. a solicitor or an advocate. These judges sit alone without the assistance of a legally qualified clerk. These judges are professional magistrates and, consequently, they receive a salary for their services. A Stipendiary Magistrate can impose a maximum prison sentence of three months or up to six months if the crime involves violence or dishonesty and the accused has relevant previous convictions. A maximum fine of £5000 can also be imposed on a guilty person. Interestingly, as we shall see, a Stipendiary Magistrate has exactly the same powers as a Sheriff under summary procedure in the Sheriff Court. It is worth pointing out that the City of Glasgow Council is the only Scottish local authority which uses Stipendiary Magistrates in its District Court.

 Key point: A lay Justice of the Peace can impose a 60-day term of imprisonment and/or a £2500 fine whereas a legally qualified Stipendiary Magistrate can impose a prison sentence of three to six months and/or a £5000 fine.

An accused on trial before the District Court will usually be represented by a solicitor. And the prosecutor will be from the Procurator Fiscal Service. The Fiscal is a civil servant who is employed by the Scottish Executive and who has responsibility at the local level for the investigation and prosecution of crimes. The accused will be given a document known as a complaint which will detail the charges that he or she is facing.

An appeal from a decision of the District Court is made to the High Court of Justiciary in Edinburgh.

Proposed reforms to the District Court

In January 2004, Sheriff John McInnes, who had been commissioned by the Scottish Executive to produce a report on summary justice in Scotland in November 2001, reported his initial findings. In its interim report, the McInnes Committee proposed that the position of Justice of the Peace should be abolished. If this proposal is implemented, all of Scotland's 700 lay magistrates will be replaced by Stipendiary Magistrates. This, of course, will lead to the professionalisation of the District Court. Furthermore, under the proposed reforms, local authorities would lose responsibility for the operation of the District Court and responsibility would pass to the Scottish Courts Service.

The Sheriff Court

In terms of work load, the Sheriff Court is the busiest criminal court in Scotland. Glasgow Sheriff Court, for instance, is the busiest criminal court in Europe dealing with approximately 330 criminal cases per day. The present Sheriff Court was established by the Sheriff Courts Act 1971.

The Sheriff Court, it will be remembered, can also hear civil cases. The organisation of the Sheriff Court in civil matters (Sheriffdoms and Sheriff Court districts) is exactly the same for the criminal court. A Sheriff Court can deal with all crimes committed within the boundaries of the Sheriffdom. In practice, however, there will be many crimes which the Sheriff Court cannot deal with. Crimes such as murder, rape, treason, incest and piracy will be tried by Scotland's supreme criminal court, the High Court of Justiciary. Furthermore, particularly serious crimes such as trafficking in drugs and armed robbery will come under the jurisdiction of the High Court.

Sheriffs will have been practising lawyers for at least ten years. They can be appointed from the ranks of solicitors or advocates.

 Key point: The Sheriff Court is the busiest criminal court in Scotland.

There are two criminal procedures in the Sheriff Court:

◆ A summary procedure
◆ A solemn procedure

Summary procedure

A trial of an accused under summary procedure means that the Sheriff will sit alone to try the case. There is no jury present and the Sheriff will decide the guilt or the innocence of the accused. The Sheriff will be the master of the facts. If the prosecution proves beyond a reasonable doubt that the accused is guilty, then the Sheriff will decide the appropriate punishment. Less serious crimes are dealt with under summary procedure. The accused will receive a document known as a complaint which details the charges that he or she is accused of.

The powers of a Sheriff under summary procedure are exactly the same as that of a stipendiary magistrate sitting in the District Court. A Sheriff can impose a three-month prison sentence and/or a fine of up to £5000. In cases where the crime involves violence or dishonesty and the accused possesses relevant previous convictions, the Sheriff may even impose a maximum prison sentence of six months. However, Sheriff's sentencing powers can often be affected by Acts of Parliament which will lay down the maximum sentence or punishment which a judge can impose.

The last Conservative Government (1992–97) introduced legislation to increase the power of a summary Sheriff. However, these provisions were not brought into force. The Crime and Punishment (Scotland) Act 1997 would have given Sheriffs the power to impose a maximum prison sentence of six months and, where the guilty party had relevant previous convictions for certain offences, a maximum prison sentence of one year could have been a possibility.

Appeals from a decision of a Sheriff under summary procedure are made to the High Court of Justiciary in Edinburgh.

Solemn procedure

More serious types of crimes are dealt with under solemn procedure. The Sheriff sits with a jury of 15 men and women. This time, the jury will be the master of the facts in that it will decide the innocence or guilt of the accused. Should the jury return a guilty verdict, then it is for the Sheriff to impose the appropriate punishment.

A Sheriff under solemn procedure can impose a maximum prison sentence of up to five years and/or an unlimited fine. If the Sheriff is of the opinion that his sentencing powers are not adequate enough to punish an offender, he can send the accused to be sentenced in the High Court of Justiciary. The High Court has unlimited powers of imprisonment and fine.

On 1 May 2004, section 13(1) of the Crime and Punishment (Scotland) Act 1997 relating to Sheriff's sentencing powers under solemn procedure, was finally brought into force. This means that a Sheriff's powers of imprisonment were increased from three to five years. These changes came about as a result of the Criminal Procedure (Amendment) (Scotland) Bill which aims to remove cases from the High Court that could easily be dealt with by Sheriffs. The result of these reforms is that certain categories of accused offenders (e.g. sex or violent) may face a prison sentence of up to five years in the Sheriff Court from 1 May 2004 onwards.

In a solemn trial, the accused will receive a document detailing the charges that he or she is facing. This document is known as an indictment.

 Key point: The Sheriff Court has two types of criminal procedure – summary (the Sheriff sits alone) and solemn (the Sheriff and a jury of 15).

An accused will usually be represented by a solicitor when the Sheriff Court is sitting under solemn procedure. However, it is not unusual for the accused to be represented by an advocate. The prosecution of the accused is normally conducted by the Procurator Fiscal, but an Advocate Depute may appear for the prosecution.

Appeals from a decision of a Sheriff under solemn procedure are made to the High Court of Justiciary in Edinburgh.

 Key point: A Sheriff under summary procedure can impose a prison sentence of three to six months and/or a £5000 fine whereas under solemn procedure he can impose a prison sentence of up to five years and/or an unlimited fine.

The High Court of Justicary

The High Court of Justiciary is the most senior and most powerful of Scotland's criminal courts. The High Court was founded by the Courts Act 1672, but it can trace its roots back much further to the medieval practice of sending judges (known as justiciars) out on circuit or ayre to various parts of Scotland to dispense criminal justice. These judges originally heard both civil and criminal cases, but eventually they became responsible for criminal trials.

As a result of the decision in the case of the **Lord Advocate v Mackintosh (1876)**, the right of any further appeal in criminal matters to an English court i.e. the House of Lords was ruled out. As shall be seen later in this chapter, the Scotland Act 1998 has given the English court known as the Privy Council the right to hear appeals from the High Court where the case involves issues relating to devolved government or human rights issues. Furthermore, the recent proposals by the Blair Government to establish a Supreme or Constitutional Court for the United Kingdom to replace the House of Lords may undermine the High Court's independence in criminal matters.

 Key point: The High Court of Justiciary is Scotland's supreme criminal court.

The High Court of Justiciary is often simply referred to as the High Court, but it should not be confused with the English High Court which is a completely different body altogether. The Lord Justice General (currently Lord Cullen) is the president of the High Court and his deputy is the Lord Justice Clerk (currently Lord Gill). In addition to the Lord Justice General and Lord Justice Clerk, the remaining 30 judges of the Court of Session also sit on the High Court. These 30 judges who, when sitting in the High Court, are referred to as Lords Commissioners of Justiciary. The judges of the High Court are overwhelmingly male and, in 2003, there were just three female members of this court, namely, Lady Cosgrove, Lady Paton and Lady Smith.

The High Court's permanent base and headquarters is in Edinburgh. The High Court, however, is not confined to holding trials in Edinburgh and one of its distinctive features is that it can sit as a trial court in the cities and the larger towns throughout Scotland. This is known as 'going on circuit' when the High Court sits outside Edinburgh and often the local Sheriff Court will play host to the High Court. Glasgow is the exception with the city having its own permanent building for the use of the High Court near Glasgow Green. Furthermore, the High Court sits in Glasgow for 11 months of the year, unlike any other circuit location in Scotland. The four circuits are Home, West, North and South.

 Key point: The High Court has its permanent base in Edinburgh, but it also sits throughout the towns and cities of Scotland – this practice is known as 'going on circuit'.

The High Court's jurisdiction extends over the whole of Scotland and over all crimes committed in Scotland. In practice, the High Court tends to deal only with the most serious types of crime such as the so-called 'pleas of the Crown' which includes murder, rape, treason and incest. Armed robbery, and serious drug crimes will also come under the jurisdiction of the High Court. Where many less serious types of crime are concerned, the High Court is often prevented from exercising its jurisdiction as a result of various Acts of Parliament which stipulate that these less serious offences should be dealt with under summary procedure. The High Court has unlimited powers of imprisonment and fine.

The procedure in the High Court is almost always solemn where one Lord Commissioner of Justiciary can sit with a jury of 15 men and women.

 Key point: The High Court deals with the most serious types of crime and the procedure is almost always solemn i.e. one Lord Commissioner of Justiciary can sit with a jury of 15. The High Court has unlimited powers of imprisonment and fine.

It should be noted that, at the trial of the two Libyans accused of planning the terrorist attack on the American passenger jet, PanAM flight 103, over the Scottish town of Lockerbie in December 1988, the services of a jury were not required and three Lords Commissioners of Justiciary formed the trial court. Lockerbie was, of course, the worst mass murder in Scottish criminal legal history and the arrangements for the trial were exceptional to say the least. The trial itself did not take place physically in Scotland, but at a former United States Air Force base called Camp Zeist in the Netherlands which was turned over to the jurisdiction of the High Court.

When dealing with appeals, the High Court sits only in Parliament House in Edinburgh. However, in 2001, the appeal of one of the Libyans involved in the Lockerbie bombing was conducted at Camp Zeist in the Netherlands before five High Court judges. The normal practice is for at least three Judges to sit to hear appeals by an individual against his conviction and two judges will sit when the appeal is against the length of the sentence imposed on a guilty person. The High Court hears appeals from the High Court when it sits as a trial court, the Sheriff Court (both summary and solemn cases) and from the District Court.

 Key point: The High Court sits in Edinburgh to hear appeals from the other Scottish criminal courts.

Cases in the High Court are prosecuted by certain advocates or solicitor-advocates (advocate deputes) who are chosen to represent the Lord Advocate, in whose name all prosecutions are brought in the public interest. It is possible, although extremely rare, for a private prosecution to be brought. The defence will usually be conducted by an advocate or solicitor-advocate. In addition a practitioner from another member state of the European Union may appear for a client in the circumstances prescribed by the European Communities (Services of Lawyers) Order 1978. An accused may conduct his own defence.

The Lord Advocate's Reference to the High Court

Under the Criminal Procedure (Scotland) Act 1995, the Lord Advocate, the most senior Scottish Law Officer, may ask the High Court to comment upon a legal point which has arisen as a result of a particular case. This procedure permits the High Court to give an opinion which will hopefully clarify the law and provide guidance to judges in future cases where the same point of law is at issue. A reference from the Lord Advocate to the High Court will not affect the outcome of the particular case for which the opinion is sought.

 A particularly interesting example of a reference from the Lord Advocate to the High Court occurred in **Lord Advocate's Reference Number 1 of 2000**. In this case, three peace protesters were accused of illegal entry to a ship which was anchored on Loch Goil in June 1999. The ship had a role in relation to submarines carrying Trident missiles. The protesters faced criminal damage and theft charges in relation to equipment which was on the ship. In their defence, the protesters claimed that their actions were justified because they were attempting to draw attention to the British Government's continued possession of nuclear weapons – a situation which the protesters argued was a crime under international law. At the trial at Greenock Sheriff Court, the Sheriff, Margaret Gimblet, directed the jury to return a not guilty verdict in relation to several of the charges. As for the remainder of the charges, the jury found the protesters not guilty. The Sheriff Gimblet was extensively criticised for the way in she had directed the jury to return not guilty verdicts. It was felt that this judgement would give the green light to other peace protesters to carry out similar acts as part of their ongoing anti-nuclear weapons campaign. The Lord Advocate, therefore, felt it necessary to refer the case to the High Court for clarification where it was held that the protesters were not justified in their actions.

 Key point: the Lord Advocate may ask the High Court to comment upon a legal point which has arisen as a result of a particular case, thus, permitting the High Court to give an opinion which will hopefully clarify the law and provide guidance to judges in future cases where the same point of law is at issue.

The Scottish Criminal Cases Review Commission

This is a statutory body established by section 194A of the Criminal Procedure (Scotland) Act 1995. The Commission consists of seven members and one of these acts as Chairman. The role of the Commission is to investigate cases where a miscarriage of justice may have taken place. If the Commission is of the opinion that a conviction in a criminal case may be unsafe, it can take steps to refer the matter to the High Court of Justiciary. Furthermore, the Commission can also investigate sentences which were handed down by the courts. Any person can make an application to the Commission in order to request that it investigate a particular case. The Commission has been given robust powers of investigation and it can force individuals and organisations to hand over documents and provide testimony.

There is no point contacting the Commission until an appeal has been heard by the High Court. The Appeals system, of course, exists to correct earlier mistakes and it would be completely inappropriate for the Commission to pre-judge the High Court's final decision in the matter. The Commission does not provide legal services to an applicant. The Commission merely investigates the circumstances of a conviction or a sentence and then makes a recommendation to the High Court. Applicants are advised to secure the services of a lawyer if it is likely that the case will be revisited by the High Court.

In September 2003, one of the most high profile referrals to be referred to the Commission so far was the conviction of Abdelbaset Ali Mohmed Al Megrahi. Megrahi was convicted of the murder of 270 people as a result of the Lockerbie Bombing in January 2001. He unsuccessfully appealed against his conviction later in 2001. Megrahi's solicitors made the application to the Commission in order for it to review their client's conviction.

The Commission is answerable to Scottish Ministers and the Scottish Parliament. It is a non-departmental body which is sponsored by the Scottish Executive's Justice Department. The Commission has its headquarters in Glasgow.

 Key point: The role of the Scottish Criminal Cases Review Commission is to investigate cases where a miscarriage of justice may have taken place.

The Judicial Committee of the Privy Council

History of the Privy Council

This court is a direct descendant of the ancient English King's Council which was a type of cabinet which advised the Crown. The court's jurisdiction is derived from the Judicial Committee Act 1833. The Judicial Committee is not part of the English Supreme Court. The Privy Council is the final court of appeal in civil and criminal matters from the courts of some Commonwealth countries and British territories. Nowadays, many Commonwealth states no longer use this court – in 1986, Australia stopped using the court, Singapore abolished the Privy Council as its highest Court of Appeal in 1994 and the Privy Council ceased to have any jurisdiction over Hong Kong in 1997 when the territory was returned to China. Interestingly, Malaysia, Bermuda, Jamaica, Gambia and Trinidad and Tobago, are among those countries which continue to make use of the court. In October 2003, New Zealand abolished appeals to the Privy Council in respect of cases heard by the Court of Appeal of New Zealand after 31 December 2003.

The Privy Council sits to hear cases in Downing Street, London.

 Key point: The Privy Council was originally an English Court that had no jurisdiction to hear Scottish cases.

Constitutional developments and the changing role of the Privy Council

Significantly, the Privy Council has recently been given a new lease of life. Under the Scotland Act 1998 and the Human Rights Act 1998, the Privy Council has jurisdiction in devolution matters and human rights issues. This means that even the decisions of the supreme Scottish criminal court, the High Court of Justiciary, can now be challenged if they appear to breach the Scotland Act or the Human Rights Act. The supremacy of the High Court appeared to be guaranteed in the nineteenth Century with the decision of the **Lord Advocate v Mackintosh (1876)**. This case ruled out any further right of appeal in criminal matters to an English court i.e. the House of Lords. Devolution and the direct incorporation of the European Convention on Human Rights and Fundamental Freedoms into British law appear to have significantly undermined this belief.

A recent example of a High Court decision being overturned by the Privy Council was that of **Brown v Stott (2000)** in which the owner of a vehicle was compelled under the Road Traffic Act 1988 to give information as to the identity of the driver at the time when the relevant offence was committed. The offence was one of drunk driving. The accused argued that the very fact that she had to admit to the police that she had driven the car in response to their questioning of her amounted to self-incrimination. Her response would, of course, be used against her at the trial and she claimed, therefore, that her right to a fair trial had been breached under Article

6 of the European Convention on Human Rights because she had self-incriminated herself (remember, it is up to the Prosecution to prove the guilt of the accused and the accused is under no duty to help the prosecution convict him or her). The accused was convicted in the Sheriff Court. The High Court of Justiciary held that the Crown had no power to rely on evidence of the admission which the accused had been compelled to make under the Road Traffic Act. The appeal was allowed. However, the Privy Council had other ideas and decided to overturn this ruling. The Privy Council confirmed the rule that an accused had to answer truthfully when the Police questioned him or her in relation to a suspected offence under the Road Traffic Act.

 Key point: As a result of the Scotland Act 1998, the Privy Council can now hear appeals from the Court of Session and the High Court of Justiciary where the case involves human rights or devolution issues.

The function of the Privy Council

The Judicial Committee (better known as 'The Board') includes the Lord Chancellor, the Lords of Appeal in Ordinary (the Law Lords) and all Privy Counsellors who have held high judicial office in the UK. These Privy Counsellors include past and present members of the Inner House of the Court of Session. The Committee still includes the Lord Chancellor, but as previously mentioned in relation to the House of Lords, the present holder of the office, Lord Falconer does not intend to act as a judge. Added to this number are Commonwealth judges who have been appointed members of the Privy Council. Admittedly, the Law Lords do most of the work of the Privy Council and, arguably, it is really just the House of Lords in another guise.

Five judges normally sit to hear appeals (except appeals from United Kingdom professional bodies) and three for other matters. The Board does not actually decide cases, but advises the Crown which implements the advice by means of an Order in Council. Since 1966, this advice does not need to be unanimous – those present may express dissent with the majority view and give their reasons.

Despite the fact that the Privy Council no longer plays such a prominent role in the legal affairs of the Commonwealth, this does not mean that it is merely a relic of the British Empire. The court is still the final court of appeal for civil and criminal appeals from the Channel Islands, the Isle of Man and Gibraltar. Strictly speaking, there is no right of appeal. It is traditional to petition the Crown for leave to appeal. In recent years, the Privy Council has courted controversy in its dealings with Caribbean states and territories which still use the court. Many of the cases which come before the Privy Council from the Caribbean have centred on individuals who have been condemned to death. The Privy Council has shown a marked reluctance to allow these executions to proceed and, accordingly, it has been severely criticised by Caribbean governments. The upside of continuing to use the Privy Council is that these Caribbean governments do not have to go to the considerable expense of maintaining and paying for their own courts of appeal.

The Privy Council is not bound by its previous decisions.

 Key point: Five judges of the Privy Council normally sit to hear appeals and the court sits in Downing Street, London.

Alternative methods of resolving legal disputes

There has been a great increase in administrative justice which is dispensed through special courts or tribunals during the twentieth century. Many legal and constitutional writers have viewed this trend as alarming because, rightly or wrongly, they feel that it undermines the jurisdiction of the longer established courts such as the Sheriff Court or the Court of Session.

These courts of special jurisdiction operate outside what we would recognise as the traditional legal system of Scotland. The increasing role which these administrative courts and tribunals have taken on is largely due to the government's greatly expanded powers in relation to important issues like pensions, social security, taxation, industrial relations, immigration, planning and compulsory purchase orders. As a result of the government's expanded responsibilities it is hardly surprising that disputes often arise between individuals and the state.

However, it would be a mistake to assume that these special courts and tribunals deal solely with disputes between private citizens and the state. The Scottish Land Court, for example, deals with disputes between landlord and tenant in crafting and agricultural matters.

Another point to note is that courts or tribunals of special jurisdiction do not always sit on a permanent basis. Some are very temporary in nature. Obviously, we cannot cover every type of special court or tribunal exhaustively so we will concentrate our efforts on the most prominent.

 Key point: Not all legal disputes are dealt with by the Scottish criminal and civil courts. There are special courts and tribunals that exist to hear certain types of dispute, for example, the Employment Tribunal.

The Children's Hearing or Panel

In Scotland, a child under the age of eight cannot be guilty of a criminal offence. In other words, a criminal prosecution cannot be brought against a child under the age of eight. Criminal responsibility in Scotland, therefore, begins at the age of eight. A child under the age of 16 cannot be prosecuted in a criminal court without the permission of the Lord Advocate. Children will only appear in the Sheriff Court and the High Court of Justiciary if they are accused of murder, assault which endangers life or driving offences which are punishable by disqualification. Private prosecutions of children would definitely not be allowed. The Lord Advocate will occasionally issue instructions to procurator fiscals which address the treatment of children in criminal matters.

The Children's Hearing was established by the Social Work (Scotland) Act 1968 and is now regulated by the Children (Scotland) Act 1995. It is an alternative to sending children to trial in an adult court. The aim of the Children's Hearing is to prevent young people from being exposed to the criminal justice system in the hope that they will be given a chance to reform before their behaviour has more serious consequences. The Children's Hearing is, therefore, deliberately not part of the Scottish criminal justice system.

Individuals who sit on the Children's Panel come from a wide range of different backgrounds. They are members of the public and volunteers aged between the ages of 18 and 60. They will have been selected by Scottish Executive Ministers on the recommendations of the Children's Panel Advisory Committee for the local council area and they will have received training to help them in their role. A Panel of three members will sit (at least one of them being a female). Cases are referred to the Hearing by the Reporter to the Children's Hearing.

 Key point: The Children's Hearing is an alternative way of dealing with children accused of committing crimes.

Employment Tribunals

The huge increase in employment law in the United Kingdom generally has led to a much more prominent role for Employment Tribunals in areas like sexual, racial and disability discrimination, equal pay cases, unfair and wrongful dismissal actions. Employment Tribunals (previously known as Industrial Tribunals) are governed by Part I of the Employment Tribunals Act 1996.

Some of the legislation which confers jurisdiction on Employment Tribunals includes:

- The Equal Pay Act 1970
- The Sex Discrimination Acts 1975 and 1986
- The Race Relations Act 1976
- The Disability Discrimination Act 1995
- The Employment Rights Act 1996
- The Working Time Regulations 1998
- The Employment Act 2002

In Scotland, the Chairperson of a Tribunal is appointed by the Lord President of the Court of Session. The Chairperson sits with two other individuals appointed by the Secretary of State at the Department of Trade of Industry. These individuals have been selected from a panel of persons compiled by the Secretary of State on the strength of them possessing detailed knowledge or extensive ability in relation to commercial or industrial matters. In some situations, the Chairperson may sit alone to decide cases. This eventuality occurs if both parties agree to this or the case is undefended.

The Employment Tribunal sits at suitable locations throughout Scotland (Edinburgh, Glasgow, Dundee and Aberdeen) in order to determine the varied issues which come before them. The hearings are very informal in style and the parties are not required to be represented by a lawyer – although this will often be the case. Since 15th January 2000, Legal Aid has been available to parties who otherwise would not have be in a position to hire the services of a lawyer. The hearing before a Tribunal will normally be held in public, unless there are compelling reasons for this not to be the case, for example, where allegations of sexual harassment will be discussed. Decisions of the Tribunal are reached by majority and it is possible for the two lay members of the panel to outvote the Chairperson. An appeal is made to the Employment Appeal Tribunal in Edinburgh on a point of law.

 Key point: Employment Tribunals sit with a legally qualified Chairperson and two lay members and they have jurisdiction to deal with employment law disputes.

The Employment Appeal Tribunal (EAT)

If an individual is dissatisfied with the decision of a Tribunal, it can be challenged by appealing to the EAT on a point of law only. It is absolutely vital, for the appellant's sake, that the facts are properly presented to the Tribunal at the original hearing. The EAT will only look at the version of events presented at the Tribunal – it is extremely rare for new evidence to be introduced.

The EAT is a superior court and has its headquarters in Edinburgh. It is regulated by Part II of the Employment Tribunals Act 1996.

Appeals to the EAT are commenced by serving the Employment Tribunal with a notice of appeal within 42 days of the original Tribunal decision being issued to the parties. Legal Aid is available to individuals for appeals to the EAT and the parties are expected to be legally represented.

Appeals before the EAT are usually heard before a judge of the Court of Session who acts as President and between two and four appointed members. The President of the EAT is appointed by the Lord President of the Court of Session. As for the lay members, they are appointed by the Queen on the joint recommendation of the Lord Chancellor and the Secretary of State for Trade and Industry. These appointed members of the EAT are not part of the judiciary, but they will have specialist knowledge or experience of industrial relations as representatives of either employers or workers. The hearing normally proceeds in public but it can be held in private for reasons of national security or trade secrets, for example.

It is vitally important that in each appeal, equal numbers of persons representing employers and workers participate. In cases of major importance, the presiding judge and four lay members (an equal balance between employers and workers) will sit. There may be one or three lay members present if the parties agree to this.

The EAT need not reach a unanimous decision and majority decisions are just as binding. Each member of the EAT has a vote and it is possible that the judge could be outvoted. This outcome, however, is extremely rare. Exceptionally, providing that the parties agree, the case could be heard by the judge and one or three members. The EAT may review or change any of its previous decisions, for example, on the grounds of new evidence.

An appeal is made to the Inner House of the Court of Session with the possibility of a further appeal to the House of Lords.

 Key point: The EAT is a superior court and has its headquarters in Edinburgh and it hears appeals from the Employment Tribunal. There is a further right of appeal on a point of law to the Court of Session and, possibly, the House of Lords.

The Lands Tribunal for Scotland

This is the body which considers whether unnecessary or oppressive conditions imposed on land should be removed in terms of sections 1 and 2 of the Conveyancing and Feudal Reform (Scotland) Act 1970. The Tribunal also considers cases where the value of land is in dispute and it can make decisions in certain disputes in relation to council house purchases by tenants. The Tribunal also has the authority to hear appeals against decisions of the Keeper of the Registers of Scotland.

The Tribunal is organised under the following statutes and rules:

◆ the Lands Tribunal Act 1949
◆ the Tribunals and Inquiries Act 1992
◆ the Lands Tribunal for Scotland Rules 1971 (as amended by the Amendment Rules of 1977 and 1985)

Other statutes also confer jurisdiction upon the Tribunal:

◆ the Feudal and Conveyancing Reform (Scotland) Act 1970
◆ the Housing (Scotland) Act 1987

Membership of the Tribunal

The membership of the Tribunal consists of suitably qualified legal members and others who have experience in the valuation of land. In 2003, the Tribunal consisted of a President (Lord McGhie) and four other members – two legal members and two surveying members.

Any one or more of its members may exercise the jurisdiction of the Tribunal. Where two or more members deal with a case, the senior legal member will normally preside. Any disagreements between members about a decision will be resolved by majority vote. In the event of an equal number of members sitting at the hearing, the member presiding will have a casting vote. The Tribunal will follow similar procedures to those operating in the Court of Session and the Sheriff Court. The Tribunal will try to be as flexible as possible in its organisation. There is a right of appeal on a point of law to the Court of Session. Further appeal to the House of Lords may be allowed with the permission of the Court of Session.

 Key point: The Lands Tribunal for Scotland considers whether unnecessary or oppressive conditions imposed on land should be removed, it considers cases where the value of land is in dispute and it can make decisions in certain disputes in relation to council house purchases by tenants. The Tribunal also has the authority to hear appeals against decisions of the Keeper of the Registers of Scotland.

The Scottish Land Court

This body was created in 1912 as a result of the Small Landholders (Scotland) Act 1911. It is now regulated under the terms of the Scottish Land Court Act 1993. The court exists to determine the outcome of disputes between tenants and landlords in agricultural and crofting matters. Its jurisdiction comes from two statutes, namely, the Agricultural Holdings (Scotland) Act 1991 and the Crofters (Scotland) Act 1993.

However, the Court's jurisdiction is limited in the sense that it cannot decide questions of land ownership which are within the jurisdiction of the Sheriff Court and the Court of Session. The title of the court is slightly misleading in that it is not authorised to deal with all legal disputes which are concerned with land. The court most certainly is not authorised to deal with land issues in a town or urban setting.

The Court consists of a Chairman and three members who will have a background in crofting and farming matters. Its Chairman Lord McGhie is also the President of the Lands Tribunal for Scotland and they share the same offices, although both bodies are completely separate as far as their functions are concerned. The Scottish Land Court has jurisdiction in the areas of agricultural disputes between landlords and tenants. The Court may sit as a Divisional Court where cases are heard by a Court member and a legal assessor. Alternatively, a Full Court can be convened where a minimum or quorum of two members is required and the Chairman. Parties have a right of appeal to the Court of Session but only on a point of law. The Chairman of the Scottish Land Court enjoys the same status and benefits as a judge of the Court of Session.

 Key point: The Scottish Land Court exists to determine the outcome of disputes between tenants and landlords in agricultural and crofting matters.

The Court of The Lord Lyon

This Court is presided over by the Lord Lyon who is a Minister of the Crown and a judge of the realm. Scotland, together with Spain, is one of the few countries to have retained the services of this type of court up until the present day. The Court deals with matters relating to heraldry and the right to use certain ancient titles. A person who wishes to claim the right to use an ancient Scottish title will, of course, have to produce evidence to substantiate his claim and the Lord Lyon will have to be satisfied before he grants such a right. Heraldic symbols and coats of arms were very important in societies where most people did not possess the skills of reading and writing – this also included the landed aristocracy. Many powerful individuals adopted symbols or coats of arms which over the years became associated with these individuals or their families. As time went on, the possession of a coat of arms marked a person out as being someone of importance and wealth. Such persons were obviously very keen to have exclusive control over these symbols and the Court of the Lord Lyon was established to deal with disputes in relation to these matters. It was common practice for these symbols to be copied and used by other individuals who had no right to use them. Amazingly, even to this day, disputes can arise regarding the rights of individuals to use certain symbols or titles. A school will have to be very careful when it decides to redesign its crest or motto that it does not infringe someone else's right to use a symbol or a coat of arms. The Lord Lyon also protects the rights of the Crown to use certain symbols and coats of arms.

The Court of the Lord Lyon has its headquarters in Her Majesty's New Register House in Edinburgh. The Court has both criminal and civil jurisdiction. It is an offence for anyone to use a coat of arms or a heraldic symbol belonging to another person. To this end, the Court can impose fines on offenders and even terms of imprisonment. The Court has a prosecutor known as Procurator Fiscal.

 Key point: The Court of the Lord Lyon is a court of special jurisdiction which has responsibility for determining who has the right to use certain heraldic symbols, coats of arms and ancient Scottish titles.

Courts Martial

The British armed services have their own tribunals or courts where members of the military who breach the services' disciplinary codes and/or commit other offences may face trial. The Army Act 1955 governs the procedure of courts martial for members of the Army. There are similar rules for courts martial in the Air Force Act and the Navy Act. The courts martial system, however, was also extensively reformed by the Armed Forces Act 1996 in order to ensure fairness to the accused. There are two types of court, a District Court Martial and a General Court Martial. The General Court Martial has more extensive powers to punish an offender and usually deals with serious offence like treason. The accused is entitled to be legally represented at the hearing. The accused is permitted to rely on witnesses and evidence in order to support his defence and his legal representative will be permitted to cross-examine the prosecution's witnesses. In fact, procedures at the court martial will be similar to that of a civilian court. Unlike civilian courts, however, courts martial are not open to members of the public. Courts martial must ensure that the accused enjoys a right to a fair trial which is protected by the European Convention on Human Rights. In peacetime, it is more likely that members of the military who commit serious crimes or who commit crimes outside military quarters would face trial in the ordinary Scottish criminal courts.

An appeal may be made to the court martial Appeal Court.

 Key point: A court martial deals with members of the armed forces who have committed crimes or who are guilty of breaches of discipline.

Ombudsman schemes

The establishment of ombudsman schemes is a very popular route which provides citizens with a safeguard against maladministration by public authorities. This is an alternative to the more traditional route of beginning a legal action for judicial review in the Court of Session. Ombudsman schemes are modelled upon the Scandinavian office of the Ombudsman.

The Scottish Public Services Ombudsman

The Scottish Public Services Ombudsman Act 2002 establishes a single Ombudsman to deal with complaints by the public which involve the Scottish Executive and Parliament, the National Health Service in Scotland, Scottish local authorities and Scottish Housing Associations. The Ombudsman scheme is all about the prevention of abuses of power by a wide range of Scottish and even British public bodies, for example, the Scottish Legal Aid Board. Professor Alice Brown is the first Scottish Ombudsman to be appointed. The Scottish Public Services Ombudsman and her three assistant Ombudsmen are appointed by the Queen on the recommendation of the Scottish Parliament.

United Kingdom Parliamentary Ombudsman or the Parliamentary Commissioner for Administration

This scheme provides a further check on abuses of power by British government departments under the provisions of the Parliamentary Commissioner Act 1967. This jurisdiction of the Ombudsman was extended by the Parliamentary Commissioner Act 1994. The current post-holder, Ann Abraham, was appointed in 2002 by the Crown and has the same security of tenure as a senior judge. The Ombudsman is also a member of the Council on Tribunals. The main function of the Ombudsman is to investigate complaints relating to the exercise of administrative functions. An investigation of a central government department is initiated only at the request of a Member of Parliament and citizens who wish to use the services of the Ombudsman must approach a Member of Parliament who may or may not want to take up their case.

Unfortunately, the Ombudsman is undoubtedly less effective than her counterparts in other countries. Britain is alone in preventing its national Ombudsman initiate her own investigations. The Ombudsman cannot investigate complaints against the police, judges and local authorities.

 Key point: The Ombudsman Scheme allows members of the public to make complaints about alleged maladministration in relation to the provision of public services.

Other Ombudsman and regulatory authorities

In the areas of banking, insurance and building societies, Ombudsmen have been appointed to deal, on a limited basis, with disputes in those industries.

The Council of the London Stock Exchange has appointed such a person to mediate in disputes between investors and stockbrokers.

Sections 150 to 160 of the Pensions Act 1995 established a Pensions Ombudsman to deal with disputes between an individual and a pension scheme or provider regarding the way in which pensions schemes are run. Complaints about the sales and marketing of pension schemes are dealt with by the Financial Ombudsman Service.

There is also a Financial Services Authority (FSA) which was set up as a result of the Financial Services and Markets Act 2000 and deals with deals with complaints concerning the United Kingdom's financial services industry such as the mis-selling of endowment mortgages in the 1980s and 1990s.

Many of the utilities industries, for example, gas, water, electricity and telecommunications have a regulator who ensures that they are acting fairly. Members of the public who are dissatisfied with, for example, an electricity provider can complain to the Ofgem, the Office of Gas and Electricity Markets.

 Key point: In the areas of banking, insurance and building societies, Ombudsmen have been appointed to deal, on a limited basis, with disputes in those industries.

Public inquiries

The Government will often to choose to set up an independent public inquiry regarding a problem over which the public has expressed concern and, more importantly, where there may be serious legal consequences if nothing is done. There are no general rules governing these inquiries and they will differ very much in shape and form depending on the situation. In October 2003, Lord Fraser of Carmyllie QC, a former Lord Advocate, began an investigation into the spiralling costs of the new building for the Scottish Parliament at Holyrood. Lord Fraser is being assisted by Mr John Campbell QC and Professor Robert Black, the Auditor General for Scotland. This investigation was launched by the Scottish Executive as a direct result of mounting public anger over the cost of the project which was originally estimated at £40 million. The cost of the project in September 2003 was a staggering £400 million. The inquiry is due to report its findings some time in 2004.

 Key point: Public inquiries are set up by the Government on a temporary basis to investigate particular problems or important issues, for example, the Hutton and Fraser inquiries 2003–2004.

Arbitration, mediation and conciliation procedures

Parties to a legal dispute may not wish to go court or a tribunal for a variety of different reasons. Instead, as an effective alternative, they may wish to use the services of a neutral third party to help them resolve the disputes. In these situations, the parties often make the choice of taking responsibility for dispute resolution upon themselves rather than relying upon a court which will impose its own judgement.

In a commercial dispute, the parties may wish to use an arbitration procedure to come to some sort of agreement. Arbitration allows the parties to appoint a neutral party, known as an arbiter in Scotland, who will hear both sides of the argument and who will then suggest a solution which hopefully will be broadly acceptable to both sides. The mechanism for appointing an arbiter is simple. The parties may have anticipated a dispute occurring and they have taken steps to address this by inserting an arbitration clause in the contract that they have formed with one another. Alternatively, when a dispute first arises, the parties may agree to use arbitration instead of the courts. Once the parties have chosen arbitration over the courts, they are committed to this procedure and they cannot withdraw unless the arbitration process is seriously flawed. Arbitration is not permitted, however, in criminal matters or in family law (divorce, separation or custody of children). Arbitration is often preferred in business as it is private (as opposed to public court hearings), it is usually faster than the courts, it may be less expensive than court and the parties can decide the most appropriate procedures that will be used.

The Advisory, Conciliation and Arbitration Service (ACAS) is a publicly-funded body established in 1974 which attempts mainly to resolve disputes in the workplace. During industrial action or strikes, ACAS can be used by both employers and Trade Unions as a neutral referee to help resolve the dispute. The input of ACAS may simply amount to the provision of a neutral meeting place for the parties in the presence of neutral conciliators who will try to bring the parties towards a solution. The parties to an industrial dispute can even approach ACAS having agreed to submit to its binding arbitration procedures.

When parties have taken a dispute to an Employment Tribunal, ACAS has a statutory duty to act as a conciliator between the parties. Both parties will attempt to solve the dispute that they now find themselves in and ACAS will suggest possible ways in which the parties can achieve this outcome. In Employment Tribunal disputes, it is very common for both parties or their solicitors to use the services of ACAS in order to negotiate an out-of-court settlement. This is often a very successful process and it can avoid the necessity of the parties going to an Employment Tribunal. ACAS now provides a voluntary arbitration scheme whereby parties to a straightforward unfair dismissal claim can use this as an alternative to proceeding to an Employment Tribunal.

 Key point: Arbitration, mediation and conciliation are procedures that can be used by parties who do not wish to go court and, as an alternative, a neutral third party can be appointed to help reach an out-of-court settlement.

The influence of European Courts

The House of Lords is no longer the only superior court for legal issues in the UK – the Court of Justice of the European Communities now has a very large say in the development of UK law.

The European Court of Justice (ECJ)

The ECJ sits in Luxembourg and its task is to ensure that the laws of the European Union are properly observed when the member states implement their Treaty obligations via their domestic legal systems. Admittedly, the vast bulk of cases coming before the ECJ will be firmly rooted in the civil system. Criminal courts, however, should be aware that certain decisions by them may infringe European law. In such a case, the court may choose to approach the ECJ for clarification of European law. In the English criminal case of **R *v* Marlborough Street Stipendiary Magistrates *ex parte* Bouchereau (1977)** the magistrate in question made a recommendation for the deportation of Bouchereau, but it was claimed that the magistrate had no power to do this as Bouchereau was a migrant worker as defined under the Treaty of Rome. The Magistrate referred the case to the ECJ in Luxembourg for a preliminary ruling.

The decisions of the ECJ must be accepted by the courts of the member states. It is important to note that the decisions of the ECJ cannot be appealed. Matters brought to the court are disposed of before all the judges, although some preliminary (interlocutory) matters can be dealt with by a division of three judges. The ECJ consists of professional judges, academic lawyers and public servants. A judge may only be removed by the unanimous decision of the other judges.

 Key point: The European Court of Justice sits in Luxembourg and its task is to ensure that the laws of the European Union are properly observed when the member states implement their Treaty obligations via their domestic legal systems.

Procedure

At the ECJ, more emphasis is placed on written submissions (pleadings) rather than on oral arguments. The proceedings are more inquisitorial in nature and the judges play a far more active role in asking questions during the proceedings. Eight Advocates-General assist the court and provide the ECJ with independent opinions before it publishes its decision. The opinions of the Advocates-General, however, are not always followed by the ECJ; but they can be extremely interesting in their own right.

The ECJ gives a single decision – dissenting views are not revealed. The enforcement of the Court's decisions will be carried out by the national courts of the member states. The language spoken at the hearing before the Court will normally be that of the pursuer, unless the pursuer is suing a member state which means that the language spoken will be that member state's.

 Key point: The ECJ gives a single decision – dissenting views are not revealed and the enforcement of the Court's decisions will be carried out by the national courts of the member states.

A particularly important role for the ECJ is its power to give preliminary rulings under Article 234 of the Treaty of Rome. A preliminary ruling concerns an application to the ECJ from any court or tribunal of a member state requesting that an area of EU law be clarified. Article 234 references were particularly important in the early days of the Community when European law was being built from the ground up.

The ECJ may also deal with the following types of actions:

- Actions against a member state by the Commission for failure to fulfil Treaty obligations (Article 189)
- Actions by one member state against another for failure to fulfil Treaty obligations (Article 170)
- Actions by a member state, an individual or a company/business association against the Council or the Commission for acting in breach of the Treaties (Article 173)
- Actions by a member state against the Council or the Commission for failure to act

The role of the ECJ at Luxembourg

The English Court of Appeal in **Bulmer v Bollinger (1974)** stated that the English High Court and the Court of Appeal had a right to interpret European law without referring the matter to the ECJ. If the case goes before the House of Lords, however, that court is **bound** to refer the case to the ECJ if either or both parties wish it. Any court or tribunal of a member state (under Article 234) may request a preliminary ruling but only the House of Lords is bound to do this if one of the parties before it requests this procedure.

In **Bulmer** (the so called 'Champagne' case), Lord Denning MR laid down certain guidelines on whether a judge should refer the matter to the ECJ:

1. The time involved to obtain a ruling – Article 234 references can take a long time to be heard. Would this lead to undue protraction of the case, delays and expense for both parties?

2. The ECJ must not be swamped with Article 234 references – all the judges of the ECJ must deliberate on a reference from a national court and they are not allowed to split into divisions to consider the matter.

3. The question must concern a matter of interpretation of the Treaty only. The manner in which a national court/tribunal interpreted the Treaty (wrongly or incompletely) can provide grounds for an Article 234 reference.

4. The difficulty surrounding the question of European law raised i.e. the complexity of the point of law. Is it entirely appropriate that a Scottish or English judge should decide the matter?

5. The national court will have to consider the wishes of the parties and this will be especially so when one of the parties does not wish the case to be referred to the ECJ for a preliminary ruling.

6. A national court should not refer a case to the ECJ for a preliminary ruling if the principal of law has already been sufficiently clarified by previous decisions.

If the area of European law is sufficiently clear then the judge will have no need to refer the case to the ECJ under Article 234. This is known as the doctrine of *Acte Claire*.

 Key point: Only the House of Lords is bound to refer a case to the ECJ for a preliminary ruling if one of the parties requests this procedure.

The European Court of Human Rights

This court sits in Strasbourg and was established by the Convention for the Protection of Human Rights and Fundamental Freedoms.

The European Court of Human Rights is a single, full-time court which deals with the enforcement of human rights and democratic freedoms which are protected by the European Convention on Human Rights (see the Human Rights Act 1998 p 23). It sits at Strasbourg in France and it should not be confused with the European Court of Justice – it is a completely separate institution. The Court of Human Rights is the court of the Council of Europe, an organisation of 44 European member states. All the member states of the European Union are members of this body. The Council of Europe is a body which aims to promote culture, the rule of law and respect for democratic freedoms.

Since 1966, the United Kingdom has accepted the compulsory jurisdiction of the European Court of Human Rights and, on many occasions, British citizens have taken cases to the court in Strasbourg. Despite the fact that the European Convention had not been directly incorporated into United Kingdom law, the decisions of the European Court of Human Rights have always been accepted by successive British governments (although, as we shall see, not always easily). It is only since 2nd October 2000, that British courts have had the right to hear cases which involve alleged breaches of the European Convention. Theoretically, this important development in British law should mean that United Kingdom citizens should not have to undertake the long, difficult and often frustrating task of making an application to the judges in Strasbourg.

The Organisation of the European Court of Human Rights

The European Court of Human Rights consists of 44 judges (although in May 2004, Bosnia and Herzegovina's seat was vacant). The number of judges is, therefore, equal to the number of contracting states to the European Convention. Each of the contracting states does not have the right to appoint one of its own citizens as judges. The power of appointment lies with the Parliamentary Assembly of the Council of Europe which elects the judges for a renewable period of 6 years. In practice, however, there is an electoral system in place which means that half of the judges must put themselves up for re-election every 3 years. In theory, it is possible for a number of judges to be citizens of the same contracting state as there is no requirement that each judge should represent an individual member state of the Council of Europe. In this regard, it is important to emphasise that the judges are expected not to promote their own national interests and they must be completely impartial and independent. Judges must retire from office when they reach the age of 70.

The full (or plenary) Court will elect a President , two Vice-Presidents and two Presidents of Section. All these individuals hold their posts for a period of 3 years. The Court is organised into four Sections, whose membership is fixed for three years. The Sections must be geographically and gender balanced and takes account of the different legal traditions of each member state of the Council of Europe. Two of the Sections are headed by the Vice-Presidents of the Court, with the remaining two Sections headed by the Section Presidents. Section Presidents have their own deputies, known as Section Vice-Presidents, who will be elected by the various

Sections. These Section Vice Presidents are entitled to stand in for their Section President when he or she is indisposed. The four Sections are further organised into committees (3 members) and chambers (7 judges). Hearings before the European Court of Human Rights are normally held in public and the proceedings are of an adversarial nature i.e. not unlike proceedings in Scottish courts where the respective parties come in and argue the merits of their cases. The judges do not have to reach a unanimous verdict and many decisions will be by majority. Any of the judges are entitled to attach their own comments to the official decision of the Court and there is nothing to prevent a judge from stating publicly that he disagrees with the majority.

When the European Court of Human rights has to deal with a very important or potentially sensitive case, a single court of **17 judges** may sit. This court is referred to as the Grand Chamber and consist of the President, Vice-Presidents and the Section Presidents.

It is always possible that applications to the Court may be settled by the parties themselves or with the assistance of one of the Registrars of the Court before the case proceeds to a full hearing. Negotiations between the parties with the aim of attempting to secure an out-of-court settlement, are necessarily of a confidential nature.

Key point: The European Court of Human Rights is an independent, full-time court which deals with the enforcement of human rights and democratic freedoms across Europe.

The margin of appreciation

It is very important to emphasise that, unlike the other European Court (i.e. the Court of Justice of the European Union), the Court of Human Rights does not seek to impose a uniform system of law upon the contracting states to the European Convention. It should be appreciated that protection and promotion of human rights and fundamental freedoms can be achieved in a variety of ways. Various states will attempt to achieve these aims in a genuine fashion in accordance with their culture, with their political systems and, to an extent, with their history. In the immediate decades after the Second World War, countries such as Germany and Italy probably displayed a far greater sensitivity to the protection of human rights in comparison with the United Kingdom. In more modern times, membership of the council of Europe has expanded to include states such as Greece, Turkey and Spain with their common histories of military rule and subsequent crackdowns on political and democratic freedoms.

When making its decision, the European Court of Human Rights will apply a doctrine or a practice known as the **'margin of appreciation'**. This doctrine or practice permits a state to argue that it should be given a certain amount of freedom to determine in what way the various human rights and freedoms guaranteed by the Convention should be implemented into its national legal system. The European Court has been much more willing to permit states like the United Kingdom to restrict free speech in relation to personal morality or religious beliefs in a way that would not be permissible if the case involved restrictions on political freedoms. An application of the margin of appreciation can be seen in the following case:

Wingrove v UK (1997) the United Kingdom was able to argue successfully that the director of a film known as *Visions of Ecstasy* should be not be entitled to receive a certificate from the British Board of Film Classification. Without this certificate, the film could not secure a video release in the United Kingdom. The film was refused such a certificate on the grounds that this would result in a breach of the Video Recordings Act 1984 because it portrayed the crucified Christ in a blasphemous way. The blasphemy laws primarily exist in the United Kingdom to protect the Christian religion (and by extension the Jewish religion). What constitutes blasphemy can often be a thorny question because it inevitably raises the issue of freedom of speech. What a Christian may find blasphemous may be seen by another person as an expression of artistic freedom. The film itself contained images of Jesus Christ on the Cross with strongly sexual imagery. Wingrove, the director of the film was arguing that his right to freedom of speech, guaranteed by Article 10 of the European Convention, had been violated.

Held: by the European Court of Human Rights that, generally speaking, a contracting state such as the United Kingdom will be entitled to a certain amount of freedom where issues such as blasphemy come before the courts.

However, states will not be entitled to plead the margin of appreciation doctrine where a serious breach of Convention rights has occurred.

 McCann v UK (1996), the United Kingdom was held to have violated the right to life of three IRA terrorists who had intended to detonate a bomb in Gibraltar which would have caused considerable loss of life and widespread property damage. The three individuals were shot and killed by members of the elite SAS regiment before the bomb could be detonated. The SAS did not give the three IRA members an opportunity to surrender first. It was this shoot-to-kill policy which fell foul of the Strasbourg judges. The right to life is guaranteed by Article 2 of the European Convention and is considered to be one of its most important provisions – contracting states are not permitted to ignore or abuse this right. As will be appreciated, the judgment in **McCann** caused considerable controversy and outrage in the United Kingdom. In fact, over many years, the United Kingdom has found itself dragged before the European Court in relation to its handling of the political situation in Northern Ireland (which was at its worst phase from the early 1970s until the first IRA ceasefire in 1994). The United Kingdom argued that it was taking legitimate measures to safeguard the lives and security of its citizens in its effort to combat terrorism. However, the European Court did not always see eye to eye with the United Kingdom.

 Key point: The European Court of Human Rights recognises that member states have a measure of discretion in the way that they give effect to general standards set out in the Convention.

Summary

- Since the introduction of devolution as a result of the Scotland Act 1998, Scotland now has its own Parliament in Edinburgh which has law-making powers.

- The Scottish Parliament's powers are restricted to devolved matters.

- Scots law has many influences and has evolved through the centuries through a combination of judge-made law, Parliamentary laws, European law, customs and practices and historical sources.

- The Westminster Parliament is still the supreme law-making body in the UK, despite the introduction of devolution.

- There are two types of lawyers who appear in court in Scotland; solicitors and advocates.

- The civil justice system mainly exists to resolve disputes between private individuals.

- The three main civil courts in increasing order of importance are the Sheriff Court, the Court of Session and the House of Lords.

- The criminal justice system exists to uphold law and order and to punish those individuals who commit criminal acts.

- In Scotland, there is a public system of prosecution and private prosecutions are extremely rare.

- The three main criminal courts in increasing order of importance are the District Court, the Sheriff Court and the High Court of Justiciary.

- The Privy Council has been given a role under the Scotland Act 1998 to hear appeals from the High Court of Justiciary and the Court of Session where cases involve devolution and human rights matters.

- There are a variety of alternatives to going to court in order to solve legal disputes: arbitration, conciliation, mediation.

- There are numerous alternative courts: the Employment Tribunal, the Scottish Land Court, Courts Martial, the Lands Tribunal for Scotland.

- Owing to the fact of the UK's membership of the European Union, European law is now a major source of Scots law.

- If there is a conflict between European law and Scots law, the European legal rule will be preferred.

Test your knowledge

Short answer questions, examination standard essay questions and case-studies.

1 List two sources of Scots law.

2 What is meant by the common law? Give at least two examples.

3 What is an Act of Parliament? Give five examples.

4 Describe in detail how the British Parliament makes new laws.

5 Explain the following:
   • A Government Bill
   • A Private Member's Bill

6 How is the European Court of Justice organised?

7 How is the Court of First Instance organised?

8 Name the main institutions of the European Community.

9 Regarding European Law, what is meant by:
   • Primary Legislation
   • Secondary Legislation

10 Describe in detail each of the following:
   • A regulation
   • A directive
   • A decision
   • A recommendation

11 How is the European Parliament organised?

12 How is the European Commission organised?

13 How is the Council of Ministers organised?

14 List the three courts which form part of the Scottish civil court structure.

15 List the civil courts in order of importance.

16 How many Sheriffdoms are there in Scotland? Name them.

17 What is meant by the term 'jurisdiction'?

18 Describe in detail the main features of the Small Claims Procedure in the Sheriff Court.

19 How is the Sheriff Court under the civil law system organised?

20 How is the Court of Session organised?

21 What is the burden of proof required by a Scottish civil court?

22 If a Scottish criminal court seeks to punish a convicted offender, what does a Scottish civil court seek to do?

23 Name the two parties involved in a dispute before a civil court.

24 What do we call people who go to court?

25 Which judges would sit in the following courts:
   • The Sheriff Court
   • The Court of Session
   • The House of Lords

26 What type of lawyer would you need to represent you in the following courts:
   • The Sheriff Court
   • The Court of Session
   • The House of Lords

27 Who is responsible for running the Sheriff Court system?

28 Where would the following cases be dealt with?
   • A divorce
   • Tenor of a lost document
   • An appeal from a summary cause

29 Why might a pursuer choose the Sheriff Court in preference to the Outer House of the Court of Session?

30 Consider the following civil disputes. Advise the aggrieved party (the victim) about the following two issues:
   • Which civil courts have jurisdiction over the action

   • To which courts they can appeal if dissatisfied with the decision of the court of first instance

   a) John Willis is owed £10,000 by Janice Long for computer equipment delivered ten weeks ago. The agreed credit period has now expired and, despite repeated reminders, Janice Long still refuses to pay this outstanding invoice. John feels that he must now go to a court of law to resolve this dispute.

⚖ b) Agnes Pratt purchased a tumble dryer from Shockz Electrical Goods Ltd for £350. One day, two weeks later, the tumble dryer caught fire causing £150 worth of damage to her kitchen and destroyed clothes worth £200. The tumble dryer was faulty but Shockz Electrical Goods Ltd is refusing to compensate Agnes in any way. She is now considering suing them for £700.

⚖ c) As a result of a breach of contract by Jack MacDonald, Dougie Fisher has suffered a loss of £1300. Jack has offered £500 compensation which Dougie thinks is unacceptable. Dougie has now decided to sue Jack for the full £1300.

⚖ d) Frank bought a new stereo costing £499. However, after a few days, Frank discovers that his advanced multi-disc C.D. player does not work. Clearly unhappy, he takes the stereo back to Livewire Electric but they refuse to change it. Frank is very angry and decides to sue the shop.

⚖ e) A company called Fly-by-Night PLC has made some very stupid business decisions. As a result of this, the company has run out of money and is about to be wound-up. The company had a share capital of £5 million pounds. Jim is owed a very substantial sum of money by the company and he wishes to know which court will deal with winding up Fly-by-Night PLC.

31 Name the three Scottish Criminal Courts.

32 What is a crime?

33 What is the level of proof required by the Scottish Criminal Courts?

34 What is the difference between summary and solemn proceedings?

35 Which judges sit in the following Courts:
- The District Court
- The Sheriff Court
- The High Court

36 In a criminal case, to which Court would you appeal if you had first appeared in the following Courts:
- The District Court
- The Sheriff Court
- The High Court

37 List the powers of the District Court.

38 List the powers of the Sheriff Summary Court.

39 List the powers of the High Court.

40 Name the Courts in which the following prosecutors will appear:
- the Procurator Fiscal
- the Advocate Depute

41 What is the name of the Government Department in Edinburgh which has responsibility for the Scottish system of public prosecution?

42 Name the three possible verdicts/decisions in a criminal court.

43 Name the Sovereign's three law officers in Scotland.

THE LAW OF CONTRACT

Introduction

The law of contract is one of the most important foundations of commercial and business law. The influence of contract can be found in almost every aspect of the business world, for example, employment contracts, contracts of sale, contracts of agency, contracts of partnership, company law. It is, therefore, vital that people in business have a sound grasp of basic rules of contract law.

This chapter covers the following areas:

- The definition of a contract
- The composition and formation of a contract
- The factors which affect the validity of a contract
- Exclusion clauses and other unfair terms
- The remedies available for breach of contract
- The ways in which a contract can be terminated

The definition of a contract?

Basically, a contract is a legally enforceable agreement i.e. an agreement which the courts will enforce. This is an important definition because it is worth bearing in mind that there are many types of agreements that the courts will have nothing to do with. In effect, a court will wash its hands of an arrangement which it considers not to be a proper contractual agreement.

 Key point: A contract is a legally enforceable agreement between two or more legally distinct parties.

A contract centres around important matters, certainly not issues which are of a trivial nature. A number of individuals living in shared accommodation may have established a rota which sets out whose turn it is to do the cleaning, the cooking and the washing-up. On a very simple level, this rota is an agreement, but it is not a contract. If a dispute arose between the parties to this rota they most definitely could not threaten one another with legal action to enforce it. The individuals involved must sort things out for themselves. Where contracts are concerned, the courts must be convinced that a failure to comply with an agreement will very often lead to one of the parties suffering prejudice or real harm. If this is so, then it is right and proper that the courts should step in to protect the innocent party to the agreement by granting a decree in his favour.

At least two legally distinct persons must be party to a contract, for example, a buyer and a seller in a contract for the sale of goods (a bilateral agreement/contract). However, it is possible for more than two individuals to be involved in a contract, for example, partners in a firm or shareholders in a limited company (a multilateral agreement/contract).

 Key point: The law of contract relates to every sort of business activity imaginable.

The law of contract relates to everything you buy or sell. It would be a mistake to assume that the study of contracts always involves an examination of very complex documents. It is only in a number of limited situations that the law will demand that contracts should be in writing or that some sort of written evidence be produced. Admittedly, businesses will often prefer to have some sort of written contract or agreement in place, but this preference usually reflects the fact that a lot of money is at stake and businesses feel more secure if the main terms of the contract are written down. In the event of a dispute occurring in relation to the agreement, it is obviously a lot easier to prove something if you can refer to some written evidence rather than by attempting to remember what someone said six months or a year ago and even what they meant by their statements.

The composition and formation of a contract

It is often surprising to learn that forming a contract is usually a very straightforward task. In fact, people enter into many different contracts every day. You make a contract when you pay for your bus or train ticket; when you buy a newspaper or a magazine; when you buy your lunch; or when you purchase an item of clothing. A contract can be written, verbal or implied and can be proved by the production of any relevant, competent evidence including witnesses or documents in the event of dispute. A legally enforceable agreement or a contract has two basic elements – an offer and an acceptance of that offer. This can be expressed in a simple formula as:

Offer + Acceptance = Contract

 Key point: Contracts are entered into everyday and are much more common than you would expect.

However, this can be a deceptively simple formula. As we will learn later, it is absolutely crucial to be able to identify a genuine offer and to see whether this is matched by an unqualified acceptance. It is only when the offer and the acceptance are in place that we can say that a contract has been formed. However, an offer and an acceptance do not miraculously appear on the table leading automatically to a contract. In most cases, contracts will be formed only after a series of negotiations between the parties have been completed.

The formation of a contract should be regarded as more of a process rather than a one-off event. Contractual negotiations will involve the parties wheeling and dealing before one individual places a definite offer on the table which the other person may or may not want to accept.

 Key point: The main elements of a contract are the offer and the acceptance.

However, it should be re-emphasised that not all agreements are contracts. In other words, there are certain types of agreements that the Scottish courts will refuse to enforce. It is important to remember that a contract in Scots law is an agreement that the courts will enforce. Most commercial agreements, which involve the sale of goods and services, will be regarded as legally enforceable.

Unenforceable agreements

So, what are these types of agreements which the courts will refuse to enforce? They fall into several categories:

- Social agreements
- Domestic agreements
- Agreements binding in honour only
- Gambling agreements

Let us look at each of these types of agreement in turn.

Social agreements

A social agreement would cover arrangements such as dinner invitations, an invitation to meet friends in the pub for a drink or if you were asked out on a date by someone. Should you choose to break such an arrangement, the consequences will be no more serious than upsetting or disappointing your friends. There is no way that the disappointed individual could raise a legal action against you in an attempt to recover damages for a new outfit that she had bought in anticipation of the social occasion or to pay for travel expenses which she has incurred. Simply put, social arrangements are not something with which the courts have either the inclination or the time to get involved.

Domestic agreements

Domestic agreements, on the other hand, involve arrangements that people put in place to regulate their private lives. Examples of this type of arrangement would include the way in which a married/cohabiting couple or a group of young people (students) run their household affairs. These types of agreements would cover various run-of-the-mill tasks like whose turn it was to prepare meals, to clean the dishes, to clean the house or to put the bins out the night before the weekly refuse collection. It is up to the individuals involved to determine responsibility for these tasks and certainly not the job of the courts. However, it should be stressed that married or cohabiting couples can enter into legally binding contracts with one another, but not usually where household tasks are concerned.

 An interesting example of a domestic agreement coming before the courts occurred in **Spellman v Spellman (1961)**. In this case, a husband bought a car for his wife. The marriage had been under strain and the husband's purpose in buying the car was to try and save the marriage. Unfortunately, this was a doomed gesture and the couple later split up and went their separate ways. However, the husband took the car – his argument being that as he had paid for the car he had every right to it now that the marriage was over. The wife argued that the husband was bound by his agreement to let her use the car. The court disagreed stating that the husband and wife had made a domestic agreement not a contract. Therefore, the wife could not enforce the agreement before the courts.

Agreements binding in honour only

Agreements binding in honour only involve situations where the parties clearly intend that they will not be bound by any agreement that they might choose to enter into. If one person decided to withdraw from such an arrangement, his honour or integrity might well be called into question, but the individual concerned could probably live with this knowing full well that he would not be facing any legal consequences.

 An example of an agreement binding in honour only can be seen in the case of **Jones *v* Vernon's Pools (1938)**. Jones had returned a football coupon which contained a winning line. The pools company denied ever having received the coupon and it refused to honour the agreement.

Held: this was agreement binding in honour only i.e. it was not legally binding and Jones was, therefore, unable to enforce it before the courts. In fact, the coupon explicitly stated that the agreement between Jones and the pools company was not legally binding.

Gambling agreements (*sponsione ludicrae*)

Gambling agreements or *sponsione ludicrae* (ludicrous promises) are contracts which people enter into usually by way of placing a bet on a variety of sporting events or other frivolous activities, for example, who will be the latest evictee from Channel 4's Big Brother or who will win Pop Idol or Fame Academy. It could be said that the state is quite hypocritical as regards gambling activities in that it is happy to impose a tax on punters, yet the courts will not referee disputes which arise out of these agreements. Again, the courts regard gambling agreements as clearly below their dignity. When punters refuse to settle outstanding debts with a bookie, this is why the bookie will have to resort to hiring 'muscle' to persuade the reluctant punter to pay up. The Scottish courts will simply not enforce the terms of a gambling contract.

 Ferguson *v* Littlewoods Pools Ltd (1997), the members of a pools syndicate had won several million pounds on a football coupon – or so they thought. The syndicate was completely unaware of the fact that the agent for Littlewoods Pools had not forwarded the stake money because he had stolen it. When the theft was discovered, the syndicate members not unnaturally demanded that Littlewoods honour the winning ticket. Littlewoods claimed that it had never received the winning ticket. In response, the syndicate members argued that Littlewoods was responsible for the actions of its dishonest agent.

Held: by Lord Coulsfield in the Outer House of the Court of Session that the contract between the syndicate and Littlewoods was an example of a gambling or gaming contract and it was, therefore, unenforceable. Lord Coulsfield refused to order Littlewoods to pay out the sum owed to the syndicate.

The courts' attitude to gambling contracts stems from the time when Christianity was a much more powerful social force. Gambling was seen as a social evil and, in no circumstances should such activities be tolerated or promoted. By denying gamblers an effective means of enforcing these kinds of agreement, the courts were warning people that they indulged in these activities at their peril.

 Robertson *v* Balfour (1938) Robertson had entered into gambling agreements with Balfour, a bookie, to place bets on two horses, 'Swift and True' and 'Scotch Horse'. Both horses won their respective races, but Robertson received a mere £10 in winnings from Balfour. In fact, Balfour owed Robertson another £33 in winnings. Robertson had agreed that he would give Balfour extra time to pay him the balance.

Held: Robertson could not enforce the agreement against Balfour to pay out the additional £33. This was a gambling debt and the courts would not enforce such an agreement.

What if an action concerning the terms of an agreement which is not a contract (social, domestic, binding in honour only and gaming agreements) is lodged before the Scottish courts? As should already be apparent, the judge or judges would quite simply refuse to give the parties a remedy when the true nature of the agreement is revealed (see **Spellman *v* Spellman** and **Ferguson *v* Littlewoods Pools**). The judges' attitude to such agreements is that they are not worthy of judicial time. Realistically, this would mean that the parties would be forced back to square one where they would have to attempt to resolve the problem themselves – something which probably is not possible. In other words, the refusal of the judges to give litigants a solution would effectively leave them high and dry or one party severely disadvantaged.

Interestingly, however, individuals who form a gambling syndicate or who have an arrangement that they will split any winnings that they make may be shocked to learn that their fellow gamblers can enforce the terms of such an agreement against them. The Inner House of the Court of Session courts re-emphasised the approach of Scots law to gambling contracts generally and to agreements between gamblers particularly in the following case:

 Robertson *v* Anderson (2002) both women were friends who regularly attended Bingo sessions together. On one occasion, both women travelled to the Mecca Bingo Hall in Drumchapel from their homes in Dunoon. That particular evening, Robertson enjoyed a huge win of over £100,000 (three prizes of £390, £8000 and £100,000 approximately). Anderson claimed that she was owed half of the National Prize of £100,000 – a claim that Robertson disputed. Evidence was heard which established that Robertson and Anderson had an agreement that they would share equally any money that they might win during a game of Bingo. It was argued by Anderson that the arrangement she had with Robertson was a gaming or gambling contract that was unenforceable. The Inner House accepted that if one of the parties had attempted to sue Mecca for the winnings this action would have been unsuccessful. The question then centred around whether the agreement between Robertson and Anderson was a collateral contract and, therefore, enforceable despite the fact that it was slightly tainted by association with the main gambling contract between Anderson and Mecca.

Held: by the Inner House that Robertson could enforce the collateral contract that she had with Anderson. Collateral contracts are linked to another contract and they often give rise to a completely separate set of rights and duties. Their contract related to gaming, but it was not itself a gaming contract. The issue before the court – whether Anderson was under an obligation to share with Robertson the winnings which she received did not involve the enforcement of a gaming contract. This was the crucial difference between this case and **Ferguson v Littlewoods Pools Ltd** (above).

 Key point: Social, agreements, domestic agreements, agreements binding in honour only and gambling agreements are not contracts and are, therefore, not legally enforceable.

Unilateral promises or gratuitous obligations

We have already described a contract as a legally enforceable agreement between two or more legally distinct parties. The traditional model of contract in both Scotland and England anticipates that the parties will bring some form of consideration to the bargain. Consideration is best understood as meaning that in order to get the benefit of an agreement a party must do something in return or more, colloquially, 'if you scratch my back, I'll scratch yours'. The parties have rights, but they also have duties. In a contract for the sale of goods, the seller's consideration would be to deliver goods to the buyer which comply with the contract, but the reverse side of the coin is that the buyer will also have to provide consideration by paying the contract price for these goods. Admittedly, the vast majority of contracts in Scotland will be supported by some form of consideration. However, unlike the situation in England, consideration is not an essential requirement of contractual formation in Scotland.

In fact, it is possible in Scotland for one party to make a unilateral promise and be legally bound by its consequences. We might begin to understand this type of obligation by turning to the old tried and trusted saying 'my word is my bond'. The *promisor* is under a legal obligation to make good on his promise, but in contrast to the traditional model of contract the beneficiary of the promise need do nothing in return. Examples of unilateral promises would include unconditional gifts, rewards, donations and promises to keep an offer open for a specified period of time. The terms of the promise must be definite and sufficiently certain, there can be nothing vague about them as this will be fatal to a beneficiary's claim.

 Key point: In Scotland, the phrase 'my word is my bond' could apply to unilateral promises.

At first glance, a unilateral promise may have many similarities to a contract. There are clear differences:

◆ A contractual offer is not legally binding until it is accepted by the other party.

◆ A unilateral promise binds the promisor as soon as it is made – even if the promise will only be performed under certain conditions, for example, the promisor will give the beneficiary £10,000 when she completes her university education securing an upper second class Honours degree in law.

◆ Written evidence supporting the existence of unilateral promises should be provided. An exception is a unilateral promise made in the course of business where a verbal promise will be more than adequate for enforcement in the courts. Additionally, unilateral promises can be enforced where the beneficiary can prove that he acted on the strength of the promise, the promisor was aware of this and if the promise is not enforced, the beneficiary will suffer severe harm or hardship. Generally speaking, the existence of contracts can be proved without having to rely on written evidence.

◆ In many cases, the beneficiary will not even have to communicate his acceptance of the promise to the promisor. Scots law makes the assumption that no reasonable person would want to turn down the benefits of a promise, for example, the offer of a gift or a donation. A beneficiary can, of course, always reject a promise and this will mean that the promisor is no longer under a legal obligation. A beneficiary can even sue the promisor in order to compel him to make good on his promise, but Scots law does not permit the promisor to enforce a promise against the beneficiary.

 Key point: A contract consists of bilateral obligations in sense that the parties owe duties to one another, but where unilateral promises are concerned, only one person (the promisor) is duty bound to do something for the other party (the beneficiary).

Although there are clear differences between contracts and unilateral promises they are related. A unilateral promise can often be used in business by an individual in the hope that this will encourage the beneficiary to enter a contract with the promisor. If, for example, a seller of goods is attempting to encourage a potential buyer (the beneficiary) to enter a contract he might promise the interested party that he will not sell the goods to a third party for a specified period of time – until the end of business on Friday afternoon. Effectively, the beneficiary is being offered first refusal for a specified period of time. If the seller later sold the goods before the deadline has passed and the beneficiary returned before the end of business on Friday with the intention of purchasing the goods, the seller could be liable to pay compensation to the beneficiary. This will most certainly be the case, if the beneficiary can show that he has suffered a loss owing to the breach of promise; for example, he has had to go to another seller in order to buy the goods and he has had to pay more for them. As we shall see, a promise can be quite costly in Scotland.

 Petrie v Earl of Airlie (1834) in 1831, a political meeting had been held in Forfarshire to debate the Reform Bill which was currently progressing through Parliament. The Reform Bill, if given the Royal Assent, would extend the franchise in Westminster parliamentary elections to many individuals who were currently denied the right to vote (the following year the Bill was passed into law becoming the Reform Act 1832). The Earl of Airlie was in the

Chair at the meeting and a vote was taken whereby the assembly was asked to approve or disapprove the Bill. The Earl was in a group that voted against the Bill, although the majority of those present voted in its favour. Some time after this meeting, notices appeared around several districts in the county which appeared to defame the Earl by suggesting that his actions at the meeting had somehow been disloyal to the King, his Government and his people. The Earl issued a proclamation stating that he would pay a reward of 100 guineas to anyone who came forward with information to reveal the identities of the people who had written and printed the notice. Such a reward would be payable on the conviction of those (as yet unknown) persons. Alexander Petrie came forward with information to say that his brother and another individual were responsible for the notice. The Earl attempted to have the two prosecuted but the Crown's law officers refused to take this matter further because no indictable offence had been committed. They informed the Earl that he had two options: he could begin a criminal action himself or he could raise a civil action for damages. The Earl chose not to prosecute the two suspects.

Held: by the Inner House of the Court of Session (affirming the judgement of the Lord Ordinary) that the Earl must pay the reward to Alexander Petrie. The Earl had obtained everything that he had asked for in his offer of the reward and he was not entitled to evade making the payment to Petrie.

 Morton's Trustee *v* Aged Christian Friend Society of Scotland (1899) Morton had written to the Society agreeing to pay the pensions of 50 individuals selected by the Society for the remainder of their lives. Unfortunately, Morton died and the executors of his estate were unwilling to continue paying out the pensions to the 50 individuals. The Society claimed that Morton's promise had bound his estate, even in death.

Held: Morton had made an enforceable unilateral promise which continued to have legal effect after his death. His executors would have to continue to pay the life pensions until every one of the 50 individuals died. This, of course, could mean that a considerable period of time might pass before the consequences of the promise were fulfilled.

Evidence for the proposition that the Scottish courts recognise the concept of binding unilateral promises can be found in the following cases:

 Littlejohn *v* Hawden (1882) Lord Fraser (in the Outer House of the Court of Session) made the point that, if an offeror made a unilateral promise to keep an offer open for a certain period of time, for example, ten days from the date of the original offer, he cannot withdraw it until this period of time has passed. If he does so, he will run the risk of the offeree raising an action against him for breach of promise. Clearly, in such a situation, there will be no contract as the offeror has taken steps to withdraw the offer before the offeree has had an opportunity to accept it. Should the offeror honour his promise, the offer will lapse when the period for acceptance has passed and the offeror has failed to take advantage of this opportunity.

A & G Paterson _v_ Highland Railway Co 1927 Viscount Dunedin, speaking obiter in the House of Lords, expressly approved Lord Fraser's approach to the question of unilateral promises in Scots law:

'... _if I offer my property to a certain person at a certain price, and go on to say: 'This offer is to be open up to a certain date,' I cannot withdraw that offer before that date, if the person to whom I made the offer chooses to accept it. It would be different in England, for ... there would be no consideration for the promise to keep the offer open._'

 Key point: Unilateral promises in Scotland are capable of being legally enforced.

The offer

An offer must be a precise and definite proposal. Anything that lacks certainty or specifics cannot be regarded as an offer. An offer must be capable of being accepted by the person to whom it is properly addressed or communicated. An area of difficulty often arises when it comes to determining whether a definite offer exists which is capable of being accepted. An offer demonstrates that the _offeror_ intends to be legally bound by the consequences of his/her undertaking if it is accepted in an unqualified fashion as the following example demonstrates:

Brian: 'I will sell my stereo to you for £700.'

Valerie: 'It's a deal!'

An offer must be sufficiently definite in its terms.

 Harvela Investments Ltd _v_ Royal Trust Company of Canada Ltd [1985] the House of Lords refused to permit the practice of referential bidding by an offeror. This practice would have allowed an offeror to contact the offeree and submit a bid say of £10,000, but he could then add the following proviso: 'or £5,000 over and above any other offer that you receive.' In **Harvela Investments**, Harvela and Sir Leonard Outerbridge were locked in a battle to take control of Harvey & Co Ltd. Harvela offered to purchase shares in Harvey for 2,175,000 Canadian dollars, whereas Sir Leonard Outerbridge made an offer to purchase shares in Harvey in the following terms: '2,100,000 Canadian dollars or 100,000 Canadian dollars in excess of any other offer'.

Held: by the House of Lords that Sir Leonard Outerbridge had not submitted a valid offer because its terms were not definite enough.

 Key point: An offer must be a precise and definite proposal.

An offer can be made to one person, a group of persons or to the world at large (for example, an automatic vending machine).

An invitation to treat

It can often be problematic when it becomes necessary to be able to tell the difference between an offer and an invitation to treat. It is important to distinguish between an offer and other representations or statements that, at first glance, appear to resemble offers. However, invitations to treat can be refused therefore resulting in a binding contract not being formed. A statement which merely suggests a willingness to negotiate or to consider offers is referred to as an invitation to treat. An invitation to treat can most effectively be explained with reference to the phrase 'make me an offer which I may or may not accept'. An alleged offer may be little more than a mere price indication.

 Key point: It is important to distinguish between an offer and other representations or statements made by someone which amount to an invitation to treat i.e. 'make me an offer'.

Examples of invitations to treat include the following situations:

◆ Goods or services which are advertised in newspapers, trade journals, catalogues and on the Internet
◆ Goods displayed in shop windows and on the shelves
◆ Price lists
◆ Goods at auctions
◆ Company prospectuses/adverts in connection with sale of securities

If you make an offer to someone, you are indicating by words, writing or by your actions that you are willing to be bound on certain terms and should these terms be accepted by another person, both of you will be locked into a legally enforceable agreement. Therefore, once your offer has been accepted and an agreement has been formed, the consequences of withdrawing from a contract can be potentially serious. If, for example, after having had your offer accepted by another individual, you wished to withdraw from it, it is highly likely that you would face a legal action for breach of contract. In most cases, this would mean that you would have to pay damages or compensation to the innocent party as a direct result of your breach of contract. In other situations, the court may force you to comply with the original terms of your offer.

 Key point: If a person makes a definite offer which is subsequently accepted by another person, a legally enforceable contract now exists between these two parties.

The acceptance of an offer will only result in a binding contract if it corresponds exactly to the essential terms of the offer. The terms of the acceptance must be identical to the original offer. Any attempt by the offeree to change the terms of the offer will mean that no contract is formed. Even simple misunderstandings between the parties can mean that no contract is formed. The parties must show that they have achieved a meeting of minds or, as expressed in the old Latin phrase, *consensus in idem*.

 Key point: The offeree is the person or party to whom the offeror makes an offer.

A good illustration of a failure to achieve a meeting of minds can be seen in the following case:

 Mathieson Gee (Ayrshire) Ltd *v* Quigley (1952) Mathieson Gee wrote to Quigley stating that they could supply mechanical equipment for the purpose of removing mould which was deposited at the bottom of Quigley's pond. Quigley responded in writing by saying that he was confirming his verbal acceptance of Mathieson Gee's offer to remove the silt and deposit from his pond. However, had both parties actually managed to conclude a contract? In other words was there a meeting of minds or agreement? Mathieson Gee had made an offer to supply equipment to Quigley to carry out the job in question – they had not offered to supply the equipment and carry out the job. Quigley had mistakenly assumed that Mathieson Gee were offering to supply both the equipment and remove the silt from his pond. The parties were, therefore, completely at cross-purposes.

Held: By the House of Lords that there was no contract between them because they were not in agreement about the same things i.e. the offer and acceptance did not mirror one another.

An offer may be communicated to an individual, a group of people or to the world at large.

Carlill *v* Carbolic Smokeball Co (1893) demonstrates an offer being made to the world at large, which Mrs Carlill impliedly accepted by purchasing the product and following the instructions to the letter. The manufacturers of the carbolic smokeball were so confident of its properties that they stated in advertisements (in various newspapers) that they would pay £100 to anyone who bought the smokeball, used it according to the strict instructions and still caught flu. They added that they had deposited £1000 in the Alliance bank to show sincerity in the matter. Mrs Carlill bought the product, followed the instructions, but still caught flu. It was held that the wording of the advert was such that it amounted to an offer. There was a clear intention that the company intended to be bound by the offer. Mrs Carlill accepted the offer by performing the actions required by the advert. Mrs Carlill was therefore entitled to the money. This case illustrates that there can be implied acceptance of an offer. It also emphasises the importance of communication of the offer. If Mrs Carlill merely chanced to buy a smokeball without having seen the advert, she would not have been entitled to the £100. Her actions constituted implied acceptance of the offer because it was in response to the offer. Offers must be definite, capable of being accepted and the offeror must intend to be bound by the consequences of it being accepted.

Hunter *v* General Accident Fire and Life Assurance Corporation Ltd (1909) Mr Hunter responded to an advertisement in a Lett's diary on 25 December 1905. The advertisement was offering up to £1,000 in insurance cover for those individuals who were killed in a train accident. A condition of the advertisement was that all applicants had to ensure that their names were registered at the company's head office. A further condition of the advertisement was that any claim made under the policy must relate to a fatal accident which occurred within one year of each applicant's registration. On the event of death, £1,000 would be paid to the deceased's executor. Hunter received a letter from the insurers dated 3 January 1906 which contained an official confirmation of his registration dated 29 December

1905. On 28 December 1906, Hunter was seriously injured in a rail accident and he died of his injuries the next day. His wife, who was executrix, lodged a claim for £1,000 in accordance with the terms of the policy on 2 January 1907. The company refused to pay this sum to her. It claimed that Hunter had been accepted for the policy on 27 December 1905. If this was the case, then Mrs Hunter's claim was several days too late as it fell outside the period of one year in which any claim should have been lodged.

Held: by the House of Lords that the company could not prove with any certainty when it had actually registered the deceased. The date of 3 January 1906 was to be regarded as the date upon which registration became effective and this meant that Hunter's wife had brought the claim within one year of his registration. The company failed to prove when registration had actually taken place and it, if anyone, should have been able to pinpoint this date exactly. Mrs Hunter was, therefore, entitled to enforce the policy. Lord Loreburn, the Lord Chancellor, made the point that every judge who had considered the case thought that the advertisement was an offer which had been accepted by every individual, including Hunter, who managed to comply with its conditions. During consideration of the case in the Court of Session, Lord Kinnear stated:

'It is suggested that this is making a contract by an advertisement, but it is none the worse for being an advertisement if it is a distinct and definite offer capable of acceptance.'

 Key point: Offers can be communicated either to a single person, to a group of people or to the world at large.

The offer and an invitation to treat contrasted

The contrast between invitations to treat and offers can clearly be seen in:

 Harvey *v* Facey (1893) The legal issue in this case centred around whether the parties had concluded a contract of sale for an estate in Jamaica or whether they were still in a state of negotiation. Events began with the pursuer contacting the defender by telegram and posed the following question: "Will you sell us Bumper Hall Pen? Telegraph lowest cash price." Bumper Hall Pen was the name of the estate in Jamaica that the pursuer was interested in purchasing. The defender duly obliged the pursuer's request for information by sending a telegram in reply which stated: "Lowest price for Bumper Hall Pen £900." The pursuer thought that this reply was a definite offer from the defender and sent an 'acceptance' in the following terms: "We agree to buy Bumper Hall Pen for £900 asked by you. Please send us your title deeds in order that we get early possession." Rather ominously the defender did not respond to this 'acceptance' by the pursuer and it soon became apparent that the defender was disputing the existence of a contract of sale. As far as the defender was concerned its response to the pursuer's first telegram was a mere invitation to treat and not a definite offer. In other words, if the pursuer wished to be regarded as a serious contender to buy the property, an offer greater than £900 would have to be made. All that the defender was indicating was the lowest cash price that it would consider selling the property for. The Supreme Court of Jamaica, however, decided the case in favour of the pursuers. The defender then appealed to the Privy Council in London.

Held: by the Privy Council that the parties had failed to conclude a binding contract. The defender's response to the pursuer's original enquiry was merely a response providing the desired information about the estate. The defender had made an invitation to treat i.e. make me an offer which must be at least £900 or above if you want to be regarded as a having a serious chance of purchasing the estate. As far the defender was concerned, their telegram was alerting the pursuer to the fact that they would not even consider offers under £900. The Privy Council stated that the pursuer had made an offer to buy the estate for £900 which the defender had quite clearly refused to consider.

Another situation where it is important to know the difference between an offer and an invitation to treat is where goods are sold at auction:

 Fenwick v Macdonald, Fraser & Co Ltd (1904) the pursuer made a bid for a bull that was part of a herd of cattle being sold at auction. In the auctioneer's catalogue, the cattle were described as being "offered for unreserved sale". The pursuer, in common with the other bidders, thought that this phrase meant that the owners had not placed a reserve price on the bull. There was certainly no mention made of any reserve price in relation to the sale of the animal. If a reserve price has been placed on goods by the owner, the auctioneer has absolutely no authority to sell for anything less than this. The owners of the bull decided to withdraw the animal from the auction on the grounds that a reserve price of 150 guineas had not been met by any of the bidders, including the pursuer. The pursuer sued for breach of contract.

Held: by the Inner House of the Court of Session that there was no contract. Lord MacDonald, the Lord Justice Clerk, stated that:

'Whatever might have been the law formerly, the law of Scotland is now that a sale by auction is complete when the auctioneer announces its completion by the fall of the hammer or in other customary manner. Until such announcement is made, any bidder may retract his bid.'

The judges of the Second Division then went on to consider whether a seller could withdraw his property for sale before the fall of the auctioneer's hammer. The seller, by putting goods up for auction, was making an invitation to treat and, by withdrawing the bull from auction, he was indicating that none of the offers was acceptable to him. Interestingly, the Court of Session did appear to suggest that the law of Scotland, before the introduction of the Sale of Goods Act 1893, would not always have permitted the seller to withdraw from the auction in similar circumstances.

 Jaeger Brothers Ltd *v* J & A McMorland (1902) the pursuers were in the market to purchase a quantity of iron which they intended to ship to Australia. They contacted the defenders and made enquiries regarding the prices of 500-600 tons of iron of various specifications. They stressed the urgency of a response from the defenders to their enquiries. The pursuers were anxious to confirm to their Australian business associates that they had managed to secure the iron and they wished to send notification of this by telegram to Australia the following day. The defenders replied the next day by telegram stating:

"Offer 600 tons half one, half three, Govan, Leith, 75s 9d; c.i.f. Hamburg 80s 9d."

The terms "half one" and "half three" referred to the specification of the goods and the amount i.e. the consignment was to consist of two different types of goods. The term c.i.f. meant the defenders would bear responsibility for all aspects of shipping the goods Hamburg i.e. the cost, insurance and freight to – obviously for an increased price. If the pursuers were not interested in this arrangement, a lower price was payable.

The pursuers replied accepting the "offer" to supply 500 tons of the iron (half one and half three) for shipment from Govan on c.i.f. terms to Hamburg. A disagreement emerged later between the parties as to the date of delivery. The defenders stated that no contract had actually been formed as their response to the pursuers' original enquiry was a mere quote expressed in general terms and could not be considered as an offer capable of acceptance.

Held: by the Inner House of the Court of Session that the pursuers' original letter addressed to the defenders was in the manner of an invitation to treat i.e. make us an offer. Unfortunately, the defenders had responded to this enquiry in a very precise fashion and they had conveyed an offer to the pursuers by telegram. They had offered the pursuers two options: either delivery of a specific quantity of iron placed aboard a ship of the pursuers' choice at Govan or Leith for a specific price or delivery of a specific quantity of iron to Hamburg at a specific price. The pursuers, of course, had accepted the second offer. The pursuers' acceptance of the defenders' offer had resulted in the formation of a contract.

Contrary to popular opinion, advertisements displayed in newspapers, magazines, trade journals and on the internet are not offers, but are regarded as invitations to treat. The offer is to be made by the consumer in response to the advertisement. The advertiser is at liberty to accept or decline any offers potential customers might choose to make. An invitation to treat can take the following forms: goods in a shop window display, on a shop shelf or in a catalogue, goods exposed for sale at an auction. The offer can be made by taking goods to the cash desk or requesting them from the shop assistant, it is then up to the advertiser or the shop assistant to decide whether to accept or refuse the offer. A shop assistant does not have to give a customer a reason for refusing to accept an offer and is not bound by the marked price on the goods. If, for instance, you happen to be under 18 years of age and you attempt to purchase alcohol from your local supermarket, the assistant will be well within her rights to refuse to accept your offer to purchase the goods.

 Pharmaceutical Society of Great Britain *v* Boots Cash Chemists (1953) the judges helpfully distinguished between an invitation to treat and an offer. The case arose as a result of a provision of the Pharmacy and Poisons Act 1933, which stipulated that the sale of certain medicines must take place within the presence of a registered pharmacist. Boots operated a self-service system whereby customers were able to place medicines that they wished to purchase in their shopping baskets. The customers would then take the medicines to the cash register in order to pay for them. The essence of the case centred around the issue of when the sale actually took place. Was the display of goods an 'offer' in the legal sense or merely an invitation to treat? If it was an offer then, on the selection of goods (articles are put in a basket) a contract would be formed and the sale would be unlawful under the Act because a pharmacist was not present at that time. However, if the display of goods was merely an invitation to treat, customers would have to make an offer to buy at the cash desk, at which point the pharmacist would accept the offer or would be present to supervise the salesperson, a contract would be formed and the sale would therefore be properly supervised and, thus, comply with the provisions of the Act.

This case established that placing goods on display in shops does not constitute an offer to sell those goods – it is merely an invitation to treat. This is why an advance indication of the price of goods or services, by notice, labelling or price tickets, is a non-binding estimate. Such advance notifications are quotations or simply an expression of a willingness to negotiate.

This may seem like a clever legal distinction which is more apparent than real, but the outcome of some cases has turned on whether a trader has been making an invitation to treat or an offer. We can see how this distinction operates in the following English High Court case:

 Fisher *v* Bell (1961) a flick-knife with a price label on it was displayed in a shop window. The shopkeeper was charged with the offence of offering such a knife for sale. He was found not guilty. Lord Parker CJ said:

'It is clear that, according to the ordinary law of contract, the display of an article with a price on it in a shop window is merely an invitation to treat. It is in no sense an offer for sale, the acceptance of which constitutes a contract.'

 Key point: An invitation to treat could take the from of an advertisement, catalogue, brochure, price list or quotation and is a means by which sellers alert potential buyers to the existence of certain goods services. It will then be up to these buyers to make an offer to purchase these goods and services which the seller may or may not accept.

Under the criminal law, a shop which has wrongly or mistakenly displayed misleading prices would fall foul of Sections 20–21 of the Consumer Protection Act 1987. However, the aggrieved consumer will still not be entitled to receive the goods at the (wrongly) marked price because it is the consumer who is making the offer to the shop – an offer which the shop has rejected and it follows that there can be no contract.

Other situations

What about vending machines? We could take the view that the machine is making an implied offer to the world and when an individual places his/her money in the machine s/he has accepted that offer. Therefore, we have a contract.

In **Thornton *v* Shoe Lane Parking (1971)** the Court of Appeal stated that the ticket machine at the entrance to the car park represented an offer to the world at large which was capable of being accepted by members of the public. Acceptance of this offer became a reality when an individual approached the machine and took the issued ticket. Lord Denning said:

'The customer pays his money and gets a ticket. He cannot refuse it. He cannot get his money back. He may protest to the machine, even swear at it; but it will remain unmoved. He is committed beyond recall. . . The contract was concluded at that time. It can be translated into offer and acceptance in this way. The offer is made when the proprietor of the machine holds it out as being ready to receive money. The acceptance takes place when the customer puts his money into the slot. The terms of the offer are contained in the notice placed on or near the machine stating what is offered for the money. The customer is bound by those terms if they are sufficiently brought to his notice beforehand, but not otherwise. He is not bound by the terms printed on the ticket if they differ from the notice, because the ticket comes too late.'

Withdrawal or revocation of offer

An offer can be cancelled at any time *before* it is accepted. In Scotland, the exception to this rule would cover a situation whereby the offeror has made a unilateral promise to potential offerees to the effect that he will keep the offer open for a specified period of time, for example, that the offer will remain valid until noon on Friday. If no one has accepted the offer by noon on the Friday, the offeror is quite free to withdraw it, but not before this (self-imposed) deadline. Once it has been accepted, an offer cannot be withdrawn and this will be the case even if the offeror has made a mistake in the terms of the offer as can be seen in the following case:

 Centrovincial Estates PLC *v* Merchant Investors Assurance (1983) a firm of solicitors, acting for a property letting company, had communicated a definite offer to the effect that their clients were willing to rent offices to potential tenants for the sum of £65,000 per year. The offerees promptly accepted this offer of the tenancy at the stated rent. However, in what turned out to be an extremely costly mistake, the solicitors realised that the landlord wished to charge the tenants a sum of £126,000 for the yearly rent. The solicitors then telephoned the tenants and invited them to regard the terms of the original offer as changed to reflect the true position of their clients. Understandably quite happy with the outcome of the negotiations, the tenants refused to take this request seriously. The landlord then attempted to have the contract with their new tenants cancelled by reason of the unilateral mistake contained in the original letter of offer.

Held: by the English Court of Appeal that a binding contract had been formed. The tenants would get the benefit of the tenancy for a very favourable price. Unfortunately for the landlord, it had learned a very harsh lesson in the sense that the law did not protect it from the consequences of its own stupidity when it made an exceptionally bad bargain with the new tenants. It should be stressed that the tenants were completely unaware of the landlord's error and that they had acted in good faith when accepting what they regarded as a very favourable offer. Had the tenants known that the landlord had made such a serious error then the case would have had a very different outcome. As something of a consolation, the landlord would have a claim for damages against the solicitors as a result of their negligence.

If the offeree knows that the offeror is mistaken, the contract may be void on the grounds of unilateral mistake.

The Scottish case of **Krupp v John Menzies Ltd (1907 SC 903)** stands in stark contrast to the decision of the English Court of Appeal in **Centrovincial Estates** (above). In **Krupp**, the parties had already made a verbal agreement that the employee, the manageress of the Mallaig Station Hotel, would receive a salary representing 5% of the profits of the business. When this agreement was formalised, the written contract contained a clerical error which stated that the employee's salary was to be 20% of the profits of the business. This, of course, was a considerably more attractive salary than the employee had originally anticipated. The employee knew that this calculation in the written contract was completely in error, but it did not prevent her from attempting to enforce this much more favourable agreement in preference to the original, verbal agreement.

Held: the Court of Session permitted the employer to have the written contract changed to reflect the true contractual position which the original verbal agreement represented. The difference between this case and the **Centrovincial Estates** decision was that the hotel manageress was not acting in good faith – she was fully aware of the clerical error in the written document. As we shall see later in this chapter, the Contract (Scotland) Act 1997 allows additional external sources of information (for example, verbal statements or documentary evidence) to be used in court in order to give true expression to the parties' intentions in a written contract. Generally speaking, of course, the 1997 Act takes the position that a written document will contain all the main terms of the agreement.

 Key point: Generally, an offer can be withdrawn at any time by the offeror (unless he has promised to keep it open for a specified time) before it can be accepted by the offeree.

How can the offeror effectively cancel any offer that he has made?

Such an intention on the part of the offeror must be communicated to the offeree before the offer can be accepted. Effective communication of a change in the offeror's intention to be bound by the offeror merely implies that the offeree has some knowledge that the offer is no longer valid. Presumably, the offeree cannot turn a blind eye to facts which strongly suggest that the offeror has had second thoughts and now intends to cancel the offer such as failure by the offeree to open a letter with the offeror's name and address stamped on the rear of the envelope.

Communication of an intention to withdraw the offer may be made to the offeree by the offeror or via some other reliable source, for example, the offeror's agent (a solicitor).

 Key point: When the offeror decides to withdraw or cancel his offer, he must communicate this decision effectively to the offeree or his agent.

The effect of the death of one of the parties

Does the death of one of the parties affect the creation of a contract or, perhaps more ghoulishly, is it possible to contract with the dead? The answer to this question would seem to depend on whether the death occurred before or after acceptance of the offer.

Death of the offeror before acceptance

The Scottish position, according to Viscount Stair and Professor Bell, concerning the death of the offeror is very clear. Generally speaking, if the offeree has not accepted the offer at the time of the death of the offeror, then no contract is formed. In other words, the offer terminates automatically upon the death of the offeror. Interestingly, the position in England is slightly less clear and it has been argued that an offer does not automatically lapse on the event of the offeror's death. English law seems to take the view that, when a contract does not require a high degree of personal involvement of the offeror, for example, when it is not an employment contract or a contract for services, death may not necessarily be a barrier to the creation of a legally enforceable agreement. If we follow this logic, then it would be possible for the estate of the deceased to be bound in contract to the offeree for the sale of land. However, this theory sits very much at odds with statements made by English Court of Appeal judge, Lord Justice Mellish, in **Dickinson v Dodds (1876)**. His Lordship was overwhelmingly hostile to the idea that that an offer does not necessarily cease to be capable of acceptance when the offeror dies. The obiter statement of Lord Justice Mellish reflects Scots law: the offer cannot be accepted after the offeror's death.

Death of an offeree before acceptance

If the offeree has not accepted the offer prior to his death, the parties have clearly failed to enter into a contractual relationship. It is very important to stress that an executor of the deceased offeree does not have the authority to accept the offer. The operation of this rule is not dependant upon the nature of the proposed contract. Quite simply, the offeree failed to accept the offer when he was alive, there is no chance of him accepting it now that he is dead. In the English decision of **Reynolds v Atherton (1922)**, Lord Justice Warrington in the Court of Appeal stated that the death of the offeree terminates the offer and not even his executor will have the authority to accept it on his behalf.

Interestingly, a case from Canada determined by the Appellate Division of the Supreme Court of Ontario considered the issue of the effect of the offeree's death before any acceptance of any offer had been made.

 Re Irvine (1928), it was held that a son had no authority to accept an offer on behalf of his deceased father. Apparently, the deceased had written a letter of acceptance in response to a offer. He asked his son to post this letter, but before the son was able to do this, the father died. Nevertheless, the son decided to post the letter despite the fact of his father's death.

Held: Sensibly, the Supreme Court of Ontario stated that no contract had been created. The offer had been personally addressed to the deceased and it ceased to have any legal effect upon his death. The offer could not be accepted by anyone other than the deceased.

There may, however, be an exception to this rule that the death of the offeree means that the offer is no longer capable of acceptance. There may be an enforceable contract in circumstances, where an agent has concluded a contract with a third party and who is completely unaware that his principal has died before the conclusion of this agreement. Such a rule was deemed to be sensible in the absence of modern and instantaneous methods of communications (see **Campbell v Anderson (1829) in Chapter 5**). It was not unusual for the principal to die in Scotland and it might take many months before this news reached his agent in, for example, Australia. It will, of course, be appreciated that, as the personal representative of the principal, the agent may have accepted many offers on the principal's behalf before news of the death reached him. Even with the advent of modern communications, this exception to the general rule may still have its uses.

 Key point: In Scots law, it would appear that the death of either the offeror or the offeree before the offer can be accepted will mean that no contract is formed as the offer lapses automatically.

Death of the parties after acceptance

Obviously, if an offer has been accepted prior to the death of one of the parties, this is a completely different situation. As Viscount Stair remarked: 'An offer accepted is a contract.' From this statement it is possible to find support for the notion that the death of either the offeror or the offeree would have no effect unless, of course, the contract involved the provision of personal services, for example, an employment contract or a contract of agency. What about the sale of heritable or moveable property? Such a contract should still be enforceable in Scotland. As we have seen in the case of **Morton v Aged Christian Friend Society of Scotland (1899)** (above), a unilateral promise to provide 50 life pensions continued to be binding and the death of the promisor mattered not one bit.

Lapse of an offer

An offer will no longer be capable of acceptance in the following circumstances:

- If it is rejected
- If the other party makes a counter-offer
- If a time limit for acceptance fixed by the offeror expires
- If the subject-matter of the contract is destroyed or materially altered
- If the proposed contract becomes illegal or otherwise becomes impossible to perform
- If either party dies or the offeror becomes insane or pronounced bankrupt
- If the offer is not accepted within a reasonable time

 Key point: An offer will be deemed to be no longer capable of acceptance in the following circumstances – if it is rejected, if it is the subject of a counter-offer, expiry of the time-limit for acceptance, if the subject matter of the contract is destroyed or materially altered, if the proposed contract becomes illegal, if either party dies, becomes insane or is declared bankrupt or if it is not accepted within a reasonable time.

The offer is not accepted within a reasonable time

An offer which is not accepted within a reasonable time is presumed to lapse. Simply put, offers have a limited shelf-life. They do not last forever. It would be quite absurd, if the offeror was placed in a position whereby he could be bound by the consequences of an offer which he made ten years previously which the offeree now wishes to accept. This, of course, is an extreme example and some offers will have an extremely short life. A reasonable time may vary on the circumstances of the case, the nature of the transaction and the nature of the market which the parties are operating in. The phrase 'a reasonable time' means different things in different situations and, therefore, it will be a matter for the court to determine what constitutes a reasonable time.

Offers involving perishable goods or commodities, for example, agricultural produce, oil and precious metals that tend to suffer fluctuating market prices will clearly leave the offeree with a shorter time to decide whether to accept such an offer than offers for goods or services which tend to experience less volatile price movements. An example of this situation can be seen in the following two cases:

 Wylie and Lochhead v McElroy and Sons (1873) an offer to carry out work which involved fitting iron decorative work on stables was not accepted for five weeks. During this time the price of iron increased significantly. By this time, the offeree had decided to accept the original offer at the much lower price. The offeror argued that the original offer was no longer capable of being accepted. A dispute ensued. It was held that because there had been no acceptance within a reasonable time the offer had been impliedly withdrawn and no contract was formed. The court took the view that where such a commodity as iron was concerned with its tendency to experience price fluctuations 'hours must suffice for a decision, not weeks or months'.

 Glasgow Steam Shipping Company v Watson (1873) Watson, the defender, had made an offer to the Glasgow Shipping Company, the pursuers, to supply coal to them for the period of a year and the price was to be based on seven shillings per ton. The defender made this offer on 5 August, but the pursuers did not accept it until 13 October. By this point, the price of coal had risen considerably to nine shillings per ton. The defender refused to supply the coal at the price stated on 5 August claiming that a reasonable time for acceptance of that offer had passed. If the pursuers wished to purchase the coal, they would have to do so at the higher price. The pursuers raised an action for breach of contract. The dispute arose because the defender had not laid down a time-limit for acceptance of the offer and this situation made it possible for the pursuers to argue that they were acting well within a reasonable time-limit when they eventually communicated their acceptance in response to the offer of 5 August.

Held: there was no contract as the defenders had failed to accept the offer within a reasonable time frame. Lord Deas made a memorable statement in the following terms:

'But as regards such an offer as this, to supply an article which at all times fluctuates in price, and which at the time in question was rapidly

*rising in price, it is altogether out of the question to hold it to have been
a continuing offer for so long a period as is here contended for. . .'*

The above cases of **Wylie and Lochhead** and **Glasgow Steam Shipping Company**
clearly demonstrate that an offeree will not be permitted to keep the offeror hanging
on until the last possible moment when he finally decides whether or not to accept
the offer. If this situation was tolerated by the courts, an offeree would have an unfair
advantage whereby he could watch price movements in the relevant market. If the
price increases in value substantially, the offeree would be able to hold the offeror to
the contract price which was originally quoted. On the other hand, if the value of the
goods decreases significantly, the offeree could demand that the price be completely
renegotiated. There is, of course, a very simple way in which the offeror could avoid
disputes surrounding the issue of what is a reasonable time for acceptance of his
offer. He could state a time for acceptance of the offer, for example, 'Your acceptance
of this offer must be in our hands by 5 p.m. on Friday 16 January'.

 Key point: Where the offer does not state a time-limit for acceptance, the
offeree must accept it within a reasonable time and what is a reasonable time
will depend on the circumstances of each case.

Acceptance

Acceptance of the offer means that a contract has been formed. Once an offer is said
to exist, the court must be satisfied that it has actually been accepted, otherwise no
contract has been created. Acceptance of an offer is an expression by the offeree of
his willingness to bind himself legally to a contract with the offeror with the
conditions stated in the offer.

 Key point: Acceptance of an offer means that a contract has been formed.

For an acceptance to result in a legally binding contract it must correspond exactly
to the essential terms of the offer. *Consensus in idem* or 'a meeting of minds' must
be said to have been achieved. Therefore to achieve *consensus in idem*,
acceptance by the offeree must be of a completely unconditional nature. An
acceptance will not be deemed to be valid if it does not mirror all the essential terms
of the offer. If an acceptance includes terms which are not contained in the offer, it
is said to be a conditional acceptance. This is viewed as a completely new offer
which must subsequently be accepted in order for a contract to come into existence.

 Key point: The acceptance of an offer must be a mirror image of the terms
of the offer.

Such a qualified acceptance will not bind the offeror and, thus, form a contract. Any
response to an offer which seeks to adapt in any way or add to the conditions of the
original offer, must be regarded as a counteroffer. A counteroffer cancels the original
offer and no subsequent acceptance of the original terms will be effective. An
acceptance is only valid when it has been effectively communicated to the offeror.

 Key point: Acceptance is only valid when it has been effectively
communicated to the offeror.

Communication of an acceptance

This could take the form of writing, verbal acceptance or by implication (for example, the fall of an auctioneer's hammer). The acceptance must comply with any requirements of the offer as to the mode of acceptance, for example, the offer may state that acceptance should be made in writing or telephone. Accepting a sum of money in response to an offer to buy, dispatching goods, issuing a ticket or putting a coin in a slot machine are all actions which are regarded as acceptance by performance. In Scots law, if the offeror fails to stipulate a particular method of communication, then the manner of acceptance must be effective and usually follows the same manner as the offer.

The offer can then only be accepted by a person to whom it is addressed. Acceptance must be communicated by a person generally authorised to do this.

 Powell v Lee (1908) Powell applied for the post of Head Master of The Cranford School. The managers of the school considered Powell's offer and decided to appoint him by three votes to two. Powell successfully beat off competition for the post from two other candidates. In what proved to be an important decision, the managers chose not to communicate their acceptance of the offer immediately to Powell. In fact, no decision had been taken as to how the results of the selection process were to be communicated to the successful applicant. Dismore, one of the managers, informed Powell that his application had been successful – this statement was, of course, completely truthful. However, Dismore, had no actual or ostensible authority to release this information to Powell (**see Chapter 5 for an explanation of an agent's authority**). The managers later changed their earlier decision to select Powell as Head Master and decided to appoint one of the previously unsuccessful candidates in his place. Powell sued the managers for breach of contract.

Held: by the King's Bench Division of the English High Court that Powell's claim for breach of contract should be dismissed. At no time had Dismore been given authority to inform Powell of the managment's decision. The statement that Powell had been accepted for the position of Head Master was, therefore, completely unauthorised and did not bind the managers into a contract with him.

 Burr v Commissioners of Bo'ness (1896) an employee received information through unofficial sources that his employer had decided to increase his annual salary from £10 to £20. This increase was never officially communicated to the employee. About a month after making the initial decision to increase the employee's salary, the employer decided not to proceed with this. The employee sued for the increased salary.

Held: by the Inner House of the Court of Session that the employee was not entitled to the increase because his employers had not communicated this decision to him.

 Key point: An offer must be accepted by the offeree, the person to whom it is addressed, or someone who is authorised to act on his behalf (an agent) for this purpose.

An offer may, however, be addressed to the world at large or to members of the public (see **Carlill v Carbolic Smokeball Company (1893)** or **Thornton v Shoe Lane Parking (1971)**).

The offer cannot state that silence shall be taken as an acceptance. It is unacceptable that the offeree should have to go to the effort of expressly refusing an offer. Silence on the part of the offeree, therefore, cannot usually be regarded as a valid means of communicating acceptance.

 Felthouse v Bindley (1862) the pursuer had been negotiating to purchase his nephew's horse and there had been problems regarding the price to be paid. Eventually, the pursuer wrote to his nephew stating that if he did not hear anything from him then the pursuer would consider the horse as his for the price specified in the letter. The nephew did not reply, but he wished to sell the horse to his uncle and for this purpose he instructed his auctioneer not to sell the horse. The auctioneer, however, inadvertently sold the horse. The uncle sued the auctioneer basing his claim on the fact that his nephew had sold the horse to him and, therefore, the auctioneer had wrongly sold his property.

Held: the action failed because although the nephew wished to sell to his uncle he had not communicated this fact. There was no contract between uncle and nephew.

Admittedly, in the case of **Carlill v Carbolic Smokeball Company (1893)** (above), Mrs Carlill did not reply to the Smokeball Company personally and communicate her intention to accept the offer, but her actions in responding to the advert by buying the product and using it according to the instructions were taken by the court as implied acceptance of the Company's offer.

The common law rule in **Felthouse v Bindley** provides an element of protection against the practice of inertia selling where goods are delivered to potential customers who have not requested delivery.

 Key point: An offeror cannot insist that the offeree's silence can indicate that he has accepted the offer as acceptance must consist of either positive words or behaviour.

The Unsolicited Goods and Services Acts 1971 and 1975 now go a long way to prevent these kinds of trade practices. The Acts put in place a system of fines which will be imposed on unscrupulous traders who make demands for payment of goods they know to be unsolicited i.e. they have not been requested by the people who have received the goods. If a demand for payment for the unsolicited goods/services is accompanied by threats, a higher scale of fines will apply.

Section 1 of the 1971 Act states that unsolicited goods may be kept by a recipient without payment after a period of 30 days providing that the recipient has given notice to the sender asking that they be collected or after six months regardless of any such notice. These Acts protect consumers **not** businesses.

 Key point: The Unsolicited Goods and Services Acts 1971 and 1975 protect consumer buyers against the dangers of so-called inertia selling by businesses.

Instantaneous communications

A contract will not have been concluded unless the acceptance is effectively communicated and the offeror has notice of this intention. When using so-called instantaneous methods of communication such as facsimiles, telexes, e-mails and text messages to send an acceptance, it is vital that the offeree ensures that the acceptance has been properly received by the offeror.

If, for example, the offeree left a message on the offeror's voicemail answering service stating that he had decided to accept the offer, this message must reach the offeror. If the message was accidentally erased by the offeror before he had listened to his messages, then no contract would have been formed because the offeree's acceptance could not be said to have been effective.

It does not take a stretch of the imagination to realise that such messages can be misdirected or even rendered unreadable when received by the offeror. The responsibility will very often be on the offeree's shoulders to ensure that the acceptance was received and actually understood. The dangers of using instantaneous communications are all too obvious from a brief examination of the following Scottish decision:

 Verdin Brothers *v* Robertson (1871) Robertson sent a telegram from Peterhead to Verdin in Liverpool. Robertson's telegram stated:

"Send on immediately fifteen twenty tons salt invoice in my name cash terms."

Owing to the fault of the clerks in the telegraph office, Verdin received the telegram in a completely different format:

"Send on rail immediately fifteen twenty tons salt Morice in morning name cash terms."

Needless to say, this led to a great deal of confusion because Verdin dispatched the goods to "Morice, Peterhead" and sent invoices to the same address. The invoices were later returned to Verdin by reason of the fact that no one of that name and address could be found. When the confusion was cleared up, Robertson refused to take delivery of the goods because he no longer required them.

Held: Lords Cowan, Benholme and Neaves (in the Inner House of the Court Session) all agreed that there was no contract because there was no true agreement i.e. the parties had failed to achieve consensus in idem. The parties had not properly communicated with one another. Lttle real sense could be made of the true intentions of the parties at a time when this was of vital importance.

 Key point: When using so-called instantaneous methods in order to communicate an acceptance, the offeree must ensure that the acceptance reaches the offeror in the form that he intended to send it.

The following cases demonstrate that acceptances sent by instantaneous methods of communication will conclude a contract when they have been received by the offeror.

 Entores Ltd *v* Miles Far Eastern Corporation [1955] the pursuers who carried on a business in London sent an offer to the defender's agent in

Amsterdam using their telex machine. The defender's agent in Amsterdam responded to the pursuers' offer by sending an acceptance via a telex machine. This acceptance was received by the pursuers on their telex machine in London. Some time later, the pursuers were attempting to serve a writ on the defender for breach of contract. The English courts would only grant them authority to commence the action against the defender if it could be proved that the contract had been concluded in England. If this was the case, the English courts would have the necessary jurisdiction to hear the pursuers' action for breach of contract. The case, therefore, centred around two issues: when and where the defender had accepted the pursuers' offer. The defender claimed that proper acceptance of the offer had taken place in Amsterdam at the time when the message of acceptance was typed into the telex machine. The pursuers, on the other hand, argued that the acceptance only became valid when it was received on their machine in London and printed out.

Held: by the English Court of Appeal that a contract had been concluded between the parties. Lord Denning stated that when the parties use instantaneous methods of communication, for example, telex machines, the acceptance is only valid when it is actually received by the offeror and the contract is made at the place where acceptance is received. The acceptance had, therefore, become valid when it was received on the pursuers' telex machine in London. The contract had been concluded in England and was subject to the jurisdiction of the English courts. Lord Denning also highlighted the dangers of using so called instantaneous methods of communication. What if, for example, a telephone line goes dead just as the offeree has made his acceptance? Did the offeror hear the vital words of acceptance? If not, then there can be no contract. Similarly, a clerk who sends an acceptance by telex must ensure that the message actually reached its destination and in the proper form. To be on the safe side, it may be advisable for the clerk to send a second communication (and a third and a fourth . . .) to ensure that the acceptance has been received and understood by the offeror. Until he receives verification from the offeree that the acceptance has been received, he cannot be certain that the contract has been successfully concluded. All sorts of accidents can and do happen with these types of communications. Better to be safe than sorry.

 Key point: When the parties use instantaneous methods of communication, for example, telex machines, e-mail, faxes and telephones, the acceptance is only valid when it is actually received by the offeror and the contract is made at the place where acceptance is received.

The House of Lords approved the decision of the Court of Appeal in **Entores Ltd v Miles Far Eastern Corporation**. In the later case of **Brinkibon v Stahag Stahl [1982]**. The facts of **Brinkibon v Stahag Stahl** were quite similar in that the offeree had sent a message of acceptance by telex. This case also involved an attempt by the English buyers to sue the sellers, who were based in Vienna, for breach of contract. The English courts would only allow a writ for breach of contract to be issued if they had jurisdiction to hear the case. The question once again arose as to where and when the contract had been formed. This time the offeree had sent the acceptance from London to Vienna. Following the decision in **Entores**, the House of Lords held that the contract had been formed in Vienna not London. In other words, the acceptance became valid when it was received by the offeror on the telex machine in Vienna. The summons could not be served because the contract had been made in Vienna and not in London and, therefore, the English courts had no jurisdiction regarding the contract.

 Key point: When using so-called instantaneous methods in order to communicate an acceptance, the offeree must ensure that the acceptance reaches the offeror in the form that he intended to send it.

Counteroffers or qualified acceptances

A counteroffer is a qualified acceptance, which contains additional or contradictory terms/conditions. A counteroffer cancels the original offer; the original offer disappears and is no longer capable of acceptance.

 This is shown in the case of **Wolf & Wolf v Forfar Potato Co Ltd (1984)** where a Scottish company sent a telex to a Dutch company offering to sell a quantity of potatoes. It was a condition of the offer that it had to be accepted by 5 p.m. the next day. The following morning the Dutch company sent a telex which appeared to be an acceptance of the offer but which contained new conditions. The Scottish company advised by telephone that these conditions were unacceptable and the Dutch company sent another telex, still within the time limit, which 'accepted' the original offer. The Scottish company ignored the second telex and the Dutch company raised an action for damages for breach of contract. The court held that no contract had been formed. The first telex was a counteroffer, which had the effect of causing the original offer to be cancelled. Therefore when the second 'acceptance' was sent there was no offer to accept.

 A similar case, **Hyde v Wrench (1840)**, also establishes a counteroffer; Hyde offered to sell his farm for £1000, Wrench offered £950. On rejection of Wrench's offer, he later advised Hyde that he would pay the original offer of £1000. Wrench's offer of £950, constituted a counteroffer, which cancelled out Hyde's original offer. Accordingly, Hyde's original offer was no longer open for acceptance.

 Key point: Qualified acceptance of the offer does not result in the creation of a contract, because the offeree has, in fact, rejected the original offer and replaced it with a new offer of his own which the offeror may or may not choose to accept.

Requests for additional information by the offeree are not necessarily counteroffers as can be seen in the following case:

 Stevenson v McLean (1880) on Saturday, the defender addressed a definite offer to the pursuers to sell them a specified quantity of iron at a specific price. The pursuers were given until the close of business on Monday to communicate their acceptance of this offer to the defender. The pursuers wished clarification of certain aspects of the defender's offer and, to this end, they addressed some questions to the defender. The pursuers primarily wished to know how long the defender was prepared to supply them with the goods at the quoted price, whether the goods could be delivered by instalment as and when required, and the terms of payment. The pursuers sent a telegram requesting this information on Monday morning, but the defender did not reply to this communication. In the early afternoon, the pursuers decided to accept the offer and sent off a second telegram to this effect. Shortly before, the defender had sent a telegram of his own withdrawing his offer, but this communication did not reach the pursuers until after they had sent their acceptance. The defender claimed that there was no contract because the pursuers' first telegram should be regarded as counter-offer. In response, the pursuers claimed that this telegram was merely a request for further information to clarify the terms of the offer.

Held: that the pursuers' first telegram should be viewed as an inquiry for further information. It was not a counter-offer. The original offer had not been rejected and the pursuers had accepted it in good time before the defender could effectively withdraw it. A legally enforceable contract had been created.

 Key point: Request for additional information in order to clarify the terms of the offer are not necessarily counter-offers, but great care will have to be taken by the offeree that his request for clarification should not be viewed as a rejection of the offer.

'The Battle of Forms'

In this electronic age, it is increasingly likely that businesses will use their own pre-printed forms (usually stored as a template on a computer's hard drive) to make an offer or to conclude an acceptance of an offer. These forms will no doubt contain terms and conditions which are peculiar to each party. Such terms might cover such issues as the law which will govern the contract, for example, Scottish or English law; which party has to bear the cost of insurance for the goods; which party has to organise delivery of the goods; or when property in the goods passes from seller to buyer.

It is highly unlikely that both parties' pre-printed forms will contain conditions which match exactly. It is probable that if the offeree responds to an offer contained in a pre-printed form by using his own paperwork or invoice he may well have unwittingly made a counteroffer which, of course, results in a rejection of the original offer. Therefore, no contract would be formed. In these situations, the courts have attempted to take a more flexible approach and this can be demonstrated in the following case.

 Butler Machine Tool Co Ltd *v* Ex-Cell-O Corpn (England) Ltd (1979)
Butler quoted a price for a machine tool of £75,535, delivery to be within ten months of order. The quotation gave terms and conditions which were stated expressly to prevail over any other conditions contained in the buyer's order. One of the terms was a price variation clause which operated if costs increased before delivery. Ex-Cell-O ordered the machine, their order stating that the contract was to be governed by Ex-Cell-O's terms and conditions as set out in the order. These terms did not include a price variation clause, but

did contain additional items to the Butler quotation, including the fact that Ex-Cell-O wanted installation of the machine for £3100 and the date of delivery was changed from ten to eleven months. Ex-Cell-O's form had a slip attached to it which Butler filled in and returned. The slip stated that Butler had to accept Ex-Cell-O's contractual terms. The machine was ready for delivery, but owing to a delay on Ex-Cell-O's part, the costs rose and Butler insisted that Ex-Cell-O compensate them. The Court of Appeal employed a traditional counteroffer analysis. Butler's original quotation was an offer, Ex-Cell-O's reply was a counteroffer which Butler had accepted by filling in the form and returning it. Ex-Cell-O did not have to pay the extra costs. If Butler had wanted the price variation clause to be enforceable, it should not have filled in the slip and returned it – this was tantamount to acceptance of Ex-Cell-O's terms.

 Key point: Great care will have to be taken by the parties when they use standard forms to communicate with each other which contain very different terms.

The postal rule

There is a special rule which will affect the creation of contracts where the offer and acceptance are sent using the Post Office. We first hear of the postal rule being established in the English case of **Adams v Lindsell (1818)** and, shortly afterwards, the rule was introduced into Scots law as a matter of convenience. Obviously, a great deal of trade was conducted between Scotland and England and it would have caused great inconvenience to have radically different rules governing the formation of postal contracts in both countries.

On the face of things, the effect of the rule is problematic and appears to fly in the face of common sense. Most people would assume that a letter of acceptance, sent in response to a letter containing an offer would only be valid when the acceptance actually reached the offeror or his agents.

When the offeror posts his letter containing the offer to the offeree, a contract will be formed as soon as the offeree responds to the offer by placing his letter of acceptance in the postbox or by handing the letter to a Post Office employee such as a counterclerk who is authorised to forward the letter for posting. This is in spite of the fact that it could take anything from a day to a couple of days for the letter of acceptance to reach the offeror who will be completely in ignorance of the offeree's decision. A contract will nevertheless have been formed. If an acceptance is sent by post, a contract is immediately formed.

 Key point: As soon as a letter of acceptance in response to a postal offer is posted a valid contract will have been formed.

 A very good illustration of the postal rule can be found in **Jacobsen v Underwood (1894)**. On 2 March, Underwood sent a letter containing an offer to Jacobsen using the Royal Mail. Underwood's letter stated that the offer must be accepted by 6 March. On 6 March, Jacobsen posted a letter of acceptance to Underwood. This letter of acceptance did not reach Underwood until 7 March. It was held that the postal rule applied and that the offer had been accepted on time i.e. by being posted on 6 March. In order to protect himself, Underwood should have insisted that acceptance would not be valid until the acceptance had physically reached him. In other words, he could have expressly excluded the postal rule.

There are two potentially problematic situations when the Royal Mail is used by the parties to communicate with one another:

◆ What if the offeror has second thoughts and decides to withdraw the original offer that he has made to the offeree?

◆ What if, on the other hand, the offeree decides to cancel the acceptance after having posted it?

We will look at these situations in turn.

 Key point: The postal rule can be problematic when a) the offeror decides to withdraw his offer or b) the offeree decides to cancel his acceptance.

Withdrawal of a postal offer

What if the offeror had second thoughts and wished to withdraw his offer? In order to ensure that any withdrawal was effective, the offeror would have to cancel the offer and communicate this new development to the offeree before the offeree was able to put his letter of acceptance in the post box and thus form a contract. So there is a real incentive on the part of the offeror to cancel his offer before the offeree accepts it by placing his letter of acceptance in the post box.

 Thomson v James (1855) James contacted Thomson by letter on 26 November offering to sell him a piece of land. Thomson sent a letter of acceptance to James on 1 December. In the meantime, James had had second thoughts about his original offer of 26 November and on 1 December he sent a letter to Thomson which contained a withdrawal of his earlier offer. James' withdrawal letter and Thomson's letter of acceptance crossed in the post. Both letters arrived on 2 December. Did James have a contract with Thomson?

Held: in order for James' letter of withdrawal to be effective, it would have to have reached Thomson before Thomson posted his letter of acceptance. Unfortunately for James, his withdrawal arrived (on 2 December) after Thomson had posted his acceptance (on 1 December) and, therefore, a contract had been formed.

 Key point: In order to make his cancellation of the offer effective, the offeror must ensure that his letter of cancellation reaches the offeree before a letter of acceptance can be posted.

The Scottish courts appear to have failed to resolve the problem of what will happen if an acceptance goes missing in the post. It has been suggested that so long as the offeree has a receipt of posting, the acceptance will be valid and the contract will stand. Such a situation occurred in the following English case and the court ruled that the offeror was bound in contract to the offeree.

 Household Fire Insurance Company v Grant (1879), the defender handed a written application (the offer) to purchase shares in an insurance company to the company's agent. The application contained a declaration to the effect that the defender had paid a deposit to the company's bankers so that he could be certain of acquiring the shares. Under the terms of the proposed contract, the defender also agreed to pay an additional sum to the company within twelve months of the shares being allotted to him. The agent posted the defender's offer to the company. Upon receipt of the defender's offer, the company secretary wrote a letter to the defender informing him that he was now a member of the company. This letter (which was the acceptance of the defender's offer) was posted to him using the Royal Mail. For some unexplained reason, the letter was never received by the defender. The defender assumed that his offer to purchase shares in the company had been unsuccessful. Completely unknown to the defender, the company listed his name on the share register and credited him with the proceeds of dividends. The company later experienced severe financial difficulties and, eventually, it was forced to go into liquidation. The liquidators began to sue those members of the company who either had not paid for their shares or who still owed the balance of their shares. This group of individuals included the defender. The defender not unnaturally objected to this unexpected development and he argued that his attempt to purchase shares in the company had been unsuccessful.

Held: by the English Court of Appeal that the defender was liable to pay for the shares. A contract had been successfully concluded when the company secretary had posted the letter of acceptance. The Post Office was the common agent of the parties and delivery to it of the letter of acceptance meant that the defender's agent had effectively received this acceptance. This view did not find favour amongst all the judges of the Court of Appeal. Lord Justice Bramwell issued a strongly dissenting judgement. His Lordship was of the opinion that the acceptance of the offer had to be properly communicated to the defender. If a letter fails to arrive at its destination, this can place the offeror at a significant and serious disadvantage as this case only too well demonstrates.

 Key point: The offeree's letter of acceptance forms a valid acceptance as soon as it is posted and this is despite the fact that the letter could go missing in the post or be destroyed.

Withdrawal of a postal acceptance

The better view in English law is that an acceptance cannot be withdrawn once it has been posted, even though it has not yet reached the offeror. This approach seems very sensible since the offeror is bound by contract as soon as the acceptance is posted. The Countess of Dunmore, however, demonstrates that the situation is radically different in Scotland. Normally, of course, an acceptance cannot be withdrawn once made unless the offeree wishes to face the possibility of an action for breach of contract.

 Countess of Dunmore *v* Alexander (1830) Lady Agnew's servant, Betty Alexander was seeking new employment. The Countess of Dunmore was sufficiently interested in the possibility of engaging Betty as her new servant that she took the trouble to write to Lady Agnew asking for a reference and she stated that she would pay Betty an annual salary of £12 and 12 shillings. This was regarded as an invitation to treat from the Countess. Lady Agnew replied on Betty's behalf with a reference recommending Betty for the position and stating that the wages the Countess was prepared to pay were acceptable to her. Betty Alexander, like many servants of the time, could not read or write, and this is why Lady Agnew wrote the letter on her behalf. This letter from Lady Agnew was, therefore, an offer from Betty to the Countess. The Countess sent her acceptance by post on the 5th November in response to Betty's offer. However, for some reason, she changed her mind about employing Betty and the next day she posted a second letter withdrawing her original acceptance. Betty received both the letters of acceptance and withdrawal at the same time. Betty then sued the Countess for breach of contract and the loss of wages for the six month period that she was without work.

Held: by the Court of Session that there was no contract between Betty and the Countess. This, of course, was a blatantly biased decision against Betty Alexander, a mere servant, who had dared to bring a claim for damages against an aristocratic lady such as the Countess. This case did establish an important legal principle in Scotland regarding the formation of postal contracts. A withdrawal of an acceptance will be effective if it reaches the offeror before, or at the same time as, the original letter of acceptance. For those with overly analytical minds, it does not matter which letter goes through the letterbox first or which letter the offeror opens first – as long as both letters arrive together. Clearly, if the letters arrived a post apart, this would make a difference to the question of whether a contract had been cancelled or not, which was a point forcefully made by Lord Balgray. In **Thomson v James (1855)**, Lord M'Neill, the Lord President referred to this decision as 'a very peculiar case', whereas Lord Deas would have gone further and abandoned the principle that it established.

This case can be criticised for a number of reasons, but it is worth bearing in mind that the Scottish courts have never overruled the decision and it remains very much in force. The case has been justified (on the rather unconvincing ground) that the second letter from the Countess should be treated as an addition to the first letter and reading the two letters together it became obvious that the Countess was totally hostile to the idea of employing Betty Alexander.

 Key point: The offeree can withdraw his letter of acceptance by sending a second letter cancelling his acceptance but, in order to be effective, this second letter must reach the offeror before or at the same time as the original letter of acceptance.

Repeal of the postal rule

The repeal of the rule was last considered in 1992 by the Scottish Law Commission, but as yet no concrete steps have been taken to change the law. Particularly astute lawyers will opt out of the rule by, for example, inserting an express term in the letter of offer to the effect that the postal rule does not apply.

 Key point: It is possible for the parties to exclude the postal rule by simply stating that it does not apply to their dealings.

When the offer and acceptance will have to be implied by the courts

So far, we have approached the formation of a legally enforceable agreement using a tried and tested formula i.e. offer + acceptance = contract. It follows from an application of this formula, that it is important to be able to identify when a definite offer is on the table and, in response to this willingness to be bound on the part of the offeror, we can say that an unqualified acceptance has been made by the offeree. When we have these two elements in place, we can say with some satisfaction that the parties are bound together in contract.

There are a number of situations where the formation of a contract will be not immediately apparent to the casual or inexperienced observer. Applying the above formula (offer + acceptance = contract) will perhaps only lead to a great deal of frustration. In these kinds of circumstances, the casual observer may well seek in vain for the more traditional and familiar features which herald the creation of a legally enforceable agreement. There may not even be a semblance of contractual negotiations between the parties indicating that a bargain is about to be concluded. The absence of these familiar contractual features, however, has not proved an insurmountable obstacle to the Scottish courts.

A court may be perfectly happy to imply or presume the existence of contractual obligations from the actions of the parties. Admittedly, the individuals concerned may not have used the words 'offer' and 'acceptance' in the course of their dealings with one another and perhaps they are completely oblivious to the fact that they have become subject to a range of legally binding obligations. In a number of situations, Scots law recognises the concept of collateral contracts that are linked to another contract and this relationship often gives rise to a completely separate range of rights and duties and to ignore these obligations is to act perilously. A recent example of a collateral contract can be found in the decision of the Inner House of the Court of Session in **Robertson v Anderson 2002** (above). In **Robertson**, it will be recalled that two friends who attended bingo together on a regular basis had an informal agreement to share their winnings. This implied agreement was capable of enforcement despite its association with gambling. The informal agreement between the friends was linked or was collateral to the main gambling contract between the winner of the National Prize that evening and Mecca Bingo.

The creation and enforcement of collateral contracts has been recognised in some of the older cases:

 Clarke v Earl of Dunraven [1897] the owners of two yachts named *Satanita* and *Valkyrie* respectively entered them in the Mudhook Yacht Club Regatta which was to be held on the River Clyde. As a condition of entry to the event, all participants had to sign a written undertaking to obey the rules of the Club. The rules imposed a duty of responsibility upon all yacht owners for any damage that they caused to other vessels competing in the Regatta. Whilst heading for the starting line, *Satanita* collided with *Valkyrie* and, consequently, *Valkyrie* sunk. The owner of *Valkyrie* sued the owner of *Satanita* for damages. *Satanita*'s owner claimed that he was only his liable in terms of statute which, in any case, permitted him to limit any sum of compensation to £8 per ton. He argued that he was in no way legally bound by the rules of the Mudhook Yacht Club. This limited sum payable under statute would in no way have adequately compensated the losses of the owner of the sunken *Valkyrie*.

Held: by the House of Lords that the participants in the Regatta had bound themselves in contract to the Club and to one another. They had no choice but to obey the rules of the event. This meant that the yacht owner who was responsible for the damage to the *Valkyrie* had to compensate its owner fully for the losses that he had suffered.

 Key point: Collateral contracts are linked to another contract and they often give rise to a completely separate set of rights and duties.

Certainty of the terms of an agreement

Contracts will not be enforced unless both parties have expressed themselves with a sufficient amount of clarity regarding the essential terms of their agreement. Sometimes, aspects of the contract are not at all clear and are very confusing. Does this situation affect the status of the contract? Indeed, can a contract even be said to exist? Courts will not go out of their way to label a contract unenforceable, but sometimes the parties do not help matters when they fail to express themselves clearly enough and it is little wonder that the validity of the contract is subject to question.

There are a variety of devices that the courts can rely upon in an attempt to salvage an agreement. Many trades and professions have well-established customs and practices of which the courts are perfectly aware and are only too happy to enforce on behalf of the parties if this means that the survival of the agreement can be ensured. As we shall see in Chapter 5, in a contract of agency, the agent is entitled to be paid at the customary rate (whatever that is) when the agreement fails to address the issue of a salary or commission. Alternatively, the agent can be paid on a *quantum meruit* basis i.e. as much as he has earned or at a reasonable rate (**see Kennedy v Glass (1890)**). In many situations, the parties themselves may have foreseen the possibility of a dispute arising in relation to particular terms of the contract. To this end, they may have put in place the machinery for resolving such a dispute, for example, an arbitration clause. Furthermore, as we shall see in **Hillas & Company Ltd v Arcos [1932]** and **Foley v Classique Coaches Ltd [1934] (discussed below)**, a previous course of business dealings by the parties can greatly assist the courts to flesh out the terms of the contract. Very often, disputes will arise concerning the certainty of contractual terms because one party (sometimes both) now wishes to cancel the agreement or to change radically the terms of the contract.

Reference to an Act of Parliament may be helpful where the price of goods is disputed or the parties have failed to address this issue. Sections 8 and 9 of the Sale of Goods Act 1979 can be very useful in this regard. Section 8 states that the parties can leave the price of goods to be fixed by the contract or by reference to a method laid down by the contract. Alternatively, the parties may have had previous dealings that can be referred to in order to calculate the price. If the contract is silent on the issue of the price or there have been no previous dealings between the parties, the buyer must pay a reasonable price for the goods and what is reasonable will depend on the facts of each situation. Section 9 permits the parties to a contract of sale to fix a price by appointing a third party to carry out a valuation of the goods. Sections

12–15 of the Sale of Goods Act also address some of the most important terms in a contract of sale (title, description of the goods, quality and fitness for purpose and sales by sample) and these can be used to determine and clarify the rights and duties of the parties (**see Chapter 4 for a fuller explanation**).

However, if such avenues do not exist, or if all these options have been exhausted without success, the court will be unable to enforce the agreement. The contract is said to suffer from uncertainty.

If a term turns out to be unworkable by reason of a lack of certainty, the courts may have no option but to remove or sever it from the contract. The risk of such an action could mean, of course, that the rest of the contract is fatally undermined. It should go without saying that the parties go to great pains to express themselves clearly and effectively.

 Key point: Contracts will not be enforced unless both parties have expressed themselves with a sufficient clarity as to the essential terms.

 Hillas & Company Ltd v Arcos (1932) the contract centred around an order for a quantity of a Russian soft wood of fair specification to be supplied over the season 1930. The contract contained an option which allowed the pursuers to order a further quantity of wood the following year. The contract was performed during 1930 without problems despite the vague wording of the contract to do with the specification of the wood. The pursuers tried to take advantage of the option for 1931, but the defenders refused to supply the wood owing to the vague wording. Where they were concerned, the contract was inchoate.

Held: by the House of Lords that this option was valid despite its vagueness. There had been a previous course of dealings between the parties which the court could use to overcome any difficulties. Indeed, the parties had not previously experienced any major difficulties in carrying out the contract.

 Foley v Classique Coaches Ltd [1934] Foley had supplied Classique with petrol at an agreed price for a period of 3 years. Classique had agreed to purchase petrol from Foley in return for Foley agreeing to sell it land of which he was the owner. The agreement operated perfectly well and the parties had agreed that any disputes could be settled by arbitration. Eventually, Classique gave notice of its intention to withdraw from the contract simply because it could purchase petrol more cheaply from an alternative supplier. Classique argued that it was entitled to take this unilateral action since there was no agreement in writing addressing the price of petrol.

Held: by the English Court of Appeal that there was a perfectly enforceable contract between the parties which had had been in existence for 3 years and which was concerned with the supply of petrol at a reasonable price and of a reasonable quality. It did not undermine the agreement that the parties had failed to agree a price beyond the initial 3 year period of the contract. Future prices could be negotiated by the parties and, if disagreements did arise, they could be resolved by a reference to arbitration.

Key point: A lack of clarity as to the material terms of the contract may mean that the agreement cannot be enforced.

Contractual terms

It is important that the parties understand the extent of their rights and duties under the contract. Unless the parties have taken the step of writing down the main terms of their agreement, how can they identify with any certainty what the main contractual terms are? 'With a great deal of difficulty' may be the most honest answer! It is highly likely that the need to identify the main terms of the agreement will only really become a matter of some urgency when the parties are heading towards a dispute.

It will be important to establish whether, by behaving in a particular way, one of the parties has breached the terms of the agreement. Clearly, if a party breaks his side of the bargain certain consequences flow from this. If someone commits a breach of contract this leaves the other party with an option to sue for damages. Where a material breach of contract has been committed, this may give a party the right to cancel the agreement in addition to the remedy of damages.

If a lack of clarity surrounds the contractual main terms this can be a recipe for disaster. By failing to communicate with one another properly, the parties may have made it impossible for an agreement to work effectively.

In the event of a dispute, courts are often left with the thankless task of trying to make sense of what the parties have said and done in the course of their dealings with one another. As a starting point, a court could examine any written evidence surrounding the contract. If this resource is not available or is, more likely, inconclusive, the court will scrutinise verbal statements that the parties have made leading up to formation of a contract. Written documents and verbal statements are known as the *express terms of a contract*. The rights and duties of the parties could also be implied from their behaviour. Additionally, various Acts of Parliament, for example, the Sale of Goods Act 1979 (as amended) automatically include certain terms into a contract of sale which address the seller's right to sell the goods, the description of the goods, the quality of the goods and their fitness for purpose and sales by sample (**see Chapter 4**). Such terms whether in reference to the parties' behaviour or to statute are referred to as the *implied terms of a contract*. As a general rule, express terms will be preferred over implied terms. However, under the Unfair Contract Terms Act 1977, an express term which attempts to exclude the seller's liability to a consumer buyer in relation to the implied terms of the Sale of Goods Act 1979 will be automatically void.

The common law also implies various rights and duties into particular contracts. In an agency relationship, the courts have gone to great pains to develop the rights and duties of the parties. An agent, for example, has the right to be paid, the right to be indemnified and the right to be compensated by his principal. The agent is also said to have a right of lien. By comparison, the agent must not delegate his functions, must render true accounts and must put the interests of his principal above his own.

 Key point: Statute and the common law can imply the existence of rights and duties in relation to the contract that the parties have entered.

Before the introduction of the Contract (Scotland) Act 1997, the courts tended not to accept verbal evidence which would contradict a contract which is entirely in written form. Following on from this, courts were also less than willing to accept previous communications between the parties as evidence, whether written or not, once the agreement had finally been committed to writing. As we shall see, in the discussion about contractual formality, the courts are now more relaxed about the range of external sources of evidence that can be used to clarify the terms of a written contract. Generally speaking, the parties are free to make up their own minds as to what form the contract will be in. However, the courts tend to prefer a written document which embodies all the rights and duties of the parties. Obviously, the courts will not have to refer to additional or external sources of evidence where the written contract is clear and precise and contains all the terms by which the terms have agreed to be bound.

When examining words or phrases that the parties have used, the court must give these their plain ordinary meaning. Words which are commonly used in a particular trade, business or profession may appear in the contract and the court may be totally unfamiliar with these. Where there is any doubt in relation to words that imply a technical meaning or where the words are not commonly used in the English language because they are foreign, the court may call upon expert assistance to determine their true meaning.

If the meaning of a word is ambiguous, the court will do its best to give it a meaning which will aid the operation of the contract. This is often expressed as the giving of business efficacy to the contract, the judge regarding himself as doing merely what the parties themselves would in fact have done in order to cover the situation if they had addressed themselves to it. This, of course, is easier said than done and frequently the careless use of certain words or phrases by the parties can make it all but impossible for the court to determine their true meaning. Ultimately, of course, the parties have no one to blame but themselves.

 Key point: Generally, the courts prefer written evidence of a contract, but there is nothing to stop the parties from relying on verbal testimony or their own actions.

 The Moorcock (1889) the contract stated that the pursuers' steamship known as *The Moorcock* was to come alongside the defenders' wharf and jetty on the River Thames in order to unload her cargo and for the purpose of having a new cargo placed aboard. These activities were supposed to be carried out at low tide on the Thames. Both parties were well aware that it was dangerous for any vessel to approach the wharf at low tide as there was real chance that it would be exposed to the risk of running aground. Neither party had bothered to address explicitly in their contract, the issue of the vessel's safety. The vessel was brought alongside the wharf, but she sustained serious damage when she came to rest on hard ground when the tide went out and left her stranded. The English Court of Appeal implied a term (that it was safe for *The Moorcock* to come alongside the wharf at low tide) to give the contract the business efficacy which the parties surely must have intended because no reasonable person would have wished to expose the vessel to the risk of serious damage. The defenders had not been asked to give any assurances about the vessel's safety, but they should have given such an undertaking to the pursuers. The defenders were, therefore, liable to pay compensation to the pursuers for the damage sustained to *The Moorcock*.

A court (according to Lord Justice Bowen in **The Moorcock**) cannot imply a term into a contract simply because it is reasonable to do so. If the parties have concluded an agreement that is simply unworkable, then this must have been their intention! It is very unusual for a court to intervene as the Court of Appeal did in **The Moorcock**. When judges do act in this way, they are often referred to as officious bystanders who are saying to the parties: 'Look, you forgot to add that term to make the agreement work,' and the parties respond: 'Yes, of course, we completely overlooked that term because it was so obvious. We both assumed that it would form part of the final contract between us.' The court takes this particular course of action so that the contract may be given business efficacy.

To paraphrase Lord McClaren, in **William Morton & Co v Muir Brothers (1907)**, the concept of an implied term relates to contracts of every description. However, the approach to this area of law shows that they are either enforced because they rely on a universal custom or the nature of the contract itself. If a reasonable person wished to include such an obvious term in an agreement for his own protection and the other party, also being a reasonable person, could have no possible objections, surely such a term should be regarded as part of the contract? The problem arises in the first place because the term is so obvious that the parties merely forgot to include it. The courts have implied terms into contracts on a number of occasions (**Robb v Green (1895)** and **Lister v Romford Ice and Cold Storage (1957)** where a duty to act in good faith and show fidelity to the employer was implied into employment contracts).

Lord Denning, the famous English judge, wanted to go further than this, admittedly, limited approach demonstrated in **The Moorcock**. In **Liverpool City Council v Irwin [1977]**, his Lordship opened himself to severe criticism when he attempted to imply certain terms into contracts by virtue of the fact that it was reasonable for a court to do so. The implied term did not have to be of vital commercial importance in order to give the contract business efficacy, it was merely reasonable to include it in the agreement. On appeal to the House of Lords, Lord Denning's approach to the incorporation of implied terms attracted little support from their Lordships. The Scottish and the English courts pointedly refused to follow Lord Denning's lead, preferring a much more limited approach.

 Key point: Generally speaking, courts will only imply a term into the contract in situations where it is commercially vital in order to make the contract effective.

Courts can also use certain rules of construction when it comes to the interpretation of contracts. The *ejusdem generis rule* allows a judge to group certain words or phrases together so that they form a particular group or subset which have characteristics in common. If a reference in a contract contained the words 'dogs, cats and other animals', the phrase 'and other animals' would be understand to mean animals of a domestic type. This would exclude animals such as lions, tigers and elephants which are most definitely not domestic in nature. Additionally, the *contra proferentum rule* arises in situations where one of the parties wishes to rely on a contractual term which they themselves have drafted and which is vague or ambiguous, for example, an exclusion clause. The court will not allow the party relying on this clause to reap full advantage of the clause if it is in any way vague or ambiguous.

 Key point: The courts can also rely on the *ejusdem generis* and *contra proferentum* rules to make sense of the contractual terms.

Contractual terms which impose duties upon the parties can be classified in various ways:

- Those which have immediate effect or those which have to be performed within a reasonable time after the formation of the agreement
- Those which are dependent upon some future, specified event
- Those which are contingent or rely upon the fulfilment of some condition

Third Party Rights

Generally speaking, third parties or outsiders have absolutely no rights in relation to a contract. To put things rather bluntly, it is not their agreement having had no involvement in its creation. Consequently, they do not enjoy any rights and they are not under a duty to do something for any other person. It follows from this general rule, that third parties do not have the right to bring a court action relating to a contract in which they do not have a legal interest.

There are certain situations, however, where third parties may be able to enforce terms of a contractual agreement that relate specifically to them or where they are entitled to claim some sort of benefit. Usually the contract will either name a specific individual or a specific class of persons who are entitled to benefit from the agreement. Such third parties are entitled to enforce eitgher a *jus quaesitum tertio* or a *jus quaesitum*. In **Carmichael v Carmichael's Executrix (1920)**, Lord Dunedin explained the difference between a *jus quaesitum tertio* and *jus quaesitum*. A *jus quaesitum tertio* would arise where A and B have made a contract and C, who is entitled to benefit from the agreement, is forced to sue because A refuses to recognise C's rights. A *jus quaesitum*, on the other hand, would occur where A and B have a contract but, this time, it is B who objects to C enforcing his third party rights.

Insurance policies are good example of this where a parent insures the life of his child. Obviously, the contract is between the insurer and the parent, but the child may become entitled to any dividends payable under the policy when he becomes an adult. Such a situation occurred in **Carmichael v Carmichael's Executrix (1920)** where a father had taken out a policy for his son who was aged 9. When the son reached adulthood, he became entitled to claim the benefits of the policy. Tragically, the son died soon after becoming an adult and, according to the terms of is will, his aunt Miss McColl was to benefit from his estate. As part of the son's estate, Miss McColl claimed a dividend that was payable under the insurance policy. The father objected to this by claiming that he was entitled to the money having paid the premium over many years.

Held: by the House of Lords that Miss McColl was entitled to enforce the third party rights (*jus quaesitum*) that she had inherited from her nephew. The money payable under the terms of the policy was rightfully hers.

Factors which affect the validity of a contract

In many situations, individuals will emerge from contractual negotiations in the belief that they have managed to form a binding contract. However, these individuals should avoid giving themselves a pat on the back just yet because there is still plenty of room for things to go wrong.

By becoming exposed to a variety of factors or situations, a potential agreement can be rendered *void* or *voidable* because in the eyes of the law there is a lack of consensus *in idem* or insufficient agreement. Furthermore, the so-called 'contract' (note the inverted commas) may be affected by such varying factors as error, misrepresentation, lack of formality, illegality, duress and undue influence.

If such situations do arise it is absolutely essential to be able to predict how any potential agreement will be affected. The main issue to consider here is whether the 'contract' will be rendered void or whether it will be merely voidable.

 Key point: A seemingly valid contract may be rendered void or voidable after it has been negotiated and this will have serious consequences for the parties.

Void contracts? This phrase is actually something of a contradiction in terms because if an agreement is said to be void this will mean that no contract actually exists. In fact, there never was a contract. The parties may have been involved in negotiations and will probably believe that they have concluded a 'contract', but this will be of little consequence since the courts will declare that there is no contract. It follows that, if there is no contract, neither party can have any rights or duties.

This situation has extremely serious consequences for third parties who may purchase property which forms the subject matter of a void contract. Unfortunately for these third parties they will be unable to enforce any legal rights to such property and any items will have to be returned to their original owners. Any such 'contract' which the courts consider to be void will, therefore, be completely unenforceable.

Examples of void contracts arise in the following situations:

◆ Where the contract is illegal
◆ Where one of the parties has been forced into the agreement by the use of force and fear
◆ Where there is substantial error
◆ Where one of the parties suffers from insanity
◆ Where the contract is with a child under the age of 16

 Key point: When a contract is declared void, the court is making a statement to the effect that a contract has never existed, despite what the parties may believe, and, therefore, no party can be said to have rights or duties.

Voidable contracts

This is a slightly more problematic area of the law. At one point, the parties have managed to conclude a legally binding contract. However, because of certain factors at play, one or both of the parties may have the option of cancelling the contract. Unlike the situation with void contracts, however, third parties can become the legal owners of property which forms the subject matter of voidable contracts. This is why it is essential for the party which has the right to cancel the agreement to act swiftly. Any hesitation on their part may mean that the other party may have transferred ownership of goods to a third party. If this turns out to be the case, it is highly unlikely that such property will be returned to its original owner. Examples of voidable contracts arise in the following situations:

- Where one of the parties has made a misrepresentation of fact
- Where there is a lack of formality
- Where one of the parties was intoxicated as a result of alcohol and/or drugs (whether prescription medicines or illegal drugs)
- Where the one of the parties was 16 or 17 years of age
- Where there has been facility and circumvention
- Where there has been undue influence

 Key point: In complete contrast to a void contract, a voidable contract remains valid until one of the parties takes steps to have it cancelled. In practical terms, this parties will continue to have rights and duties under the agreement until such time as it is cancelled.

Error

When a party to a contract is influenced by some sort of error, they have a mistaken or distorted view of the facts surrounding the agreement.

When we speak about error or mistake in relation to contracts, we are entering an area which is particularly complex. There are different categories of error in Scots law which may or may not undermine the validity of a contract. Clearly, we are particularly interested in those categories of error which undermine the formation of a contract. It is important to determine whether the error in question renders the contract void or voidable.

There are three key questions which must be asked when dealing with the issue of error in relation to contracts:

- Did the error or mistake directly influence the party to enter the contract?
- Was the error caused by the ignorance of one of the parties?
- Did one of the parties, knowing the other party to be in error, actively encourage this mistaken belief as to the facts?

It may seem a very harsh rule, but the law will not protect people from the consequences of their own stupidity or ignorance. It is only where the error or the mistake has been actively encouraged by one of the parties, who is fully aware of the true factual situation, that the courts will show a willingness to intervene. Such a situation may lead to the cancellation of the contract.

 Key point: It is particularly important to distinguish between mistake and misrepresentation because a contract affected by mistake is void, whereas a contract affected by misrepresentation is voidable. In void contracts, third parties cannot acquire good title to contractual goods, whereas in voidable contracts third parties can enforce their right to property acquired.

Induced or uninduced error

Uninduced error arises in situations where a person has entered a contract owing to their ignorance of the true facts. Such a person has not been influenced or encouraged by statements or representations of another party. Usually, the contract has been formed as a result of stupidity or ignorance. It is unlikely that the courts will intervene to remedy such a situation.

Induced error means that you have been encouraged to enter a contract because of something that the other party has told you whether by accident or design on their part. This piece of (false) information has directly influenced you to enter the contract. Perhaps you asked a seller of goods a direct question and his answer has encouraged you to make a contract with him. In these situations, the court is much more likely to provide some sort remedy to the innocent party, for example, cancellation of the contract and/or financial compensation.

 Key point: Induced error means that the other party has actively encouraged your mistaken view of the facts, whereas uninduced error relates to situations when the mistaken view as to the factual situation is entirely of your own making.

It must be stressed that the law does absolutely nothing to protect people from making a bad bargain which will leave them at a disadvantage, for example, making a financial loss if this is a result of their own stupidity or lack of business experience. The law will only provide assistance where someone has entered into a bad bargain where there has been some flaw in the agreement or, upon further investigation, it becomes obvious that there really is no agreement between the parties. Such types of agreement are usually void or voidable.

Mistakes which affect the status of the contract must relate to factual situations and not mistakes about the law. Furthermore, 'mistake' has a technical meaning and does not cover, for example, errors as to value. When a person makes a mistake due to his own stupidity or negligence, the rule expressed as *caveat emptor* (let the buyer beware) normally applies.

 Key point: The law does not usually protect people from the consequences of their own stupidity or negligence which, in turn, influences them to make a bad bargain.

Types of error

There are three types of error which can, potentially, undermine a contract:

♦ Common bilateral error
♦ Mutual bilateral error
♦ Unilateral error

 Key point: Errors may be common bilateral, mutual bilateral or unilateral.

We will examine each of these in turn.

Common bilateral error

Such a situation will occur when both contracting parties make an identical mistake. Where common bilateral error is present, it cannot be said that the parties lack agreement. The only exception to this may be a situation where the error affects the *substantials* of the contract. In fact, a contract affected by common bilateral error will be rendered void if the error relates to the existence of the subject matter of the contract. We can see the effects of this type of error in the following cases:

 Dawson v Muir (1851) the contracting parties had concluded the sale of sunken vats being sold by Dawson to Muir. Both parties believed that the vats were empty. This was not the case and later it was discovered that the vats contained white lead, a very valuable substance.

Held: that the contract was valid and the seller was not entitled to have the goods returned and certainly not the contents of the vats.

 Couturier v Hastie (1856) Hastie placed a cargo of corn aboard a ship in the Greek port of Thessalonikki. The documents of title to the goods were sent in advance to his London agents so that contracts of sale for the goods could be negotiated with buyers in advance of the ship's arrival at London. The London agents engaged Couturier to approach prospective buyers, one of whom entered a contract for the goods. At this point, the parties were unaware that the cargo had started to overheat while the ship was sailing through the Mediterranean. The Master, seeing that this was an emergency, put the ship in at the port of Tunis in North Africa and sold the remaining goods. In this way, the Master was acting as an agent of necessity (**see Chapter 5**) This meant that when the contract of sale had been concluded in London, the subject matter had ceased to exist. When this situation became common knowledge, the buyer communicated his intention to cancel the contract. Hastie sued Couturier because as a *del credere* agent he had given an undertaking to his principal that he would compensate him for any losses if the contract failed to go ahead.

Held: by the House of Lords that the action against Couturier should be dismissed because the contract with the buyer was totally dependent upon the continued existence of the goods.

 Key point: Common bilateral error occurs when both contracting parties make an identical mistake, but a contract is still said to have been formed despite the parties' error. The contract may be set aside if the error affects the material terms of the agreement.

Mutual bilateral error

This is a more serious situation because there are real grounds for questioning the very existence of any agreement. It should be remembered that, if there is no agreement, there is no contract. The courts will have to be very careful here and any vagueness surrounding the parties' intentions could fatally undermine any agreement. The parties must have expressed a certain level of clarity with regard to all the important terms of the contract. If this is not the case, then the agreement will be void on the grounds of uncertainty. If, for example, X offers to sell his desktop PC and Y agrees to buy thinking that X means to sell his laptop computer, there is a bilateral mistake which is non-identical or, in other words, a mutual misunderstanding. It will be remembered that in the previous category the mistake of error was bilateral but both parties had made an identical mistake. Confusion of this non-identical bilateral kind generally exists in the mind of one party only and may, therefore, have no effect on the contract.

Key point: Mutual bilateral error is a much more serious situation because there are real grounds for questioning the very existence of any agreement.

Unilateral error

With this type of error, one of the parties will have a mistaken view of the contract. The quality of this error will determine whether the contract is ultimately rendered unenforceable. The law can be quite strict here because, generally, people are supposed to be able to look out for their own interests and the courts cannot be expected to offer protection to those who suffer the consequences of their own stupidity. If, however, the other party misrepresented certain facts and this misrepresentation encouraged an individual to enter the contract then the agreement could be voidable. In other words, the innocent party would be able to petition the court and request that the contract be cancelled, but he would have to act extremely quickly before the property could be transferred to an innocent third party.

 Macleod v Kerr (1965) a rogue named Galloway approached Kerr and offered to purchase his Vauxhall Cresta car which had been advertised in the *Edinburgh Evening News*. Both parties agreed terms and, in return for a cheque signed in the name of L. Craig, Kerr permitted Galloway to take away the car and its registration book. Kerr then discovered that the cheque had been stolen. Galloway, in the meantime, had been busy selling the car to an innocent third party named Gibson. Kerr attempted to have his property returned to him from Gibson.

Held: by the Inner House of the Court of Session that property in the goods had passed to Gibson. The contract between Kerr and Galloway was voidable on the grounds of Galloway's fraud. Kerr had acted too slowly to recover his property by cancelling the contract with Galloway and Gibson was now the owner of the vehicle. The question of Galloway's identity was not an issue in the sense that it did not influence the creation of the contract. Kerr was not the slightest bit interested in the Galloway's identity – only his ability to pay for the car.

 Phillips v Brooks [1919] Phillips, the pursuer, carried on a business as a jeweller. On April 15 1918, a well-dressed man had entered Phillip's premises and stated that he was interested in purchasing some pearls and a ring. Phillips offered this individual some items in his stock for inspection. The customer entered a contract with Phillips to purchase pearls costing £2550 and a ring costing £450. The customer paid for these items by cheque. Normally, Phillips would not have permitted a customer paying by cheque to take items purchased from the shop until confirmation had been received by him that the customer had adequate funds in his bank account to pay for the goods. While the customer was writing the cheque, he had claimed to be Sir George Bullough of St James' Square. Phillips consulted a telephone directory and his enquiries confirmed that there was such an individual living at that particular address. On the strength of the stranger's claim, Phillips allowed him to take the ring away. The customer had claimed that it was his wife's birthday the following day and he was particularly anxious to take the ring home to her. Unfortunately for Phillips, his customer turned out to be a fraudster called North and the cheque was subsequently dishonoured. Phillips then took steps to retrieve the ring. The fraudster, however, had wasted little time because on 16 April, he had pledged the ring to Brooks, who was a pawnbroker, to secure a loan of £350. Phillips attempted to force the pawnbroker to return the ring to him. The pawnbroker replied that he had acted in good faith and he refused to return the ring or pay over its value to Phillips.

Held: the issue of North's identity was not a material factor in relation to the formation of the contract of sale. Phillips was not the slightest bit interested in North's identity until the issue of payment for the jewellery arose. Until this point, Phillips would have entered a contract with anyone who wished to purchase the jewellery. In other words, ownership of the ring had passed to North, the fraudster, when the sale had been concluded. The problem, as Phillips was to discover later, was that North was not in a position and had no intention of paying for the goods. The only solution open to Phillips was to sue North for the price of the goods and he could not force Brooks, the pawnbroker, to return the goods to him. This was an example of a voidable contract and the attempts by Phillips to cancel the contract for the sale of the ring were too little, too late.

The difference between the outcomes in **Macleod v Kerr** and **Phillips v Brooks** compared with that of **Morrisson v Robertson (1908) (discussed below)** was the fact that the identity of the buyer in **Morrisson** was a crucial factor right from the outset which determined the seller's decision to form a contract with the buyer (a rogue called Telford). The legal issue in **Macleod v Kerr** and **Phillips v Brooks** is, therefore, identical to the case of **Lewis v Averay [1972] (see Chapter 4 for the details of this case**). In **Lewis**, the identity of the buyer only became an important issue where the seller was concerned *after* a contract of sale had been formed and the question of the buyer's ability to pay for the goods arose.

 King's Norton v Edridge Merret (1897) Wallis, a rogue set up a company called Hallam & Company. He had stationery printed in such a way that it made the company appear very creditworthy. Using this stationery, he wrote ordering goods on credit from King's Norton. King's Norton supplied the goods.

Held: by the English Court of Appeal that the contract should not be rendered void on the grounds of unilateral mistake. The mistake in question concerned a minor term only i.e. the creditworthiness of one of the parties – a 'mere attribute.'

 Cundy v Lindsay (1878) a rogue called Blenkarn, based at 37 Wood Street, wrote to Lindsay ordering goods on credit. He made his order look as though it had come from a creditworthy firm called Blenkiron & Company, based at 123 Wood Street. Lindsay supplied the goods.

Held: by the House of Lords that the unilateral mistake concerned a material term of the contract i.e. the true identity of one of the parties to the contract.

In both the above cases, the rogues (Wallis and Blenkarn) sold the goods to innocent third parties (Edridge Merret and Lindsay). When the frauds were discovered, the sellers attempted to recover the goods from the third parties on the grounds that the identity of both rogues was absolutely central to the formation of the contracts.

The difference in outcomes between **King's Norton** and **Cundy** is that, in the first case, the pursuers intended to deal with the person who had written the letter offering to purchase goods. Wallis, the rogue, had set up a front company trading as Hallam & Co and he had used the front company's headed notepaper on which to write to the pursuers to place an order for goods. The pursuers only became concerned about his identity when it became obvious that he was not going to pay for the goods. In **Cundy**, on the other hand, the pursuers had always clearly intended to deal with a particular party (Blenkiron) and the issue of identity was, therefore, vitally important to the formation of this contract. The pursuers would not have entered the contract had they known the true identity of the rogue, Blenkarn.

 Key point: To render a contract void, a unilateral mistake must be related to a crucial term and not a minor term; the very fundamentals/material terms of the contract.

To summarise, if a situation indicates that there has been a unilateral mistake, a court will not consider declaring the contract void *ab initio* i.e. from the very beginning, unless all the following conditions are met:

1 The mistake must be about a crucial term of the contract, not a minor term

2 The mistaken party must have established that s/he was in no way to blame for the mistake

3 It must be shown that the other party knew (or, perhaps, ought to have known) of the mistake

The effect of these three preconditions, taken together, is that it is a rare event for a contract to be held void at common law for unilateral mistake. One reason for this judicial reluctance is that, if a contract is declared void *ab initio*, third parties may lose rights to property that they acquired innocently and in good faith.

 Key point: It is very difficult for a party to convince a court that a court should be declared void *ab initio* on the grounds of unilateral mistake.

Error in the substantials

When we talk about an error we usually mean that someone is labouring under a mistaken view of the facts. Substantial error, however, is an extremely serious problem because it usually means that the mistaken belief goes to the very roots of the contract and, therefore, completely undermines any potential agreement. In such situations, the mistaken beliefs of the parties do not centre around trivial matters which can easily be resolved. Error in the substantials concerns one or more of the important aspects of the agreement. In situations where an agreement is affected by substantial error there can be no true consensus *in idem* or agreement. In fact, the actual contract is radically different from the one that the parties originally intended to create.

Any 'contract' will be considered null and void from the beginning. In other words, there never was a contract despite what the parties might otherwise believe in their own minds. Practically speaking, this will mean that any property or money that has been transferred to the other party under the 'contract' must be returned to the original owner. Neither party can be said to acquire any rights or duties in such instances.

 Key point: Substantial error is a mistake that is so serious that it strikes at the very heart of the contract i.e. the material terms to the effect that there can be no real agreement between the parties thus rendering the contract void.

Professor Bell, one of the institutional writers, identified four types of substantial error in respect of the following issues which the House of Lords affirmed in **Stewart v Kennedy (1890)**.

Identity of one of the contracting parties

This will usually occur where one person is operating under a mistaken belief as to the identity of the other party with whom they are attempting to form a contract. However, the issue of mistaken identity must be fundamental to the formation of a contract. In order to convince a court that mistaken identity should render the agreement void, a person would have to demonstrate that he intended to enter into a contract with a particular person and no other.

 Morrisson v Robertson (1908) Robertson, a farmer, was approached by an individual (later discovered to be named Telford) who wished to buy two cattle from him. This individual wished to buy the cattle on credit. Morrisson was unhappy about this, but Telford stated that he was the son of a man called Wilson with whom Morrisson had dealt with previously. Morrisson knew Wilson to be a man of good credit. Morrisson gave the cattle to Telford who promptly sold the cattle to an innocent third party, Robertson who was ignorant of the fraud. Telford disappeared and Morrisson, who was still awaiting payment, sued for the return of the cattle.

Morrisson thought that he was contracting with Wilson's son, but unknown to him he was in fact contracting with Telford. In a credit transaction like this, Telford's identity was absolutely vital to the formation of a contract. Morrisson would never have contracted with Telford had he known Telford's true identity. Telford, therefore, did not have good title (i.e. ownership) to the cattle.

Held: the cattle had to be returned to Morrisson, the true owner.

Generally, in cases of mistaken identity as in **Phillips v Brookes (1919)** above, the court starts from the presumption that the claimed identity of each party is a crucial factor where the contracting parties are at a distance from one another. Where the parties are face-to-face, the court presumes that the each party intended to contract with the person present and therefore, the claimed identity is only a minor term and will, therefore, not affect the formation of a contract. Although in **Morrisson v Robertson (1908)** the parties were dealing face to face, the nature of the contract (a credit transaction) made Telford's statements about his identity an essential or material term of the contract.

 Key point: In **Morrisson v Robertson**, Telford's identity was an absolutely material term of the contract because Morrisson would not have entered the agreement had he been aware of the deception.

The subject matter of the contract

Such a situation is likely to arise where the parties are completely confused and mistaken as to the subject matter of the agreement. One party (the potential buyer) believes that a particular item is being offered for sale whereas the other party (the potential seller) believes that she has made an offer to sell a completely different item. Both parties are completely at cross purposes. There can be no real agreement between them and, therefore, no contract.

 Raffles *v* Wichelhaus (1864) the case involved two ships named Peerless both sailing from Mumbai in India carrying a cargo of cotton. This situation was the subject of much confusion as it will doubtless be appreciated. To complicate matters further, the ships were sailing from Mumbai two months apart. The defenders thought that they were purchasing the cotton aboard the first Peerless, whereas the pursuer thought that they were selling the cotton on the second Peerless. The defenders refused to take delivery of the second cargo when it arrived and were sued for breach of contract.

Held: that since there was a mistake as to the subject matter of the contract, there was in effect no contract or at least no contract which corresponded with the so-called agreement that both parties had supposedly concluded. Consequently, the pursuer's action failed.

 Key point: In **Raffles *v* Wichelhaus**, there was complete confusion in respect of the subject-matter of the contract and this totally undermined the agreement.

The price

The price that one party expects to pay and the price that the other party expects to receive will, obviously, be a very important term of the contract. Any confusion surrounding the price will render the contract void. Admittedly, it is possible for the parties not to fix a price and still have a valid contract as long as some mutually agreed system or mechanism exists for determining the price (Sale of Goods Act 1979 (as amended)).

 Wilson *v* Marquis of Breadalbane (1859) both Wilson and Breadalbane had intended to enter into a contract for the sale of cattle. However, both men had misunderstood at what the price the cattle were to be sold. Breadalbane took delivery of the cattle and paid what he assumed to be the correct price of £13 per head. Wilson informed Breadalbane that £13 per head was not the correct price and he later sued for the alleged balance. Clearly, both individuals had failed to conclude a mutually satisfactory price and, therefore, they had failed to form a contract.

An important matter to consider in this case is that it was not physically possible for the Marquis of Breadalbane to return the cattle to Wilson as they had been slaughtered and the carcasses eaten. Therefore, the court had to do the next best thing which was to order the payment of compensation to Wilson. This sum was fixed at an appropriate amount to reflect the loss suffered by Wilson.

 Key point: Wilson *v* Marquis of Breadalbane demonstrates that the price is a material term of the contract.

The type or nature of contract

This may occur where both parties misunderstand the nature of the contract. They may both be in agreement as regards the identity of the contracting parties and the subject matter of the contract. However, a mistaken belief as to how the contract will operate may completely undermine matters. An individual may believe that he will have use of an item under a contract of hire (or rental agreement) whereas the owner of the goods may well believe that she is agreeing to sell the goods. Clearly, a contract of hire and a contract of sale are legally distinct and have very different consequences.

 Foster v Mackinnon (1869) Foster, an old man of feeble sight was induced to sign a document which he thought was a guarantee for £3000. In fact, the document was a bill of exchange for £3000. A guarantee was a completely different type of agreement from a bill of exchange. The bill of exchange became immediately payable whereas the guarantee only became payable upon the event of someone becoming insolvent – an event which might not happen. The old man would not have signed the bill of exchange had it known its true nature. The document was, therefore, void.

 Key point: In **Foster v Mackinnon**, the old man thought he was entering a completely different type of contract than the one which was presented to him for signing.

 Key point: Substantial error occurs when there is error as to the identity of the contracting parties, error as to the subject matter of the contract, error as to the price and error as to the type of contract the parties are entering.

Force and fear

A contract will seldom be formed as a result of actual violence but threats of violence are more probable. Violence or the threat of violence must be such that they are enough to overwhelm a mind of ordinary firmness. Force and fear will have the effect of making the contract void. Threats to take legitimate legal action against someone do not fall into the category of force and fear. The following case gives a particularly vivid example of the effect of force and fear on a contract.

 Earl of Orkney v Vinfra (1606) the Earl summoned Vinfra to his castle and presented him with a written contract which he was to sign. The effect of this agreement was that Vinfra would have to pay the Earl a sum of money. Vinfra refused and the Earl turned nasty. The Earl started to curse and laying his hand on the hilt of his dagger threatened to kill Vinfra if he did not sign the document. Vinfra had no reason to believe that the Earl was anything but serious in his intentions and he wisely signed the document in order to save his life. Later, Vinfra refused to pay the money that he supposedly owed to the Earl claiming that he had only entered the agreement because he had feared for his life. The Earl claimed that he had been joking and that Vinfra's fears were misplaced.

Held: Vinfra's fears were all too real and the contract was, therefore, declared void.

Key point: Violence or very real threats of violence that are used to pressurise a party to enter an agreement will have the effect of rendering the contract void.

Contractual capacity

A valid contract requires that the parties must have capacity. A person of full capacity is capable of taking on duties which the law recognises and will force them to comply with. Additionally, the law will recognise any rights that these individuals are entitled to and will enforce these rights on their behalf. Most *natural legal persons* i.e. human beings, have full capacity.

Certain groups have no capacity or limits placed on their ability to enter contracts. These are:

- Young people under the age of 18
- Adults with incapacity
- Intoxicated persons
- Enemy aliens

 Key point: In order to enter a contract that the law will recognise, a person must have the power or ability to do this. This power or ability is known as contractual capacity.

Children and young persons

The law relating to young people and children was changed by the Age of Legal Capacity (Scotland) Act 1991. By young people and children, we mean those individuals who have not yet reached the age of 18 (the age of their majority). When a person reaches his eighteenth birthday, he will be regarded as an adult with powers of full capacity in the eyes of the law.

The 1991 Act draws a distinction between children aged under 16 and those who are 16 and over.

Children under 16

The general rule is that a child under 16 has no capacity to enter into any legal transaction. Technically, this means that any transaction entered into by an individual under the age of 16 will be void. However, the law in this area is capable of flexibility and there are exceptions to this rule. The contract that an under 16 has entered into will be enforceable if it satisfies two tests. The contract must be:

1 Of a kind usually entered into by persons of his age and circumstances

2 On terms which are not unreasonable

 Key point: The general rule is that a child under 16 has no capacity to enter into any legal transaction.

We are really talking about everyday types of contracts that a child would be a party to such as buying sweets. Obviously, as the child becomes older, the range of goods and services that he can purchase will increase dramatically. However, any doubts about the child's capacity should be referred to the child's guardian.

Young persons aged 16 and 17

These individuals are regarded as having full legal capacity in much the same way as an adult would. However, the 1991 Act does explicitly recognise that this group of young people will perhaps require some protection. It should be remembered that young people will have less experience of life and could be taken advantage of by unscrupulous older people. The courts will, therefore, cancel a contract that a young person has entered into if it can be shown that the agreement was harmful/prejudicial to the young person's interests. Potentially, a contract made with a young person aged 16 or 17 could be declared voidable by the courts.

 Key point: Contracts involving young persons are capable of being enforced, but they could be declared voidable by the courts.

However, the young person must satisfy two conditions if he is to demonstrate that the agreement was prejudicial/harmful to his interests. These two conditions are that:

1   It is highly unlikely that a sensible/reasonable adult would have entered into the contract under the same circumstances

2   The contract is likely to cause substantial prejudice/harm to the young person

Only the young person can use the protection that the 1991 Act provides. Other people (usually older persons) cannot use it to get out of the contract.

However, the protection offered to young persons under the 1991 Act has limitations. The young person must use this defence before he reaches the age of 21. Furthermore, the young person cannot use this defence to get out of a contract he has made in the course of his business or to which he has now agreed (ratified) after reaching the age of 18. It is also important to bear in mind that the young person will have no protection under the 1991 Act if he pretended to be 18.

Given the problems surrounding contracts and young persons, businesses may be very reluctant to enter contracts if they think the young person will use this defence. If there are doubts about the agreement's fairness, it may be worth approaching the Sheriff Court and requesting a Sheriff to decide whether the proposed contract could be harmful to the young person's interests. The Sheriff's decision cannot be challenged later.

 Key point: A young person may be able to have a contract cancelled if he can show that no sensible or reasonable adult would have entered the agreement and, furthermore, the agreement will cause him real harm if it is allowed to stand.

Some of the older cases concerning the capacity of young people can still provide useful illustrations.

 Wilkie _v_ Dunlop (1834) Wilkie, a young man who was just short of becoming an adult, ran up a bill when he stayed at an inn for three weeks. Wilkie was accompanied by an adult friend who had promptly paid his bill. Wilkie, however, failed to pay his part of the bill. His guardians also refused to pay the bill arguing that they had not authorised Wilkie's contract with the innkeeper. Part of their refusal to pay stemmed from the fact that his guardians were claiming that Wilkie was already adequately supported by them. The court was extremely unsympathetic towards Wilkie and his guardians stating that the amount of the bill was reasonable and that it would be unreasonable for someone to stay at an inn for three weeks and not pay for his board and lodging.

Held: Wilkie may not have been adult, but the contract that he had entered into was in way harmful or prejudicial to his interests.

 In the English case of **Chaplin *v* Leslie Frewin (Publishers) [1965]** the pursuer, who was the son of the silent film star Charlie Chaplin, entered a contract with the defender for the purpose of publishing a book that was to be written on his behalf and which would recount his life story. The book was entitled *I Couldn't Smoke the Grass on My Father's Lawn*. At the time the contract was made, Chaplin junior was not yet an adult and, therefore did not have full contractual capacity. He later sought to have the contract cancelled on the grounds that the book had caused him to suffer prejudice or severe harm. In the book, he had been portrayed in a very unflattering light and he felt that his reputation had suffered as a result.

Held: Chaplin failed to have contract cancelled. The book had actually benefited him at the time he had signed the contract because it had helped to establish his career as a writer. It is worth pointing out that the dispute between Chaplin and the publishers was not about money. In fact, Chaplin had made rather a lot of money from the publication of the book. In terms of the Age of Legal Capacity (Scotland) Act 1991, Chaplin's contract with the publishers would be regarded as a business contract and, as a young person, the defence that he had suffered prejudice because he had proceeded with it would not be available to him.

 Key point: Any adult entering into a contractual agreement with a child or a young person will have to be particularly careful.

Adults with incapacity

This category of people would include, for example, the insane, people with dementia and people who suffer from some sort of mental disability such as Downs Syndrome and are, therefore, incapable of entering into contracts which would be recognised by the courts. The Adults With Incapacity (Scotland) Act 2000 allows a guardianship to be declared where someone can act for a person who lacks capacity. The guardian may act for the incapable person in one transaction only, in a series of transactions or in relation to all the incapable person's affairs. The 2000 Act recognises various means by which a guardianship can be established.

 Key point: The Adults With Incapacity (Scotland) Act 2000 permits a guardian to be appointed to act for an individual who has been declared mentally incapacitated.

Insanity

Many of the older court cases involving an individual's mental incapacity deal with the issue of insanity. Insane persons have no capacity. A contract entered into by an insane person is, therefore, void. However, there could be an exception during a 'lucid interval' i.e. when the insane person regains sanity for a short period.

Someone who supplies essential items or necessaries to an insane person is entitled to be paid for these items (Section 3(3): Sale of Goods Act 1979). Clearly, the courts would be unlikely to view luxury sports cars as an essential item. By necessaries we mean, for example, food and clothing or the basic items necessary for a person's survival.

Someone can be appointed to a guardianship to act for an insane person. There are different levels of guardianship depending on the severity of the illness. A guardian can, of course, make contracts and enter into agreements on the insane person's behalf. This is particularly useful where the insane person has business or financial interests. A guardian can be appointed in a variety of different ways. Before the introduction of the Adults With Incapacity (Scotland) Act 2000, a guardian was known as a *curator bonis*.

 Loudon v Elder's Curator Bonis (1923) on 23 and 28 March, Elder, a wholesale meat merchant, placed orders with Loudon & Co for supplies of frozen meat. On 31 March, Elder was certified insane. The meat had not yet been delivered by Loudon to Elder. On 1 April, Thomas Hunter, Elder's legal guardian or *curator bonis* informed Loudon that the contracts were void on the grounds of Elder's insanity. Loudon refused to accept this situation and sued for breach of contract. Hunter in turn argued that, although the contracts had been made before Elder's insanity became public knowledge, medical evidence would prove that Elder was insane when he entered into the contracts with Loudon.

Held: the contracts were void on the grounds of Elder's insanity and, consequently, no damages for breach of contract were payable.

 Key point: Contracts entered into with an insane person will generally be declared void.

Intoxicated persons

This category would include people under the influence of drink, drugs or medication. However, the individual must be so intoxicated that s/he does not know what they are doing and cannot give true consent. Viscount Stair, the institutional writer, remarked that those who through fear, drunkenness or disease have not for a time the use of reason do not legally contract.

The intoxicated individual would have to take immediate steps to get out of the contract and the level of intoxication will matter, for example, a few after-dinner drinks which put a person in a good mood will rarely affect the validity of an agreement. A contract which has been formed as a result of one of the parties being under the influence of alcohol or drugs may be voidable.

 Taylor v Provan (1864) Provan offered to buy cattle from Taylor at £14 per head. Taylor, however, demanded that Provan pay a price of £15 per head for the cattle. No contract, therefore, was formed. Later that evening, Provan returned and offered Taylor £15 per head and Taylor accepted this offer. Provan later attempted to have the contract declared voidable on the grounds that he had been drunk when he had made the second offer to Taylor. Provan argued that his drunken state had prevented him from realising what he was doing when he made the second offer.

Held: Provan had failed to provide evidence that he was so drunk that he had lost his reason and was, therefore, completely unaware of the consequences of his actions. The mere fact that he had been under the influence of alcohol when he entered the agreement was not sufficient to have it cancelled.

 Key point: A contract with a drunken person must in effect always be voidable by him because presumably the fact that he is drunk will be known to the other party. This is not so in cases of unsoundness of mind which might not be known to the other party. However, a drunk person will have to take immediate steps to cancel the contract because delay may give the impression that he has agreed to stand by the agreement.

Enemy aliens

Those citizens of countries that the United Kingdom is at war with are known as enemy aliens. Such individuals continue to live in territory controlled by the United Kingdom during hostilities. It is, therefore, illegal for British citizens to enter into contracts with enemy aliens or with businesses controlled by them. Any contract with enemy aliens is generally regarded as being void. Interestingly, however, the contract becomes enforceable in the British courts when hostilities cease upon conclusion of a peace treaty or armistice and it is possible for the former enemy aliens to assert any rights that they have or may have had under the contract with British citizens and businesses. During the First and Second World Wars, German citizens and businesses controlled by them would have been regarded as enemy aliens. More recently, Iraqi citizens and businesses would have been regarded as enemy aliens. Sometimes the British government takes a hostile stance towards various countries and imposes sanctions on those states. Countries such as Libya, the former Yugoslavia and Iraq have all been the subject of international sanctions and it would have been illegal for any British citizen to do business with any of the citizens of these countries. An example of a contract with enemy aliens can be seen in the following case:

 Cantiere San Rocco SA *v* Clyde Shipbuilding and Engineering Co Ltd (1923) a Scottish shipyard had entered into a contract with an Austrian business just before the First World War began. Austria entered the First World War as an ally of Germany and declared War on the United Kingdom. This meant that Austrian citizens and businesses were now to be regarded as enemy aliens and any contracts that had been entered into were null and void and, consequently, unenforceable. After the War had ended, the House of Lords stated that the contract between the Scottish shipyard and the Austrians was capable of being enforced.

Corporate bodies

Registered companies and local authorities fall into this category and are known as *artificial legal persons*.

Local authorities are governed by the Local Government (Scotland) Act 1994. They enjoy powers given to them by this Act and other pieces of legislation. They must not act outside these powers (*ultra vires*). Any contract which is not within their powers will be void.

Registered companies are governed by the 1985 Companies Act. Section 3A of this Act allows a company to carry on business as a general commercial company in any trade or business whatsoever. No act done by a company may be questioned by the fact that it was beyond its legal capacity as stated in its memorandum of association.

A person dealing with a company does not have to check to see whether there are any limits on the company's capacity. Practically speaking, all contracts are enforceable against the company. The abolition of the *ultra vires* does not allow directors to escape liability in situations where they have acted beyond the authority given to them by the company's Memorandum of Association (see Chapter 5). The harshness of the *ultra vires* rule can be seen in the following case:

 Ashbury Railway Carriage & Iron Co *v* Riche (1875) According to its Memorandum of Association (i.e. its constitution) the company had been set up in order to manufacture and sell railway wagons, other railway equipment and to carry on the business of mechanical engineers and general contractors. The company took on a project to build an entire railway system in Belgium and it sub-contracted the building of the actual railway line to Riche. Riche began work and the company paid him for this. Problems arose when the company experienced a number of financial problems and the shareholders made it clear that the company should cease to play a further role in the construction of the railway. The directors then informed Riche that the company was withdrawing from the project. Riche promptly raised an action for breach of contract.

Held: by the House of Lords that the company could withdraw from the contract because the directors had acted *ultra vires* i.e. beyond their powers when they took over responsibility for constructing the railway. According to the company's objects clause in the Memorandum of Association, the contract with Riche was void. The objects clause, which listed *all* the business activities of the company, did not permit the company to construct an entire railway. The company was only permitted to supply materials for railway construction, but had no power to take on overall responsibility for a major project like the one in Belgium. Riche was deemed to have notice of this limitation on the company's powers because the Memorandum of Association was a publicly available document. It did not matter if he had not read this document.

The *ultra vires* rule was a Victorian device which allowed members of a company to restrict the powers of the company and the directors. This meant that directors would be prevented from acting in an unauthorised way so that they could not enter a transaction which was not included in the objects clause of the Memorandum of Association. This was a device to protect present and future members of the company by ensuring that the directors could only enter contracts which had been pre-approved by the members. An added protection of the rule was that it prevented a company from approving the unauthorised acts of its agents after the fact by passing a special resolution. Nowadays, of course, the company is permitted to pass a special resolution of the members in order to approve an action which is, strictly speaking, *ultra vires*. In to get round the restrictive nature of the *ultra vires* rule, it was not unusual for a company to draft a huge objects clause covering almost every sort of legitimate business activity imaginable.

Key point: Certain bodies such as local authorities must act strictly within their powers otherwise any transaction entered into which goes beyond these powers will be declared void.

Formality

Many people believe that it is a legal requirement that all contracts must be in writing and witnessed. Under Scots Law, many contracts do not require formalities i.e. the need to have written terms and conditions. The majority of contracts will be verbal agreements or their existence can be proved by looking at the parties' behaviour or by implication (see **Carlill v Carbolic Smokeball Company (1893)** or **Thornton v Shoe Lane Parking (1971)**). The existence of contracts can be usually proved by any type of evidence (statements from parties' testimony and their witnesses). Some contracts, however do need to be in written form.

 Key point: Many people believe that it is a legal requirement that all contracts must be in writing and witnessed. Under Scots Law, many contracts do not require formalities i.e. the need to have written terms and conditions to prove the existence of the contract.

The Requirements of Writing (Scotland) Act 1995

In modern Scots law, contracts involving land and buildings (heritable property) are covered by the Requirements of Writing (Scotland) Act 1995. A contract for the sale of land has to be in writing and must contain all the terms expressly agreed by the parties and each of those terms must be set out in the written document. The Act does allow terms of the agreement to be incorporated in the document where it refers to some other document or documents containing the terms. Failure to draw up a written contract has the effect of making such an agreement voidable. In other words, one or both of the parties could withdraw by justifying their actions on the basis that there was no written agreement. Both parties may have a verbal agreement and, normally, in many other situations this would be enough, but not if the contract concerns land or buildings.

 Key point: Land and buildings and things attached to land and buildings are referred to as heritable property. Leases and rents are also classified as heritable property.

The Requirements of Writing (Scotland) Act 1995, which came into force on 1 August 1995 changed the law here with regard to the evidence required to prove the existence of gratuitous obligations and bilateral contracts.

As previously discussed in this chapter, it is still the general rule that contracts or unilateral promises do not have to be in written form. However, certain types of legal obligations must be in written form. These include the following:

- Contracts or unilateral promises which involve transactions in relation to heritable property i.e. land and buildings and anything which is attached to or forms part of land
- Unilateral promises except those which are made in the course of business
- A trust where a person declares himself to be the sole trustee of his own property or property that he acquires
- Where a person makes a will

The Consumer Credit Act 1974 insists that all the main terms of a regulated credit agreement must be in writing, otherwise the creditor will only be able to enforce the agreement with a court order. Furthermore, the Bills of Exchange Act 1882 insists that all negotiable instruments, for example, a bank cheque or promissory note must be in written form.

 Key point: In situations where the law demands that the parties draw up a written contract, an informal agreement will regarded as voidable.

In terms of the Requirements of Writing (Scotland) 1995, what type of evidence is required to prove the existence of a contract?

All that is necessary is that the document is signed by the relevant persons (i.e. the parties or their agents). Only one witness is required under the 1995 Act and the document will be perfectly valid. Unless the court has any reason to be suspicious about the validity of the document, it will take the witness's signature at face value. Should the parties to the written document fail to get it witnessed, the court will demand evidence from the parties that the agreement is, in fact, an accurate statement of their intentions. Such evidence will be in the form of sworn affidavits (statements). A court can also issue a certificate which authenticates the validity of a document. The Contract (Scotland) Act 1997 clarified the law in this area and additional external sources of information whether consisting of verbal statements or documentary evidence can be used in court to flesh out additional express terms in relation to a written contract. Otherwise, the 1997 Act assumes that a written document will contain all the main terms of the agreement.

 Key point: The Requirements of Writing (Scotland) Act 1995 states that the signature of one witness will be all that is required to validate a written contract and the Contract (Scotland) Act 1997 now allows external evidence to clarify the terms of the written agreement.

Electronic signatures

Section 7 of the Electronic Communications Act 2000 states that electronic signatures incorporated in electronic documents will now be admissible as evidence in a court.

Failure to draw up a written agreement

What if the parties fail to provide a written agreement or document when the 1995 Act places a duty on them to do so?

It might be thought that if the parties have a purely verbal contract involving heritable property, the courts would refuse to enforce it. However, this is not the case. Despite the fact that the 1995 Act states that all contracts involving heritable property should be in writing, there are situations where the courts will enforce unwritten contracts. A contract (and for that matter a unilateral promise) can be enforced where there have been 'significant actings'.

If one party attempted to withdraw from an informal contract involving heritable property on the grounds that there was nothing in writing, they might be in for something of a shock. It will not be possible to use the argument that as there is no written contract then the agreement can be cancelled if:

1   The other party has relied on the contract

2   The other party knew of their actions and agreed to them

3   The actions of the party wishing to honour the contract were material (not trivial) so that they would be prejudiced or severely disadvantaged if the other party pulled out

 Key point: In situations where the law imposes a duty on the parties to have a written contract and they have failed to draw one up, an unwritten agreement may still be enforced if one or both of the parties can demonstrate that there have been significant actings.

Effect of undue influence on the parties to the contract

Undue influence renders the contract voidable so that it may be rescinded or cancelled. However, if rescission is being sought by one of the parties to the contract as a remedy, there must be no delay in claiming relief after the influence has ceased to have an effect. Delay in claiming relief in these circumstances may bar the claim since delay is evidence of affirmation or agreement.

Undue influence can perhaps occur in the following relationships: parent and child and husband and wife. There will, of course, be other relationships where a stronger party may exert a particularly negative influence on the weaker party, for example, members of a religious cult who unquestionably obey the orders of their spiritual leader.

 Key point: Undue influence renders the contract voidable so that it may be rescinded or cancelled.

 Allcard _v_ Skinner (1887) in 1868, Allcard, the pursuer, became a novice in an all female religious order called St Mary at the Cross, which had a particular emphasis on works of charity. In 1871, Allcard became a full member of the order. All members of the order had to take a vow of obedience to Skinner, the Superior (head) of the order. The order was run along very oppressive lines and in the modern age might be regarded as something of a religious cult. The Superior was to be regarded as one of God's personal representatives on earth and this person's word was effectively law. Furthermore, all issues and problems affecting the members had to be discussed with the Superior and members were absolutely forbidden to seek counsel or advice from outsiders. Shortly after becoming a full member of the order, Allcard drew up a will leaving all of her possessions to the group. Allcard was a wealthy young woman and, over the next few years, she came into possession of large sums of money and shares in various companies. She transferred large amounts of her wealth to the order. In May, 1879, Allcard decided to leave the order and she took immediate steps to change her will to reflect the fact that she no longer wished the order to be her beneficiary. Unfortunately, Allcard failed to raise an action to recover the money and shares that she had transferred to the order until 1885. Allcard alleged that she had only handed over her property to the order, without taking independent advice, because of the Superior's undue influence.

Held: by the English Court of Appeal that Allcard's action to recover her property should be dismissed. The Court of Appeal was strongly of the opinion that the pursuer's claim was time-barred by the fact that she did not bring a claim against the order until nearly six years after she ceased to be a member. Clearly, the pursuer's claim against the order may have succeeded if only she had commenced legal action much sooner.

 Anderson *v* The Beacon Fellowship 1992, Lord McCluskey (in the Outer House of the Court of Session) considered whether the defenders, a religious group, had used undue influence in relation to the pursuer to procure donations of money from him. Representatives of the Fellowship regularly visited the pursuer and exerted a very strong influence over him. The pursuer suffered from a number of psychiatric illnesses and had been taking medication from time to time to control his various ailments. He was, therefore, somewhat vulnerable to the overtures of the Fellowship i.e. that money was worthless and that it should be given away. The pursuer eventually raised an action to recover the various donations that he had made to the Fellowship. Lord McCluskey felt that there was sufficient evidence to suggest that there had been undue influence and allowed the case to proceed to a proof.

Husbands and wives: a presumption of undue influence?

In Scotland, the issue of undue influence has been reconsidered in connection with the relationship of husband and wife. During the 1990s, several cases were brought before the Scottish and English courts regarding the issue of undue influence. All these cases had remarkably similar facts, whereby the pursuers, a number of wives, alleged that they had agreed to re-mortgage the marital home so that a bank would lend money to their husbands (usually, but not always, for business purposes). These wives claimed that they had not been given sufficient information by their husbands when they had agreed to approve what later turned out to be very risky transactions. Some of the pursuers had not sought independent legal advice before agreeing to take out the second mortgage.

The House of Lords, in **Barclays Bank plc *v* O'Brien [1993]**, stated that a married woman (or cohabitee) must be regarded as a special, protected class of guarantor when agreeing to guarantee her husband's (or partner's) debts because of the nature of the relationship. The bank should be on alert for signs of undue influence which would undermine the validity of the transaction. The bank is under a duty to ensure that the wife or the cohabitee has the benefit of independent advice. Their Lordships, however, did make a distinction in these types of cases. In **CIBC Mortgages *v* Pitt [1994]** a wife was not allowed to succeed in her claim of undue influence because the mortgage was in the names of both husband and wife and, therefore, she was benefiting from it.

However, the decision of their Lordships in **Barclays Bank plc *v* O'Brien** was not followed by the Inner House of the Court of Session in **Mumford *v* Bank of Scotland** where it was held that banks are not under a general duty to explain all the material circumstances of a loan to someone who has guaranteed it. In **Smith *v* Bank of Scotland (1997)**, the House of Lords attempted to bring Scots law into line with English law. In a further English case, **Royal Bank of Scotland PLC *v***

Ettridge (No.2) (2001), the House of Lords has stated that undue influence will not be presumed merely because the parties to a transaction are husband and wife. It will be for the wife to show that there was undue influence on the part of the husband and that the bank should have been aware of this fact. The bank is then free to disprove this allegation – if it can.

In a series of recent cases (**Forsyth v The Royal Bank of Scotland PLC 2000** and **Royal Bank Scotland PLC v Wilson & Ors [2003]**), the Inner House of the Court of Session has refused to accept that wives were unduly influenced by their husbands. Misrepresentations by the husband were more likely to have induced the wives to agree to become guarantors rather than any hint of undue influence. In **Forsyth**, the creditor was able to show that it had acted in good faith because it was aware that the wife had access to independent, professional legal advice. This permitted the creditor to enforce the standard security against the couple's house. The extent of any duty which is placed upon the creditor to enquire whether the wife is fully aware of the obligation that she is taking on is not as well developed in Scotland as in England. In **Royal Bank of Scotland PLC v Ettridge (No.2) (2001)**, the House of Lords stated that a creditor owes a duty of care to a wife if it has constructive notice that the husband's undue influence induced the wife to guarantee the transaction. It has to be said that the duty placed upon a bank in Scotland is not as demanding as the test imposed in England.

Facility and circumvention

An individual may be able to withdraw from what appears to be a perfectly valid contract if he can later prove that at the time of entering the agreement, the other party took advantage of some personal weakness such as old age or physical weakness. This leaves the individual in a vulnerable position in the sense that he is more open to persuasion, advice or intimidation usually coming from the other party. The affected individual is not suffering from some form of mental incapacity, but his condition will have been taken advantage of by the other party.

 Cairns v Marianski (1852) a father had two daughters. One of the daughters was married to Marianski, the other to Cairns. The father had lived with the Marianskis from just after their wedding until his death at the age of 90. The Marianskis had looked after the old man and he felt under an obligation to them which they were later to exploit. Upon the father's death, it emerged that certain documents signed by the father conferred benefits on Marianski. Cairns was convinced that the Marianskis had taken advantage of the old man's frail health and their close personal relationship in order to persuade him to give them certain rights over his estate when he died.

Held: by the House of Lords that there had been facility and circumvention and that the documents drawn up in Marianski's favour were to be cancelled.

 Key point: Facility and circumvention involves situations where someone's weakness of will or ill-health is used by another person to gain advantage in relation to property or contracts.

Misrepresentation

A misrepresentation occurs when one party, during negotiations leading to the formation of a contract, makes a materially false statement of fact which has the effect of encouraging or inducing the other party to enter the agreement. It is usually after the contract has been formed that the party who relied on the statement will discover that it factually false. The innocent party must be able to prove that, if he had been aware that the statement was in fact false, he would never have entered the contract in the first place. In the course of making a misrepresentation, a party does not have to be aware that the statement was false. A misrepresentation is not necessarily a deceitful or dishonest statement.

The nature of the misrepresentation

Since the decision of the House of Lords in **Hedley Byrne & Co Ltd v Heller & Partners Ltd (1963)**, three categories of misrepresentation are recognised by the Scottish Courts:

1 Innocent

2 Fraudulent

3 Negligent

With an innocent misrepresentation, the party who made the statement genuinely believes what he is saying to be the truth. There is no intention to deceive, but the statement is still factually incorrect and it may have encouraged another individual to enter the contract.

Fraudulent misrepresentation, on the other hand, is a deliberate attempt by the party making the statement to deceive another person and, therefore, influence the innocent party to enter the contract. The party who made the fraudulent statement is fully aware of the falseness of his statement. In other words, he is being consciously dishonest when he makes the misrepresentation to the other party.

Lord Herschell, a former Lord Chancellor, described fraudulent misrepresentation in **Derry v Peek (1889)** as:

'*A false representation of fact, made with a knowledge of its falseness or in utter disregard if it be true or false, with the intention that it should be acted upon and actually inducing the other party to act upon it.*'

The facts of **Derry v Peek (1889)** are as follows:

 A special Act of Parliament permitted a tramway company to be created. The Act stated that the new company's carriages might be moved by animal power, for example, by using horses and mules. If the company wished to use steam power to move the carriages using steam power, it had to obtain the consent of the Board of Trade (a British government department). The company directors issued a prospectus containing a statement claiming (falsely as it later turned out) that the special Act of Parliament permitted the company to use steam power instead of horses. There was no mention that the consent of the Board of Trade was required to authorise this activity. The pursuer, however, decided to invest in the new company on the basis of this statement in the prospectus. The Board of Trade afterwards refused to give its consent authorising the use of steam power and the company was wound up. The pursuer claimed that the directors had made a fraudulent misrepresentation that had encouraged him to enter the contract and he sued for damages.

Held: by the House of Lords, reversing the decision of the English Court of Appeal and restoring the decision of the trial judge, that the directors were not liable. They had included the statement regarding steam power in the honest belief that it was true. They had made an innocent misrepresentation and no damages were payable.

It can be difficult for an innocent party to prove that someone has made a fraudulent misrepresentation. Conscious dishonesty must be proved according to the criminal standard i.e. beyond a reasonable doubt, and not according to the civil standard of proof i.e. on the balance of probabilities.

Negligent misrepresentation is a relatively recent concept. Prior to **Hedley Byrne**, a misrepresentation was either of an innocent or fraudulent nature. This position meant that there was no middle ground for the innocent party. The party making the statement may not have been dishonest, but he may have been reckless. Fraud, as we have seen, can be difficult to prove and, in many cases, the courts found that the misrepresentation was of the innocent variety. This approach by the courts did not always favour the victim because damages were not payable for innocent misrepresentation in Scotland and the parties could not always be returned to their original pre-contractual positions. As a result, a finding of even innocent misrepresentation did not necessarily leave the innocent party any better off. As we shall see when we come to a discussion of the remedies available for misrepresentation, the decision in **Hedley Byrne** strengthens the position of the innocent party.

A negligent misrepresentation is very different from innocent and fraudulent misrepresentation. Someone who makes a negligent statement does not intend to deceive the other party but, at the same time, he cannot prove that he had reasonable grounds for believing the truth of his statement. In other words, he has made the statement recklessly without verifying its accuracy. Generally, negligent misrepresentation will occur in situations where the parties have a special relationship and the party making the statement will owe the other party a duty of care. Negligent misrepresentation is also very much part of the law of the delict and is discussed in detail in Chapter 3. Clearly, where a contract is concerned, the parties have a special, legal relationship and they will owe duties (of care) to one another.

Did the misrepresentation influence the innocent party?

In order to be able to raise an action against the party who made the misrepresentation, the innocent party must prove that the false statement influenced his decision to proceed with the contract. If the innocent party fails to show that the misrepresentation had no influence on his decision and that he would have entered the contract in any case, his claim will fail.

 Smith *v* Chadwick (1884) an action was brought by Smith, a steel manufacturer, against Messrs Chadwick, Adamson and Collier who were accountants and promoters of a company. Smith claimed an amount of money as losses caused as a result of his decision to buy shares in the company which were worth much less than the price he had paid for them because of certain misrepresentations contained in the company prospectus issued by the defenders. Among the misrepresentations alleged by Smith was the statement that a certain Member of Parliament was a director of the company. In fact, this Member of Parliament had withdrawn from the company on the day before the prospectus was issued.

Held: the statement about the Member of Parliament was false but not material, because Smith had never heard of him and his decision to buy shares in the company had not been influenced by this piece of information. Smith's action for damages was, therefore, unsuccessful.

 Attwood *v* Small (1838) during negotiations for the sale of a mine, the defender made false statements to the pursuer about the mine's potential. The pursuer, however, appointed his own surveyor who broadly confirmed what the defender had said about the mine's potential. On the strength of the surveyor's report, the pursuer then proceeded to purchase the mine.

Held: the pursuer's reliance on his own survey clearly demonstrated that he had not been influenced in respect of his decision to purchase the mine by the original misrepresentation of the defender.

The effect of misrepresentation

Generally, misrepresentation has the effect of making a contract voidable. In other words, it will be up to the party who is the victim of the misrepresentation to take effective steps within a reasonable period of time to have the contract set aside or cancelled (the remedy of rescission). If the victim of the misrepresentation fails to cancel the contract within a reasonable time, the courts will treat this failure as evidence that he has decided to ratify or approve the agreement and he will have lost his right to cancel.

In order to cancel the contract, the court must be able to return the parties to their pre-contractual positions (*restitutio in integrum*). As shall become apparent, this remedy is not always available to the courts because of the impossibility of returning the parties to their original positions. Returning the parties to their original positions, for all practical purposes, means that any money or property that has been transferred must be returned to the original owners.

We can contrast the approach taken by the courts towards the remedy of rescission in two cases: **Boyd & Forrest *v* Glasgow & South-Western Railway Co (1915)** and **Erlanger *v* New Sombrero Phosphate Co (1878)**.

 Boyd & Forrest, a misrepresentation (innocently made) by the Glasgow & South-Western Railway's engineer as to the hardness of a section of subsoil, which was to be removed for the purpose of building a railway, cost the contractors £136,000 in additional costs. The House of Lords refused to return the parties to their original positions. What could be realistically achieved by ordering the parties to be returned to their pre-contractual positions? Tear down the brand new railway and replace all the rock and soil which had been extracted? This was a ridiculous suggestion on the part of the contractors and the court rightly refused to order this course of action. When the contractors realised that the information that they had received from the Railway was wrong, they should have stopped work immediately and informed the Railway of this problem. Instead, the contractors foolishly decided to proceed with the work.

 Erlanger, the pursuer was induced to buy an island containing mines on the basis of representations made by the other party as to their production capacity. It was held that although the mines had been substantially worked by the pursuer, he was entitled to rescind the contract on condition that both the mines and all the profits received from working it were returned to the other party. The pursuer, of course, would be entitled to reclaim the price that he had paid for the island and the mines.

It is also worth appreciating that the remedy of damages may not available to the victim who has suffered loss as result of the misrepresentation. Where the misrepresentation is of an entirely innocent nature, the Scottish courts will not award damages and the only course of action (which may not provide much of a consolation) would be to attempt to have the contract rescinded or cancelled – if indeed this is a realistic possibility. In **Boyd & Forrest**, the misrepresentation was of an innocent nature and, consequently, the contractors were not awarded damages.

In situations involving negligent and fraudulent misrepresentation, there are a number of options available to the victim. The following remedies or combination of remedies is available to the victim:

1 Rescission or cancellation of the contract

2 Rescission or cancellation of the contract and an award of damages

3 Retention of the contract and an award of damages

In England, as a result of the Misrepresentation Act 1967, it is possible for the victim of an innocent misrepresentation to obtain damages.

Silence as a misrepresentation

By contrast, in the face of silence, the court normally applies the maxim *caveat emptor* – let the buyer beware. During contractual negotiations, the parties are allowed to keep their cards close to their chests in an attempt to obtain the best bargain for themselves. Obviously, when a party is asked a direct question during negotiations which concerns some aspect of the future contract, that question should receive an honest answer. As a matter of policy in these cases, the onus is placed on a party to discover the truth by means of interrogation, inquiry and examination. The law does not protect a party from the consequences of his own stupidity and which will lead him to make a bad bargain with the other party.

 This approach can be seen most clearly in the case of **Gillespie v Russel (1856)** where an individual who had taken out a lease on a gold mine discovered that the mine also contained a very valuable seam of coal. This fact was not communicated to the owner. The owner of the mine was completely unaware that the property also contained coal. Upon this discovery, the owner attempted to have the contract cancelled.

Held: the contract had already been concluded and it was up to the owner to keep a proper record of his assets.

If a party uses half-truths to conceal material facts, this may be regarded as a misrepresentation.

 Couston v Miller (1862) Miller had read out the contents of a deed that Couston intended to sign – Couston did not read the document. What Miller failed to do was to read out the most important part of the deed which, if he had done so, would have prevented Couston from going ahead and signing it. Miller had not told any lies, but his conduct was dishonest and amounted to a misrepresentation (see also **Chemical Cleaning and Dyeing Co (1951)** in relation to exclusion clauses below).

The difference between an opinion and a misrepresentation

An opinion is just an opinion and everyone is entitled to his opinion for what it may be worth. This may sound very democratic, but in practice the person who voices his opinion may be viewed as an expert or someone who possesses specialist knowledge. If this is the case, it may be that the person who got the benefit of the opinion may attach greater significance to it if it came from an expert. Sometimes, the dividing line between an opinion and a misrepresentation will be a very fine one.

 Hamilton v Duke of Montrose (1906) an advertisement in a newspaper of 'hill grazing capable of keeping about 2000 black faced sheep and summering 100 cattle' was not a misrepresentation. It was held to be a statement of opinion.

 Bisset v Wilkinson (1927) the buyer had purchased land in New Zealand, but he later wished to cancel the contract because he claimed that the seller had made a false statement as to how many sheep the land could accommodate.
Held: by the Privy Council, on the evidence, that the statement made by the seller of land was merely an opinion that he honestly held and, consequently, the buyer's action to have the contract cancelled or rescinded failed.

Innocent misrepresentation

 Boyd & Forrest v Glasgow & South-Western Railway Co (1912) the railway company had invited tenders from various contractors for the purpose of building part of a railway line. All the contractors had been shown the findings from various studies which indicated the type of soil that would have to be dug up along the proposed stretch of line. On the basis of the information supplied by the railway, Boyd & Forrest submitted a successful bid to carry out the work for £243,000. The work commenced, but Boyd & Forrest discovered that the ground contained a much larger quantity of rocky subsoil than the original studies had indicated. Instead of stopping the work and querying the findings studies, Boyd & Forrest pressed ahead with the work and completed it at a total cost of £379,000 (£136,000 more than had been originally anticipated – a truly colossal figure). It later emerged that one of the railway engineers, Melville, had altered the findings of the studies because he honestly believed that they were mistaken. Boyd & Forrest attempted to recover the extra figure of £136,000 from the railway alleging that Melville had fraudulently altered the information. Boyd & Forrest claimed that Melville's alleged fraud had encouraged them to enter the contract.

Held: by the House of Lords that Melville's actions had been completely honest – there was no attempt on his part to make a fraudulent misrepresentation. He had made an innocent misrepresentation. The action by Boyd & Forrest, therefore, failed.

Fraudulent misrepresentation

Edgington *v* Fitzmaurice (1885) the directors of a company issued a prospectus inviting investors to take out debentures in the company. A debenture is effectively a loan made to the company. The prospectus stated that the proceeds raised from the debentures would be used to expand and develop the company's business. The real object of the loan was to enable the directors to pay off financial debts that had been run up and which the company's creditors were now demanding should be paid. The pursuer advanced money on some of the debentures under the mistaken belief that the prospectus offered a security over the property of the company, and stated in his evidence that he would not have advanced his money but for such belief. Furthermore, he also relied upon the statements contained in the prospectus. The company became insolvent.

Held: by the English Court of Appeal (affirming the decree of Denman J), that the directors had made a fraudulent misrepresentation in the prospectus which had partly influenced the pursuer to advance loans to the company. However, this partial reliance on the misrepresentation was enough to allow the innocent party to raise a claim for damages.

Negligent misrepresentation

The leading case is **Hedley Byrne & Co Ltd *v* Heller & Partners Ltd (1963)** and is discussed in greater detail in Chapter 3. An advertising agency had relied on statements made by a bank about the financial solvency of a mutual client. The bank had assured the agency that the client had enough money in a bank account to pay for advertising contracts that the agency had entered into on the client's behalf. The bank, however, had made this statement negligently. The client did not have sufficient funds in the bank account to pay the advertising costs. Consequently, the agency lost £17,000 as a result of the bank's negligent misrepresentation. The agency sued the bank for the losses it had suffered. The bank argued that it had excluded its liability for negligence by issuing a statement to the effect that the information provided should not be relied upon by the agency. The bank's disclaimer was issued together at the same time as it had provided the financial advice in respect of the client.

Held: that in the present case, the presence of the disclaimer excluded a duty of care owed by the bank to the agency. However, if the bank had failed to issue the disclaimer, it would have been liable to the agency for the losses caused by its negligence for making a false statement. This was in spite of the fact that the bank did not have a fiduciary relationship (relationship of trust) or a contract with the agency. The House of Lords effectively introduced a new type of misrepresentation into the law i.e. negligent misrepresentation as a result of this case.

The House of Lords stated that the duty of care arose where there was a special relationship requiring care. It has been argued that a duty of care will be owed by the parties in a contractual relationship. The boundaries of **Hedley Byrne**, even to this day, are still not firmly settled, but the existence of a special relationship between the parties is a useful starting point. Lord Devlin said that when one party pays for information or advice this strongly indicates that the party requesting the information will be using it to make important decisions and the adviser will not to be able to argue, convincingly, that he did not know this. Furthermore, the fact that the information was not paid for by the person who requested it does not mean that an adviser can be reckless or negligent when issuing it. If the existence of a special relationship between the parties can be proved between the parties, the adviser will still have to take care if he is aware that the other party will be relying on this information regardless of whether he received payment or not.

There is a more detailed discussion in Chapter 3 concerning the types of special relationship that the courts have recognised give rise to a duty of care in respect of negligent misrepresentation.

Requirements of disclosure

Sometimes the law imposes a duty on one or both of the parties to disclose all material facts that may have an effect on a contractual relationship.

Fiduciary relationships

A fiduciary relationship is a relationship of confidence that imposes a special duty of care on one or both of the parties. Examples of such relationships include those of solicitor/client, principal/agent, doctor/patient, parent/child and the partners in a firm. If a party owes a fiduciary duty to someone else this means that he must disclose all material facts to the other person. The duty arising from these types of fiduciary relationships are different from the duties that arise under contracts *uberrimae fidei* i.e. of the utmost good faith. In contracts *uberrimae fidei*, it is the nature of the contract, for example, an insurance contract which requires disclosure in spite of the relationship between the parties. In the fiduciary situation it is the relationship of the parties and not the particular contract which gives rise to the need to disclose. Fiduciary duties are discussed in relation to the law of agency in Chapter 5.

 McPherson's Trustees *v* Watt (1877) Watt, a solicitor or law agent who represented the interests of the trustees, had been given instructions to sell four houses for the trustees. Watt entered into an arrangement with his brother that he would sell the properties to his brother. Watt did not disclose this arrangement to the trustees. This arrangement was to operate on the condition that Watt's brother would later sell two of the houses to him at half the purchase price. The trustees discovered this arrangement between Watt and his brother and, before they could carry out the contract, the trustees obtained an interdict or court order to prevent it going ahead.

Held: the contract for the sale of the houses was invalid. A solicitor, as a law agent, has a duty to act in good faith and there must be no conflict of duty and interest.

 Pillans Brothers *v* Pillans (1908) the three Pillans brothers carried on a partnership business as rivet, bolt and nut manufacturers mainly in the Motherwell area. Richard Pillans, one of the brothers, later bought a business at Greenfield, four miles outside Motherwell, in which was involved in the same line of trade as the business that he ran with his brothers and which had directly competed against the family firm. Richard did not disclose to his brothers the fact that he was now the owner of a rival business. His brothers discovered this fact and raised a legal action against him.

Held: Richard had to disclose to his brothers all the profits that his rival business had made and, furthermore, he had to give them a share of these profits. Effectively, Richard had to surrender control of his business at Greenfield to the family firm.

Contracts *uberrimae fidei*

In a small number of situations, the law demands that, during pre-contractual negotiations, a party must act with the utmost good faith (*uberrimae fidei*). The example of insurance contracts are often used to demonstrate how this duty to act with the utmost good faith works in practice. The proposer (the person intending to take out the policy) is under a positive duty to bring all material facts to the insurer at the time of making the contract of insurance. If the proposer is in any doubt about the importance of a fact, for safety's sake and to protect his own position, he should bring it to the attention of the insurer. Failure by the proposer to do so may allow the insurer to treat the contract as voidable and refuse to pay out under the policy as the House of Lords made it quite clear in **Pan Atlantic Insurance *v* Pine Top Insurance (1994)**.

 The Spathari (1925) the owners of a ship deliberately concealed from the insurance company that the vessel was Greek owned. The ship later sank and the owners attempted to make a claim under the insurance policy. The insurance company at that time, in common with many other insurers, was refusing even to consider insuring Greek ships because they were regarded as such a bad risk. The insurance company later discovered the true facts concerning the vessel's ownership and informed the proposer that it would not honour the contract.

Held: by the House of Lords that the contract was voidable because the proposer had not disclosed all material facts as he was duty bound to do. The insurance company was entitled not to honour the contract.

The law is very strict with regard to insurance contracts because the proposer is could quite easily conceal material facts and the insurance company would be none the wiser. This would result in the insurers agreeing to take on a risk, without full knowledge on their part. However, if the insurance company decides to treat the contract as voidable, it must return the premiums paid to the proposer (**Banque Keyser Ullmann SA *v* Skandia (UK) Insurance Co (1989)**). In other words, the contract is rescinded or cancelled and the parties must be returned to their pre-contractual positions. Admittedly, most proposals for insurance require a proposer to sign a declaration in which he is stating for the record that the information he has provided is, to the best of his knowledge, truthful and accurate. This declaration by the proposer becomes part of the contract and, later if the proposer's failure to reveal all material facts is discovered, the insurers can treat the contract as void.

 Dawsons Ltd *v* Bonln (1922) the pursuers insured a lorry against loss by fire and stated on the proposal form that the lorry would be garaged at their business address. However, there was no garage at this address and the lorry had to kept elsewhere. The insurance company had insisted that the pursuers sign a declaration that all information provided was factually correct. The pursuers' secretary, who signed the proposal form on behalf of the company, knew that this statement was a mistake, but she failed to bring it to the attention of the insurers. The lorry was destroyed by fire and the pursuers tried to enforce the policy.

Held: by the House of Lords that by signing a declaration stating that all information provided to the insurers was accurate, the false statement regarding the lorry's whereabouts rendered the insurance contract null and void.

Where statute requires disclosure

When a company has a full listing on the London Stock Exchange, the **Financial Services Act 1986** imposes a requirement that certain types of information must be disclosed in an advert or prospectus issued by a company which is for the purpose of inviting members of the public to subscribe for shares or debentures. This advert or prospectus must be detailed enough so that essential information is given to investors and professional advisers so that they can make a reasonably informed decision about purchasing the shares or taking up the debentures. The provisions of the **Financial Services Act** apply to companies that have a full listing on the Stock Exchange.

Where unlisted securities are concerned i.e. companies which are listed in the **Alternative Investment Market**, the legal requirements relating to disclosure of material facts to members of the public are contained in the **Public Offers of Securities Regulations 1995** as amended by the **Public Offers of Securities (Amendment) Regulations 1999**. Regulation 4 of the 1995 Regulations requires the publication and registration of a prospectus before securities are offered to the public in the UK for the first time. Regulation 5 states that a person is to be regarded as offering securities if, as principal, he makes an offer which, if accepted, would give rise to a contract for the issue or sale of securities, or if he invites a person to make such an offer. The securities must be offered to the public in the UK. Admittedly, many companies will be exempted from the rules contained in the1995 Regulations as a result of the **Financial Services and Markets Act 2000** and the **Financial Promotion Order 2001**.

Clearly, a false statement in a company prospectus may amount to a misrepresentation of some variety or other which may the give the innocent party a right of action against the person who was responsible for it (**but see Smith *v* Chadwick (1884)**).

Concealed fraud

Silence can amount to misrepresentation in the case of concealed fraud.

 Gibson v National Cash Register Co Ltd (1925) the seller of cash registers had work carried out on the goods to make them appear as if they were brand new items. The goods were, in fact, second hand, but the buyer was not aware of this and the basis of the appearance of the goods he entered a contract with the seller thinking that he was purchasing brand new goods. The seller, of course, did not inform the buyer of the true facts. The buyer later discovered the truth about the goods and sued the seller for damages on the grounds of fraudulent concealment.

 Gordon v Selico Co Ltd (1986) a block of flats which had recently been converted by a developer was leased to the pursuer for 99 years. Not long after the pursuer had moved into the property, dry rot was discovered.

Held: by the English Court of Appeal that deliberate concealment of dry rot by the developer could be regarded as fraudulent misrepresentation and damages were awarded to the pursuer.

Failure to disclose a change in circumstances

Parties have a duty to disclose any change in circumstances.

 Shankland v Robinson (1920) the seller of a traction engine reassured a potential buyer that the item was not going to be requisitioned by the Government. It later emerged that the Government now intended to requisition the machine.

Held: by the House of Lords that, if the seller had definitely been aware that the machine was going to be requisitioned, and had attempted to conceal this from the prospective buyer this would have amounted to fraudulent concealment. A seller in these circumstances was under a duty to reveal a change in circumstances to a buyer as soon as he became aware of the relevant facts.

 With v O'Flanagan (1936) the seller of a medical practice informed the prospective purchaser that the practice was a profitable business. This statement was quite true when it was originally made. Time passed and the practice ceased to be profitable, but the seller chose not to inform the purchaser of this change in circumstances before the sale took place. The sale went ahead and the purchaser discovered the true state of the business.

Held: by the English Court of Appeal that the seller's failure to notify the change in the circumstances of the business amounted to a misrepresentation.

Illegality

When we talk about illegal contracts, it is worth emphasising as Lord Wheatley did in the case of **Dowling & Rutter and Others v Abacus Frozen Foods Limited (2000)** (Outer House of the Court of Session) that a distinction should be made as to the illegal creation of a contract and the illegal performance of a contract. If performance of a perfectly legal contract is carried out in a way which involves a breach of statute, the courts may be prepared to overlook this by taking the view that it involved such a minor degree of illegality as to be irrelevant to the main purpose of the contract; or that the breach was outwith the scope of the statute in question. In such cases, it would be extremely harsh if the courts prevented one or both of the parties from enforcing the contract as a result of a very minor breach of statute. The parties to an agreement which breaches statute may not escape completely. They may find that breaches of the statutory provisions result in fines or some other punishment being imposed.

Lord Wheatley made it very clear, however, that if the creation of a contract is forbidden by statute it would be very difficult, impossible even, for the courts to enforce it. It would be ridiculous if a party attempted to form a contract to do something which was forbidden by statute law and then turned to the courts for assistance in order to enforce the illegal agreement.

As a general rule, the doctrine of illegality penalises those parties who create particular contracts that are regarded as illegal (sometimes referred to as *pacta illicita*). The greatest sanction that the court has is to refuse to enforce the agreement if its creation breaches the common law or statute. Such an agreement is void from its creation. This means that, in the event of a dispute, the parties will not have any rights or duties under the agreement – the courts will simply not recognise its validity. The general rule regarding illegal contracts is often expressed as *ex turpi causa non oritur actio* i.e. a party can have no right of action when the dispute involves an immoral or illegal situation.

 Key point: The creation of a contract may be illegal either at common law or as a result of statute.

What would be the situation if, for example, a man hired a contract killer to murder to his wife, he paid the killer in advance to go ahead and carry out the murder, but at the last the killer decided to pocket the money and not carry out the job? Firstly, the husband would be unable to sue for the return of his money and, secondly, he could not sue the contract killer for breach of the agreement and even begin to convince a judge that he should be awarded damages as compensation. If the husband brought this agreement to the attention of the courts, it would mean exposing the whole scheme to the criminal authorities. This example of illegal contracts is a particularly dramatic one, but not all illegal contracts will involve breaking the criminal law.

 Key point: An illegal contract will not necessarily involve breaches of the criminal law but such contracts often breach civil law.

An example of an illegal contract and the attitude of the courts can be seen in the following case:

 Cowan *v* Milbourn (1867) a person hired a hall for lectures which were illegal under the blasphemy laws. When the purpose of the lectures was revealed, he was then refused possession of the hall. His action claiming possession was refused on the grounds that the court could not enforce the contract when its purpose was illegal.

If the parties have exchanged property or money under such an illegal agreement, there is very little chance of it being returned to the original owners. Any contract which is illegal will be null and void.

Key point: Neither party can enforce an illegal contract as it has no legal force whatsoever i.e. it is completely void.

In situations where a pursuer can argue that he is not equally to blame or in the wrong (*in pari delicto*), he may be able to recover damages or money paid under the contract. Where the contract is unlawful on the face of it, equal guilt is presumed but this may be disproved if the pursuer can show that the defender is to blame and that he is an innocent party.

 Cuthbertson *v* Lowes (1870) the contract involved the sale of potatoes and the price had been calculated using Scottish measurements. On the face of it, there was nothing wrong with this agreement, but the Weights and Measures Acts prohibited the use of Scottish measurements – the imperial measure should have been used to calculate the price of the goods. The Weights and Measures Acts stated that if parties used a measure other than the imperial measure, the contract would be void. The seller delivered the goods, but the buyer refused to pay for them. The seller raised an action for the price, but the statutes had declared the contract void.

Held: if the seller was prevented from suing for the price of the goods this would result in a totally unjust situation as the buyer would get the goods for nothing. The buyer had to pay the value of the goods at the time of their delivery.

 Key point: In exceptional circumstances, the courts may enforce an agreement tainted by illegality if one of the parties can show that he was an innocent party and, therefore, unaware of the illegal nature of the agreement.

Illegality in terms of statute

Parliament (either Westminster or the Scottish Parliament) will have passed legislation (statute law) in order to make certain types of contracts illegal. In situations where the creation of some contracts are forbidden by statute with the effect that they are rendered illegal, the word 'unlawful' will appear in the statute to describe these types of agreement. Statute includes orders, rules and regulations that ministers of the Crown and other persons authorised by Parliament can issue. Statutory prohibitions may be expressed or implied.

Under the Consumer Credit Act 1974, for example, it would be illegal for an individual to operate a consumer credit business without having first secured a licence from the Office of Fair Trading. Any transactions entered into with consumers by the creditor would, therefore, be tainted with illegality. The aim of the Consumer Credit Act 1974 is to protect debtors and to ensure that those who engage in a credit business are fit and proper people. This is primarily achieved through the operation of the licensing system (see Chapter 4).

 Bigos *v* Bousted (1951) a contract to supply lire in Italy in exchange for payment in sterling in the UK contravened the Exchange Control Act 1947. One of the parties refused to supply the Italian currency and the other party sued for breach of contract. This was a deliberate attempt by both parties to circumvent United Kingdom currency regulations and, since both parties were equally to blame, neither could enforce the contract.

Implied statutory prohibition

The statute, in such a situation, may not provide a great deal of detail as to the types of conduct it considers to be illegal. The courts will have to make sense of Parliament's intention regarding this matter i.e. whether there is an intention to prohibit certain types of behaviour or whether the statute is designed to achieve some other purpose. The statute may have an indirect effect on a contract thus rendering it illegal in some way.

Illegality at common law

Some agreements will be illegal because judges have developed common law rules over the years which have forbid the formation of such agreements.

Examples of illegal contracts at common law include the following:

- Contracts to commit crimes or civil wrongs
- Contracts promoting sexual immorality
- Contracts harmful to good foreign relations
- Contracts harmful to the administration of justice
- Contracts promoting corruption in public life
- Contracts entered into with enemy aliens
- Contracts to avoid (by illegal means) the payment of taxes
- Contracts in restraint of trade or restrictive covenants

Contracts promoting sexual immoral behaviour

 Pearce v Brooks (1866) the pursuers hired a carriage to the defender for a period of 12 months. The defender was to pay the price by instalments. The defender was a prostitute and the carriage was of a very attractive design in order to attract customers. It was established that one of the pursuers knew what use the carriage was to be put to and that, consequently, their claim for sums owed under the contract of hire failed due to the illegal nature of the contract. The contract would have been valid had the pursuers not known how the carriage was going to be used.

Contracts which harm good foreign relations

 Regazzoni v Sethia (1958) a contract to supply jute to Apartheid-era South Africa which was legal under English law, was not enforceable in the English courts because it was in breach of anti-Apartheid regulations in India, the country where the contract was to be performed. India was a country that the United Kingdom had friendly relations with and it is not usually the practice of the British courts to enforce contracts which break the laws of friendly countries. The jute was to be shipped from India to Italy and then on to South Africa. The defenders had failed to deliver the jute bags as agreed and this is why the action was brought before the courts.

Contracts which promote corruption in public life

 Parkinson v College of Ambulance (1925) Parkinson donated a large sum to the College on the understanding that by doing so he would be given a knighthood. However, Parkinson did not receive his knighthood and he demanded that the donation be returned to him. The College refused to return the donation and Parkinson sued for its return.

Held: Parkinson's action failed because the court felt that the buying and selling of knighthoods and other honours was clearly corrupt. The court did not wish to enforce an agreement that would clearly lead to greater levels of corruption in public life. The agreement was void and Parkinson did not get his money back.

Contracts involving trading with the enemy

 Cantiere San Rocco SA *v* Clyde Shipbuilding and Engineering Co Ltd (1923) the pursuers were an Austrian firm which had entered into a contract with a Scottish company, the defenders. When the First World War began on 4 August 1914, the Austrian firm became an enemy alien owing to the fact that Austria and her ally, Germany, were now at war with the United Kingdom.

Held: by the House of Lords that the contract was to be regarded as void and unenforceable during the course of the War, but when hostilities ended the contract would be capable of enforcement. The defenders could not continue to have a contractual relationship with the Austrians during wartime because this would have amounted to trading with the enemy.

Restrictive covenants or contracts in restraint of trade

A restrictive covenant is used by one party in a contractual relationship to protect his legitimate business interests from unjustified exploitation or interference by another person, for example, ex-employees who are now employed by business rivals and former owners of a business who are now attempting to set up rival businesses. Legitimate business interests might include the following:

- Trade secrets

- Designs for new products

- Manufacturing processes

- Business expansion plans

- Investments

- Customers and other business connections

These types of contractual terms are restrictive in the sense that they limit the freedom of one of the parties to the contract to do certain things. They are particularly common in contracts of employment and are often inserted at the employer's insistence. By using them, the employer is attempting to prevent an employee from working for a business rival after his current employment has ended. However, such contractual terms are potentially abusive and they are usually scrutinised very strictly by the Scottish courts. Scottish judges will tend to display an almost instinctively suspicious attitude when asked to consider contracts in restraint of trade. After all, they are first and foremost anti-competitive agreements. Why should employees be prevented from taking up an offer of alternative employment which is more lucrative and satisfying if they so choose? If an employer cannot retain the services of a valuable employee then perhaps, as a consequence, he deserves his business to suffer. Similarly, why should a person who has just sold a business at a large profit be prevented from establishing a new business in the same trade or profession?

Key point: A restrictive covenant may be used to protect legitimate business interests such as trade secrets, designs for new products, manufacturing processes, business expansion plans, investments and customers and other business connections.

Restrictive covenants or contracts in restraint of trade, as they are alternatively known, are contractual terms commonly found in the following types of agreement:

- Employment contracts

- Contracts involving the sale of a business

- Solus (exclusive supply) and franchise agreements

- Agreements between trade associations and their members

 Key point: Restrictive covenants are commonly found in employment contracts, sales of businesses, solus and franchise agreements and trade association agreements.

Free and fair competition

The statement that free and fair competition makes for a healthy economy is a self-evident truth. This statement begs the question as to whether restrictive covenants should be tolerated in a free market economy. Surely, employees have an absolute right to work and businesses have an absolute right to trade on terms which promote their interests? However, competition must be fair if it is to be effective. The former employer of a particularly competent employee may have legitimate business reasons for wanting to restrict the employment opportunities of the individual in question. On a similar theme, the new owner of a business may be less than delighted to discover that the person, from whom he has just purchased the concern, has set up a new establishment in the same trade or profession a few hundred yards down the street. Although the motives of those individuals seeking to rely on these types of contractual arrangements may be entirely understandable, it is worth bearing in mind that anti-competitive agreements (no matter how well intentioned) may actually breach the provisions of the Competition Act 1998 and European Union competition policy (**Articles 81 and 82: Treaty of Rome 1957**).

A useful rule of thumb for an individual wishing to enforce a restrictive covenant is to remember not to impose unduly excessive terms on a weaker party and to do nothing more than is absolutely necessary to protect legitimate business interests. Ultimately, however, the Scottish courts will determine what is reasonable by carefully examining all the circumstances of the case.

 Key point: Anti-competitive agreements (no matter how well intentioned) may actually breach the provisions of the Competition Act 1998 and European Union competition policy (Articles 81 and 82: Treaty of Rome 1957).

The judicial approach to contracts in restraint of trade

The role of the courts in all of this is to weigh up the competing interests of the parties and determine whether the party who wishes to rely on the contract in restraint of trade has a legitimate interest which should be protected. If such an interest is deemed worthy of protection, then the court will issue an interdict to prevent a former employee from taking up alternative employment with a business rival or the new owner of a business may win an interdict which prevents the former owner setting up in competition just down the road (or even next door as has occurred on occasion). When relying upon a restriction in the contract, an individual must show that he is taking legitimate measures to protect his position. After all, these restrictions are anti-competitive and the courts are right to treat them with suspicion. Employees should have the right to seek alternative employment and businesses should have the right to compete against one another. The courts are, therefore, placed in a position where they will have to perform a delicate balancing act, weighing up, for example, the employer's right to protect legitimate business interests such as trade secrets and, on the other hand, the employee's right to seek profitable work wherever he can find it.

A contractual restriction may be challenged in a number of ways:

◆ The restraint is unreasonable between the parties i.e. it is an illegitimate attempt to limit a person's freedom. The restriction may not be an honest attempt by the party relying on it to protect his legitimate business interests. In short, the clause may be nothing more than a blatant attempt to stifle competition by preventing an employee from seeking alternative employment.

◆ The length of the restraint is unreasonable i.e. it lasts for a period of time which is longer than is absolutely necessary. The new owner of business may attempt to prevent his predecessor from starting a rival business for a period of ten years. This could be excessive in a situation where a two year restriction would have been more than adequate.

◆ The geographical area of the restraint is unreasonable i.e. United Kingdom, European or global restrictions may immediately excite suspicion and may be viewed as excessively wide. Excessively wide local restrictions can also be struck down by the courts. It would not be reasonable for someone to impose a term in a contract for the sale of a business which stated that the previous owner could not establish a similar business anywhere within a twenty-five mile radius of Hamilton. If the business was purely local in nature and confined largely to the Hamilton area, the new owner has no right to prevent the previous owner from setting up another business in Edinburgh.

◆ The restraint is not in the public interest – restrictive business practices clearly do not benefit the public and can restrict consumer choice.

A court, when reaching its decision, may also take into account any other relevant factors such as trade customs and practices, the ease with which an employee will be able to secure new employment and the employee's need to continue working in order to gain valuable experience and to keep his skills updated. It will be appreciated that trade customs and practices must be reasonable and must be essential for the protection of legitimate business interests.

 Key point: A restrictive covenant must be reasonable between the parties, in terms of its duration, its geographical area and its enforcement must be in the public interest.

The consequences of an unreasonable restraint of trade

A party who wishes to enforce a restraint of trade must realise that if the court regards it as anti-competitive and abusive, it will be struck down. In other words, such a contractual term will be regarded as automatically null and void. The offending clause will be removed or severed from the contract. Furthermore, the Scottish courts will not redraft the clause in more reasonable terms. This means that the party who sought to enforce the restraint is now left completely unprotected and there is nothing to stop the other party doing pretty much what he pleases (**see Dumbarton Steamboat Co *v* MacFarlane (1899) discussed below**). It is worth bearing in mind that a judge's decision to render a restraint void and unenforceable will not affect the functioning of the other terms of the contract. The court will usually delete only as much of the invalid part of the clause as is strictly necessary, for example, a line or a word. It is not usual judicial practice to treat the whole clause as void unless it has no other option (**see Nordenfelt *v* Maxim Nordenfelt Guns and Ammunition Co [1894] discussed below**). The remaining contractual terms are very much capable of enforcement by both parties. It is only in very unusual circumstances, that the removal of the offensive term from the agreement will completely undermine the operation of the remainder of the contract.

 Key point: If a restrictive covenant is found to be excessive and completely unreasonable in the sense that it goes beyond what is adequate to protect legitimate business interests, it will be automatically void and the party relying on it will be left completely vulnerable as the courts will refuse to replace it with something more reasonable.

Employment contracts and restraints of trade

One of the greatest fears that many employers have is that a high-flying or extremely competent employee might be tempted to go and work for a business rival or set up in business on his own account. Generally speaking, however, a court will not prevent an individual from using skills or information gained in the course of previous employment (**see Centre for Maritime Industrial Safety Technology Ltd *v* Crute [2003] below**). The dangers for an employer of failing to insert some sort of restraint in the employment contract becomes all too obvious upon an examination of the following case:

 Faccenda Chicken Ltd *v* Fowler [1986] Fowler was employed in the position of sales manager with Faccenda Chicken Ltd. He had worked for the company for seven years and had played a very prominent role in the creation and expansion of the company's refrigerated poultry selling operations. The company operated a fleet of refrigerated vans which travelled around various retailers and wholesellers in the local area selling products directly to these individuals. Fowler eventually decided to leave his employment with Faccenda. He set up his own business which competed directly with his ex-employer. Fowler had also persuaded some of his former colleagues at Faccenda to come and work for him at his new business. Not surprisingly, Faccenda was extremely alarmed at this development and attempted to obtain damages from Fowler alleging that he had breached his contractual duty not to use confidential information in a way that harmed the interests of his former employer.

Held: by the English Court of Appeal that Faccenda's attempt to sue Fowler for damages should be dismissed. The information that the company claimed was confidential (names of customers, delivery routes, times of deliveries) was widely known. By no stretch of the imagination could this information be described as a trade secret. Faccenda had no one to blame but itself for its failure to include restraints in the employment contracts of Fowler and other former employees.

A business rival will obviously be eager to recruit such an individual because of the kind of information that they will possess: knowledge of trade secrets, designs, business expansion plans, lists of customers and other investments. The ex-employee will doubtless have gained invaluable skills and experience in his last job and, furthermore, he may have benefited from a range of training and educational opportunities which were all provided to him courtesy of his ex-employer. All these features, which made the employee so valuable, are now, potentially, at the service of the new employer. It is not uncommon for a business rival to attempt to headhunt highly rated employees from their current employers by offering them much better terms and conditions (and various other incentives). It is not stretching the imagination to suggest that an ex-employee will be only too eager to get off to a flying start in his new job by divulging confidential information, gained in his previous employment, to his new employer and that the ex-employer will have real concerns about this.

 Key point: An employer would be well advised to insert a restrictive covenant in an employee's contract of employment in order to protect legitimate business interests as failure to do so can often be catastrophic.

In certain trades or professions, for example, information technology, the law and banking and financial services, the defection of valuable employees is always a very real threat. Faced with the realisation that they are not able to retain the services of such individuals, many employers will have made sure that a damage limitation mechanism is in place. Employers will, therefore, attempt to restrict the immediate and future employment opportunities of their ex-employees – albeit for a fairly limited period of time. The theory goes that, by the time the ex-employee is ready to take up a position with a new employer, most of the knowledge gained may be outdated or even redundant. This would clearly make the employee less attractive to prospective employers. There is also the question of how a restraint may harm the ex-employee's skills – he may work in an industry or profession where continued updating of skills and experience is both necessary and expected. Effectively forcing the ex-employee to pursue an alternative career (even for a relatively short period of time) may do irreparable harm to his long-term career prospects. The age of the employee may also be an important factor for the courts to consider when deciding whether or not to enforce the restraint.

 Key point: Restrictive covenants are basically anti-competitive devices and may actually do irreparable harm to an ex-employee's long-term career prospects so the courts will have to be particularly careful when deciding whether or not to enforce such a term of the contract.

 Bluebell Apparel *v* Dickinson [1978] Dickinson was a management trainee who worked for a subsidiary of an American company that was involved in the production of "Wrangler" jeans. As a management trainee, Dickinson had access to trade secrets and information about business connections and customers. There was a term in Dickinson's employment contract that, if he left the company's employment, he would not seek employment with any business rival of his employer anywhere in the world for a period of two years. Later, Dickinson left his employment and, in breach of this restriction, he accepted an offer of employment with Levi Strauss & Co who were also involved in the global business of manufacturing denim jeans. Dickinson's former employers sought an interdict to prevent him from continuing to work for Levi Strauss.

Held: the restriction was reasonable in terms of time and geography and that Dickinson's former employer was taking reasonable steps to protect its legitimate business interests. The court granted an interdict to Dickinson's former employers and he had to give up his new job with Levi Strauss.

 Centre for Maritime Industrial Safety Technology Ltd *v* Crute [2003]
Clive Crute, the defender, had worked as a manager for the pursuer, Centre Maritime Industrial Safety Technology (known as C-MIST). He had commenced employment with the pursuer on 4 April 2002. Crute had previously been employed as a Master Mariner for over 30 years. C-MIST was involved in the provision of a wide range of services relating to health and safety issues in connection with the operation of marine terminals and jetties. Crute was offered new employment with Briggs Marine Contractors Ltd, a client of C-MIST's on 11 November 2002 (with 1 February 2003 envisaged as a starting date). Briggs operated the Coryton Terminal in Essex for British Petroleum. The new post with Briggs was described as Contractors Manager for jetty operations at the Coryton Terminal. On 25 November 2002, Crute submitted a letter of resignation to C-MIST and he explained that he was going to work for Briggs. He was informed by a one of C-MIST's directors that he was prevented from working for Briggs due to a restrictive covenant and confidentiality clause in his contract. The restrictive covenant stated that Crute could not provide services (whether paid or unpaid) to clients of C-MIST for a period of 18 months after the termination of his contract. The confidentiality clause stated that Crute was prevented from using skills in his new employment that he had acquired while working for C-MIST. C-MIST was fearful that if Crute was allowed to take up employment with Briggs it would mean that he would be in a position to establish in-house health and safety training courses so that Briggs would eventually dispense with their services.

Held: by Lord Mackay of Drumadoon (in the Outer House of the Court of Session) that the restrictive covenant of 18 months was excessive and went far beyond what was required to protect C-MIST's legitimate business interests. His Lordship balanced C-MIST's interests against those of Crute and was strongly of the opinion that the employee would be harmed if the restriction was enforced. A number of factors were taken into account: Crute was 57 and, at his time of life, his future employment prospects might be harmed if he was restrained from working for Briggs or any other prospective employer covered by the restriction in his contract. Furthermore, C-MIST's fears that Crute would be able to provide in-house health and safety training for Briggs at its expense was completely unfounded. C-MIST and Briggs still had the better part of 2 years of a 3 year contract remaining in relation to the provision of consultancy services. As for the confidentiality clause in Crute's contract, an employee is permitted to use skills that he has acquired in the service of a new employer. As we shall see, an employee will commit a breach of his implied duty of good faith and fidelity if he divulges confidential information, gained in the course of his previous employment, to his new employer.

An employer would argue very strongly that he has a right to protect his business and very few people would take issue with such an argument. What the courts will not tolerate is a blatant attempt by the employer to ruin the future employment prospects of an ex-employee. Employees, after all, have the right to seek better employment opportunities. This is particularly the case when we remember that the modern United Kingdom labour market is characterised in the main by the high dependency shown by employers on short-term, temporary employment contracts. It is little wonder that today many employees have no concept of company loyalty. Given the short-term nature of many employment contracts, it may now be even more unreasonable for an employer to attempt to impose a lengthy time restriction on the employee. As we have seen in **Centre for Maritime Industrial Safety Technology v Crute [2003]**, Lord Mackay of Drumadoon was strongly of the view that an eighteen month restriction went much further than was strictly necessary to protect the interests of the employer.

 Key point: The decisions in Bluebell Apparel and Centre for Maritime Industrial Safety Technology demonstrate very clearly that the courts examine the time limit in the restrictive covenant very much on its individual merits and what is a reasonable time in one situation may be completely unreasonable in other circumstances.

Restrictive covenants and junior employees

It would be a mistake to assume that these restrictions appear only in the employment contracts of senior executives and highly skilled professionals. In **Scottish Dairy Farmers Company (Glasgow) Ltd v McGhee (1933)** and **Home Counties Dairies v Skilton [1970]** the employees in question were both milkmen who were successfully restrained from approaching the customers of their former employers. McGhee and Skilton had left their previous employers to go and work for rival dairies. It should be understood that both employees were, therefore, in a very strong position to approach their ex-employers' customers and persuade them to use the services of their new employers. This practice is often simply referred to as poaching customers. McGhee and Skilton had both set out to commit a deliberate breach of contract by approaching the customers of their former employers in complete defiance of the restriction to which they had voluntarily agreed. The Inner House of the Court of Session in **McGhee** and the English Court of Appeal in **Skilton** found in favour of the employers. Neither restriction was excessive in terms of the time limit (both lasted for a year after termination of the employment), the employers were protecting legitimate business interests (their customer base) and the geographical area of the restrictions was not unreasonable (both milkmen were forbidden from approaching customers that they had previously dealt with who lived in the area of their former rounds). Furthermore, in **Skilton**, the English Court of Appeal did not think that the phrase 'dairy produce' as it appeared in the milkman's contract applied to an excessively wide range of products. Dairy produce covered all the items that that a milkman ordinarily sold to customers as part of his rounds. There was something of a crumb of comfort for the employee in **Skilton**, as the Court of Appeal did concede that he would be allowed to approach those individuals who had ceased to be customers of his ex-employer in the 6 month period prior to the termination of his employment contract. It had been a condition of the restrictive covenant that he could not approach those individuals who had been customers of his ex-employer during the 6 months before his contract had ended.

 Key point: Although restrictive covenants will often be found in the contracts of high-flying and more senior employees, many employers may wish to seek the protection of such a term in relation to more junior employees.

The consequences of divulging confidential information to a new employer

In **PSM International and McKechnie v Whitehouse and Willenhall Automation [1992]** the English Court of Appeal has stated that any attempt by a former employee to divulge confidential information acquired in the course of his previous employment should be regarded as a material or extremely serious breach of that contract. The previous employer may even be able to obtain an interdict in order to prevent the new employer from capitalising on this information if he can show that the ex-employee's breach of contract has caused him to suffer loss. The effect of this interdict would mean that the new employer would be unable to derive any benefit from the information given to him by his new employee. However, the burden of proof will clearly be placed upon the ex-employer to demonstrate that there is a direct link between the breach of confidence and the losses that he has sustained.

Individuals will not be permitted to use trade secrets or confidential information acquired during the course of their employment for their own benefit. Therefore, a deliberate attempt by an individual to use trade secrets or confidential information in this way can be subject to legal challenge. It does not matter whether the contract of employment contained a restraint or not. In **Robb v Green [1895]**, a manager quite deliberately, and in an extremely calculated fashion, copied the names of his employer's customers. The manager's intention was to canvas these customers at a later date with a view to persuading them to use the services of the business that he was setting up.

Held: by the English Court of Appeal that, although there was no restrictive covenant in the manager's contract of employment, he owed an implied duty of good faith and fidelity. By acting deliberately in a way that harmed his employer's interest, the ex-employee had breached an important term of his contract and he was not permitted to approach this group of customers.

It will be recalled in **Faccenda Chicken Ltd v Fowler (above)**, that the employer attempted to argue (unsuccessfully) that Fowler, its former manager, had breached his duty of confidentiality which he continued to owe to the company despite leaving its employment. Information may be regarded as confidential if it can be regarded as a trade secret and the employer has continually stressed its confidential nature. The information will not be treated as confidential if it was readily available to members of the employer's staff in the course of their ordinary duties.

There is always the danger for an employer that the employee will build up personal relationships with customers who may wish to follow the employee if he leaves his current employment for a new position in a competing business undertaking. An added danger may be that the ex-employee may approach these customers directly in a brazen attempt to secure their business. This is why it is vital for an employer to include a restrictive covenant in the employee's contract of employment.

 Key point: Any attempt by a former employee to divulge confidential information acquired in the course of his previous employment should be regarded as a serious breach of that contract. The previous employer may even be able to obtain an interdict in order to prevent the new employer from capitalising on this information.

Extended notice periods

An employer can always use an alternative approach to the problem of protecting trade secrets and business connections. Some employers, rather than including a restrictive covenant in the employment contract – which can always be challenged on the grounds that it is unreasonable, will insist that an employee has to give an extended period of notice if he wishes to terminate his employment. Eighteen-month notice periods are not unknown in some trades and professions where the employee is in a very senior position within the organisation. This gives the employer time to prepare for the employee's departure by taking precautions to protect trade secrets or business connections. Furthermore, the current employer may actually state that it is not necessary for the employee to turn up for work – he may as well tend his garden (hence the phrase 'garden leave'). The beauty of these contractual notice periods is that the employee cannot work for any other employer who is competing against his current employer.

This arrangement effectively prevents the employee from gaining access to any trade secrets or having any dealings with customers of the employer. By the time that the extended notice period is at an end, the employee will represent less of a threat to his former employer if he goes to work for a rival business. These extended notice periods will not escape examination by the courts. These arrangements can stifle or prevent genuine competition and employers would be well advised to act reasonably when incorporating these types of terms in employment contracts. They can be used to get round some of the problems that restrictive covenants pose, but they are not without their problems. Employees who are affected by these 'garden leave' clauses can challenge them by putting forward the argument that it is important that they are allowed to continue to work in their chosen profession in order to keep vital skills updated and current. A software engineer could argue that an 18-month 'garden leave' clause was excessive in that it prevented him from developing his skills and gaining valuable work experience in an industry which is notoriously susceptible to rapid changes in technology.

In **William Hill Organisation Ltd _v_ Tucker (1998)** (discussed below), the

English Court of Appeal criticised the growing use by employers of garden leave clauses in employment contracts. The Court was particularly concerned that this was little more than an attempt to get round the strict rules governing the use of restrictive covenants in employment contracts. It was felt that garden leave clauses should be scrutinised carefully and, furthermore, the rules surrounding these types of clauses should be considerably tightened to prevent abuse by employers.

 William Hill Organisation Ltd *v* Tucker (1998) William Hill, the pursuers and appellants, attempted to prevent Tucker, the defender, from going to work for a business rival, City Index Ltd, during his notice period. The contractual notice period was for six months. The notice period had originally been for one month, but the defender had later agreed to extend it to six months. The defender worked for a subsidiary of the pursuers called William Hill Index Ltd which operated a gambling business known as 'spread betting'. This type of gambling activity is regulated by the Securities and Futures Authority (SFA) and William Hill Index Ltd was one of only five companies authorised by the SFA to carry on such a business. One of the other four was City Index Ltd. The defender commenced employment with the pursuers in 1995 as the senior dealer. There was a term in the defender's employment contract that stated:

'Whilst in employment, you must not undertake any other employment, or hold office, which creates a conflict of interest with the Company, or any company within the Group. You should declare to your Manager any interests/connections with existing/potential suppliers or customers of the Company. If so directed, you will sever the interest/connection immediately or render yourself liable to disciplinary action.'

On 2 February 1998, the defender decided to leave his employment with the pursuers and go to work for City Index Ltd – a rival of the pursuers. The defender gave one month's notice despite the fact that he had agreed to extend it to six months in return for an enhancement to his conditions of employment. The defender argued that the pursuers had not made good on the promises made to him and that they should not stand in the way of his attempt to further his career with another employer. The pursuers attempted to obtain an interdict to prevent the defender from doing this, claiming that they were concerned that the defender would divulge confidential information to his new employer. It was also confirmed by the pursuers that the defender did not have to turn up to work during his extended notice period and that he would continue to enjoy his salary and other benefits during this period. The defender argued that he wanted to continue working in order to develop his skills and, in any case, he longer possessed confidential information to pass on to his new employer.

Held: by the English Court of Appeal that the defender's post of senior dealer was a special and unique one. It was important that the defender continued to develop his skills in this area by being permitted to continue to work in the specialised field of spread betting. The interdicts were, therefore refused.

Key point: Very often it will be better for the employer to insist on an extremely long notice period (a garden leave clause) whereby the employee is paid but does not have to turn up to work and, during this period, the employer knows that the employee has no access to trade secrets or dealings with customers.

Informal arrangements between employers

In certain situations, a group of employers may enter into informal arrangements with the aim of preventing their employees from seeking alternative employment.

Kores Manufacturing Co Ltd *v* Kolok Manufacturing Co Ltd (1958)
the premises of the two companies were located next to one another and they were both in a similar line of business. They had an informal agreement whereby Kores would refuse to offer employment to an individual who had worked for Kolok in the last five years and vice versa. A former employee of Kores sought employment with Kolok and Kores took steps to prevent this.

Held: by the Court of Appeal that the attempt by Kores to obtain an interdict to prevent its former employee from taking up employment with Kolok should fail. Kores and Kolok were operating a completely unreasonable agreement which was not in their employees' interests nor in the wider public interest. If Kores and Kolok wished to take proper steps to protect their interests, it would have been more appropriate and more reasonable to include a restrictive covenant in the contracts of their employees.

Restraints imposed on the seller of a business

Such a restraint would be void, unless it is necessary to protect the goodwill of the business sold and not to stifle competition. Sometimes, the sale of a business can involve a global restraint. However, these global restraints will be very strictly examined by the courts and, more often than not, they will be unsuccessful.

Nordenfelt *v* Maxim Nordenfelt Guns and Ammunition Co (1894)
Nordenfelt was the manufacturer of machine guns and other armaments. When he sold the business to a company he agreed to a restriction that would severely restrict the scope of his business interests. Nordenfelt had, in fact, agreed that he would not set up another business in any part of the world for the purpose of producing armaments for a period of 25 years and, furthermore, that he would not compete with the new venture in any trade or business whatsoever that it was involved in.

Held: by the House of Lords that the global restriction lasting 25 years regarding the sale of the armaments business was valid and enforceable, even though it was very wide. The armaments industry was highly specialised and the pool of potential customers was very small. The new company needed the time to build up a relationship with Nordenfelt's former customers in order to establish itself in this particular market. However, the court was able to remove the other part of the clause which attempted to prevent Nordenfelt from competing against the new company in any other trade or business whatsoever. This part of the agreement was void because it was plainly anti-competitive and was completely unnecessary to protect the business interests of the new company.

159

British Reinforced Concrete Co v Schelff (1921) the seller of a local business producing 'loop' road reinforcements, at the insistence of the buyer, promised not to manufacture or sell any road reinforcements as part of any other business that he might establish at a later date. The buyer was a large manufacturer and seller of all types of road reinforcements who sold these products on a United Kingdom-wide basis. The clause that the seller had agreed to prevented him from competing against the buyer in the manufacture or sale of such products anywhere in the United Kingdom.

Held: the new owner of the business could not enforce the clause in the contract of sale because it went further than was necessary to protect legitimate business interests. The buyer had manufactured and sold just one type of product. The clause attempted to prevent the buyer from manufacturing other types of products. This clause was, therefore, unreasonable and anti-competitive.

 Dumbarton Steamboat Co v MacFarlane (1899) MacFarlane had operated a carrier business on the River Clyde running between Glasgow, Greenock and Dumbarton. He later decided to sell the business and the buyer insisted upon the inclusion of a clause in the contract sale that effectively prevented MacFarlane from establishing a similar business anywhere in the United Kingdom for a period of ten years. MacFarlane's business operations were of a purely local nature being confined to the River Clyde. Some three years later, after selling the business, MacFarlane set up another carrier business operating between Glasgow and Dumbarton. The buyers applied for an interdict to prevent MacFarlane from carrying on his new business.

Held: the restriction in the contract of sale was totally excessive and the court refused to replace it with a more reasonable alternative. This meant that MacFarlane was totally free to run his business with complete impunity much to the buyers' anger and frustration.

Restrictions on shareholder-employees

The courts will generally allow wider restraints on the sellers of businesses than in the case of employees. An interesting question for the courts to deal arises in situations where the person affected by the restrictive covenant is both an employee and a shareholder i.e. a part-owner of the business.

 Systems Reliability Holdings plc v Smith (1990) Smith, the defender, was employed as a computer engineer and he developed his skills to an extremely high level. It was Smith's involvement in the business that greatly contributed to its expansion. However, Smith's employer was taken over by another company and his contract was terminated. Smith also held a small amount of shares in his former employer, but the new owner of the company paid Smith a very large sum of money for these shares. The new owner of the company attempted to rely on a clause in contract of sale that restrained Smith from working for a period of 17 months for any business rival or involvement in a business competing against the company. Smith was also expected not to divulge any confidential information or trade secrets that he had gained access to during the course of his employment. Smith decided to set up a business which competed against his old company. The new owners of the company sought an interdict to prevent him doing this.

Held: by the English High Court that the restraint satisfied the requirement of reasonableness and it could be used to prevent Smith from running a rival business. Seventeen months was not an unreasonable length of time for a restraint of this nature to run. The restraint was more in line with what would normally appear in a contract for the sale of a business rather than an employment contract. The High Court was, therefore, prepared to be more flexible in allowing the new owner of the business to enforce it. Admittedly, Smith had not been a major shareholder in his old company, but the new owner had been very generous when they bought out his shares.

Solus or exclusive supply agreements

This type of agreement is known as a *solus* or exclusive supply agreement whereby an individual, for example, a pub landlord is 'tied' to a brewery or someone who runs a petrol station has to stock the products of a particular petrol company. In other words, the pub is not a 'Free House' because the landlord will have to sell the brewery's products and the person who runs the petrol station will have to sell the petrol company's products. These types of agreements are void if they are unreasonable. Where a garage owner is concerned, the cases which have involved challenges to *solus* agreements have centred around mortgages that a petrol company has granted to the garage owner. One of the terms of the mortgage is that the owner promises not to stock the products of the company's business rivals. The rules about *solus* agreements do not apply where the garage and the land upon which it is situated are owned by the petrol company. In this situation, a tenant will have no choice but to supply the company's products.

 Esso Petroleum Co Ltd *v* Harper's Garage Ltd (1967) two solus agreements were involved preventing Harper, a petrol station owner, from stocking the products of any competitor of Esso. Harper had agreed to this arrangement because Esso were prepared to lend him money in order to modernise his property. The owner had to grant Esso a mortgage in relation to his two filling stations in order to secure the loan. The first *solus* agreement was to last for four years and five months and the second was to last for 21 years. Harper attempted to pay off the second mortgage of 21 years early, but this course of action was not permitted by reason of a clause in the mortgage which stated that the agreement had to run for the specified period. Harper broke his agreement with Esso when he began to sell another petrol company's products. Esso tried to prevent Harper from doing this and, therefore, tried to obtain an interdict.

Held: by the House of Lords that the rule of public policy against unreasonable restraints also applied to the *solus* agreements and the mortgage. The shorter period of four years and five months was reasonable, but the longer period of 21 years was totally unreasonable and unenforceable.

 Texaco *v* Mulberry Filling Station (1972) the owner of a garage under a *solus* agreement for the exclusive supply of Texaco petrol broke the agreement during a tanker drivers' strike by obtaining and supplying Jet petrol. Since the duration and the extent of the restraint were reasonable, Texaco were entitled to enforce the agreement. The court would not accept that the agreement was contrary to the public interest.

Trade associations

A trade association or professional body may decide to impose certain practices or restraints on its members without their prior consent. Such restraints would be void if they are unreasonable. Many members of trade associations or professional bodies will have little choice but to accept the rules because this is the price of membership. In many trades or professions, an individual will have to be approved by the relevant body if he is to be regarded as a fully practising member. This puts the relevant professional body in a very powerful position and abuses of this power have been known to occur.

 Pharmaceutical Society of Great Britain *v* Dickson (1968) the Society passed a resolution that any new pharmacies that were opened by its members would be required to provide a very narrow range of predetermined services. This would mean that new pharmacies were not free to decide for themselves which services they wished to develop. Furthermore, members who ran existing pharmacies would have to obtain the prior approval of the Society's Council if they wished to expand the range of services that they were currently offering to members of the public. Dickson brought an action against the Society on the grounds that the proposed new rule was *ultra vires* i.e. beyond or outwith its powers as an unreasonable restraint of trade. A declaration was made by the court to this effect and the Society appealed to the House of Lords. The appeal was dismissed.

The House of Lords made a number of observations about this type of restrictive agreement:

- If a professional association passes a resolution, even if binding in honour only, its validity is a matter for the courts since failure to observe it is likely to be seen as misconduct and disciplinary action will follow.

- A professional association's resolution is *ultra vires* if it is outwith the main objects (aims) of the organisation. The resolution in this case was quite clearly *ultra vires*.

- A professional association's resolution regulating the conduct of its members will be void if it is an unreasonable restraint of trade.

The consequences of an illegal restraint of trade

The offending clause will be removed or severed from the contract. Crucially, the courts will not substitute it with a more reasonable alternative. It is not for the courts to do a party's job for him in this regard (see **Dumbarton Steamboat Co *v* MacFarlane (1899)**). It is important to note that the court will usually delete only the invalid part of the clause, for example, a line or a word. The court will not generally treat the whole clause as void unless it has no other option (see **Nordenfelt *v* Maxim Nordenfelt Guns and Ammunition Co (1894)**).

Exclusion clauses and other unfair terms

Parties to a contract have rights under the agreement, but they also are under a duty to do something for the other party. If a party fails to honour a duty i.e. commits a breach of contract or performs the duty in a negligent fashion this may cause the innocent party to suffer loss, damage or injury. Naturally enough, the innocent party would wish to raise an action for damages against the other party who was in breach or who had been negligent in some way. In certain situations, however, this course of action by the innocent party may become problematic because there are ways in which the offending party can limit or exclude his liability. The offending party may have insisted, before or at the formation of the contract, that a term should be included in the agreement which allows him to limit or exclude his liability for contractual breaches or acts of negligence on his part. Such contractual terms are popularly referred to as exclusion and limitation clauses. Exclusion and limitation clauses are, admittedly, very narrow definitions. Other examples of potentially unfair terms include exemption/exception clauses and indemnity clauses. The former category of term is used by a party to escape liability in certain situations. An indemnity clause, on the other hand, (**see British Crane Hire Corporation *v* Ipswich Plant Hire Ltd [1975]**) is used by one party to claim compensation from another individual for losses sustained while performing the contract

Exclusion and limitation clauses are widely used in pre-printed or standard form contracts and they are also found on tickets such as train, plane and bus tickets. However, it is possible for one party to insist upon an inclusion of a term in a verbal contract that would allow him to limit or exclude his liability. Exclusion and limitation clauses can also be found in non-contractual notices, for example, a notice in a park that states the local authority will not be liable for any injuries suffered by persons using the park. It is important to note that the individual who has suffered an injury will not have a contractual relationship with the local authority and, prior to 1 April 1990, would not have been able to raise an action under the Unfair Contract Terms Act 1977. Such notices are now covered by the Unfair Contract Terms Act 1977 as a result of Section 68 of the Law Reform (Miscellaneous Provisions) (Scotland) Act 1990.

If the offending party was able to rely on some term of the contract which allowed them to walk away from the consequences of their breach of contract or negligence, this would clearly give them an unfair advantage. We might like to think of exclusion and limitation clauses as a 'get out of jail card'. As discussed above, in such situations where the contract has been breached, the innocent or aggrieved party would wish to sue the person who broke the agreement. However, the existence of a limitation or exclusion clause in the contract might make this action impossible or much less effective than might otherwise have been the case.

 Key point: The common law of contract permits a party to exclude or limit his liability for loss, damage, personal injury and even death caused by his negligence or breach of contract.

An example of an exclusion clause is:

'All cars are parked at the owners' risk. Wylie and Crossan Car Parks Ltd accept no liability whatsoever for any loss, damage or injury caused to vehicles, property or persons that occurred on our premises.'

The courts can often take a very tough line towards exclusion clauses because realistically it is an attempt by one party (usually the stronger one) to escape liability completely.

An example of a limitation clause, on the other hand, is:

'Our liability for loss or damage in relation to passengers' luggage and personal belongings carried by us or by our agents shall in no circumstances exceed the sum of £100.'

Limitation clauses come in a wide variety of shapes, in that they restrict rather than totally exclude liability. The person who relies on a limitation clause is admitting his responsibility for the breach of contract or for negligence, he just wishes to reduce that liability to a very small amount of compensation which in no way reflects the losses suffered by the innocent party.

 Key point: An exclusion clause attempts to exclude a party's liability for loss, injury, damage or death caused by his negligence or contractual breach, whereas a limitation clause attempts to restrict liability, for example, by restricting the compensation payable to the innocent party to a very small sum of money.

The law here is complex and there are three areas of it which apply to exclusion and limitation clauses:

◆ Unfair Contract Terms Act 1977
◆ Unfair Terms in Consumer Contract Regulations 1999
◆ Enterprise Act 2002

The situation before the Unfair Contract Terms Act 1977

Before the Unfair Contract Terms Act 1977, it was possible for a person to exclude his liability for negligent performance and non-performance of the contract as long as he gave the other party adequate notice of the existence of an exclusion clause. The law before 1977 meant that it was possible for someone to exclude his liability for death and personal injury caused by his negligence or by failing to perform the contract. Now, the case law before 1977 will largely be of historic interest. However, if an exclusion clause survives the tests laid down by both the Unfair Contract Terms Act 1977 and the Unfair Terms in Consumer Contract Regulations 1999, the old case law could still be relevant. In other words, the parties would have to argue whether adequate notice of the existence of the clause had been given by the party who wishes to rely upon it to escape or limit his liability.

Clearly the old common law was very unsatisfactory because exclusion clauses tended to encourage people not to perform their contractual duties properly. The common law positively encouraged abuses of the contract. You might have a situation where someone had put their car into a garage to have the brakes tested by a mechanic. What if the mechanic insisted that the car owner sign a document which stated that the garage would not be responsible for death or personal injury caused by the mechanic's failure to carry out the job properly? This would be an outrageous situation, but the mechanic might yet escape liability for the death of the owner if he drew such a clause to the attention of the car owner. The owner would be regarded as having accepted this clause if he signed the document or went ahead and put his car into the garage without bothering to raise a protest.

The widespread use of exclusion clauses, therefore, encouraged people to be lazy, complacent and careless. Why bother to go the extra mile when you always had the protection of an exclusion clause to fall back on? However, Parliament had other ideas and decided that this situation could no longer be tolerated. The Unfair Contract Terms Act 1977 was an attempt by Parliament to prevent the worst abuses which had been encouraged by the use of exclusion clauses.

 Key point: Before the introduction of the Unfair Contract Terms Act 1977, it was possible for a party to exclude his liability completely for loss, injury, damage or even death.

An example of the worst type of exclusion clause before 1977 can be found below:

'Wylie and Crossan Ltd accepts no responsibility for the death or any personal injury, damage, loss, delay or accident wheresoever and howsoever caused and whether by the negligence of our employees or otherwise.'

The Unfair Contract Terms Act 1977

Part II of the Unfair Contract Terms Act 1977 applies to Scotland only and Part III of the Act applies throughout the United Kingdom generally (Part I of the Act has application to England, Wales and Northern Ireland only). The strongest possible protection is given by the Unfair Contract Terms Act 1977 to those individuals who are classed as consumers. However, there are situations where it may still be possible for those individuals who are not consumers to claim the protection of the Act. It will be much more difficult for businesses, but by no means impossible for them, to use the Act in order to strike down exclusion and limitation clauses.

Section 17 of the Act describes a consumer contract as consisting of one party who is dealing in the course of his business and another party is who *not* dealing in the course of business (a consumer). Such a contract must involve the sale or the hire of goods and these goods are usually supplied for the private use and consumption of the non-business party to the contract.

Section 25(1) of the Unfair Contract Terms 1977 Act states that a consumer contract is where 'one party to the contract deals and the other party to the contract (the consumer) does not deal or hold himself out as dealing in the course of business'.

In **Chapman *v* Aberdeen Construction Group Limited (1991)** Lord Caplan made the following remarks in relation to the distinction between consumer and non-consumer contracts:

'The word "business" is notoriously difficult to define precisely but in my view in its ordinary sense it implies not only activity for gain but a degree of organisation of activity for gain.'

It will, therefore, be possible for a business to act outwith its ordinary trade or profession and enter into contracts with other parties. Merely because this contract involves, at first glance, two businesses does not mean that the transaction should be treated as a non-consumer sale.

 R & B Customs Brokers Co Ltd *v* United Dominions Trust (1988)
R & B Customs Brokers bought a car so that one of its directors could use it.

The contract of sale contained an exclusion clause whereby the seller of the car, United Dominions Trust, attempted to escape liability in relation to Section 14(3) of the Sale of Goods Act 1979. Section 14(3) imposes a duty on the seller to supply goods that must be fit for their purpose. An exclusion clause like this would have been automatically void and ineffective in a consumer transaction in terms of Section 20 of the Unfair Contract Terms Act 1977 in Scotland. The key question was whether this contract, which undoubtedly involved two business parties, could be regarded as a consumer contract for the purposes of the Unfair Contract Terms Act 1977?

Held: by the English Court of Appeal that when a business buys goods from another business, the transaction will not always be a straightforward non-consumer contract. The business buyer in certain situations may actually find that it may have the protection of consumer law in common with ordinary members of the public if the transaction is not a regular business contract. In this particular case, R & B Customs Brokers must be regarded as a consumer. The purchase of the car was not a frequent business transaction and unless United Dominions Trust could prove anything to the contrary, R & B Customs Brokers should have the benefit of the law protecting consumers in relation to exclusion clauses. The clause was, therefore, void and ineffective.

As should now be apparent, the vast majority of exclusion and limitation clauses will be contained in standardised contracts. Unfortunately, there is no definition of 'written, standard terms' or 'standard form contracts' in the 1977 Act, but these definitions would obviously cover cases in which the seller insists that all (or nearly all) of his customers buy or hire goods on the same terms with no change from one contract to another.

It is worth emphasising that a private transaction between a private seller and a private buyer is not to be regarded as a consumer transaction.

 Key point: The Unfair Contract Terms Act 1977 gives the strongest possible protection to consumers in relation to the use and abuse of exclusion and limitation clauses.

What types of contract does the Unfair Contract Terms Act cover?

Section 15 lists the types of contract which the Act covers. These include:

- Contracts for the sale of goods
- Contracts of hire
- Contracts of hire purchase
- Contracts of employment or apprenticeship
- Contracts for the provision of services
- Contracts relating to occupier's liability (where the occupier is a business, for example, a cinema, pub, theatre or fairground)
- Contracts which grant a right to enter or to use land

The Unfair Contract Terms Act does not apply to the following types of agreement:

- Insurance contracts
- Contracts for the transfer of an interest in land

- Auction sale contracts
- Contracts for the sale of goods on an international basis
- Contracts involving the creation, membership and termination of partnerships and companies

House purchases will not be covered by the Act, although liability for misrepresentations made in the course of a sale of a house by a surveyor, where he has been employed by a bank or building society, cannot be excluded unless such a term can pass the test of reasonableness. Nor does the Act apply to certain contracts for the sale of goods on an international basis because these are covered by international conventions, for example, the Vienna Convention 1980. Furthermore, it should be noted that a written arbitration agreement will not be treated as excluding liability or restricting liability for the purposes of the Unfair Contract Terms Act and such an agreement is valid.

 Key point: There are certain types of contracts that are not covered by the Act: insurance contracts, contracts transferring an interest in land, auction sales, international sales of goods, the creation, membership and termination of partnerships and companies.

Void exclusion and limitation clauses under the Unfair Contract Terms Act 1977

The Act has the effect of rendering some types of exclusion and limitation clauses void and ineffective. It will not matter whether adequate notice of the existence of the clause was given by the party relying on it to the other party. Any attempt to include the clause in the contract will quite simply fail.

Under section 16 of the Act, any clause where a party attempts to escape or limit his responsibility for having caused death or personal injury to another as a result of his actions will be automatically void. The clause cannot be relied upon and will not be enforced by the courts.

 Key point: As a result of the Unfair Contract Terms Act 1977, any attempt to exclude liability for personal injury or death will be automatically void.

In terms of Section 19 of the Act, a manufacturer's guarantee cannot exclude or restrict his liability for loss or damage arising from defects in goods used by a consumer which was caused by negligence in the manufacturing or distribution process. Any such attempt by the manufacturer will be void and ineffective.

 Key point: Attempts by manufacturers to exclude or limit their liability to consumers in relation to defective goods will be void and ineffective.

Very often, a business seller will attempt to exclude or limit his liability to a consumer buyer in a sale of goods transaction. Sections 12 to 15 of the Sale of Goods Act 1979 gives a consumer buyer extensive protection in respect of the following:

- The buyer is entitled to assume that the seller will have the right to sell the goods (Section 12)
- If the seller uses a description in relation to the goods, this description must comply with the goods (Section 13)
- The goods supplied by the seller must be of satisfactory quality and fit for their purpose (Section 14)

◆ If the transaction is a sale by sample, the goods supplied must comply with the sample in terms quality and fitness for purpose (Section 15)

Sections 12 to 15 of the Sale of Goods Act 1979 are referred to as the *implied terms* which form part of every contract involving the sale of goods. They are material terms of the contract i.e. they are at the very heart of the agreement and, obviously, any attempt to exclude or limit their operation should be treated with extreme suspicion by the courts.

Section 20 of the Unfair Contract Terms Act 1977 states that any attempt to exclude or limit the implied terms of the Sale of Goods Act in a consumer sale will be automatically void. In a non-consumer sale, Section 20 of the Unfair Contract Terms Act makes it clear that any attempt by a seller to limit his liability in terms of Section 12 of the Sale of Goods Act, will be automatically void.

In a non-consumer sale, a seller may be able to exclude or limit his liability in relation to Sections 13 to 15 of the Sale of Goods Act, but Section 20 of the Unfair Contract Terms Act states that this will only be permitted if this is fair and reasonable.

 Key point: Any attempt by a seller to exclude or limit his liability in terms of Section 12 of the Sale of Goods Act 1979 regardless of whether it is a consumer contract or a non-consumer contract will be automatically void. In a consumer sale, a business seller will not be permitted to exclude or limit his liability in relation to Sections 13 to 15 of the Sale of Goods Act 1979.

A manufacturer's guarantee cannot exclude or restrict his liability for loss or damage arising from defects in goods used by a consumer which was caused by negligence in the manufacturing or distribution process. Any such attempt by the manufacturer will be void and ineffective.

The enforcement of exclusion and limitation clauses

Under Section 16 of the Unfair Contract Terms Act, exclusion or limitation clauses will now only be capable of enforcement in situations involving liability for loss or damage caused to another person's property and this clause is regarded as fair and reasonable.

However, determining when a clause will be fair and reasonable has caused a fair amount of legal debate and argument.

Section 17 of the Act addresses a number of situations regarding any term in either a consumer contract or a standard form contract which would allow the party relying on such a clause to do any of the following:

1   To exclude or limit his liability for breach of contract

2   To avoid performance of his contractual obligations completely

3   To perform the contract in a totally different way from that which was reasonably anticipated by the other party

Section 17 goes on to state that any term falling into the three categories listed above will be completely ineffective unless the party who wishes to rely on it can demonstrate that it was fair and reasonable to insist that it should form part of the contract. Although consumers receive the maximum amount of protection under the

Act, Section 17 leaves it open to a business to argue that its attempt to escape or limit liability in relation to consumer contracts should be regarded as fair and reasonable.

It should be remembered that some exclusion and limitation clauses will be automatically void in relation to death and injury generally and in respect of Sections 12 to 15 of the Sale of Goods Act 1979 in a consumer transaction (and Section 12 in a non-consumer sale). Any other type of exclusion or limitation clause will have to pass the test of reasonableness. Obviously, an attempt by the seller to exclude or limit liability will only be really worth attempting in respect of some of the less important terms of the consumer contract.

Furthermore, in terms of Section 18, an indemnity clause in a consumer contract will be ineffective if it fails the test of reasonableness. Such clauses are used where a business may agree to perform work for a consumer, but only if the consumer will indemnify (compensate) the business in relation to any liability which it may incur during the performance of the contract. An employee of the business, for example, may injure a third party as a result of his negligence and the business will turn to the consumer for compensation when it is sued by the victim. Generally, a business should take responsibility for its negligence and this exposure to risk can always be reduced by means of an insurance policy. Such indemnity clauses in consumer contracts will, therefore, be treated with suspicion by the courts.

 Key point: In terms of the Unfair Contract Terms Act 1977, a person relying on an exclusion or limitation clause in order to escape or limit his liability for damage caused to another person's property must demonstrate that the clause is fair and reasonable.

The reasonableness of exclusion and limitation clauses

One of the key questions that the Unfair Contract Terms Act poses is whether an exclusion or limitation clause can be regarded as reasonable. Although the matter of reasonableness is primarily a question for the courts to answer, there are guidelines which appear in Section 24 and Schedule 2 of the Act.

Section 24 states that the matter of reasonableness must be decided by referring to the circumstances surrounding the contract when it was made and exactly what facts the parties were aware of or should have been made aware of. Where a clause limits the amount of compensation payable, the courts should examine the resources of the person who is relying upon the clause and whether he could have reduced the risks that he was exposed to by taking out an insurance policy. The purpose of this rule is to encourage businesses to take out insurance wherever possible in order to safeguard themselves against liability. A failure to do so would doubtless play very badly with the court. However, the court will be well aware that there are some risks that insurers will simply not entertain.

Where the contract is for the supply of goods i.e. under a contract of sale, hire-purchase, hiring or work and materials, Schedule 2 of the Act states that the following factors must be examined:

a) The strength of the bargaining position of the parties i.e. a stronger party may not be allowed to rely upon the exclusion or limitation clause where it is quite obvious that this would permit an abuse of power. This, of course, depends upon the circumstances of the situation.

b) The availability of alternative supplies. If a seller who holds a dominant position in the marketplace and attempts to use a clause he may well be prevented from doing so because the opportunity for the buyer to secure the goods from another source is severely restricted.

c) Inducements that encourage the buyer to accept the inclusion of the clause in the contract. This would occur for example, if the buyer benefits from lower prices or where he was offered a gift from the seller which persuades him to agree to the clause. Behaviour like this on the part of the buyer may persuade the court that the seller has attempted to be reasonable as regards the clause.

d) The buyer's knowledge of the extent of the clause. Has adequate notice of the clause's existence been given? Is the buyer fully aware that his rights have been reduced under it? If these conditions are satisfied, the court may hold the clause reasonable.

e) Customs of trade and previous dealings. It seems to be the position that previous dealings in consumer contracts do not appear to be relevant, unless they occur on a frequent basis.

f) Whether the goods have been made, processed or adapted to the order of the buyer. Obviously, if the seller has been required by the buyer to produce goods to order, then it may be fair and reasonable for the seller to exclude liability which might arise because of faults in the buyer's design which he insisted should be followed. In such a business transaction, it is probably the case that the seller would be acting in a completely reasonable way if he insisted upon excluding the implied term (contained in Section 14 of the Sale of Goods Act 1979) that the goods should be of satisfactory quality or fit for purpose.

 Key point: The issue of whether an exclusion or limitation clause is reasonable will be primarily a matter for the courts based on the evidence presented to them by the parties.

We can see below how the courts have developed the test of reasonableness in relation to the Unfair Contract Terms Act 1977:

 Woodman v Photo Trade Processing Ltd (1981) Woodman had been the only photographer present at the wedding of his friends. It was his intention to have these photographs developed and have them included in an album which he would then give to his friends as his wedding gift to them. He put his roll of film in to be developed by the defenders. The film quite obviously had a unique value, but, unfortunately, due to the defenders' negligence the film was lost and it was never recovered. Woodman sued the defenders for the loss of the film. They attempted to limit their liability to the cost of a replacement roll of film. The defenders claimed that they were merely relying upon a standard limitation clause which was widely used in their particular line of business. Furthermore, the defenders argued that Woodman had been given adequate notice of the existence of such a clause and there could no dispute that it formed part of the contract. The defenders did concede that customers were taking a risk when they entrusted their films to them – accidents can and do happen. However, the defenders were able to offer customers a very valuable and efficient service at highly competitive prices. They would not be able to do this if they were forced to operate their business without the protection of such limitation clauses. Expensive legal action, the likes of which Woodman had commenced, would eventually be passed on to the consumer in the shape of much higher prices. Woodman argued that, although he had been given adequate notice of the clause, it was not fair and reasonable in the circumstances. The developers were only too well aware that customers attached an extremely high value to their films which were records of important events in their lives. The clause read as follows:

'All photographic materials are accepted on the basis that their value does not exceed the loss of the material itself. Responsibility is limited to the replacement of film. No liability will be accepted consequently or otherwise, however caused.'

Held: by Judge Clarke QC in the English County Court that the customer had no means of challenging such a clause. He had to take it or leave it. Practically speaking, there was no real alternative as most, if not all, businesses in this particular line would have operated according to similar or identical conditions. Woodman, being a consumer, was the much weaker party in the contractual relationship and the developers were in a much stronger position in that they could impose highly unfavourable terms. The film clearly had a unique or sentimental value (it was irreplaceable) and the defenders were only too aware of this fact. The clause placed an unacceptably high degree of risk on the weaker party i.e. the consumer. The clause was unfair and unreasonable and Woodman was awarded damages of £75.

 Smith *v* Eric S Bush (1990) a surveyor attempted to rely on an exclusion clause which effectively allowed him to escape liability for any negligence on his part. The surveyor had been instructed by a building society to carry out an inspection of the property in order to have it valued. The cost of the survey was to be paid by the prospective buyer. The surveyor was aware that the prospective buyer would rely on this report and it was highly unlikely that the buyer would consult another surveyor for the purpose of obtaining a second opinion in relation to the property. The sale of the house went ahead, but it soon became apparent that the property suffered from serious defects and, consequently, it was not suitable for habitation. The buyers raised an action against the surveyor who attempted to rely on the exclusion clause in order to escape liability.

    Held: by the House of Lords that, in terms of the Unfair Contract Terms Act, it was unreasonable to allow the surveyor to rely on such a clause. The building society and the surveyor could not be permitted to pass on the risk of loss due to their incompetence or carelessness when the high cost of houses and the high cost of interest rates were taken into account.

 St Albans City and District Council *v* International Computers Ltd (1996) the pursuers, the Council, had entered into a contract with the defenders, International Computers, for the purchase and installation of a software package. The software package would permit the Council to set up a database of eligible poll tax payers. The software package contained some sort of error which led to the pursuers to over-estimate the number of eligible tax payers. This meant that the pursuers received a less generous grant from central government. The pursuers sued the defenders for damages for the losses suffered. The defenders attempted to rely on a limitation clause which reduced their liability to a sum of £100,000.

Held: by the English High Court that reliance by the defenders on such a clause was unreasonable in terms of the Unfair Contract Terms Act. The defenders were a very large business concern being part of a multinational company which had a great deal of financial resources. The defenders had taken out insurance in relation to their products and this policy covered them for up to £50 million. Finally, the defenders were one of a very limited number of businesses who could meet the pursuers' requirements and all of these rival businesses used very similar clauses in their standard terms and conditions. This put the defenders in a very strong position in comparison to the pursuers. The defenders appealed, but the English Court of Appeal ruled against them.

Unfair Terms in Consumer Contract Regulations 1999

These Regulations replace the Unfair Terms in Consumer Contracts Regulations 1994. The original Regulations of 1994 implement the EC Directive on Unfair Terms in Consumer Contracts. The 1999 Regulations (like their predecessor) are entirely separate from the Unfair Contract Terms Act 1977 and, therefore, it is possible to challenge an exclusion clause under both pieces of legislation. As the title of the Regulations suggests, the law in this area applies only to consumer contracts. They create an entirely separate regime from the Unfair Contract Terms Act 1977.

 Key point: The Unfair Terms in Consumer Contracts Regulations 1999 as the title suggests provide protection to consumers not businesses and, furthermore, the Regulations are completely separate from the Unfair Contract Terms Act 1977.

There is a clear difference in approach between the Regulations and the Unfair Contract Terms Act 1977. The Unfair Contract Terms Act deals with exclusion and limitation clauses rather than unfair terms generally. The Regulations will, therefore, have a much wider application than the Act. The Act does, however, have a major strength in the sense that some contractual terms are considered to be automatically void in all situations (death or personal injury generally and Sections 12 to 15 of the Sale of Goods Act in relation to consumer contracts specifically). The Regulations, on the other hand, apply a test of fairness before an exclusion or limitation clause can be regarded as void and unenforceable. With regard to the issue of excluding or limiting liability for death or personal injury, the Regulations state that such terms may be unfair whereas the Act makes these automatically void.

When dealing with the question of unfair terms, it is important to realise that the Unfair Contract Terms Act and the Unfair Terms in Consumer Contracts Regulations do not always cover the same types of contracts. This means that particular care will have to be taken when dealing with unfair terms and it will be sensible to keep a copy of both the Act and the Regulations at hand.

 Key point: The Unfair Contract Terms Act 1977 applies only to exclusion and limitation clauses in consumer and business contracts whereas the Unfair Terms in Consumer Contracts Regulations 1999 applies generally to unfair terms in consumer contracts.

Unfair terms

Schedule 3 of the Regulations provides 17 examples of terms in consumer contracts that *may* be unfair. These examples cover the following issues:

a) An attempt by the seller or the supplier to rely on a clause that excludes or limits his liability for death and/or personal injury to a consumer resulting from the seller or supplier's negligence.

b) An attempt by the seller or the supplier to force a consumer to pay an unfair penalty as compensation if the consumer breached the contract in some way. This would cover situations involving non-refundable deposits.

c) An attempt by the seller or the supplier to change the terms of the contract without first having sought the consumer's consent.

d) An attempt by the seller or the supplier to limit the range of actions available to the consumer in the event of the business not being able to perform its duties under the contract or where there is partial performance by the business.

 Key point: One of the features of the Regulations is that they apply a test of fairness to a term in a consumer contract rather than render the term automatically void as is the case with the Unfair Contract Terms Act 1977.

What types of contractual terms do the Regulations cover?

Regulation 3(1) makes it clear that the Regulations apply to all contracts concluded between a seller or a supplier *acting in the course of business* and a consumer where terms are not individually negotiated. This, of course, means that the terms are standardised or uniform and the buyer will have to take them or leave them. These types of standard or uniform terms will most often be found in pre-printed documents, but standard terms can be found in contracts of a purely verbal nature.

A court is unlikely to be impressed by a seller or supplier's argument that the term must be fair because token negotiations have taken place with the buyer if it soon becomes apparent that the seller or supplier has managed to impose most of his standard conditions on the buyer. The burden of proof will be on the seller to prove that the term, which is at the centre of the dispute, was individually negotiated and not imposed on the buyer by way of a standard condition.

 Key point: The Regulations apply to standard terms in written or verbal contracts used by a business seller or supplier, these terms are imposed on a consumer buyer and, generally, the buyer will not be in a position to negotiate with the seller or the supplier.

Generally, the Regulations do not apply to terms which address the price to be paid by the consumer for goods and services or those terms which describe the subject-matter of the contract. It must be remembered, however, that the Regulations impose a general requirement that every standard term of a consumer contract must be written in plain and intelligible language so that they can be easily understood by the buyer. Traders could be challenged by a consumer if the meaning of a term is difficult to understand and, if this situation does arise, the meaning most favourable to the consumer will be the one favoured by the court (Regulation 6).

Regulation 3 states that a number of contracts will not be covered by the Regulations:

- ◆ Contracts of employment
- ◆ Business contracts
- ◆ Contracts between private individuals
- ◆ Contracts relating to succession rights
- ◆ Contracts relating to rights under family law
- ◆ Contracts relating to the incorporation of companies or partnerships
- ◆ Any contractual term incorporated in order to meet United Kingdom statutory or regulatory provisions or international conventions
- ◆ Contracts made before 1995

Despite these exclusions the Regulations are still wider than the Unfair Contract Terms Act 1977 because they include contracts for the transfer of interests in land, contracts involving the transfer of securities, auction sales and contracts of insurance.

 Key point: Despite the fact that the Regulations will not apply in every situation, their application is potentially wider than the Unfair Contract Terms Act.

The test of fairness

Regulation 4 contains a test of fairness which will be applied to contractual terms. A term will be considered to be unfair if it can be demonstrated that a business has not acted in good faith and it causes a significant imbalance in the parties' rights and obligations under the contract and, as a result, a consumer is placed at a serious disadvantage.

The requirement of good faith means that traders must deal fairly and openly with consumers. Although traders may have very good reasons for using standard terms and conditions in contracts, any provision that exploits or harms the consumer could be potentially unfair.

Regulation 4 also states that an examination of the unfair nature of the term should take into account the following:

a) The nature of the goods or services for which the contract is concluded

b) The circumstances surrounding the conclusion of the contract

c) Other terms of the contract or of another contract on which it is dependent

Schedule 2 of the Regulations lists the kinds of factors that a court will consider when deciding whether a clause is unfair:

a) The relative bargaining positions of the parties (did a business impose unfavourable terms on the consumer, the weaker party?)

b) Whether the consumer has an inducement to agree the term (did the consumer accept a discount or a gift or some other benefit in exchange for agreeing to include certain terms in the contract?)

c) Whether the goods or services where sold or supplied to the special order of the consumer (was the seller or supplier contractually bound to provide custom-made goods in order to comply with requirements laid down by the consumer?)

d) The extent to which the seller or supplier has dealt fairly and equitably with the consumer (did the seller or the supplier attempt to take advantage of the consumer's inexperience, naivety or age?)

 Key point: When relying on exclusion clauses in its dealings with consumers, a business must act in good faith and such a clause will be probably be unfair if it causes consumers to be placed at a serious disadvantage.

The consequences of including unfair terms in a contract

According to Regulation 5, an unfair term will not be capable of enforcement against the consumer – it is not binding. This does not mean that the consumer can refuse to honour all of his duties as the contract will continue to be in force provided that the unfair term does not undermine the whole contract.

Additionally, the Regulations do not apply to contractual terms which determine the price or define the product or service i.e. the subject-matter of the contract. Terms in consumer contracts that set the price or define the product or service being supplied are the material terms of the contract and are exempt from the test of fairness as long as they are expressed in plain language.

 Key point: The Unfair Terms in Consumer Contracts Regulations 1999 do not apply to the following agreements – contracts made before 1995, private contracts, business contracts, non-consumer contracts, where the contract is the result of genuine negotiation between the parties and where the law imposes a duty to include particular terms in the contract.

Enforcement of the Regulations (Regulation 8)

A number of organisations or 'qualifying bodies' have been given enforcement powers under the Regulations, including the Office of Fair Trading, the utilities regulators (gas, telecommunications, water and electricity), the Information Commissioner, the Consumers' Association, the Department of Enterprise, Trade and Investment in Northern Ireland, the Financial Services Authority, and all trading standards services.

It is not up to the various bodies that have been given powers under the Regulations to decide whether a term is or is not unfair or whether any individual consumer is entitled to compensation. It is their duty to consider any complaints about the unfairness of a contract term and if they believe that a term is unfair, the courts can be approached and asked to issue an interdict to prevent the term being used or recommended for use. However, only the courts can finally decide whether a term is or is not unfair.

Alternatively, it may be acceptable on the part of the trader to give a promise not to use the term and, therefore, court action will be unnecessary.

Key point: The Regulations give powers to certain agencies, for example, the Office of Fair Trading in order to take action against sellers or suppliers who use unfair terms in their contractual dealings with consumers.

The Enterprise Act 2002

This Act gives the Office of Fair Trading the power to investigate the use of exclusion clauses and other unfair terms being used in consumer transactions. The Office of Fair Trading is supposed to investigate consumer trade practices and, in particular, terms and conditions on which or subject to which goods or services are supplied. If after the investigation, the Office of Fair Trading feels that a particular practice in terms of exemption clauses should cease it can make a report to the Minister who may introduce a statutory instrument to stop the practice, for example, the **Consumer Transactions (Restrictions on Statements) Order 1976** makes it a criminal offence to sell or supply goods and purport that the implied terms in sale of goods and hire-purchase legislation can be excluded in a consumer sale since this might suggest to the consumer that he has no rights so that he will not bother to enforce them.

 Key point: The Enterprise Act 2002 gives power to the Office of Fair Trading to investigate and challenge the use of exclusion clauses and other unfair terms by businesses.

The attitude of the courts to exclusion and limitation clauses

One of the ways that the courts have dealt with the use of such clauses in contracts is by examining the type of contract. Over the years, the courts have tended to take a much tougher approach to the use of these clauses in consumer contracts. A consumer contract is one where the seller is selling in the course of a business and the buyer is purchasing the goods or services for his own personal use. Normally, a consumer will not have the bargaining power to impose contractual conditions on the seller. Very often, a business seller will be in the position of being able to impose his standard conditions on the buyer. In other words, the buyer will have to like or lump the seller's conditions. In a consumer contract, there will be little prospect of the buyer entering into complex negotiations with the seller. Here lies the danger because an unscrupulous seller, who is perfectly aware that the buyer is in a much weaker position may seek to take advantage. Ultimately, this will mean that the seller could impose all sorts of negative conditions on a consumer and there is very little that the consumer can do.

 Key point: The common law could still be used to attack an unfair term in a contract in situations where the term satisfies the tests laid down by the Unfair Contract Terms Act and the Unfair Terms in Consumer Contracts Regulations 1999.

Lord Diplock, in **Schroeder v Macaulay (1974)**, made a powerful argument when he highlighted the weakness of consumer buyers in comparison with business buyers. The seller is effectively saying to the consumer buyer 'if you want these goods or services at all, these are the only terms on which they are obtainable. Take it or leave it.'

It is true to say, however, that the courts have taken a less sympathetic attitude towards those individuals who have fallen foul of such clauses in commercial or business contracts. The courts often expect business parties to a contract to have conducted serious negotiations, where both of them have had a real chance to determine the shape of the final agreement and where both parties will be fully aware of the consequences of each individual term.

In a business, the theory (rather than the practice) suggests that both parties will have had a fair chance to insist that contractual terms which are favourable to them are included in the final deal. If, later on, one of the parties discovers or realises that negative terms have been imposed on him, the courts may take the view that this individual had ample opportunity to object to these being included in the contract and, ultimately, he could have refused to enter the contract if the offensive terms were not removed. Therefore, any losses suffered by a party who is the victim of an exclusion clause will have to be offset by an insurance policy (if he has one which covers this situation) or it may have to come out of that party's own pocket.

The concept of equal bargaining power

The approach that the judges have taken towards exclusion clauses in business contracts, however, is very much based on an assumption that both parties are coming to negotiations with equal bargaining power. Just as the consumer is often the weaker party in a consumer contract, it is perfectly possible that one business will be stronger than another and this situation will lead the stronger party to impose all sorts of unfavourable conditions on the weaker party. Very often the concept of equal bargaining power in business negotiations is nothing less than an illusion.

 Key point: The courts tend to treat parties to a business contract less sympathetically when they have fallen foul of an exclusion clause.

The courts have protected consumers of goods in two ways by:

- Deciding that the exclusion clause was never part of the contract
- Examining the wording and the likely impact of the clause in such a way as to prevent its use

Was the clause part of the contract?

The court will demand that the person wishing to rely upon the clause bring evidence to show that the other party agreed to include the term in the contract, otherwise it will not form part of the agreement. A number of issues will arise:

1   What if an agreement is formed by the parties signing a written contract containing potentially unfair terms?

The party who signs such an agreement will, generally, be bound by all the terms which the document contains. This will be the case even if he has not read the contract properly, unless he was encouraged to enter the contract as a result of a misrepresentation made by the other party as to the legal effect of the document and its terms.

 Curtis v Chemical Cleaning and Dyeing Co [1951] the pursuer took a white satin wedding dress with beads and sequins to the defender's shop for cleaning. She was asked to sign a receipt which contained the following clause:

'This article is accepted on condition that the company is not liable for any damage howsoever arising.'

The pursuer claimed in evidence that she had asked why she had to sign the document and the assistant said that the clause excluded the company's liability for damage that occurred to beads and sequins only. The clause did not, therefore, apply to damage caused to the dress itself. She did not read all of the receipt before she signed it. The dress was returned with a stain and the pursuer sued for damages. The company relied on the clause.

Held: by the English Court of Appeal that the company could not enforce the exclusion clause because the assistant had innocently misrepresented the legal consequences of the document. As a result of the assistant's response to her query, the pursuer was entitled to believe that damage to the beads and sequins was covered by the exclusion clause, but not damage to the dress itself.

 Key point: Generally, the courts take the attitude that those individuals who voluntarily enter contracts which contain an exclusion clause, for example, by signing a document will be bound by the consequences of this action on their part.

2   What is the legal effect of potentially unfair terms contained in documents like tickets, receipts or vouchers?

If the primary purpose of such a document is merely to provide basic evidence that the parties have a contract, it can hardly be argued that it should be treated as an important contractual document containing all the terms of the agreement. The person seeking to rely on the clause must prove that the other party should have realised that the document would contain the essential terms of the agreement. If this can be proved, the clause will apply even though the other party was not aware of its existence because he failed to read the document properly.

 L'Estrange Ltd *v* Gracoub (1934) the pursuer, a café owner, purchased a cigarette slot machine from the defender. The defender had presented a written contract for the pursuer to sign. Unknown to the pursuer, the defender had included a clause which stated:

'Any express or implied condition, statement or warranty, statutory or otherwise, is hereby excluded.'

The pursuer did not bother to read the part of the contract which contained the exclusion clause and went ahead and placed her signature on the written contract. The machine was later found to be defective and unsatisfactory and the pursuer sued the defender for damages in respect of the now unusable machine.

Held: the exclusion was enforceable against the pursuer and her arguments that she had not read the written contract because she thought it was merely an order form did not impress the court. Furthermore, despite the fact that the defender had not drawn the pursuer's attention to the clause nor had he read it to her, no misrepresentation or fraud had been committed.

 Chapelton v Barry UDC [1940] Chapelton wished to hire deck chairs and went to a stack of chairs owned by the defenders, behind which was a notice stating:

'Hire of chairs 2d per session of three hours.'

The pile of deck chairs was regarded as a general offer to members of the public that Chapelton had accepted when he selected two chairs. He paid for them and received two tickets which he put into his pocket after merely glancing at them. One of the chairs collapsed and he was injured. A notice on the reverse of the ticket stated that:

'The Council will not be liable for any accident or damage arising from the hire of the chairs.'

Chapelton sued for damages and the Council attempted to rely on the clause.

Held: by the English court of Appeal that the clause could not be relied on by the Council to escape its liability towards Chapelton for his injuries. The board by the chairs made no attempt to limit the Council's liability because it did not alert the pursuer to the existence of the exclusion clause. In any case, Chapelton had accepted the offer by selecting the deck chairs and it could be argued that the attempt to rely on the exclusion clause was an attempt to introduce new terms into the contract. However, the ticket was a mere voucher and not a document that an ordinary member of the public would suspect contained all the terms of the contract.

 Taylor v Glasgow Corporation 1952 Mrs Taylor, the pursuer, had suffered injury when she fell down a staircase inside Glasgow Woodside Public Baths and she brought a subsequent action for damages against Glasgow Corporation. She alleged that the accident had been caused by the negligence of the Corporation's employees. When Mrs Taylor had paid the entrance fee to the Baths, she had been given a ticket. On the front of the ticket there was the following statement: 'For conditions see other side.' The statement on the back of the ticket said the following:

'The Corporation of Glasgow are NOT responsible for any loss, injury or damage sustained by persons entering or using this establishment or its equipment '

Mrs Taylor admitted that she had seen the printing on the ticket, but she had not bothered to stop and read the statements.

Held: by the Court of Session that the ticket was a voucher and not an important contractual document containing all the terms of the agreement of which a person in Mrs Taylor's position should have been made aware. Lord Thomson, the Lord Justice Clerk, stated:

'My view of the evidence is that this voucher aspect of this 'ticket' was the significant aspect, and that the purchaser regarded it as a pass or voucher or as a receipt for sixpence which entitled her to be given a hot

bath, she was entitled so to regard it . . .'

The exclusion clauses in **Chapelton and Taylor** would now fall foul of both the Unfair Contract Terms Act 1977 and the Unfair Terms in Consumer Contracts Regulations 1999.

Lord Denning in **Spurling v Bradshaw [1956]** did make a very interesting comment regarding the incorporation of exclusion clauses into contracts. He said that they would 'need to be in red ink with a red hand pointing to it – or something equally startling.' Lord Denning expressed this view again in **Thornton v Shoe Lane Parking [1971]** a case which demonstrates very clearly the attitude of the courts towards attempts by individuals to incorporate exclusion clauses after an agreement has been concluded between the parties.

Thornton v Shoe Lane Parking (1971) demonstrates that the requirement of adequate notice will be strictly enforced by the courts. In the English Court of Appeal, Lord Denning remarked that such a clause would 'need to be in red ink with a red hand pointing to it – or something equally startling.'

 Key point: If additional documents contain exclusion clauses such as tickets, it is a sensible precaution for the party relying on the clause to bring it to the other party's attention so that it can be said to be fully incorporated into the contract.

3   What if the parties have dealt with one another previously and on a regular basis and the pursuer, being a reasonable person, would know that the defender always contracts on identical or very similar terms?

 Hardwick Game Farm v Suffolk Agricultural Poultry Producers Association [1969] a farmer was in the habit of purchasing feeding stuff for his poultry from the same supplier. On the first occasion that the farmer had done business with the supplier, the goods, when they were delivered, were accompanied by a sold note which contained an exclusion clause. This exclusion clause had no legal effect, of course, because the supplier had not drawn it to the farmer's attention before the contract had been formed. It was, therefore, an attempt to introduce a new term after the original agreement had been formed. Over the next few years, the farmer entered into a regular series of contracts of sale with the supplier (on average 3 or 4 a month). Every consignment of goods was accompanied by a sold note which contained the same exclusion clause – there was never any variation. In total, the farmer received over 100 of these sold notes as a result of his dealings with the supplier. Problems occurred when the supplier attempted to rely on the exclusion clause in the sold note. A consignment of the goods had been contaminated and this had resulted in much of farmer's livestock being poisoned.

Held: by the House of Lords that the seller was permitted to enforce the clause because a consistent course of dealings between the parties had incorporated the clause into the contract. The farmer's protests that he had never bothered to read the sold note and was, therefore, completely unaware of the consequences of the exclusion clause were irrelevant. The parties had now established a regular and consistent course of dealing. The farmer was well aware by now that every delivery was accompanied by a sold note which contained an identical exclusion clause. In other words, the supplier always contracted on the same terms. The farmer was under a duty to discover what these terms were and to raise objections if they were not to his liking. The farmer had never bothered to do this and, by implication, it was the supplier's terms (including the exclusion clause) which governed the contract.

The person relying on the incorporation of the exclusion clause must demonstrate that the clause was always included in the contract if there has been a course of dealing between the parties. In other words, there must be a consistent pattern whereby the clause is always included in the contract – not most of the time or some of the time, but all of the time. The party against whom the clause will be enforced against must be left in no doubt whatsoever that the clause forms part of the standard terms of the contract.

 In the leading Scottish case of **McCutcheon *v* David MacBrayne Ltd [1964]**, the House of Lords was asked to consider whether or not there had been a consistent course of dealings between MacBrayne, a ferry operator, and an individual who had used the ferry service to transport a relative's car from Islay, one of the Western Isles, to the Scottish mainland.

The car owner (McCutcheon) had asked his brother-in-law, McSporran, to arrange to have the vehicle placed aboard the ferry, *Lochiel*. McSporran had previously used the services of the ferry operator to transport goods. On several of these previous occasions (but not on every occasion as it turned out), McSporran had been asked to sign what MacBrayne described as a 'risk note'. This 'risk note' contained a statement that goods were shipped at the owner's risk. Due to the negligence of MacBrayne's employees the ferry hit a rock during the crossing and sank. Nothing of value could be salvaged from the wreck. The owner sued MacBrayne for damages for the loss of the car. MacBrayne then attempted to escape liability by relying upon an exclusion clause. The ferry operators claimed that the exclusion had been incorporated into this particular contract of carriage. On this occasion, however, McSporran had not been asked to sign any 'risk note'. As Lord Reid pointed out:

'This time he (McSporran) was offered an oral contract without any reference to conditions, and he accepted the offer in good faith . . .'

A particularly significant fact of this case was that, in the course of previous dealings, MacBrayne had sometimes failed to insist that McSporran sign such a 'risk note' when he used the ferry service. On some occasions he might be asked to sign it and on other occasions the 'risk note' was not even mentioned. There was no consistency on MacBrayne's part. In his evidence, furthermore, it was stated by McSporran that, on those occasions when he signed the document, he had never bothered to read it.

Held: by the House of Lords that MacBrayne had failed to demonstrate that there was a consistent business practice which would have allowed the incorporation of this clause into this particular contract. If anything, the ferry company's approach to the incorporation of exclusion clauses was extremely haphazard and the fact that McSporran sometimes signed a 'risk note' owed more to luck than the application of a consistent policy.

Hollier v Rambler Motors (AMC) Ltd [1972] Hollier's car had an oil leak and he left the vehicle to be repaired at a garage owned by the defenders, Rambler Motors. While the car was at the garage, it was destroyed in a fire caused by the negligence of the defenders. Rambler Motors attempted to escape liability by relying on an exclusion clause which allegedly formed part of its contract with Hollier. The clause excluded liability, amongst other things, for damage caused by fire to cars left at the garage by their owners. As part of its argument to have the clause enforced, Rambler Motors claimed that Hollier had previously dealt with them on 3 or 4 occasions over a five year period and that, consequently, he was perfectly aware that the exclusion clause was part of the garage's standard business conditions. Every time that Hollier had booked his car into the garage, he had been asked to sign a form containing the exclusion clause and he had not raised any objections. The problem for Rambler Motors was that, on this occasion, it had failed to ask Hollier to sign the form containing the clause. Unfazed by this problem, Rambler Motors argued that it should still be permitted to enforce the clause against Hollier because there was an established custom and practice on its part with regard to the incorporation of the exclusion clause in its contracts with this particular customer. In other words, there was a consistent course of dealings between the parties.

Held: the defenders were not entitled to enforce the clause against Hollier. The English Court of Appeal was unconvinced that Hollier's previous dealings with Rambler Motors represented a regular and consistent course of dealing. Lord Denning MR (speaking in the later case of **British Crane Hire Corporation v Ipswich Plant Hire Ltd [1975]**) also stressed the fact that this was a consumer transaction and that the parties did not have equal bargaining power i.e. the garage was clearly the stronger party in the contract and was, therefore, in a position to impose unfavourable terms (exclusion clauses) upon Hollier.

A point worth noting is that in certain trades or professions, the incorporation of potentially unfair clauses into contracts will be a well-established and well-publicised business practice. Any member of that trade or profession dealing with a colleague will, therefore, be presumed to possess knowledge of the existence of terms peculiar to their area of industry or commerce.

British Crane Hire Corporation v Ipswich Plant Hire Ltd [1975], both parties were in the business of hiring out heavy earth moving equipment. The defenders had hired special equipment from the pursuers, which they urgently required. After the contract had been formed, the pursuers had asked that the defenders sign a printed form containing their conditions of hire. One of the conditions was that the defenders would compensate or indemnify the pursuers for all expenses incurred while using the equipment. The defenders failed to sign this form but, in meantime, the equipment had sunk into marshy ground suffering damage as a result. The pursuers attempted to enforce the clause claiming that any reasonable person involved in this particular area of business would have been aware of the existence of such a clause in the contract and, furthermore, the defenders would have been only too aware of the fact that the pursuers would have absolutely refused to hire the equipment out if this term had not been included in the agreement.

Held: by the English Court of Appeal that the clause had been incorporated into the contract because the defenders were well aware that their particular line of business operated on standard conditions which were, according to Lord Denning MR: 'habitually imposed by the supplier of the machines and both parties knew the substance of those conditions.' The defenders, in fact, admitted that variations of a form containing similar terms and conditions of business (known as the Contractors' Plant Association Form) were widely used in their business. Lord Denning also made the point that facts in this case were quite different from **Hollier *v* Rambler Motors (AMC) Ltd [1972]** because in this case the parties enjoyed equal bargaining power.

Key point: If the parties deal with one another on a regular basis, the party relying upon the exclusion clause must be able to show that it has consistently formed part of the contract and the other party is either aware of this or should have been aware of this fact.

4   Any attempt to introduce an exclusion clause after the contract has been made will be ineffective because it is an attempt to introduce additional terms to the agreement.

Olley *v* Marlborough Court Ltd [1949] Mr and Mrs Olley arrived at a hotel where they had pre-booked a room. At the reception desk, they finalised their booking and were given the keys to their room. On one of the walls of the room was the following exclusion notice:

'The proprietors will not hold themselves responsible for articles lost or stolen unless handed to the manageress for safe custody.'

The wife locked the room and took the key down to leave it at the reception desk. An unidentified third party stole the key from behind the reception desk, used it to gain access to the Olleys' room and stole some of the wife's furs. This theft should have come as no surprise because the hotel staff had not taken reasonable precautions to prevent unauthorised third parties from having access to the room keys held behind reception. The hotel now sought to escape liability by arguing that the exclusion notice in the bedroom had been successfully incorporated into the contract with the Olleys.

Held: by the English Court of Appeal that the contract was completed at the reception desk and the attempt by the hotel to rely on the exclusion clause was nothing less than a blatant attempt to incorporate new (and unfavourable) terms into the contract. The exclusion clause should have been prominently displayed at reception if the hotel wished it to form part of the contract with guests. The guests, on seeing such a notice, would have received adequate warning of the existence of the clause.

In **Spurling *v* Bradshaw [1956]**, the Court of Appeal did suggest that if the Olleys had been previous visitors to the hotel, the exclusion may well have been enforceable against them because it would have been possible to argue that they now had adequate notice of its existence. This suggestion has been criticised and, has indeed to a certain extent, been contradicted by the Court of Appeal's later decision in **Hollier v Rambler Motors [1972]** (the facts of which are discussed above) where a garage's attempt to rely on a exclusion clause against a customer who was private individual failed. It had been argued in **Hollier** by the garage that the exclusion clause had been successfully incorporated into the contract because the customer had used the garage on 3 or 4 occasions over a 5 year period.

Thornton, the Court of Appeal decided that the conditions releasing the company from certain liabilities on a ticket issued by an automatic barrier at the entrance to the car park were communicated too late. The contract was made in the following way: the ticket machine at the entrance to the car park was to be regarded as an offer to provide services to members of the general public. This offer was accepted when the pursuer drove his car to the ticket machine which issued him with a ticket and then the barrier rose and the pursuer was given access. The exclusion clause was on the back of the ticket, but this was too late because the physical act of driving up to the machine and taking the ticket implied acceptance of the offer. This had all happened before the pursuer had even read the conditions on the back of the ticket. In any case, most drivers would have regarded the ticket as a mere voucher and not an important contractual document. If the defender had wanted to incorporate the exclusion into the contract, it should have displayed a large notice at the front of the car park that clearly informed customers about the existence of the exclusion clause. This would have given drivers the opportunity to decide whether or not to enter into a contract with the car park owners.

Key point: As a general rule, new terms (including exclusion clauses) cannot be introduced by one party after the contract has been finalised.

5   A party may be prevented (personally barred) from claiming the protection of an exclusion clause where he has made a verbal promise that is in direct contradiction to the clause.

J Evans & Son (Portsmouth) Ltd v Andrea Merzario Ltd (1976) the parties had contracted with one another since 1959. In 1967, the defenders, who were forwarding agents, gave certain assurances to the pursuers that machines which had to be transported by ship would be carried below deck. This had been standard practice on the previous occasions when the pursuers had used the defenders' services. From 1967 there had been a change in the way that the contract was performed in that containers were used to transport the goods as opposed to storing them in crates. The standard conditions used by the defenders contained a condition that the goods could be stored on the deck of the ship. This was clearly inconsistent with the practice on board the ship and contrary to the promise given by the defenders to the pursuers. Some of the pursuer's machines (precision equipment) were carried on deck and were lost when the container in which they were stored went overboard during bad weather.

Held: the court found that the defenders' statement that the goods would be carried below deck was a term of the contract. This contractual term had been breached by the defenders' decision to store the goods on the deck.

The defenders' actions were in direct contradiction to the promise given to the pursuers and the standard practice that had been followed over many years. This verbal promise was part of the contract and any attempt by the defenders to rely on inconsistent exclusion clause had to fail.

 Key point: If the party relying on the exclusion makes a statement to the other party to the effect that the exclusion clause is not part of the contract, he will be prevented form enforcing the clause in his favour.

Judicial control of exclusion and limitation clauses

It should be obvious from the previous discussions that, from the 1970s onwards, potentially unfair terms have generally become subject to a range of statutory controls with the introduction of the Unfair Contract Terms Act 1977, the Unfair Terms in Consumers Contracts 1994 and 1999 and the Enterprise Act 2002. It would be misleading to suggest, however, that prior to more effective Parliamentary regulation in this area, there was a complete absence of control regarding the use (and abuse) of such clauses. Over many years, the Scottish courts, together with their English counterparts, had developed a number of mechanisms or rules of interpretation that sought to control some of the blatant injustices and abuses that the use of unfair terms appeared to encourage. The two major control mechanisms or rules of interpretation developed by the courts are:

◆ The *contra proferentum* rule
◆ The doctrine of fundamental breach

It must be stressed, however, that the above control mechanisms are merely guidelines to assist the courts to determine whether such clauses are capable of being enforced. They are not rules of law.

The *contra proferentum* rule

This rule is based on a very simple principle. A party who wishes to rely upon potentially unfair term in a contract must be able to demonstrate that such a provision clearly and unequivocally allows him to escape or reduce his liability in respect of breaches of contract or acts of negligence committed by him (or by his servants or employees). If the wording of the clause creates confusion or ambiguity, this may be absolutely fatal to a party's attempt to escape or limit his liability. In situations, where a clause lacks sufficient clarity, the court will punish the party relying on it by refusing to enforce it.

 Smith *v* South Wales Switchgear; UBM Chrysler (Scotland) Ltd [1978], in a decision of the House of Lords, Lord Keith singled out for approval remarks made by Lord Justice Sellers in **Walters *v* Whessoe [1968]** that attempts to limit or exclude liability must use 'adequate or clear words' or such a contractual term 'could have no reasonable meaning or application unless so applied.' Lord Keith went on to say that when applying the contra proferentum rule:

'the matter is essentially one of the ascertaining the intention of the contracting parties from the language they have used, considered in the light of surrounding circumstances which must be taken to have been within their knowledge.'

An example of the *contra proferentum* rule in operation can be seen from the following case:

Houghton *v* Trafalgar Insurance Co Ltd [1954] This involved an attempt by an insurance company to escape its liability under an insurance policy. A car had been involved in a crash and its owner submitted a claim to the insurers. The insurance company discovered that, at the time of the accident, the car was carrying six people (the driver and five passengers). Strictly speaking, the car had a maximum seating capacity for a driver and four passengers at any one time. Armed with this information, the insurers argued that a term in the policy relieved them of any liability when the driver was carrying more than four passengers. The relevant clause stated that the insurers were entitled to exclude liability for damage:

'caused or arising whilst the car is conveying any load in excess of that for which it was constructed.'

The dispute, therefore, boiled down to the meaning of word 'load' in the above clause and whether it could be interpreted to cover the transport of passengers.

Held: by the English Court of Appeal that the word 'load' did not apply to passengers travelling in the car. Lord Justice Romer stated that he 'had not the least idea' what the word 'load' meant 'if applied to a private motor car'. The insurers had failed to use sufficiently clear and precise language when they drew up the policy and, unfortunately for them, they were liable to the assured.

Hopefully, it should now be obvious that attempts to construct overly elaborate clauses will often end in disaster for the party seeking to rely upon them.

The doctrine of fundamental breach and consumer contracts

The courts (in particular the English courts) have also developed the doctrine of fundamental breach as an aid to the interpretation of exclusion and limitation clauses. The doctrine is particularly useful where one of the parties has committed a material breach of contract. The party in breach will then attempt to rely upon a clause in the agreement in order to escape or limit his liability. The problem with this is that the material breach contract has effectively destroyed the whole agreement as originally concluded by the parties (including the exclusion or limitation clause). Following on from this, the innocent party will argue that enforcement of the clause would result in a grave injustice being suffered by him. Such a result would clearly be in direct contradiction to the original purpose of the contract. As we shall see, it is possible for these types of clauses to be enforced, but very precise words must be used. Clauses written in very general terms which attempt to exclude or limit liability for material breaches of contract will also certainly not be enforced by the courts. Clearly, the courts do not wish to encourage widespread use of terms that allow people to escape or limit their liability for what are extremely serious breaches of contract.

The decision of the House of Lords in **Pollock & Co *v* Macrae [1922]** encouraged a mistaken view (promoted especially by Lord Denning) that the courts would not enforce a clause allowing a party who had committed a material breach of contract to escape or limit his liability. The facts of **Pollock** are as follows:

The defenders were in the business of building and supplying marine engines. They entered into a contract to supply engines for use in the pursuer's fishing vessels. The defenders had included an exclusion clause in the contract which permitted them to defeat any claims by the pursuer if the engines did not meet the required standard of quality owing to defective materials and workmanship. The pursuer was supplied with engines that were so defective as to be entirely useless.

Held: by the House of Lords that the exclusion clause was so repugnant that it was in direct contradiction to the essence of the contract i.e. that the defenders were under a duty to manufacture and to supply working engines. In this case, the defenders had committed a material or fundamental breach of contract. Lord Dunedin did concede that it was possible for a party to exclude his liability for material breach. However, he went on to say that such conditions to be effective 'will be most clearly and unambiguously expressed.' Following a thorough examination of the exclusion clause, the House of Lords was of the opinion that it was not sufficient to exclude liability for a material breach of contract. The pursuer's claim for damages was allowed to proceed.

In the following two cases, the House of Lords decided that the defenders were able to exclude their liability for material breaches of contract because the clauses that they were relying upon happened to be clearly and unambiguously expressed.

 Photo Production Ltd *v* Securicor Transport Ltd (1980) the pursuer's premises were burned down when the night security guard provided by Securicor deliberately started a fire on the premises. Securicor had no reason to suspect that its employee would have behaved in such a fashion – the guard's actions could not have been predicted i.e. they were not reasonably foreseeable. Furthermore, the guard had come to Securicor with good references. Securicor had an exclusion clause in the contract which permitted it to escape liability for all deliberate acts and negligence which were not reasonably foreseeable. The House of Lords found that the terms of the contract were wide enough and sufficiently precise to exclude deliberate acts as well as negligence.

 Ailsa Craig Fishing Co Ltd *v* Malvern Fishing Co Ltd (1983) where the negligence of another Securicor employee caused two vessels in Aberdeen harbour to collide with another and one of the ships sank to the bottom of the harbour. One of the ships had slipped from its moorings and drifted off. The employee in question had left his post and gone off to join the New Year celebrations. The employee's actions, which led to the accident, were quite clearly a fundamental i.e. material breach of contract, but Securicor attempted to limit its liability to £1000.

Held: by the House of Lords that the clause had been drawn up in wide enough terms to include events such as this. Securicor was, therefore, able to limit its liability to £1000 by relying on the exclusion contract. The trial judge had awarded damages of £55,000, but this of course was overturned.

As we have seen, it will be consumers who benefit most from the provisions of the Unfair Contract Terms Act 1977 and the Unfair Terms in Consumer Contracts Regulations 1999. Attempts by businesses to exclude or limit their liability for fundamental breaches of contract in relation to consumer transactions will almost certainly fail.

Remedies for breach of contract and limitation of actions

By breach of contract, we mean that one of the parties has broken the agreement in some way. In other words, someone has failed to carry out their side of the bargain. The innocent party – the victim of the other party's breach – will then have to approach the courts and request a remedy. A remedy for breach of contract should hopefully be capable of putting the victim in the position that he would have been in had the breach not taken place.

 Key point: A breach of contract means that one of the parties has broken the agreement in some way.

Examples of breaches of contract would include a seller supplying goods which were not of satisfactory quality; a buyer wrongfully refusing to accept goods; the buyer failing to pay for goods on the agreed date for payment; or the seller failing to deliver goods on the agreed delivery date.

It should also be remembered that breaches of contract have different consequences. Some breaches will be regarded as material which means that they are so serious that they strike at the very heart of the agreement and completely destroy it. Other breaches will not be as serious and the consequences will be less severe. Late delivery of goods by the seller, for example, may or may not be a material breach of contract. The courts will look at the circumstances of the case and draw the appropriate conclusions. Having done so, the courts will then decide the most appropriate remedy to award to the pursuer. We can see an example of how the courts decide whether a breach is material or not in the following case:

 Simpson v London & North Western Rail Co (1876) the pursuer had entered into a contract of carriage with the defenders for the purpose of transporting product samples to an agricultural exhibition which was taking place at Newcastle. The pursuer expressly communicated his wishes to the defenders by writing on the packages containing the goods: 'Must be at Newcastle on Monday certain.' The defenders failed to deliver the goods to Newcastle in accordance with the pursuer's strict instructions and were, therefore, liable in damages for the potential loss of profits. The defenders were fully aware of the pursuer's special instructions and they had agreed to be bound by them when they accepted the goods for transport to Newcastle.

In the Scots law of contract, there are four possible remedies available to a party who has suffered a breach of contract. These are:

◆ Damages
◆ Specific implement
◆ Retention and lien
◆ Rescission

Key point: The main remedies for breach of contract are damages, specific implement, retention and lien and rescission.

Damages

Damages will usually be the most common type of remedy which an aggrieved party will seek. Generally, damages are awarded to compensate the pursuer for his loss and not to punish the defender. In situations where the pursuer has not suffered loss, for example, the seller fails to deliver goods on time but the buyer is able to purchase the goods elsewhere at no extra cost, the court will award nominal damages. Nominal damages is an award of a small sum of money, for example, £75, to reflect the view that the issue of loss or damages is of a purely technical nature.

Key point: In situations where one of the parties has not suffered a loss due to the other party's breach of contract, the courts will often award nominal damages i.e. a very small sum of money which emphasises that the breach is of a minor nature.

General and special damages

General damages are awarded to the pursuer when the loss he has suffered is a reasonably foreseeable and direct result of the defender's breach of contract. The amount of damages will ensure that the pursuer is placed in the position that he would have been had it not been for the defender's actions. General damages, therefore, compensate the pursuer for loss caused in the ordinary way of things.

Special damages, on the other hand, are awarded to the pursuer when the defender's breach of contract causes abnormal loss or loss which was not reasonably foreseeable. In these situations, the pursuer will have to take steps to inform the defender that there are special circumstances that would cause him to suffer losses far in excess of what might ordinarily be the case. If the pursuer fails to inform the defender about these special circumstances, there can be no award of special damages.

Victoria Laundry v Newman Industries (1949) the pursuers, a laundry, had ordered a new boiler for the purposes of taking on more business. The boiler was delivered some 20 weeks late – a clear breach of contract by the defenders. The defenders were perfectly aware that delivery of the new boiler was a matter of urgency because, at the time, there was an extremely high demand for laundry services. The pursuers had hoped to benefit from this demand by being able to use the new boiler. The loss of this business (£16 per week) was reasonably foreseeable in the ordinary course of things and the pursuers were awarded general damages on this basis. The pursuers, however, also claimed special damages for the loss of special government contracts which would have made them £262 per week. The pursuers lost their claim for special damages because from the defenders point of view, it was not reasonably foreseeable that their breach of contract would result in the loss of these special government contracts. The pursuers had never taken steps to warn the defenders that their breach of contract would cause them to suffer abnormal losses. The defenders were in complete ignorance of the existence of these special contracts and, therefore, were not in a position to predict fully the consequences of their breach of contract. The pursuers' loss in relation to the special contracts was simply too remote and not something that would have entered the defenders' consciousness.

Hadley v Baxendale (1854), which is discussed below, is another good example of the judicial approach to awards of general and special damages.

What can be claimed as damages?

When the pursuer raises a claim for damages, the compensation awarded will normally cover personal injuries, damage to property and financial losses suffered by him. It is only in exceptional circumstances, however, that damages will include an element for disappointment and mental distress experienced by the pursuer as a result of the defender's breach of contract.

In **Jarvis v Swans Tours Ltd (1973)** Swans promised Jarvis a 'Houseparty holiday in Switzerland'. All sorts of things were promised as part of the holiday package (good food, entertainment and companions) and the hotelier was said to speak English – this was untrue. During, the first week of the holiday there were 13 people at the hotel, but the during the second week Jarvis was left on his own. The food and entertainment were, however, seriously substandard.

Held: by the English Court of Appeal that the pursuer was entitled to an award of £125 in damages (the holiday had cost £63).

The Jarvis case is exceptional because, generally speaking, damages for disappointment, inconvenience or loss of enjoyment are not awarded. The nature of the contract was different from ordinary commercial contracts in that the pursuer's pleasure had been ruined and his expectations had not been met.

The issue of damages for disappointment, anxiety and vexation has been examined, once again, in a number of cases before the House of Lords. In **Johnson v Gore Wood & Co [2001]**, Lord Cooke of Thorndon stated the familiar rule that:

'Contract-breaking is treated as an incident of commercial life which players in the game are expected to meet with mental fortitude.'

However, this general rule may be ignored where the contract is concerned with or connected to the provision of pleasure, relaxation or peace of mind.

Farley v Skinner [2001] the pursuer had engaged the surveyor to investigate a property, Riverside House, situated in the Sussex village of Blackboys, which he was interested in purchasing. The property lay some 15 miles from Gatwick Airport and the pursuer was understandably concerned with potentially unacceptable levels of noise from aircraft flying over the property. The pursuer specifically asked the surveyor to investigate the possibility of unacceptable levels of noise pollution. He did not want to purchase a property on a flight-path. In that sense, the contract was, according to Lord Clyde, not an 'ordinary surveyor's contract'. The request for the report on aircraft noise was an additional requirement above and beyond what was usually asked of a surveyor. No doubt the surveyor could have charged an extra fee if he had bothered to spend the extra time researching the issue of aircraft noise. The surveyor informed the pursuer that the noise levels were not particularly bad. The pursuer proceeded to purchase the property which he considered to be a dream home to be used, primarily, for the purposes of relaxation. Unfortunately, the property was situated close to a navigation beacon where, during busy times at Gatwick Airport, aircraft would circle before they were permitted to land. Obviously, there were times when significant numbers of aircraft were circling the beacon. This fact completely ruined the character of the property and the pursuer's enjoyment of it. He could not raise an action against the Airport authorities because the Civil Aviation Act 1982 authorised these activities. The pursuer raised an action for damages against the surveyor for failing to alert him to the huge levels of noise generated by aircraft circling the navigation beacon.

Held: the House of Lords awarded damages of £10,000 to the pursuer in relation to disappointment and anxiety caused by the negligent report of a surveyor. Lord Clyde stated that:

'. . .*it is possible to approach the case as one of the exceptional kind in which the claim would be for damages for disappointment. If that approach was adopted so as to seek damages for disappointment, I consider that it should also succeed.*'

It was the specific provision in relation to the peacefulness of the property in respect of aircraft noise which made this an exceptional case.

 Key point: Generally, damages for disappointment, inconvenience or loss of enjoyment are not awarded to the victim of a breach of contract.

The calculation of damages

The courts use two tests when comes it to calculating the amount of damages that the aggrieved party will receive. These tests are remoteness of damage and minimisation of loss.

Remoteness of damage

The effects of a breach of contract may be far ranging but, as a matter of public policy, the courts must draw a line and say that the damages incurred beyond a certain limit are too remote to be recovered. The proximate cause of the loss will, therefore, be uppermost in the minds of the judges.

Remoteness of damage means that damages in a contract will not be recovered by the pursuer unless they are proved to be a direct and natural consequence of the defender's breach i.e. the losses caused to the pursuer occurred because of the defender's actions. If the losses have not occurred directly owing to the defender's fault, then it is likely that the defender, as a reasonable man, did not realise that such an outcome was likely to occur. Damage which does not arise naturally and which is not in the contemplation of a reasonable man can only be recovered if the defender was made aware of it and agreed to accept the risk of the loss.

We can see how this test operates in the following case:

 Hadley *v* Baxendale (1854) the pursuer owned a flour mill. The crank shaft of the pursuer's mill had been broken and was completely useless. The pursuer had asked a manufacturer in Greenwich to make him a new piece of machinery. The broken shaft had to be taken Greenwich so that it could be examined by the manufacturer in order to make the new piece of machinery. The pursuer hired the defender, a carrier, to take the shaft to Greenwich. The delivery of the machinery to the manufacturer was subject to unreasonable delay caused by the negligence of the carrier. This meant that operations at the flour mill literally ground to a halt and the pursuer began to suffer financial losses. The pursuer raised an action against the carrier for the loss of profits during the unexpected period of delay.

Held: the pursuer's claim for damages for loss of profits for the entire period that his mill was forced to stop operating was dismissed. The pursuer had failed to notify the carrier that he did not possess a spare crank shaft and that he was utterly dependent on the new piece of machinery being manufactured and dispatched to him as quickly as possible. The carrier was entitled to assume that most mill operators would have had a spare crank shaft for just such emergencies. There was no explanation by the pursuer of his predicament. Clearly, the carrier had committed a breach of contract because he would know that his failure to deliver the crank shaft to the manufacturers would cause the pursuer some inconvenience i.e. the mill would have been prevented from operating until a spare crank shaft was fitted – even if this was for a short period only. Unfortunately, as we have seen, the pursuer did not have a substitute item of machinery, but how was the defender to know this when the pursuer failed to inform him?

Mitigation of loss

The injured party has a duty to mitigate or to minimise his loss i.e. he must take all reasonable steps to cut his losses. Thus, a seller whose goods are rejected must attempt to get the best price for them elsewhere and the buyer of the goods which are not delivered must attempt to buy as cheaply as possible elsewhere. Should the parties in both these situations fail to cut their losses, they cannot rely upon the courts to award them full damages in respect of their losses. However, a pursuer only has to show the courts that he has taken reasonable steps to cut his losses. Superhuman efforts on the part of the pursuer are unnecessary.

 Gunter & Co v Lauritzen (1894) the pursuer had entered into a contract to purchase a consignment of hay. The pursuer intended to sell these goods at a profit. However, this was not possible because the defender delivered goods which did not meet the requirements of the contract and the pursuer rightfully rejected them. The pursuer then raised an action for damages against the defender. The defender claimed that the pursuer had failed to mitigate its losses. The defender stated that it had been possible for the pursuer to obtain substitute goods and this the pursuer had failed to do. The pursuer in turn pointed out that this would have meant approaching three different sellers from different parts of Scotland and negotiating with each of them in turn for the sale of the goods. The original contract was to have been performed in Aberdeen.

Held: it would have been completely unreasonable to force the pursuer to negotiate the sale of three separate consignments of goods from three different sellers throughout Scotland. The pursuer was awarded the damages for loss of profit.

Key point: When it comes to the calculation of damages, the innocent party must show that he has taken reasonable steps to reduce (mitigate) his losses and that the losses suffered are not too remote.

Liquidated damages or penalty clauses

The parties to an agreement may actually be far-sighted enough to insert a remedy into their contract which addresses the issue of the amount of damages payable should one of them break the contract. These damages are known as liquidated damages and sometimes such a clause is known as a penalty clause. The phrase penalty clause can be misleading because the courts will not enforce the provision for liquidated damages if the amount is not a genuine pre-estimate of loss. The courts, in other words, will not allow one party to punish the other – even if one of the parties is in breach. The courts will then award damages in the usual way i.e. by applying the tests of remoteness of damage and mitigation of loss.

Hugely extravagant sums in penalty clauses will usually invite judicial suspicion and may be not be enforceable. Very often, damages can be accurately assessed and the party hoping to take advantage of the extravagant penalty clause will be left exposed. If the sum provided for in the contract is payable on the occurrence of any one of several events, it is probably a penalty for it is highly unlikely that each event can produce the same level of losses. Penalty clauses will not be enforced by the courts in the pursuer's favour if the breach of contract was the pursuer's fault.

 One of the leading cases illustrating the approach of the Scottish courts to the enforcement of penalty clauses is **Clydebank Engineering & Shipbuilding Co v Yzquierdo y Castaneda (1904)**. The House of Lords was asked to determine whether a clause in a contract fixing damages at £500 per week for every week of late delivery of 4 torpedo boats was a penalty or if the sum was liquidate damages capable of enforcement.

The contract involved the construction of four torpedo boats for the Spanish navy. The Scottish shipyard was unable to complete the vessels in accordance with the completion date set down by the contract. In the interim, the Spanish-American War had occurred in which Spanish forces were decisively defeated on land and at sea. Especially galling for the Spaniards was the loss of the Island of Cuba (the richest province in its Empire) and the Philippine Islands. The Spanish Government alleged that the Scottish shipbuilders' failure to perform their obligations, as demanded by the contract, had contributed directly to the huge losses suffered by Spanish forces at the hands of the Americans during hostilities in the Cuban theatre of operations (the entire Spanish fleet had been sunk off Cuba). The Spaniards argued that they would not have lost the War had the shipyard delivered the four torpedo boats on the due date in accordance with the terms of the contract. The Spaniards sued for £75,000 to which they claimed that they were entitled in terms of the penalty clause. The shipyard argued that this was not a genuine pre-estimate of loss and that compensation should be calculated according to the ordinary rules of damages i.e. minimisation of loss and remoteness of loss.

Held: by the House of Lords that the Spaniards' demand for £75,000 did not represent a genuine pre-estimate of loss and that this sum should be instead regarded as liquidate damages. Clearly, no one could have calculated the extent of the losses suffered by the Spaniards before the war and, therefore, it would have been impossible to make a genuine pre-estimate of loss. However, the shipyard had committed a breach of contract and would, therefore, have to pay compensation. The House of Lords set a figure of £67,000 as the compensation payable to the Spanish government.

The Scottish courts will enforce penalty clauses if the party relying on it can prove that the clause is a genuine pre-estimate of loss as can be seen in the following case:

 Cameron-Head *v* Cameron & Co (1919) in April 1919, the pursuer, the owner of the Inverailort estate in Inverness-shire, brought a claim against the defenders who were timber merchants. The contract involved the sale of a forest which was to be cut down and the timber removed by the defenders. Failure by the defenders to perform their part of the contract by 1 April 1918 would result in them being liable to pay a daily penalty of 10 shillings for as long as they were in breach of contract. By the following April of 1919, the defenders had not yet managed to cut down all of the forest and clear the timber away. The claim brought by the pursuer was, therefore, for one year's penalty at the daily rate of 10 shillings.

Held: by the Court of Session that the penalty accrued on a daily basis from 1 April 1918 onwards and that the pursuer could bring an action to claim this at any time, despite the fact that full contractual performance by the defenders had not yet been achieved. Upon examination of the daily sum of 10 shillings, it was decided that this was a genuine pre-estimate of loss. The pursuer had not dreamt up this figure and it accurately reflected her losses on a day-to-day basis.

Reforming the law on penalty clauses

In 1999, the Scottish Law Commission published a Report on Penalty Clauses (**Scot Law Com No 171**). The main reform to this area of law proposed by the Commission is that a judge should be permitted to modify an excessively high penalty clause in order to make it enforceable. Currently, if the penalty clause is not a genuine pre-estimate of loss, a judge will have no option but to assess compensation in accordance with the ordinary rules of damages. The current test, centring on the concept of a genuine pre-estimate of loss, should be replaced. The proposed reforms would allow a judge to enforce a clause which was 'not manifestly excessive' even if the sum claimed is not a genuine pre-estimate of loss. The burden of proof will be on the party against whom the clause is being enforced to demonstrate that the clause is 'manifestly excessive'. Whether or not a clause is 'manifestly excessive' should be the new test applied to penalty clauses.

Specific implement (or a decree *ad factum praestandum*)

This is a very limited remedy in the sense that it will only be granted to the pursuer if the court thinks that it is appropriate. Basically, the pursuer is asking the court to make an order (a decree) which will force the defender to carry out his contractual obligations. In a small claims action in the Sheriff Court, for example, a pursuer could ask the court to force a builder who has only half-completed a patio to finish the job.

A recent example of the remedy of specific implement being granted to a pursuer by the Scottish courts can be seen in the following example:

John Anderson *v* Pringle of Scotland (1998) the employer attempted to ignore parts of its redundancy policy which formed part of a collective agreement that had been incorporated into the employees' contracts. One of the employees raised an action for specific implement in order to force the employer to obey the terms of its own redundancy policy.

Held: by the Court of Session that the employer must follow the provisions of its redundancy policy. This was something of a hollow victory for the employee because, subsequently, he was made redundant by the employer who used the proper redundancy procedures this time.

The remedy of specific implement will not be appropriate in the following circumstances:

◆ Where the court is of the opinion that an award of damages is a more than adequate remedy.

◆ Where the defender owes the pursuer money, the court will not grant specific implement because the appropriate action on the pursuer's part is to sue for damages. On a technical point, a decree of specific implement is a court order and failure to comply with it would mean that the defender was in contempt of court. This means that the defender would face imprisonment, but being sent to prison for a civil debt is no longer available to the courts in Scotland.

◆ Where the pursuer can obtain goods or services from a variety of alternative sources and there is no great inconvenience caused. If the pursuer had to pay a greater price than the contract price for these goods and services, he could sue the defender in damages for the difference. It is only where the goods or services have some unique value that the courts will grant an order for specific implement.

◆ Where the grant of an order would cause injustice or harm to someone.

◆ Where the contract in question involves a high degree of personal contact, for example, an employer cannot be compelled by an Employment Tribunal to reinstate or re-engage an employee that has been dismissed. Even if the employee wins his unfair dismissal claim and the Employment Tribunal grants a Reinstatement Order, the employer cannot be forced to take him back.

◆ Where the defender is outwith the jurisdiction of the Scottish courts.

◆ Where the granting of an order would, in effect, be ordering the defender to do something which was impossible to carry out.

 Key point: Specific implement is an order from the court that forces the party in breach of contract to carry out his duties under the agreement, but it is not always an appropriate remedy and, therefore, the courts will not always grant it.

Retention and lien

The right of retention (or lien as it is known as in England) allows an innocent party to suspend his contractual duties as a result of a breach of contract by the other party to the agreement. This does not mean that the innocent party is freed from his contractual duties. Retention simply allows the innocent party to retain property, goods or money that belong to the contract-breaker until such time as the other party carries out his side of the agreement. However, it should be noted that the innocent party can only use this remedy in relation to property, goods or money of the contract-breaker that he rightfully possesses at the time of the breach. A solicitor, for example, could refuse to hand over documents that she holds for a client until the client pays her legal bill. A hotel can also exercise its right of retention by refusing to release a guest's luggage until the guest pays his hotel bill.

The innocent party is under a duty of care to the contract-breaker, however, to ensure that any property, goods or money which is subject to the right of retention is properly safeguarded. The right of retention is a very useful remedy because it is likely that the contract-breaker will need to use his property, sell the goods on to a third party or have need of the money to meet all sorts of bills. To say that the innocent exercising his right of retention will cause the contract-breaker all sorts of inconvenience is something of an understatement. There is a very real incentive for the contract-breaker to carry out his side of the bargain.

 Haig-Boswell *v* Preston (1915) a tenant refused to pay rent to his landlord until such time as the landlord completed repairs to the tenant's roof which was letting in substantial quantities of rainwater. It was the duty of the landlord to ensure that the tenant had a suitable property which was windproof and watertight. Clearly, the landlord was in breach of contract and the tenant decided to suspend his duty to pay rent on a temporary basis until the repairs were carried out.
Held: the tenant was entitled to take this action against the landlord.

 Key point: Where one party is in breach of the agency contract, the innocent party is entitled to exercise his right of lien which allows him to retain possession of property or money that he holds in trust for the party in breach.

Rescission

This remedy will be sought by the pursuer when the defender has committed a material breach of contract. A material breach of contract is such a serious breach that it goes to the very roots of the agreement and completely undermines the contract. The practical effect of rescission is that the pursuer wishes the court to cancel the contract.

Minor breaches of contract will rarely allow the pursuer to cancel the contract and very often the court will grant damages to the pursuer as an alternative. The parties to a contract could state, however, that certain breaches of the agreement will be regarded as material and this will allow the innocent party to apply to the courts for rescission.

 Shaw, Macfarlane & Co. *v* Waddell & Sons (1890) the buyers were supposed to send a ship to pick up a cargo of coal during the period 12 to 16 April. Unfortunately, due to the fault of the buyers, the ship was delayed and could not uplift the cargo on the dates specified. In fact, there was a delay of almost eleven days. The sellers were caused great inconvenience by this delay caused by the buyers that they decided to cancel the contract.
Held: the sellers were entitled to cancel the agreement because the time

for loading the ship was a material term of the contract and the buyers had committed a material breach by failing to load the cargo between 12 and 16 April.

According to Section 15B(2)(a) of the Sale of Goods Act 1979, in a consumer contract, any breach by the seller of an express or implied term as to the quality of the goods or their fitness for purpose, for example, shall be regarded as a material breach. Consequently, Section 15B(1)(b) of the 1979 Act allows the buyer to reject any goods delivered under the contract and to treat the contract as cancelled (or repudiated).

 Key point: The remedy of rescission allows the innocent party to have the contract cancelled where the breach committed by the other party amounts to a material breach of contract.

Termination of contract

Obviously, contracts and the rights and duties established by them do not exist forever. With this thought in mind it is now time to examine the various ways in which a contract is discharged or terminated.

Performance and payment

Most contracts will come to an end simply by the parties performing their duties under the agreement, for example, a supplier of goods will deliver the goods conforming to the contract to the buyer and the buyer will, in turn, make payment to the seller for this property.

Acceptilation and discharge

An individual will effectively waive or give up his rights under the agreement which means that the other party is released from his contractual duties. One party could choose to inform the other party that payment of his debt of £10,000 is no longer required.

Delegation

An individual agrees that the other party can be released from his contractual duties and be replaced by another party. All the parties to the agreement must consent to this new arrangement. This type of arrangement is very common where the original debtor is released from his obligation to pay a debt to a lender or creditor because a new debtor has agreed to take responsibility for payment of the debt. The benefit of this kind of arrangement from the creditor or lender's point of view is that he is far more likely to see the debt repaid than if he insisted on payment by the original debtor.

Novation

A new agreement is formed with the mutual consent of the parties and this new contract replaces any previous agreement that the parties may have had.

Compensation

This allows one of the parties to a contract to make a counter-claim against the other party which has the effect of reducing his overall liability. If, for example, A owes B £10,000 and B lodges a counter-claim against A for £8000, B's overall liability will be reduced to £2000 (assuming that his counter-claim is valid). This is often a very common situation in wrongful dismissal claims where an employee sues the employer for compensation in respect of breach of contract, the employer can launch a counter-claim for compensation. If the employee is found liable to the employer in terms of the counter-claim, he may find that his compensation for wrongful dismissal is reduced dramatically.

Confusion

This situation arises when someone owes to a debt to himself. This seems a rather ridiculous situation, but it could easily arise. If, for example, a person had borrowed £10,000 from her mother and her mother later died making the daughter beneficiary of her estate, the daughter would inherit the debt of £10,000 owed by herself to her mother. Clearly, any court action raised by the daughter to sue herself for £10,000 is would result in a farcical situation. The daughter's debt is now cleared.

Material breach of contract

A material breach it will be remembered is an extremely serious breach of contract which leaves the aggrieved party with the option of using the remedy of rescission. Rescission effectively allows the aggrieved party to cancel the contract. If the contract is cancelled, all rights and duties under the original agreement are wiped out.

Lapse of time – prescription

The Prescription and Limitation (Scotland) Act 1973 has the effect of ensuring that contractual rights and duties must be exercised within certain periods of time. Failure to enforce rights or duties by the parties to the agreement within these periods has the effect of terminating the agreement. If someone owes you a debt and you do not take legal action to enforce the debtor's obligation within five years, you will lose your rights to any money owed. If a pursuer does not bring a legal action against the defender within a time laid down by the Prescription and Limitation (Scotland) Act 1973, he may find that his claim is time-barred i.e. he has had enough time to raise an action and he has failed to do so.

 Key point: Contracts do not last forever and can be terminated in a variety of ways. In the vast majority of situations, a contract will come to an end when the parties perform their obligations under the agreement.

Impossibility, frustration and illegality

Since the formation of the contract, the circumstances surrounding the agreement may have changed dramatically. The contract may now be impossible to perform or the contract may have been rendered illegal by changes in the law.

Physical destruction of the subject-matter of the contract operates to frustrate the agreement.

Taylor *v* Caldwell (1863) the Surrey Gardens and Music Hall was hired by the pursuers from the defenders for the purpose of holding four grand concerts and fêtes. Before the first concert on 17 June 1862 could took place, the hall was completely destroyed by fire. Neither party was responsible for this incident. The pursuers, however, brought an action for damages against the defenders for wasted advertising costs.

Held: By the English High Court that it was clearly impossible for the contract to be performed because it relied on the continuing existence of the venue. The pursuers claim for damages was dismissed on the grounds that the purpose of the contract had been frustrated.

 Vitol SA *v* Esso Australia 1988 a contract for the sale of petroleum was discharged on the grounds of frustration when both the ship and its cargo of petroleum were completely destroyed in a missile attack in the Persian Gulf during the Iran-Iraq War of the 1980s. The sellers had attempted to sue the buyers for the price of the goods, but this claim was dismissed.

 Key point: If the subject matter of the contract is destroyed, the contract will be considered to have been frustrated.

Does the cancellation of an event result in frustration of contract?

In **Krell *v* Henry [1903]**, Lord Justice Vaughn-Williams was of the opinion that frustration of contract was not limited to either the destruction or non-existence of the subject matter of the contract. It will be important to identify the substance or the purpose of the agreement. The cancellation of an event can frustrate the performance of a contract where that event is an absolutely material term of the agreement.

 Krell *v* Henry [1903] the pursuer was the owner of a flat in the central London district of Pall Mall. The pursuer's flat was on the route of the proposed coronation procession of the new King, Edward VII, which was scheduled to take place on 26 and 27 June 1902. The pursuer had advertised his flat for rent during the daytime on 26 and 27 June for the purpose of viewing the procession. The defender, who was anxious to view the procession, responded to the advertisement and entered into an agreement to hire the flat on the days specified. An announcement was made on 24 June stating that the procession was to be cancelled owing to the King's illness. The defender refused to pay the balance of the rent for the flat by reason that events had frustrated performance of the contract. The pursuer brought an action against the defender for payment of the balance of the rent.

Held: by the English Court of Appeal that the cancellation of the event frustrated the contract and discharged the parties from their obligations under it. The clinching argument in the defender's favour was that both parties clearly entered into the contract with the same intention. The reason behind the hire of the flat was, therefore, a material term of the contract. Had the defender failed to communicate his motivation for hiring the flat, then the contract would have remained capable of enforcement by the pursuer. Lord Justice Vaughn-Williams was of the opinion that frustration of contract was not limited to either the destruction or non-existence of the subject matter of the contract. It was also important to identify the substance or the purpose of the agreement. In other words, did the parties share the same intentions?

The illness of King Edward resulted in a second legal action. This time, however, the English Court of Appeal took a completely different approach to the issue of frustration of contract.

The decision in **Krell v Henry** can be contrasted with the decision below:

 Herne Bay Steamboat Co v Hutton [1903] the pursuers had entered into a contract to hire a steamship to the defender for two days. The Royal Navy was assembling at Spithead to take part in a naval review to celebrate King Edward's coronation. The King was to review the fleet personally. The defender wished to transport paying guests from Herne Bay to Spithead to see the naval review. Due to the King's illness, an official announcement was made cancelling the review. It would still have been perfectly possible for the defender to take his passengers on a cruise to see the assembled fleet. The defender, however, refused to use the vessel claiming that the contract had been frustrated. The pursuers brought an action against the defender for the balance of the fee of £250 owed by the defender who was refusing to pay for the hire of the boat.

Held: the contract was not discharged by reason of frustration. The main purpose of the contract could still be achieved i.e. to take paying guests for a cruise around the fleet.

The difference in approach taken by the Court of Appeal in both cases is sometimes difficult to understand. In **Krell v Henry**, both parties had clearly intended that the purpose of the contract was to view the procession. Reinforcing this fact, was the fact that the defender was only entitled to use the flat during the daytime. In **Herne Bay Steamboat Co v Hutton**, the purpose of the defender in hiring the steamship was to see the naval review, but this was not the purpose of the owners who were not the slightest bit interested why the vessel had been hired. Lord Justice Vaughn-Williams compared the situation to someone who hires a carriage to go and see the Epsom Derby, but the outbreak of some unforeseen epidemic means that the races are cancelled. This makes no difference to the owner of the carriage who will still expect to be paid for the hire of his vehicle.

 Key point: Cancellation of an event may mean that the contract could be regarded as frustrated, but it will be important to examine the terms of the agreement.

Frustration can only be used to have the contract discharged in situations where neither party is to blame. When one party is to blame for the failure to perform his obligations under the agreement, this represents a breach of contract and the innocent party can raise the appropriate action.

 Tsakiroglou v Noblee Thorl GmbH [1961] the sellers had agreed to transport Sudanese ground nuts from Port Sudan in the Red Sea to Hamburg in Germany. The ship was to take the fastest route to Europe through the Suez Canal. This proved to be impossible because the Canal was closed as a result of military hostilities following the Anglo-French-Israeli invasion of Egypt causing the Suez Crisis in late 1956. The sellers would have to ship the goods around the alternative route of the Cape of Good Hope in South Africa. This meant that the distance the ship had to travel from Port Sudan to Hamburg was greatly increased and this would also mean a dramatic increase in the costs of carriage in respect of the goods.

Held: by the House of Lords that a party will still have a duty to perform a contract even if this means that performance is more difficult or expensive than was originally intended by the parties. The closure of the Suez Canal did not mean that the sellers' duties were discharged by reason of frustration of contract.

 Key point: Merely because the contract becomes more difficult or more expensive to perform does not mean that the contract is to be regarded as frustrated.

Contracts for personal services

Such a contract is discharged by the death of the person who was to perform it. The incapacity of a person who is to perform a contract may discharge it. However, temporary incapacity is not enough unless it affects the performance of the contract in a really serious way. If an employee is killed or permanently incapacitated, it will be very difficult to argue that the employment contract should be allowed to continue.

The purpose of the contract becomes impossible to perform

As we have seen, a situation involving the physical destruction of the subject-matter of the contract will discharge the parties from performance of their duties by reason of frustration. However, frustration can also occur in situations where physical destruction of the subject-matter of the contract may not be the issue.

 In **Jackson v Union Marine Insurance Co (1874)** the pursuer owned a ship which had been chartered to go with all possible speed from Liverpool to Newport for the purpose of loading a cargo bound for San Francisco. The pursuer had insurance with the defenders to protect himself in the event that the charter might be prevented from being carried out. The vessel was stranded whilst on its way to Newport. It was not refloated for over a month and could not be properly repaired for some time. The charterers hired another ship and the pursuer turned to the insurers. They suggested that the pursuer should sue the charterer for breach.

Held: the fact that the ship was stranded effectively frustrated the agreement's commercial purpose and, therefore, the charterers were free to go elsewhere. The pursuer had no remedy against the charterers and was in turn entitled to seek compensation under the insurance policy.

 Key point: A contract may be impossible to perform or its essential commercial aim becomes impossible to achieve and, therefore, it has to be regarded as discharged due to frustration.

Illegality

 Stevenson & Sons Ltd *v* AG für Cartonnagen Industrie (1918) an English company, Stevenson, was in partnership with a German company acting as a sole agent to sell the German company's goods. By continuing to carry on business with an enemy during wartime, Stevenson would be committing a criminal act and there was no alternative but to have the partnership dissolved. (See also **Cantiere San Rocco SA *v* Clyde Shipbuilding & Engineering Co Ltd (1923)**.)

In other situations, contracts can become illegal because Parliament introduces legislation to this effect. After the murder of schoolchildren and a teacher at Dunblane Primary School in 1996 by Thomas Hamilton, the British government made it illegal to own particular models of firearms. Therefore, anyone who entered a contract to purchase firearms shortly before the legislation was introduced could not force the supplier to perform the contract. If the buyer insisted on performance of the contract by the seller, the seller would be complying with his contractual duty, but he would also be breaking the law as the contract would be illegal.

 Key point: If a contract later becomes illegal, it will be regarded as void and the parties will not be able to enforce it.

Termination of the contract as a result of breach

Breach of contract can arise in a number of situations:

- Failure to perform the contract
- Express repudiation of the contract
- Unsatisfactory performance of the contract

It is worth re-emphasising at this stage that a breach of contract does not automatically give the innocent party the right to terminate the agreement. The seriousness of the breach will largely determine this question. The only remedy available to the innocent party may be to raise an action for damages. The innocent party may find this rather galling, but a failure by him to perform his duties in response to an earlier breach by the other party will mean that he is now in breach of contract.

Anticipatory breach

This situation will arise when one party gives advance warning (either by express communication or by his behaviour) that he has decided not to comply with his duties under the contract when performance is due. This means that the breach of contract will be anticipated by the innocent party and will, therefore, be far less of a shock. The innocent party has one of two possible courses of action open to him: he is entitled to raise an action for damages immediately therefore anticipating the breach or he may choose to wait and see what the other party will actually do when the time for performance actually arrives. Clearly, which of the two options is chosen may be influenced by personal circumstances. The concept of anticipatory breach where it involves the defender expressly communicating his intention to repudiate or cancel the contract has been criticised as illogical. After all, this individual could change his mind regarding his refusal to perform the contract. Furthermore, the innocent party can still insist on performing his obligations even in the face of overwhelming evidence that the other person has no intention of performing his side of the agreement.

In **White and Carter (Councils) Ltd *v* McGregor [1961]**, a decision of the House of Lords discussed below, Lord Reid used the example of someone who has been commissioned to go to Hong Kong for the purpose of compiling a report. This individual has agreed to pay his own expenses, but he expects to be paid £10,000 in exchange for the report when he returns to the United Kingdom. Prior to his departure to Hong Kong, the person is given notice that his report is no longer required. Owing to the concept of anticipatory breach, this individual would be entitled to go Hong Kong and compile the report (even when it is clearly no longer required). There is something highly illogical and unsatisfactory about this result. Lord Hodson drew attention to the fact that an anticipatory breach does not mean that the contract should be regarded as automatically terminated. He went on to state that either the innocent party can sue for damages immediately (as a consequence of the anticipatory breach) or he can await performance of the other party's duties. When it becomes clear that the other party will not perform his duties, the innocent party can then take action and this delay will not be regarded as fatal to his claim. In **White**, the House of Lords appeared to place limits on the concept of anticipatory breach. These limits were best summed up by Lord Reid's remarks:

'It may well be that if it can be shown that a person has no legitimate interest, financial or otherwise, in performing the contract rather than claiming damages, he ought not to be allowed to saddle the other party with an additional burden with no benefit to himself.'

This statement would appear to suggest that an innocent party may have no option but to raise a claim for damages when the other party has indicated that he has no real intention of performing his obligations.

An important point worth noting is that when an anticipatory breach of contract occurs, the innocent party will only have the right to treat the agreement as terminated when the breach is material in nature.

Title to sue

 Carmichael *v* Carmichael's Executrix 1920 SC (HL) 195 Mr Carmichael, the pursuer, had taken out a life insurance policy in relation to his son, Ian, who was 9 years old. It was a condition of the policy that, until such time as Ian reached adulthood, Carmichael was entitled to the surrender value of the policy. Furthermore, if Ian died before becoming an adult, the insurers would have to repay the premiums paid under the policy to his father. Assuming, however, that Ian actually survived to become an adult, he would be entitled to the benefits of the policy if he or his representatives continued to pay the premiums. If Ian died, the sum assured should be paid to the executors of his estate. There were also a number of other options that Ian was entitled to take advantage in relation to the policy. Ian did reach adulthood, but unfortunately, he died before the next premium became due for payment. A dispute arose concerning Ian's will. He had left his estate to his aunt, Miss McColl, and she claimed that she was entitled to the proceeds of the insurance policy.

Held: by the House of Lords that Ian had known of the existence of the insurance policy. His father had not delivered the policy to him or communicated the fact that the policy was held in his name. However, the situation clearly demonstrated that Carmichael senior had fully intended his son to have rights in relation to the contract of insurance. In this respect, Ian had acquired a *jus quaesitum* under the contract of insurance and, therefore, Miss McColl, being the beneficiary of Ian's estate, was entitled to assert her rights to the proceeds payable under the policy.

 Hochster *v* De la Tour (1853) the defender agreed to engage the pursuer as a courier for European travel, his duties to commence two months later. Three weeks before the pursuer was due to begin the job, the defender wrote to him stating that his services were no longer required. The pursuer commenced an action for breach of contract a week before his starting date and the defence claimed that there was no cause of action until the date due for performance.

Held: the defender's express repudiation enabled the innocent party to raise a claim for breach of contract before the date for the performance of the contract.

 White and Carter (Councils) Ltd *v* McGregor (1961) the respondent had entered into a contract for advertising services. However, the respondent quickly repudiated the contract, writing to the appellants asking them to cancel the contract and, at this stage, the appellants had not carried out any work. The appellants, however, refused to cancel the agreement and prepared the advertisements. The advertisements were publicly displayed several months later. These adverts were continually displayed for the next three years. Eventually, the appellants demanded payment, the respondents refused to pay. The appellants sued for sums owed under the contract.

Held: by the House of Lords that the appellants were entitled to recover the contract price. Even though the respondents had repudiated the contract, the appellants were not bound to accept this. The contract survived and the appellants had completed it. There was no duty to minimise loss until there was a breach which the appellants had accepted and they had not accepted this one. This decision has been criticised because it appears to allow the innocent party to continue to perform the contract when it is quite clear that the other side has no intention of performing their contractual duties.

More recently, the Inner House of the Court of Session re-examined the right of the innocent party to treat the contract as discharged or repudiated by reason of the other party's breach of the agreement.

 Macari *v* Celtic Football and Athletic Company Ltd (1999) Macari, the pursuer, had been appointed as the manager of Celtic Football Club. There was an express term in his employment contract to the effect that Macari would have to reside within a 45-mile radius of George Square in Glasgow. Furthermore, it was expected that Macari would attend regularly at Celtic Park and provide the Chief Executive with weekly reports on the progress of the Celtic team. When Macari accepted the appointment he was currently living in England and his contract envisaged that he would move to Glasgow with his family by Easter 1994. By June 1994, Macari had still not moved to Glasgow and, on 10 June, Celtic's Chief Executive ordered him to comply with his contract and move to Glasgow. Macari responded by sending an undated fax to the Chief Executive in which he stated that he had no intention of complying with this part of his contract at the present time owing to personal circumstances. Together with a subsequent telephone conversation with the Chief Executive, Macari made it quite clear that he was opposing his employer's lawful authority and he was perfectly aware that he was flouting his employer's instructions in respect of the residency requirement, regular attendance at Celtic Park and his duty to provide weekly reports. In response to Macari's refusal to abide by the terms of the contract, Celtic dismissed him from his employment. Macari claimed that he had been wrongfully dismissed in that he had not been given the proper notice period by Celtic in accordance with the terms of his contract.

Held: in June 1994, the pursuer was in material breach of contract by reason of his failure to comply with the residence clause, by reason of his failure to comply with the instruction to attend more regularly at Celtic Park and by reason of his failure to comply with his undertaking to report to the Chief Executive on a weekly basis. Quite simply, the pursuer's behaviour indicated that he was repudiating his contract with Celtic and, as a result, his employer was entitled to treat the contract as discharged. The pursuer was, therefore, not entitled to treat himself as having been wrongfully dismissed and he was not entitled to receive a compensation payment.

 Key point: Discharge of a contract owing to a breach by one of the parties can occur where the party in breach fails to perform it lawfully by breaking one or more terms of the contract or by expressly repudiating the agreement or by making it impossible to perform.

Summary

- A contract is a legally enforceable agreement, which consists of an offer and an acceptance.

- Without both an offer and an acceptance, a contract is not formed.

- Before the contract is formed, both the offer and acceptance must reach *consensus in idem*.

- A contract is formed by a definite offer and an unqualified acceptance, thus achieving *consensus in idem* or a legally enforceable agreement.

- If a counter-offer is made, it cancels out the original offer, which is then no longer capable of acceptance.

- Offers and acceptances can be either express or implied.

- A clear distinction must be identified in the contrast between an offer and an invitation to treat.

- An offer is capable of acceptance and therefore able to form a contract, whereas an invitation to treat cannot be accepted and is merely an indication of a willingness to negotiate.

- Communication of offers, acceptances and revocations are also particularly important and can be crucial to whether or not a contract is actually formed

- Contracts can be invalidated in a variety of ways: substantial error, lack of capacity, lack of formality, misrepresentation, error, facility and circumvention, force and fear and illegality.

- The parties can attempt to exclude or limit their liability under the contract but the Unfair Contract Terms Act 1977 and the Unfair Terms in Consumer Contracts Regulations 1999 will often determine how successful these attempts are.

- Contractual obligations do not last forever; all contracts come to an end sooner or later.

Test your knowledge

Short answer questions, examination standard essay questions and case studies.

1 'A contract is an agreement, but not every agreement is a contract.'
Explain this statement.

2 Examine the advertisement below:

The latest innovation from Wylie & Crossan
Beauty Products

Ladies!

What is your trouble? Is it unseemly facial wrinkles? Do you despair about your rapidly ageing looks? Fear not! Help is at hand.

In no time at all, not a wrinkle in sight and that's a promise!

Thanks to our new, revolutionary facial gel, Plastere de Paris, wrinkles can be a thing of the past. All you have to do is apply the cream regularly each day.

Many of our clients who have already used this epoch-breaking product have been truly amazed by its qualities.

Catriona Campbell of Tobermory, Isle of Mull (aged 29) says: 'Plastere de Paris has completely changed my life. Thanks to Wylie & Crossan Beauty Products I now feel that I can face the day with renewed confidence. I no longer feel that I have to wear a head scarf and dark glasses when I'm out tending the sheep. I've definitely rediscovered my zest for life!'

So ladies, try Plastere de Paris today – what have you got to lose but your wrinkles?

Because you shouldn't have to suffer alone!

This product is available from all good retailers of beauty treatments.

---

3 **a)** In order to form a contract, the parties must achieve consensus *in idem*.
What is 'consensus *in idem*'?

   b) Sandeep has offered to sell her mobile phone to her friend, Balinder, for £50. Balinder quickly responds to this offer and sends her acceptance to Sandeep by e-mail. Sandeep replies and promises to bring the phone into work the following day. However, when Sandeep brings the phone into the office Balinder is not best pleased. She informs Sandeep that she thought she was purchasing a phone with a camera not just an ordinary mobile phone. Sandeep informs her that she had no intention of selling a mobile phone with a camera as she does not own one. Sandeep and Balinder are totally at cross-purposes.

What is the legal position?

4 In order for an acceptance to be valid, the offeree must ensure that she communicates it effectively to the offeror.

Assess the accuracy of this statement.

5 On 6 June, Suhail Ahmed posted an application form offering to buy shares in a highly successful company called McCannell Ltd. Suhail, a keen investor, knows that the company's shares are likely to be highly sought after. McCannell Ltd received Suhail's application on 8 June and the company's Chief Executive drafted a letter of acceptance which was posted on 20 June to Suhail. Suhail never received the letter of acceptance from McCannell Ltd. Some months later, Suhail is reading the financial section of his newspaper and he discovers that McCannell Ltd has gone into liquidation leaving a huge trail of debts behind. Suhail feels that he has had a lucky escape. Unfortunately, McCannell Ltd entered Suhail's name on the share register and credited him with dividends from the shares after it had issued the letter of acceptance. The liquidator is intent on bringing an action for the balance of £50,000 against Suhail for payment of the shares allotted by the company.

What are the legal consequences of this situation?

6 Creative Designs Ltd offered to design and supply Asma with business stationery for £8000. Asma is very keen to accept this offer and, to this end, she faxes a letter of acceptance to Creative Designs Ltd. There was a problem with Creative Designs' fax machine and Asma's letter of acceptance was never received.

Does Asma have a contract with Creative Designs Ltd?

7 In situations where the offeror has either forgotten or declined to impose a time limit for acceptance of his offer, the offeree will have to communicate his acceptance within a reasonable time if he wishes to form a contract with the offeror.

In relation to the acceptance of an offer, what is a reasonable time?

8 McCracken, a self-employed builder, offers to build Anne-Louise, a patio, a garden wall and conservatory for £15,000. Anne-Louise has been thinking about making these improvements to her home for some time. She thinks that McCracken's offer is just a bit on the pricey side and she accepts the offer on the condition that McCracken carries out the work for £13,500. McCracken is not prepared to do this and, in any case, he has managed to line up another lucrative building job with Anne-Louise's neighbour, Marion. Anne-Louise then says that she will accept McCracken's original offer and that she expects him to turn up to start work at her house early on Monday morning. McCracken is starting work for Marion on Monday morning.

Can Anne-Louise sue McCracken for breach of contract if he refuses to start work for her on Monday morning?

9 **a)** In Scotland, the law recognises the class of obligations known as gratuitous or unilateral promises.

What is this type of obligation and does the Scots law differ from English law?

b) Craig phones Katy offering to sell her a second hand Volkswagen Lupo 1.4, Special Edition, registration number SO52 BBX. Craig has promised that he will keep this offer open for ten days. Katy is not sure whether she wishes to accept this offer and she decides to take time to think about this. Five days later, Katy contacts Craig to inform him that she has decided to accept his offer, but Craig has sold the car to someone else. Katy has to spend at least £600 more on a similar type of car as Craig's offer was an exceptionally favourable one.

Advise Katy.

10 Gavin is walking down Sauchiehall Street one Friday afternoon when he stops to look at plasma televisions in the window of White Lightning, a well-known Glasgow electrical retail outlet. Gavin notices that one of the televisions is priced at £200. He is astonished at the low price marked on the television and he immediately rushes into to the shop where he heads straight

for the cash desk so that he can purchase the goods. On reaching the cash desk, Gavin is incredibly annoyed to be told by the cashier that the goods have been incorrectly priced and that he must pay £2000 for the television. Gavin insists that White Lightning has made him a definite offer and that he has accepted that offer – there is a legally enforceable contract between him and the store. The cashier is not sure about this. She knows that it is store policy to give customers goods at the price on the ticket when the shop has made an error, but she is pretty certain that, in this situation, her supervisor would be most unhappy if Gavin was able to obtain the goods for £200. Gavin begins to rant and rave and the other customers in the store are beginning to look ill at ease and some are even heading for the doors. However, the cashier still refuses to sell the television to Gavin for £200.

Do you think that Gavin is correct?

11 Netta and Annie are regulars at the local bingo hall. Both women are in the habit of sharing their winnings on a equal basis. One night, Netta wins £120,000 while playing the National Game. The bingo hall manager comes over to congratulate Netta on her win and to present her with flowers and a bottle of champagne. He asks Netta what she intends to do with the money. Netta replies that she will give some of the money to her family and close friends, but first of all she is going to write a cheque for £60,000 made out to Annie. Netta goes on to explain that she and Annie always go halves on anything that they win at bingo. The manager is deeply impressed by this attitude. Some weeks later, however, Netta has second thoughts about writing Annie a cheque for £60,000 – after all it's her money. As an alternative, she gives Annie a cheque for £1000. Annie is not best pleased and she decides to sue Netta for the remaining £59,000 that she feels is hers by right.

What are Annie's chances of success?

12 **a)** In order to have an enforceable contract, there are certain situations where Scots law demands that the parties have put their agreement in writing.

Is this statement correct?

b) Lisa made a verbal offer to purchase a piece of land on South Uist that belongs to Suzanne. The plot of land is just the ideal size for building a holiday home. Lisa has put forward a very fair price for the land and Suzanne telephones Lisa to accept the offer. Suzanne states that there is no need to put anything in writing because it would mean having to pay ridiculous fees to lawyers and, quite simply, it would cause them too much trouble. This is an agreement between friends and they are both perfectly capable of taking care of things. Lisa has given Suzanne the money for the land and the builders are currently on the land to start work on the new house. To begin with, Lisa had some problems with the local council over planning permission, but Suzanne asked her cousin, a prominent solicitor, to attend the council's planning sub-committee meeting in order to argue Lisa's case. The solicitor was successful and the council has given Lisa permission to proceed with the building work which is now at an advanced stage. However, just when Lisa thinks everything is going well, Suzanne contacts Lisa to inform her that she will have to give back the land. Lisa protests, but Suzanne says there is nothing in writing and, therefore, a legally enforceable contract was never concluded. In any case, Suzanne will return the money that was paid for the land. Lisa later finds out that Suzanne has received a much better offer for the land.

Evaluate the situation.

c) What is the effect of the Contracts (Scotland) Act 1997?

13 **a)** What is contractual capacity?

b) Simon is a record producer with a history of signing young unknowns who later go on to enjoy a high degree of success in the pop charts. Simon was having a drink in a local nightclub one evening when a young singer called Hugh (age 16) appeared on stage and performed a terrific vocal set for the regulars at the club. Simon thinks that Hugh has got a great future in pop music and is determined to sign him to his record label. Hugh seems very keen to develop his career with Simon's label and signs a contract on the spot. Just before signing the agreement, Hugh asked Simon if it would be a good idea if he sought some legal advice in order to clarify a couple of issues. Simon, however, brushes these concerns aside and tells Hugh that he has nothing to worry about. The contract entitles Simon to 60 per cent of Hugh's future earnings, ten albums over the next ten years and touring twice a year. Furthermore, Simon is entitled to claim back all expenses incurred by him in relation to promoting Hugh's career. Hugh feels that this is a once in a lifetime opportunity

and, carried away by a rush of excitement (or could that be the after effects of the ecstasy tablet that he took before going on stage?), he decides to sign the contract. Some months later, Hugh starts to have second thoughts about his business relationship with Simon.

What legal options should Hugh explore?

c) How does the Adults with Incapacity (Scotland) Act 2000 affect the Scots law of contract?

14 Explain the terms void and voidable in relation to contracts. Provide one example of a void contract and one example of a voidable contract.

15 **a)** Some contracts are unenforceable because they contravene public policy in a variety of ways.

Explain this statement with examples of *pacta illicita*.

b) Henry hates his wife, Julie. He has hired a very shady individual whom he met in the local pub to kill Julie. Henry overheard this individual bragging to a friend about the number of murders he had committed. Henry has paid the killer £60,000 to carry out the murder, but after accepting this sum of money, the killer dupes Henry and runs off with the cash leaving Julie very much alive. Henry is very bitter and £60,000 poorer – after all he had a legally enforceable contract with the killer didn't he?

Can Henry enforce his agreement with the contract killer?

16 Explain the meaning of the term error in the substantials.

17 Ruaridh is a local farmer and recently he has encountered a number of problems and he seeks your advice.

a) Ruaridh entered into an agreement with Gary who runs a local brewery to sell hops and barley to be used in the brewing process. Gary, however, thinks that he is paying a price of £50 per ton for the goods. Ruaridh swears blind that the price is £60 per ton. However, the goods have already been delivered to Gary and he has used them in the brewing process.

b) Ruaridh was approached by an individual who made him an offer to buy his flock of prize sheep for £100 per head. The individual had asked Ruaridh to sell him the sheep on credit, but Ruaridh was not keen to do this. This individual claimed to be the son of another local farmer, David Campbell, who Ruaridh has had previous business dealings with and knows to be a man of good credit. Swayed by this knowledge, Ruaridh enters a contract with Campbell's son and lets him take the sheep away with him. It later turns out that the individual is a well known fraudster called O'Donnell who sold the sheep to an innocent third party called McDonald who is refusing to return the sheep.

c) Ruaridh remortgaged a house that he owns for the purpose of raising money to invest in the expansion of his organic produce business. The bank has recently contacted Ruaridh to inform that his endowment mortgage will not raise enough money to pay off the mortgage. Ruaridh is puzzled because he stated explicitly that he wished to take out a capital and interest mortgage to repay the bank. Ruaridh would not have taken out an endowment policy because they have an extremely poor reputation.

d) Ruaridh entered a contract to sell potatoes to FreshFields, a local food store that specialises in organic produce. Ruaridh is under the impression that an agent of FreshFields would pick the goods up at the end of the month. Freshfields have sent an agent along to the farm to pick up the goods. The agent is convinced that a consignment of potatoes currently lying in Ruaridh's warehouse are the goods that Freshfields contracted for. It is not yet the middle of the month. Ruaridh informs Freshfields that the potatoes have not yet been harvested.

Advise Ruaridh.

18 a) Explain the effects of misrepresentation upon a contract. Your answer should distinguish between innocent, fraudulent and negligent misrepresentation.

b) Robin, an antique dealer, says to Alasdair who is interested in buying a painting which is unsigned: 'I've had this item looked over by a leading art expert who assures me that it is the work of the up and coming Scottish artist, John Mitchell. Mitchell's work is now highly sought after by collectors and is fetching very favourable prices at auction. The painting is an absolute steal at just £3000.' Alasdair is completely swayed by Robin's statements and he proceeds to write a cheque for £3000. Robin has never bothered to have the painting examined by an expert. One evening, Alasdair has a friend over for dinner. This friend is acquainted with the work of John Mitchell and he asks to see the painting. The friend informs Alasdair that the painting is not by Mitchell, but by one of Mitchell's pupils, Stuart Findlay.

What steps should Alasdair take?

19 Provide examples of the following:

a) A contract *uberimae fidei*

b) A fiduciary relationship.

20 a) What is meant by a contract in restraint of trade?

b) Iain is a highly skilled computer engineer who has been responsible for expanding the business of his employer, Global Communications Networks PLC, over the last five years. The company is based in Glasgow, but it has a strong, international profile. Iain's area of work is highly specialist and he is one of only five computer engineers in the UK who possesses the kind of skills vital to the continuing success of his employer. Iain is becoming somewhat disenchanted with his job at Global Communications Networks. He has recently had an offer to take up a new post with a rival company. This offer is very tempting because it means that Iain will effectively double his current salary. However, there is a term in Iain's contract of employment to the effect that he must not divulge any information about trade secrets or customers to rivals of is current employer. Furthermore, Iain cannot take up employment with a business rival of his current employer for a period of 12 months. This restriction applies to business rivals who operate anywhere in the world.

Will Iain be able to accept the offer of new employment with the rival business?

c) What is a 'garden leave' clause and where would you be most likely to encounter it?

21 Susan is a young, impressionable woman who also happens to be extremely wealthy. At University, she became deeply involved with a fanatical religious cult. Over a number of years, Susan got more deeply involved with the group to the extent that she had no contact with her family. The rules of cult demanded that members must hand over all of their possessions to the cult's leader, a mysterious individual who styles himself 'The Enlightened One'. The cult's leader is later convicted on charges of tax evasion and he is imprisoned for five years. Consequently, the cult breaks up and the members go their separate ways. Unfortunately, Susan suffers a breakdown and she is placed in psychiatric care. It is only after successful course of treatment that the full extent of her experiences with the group is revealed. Susan is now anxious to reclaim the money and the property that she donated to the group.

What is the likelihood of Susan succeeding in her claim?

22 Look carefully at the following notice which is prominently displayed at the cash desk of a store:

IMPORTANT NOTICE

THE STORE EXCLUDES ALL LIABILITY IN RELATION TO ANY UNSATISFACTORY GOODS PURCHASED BY CUSTOMERS. FURTHERMORE, WE REFUSE TO ACCEPT ANY RESPONSIBILITY WHATSOEVER FOR LOSS, DAMAGE OR INJURY CAUSED BY DANGEROUS OR DEFECTIVE GOODS PURCHASED AT THIS STORE BY CUSTOMERS.

How effective is this notice?

23 How does the law regulate the use of exclusion and limitation and unfair terms generally in contracts?

24 What are the main remedies for breach of contract?

25 **a)** Explain fully why the Scottish courts will not always grant the remedy of specific implement to a pursuer in a breach of contract claim.

b) Mary owes Chapelhill Housing Association £735 in unpaid rent. The Association has taken Mary to the Sheriff Court and requested that the Sheriff grant it the remedy of specific implement.

Will the Sheriff grant the Housing Association the remedy of specific implement in this case?

26 Explain the following terms:

a) Minimisation of loss

b) Remoteness of loss

27 **a)** What is a penalty clause and how does it function?

b) Davinder and Tommy had entered into an agreement whereby Tommy's construction company was to build a set of smart new offices for Davinder's graphic design business. The offices should have taken 18 months to build. However, Tommy is now six months behind with the project and it will take a further six months at this rate to complete the contract. Davinder is not best pleased and he points to a clause in the contract to the effect that Tommy will have to pay £10,000 per month to Davinder representing every month that completion of the building project is overdue. This figure of £10,000 is based on Davinder's calculation of how much business he is likely to lose if the offices are not completed on time. Tommy finds out, however, that Davinder's monthly losses are more in the region of £2000 to £3000. Davinder is demanding that Tommy pay out £120,000 in total which he claims will represent his final, overall losses.

How realistic are Davinder's chances of being able to enforce the penalty clause against Tommy?

28 Explain the difference between general and special damages.

29 Some breaches of contract will be much more serious than others.

With the above statement in mind, what is a material breach of contract?

30 Contracts do not last forever and they will all come to an end sooner rather than later.

Discuss the ways in which a contract can be terminated.

CHAPTER
3

THE LAW OF DELICT

Introduction

This chapter introduces the law of delict. The law of delict is concerned with a variety of situations where the pursuer suffers loss, injury or damage which has occurred as a result of the defender's actions or failure to act when the law imposes a duty not to harm other people or their legally protected interests. The harm caused by the defender can be intentional or unintentional.

This chapter covers the following areas:
- An introduction to the law of delict
- Duty of care and negligence
- The law of delict and landownership
- Strict liability

The law of delict

The word delict comes from the same family as that of delinquent. Obviously, if a person is referred to as a delinquent they are most definitely not being paid a compliment. Delict is, therefore, concerned with the law of wrongs. When we talk about certain types of behaviour being wrong, we can mean a number of things. The behaviour in question may be of a criminal nature or the act may be a civil wrong or it could have both criminal and civil consequences. If a person assaults another individual, this action results in both a crime and a civil wrong having been committed. The person who committed this act could, potentially, face two trials – a criminal prosecution which could result in a term of imprisonment or a fine being imposed and a civil action where the victim will sue for compensation.

It is perfectly possible for the prosecution in a criminal trial to fail to meet the necessary standard of evidence needed to secure the conviction of the accused. It should be remembered that it is necessary to prove the guilt of the accused beyond a reasonable doubt in a criminal trial. If the accused is acquitted at the conclusion of his criminal trial, this is not necessarily the end of the legal process. The accused may then have to face a civil trial where the burden of proof required by the pursuer to win the case is much lower than in a criminal trial. In fact, all the pursuer will have to do is to prove on the balance of probabilities that the defender assaulted him and caused him to suffer loss, injury or damage. With the law of delict, however, we are only interested in the civil consequences of a wrongful action.

A delict can be defined as a situation where the defender voluntarily commits an act or fails to act when the law imposes a duty of care and this failure to implement the legally required standard care causes the pursuer to suffer a personal injury or loss or damage to his property. If, for example, a motorist hits a pedestrian while driving his car the question that would have to be asked is whether the motorist was paying due care and attention when the accident happened.

If the road accident occurred as a direct result of the motorist's failure to drive carefully then the victim would have a potential claim in terms of the law of delict against the motorist. The motorist owed a duty of care to pedestrians and other road users but he has failed to meet the necessary standard when he caused the accident. Put simply, the accident can be blamed on the motorist's actions or his failure to act properly – it is the motorist's fault that the victim has been injured. It is worth stressing that the motorist cannot get into his car and decide that he is not going to drive safely today. He has no choice in the matter because the law expects him to show all necessary care when he gets behind the wheel. The motorist may, of course, also have to face criminal charges of dangerous driving, but this aspect·of the incident need not concern us.

 Key point: The law of delict imposes civil liability upon those individuals who commit acts that are regarded as being wrongful (but not necessarily in the criminal sense).

Delict is a very different area of law from contractual obligations. With contracts, the parties enter the agreement of their own free will – they are not forced to contract with one another. The law of delict is not about personal choice – we all owe a duty of care to other people and we are expected to comply with this duty. Failure to do so will result in potential liability to the victims of our actions or our failure to act properly. Delict is not just about wrongful acts. Injuries, loss or damage can also be caused by the defender's failure to act.

 If, for example, as occurred in the case of **Taylor *v* Glasgow Corporation (1922)** the council failed to put up fencing around bushes in a public park in order to prevent young children from eating the poisonous berries growing on the bushes. A young child ate the berries and died as a result. The House of Lords held that the council's failure to safeguard particularly vulnerable people, like children, from harm made it liable to the child's parents. A failure to act (an omission) is, therefore, potentially as bad as the consequences of someone committing a wrongful act. It is also worth bearing in mind that delicts can either be committed intentionally or unintentionally.

 Key point: Delictual liability arises from duties that the law imposes on us, unlike contractual obligations which are voluntarily assumed.

Delicts which are committed unintentionally by the defender resulting in loss, injury or damage to the pursuer are the most common type of civil wrong. In these situations, the defender is said to have been negligent or careless. The law, therefore, imposes a duty on each of us not to cause harm to others. Each of us has interests which the law protects, for instance, the right to personal security and the right to enjoy a good reputation.

Harmful conduct may be intentional, for example:

- Assault
- Dangerous driving
- Defamation of character
- Fraud
- Intimidation
- Conspiracy
- Inducing a breach of contract
- Trespass
- Unlawful imprisonment
- Wrongful arrest
- Passing off
- Nuisance
- Enticement
- Seduction
- Non-natural use of land and water

Remedies

The civil remedies that are available to the injured party are:

- Reparation
- Interdict

Reparation

This covers the issue of compensation or damages for the harm caused. Damages for personal injury can address a number of different issues such as the pain and suffering which the pursuer has experienced (*solatium*) and financial loss suffered by the pursuer caused as a result of the injury (patrimonial loss). Financial losses, including loss of wages and reasonable expenses, could cover the period between the time of the accident and when the pursuer's civil action is finally heard in court. The pursuer could even receive damages for future losses such as ongoing medical treatment and future earnings. It is also possible that the pursuer can receive interest in addition to the damages that he receives from the defender. If the defender's negligence results in the death of the pursuer, the pursuer's family or executor of his estate are entitled to maintain a claim for damages against the defender.

The Criminal Injuries Compensation Scheme

The Criminal Injuries Compensation Act 1995 is for compensating victims of crimes of violence. Its object was to put qualifying victims in the same position financially as they would have been in had they not been injured but not to make them better off. A Scottish criminal court can make a compensation order making the offender pay a sum compensating the victim of the crime as well as a fine or sentence which may also be imposed. This would only occur in the case where the injuries are minor and compensation orders cannot be made in the case of motor accident cases. If the offender cannot be traced or is not worth suing, a claim can be made instead to the Criminal Injuries Compensation Board.

The pursuer must show that there is a direct connection between the wrongful actions of the defender and the harm that was caused. It is important to stress that the defender's actions must cause the pursuer to suffer loss, injury or damage. If this is not the case, then the pursuer does not have a claim in terms of the law of delict. If, for example, a person attempted to punch you, but missed and as a result you suffered no harm, you have would no claim for compensation. If, however, the person managed to assault you physically and caused you to suffer injury this would be a completely different matter.

In many situations, people will suffer loss but this does not necessarily mean that they will have a bring a claim under the law of delict. If, for example, an individual invests money in companies listed on the London Stock Exchange, there is always a possibility that the value of the investment can go down as well as go up. The companies in which the investor choose to invest may hit a rough patch through no fault of their directors and may suffer losses which affects their value.

Key point: The main aim of the law of delict is to compensate the pursuer/victim for loss, injury or damage caused by a wrongful act committed by the defender.

Interdict

The pursuer applies for a court order which should stop the wrong recurring where it is likely to be repeated.

Key point: The main remedies in a delictual action sought by the pursuer are reparation and interdict.

Culpa/fault

For a delictual liability to exist, there must be harm, loss or injury which is caused by fault on the part of the wrongdoer. The pursuer must establish that the wrongdoer was to blame for what happened. The fault is called *culpa* and, generally, there can be no liability without *culpa*. The general rule in Scotland is that there can be no delictual liability without fault. Quite simply, this means that the pursuer must prove, on the balance of probabilities that the defender's actions caused him to suffer loss, injury or damage. If the pursuer cannot prove to the court that the defender was responsible for his loss or injury, then the pursuer's case will collapse. Very often, all the defender has to show is that he has taken reasonable care to prevent the harm from occurring (see **Bolton v Stone (1951)** and **Paris v Stepney Borough Council (1951)** both discussed below) and if the court is satisfied that all reasonable precautions were taken, the defender will escape liability. *Culpa* or fault is very different from intentional wrongdoing (*dolus*) where the defender has set out deliberately to cause loss or injury to the pursuer.

Key point: The general rule in Scots law is that there can be no liability without fault (*culpa*) in Scotland.

Strict liability

Admittedly, there are situations where the pursuer does not have to show that the defender was to blame for the injuries or the losses caused. In certain situations, the defender's liability is said to be strict. In other words, the law automatically presumes that the defender is to blame for the harm caused to the pursuer. This means that the defender will have to bring evidence to show, on the balance of probablities, that he was not responsible for the injuries or losses caused to the pursuer. A defender will be strictly liable for injuries or losses caused to the pursuer for dangerous products (Part 1 of the Consumer Protection Act 1987) and where animals that he is responsible for cause loss or injury to the pursuer (Animals (Scotland) Act 1987). Situations of strict liability favour the pursuer as the burden of proof is on the defender to show that he is not liable for the harm that occurred.

 Key point: In situations of strict liability, for example, the keeper's responsibility for animals, the pursuer does not have to prove fault, it is the defender who will have to show that he is not at fault.

Duty of care and negligence

Negligence is harm caused unintentionally and is, by far and away, the most likely type of delictual action that the Scottish courts will have to deal with. Negligence claims arise because the defender owes what is known as a duty of care to the pursuer and, unfortunately, a breach of this duty occurs and, as a result, the defender suffers loss, injury or damage. The leading case for negligence claims is **Donoghue v Stevenson (1932)**. The facts of **Donoghue** are as follows:

 Mrs Donoghue and her friend went into a Paisley café owned by Mr Minchella. Mrs Donoghue's friend ordered two ice creams and two bottles of ginger beer. The bottles of ginger beer were not of the clear glass type where it was possible to see the contents. Mrs Donoghue poured the contents of her bottle of ginger beer over ice cream. To her horror, the remains of a decomposed snail slid out from the ginger beer bottle. Mrs Donoghue later claimed that she had suffered gastro-enteritis as a result of consuming parts of the snail. Mrs Donoghue also claimed that she had suffered a psychiatric injury as a direct result of her experience. The question then arose as to whom Mrs Donoghue could bring a civil action for damages against. She did not have a contract with Mr Minchella, the café owner, as her friend had purchased the ginger beer. Furthermore, Mr Minchella was not aware of any impurities contained in the bottle as it had been sealed from the time that it had left the manufacturer's factory and it was not a clear glass bottle. Mr Minchella could hardly be blamed for Mrs Donoghue's unpleasant experience. Who then could Mrs Donoghue sue? The manufacturer of the product was the most obvious target. Mrs Donoghue argued that a manufacturer of goods owed to a duty of care to anyone who might use the products.

Held: manufacturers owed a duty of care to anyone who might use their product and suffer loss, injury or damage as a direct result. Manufacturers must make sure that their products are safe when they left the factory. The ginger beer manufacturers did not have to predict that Mrs Donoghue personally would use their product, but they knew that someone would use the product and be harmed if it contained impurities like the remains of a decomposed snail.

In order to succeed when bringing a negligence claim before the courts, the pursuer must show that the defender owed him a duty of care, that the defender was in a position to cause harm and that the defender failed to prevent this foreseeable kind of harm from occurring. Additionally, the pursuer must show that the defender's breach of duty was the effective cause of the loss or harm suffered by him.

 Haley v London Electricity Board (1965) workmen employed by the Electricity Board had dug up part of the street. The pursuer, a blind man, fell into the hole and was injured because it had not been properly fenced off. The Electricity Board claimed that it could not foresee or predict that a blind person would be walking about on his own along the street. In any case, the vast majority of people who could see the hole would walk round it and, therefore, avoid any injury being suffered to themselves.

Held: the Electricity Board was liable for the pursuer's injuries. It was not beyond the realms of possibility that a blind person would come walking along the pavement without being accompanied by a fully sighted person. It was not uncommon to see blind people walking along the street and the appropriate safety measures should have been taken to protect people such as the pursuer from suffering injury as result of the failure of the Electricity Board to take proper precautions.

 Bourhill v Young (1942) Young was speeding along Collinton Road in Edinburgh on a motorcycle when he collided with a car and was killed. The occupants of the car were injured as a result of the crash. Mrs Bourhill, a pregnant fishwife, was getting off a tramcar which Young had passed just minutes before he hit the car further up Collinton Road. Mrs Bourhill did not personally witness the accident happening. However, rather foolishly, after hearing the noise from the crash, Mrs Bourhill made her way up the road to see what had happened. Mrs Bourhill saw the wreckage from the crash and bloodstains on the road. She claimed this sight and the noise had caused her to suffer a psychiatric injury (post traumatic stress disorder) which resulted in her miscarrying her pregnancy.

Held: Young did not owe a duty of care to Mrs Bourhill. Young was certainly negligent the way in which he drove his motorcycle at a dangerous speed along Collinton Road. Any reasonable person ought to have known that if Young lost control of his vehicle there was a very great risk of him colliding with other road users who were nearby. Furthermore, there was every chance that these road users who were in the path of the collision would suffer injury or, at the very least, suffer damage to their property as a result of Young's failure to drive his vehicle safely. Mrs Bourhill was nowhere near the scene of the accident and was, therefore, not placed in immediate danger by Young's behaviour. A person as sensitive as Mrs Bourhill claimed to be should not have rushed up the road to see the aftermath of the accident. This was asking for trouble and, arguably, Mrs Bourhill had placed herself in a dangerous position as a direct result of her own actions and not those of Young.

 Key point: The leading case in respect of negligence actions in Scotland is **Donoghue v Stevenson (1932)**.

The neighbourhood principle

Lord Atkin who gave the leading speech in **Donoghue v Stevenson (1932)** went to great pains to stress a concept which has since become known as the neighbourhood principle:

The rule that you are to love your neighbour becomes, in law, you must not injure your neighbour, and the lawyer's question, 'who is my neighbour?' receives a restricted reply, 'you must take reasonable care to avoid acts or omissions which you can reasonably foresee would be likely to injure your neighbour'. Who then, in law, is my neighbour? The answer seems to be persons who are so closely and directly affected by my act that I ought reasonably to have them in my contemplation as being so affected when I am directing my mind to the acts or omissions which are called into question.

Lord Atkin's statement is initially misleading in that he deliberately uses the language of the Christian Gospels by referring to your neighbour. When Jesus Christ was asked the question by one of his followers: 'Lord, who is my neighbour?' the fairly daunting reply that the disciple received is that 'Everyone is your neighbour'. To lawyers, however, the above question receives a much more restricted answer. The defender does not owe a duty of care to the whole wide world, but only to those individuals whom the defender, if he were a reasonable person, would realise that his actions might cause them to suffer loss, injury or damage. Basically, the defender should have realised that his actions or failure to act will result in certain negative consequences being suffered by the pursuer.

 Key point: The rule in **Donoghue v Stevenson** states that the defender owes a duty of care to those individuals whom the defender, if he were a reasonable person, would realise that his actions might cause to suffer loss, injury or damage.

The standard of reasonable care

If the pursuer can show that he is owed a duty of care, the defender can escape liability in many situations by demonstrating that he took the appropriate standard of care which the law expects of him in order to reduce the risk of loss or injury being suffered by the pursuer. The standard of care which is expected of the defender is one of reasonable care. Reasonable care is the standard of care expected of the 'hypothetical' reasonable man or woman who is a person of ordinary care and prudence and who is neither overcautious nor overconfident. This is an objective test and is not based on the defender's personal characteristics. Very often, a reasonable person will foresee or predict that there are particular individuals who are especially vulnerable in some way and this means that they may suffer a greater degree of harm if the defender fails to take reasonable care.

 Paris v Stepney Borough Council (1951) a mechanic was blind in one eye as a result of active service during the Second World War. His employer was not aware of this disability. Later, however, one of the Council's doctors discovered the disability during a medical examination. Incredibly, the employee was not given protective goggles by his employer to protect his one good eye. During the course of his work, the employee was hammering on a piece of metal and a splinter broke off and lodged itself in his remaining good eye. This accident meant that the employee was blind in both eyes. The court heard evidence that it was not normal practice in the industry to supply protective goggles to employees. The question then arose as to whether or not the Council had been negligent by failing to protect someone it knew to be particularly vulnerable.

Held: by the House of Lords that the employer had been negligent in that it had fallen far short of the standard of reasonable care which would be expected of a reasonable man or woman.

If the defender is a child, the standard of care expected of this person is that of an ordinarily careful and reasonable child of the same age.

 Mullin v Richards (1998) the pursuer and the defender were both 15-year-old school girls. They were playing around during a school lesson by hitting one another with plastic rulers. One of the rulers snapped and a piece of plastic lodged itself in the pursuer's eye. The pursuer was effectively blind in this eye as a result of the injury that she had suffered.

Held: by the English Court of Appeal that the correct test was whether an ordinarily careful and reasonable 15-year-old could have predicted or foreseen that the behaviour in question might result in someone suffering an injury. The Court considered the fact that fencing with rulers was not an activity that had been banned by the school, it was a very common activity and the girls had received no warnings from the teachers that the activity was in any way dangerous. The injury was, therefore, not foreseeable and the defender was not liable to the pursuer for the injuries that she had suffered.

What if the defender has some special skill, knowledge or expertise? In such cases, the courts will judge the defender according to the standard that is expected of a member of that particular trade or profession. So, in a medical negligence case, the standard of care expected of a doctor would be that of an ordinary skilled member of the medical profession who is performing his duties properly in relation to his patients. However, particularly in the area of medicine, the courts have accepted that members of the profession may have different opinions about how best to treat patients. One doctor may apply a particular procedure in order to treat a patient, whereas another doctor may rely on a completely different course of treatment.

 Bolam v Friern Barnet Hospital Management Committee (1957) a patient with psychiatric problems had been undergoing electric shock treatment and, as a result, of being given relaxant drugs before the treatment, had suffered from broken bones. It was not always the practice of every doctor to give patients these drugs before electric shock treatment. Some doctors felt that by giving patients these drugs, the risk of damage to bones was greatly increased. Other doctors, however, felt that the drugs benefited the patients. So, which group of doctors was correct and how was the court to decide whether the doctor in this case had failed to meet the standard of care expected of a reasonable doctor?

Held: the court decided to give doctors and by extension other professions a certain amount of leeway to determine their own professional rules. A doctor would not be negligent if he used a medical procedure which

219

was accepted as being a proper procedure by a responsible body of doctors who are skilled in a particular field of medicine.

 In **Bolitho v City & Hackney Health Authority (1997)** admittedly, the above decision in **Bolam** was criticised because it seemed to give too much power to the medical profession and other professions to set their own standards. In **Bolitho**, the House of Lords looked at the issue of professional negligence once again. A two-year-old boy was admitted to hospital suffering from breathing difficulties. He had not been examined by a doctor. Shortly after being admitted to hospital, the boy suffered a further breathing problems which caused him to stop breathing completely whereupon he had a heart attack and died. The boy's mother sued claiming that he should have been examined by a doctor and that a tube should have been inserted into the boy's throat to assist him with his breathing. The hospital had failed to do any of these things and was, therefore, responsible for the boy's death. It was claimed that even if the boy had been examined by a doctor, she would not necessarily have gone ahead and had a tube inserted into his throat to assist him with his breathing. The doctor was able to produce one expert witness who backed her claim, whereas the mother produced another expert witness who stated that the doctor should have carried out the procedure.

Held: the pursuer's claim failed. Lord Wilberforce stated that the **Bolam** test was still the correct one to apply. However, doctors could not expect to escape liability for negligence by pointing out that their decision was backed by accepted medical procedures. A court would have to be certain that these procedures and the opinions of medical experts were reasonable. However, the fact that many medical experts backed a particular procedure would often be taken to mean that the doctor had behaved reasonably by relying on the procedure in the question. Only rarely would a court be entitled to reject the views of a body of medical experts.

The test in **Bolam** also establishes the fact that if a defender is exercising a skill in the course of his profession, he will be judged according to the standard expected of a reasonably competent member of that profession. His actual experience will not be taken into account by the courts. Admittedly, a recently qualified doctor will not have the same level of skill that would be expected of a consultant. However, the public has a right to expect that the new doctor is trained to a level which allows him to treat patients safely.

 Djemal v Bexley Health Authority (1995) the standard of care expected was that of a senior houseman. The defender who was employed in the Accident and Emergency Department was a senior houseman and was judged according to the standards of this post and the issue of how long the defender had been employed in this position was not a matter for debate.

When deciding whether a defender has failed to meet the necessary standard of care, it is important not to use hindsight. After all, since the mid-1990s, we now know that the condition BSE (popularly known as Mad Cow Disease) found in animals can affect humans through the food chain who then might go on to show signs of Creutzfeld Jakob Disease (CJD). During the 1980s, the risks from eating animals infected by BSE could not be predicted. Should farmers, therefore, be held liable when it became apparent that the risks from BSE infected animals had extremely serious consequences for humans? Defenders can only be judged according to the knowledge that they actually possessed or could have gained access to at the time when the pursuer suffered loss or injury.

 Roe v Ministry of Health (1954) a patient had undergone surgery under anaesthetic. The anaesthetic had been stored in such way that meant that it had become contaminated. The capsules containing the anaesthetic were stored in disinfectant. The disinfectant leaked through microscopic cracks in the glass containers containing the anaesthetic which caused the contamination. The anaesthetic had been injected into the patient's spine and, as a result, it caused permanent paralysis. Expert medical evidence was heard that the method of storage for the anaesthetic was a standard one and there was no way that it could be considered dangerous – at the time of the injuries to the pursuer. The injuries suffered by the pursuer had revealed the risks caused by this method of storage.

Held: the pursuer's personal injury claim failed. Lord Denning stated that 'we must not look at the 1947 accident with 1954 spectacles'.

 Key point: In many situations, a defender will be able to escape delictual liability by proving that he took reasonable care to avoid causing loss or injury to the pursuer.

Reasonable foreseeability

An important question that the court will have to look at when it is deciding whether the defender is liable for loss or injury that the pursuer has suffered is whether or not the harm was reasonably foreseeable. In other words, if the defender is judged according to the standard expected of a reasonable person, it should have occurred to him that his actions or failure to act in a particular situation are likely to cause the pursuer to be harmed in some way.

 Hughes v Lord Advocate (1963) the defenders had statutory authority to open a manhole in an Edinburgh street for the purpose of carrying out repairs to telephone cables located below the street. The defenders' workers placed a brightly coloured tent over the manhole and surrounded it with paraffin warning lamps. The workers left the manhole unattended at approximately 5 p.m. on a winter's evening. The pursuer, who was aged 8 years old, and his uncle, who was 10, decided to enter the tent and go down the manhole. They took one of the paraffin lamps to light their way. When they re-emerged from underground, one of the boys knocked the lamp into the hole which caused a huge explosion (it was reported that flames had shot some 30 feet into the air). The force of the explosion caused the pursuer to fall back into the hole and, as a result, he suffered several serious injuries. Both the Court of Session at first instance and on appeal dismissed the pursuer's claim for damages. The pursuer appealed to the House of Lords.

Held: by the House of Lords that the defenders were liable to the pursuer as the accident was completely foreseeable and reasonable precautions had not been taken to guard against the harm which had occurred. Lord Pearce referred to the tent and the paraffin lamps as a 'dangerous allurement' which had been 'left unguarded in a public highway in the heart of Edinburgh. It was for the defenders to show that, although this was a public street, the presence of children there was so little to be expected that a reasonable man might leave the allurement unguarded. But in my opinion, their evidence fell short of that ...' Lord Pearce went to say that although the exact shape of the disaster was hard to predict, all the elements were present. a partially closed tent, the lamps, the ladder, a cavernous hole – 'a setting well fitted to inspire some juvenile adventure that might end in calamity.'

 Home Office *v* Dorset Yacht Co Ltd (1970) a group of borstal boys (who would be known as young offenders today) were camping on an island. The boys were accompanied on the island by their guards. A chain of events then unfolded with the end result being entirely foreseeable or predictable. The guards went to their beds and soon fell asleep leaving the boys completely unsupervised. The boys decided to escape from the island. They couldn't swim from the island because it is too far to the mainland, so they had to steal a yacht. None of the boys had ever sailed a yacht before. The yacht that the boys were attempting to sail from the island ended up colliding with another yacht owned by Dorset Yacht and a substantial amount of damage was caused as a result.

Held: by the House of Lords that the guards had failed in their duty of care to supervise the boys properly. This failure resulted in damage to property which was entirely foreseeable.

 Key point: Reasonable foreseeability is a test that the courts apply to assess whether a reasonable person in a similar position to the defender would have realised that his actions or failure to act in a particular situation were likely to cause the pursuer to be harmed in some way.

The seriousness of the risk

This issue deals with the likelihood of damage occurring and, if so, how serious the damage will be that the pursuer suffers.

 Bolton *v* Stone (1951) the pursuer was standing outside her house which was situated in a quiet street which lay next to a cricket ground. The pursuer was struck by a cricket ball that had been hit out of the cricket ground and over the fence. The pursuer suffered injuries as a result of being hit by the cricket ball and she brought an action against the ground authorities. The pursuer claimed that the cricket ground authorities had not taken adequate steps to protect members of the public from being struck by cricket balls. It was reasonably foreseeable that some cricket balls would be hit out of the ground and that these might end up striking people and thus cause injury. In fact, cricket balls had been hit out of the ground some six times in the last 30 years, but no one had ever been hurt as a result. The cricket ground authorities had erected a 17-foot fence, there was a considerable distance from the cricket oval to the edge of the ground and the ground sloped upwards in the direction that the ball had travelled.

Held: by the House of Lords that the chance of anyone being injured where the pursuer was standing was extremely unlikely. The cricket ground authorities had not been negligent in allowing the game to be played. They had taken proper precautions and, therefore, demonstrated the fact that they had taken reasonable care to avoid loss or injury from occurring. Was the pursuer seriously suggesting that an extremely high fence should be erected or that a roof should be constructed over the cricket ground? Clearly, these types of safety measures would have been extremely expensive for the cricket ground authorities and, realistically, they would have been completely over the top in order to safeguard individuals from what was a relatively low risk activity.

As we have seen, the cost and trouble of reducing the likelihood of the risk of loss or injury which the defender must bear is an issue which the courts take into consideration.

Latimer *v* AEC (1952) a factory had been flooded as a result of heavier than usual rainfall. The excess water combined with oil and grease on the factory floor which made walking on the floor extremely treacherous. The defenders, the factory owners, attempted to reduce accidents from occurring by putting sawdust down. However, the defenders did not have enough sawdust to cover the whole floor. One of the workers slipped on an untreated part of the floor and suffered injury as a result. The injured party brought an action against the defenders for damages claiming that they should have shut down the factory in order to prevent any accidents from happening.

Held: the House of Lords stated that closing the factory would certainly have prevented any accidents. However, the dangerous patches which had been left uncovered were clearly visible and could be avoided. Closing the factory would be a solution that was out of proportion to the actual risks involved of continuing to work there.

Key point: In assessing whether the defender has taken reasonable care to prevent loss or injury to the pursuer, the seriousness of the risk of the defender's actions will be examined by the courts.

Causation

Where there is an alleged breach of a duty of care, the actual breach must be the *causa causans* (the direct cause) of the harm to the pursuer. This means that the pursuer must be able to show, on the balance of probabilities, that the defender's negligence caused him to suffer loss or injury. The defender will be able to escape liability if he can show that his negligence should be regarded as the *causa sine qua non*. This means that the defender may have behaved negligently, but his actions should not be regarded as the direct cause of the loss or injury suffered by the pursuer. The *causa sine qua non* should be seen as part of the background and not a primary cause of harm to the pursuer. As the following cases demonstrate, it is not always obvious whether the defender's actions caused the pursuer to suffer loss or injury.

Kay's Tutor *v* Ayrshire & Arran Health Board (1987) a child was admitted to hospital suffering from meningitis and was given an overdose of penicillin from which he recovered as a result of quick medical intervention. The child did, however, become deaf. Clearly the doctor had been negligent by giving the child an overdose of penicillin and this was admitted by the hospital. However, the hospital refused to take responsibility for the child's deafness. It was the hospital's belief that the overdose of penicillin had not caused the child to suffer from deafness. There was no known medical case of a patient developing deafness as a result of a penicillin overdose. There were, however, plenty of cases where patients had developed deafness as a result of suffering from meningitis.

Held: it was probably the case that the meningitis had caused the child's deafness. The child's illness was, therefore, the *causa causans* or the main reason for the child's deafness.

 Barnett *v* Chelsea & Kensington Hospital (1969) the pursuer's husband drank a cup of tea. He began to vomit and was rushed to hospital. The hospital doctor who dealt with the husband told him to go home and make an appointment to see his own doctor in the morning. The husband, however, died as the result of poison having been administered to him. The doctor had no doubt been negligent in the way that he had treated the pursuer's husband. If the doctor had given the victim a proper medical examination this would not have prevented the victim's death. The poison was fast acting and there was no antidote.

Held: the defender may have been negligent, but this in itself did not cause the victim's death. It was the nature of the poison that was the cause of death. Medical attempts to save the victim's life would have been utterly futile.

 Mount *v* Barker Austin (1998) the pursuer had entered a contract to which a bank was one of the parties. The pursuer made an allegation that the bank had breached its duty towards him and he raised an action for damages against it. The pursuer appointed solicitors to represent him in this action. The solicitors, however, failed to raise the action within the proper time limits. The pursuer then appointed a second firm of solicitors to pursue a claim against the first firm of solicitors. Unbelievably, the second firm of solicitors also failed to raise the action in time and the pursuer brought an action against them. The pursuer's claim was based on the argument that he would have won the original action against the bank and that he had suffered loss as a result of the negligence of the two firms of solicitors. The trial judge was deeply unimpressed by the pursuer's claim and he found that the action against the bank would have failed. There was not even an outside chance that the action would have succeeded. All the pursuer was entitled to were the costs of the actions against the bank and the first firm of solicitors. The pursuer appealed.

Held: by the English Court of Appeal that the pursuer would never have won the action against the bank and, consequently, the bank's alleged negligence had not caused the pursuer any loss. The pursuer could always bring evidence to show that he had a realistic chance of success against the bank, but he had not been able to do this.

Key point: Where there is an alleged breach of a duty of care, the actual breach must be the causa causans (the direct cause) of the harm to the pursuer and not the causa sine qua non i.e. a factor which is merely superfluous to the direct cause of the harm.

Multiple causes of harm

Sometimes there will be many possible reasons to explain why the pursuer suffered loss, injury and damage and the defender's behaviour may only be one of the possible reasons. The explanations that the courts have used to make their decisions have not always helped matters.

 McGhee v National Coal Board (1972) the pursuer had developed an allergy in relation to brick dust that he was exposed to at his place of work. The pursuer normally finished his shift covered in the dust and he did not have an opportunity to wash it off until he got home. This allergy caused the pursuer to suffer from dermatitis. It was known that people who carried out the type of work that the pursuer was employed to do could develop dermatitis. The pursuer argued that the defender's failure to provide showering facilities for workers at the end of the shift had increased the likelihood of him developing dermatitis. The defender, in turn, argued that the pursuer might have developed his allergy even if the showers had been installed. Had the employer's negligence, therefore, caused the pursuer's condition?

Held: by the House of Lords stated that where a defender's negligence had made a substantial contribution to the pursuer's injuries, the defender could be liable. It was not essential to prove that the defender's negligence was the only cause of the pursuer's loss or injury.

The House of Lords took a different and contradictory approach in the following case:

 Wilsher v Essex Area Health Authority (1988) the pursuer, Martin Wilsher, had been born three months prematurely. His premature birth had caused him to suffer from all sorts of health problems. The pursuer had to be helped with his breathing and, to this end, he received oxygen. On two occasions, however, the pursuer was given too much oxygen which caused him to go blind permanently. The doctor in question admitted that the oxygen had been administered negligently. The hospital then faced a legal action raised by the pursuer's family. Medical evidence showed that the pursuer's blindness could have been caused by him receiving too much oxygen, but his situation could also have been caused by the five separate medical conditions that he was currently suffering from.

Held: by the House of Lords that the pursuer would have to prove that the defender's breach of its duty care would have to be a material cause of the harm suffered by the pursuer. It was not enough for the pursuer to show that the defender's actions had increased the risk of harm occurring. The defender's actions was only one possible cause of the pursuer's condition and this was not enough to prove that the defender had caused the pursuer to suffer loss or injury.

225

McGhee is obviously a case which favours the pursuer, whereas **Wilsher** is much more restrictive in its scope. Lately, however, the test in **McGhee** seems to be making something of a comeback.

 Key point: In cases involving multiple causes of harm, the pursuer may be successful if he can demonstrate that the defender's breach of a duty of care substantially contributed to his loss or injury.

Intervening events (*novus actus interveniens*)

On certain occasions, the courts will have to consider situations where the defender has breached his duty of care, but after this event some new factor is introduced into the picture which can also cause harm to the pursuer. This new cause of loss or injury will not have been the defender's fault. The introduction of this new factor can have effect of breaking the chain of causation. This means that the defender will only be liable for the harm that he has caused and he will not be liable for any harm caused to the pursuer by the introduction of the new factor to the equation.

 Rouse *v* Squires (1973) Allen was driving his lorry along a three-lane motorway. He lost control of the lorry with the result that it ended up blocking two of the motorway lanes. The driver of a car crashed into Allen's lorry. Rouse who was driving another lorry witnessed the accident and brought his vehicle to a halt on the motorway just in front of Allen's lorry. It was Rouse's intention to help the victims of the accident. Another driver, Franklin, appeared on the scene and parked behind Rouse's lorry. Franklin thought that by training his headlights on the scene of the original crash that this would assist Rouse. However, by this time, another driver, Squires, appeared on the scene. Squires did not realise that there had been an accident and he decided to move from the inside lane to the outside lane in order to get round the obstructions which he thought were slow moving traffic. Unfortunately, it was too late by the time that Squires discovered that he was in the middle of a serious accident. He hit both the car and Allen's lorry which had been involved in the original collision. The lorry moved forward and killed Rouse who had been standing in front of it.

Held: the trial court decided that Squires was fully to blame for the death of Rouse. Squires should have been alerted to the accident by the fact that Franklin's headlights were pointed towards the scene. The English Court of Appeal was unhappy with this decision. After all, this let Allen, the lorry driver who had caused the accident in the first place as a result of his negligent driving, completely off the hook. Undoubtedly, Squires had been negligent, but should he be held totally responsible for Rouse's death? Allen, therefore, was partly responsible for the death because his actions were partly to blame for the dangerous conditions encountered by Squires. Squires could not be blamed totally for the death. The chain of causation from the original accident to Rouse's death had not been broken by Squires' actions and Allen was one-quarter to blame for the death.

Section 4 of the Law Reform (Miscellaneous Provisions) (Scotland) Act 1940 allows a court or jury to divide the responsibility between a number of defenders for acts or omissions that cause loss or injury. The court or jury are given considerable discretionary power to determine what sum the defenders will have to pay to the pursuer when deciding the question of damages. The 1940 Act, therefore, allows two or more defenders to be found jointly or severally liable. This means that the defenders can be sued as a group by the pursuer or they may be sued individually. In these situations, if one defender has had to pay all the damages to the pursuer, he is entitled to approach other individuals who could have been sued by the pursuer and demand that they also contribute to the damages.

 Reeves v Commissioner of Police for the Metropolis (1999) a prisoner hanged himself whilst being held in custody in his police cell. The police were only too well aware that this particular prisoner was a suicide risk, although he had not been diagnosed as suffering from a specific psychiatric illness. The police admitted that they owed the prisoner a duty of care, but they went on to argue that they should be allowed to escape liability because the suicide should be considered as an intervening act that broke the chain of causation. In other words, it was the prisoner's actions that caused him to die, not the police's breach of their duty of care towards the prisoner.

Held: the House of Lords stated that the suicide was not a new intervening factor which broke the chain of causation. This was precisely the sort of act on the part of the prisoner that the police were supposed to guard against and prevent. The police owed the prisoner a duty of care to make sure that he was not given an opportunity to commit suicide. The police had, obviously, failed to perform this duty.

 MacFarlane v Tayside Health Board (1999) the pursuer had become pregnant after her partner had undergone an operation to be sterilised. The pursuer refused to have an abortion and later gave birth to a perfectly healthy baby girl. The parents sued the Health Board on the grounds that the botched sterilisation procedure had resulted in an unwanted pregnancy which meant that the couple were put to the not inconsiderable expense of bringing up a child.

Held: by the House of Lords that the refusal by the mother to have an abortion was not unreasonable on her part and could not be regarded as an intervening factor which broke the chain of causation. The parents were not entitled to claim damages for the expenses involved in bringing up the child, but the mother was entitled to sue for damages for the pain and discomfort that she had suffered as a result of her unexpected and unwanted pregnancy.

 Sabri-Tabrizi v Lothian Health Board (1999) the facts of the case were very different from **MacFarlane**. The pursuer had undergone a sterilisation procedure that she knew had been a failure – she was still able to become pregnant. The pursuer had sexual relations but she did not use any contraception to prevent her from becoming pregnant. She later discovered that she was expecting a child. The pursuer sued the Health Board for breach of its duty of care to carry out the sterilisation procedure properly.

Held: the pursuer's knowledge that the operation had failed and her decision to have sex without taking the appropriate contraceptive precautions were intervening factors which broke the chain of causation. The Health Board's negligence had not caused her to conceive an unwanted pregnancy.

Key point: The introduction of a new factor can have the effect of breaking the chain of causation meaning that the defender will only be liable for the harm that he has caused and that he will not be liable for any harm caused to the pursuer by the introduction of the new factor.

The facts speak for themselves (*res ipsa loquitur*)

There are situations where the only possible explanation for the harm suffered by the pursuer is that the defender's actions or failure to act caused it. There is no other credible explanation – the defender's negligent actions or omissions must have caused harm to the pursuer. The defender is then forced to bring evidence before the court to show why he is not liable to the pursuer. If the defender can show that there is a plausible explanation that demonstrates that he is not to blame, then the pursuer's claim will fail. However, the defender's explanation must be a plausible one and not one which is only theoretically possible. It should be remembered that the principle of the facts speaking for themselves does not remove the burden of proof from the pursuer to show that the defender was at fault. The pursuer must show that the facts are credible and that they do speak for themselves.

The pursuer can only make use of this legal rule in the following circumstances:

1   The events which led to the pursuer suffering harm must have been controlled by the defender or his employees.

2   Loss or injury does not usually happen when reasonable care is taken by a responsible person.

3   The defender must not be able to provide an alternative and credible explanation for the harm suffered by the pursuer which effectively gets him off the hook.

 Scott *v* London and St Katherine's Docks (1865) the pursuer was walking by the defender's warehouse when a six sacks of sugar fell out of an open door above him. The sacks landed on the pursuer and, as a result, he suffered injury. The defender had had been in the process of lowering the sacks to the ground through the use of a crane. There were no warning signs and the area in front of the warehouse had not been blocked off to prevent pedestrians from passing directly beneath the open door from where the sacks had fallen into the street.

Held: by the English Court of Appeal stated that although there was no actual evidence of negligence, this could be implied because sacks of sugar do not fall out of open doors by themselves.

 Gee *v* Metropolitan Railway (1873) the pursuer was injured as a result of falling out through the door of a railway carriage just after the train had pulled out of the station. The pursuer had been standing against the door when it somehow opened. The staff at the station had a duty to make sure that railway carriage doors were properly shut before the train left the station.

Held: the court implied that because the accident had happened so soon after the train had left the station that the staff had been negligent by not checking to make sure that the door had been shut properly.

Cassidy v Minister of Health (1951) the pursuer was admitted to hospital so that two of his fingers could undergo a surgical procedure. After the surgery was completed, it was discovered that the pursuer could not use four of his fingers on the hand that had been operated upon. The trial judge dismissed the pursuer's claim stating that negligence on the part of the hospital staff had not been proved. The pursuer appealed.

Held: by the English Court of Appeal that the only plausible explanation for the pursuer's injuries was that the hospital staff had been negligent when they performed the surgical procedure on the pursuer.

 Radcliffe v Plymouth and Torbay Health Authority (1998) the pursuer had been admitted to hospital for the purpose of an operation to his ankle. While in hospital he developed a serious neurological condition which it was agreed had occurred as result of an injected spinal anaesthetic that the pursuer had been given before the operation. The pursuer argued that the injection must have been administered negligently and that this had caused him to suffer an injury. The Health Authority relied on expert evidence to show that the pursuer had a susceptibility to spinal cord damage and although the injection may have caused this condition to occur there had been nothing negligent about the way in which it was administered.

Held: by the English Court of Appeal that the defender had provided a plausible explanation as to why it had not been negligent. The pursuer could not come up with an explanation to prove that the defender had been negligent and, therefore, his claim failed.

 Key point: *Res ipsa loquiter* works on the presumption that the only possible explanation for the harm suffered by the pursuer is that the defender's actions or failure to act caused it.

Remoteness of damage

If the court decides that the defender has breached his duty of care towards the pursuer there still remains the issue of the extent of the defender's liability for the loss or injury caused. The defender's negligence can unleash a chain of events which can very quickly have all sorts of unintended consequences. Should the defender be liable for all the harm that has been caused by his acts or omissions even if this is not reasonably foreseeable or should the extent of the defender's liability be restricted to those consequences that he ought to have realised were likely to occur? There are two opposing viewpoints: either the defender should be liable for all the consequences of his negligence even if this is not reasonably foreseeable or the defender's liability should be limited to those consequences that were reasonably foreseeable. Unfortunately, until recently, the case law was somewhat contradictory and confusing in this area of delictual liability. The following two cases provide dramatic examples of the serious consequences of the defender's initial negligence and show very different approaches as to how the courts may decide the extent of the defender's liability.

 Re Polemis and Furness, Withy and Co Ltd (1921) a ship had substantial quantities of petrol stored in its hold. The ship had docked at Casablanca where it suffered a most unfortunate and dramatic accident. The dockworkers negligently dropped a wooden plank into the ship's hold. It was reasonably foreseeable that damage to the ship or some of the goods stored in the hold would have occurred. The consequences, however, were much more serious than this and far less foreseeable. When the plank hit the bottom of the hold and it caused sparks. These sparks ignited petrol vapour causing a fire and the ship was destroyed as a result. Should the dockworkers be held responsible for all the consequences of the accident? Clearly, the dockworkers had been negligent by allowing the plank to fall into the hold, but should they be held liable for everything that followed as a result?

Held: the English Court of Appeal awarded full damages to the pursuer. The key question to ask was whether the harm caused to the pursuer was a direct result or consequence of the defender's negligence.

 Overseas Tankship (UK) Ltd *v* Morts Dock & Engineering Co (the **Wagon Mound No. 1**) **(1961)** a ship was being loaded with oil at a dock in Sydney. As a result of carelessness of Overseas Tankship, some of the oil ended up spilling into the harbour. While this spillage was occurring, some employees of Morts Dock, who were welders, were carrying out repairs on another ship at a neighbouring dock. This job was stopped for a while in order to make sure that the oil floating in the harbour could not be ignited by stray sparks from the welders' blowtorches. The oil did cause some damage to a slipway. Several days later, when the danger appeared to have passed, the welders started their job again. There was still oil floating in the harbour and sparks from the welding equipment ignited it causing a very serious fire which spread to the dock which was burned down.

Held: by the Privy Council that the damage to the slipway was reasonably foreseeable, but the damage caused by the fire was not. In order to catch fire, the oil had to be heated to a very high temperature. The Privy Council overruled the trial judge who had followed the reasoning laid down in **Re Polemis (1921)** and awarded damages for both the damage to the slipway and the fire damage to the dock. Interestingly, Viscount Simonds, one of the judges of the Privy Council, wrongly stated that the Scottish courts had rejected outright the reasoning laid down in **Re Polemis (1921)**.

In a much quoted statement from **Allan *v* Barclay (1864)**, Lord Kinloch suggested that the extent of the defender's liability should be based on the consequences which arise directly and naturally from his breach of duty to the pursuer and that the harm caused should be reasonably foreseeable. Arguably, this reasoning would seem to favour **Overseas Tankship** over **Re Polemis**. Despite Lord Kinloch's statement (which did not form part of the actual judgement in **Allan *v* Barclay**), the tension between **Re Polemis** and **Overseas Tankship** lay unresolved in Scotland for many years. This has led to a considerable amount of confusion. In England, however, the courts have favoured the reasoning laid out in **Overseas Tankship** and this led to this case being established as the standard test for remoteness of damage in negligence cases.

Recently, the House of Lords has reconsidered the issue of remoteness of damage in relation to the Scots law of delict. In **Simmons v British Steel PLC [2004]**, an appeal from the Inner House of the Court of Session, Lord Hope of Craighead stated that:

'I would not accept the Second Division's observation that the principles governing remoteness of damage are still not finally resolved in Scots Law. In my opinion the basic principles are well settled.'

Lord Rodger of Earlsferry stated that the reasoning of the Privy Council in **The Wagon Mound No 1** '. . . was entirely consistent with the trend of Scottish authority, including **Allan v Barclay** as interpreted in subsequent cases.' His Lordship went on to say that:

'The English courts quickly adopted the new test in **The Wagon Mound**. Since the Scottish courts had not subscribed to the rule in **Re Polemis**, they might have been expected to welcome the repentance of the Privy Council and the English courts and to make common cause with them in applying the approach in **The Wagon Mound**. It was not to be . . . there is a line of Scottish authority, stretching back to **Allan v Barclay**, that is consistent with **The Wagon Mound** in that it limits a defender's liability to damage that was reasonably foreseeable."

It would now appear that this recent decision of the House of Lords has brought Scots and English law into line as regards the question of remoteness of damage. This means that **The Wagon Mound No 1** is the standard test for remoteness of damage in the Scotland.

 Key point: It is now the case that the defender's liability should be restricted to those consequences that he ought to have realised were likely to occur.

The thin skull rule

The thin skull rule comes into operation when the pursuer has proved that the defender has been negligent and this negligence has caused the pursuer to suffer a personal injury i.e. physical and mental injuries. It should be noted that this rule does not apply to situations where the harm suffered by the pursuer merely amounts to damage to property or pure economic loss (**Liesbosch Dredger v SS Edison (1933)**). The thin skull rule has potentially serious consequences for the defender in the sense that he will be responsible for the pursuer's injuries even if these were not reasonably foreseeable. If, for example, the defender delivered a blow to the pursuer's head, some physical damage would surely be expected to occur. What if, however, the pursuer collapsed and died as a result of the defender's assault because of some physical condition that he suffered from which caused a massive haemorrhage? According to the thin skull rule, the defender should be held responsible for the pursuer's death. This may seem an extremely harsh situation, but the law expects the defender to take his victim as he finds him.

 Smith v Leech Brain & Co (1962) the pursuer was splashed with molten metal as a result of the defender's negligence and he suffered a serious burn to his lip. The pursuer had a pre-cancerous condition which the burn triggered off and he went on to develop cancer. The pursuer later died as a result of the cancer and his widow raised an action against the defender for negligence.

Held: the defender was held liable for all the consequences of his negligence to the pursuer.

In **Page *v* Smith (1995)** the pursuer had been injured in a car crash due the defender's negligence. The pursuer claimed that he had also suffered psychiatric injuries as a result of the crash which had caused the condition known as ME (myalgic encephalomyelitis) to reappear. The pursuer had suffered from ME for approximately 20 years, but when the accident had occurred it appeared that he was making a recovery.

Hold: the House of Lords decided in favour of the pursuer's claim.

Simmons *v* British Steel PLC [2004] the pursuer, Christopher Simmons, was employed as a burner at the defender's Clydebridge Works at Cambuslang. While using a hand-held burning torch, the pursuer's legs became entangled in the equipment's fuel cables. This accident caused the pursuer to fall heavily and he struck a metal stanchion, shattering the visor of his protective headgear in the process. The pursuer sustained a number of injuries. The defender was aware that the cables represented a health and safety hazard and, at two other work stations, reasonable precautions had been put in place to minimise the risks to employees. In fact, the pursuer and his colleagues had often complained about these dangers, but the defender had failed to introduce appropriate safety measures to the workstation at which the pursuer suffered injury. In the immediate aftermath of the accident, the pursuer was dazed, sweating profusely and he developed swelling at the top right-hand side of his head and above his right ear. Later, the pursuer complained of severe headaches and his vision deteriorated badly. The pursuer took a successful action for damages to the Court of Session in relation to his physical injuries. This was not the end of the matter. The pursuer went on to develop the severe skin condition known as psoriasis and also began to suffer from a serious depressive illness. Admittedly, he had suffered from psoriasis in the past, but he was now alleging that his accident had, in fact, made things much worse. As a result of his additional injuries, Simmons was unable to return to work (in fact he did not return to work at all). The pursuer raised a second action for damages in relation to his skin condition and the depressive mental illness. The defender countered by arguing that these conditions had been brought on by the anger that the pursuer felt because he was the victim of an avoidable accident and the subsequent (negative) treatment that he had received from his employer. The defender should not, therefore, be held liable for the severe skin condition and the mental illness which the pursuer had developed.

Held: by the House of Lords that the aggravated skin condition and mental illness suffered by the pursuer had been caused by the defender's negligence. Applying the thin skull rule, the defender must take the victim as he finds him. It made no difference to the result that the pursuer had a predisposition to psoriasis. The defender was liable to pay compensation of £498,221.77 to the pursuer. Their Lordships also pointed out, in situations where it is reasonably foreseeable that a working practice would result in an employee suffering physical injury, the pursuer is entitled to bring a claim for damages for psychiatric injury even if the employer could not reasonably foresee that the pursuer would develop such an illness.

Key point: The thin skull rule has potentially serious consequences for the defender in the sense that he will be responsible for the pursuer's injuries even if these were not reasonably foreseeable.

Pure economic loss

It is important to stress that, generally speaking, the courts tend to award damages to a pursuer who has suffered some sort of harm in the shape of personal injuries (whether physical or psychiatric) or for damage to property which has been caused by the defender where the defender has been negligent. The courts do not have a problem with awarding damages for pure economic loss where the defender has acted in a deliberately harmful fashion. We have to be very clear when we talk about damage in terms of delictual liability. Where the pursuer has suffered financial or pure economic loss as a result of the defender's negligent actions, the courts are much more reluctant to grant compensation. Defects in property will not be regarded as providing a pursuer with an opportunity to sue the defender for damages. The defects in the property must actually cause damage to other property or cause injuries to other people. The courts have not always been consistent on this point as can be seen in the case discussed below:

 Anns v Merton London Borough (1978) large cracks in the walls of pursuer's house started to develop because the house had been badly built. Were the cracks in the wall to be treated as property damage or merely as pure economic loss because they would cause the house to lose value? However, it should be remembered that property damage must be able to cause harm to the pursuer.

Held: by the House of Lords that the cracks in the walls should be regarded as property damage and, therefore, the pursuer could be receive compensation. This approach by the House of Lords went against long established legal principles.

In **Murphy v Brentwood District Council (1991)** the House of Lords overruled **Anns v Merton London Borough (1978)**. The case also involved defects that had developed in a building and the same question arose as to whether the pursuer could claim compensation. As a result of **Murphy**, defects in products are not to be classified as damage to property and should be treated by the courts as an issue of pure economic loss. The House of Lords did not, however, overrule **Junior Books** (see below), but generally the courts have refused to follow it.

Traditionally, the courts attempt to restrict the number of cases which can be brought before them and they are very wary of opening the floodgates which would mean them being overwhelmed by large numbers of new cases being brought before them. In cases where the pursuer has suffered pure economic loss, the courts will often state that an insurance policy should be used to make good the losses (assuming, of course, that the pursuer has one). Alternatively, the parties may have a contractual relationship. If so, a breach of a duty of care by the defender may be more appropriately dealt with under a contractual claim for damages rather than by raising a delictual action.

It should be stressed, of course, that the courts will award damages for pure economic loss to a pursuer when the defender has intentionally committed a wrongful act.

 Key point: The courts will award damages for pure economic loss to a pursuer when the defender has intentionally committed a wrongful act.

The following case shows the correct judicial approach to the issue of pure economic loss:

 Spartan Steel & Alloys Ltd *v* Martin & Co (Contractors) (1972) the defenders who were contractors negligently cut the power cable that supplied the pursuers' factory. The resulting power cut lasted for 14 hours. The pursuers' furnace which was used to produce molten metal could not be operated without electrical power. Consequently, the metal which was already in the furnace when the power cut occurred solidified and had to be completely written off. The pursuers were forced to shut down their factory while the power lasted and this, of course, meant that they were not able to carry out any of the industrial processes. The pursuers based their claim for damages on the following three factors:

1   Damage caused to the metal in the furnace when the power cut occurred i.e. physical damage to property.

2   Loss of the profit that would have been made if they had sold the metal had it not been damaged (economic loss as a result of damage to property).

3   Loss of profit in relation to the metal which would have been put into the furnace but for the power cut (pure economic loss).

Held: by the English Court of Appeal that the pursuer could be awarded damages for the first two claims for compensation, but the third claim was to be regarded as pure economic loss and, therefore, no damages were payable.

 Simaan General Contracting Co *v* Pilkington Glass (1987) the pursuers were involved in a building project in Abu Dhabi. The building owner stated to the pursuers that he wanted the windows to be a particular shade of green. Green is the colour which represents the Muslim religion. The pursuers entered a contract with a firm who would purchase the glass for the windows and fit it. This firm entered into a contract with the defenders who were to manufacture the glass and supply it. The glass turned out to be the wrong colour and it was rejected and new glass had to be manufactured. This resulted in the building project being delayed which caused the pursuers to suffer economic loss. Normally, the pursuers would have sued the firm who supplied and fitted the glass. Unfortunately, for the pursuers this firm had gone into liquidation, so the pursuers sued the glass manufacturers for damages.

Held: the pursuers' claim for damages failed because the case centred around pure economic loss. The glass to be used in the windows was not defective, it was simply not fit for its purpose. Furthermore, there was no contract between the pursuer and the defender.

Key point: Generally speaking, the courts tend to award damages to a pursuer who has suffered some sort of harm in the shape of personal injuries (whether physical or psychiatric) or for damage to property which has been caused by the defender where the defender has been negligent.

The strange case of Junior Books

Junior Books _v_ Veitchi Co (1982) is a most unusual case and it is very unlikely that it will ever be followed. It goes against the generally accepted rules that govern pure economic loss. Later cases have tended not to rely upon this decision.

The facts of the case were as follows:

The pursuers had entered a contract with builders who were engaged to build a new factory. The floor of the new factory had to be of a special construction because it was required to support the type of machinery that the pursuers would be using in the factory. The builders recommended a specialist flooring company to the pursuers who they said could carry out this task. The pursuers relied upon this recommendation and used the flooring company. After the new floor had been laid down, however, it was found to be defective, although it was not dangerous. The pursuers had to spend money in order to repair the defective floor. This, of course, meant that they had suffered a pure economic loss as a result of the builder's negligence in recommending the flooring company.

Held: by the House of Lords that despite the fact that the loss was a pure economic one, the pursuers could recover damages from the builders because the builders owed a duty of care to the pursuers.

Junior Books appears to suggest that a defender could be liable for causing pure economic loss if the pursuer relied on negligent advice supplied by the defender. It has been argued that courts will still continue to refuse to grant compensation where a negligent act committed by the defender causes pure economic loss to the pursuer. If this reasoning is correct, it would make **Junior Books** much more closely related to the line of cases which started with **Hedley Byrne & Co Ltd _v_ Heller & Partners Ltd (1963)** (see below).

Key point: The decision in **Junior Books** seems very much to go against the rule that damages for pure economic loss caused by the defender's negligence will not be recoverable by the pursuer.

Liability for negligent statements or negligent advice

The parties to a contract will owe one another a duty of care not to make negligent statements which could result in one of them suffering financial loss. It was previously thought that the courts would not grant damages to a party who suffered financial losses as a result of relying on a negligent statement in the absence of a contractual agreement. This position has been altered by the decision of the House of Lords in **Hedley Byrne & Co Ltd _v_ Heller & Partners Ltd (1963)**. The facts of the case were as follows:

Hedley Byrne were advertising agents and Heller were merchant bankers. Hedley Byrne had a client, Easipower who was a customer of Heller. Hedley

Byrne had contracted with Easipower to run an expensive advertising campaign and they wished to know if Easipower had funds in the bank to meet the advertising bill. Hedley Byrne approached Heller, as Easipower's bankers, to confirm that it had the money to pay the bill in its bank account. Heller confirmed that Easipower was solvent. Admittedly, Heller did say that the value of the work that Hedley Byrne was proposing to carry out on Easipower's behalf was bigger than anything it had ever seen in the account. Heller also said that the reference was given without any liability. Relying on the reference, Hedley Byrne went ahead with the campaign and assumed personal liability for the advertising costs. Later, Easipower became insolvent leaving £17,000 in advertising costs still owed to Hedley Byrne. Heller was sued by Hedley Byrne for issuing negligent advice.

Held: luckily for Heller, the disclaimer excluded the duty of care that it would normally have owed to Hedley Byrne. However, if Heller had failed to issue the disclaimer it would have been liable to Hedley Byrne despite the fact that there was no contract or fiduciary relationship between them.

The House of Lords in **Hedley Byrne v Heller & Partners Ltd** stated that the duty of care resulted from the existence of a special relationship between the parties. Obviously, a duty of care will be owed by the parties to a contractual relationship, but it is worth emphasising that Hedley Byrne and Heller were not parties to a contract. How far **Hedley Byrne** goes is still an open question, but the presence of a special relationship between the parties is useful guide. Lord Devlin said that payment for information or advice is very good evidence that one of the parties is relying upon the statement. In situations where there is no consideration, it will be necessary to exercise greater care.

In a number of situations, the pursuer has been able to show that he has a special relationship with the defender who made the negligent statement and that he relied upon the information supplied by the defender. As a result of satisfying these conditions, the courts have awarded damages to the pursuer for pure economic loss caused by the defender's negligent statement.

 Key point: Until the House of Lords' decision in **Hedley Byrne**, it was previously thought that the courts would not grant damages to a party who suffered financial losses as a result of relying on a negligent statement in the absence of a contractual agreement.

Applying the **Hedley Byrne** principle to claims for pure economic loss

The principle in **Hedley Byrne** has been raised in a number of relationships where negligent advice or the negligent provision of services has been an issue.

Solicitors and beneficiaries of a will

 White v Jones (1995) a father had initially fallen out with his daughters and changed the terms of his will in order to prevent them from inheriting any of his property. The father later changed his mind about this action and instructed his firm of solicitors to rewrite his will to include the daughters once more. The solicitors failed to draft a new will according to the father's instructions – despite the fact that he told them to do this on a second occasion. At the time of the father's death, the new will had not been drawn up and the daughters got nothing. The daughters sued the solicitors for breach of their duty of care towards them.

Held: by the House of Lords that the solicitors owed the daughters a duty of care because they had given assurances to the father that his will would be rewritten to include his daughters.

Surveyors who issue negligent survey reports

 Smith *v* Eric S Bush (1990) it was held that it was unreasonable to allow a surveyor to rely on a general disclaimer to exclude the consequences of his negligence where he had been asked by a building society to carry out a reasonably careful visual inspection of the property for valuation purposes (to be paid for by the prospective buyer) The surveyor knew that the buyer would rely on this report and was not likely to get another one. The house was purchased, but because of the defects, turned out to be unfit for habitation. The surveyors when sued by the buyers attempted to rely on the disclaimer to escape liability.

Held: by the House of Lords that it would not be fair and reasonable to allow the surveyor to exclude his liability in terms of the Unfair Contract Terms Act 1977. The case suggests that in so far as disclaimers are used by professional persons they may not be effective, at least as regards ordinary consumers of professional services.

Employers who provide references to third parties regarding ex-employees

 Spring *v* Guardian Royal Assurance PLC (1994) the pursuer, an ex-employee of Guardian Royal Assurance, was prevented from gaining new employment in the insurance industry because Guardian Royal provided a prospective employer of the pursuer with a negligent employment reference. The reference claimed that the pursuer had committed fraud while he had been working for Guardian Royal. This was not true, the pursuer had merely been incompetent in carrying out his duties for Guardian Royal.

Held: by the House of Lords that Guardian Royal owed the pursuer a duty of care and it was foreseeable that he would suffer harm as a result of the negligent reference. Clearly, the pursuer and Guardian Royal had a special relationship – that of employer and employee.

Accountants and auditors who draw up accounts for shareholders in a company

 Caparo Industries PLC *v* Dickman (1990) Caparo owned a large number of shares in a company called Fidelity. Caparo wished to take over Fidelity and bought more shares in the company. When the takeover bid had succeeded, Caparo discovered that Fidelity was practically a failed company. Caparo claimed that it only launched the takeover bid because it relied on figures provided by Fidelity's auditors in their annual report which, by law, has to be carried out. This report claimed that Fidelity had made a good profit, but this was, in fact, not the case. Caparo sued the auditors for not exercising reasonable care when drawing up their report.

Held: by the House of Lords that the auditors' report was drawn up as requirement of law to provide existing shareholders with important information about the company. The report was not for the benefit of outsiders who wished to invest in the company, nor those existing shareholders who wished to increase their holding in the company. Lord Bridge stated that there was no special relationship between Caparo and the auditors. The auditors did not know that their report was being relied upon by Caparo to guide it in its decision to buy more shares in Fidelity. Lord Bridge admitted, however, that there may be situations where the defender knows the information that he has provided will reach the pursuer and that the pursuer will rely upon it for a specific purpose and that it will be reasonably foreseeable that reliance upon this information will cause loss to the pursuer.

 Key point: In order to bring a successful claim for pure economic loss, the pursuer must show that he has a special relationship with the defender who made the negligent statement and that he relied upon the information supplied by the defender.

The defender's liability for psychiatric injuries

The vast majority of claims that involve personal injuries will centre around the issue of whether the defender's negligence caused the pursuer to suffer physical harm. In contrast to this, there will be occasions when the defender's negligence causes the pursuer to suffer from physical *and* psychiatric injuries. It is even possible that the pursuer's injuries may be purely of a psychiatric nature. In the past, such a medical condition was unhelpfully referred to as 'nervous shock'. The term nervous shock did not really convey the seriousness of the pursuer's psychiatric injuries. In modern times, the term post-traumatic stress disorder (commonly referred to by the initials PTSD) may be a more useful label to describe the pursuer's medical condition.

In Scotland, it is always possible for the pursuer to bring an action against the defender who has been negligent if this results in psychiatric injuries being suffered by the pursuer. In **Bourhill v Young (1942)**, the House of Lords did recognise that a defender's negligent actions could cause a pursuer to suffer psychiatric injury. Unfortunately, for Mrs Bourhill it will be remembered that her claim did not succeed.

A recognised medical condition

Before proceeding further, it should be stressed that we speak of psychiatric injury the pursuer must show that he is suffering from a medically recognised condition. It is true to say that the pursuer will be able to show that he has suffered from fear, stress, grief or a range of other emotional conditions of varying levels of intensity caused by the defender's negligence. This is not enough to sustain a claim for psychiatric injury against the defender. The defender's negligence must result in the pursuer developing a medically recognised psychiatric condition.

 Simpson v ICI (1983) a large explosion occurred at the pursuer's place of employment. The pursuer was present when the incident took place and it was fair to say that he certainly got a fright as a result. The defenders admitted that their negligence was the cause of the explosion. The pursuer attempted to claim damages for psychiatric injury as a result.

Held: the pursuer had experienced a state of fear as a result of being within the vicinity of the explosion, but he had not gone on to develop a medically recognised condition where it could be said that he was suffering from psychiatric injuries as a result of the defender's negligence.

The pursuer must also be someone who will possess a reasonable level of mental or psychological strength that would not normally be undermined or overcome by exposure to the often shocking, even horrific, consequences of the defender's negligence. In **Bourhill v Young**, the pursuer admitted that she had a naturally nervous disposition, yet she still went up the road to view the scene of the accident where the defender had been killed. Obviously, someone of the pursuer's temperament should not have placed herself in a position where she might later suffer psychiatric injuries.

However, if the pursuer is an ordinary person who possesses a reasonable level of emotional and psychological strength it is perfectly possible for him to go on and develop a more serious medical condition than the defender might have expected. In these situations, the defender will have to take the pursuer as he finds him.

 An interesting illustration of the 'thin skull rule' in operation can be found in the case of **Page v Smith (1995)** where the pursuer was involved in a car crash caused by the defender's negligence. The pursuer did not suffer from any physical injury as a result of his involvement in the car accident. However, he went on to develop psychiatric injuries. Admittedly, the pursuer had suffered from psychiatric problems in the past, but it had been many years since his last illness.

Held: by the House of Lords that the defender was liable for the psychiatric injuries suffered by the pursuer – he had to take his victim as he found him.

 Key point: Psychiatric injuries are a recognised medical condition, for example, post-traumatic stress disorder – fear, stress and anxiety are emotions which may fall outside this category.

A sudden and unexpected shock

It is also important to appreciate that the pursuer must prove to the court that his psychiatric injuries were caused as the result of suffering a sudden and unexpected shock. When a relative or friend dies after an illness, a pursuer will not be able to bring a successful action for the grief and distress caused by this bereavement.

 In **Sion v Hampstead Health Authority (1994)** the pursuer had witnessed his son slowly dying in an intensive care ward. The boy had been the victim of medical negligence. The strain was too much for the father and he developed psychiatric injuries.

Held: the pursuer's psychiatric injuries had not been caused by him experiencing a sudden and unexpected shock. Therefore, his claim for compensation failed.

 Key point: The pursuer must prove to the court that his psychiatric injuries were caused as the result of suffering a sudden and unexpected shock.

Who can be affected by psychiatric injuries?

The law recognises two kinds of victim who can develop psychiatric injuries as a result of the defender's negligence:

- Primary victims
- Secondary victims

Primary victims are those individuals who have been directly involved in an accident caused by the defender's negligence. They may have suffered both physical and psychiatric injuries or their injuries may be limited purely to psychiatric damage.

Secondary victims, on the other hand, are not directly involved in the initial accident that occurred as a result of the defender's negligence. In fact, they may not have witnessed the occurrence of the accident at all. This category of victim often appears on the scene during the aftermath of the accident as in **Bourhill v Young (1942)** when the important events had already taken place. Alternatively, secondary victims are related or connected to the primary victims and as such it would be reasonably foreseeable that they would suffer some sort of distress. Whether or not secondary victims can claim compensation for their psychiatric injuries is another matter altogether.

Primary victims have always had an easier task when it comes to convincing the courts that they should be awarded damages for the psychiatric injuries that they have suffered. However, as we shall see, strict rules are now in place that will determine whether a secondary victim should succeed in his claim for damages against the defender.

 Key point: The law recognises two kinds of victim who can develop psychiatric injuries as a result of the defender's negligence – primary victims and secondary victims.

Secondary victims

 McLoughlin v O'Brian (1983) the pursuer's husband and three children were all victims of a serious car accident which had been caused as a result of the defender's negligence. One of the pursuer's daughters was killed in the accident and the surviving family members were all seriously injured. It is important to realise that the pursuer was not physically present at the scene of the accident and she was not informed about the accident until several hours after it had occurred. When the pursuer reached the hospital she saw for herself the graphic and serious nature of the injuries that her family had suffered. This all proved too much for the pursuer to deal with and she developed a long-running and serious psychiatric condition which she claimed had been caused by the defender's negligence. The difficulty for the pursuer was that she was clearly a secondary victim and the law relating to psychiatric injuries was quite clear – only primary victims could be granted compensation for the psychiatric injuries that they had suffered as a result of the defender's negligence. The House of Lords, therefore, had to consider the issue of whether the pursuer was someone that the defender could reasonably foresee would suffer harm as a result of his negligence. Furthermore, some of the Law Lords felt reasonable foreseeability of harm was not enough and the strength of the pursuer's relationship with the primary victims had to be examined.

Held: the psychiatric injuries suffered by the pursuer were reasonably foreseeable. The ties of love and affection were clearly a crucial feature of her relationship with the primary victims. She was, therefore, entitled to compensation from the defender.

McLoughlin v O'Brian is not without its critics and it did not entirely settle the question of whether secondary victims were entitled to sue for psychiatric injury. Lord Bridge suggested that reasonable foreseeability of the pursuer suffering harm should be enough to establish liability. Lords Wilberforce and Edmund-Davies felt that reasonable foreseeability was only one part of the story. The strength of the pursuer's relationship with the primary victims was a very important factor in determining whether any claim for psychiatric injury should be allowed.

 McFarlane v E E Caledonia Ltd (1994) the pursuer had witnessed the fire that swept and destroyed the Piper Alpha oil rig in the North Sea in 1987. The fire had started as result of the rig operator's failure to take proper fire safety precautions. The pursuer was a painter who had been working on the rig, but when the fire occurred he was on board a rig support vessel. The support vessel was very near to the rig for the purposes of rescue and fire fighting activities. As a result of witnessing the fire, the pursuer claimed that he had developed psychiatric injuries.

Held: by the English Court of Appeal that the pursuer could not be regarded as a primary victim. He was a secondary victim who could not prove that he had close ties of love and affection with those individuals who were directly affected by the tragedy. It was not reasonably foreseeable that a man in the pursuer's position would go on to develop psychiatric injuries. The pursuer, therefore, had to be treated as a mere bystander who was not in any immediate danger and had no expectation of being placed in such a position.

 Robertson and Rough v Forth Road Bridge Joint Board (1995) the pursuers were workmen who had been carrying out work on the Forth Road Bridge when one of their colleagues had been blown off the Bridge during a heavy gale. The pursuers had witnessed this tragedy and they had both seen their colleague's dead body minutes after the accident took place. The pursuers brought claims for psychiatric injuries.

Held: the actions failed because neither pursuer had sufficiently close ties of love and affection with the deceased. Furthermore, it was not reasonably foreseeable that both pursuers would suffer psychiatric injuries as a result of witnessing the victim falling to his death.

 Key point: Some of the most difficult cases involving liability for psychiatric injuries have involved so-called secondary victims.

Important developments relating to secondary victims

It was not until the decision of **Alcock and Others v Chief Constable of the Yorkshire Police (1992)** that the approach that Lords Wilberforce and Edmund-Davies had taken in **McLoughlin** was confirmed as correct. **Alcock** was regarded as a special case because the pursuers represented a group of individuals who had a broad range of relationships with the primary victims. The pursuers included parents, children, siblings, grandparents, in-laws, fiancés and friends. All these individuals were claiming that they had suffered psychiatric shock as a result of the harm that had been suffered by the primary victims to whom they were connected. The House of Lords was left with the task of deciding which of these secondary victims was entitled to claim compensation for psychiatric injuries.

The facts of **Alcock and Others v Chief Constable of the Yorkshire Police (1992)** are detailed below:

The events surrounding this case relate to the English FA Cup semi-final which was being contested by Liverpool and Nottingham Forest. The match was being played at the neutral venue of Hillsborough (the Sheffield Wednesday ground) and it was a sellout. The game was also being televised live on the BBC – although individuals who were caught up in the crush could not be identified from the live television pictures. The South Yorkshire Police force which was responsible for policing the match was accused of negligence for the way in which it operated its crowd control procedures. The game had to be stopped after six minutes of play because too many fans had been allowed into a section of the terraces and many of these individuals were crushed against the fencing which prevented access to the pitch. Ninety-five people died as a result of the incident and at least another 400 had to be treated in hospital for the injuries that they received. The police paid compensation to the primary victims of the incident i.e. those had suffered physical and psychiatric injuries as a result of being directly involved in the accident. This compensation payment, however, did not settle the claims of a group of secondary victims, consisting mainly of relatives of the primary victims. These secondary victims, of course, had not been directly caught up in the incident. Many had, admittedly, been present at Hillsborough and had witnessed the terrible scenes from a distance. Others in the group of secondary victims had witnessed the incident on live television, had been told about the incident by third parties or had gone directly to the ground after hearing the information in order to search for family and friends who were missing presumed injured or dead.

The pursuers attempted to rely upon Lord Bridge's test in **McLoughlin v O'Brian** that their psychiatric injuries were reasonably foreseeable and, therefore, they could claim compensation. The House of Lords felt that although the secondary victims had suffered as a result of the incident at Hillsborough, stricter rules had to apply to their claims than was the case with the primary victims. The starting point of any secondary victim's claim for damages the psychiatric injuries must be reasonably foreseeable. This is only the first hurdle placed in the pursuer's way. There are a further three tests that the pursuer must satisfy:

◆ Do they belong to a group of individuals that the courts should recognise are capable of suffering psychiatric injury as a result of the defender's negligence?
◆ How close to the accident was the pursuer in terms of time and space?
◆ How was the psychiatric injury caused?

The pursuer will find the above tests very difficult to satisfy in order to succeed in his claim.

Held: all the pursuers failed to meet one of the three tests listed above.

 White and Others *v* Chief Constable of the South Yorkshire Police (1998) also arose out of the events which took place at Hillsborough. The pursuers in this case were police officers who had been on duty that day at the Hillsborough ground and who had been involved in attempts to rescue people from the crush on the terraces. The pursuers claimed that their employer, the South Yorkshire Police force, owed them a duty of care for the psychiatric injuries that they had suffered in the line of carrying out their duties and in their role as rescuers. Undoubtedly, these officers had been exposed to horrific scenes where they had pulled the dead and the severely injured from the crush. They could not fail to have been affected in some way by what they had experienced. The pursuers argued that because they had been directly involved in the incident they should not be looked upon as secondary victims. They should be treated as primary victims. Should these officers, therefore, be allowed to claim compensation?

Held: the English Court of Appeal agreed that the pursuers should not be regarded as secondary victims and their claims succeeded. On appeal to the House of Lords, however, all the claims failed. A primary victim was a person caught up in a dangerous incident and who was either in danger of suffering a serious physical injury or reasonably believed that he would suffer serious physical harm. Anyone not in this situation was, therefore, a secondary victim and had to satisfy the tests laid down in **Alcock**. The House of Lords stressed the fact that the pursuers lacked a close relationship with the primary victims (often expressed as the ties of love and affection). Their Lordships were at great pains to stress the fact that rescuers should not expect to receive preferential treatment when claiming compensation for psychiatric injuries that they had suffered.

 Key point: Secondary victims claiming damages for psychiatric injury will have to show that the injury was reasonably foreseeable and also satisfy the tests laid down in **Alcock** – membership of a group of individuals capable of suffering psychiatric injury due to the defender's negligence; closeness to the accident in terms of time and space; and the manner in which the injury was caused.

Rescuers

It is now clear from the judgement of the House of Lords in **White and Others *v* Chief Constable of the South Yorkshire Police** that rescuers are not to be treated more favourably than other individuals when the issue of psychiatric injury arises. Rescuers can be primary victims if, by placing themselves in a dangerous situation, they suffer serious physical harm or they have a reasonable belief that by being exposed to the danger they may suffer physical harm. Later on, these rescuers may develop psychiatric injuries as a result of their physical injuries. Where rescuers are involved in dangerous situations where they are very unlikely to suffer physical harm, they will be regarded as secondary victims if they claim that they suffered psychiatric injuries.

White clearly overrules the earlier case of **Chadwick v British Railways Board (1967)** where the pursuer was involved for more than 12 hours helping the victims of a horrific train crash where over 90 people had been killed The accident had occurred near to where the pursuer lived and he had gone to the scene to offer assistance. The pursuer won damages for the psychiatric injuries that he had suffered as a result of his involvement in the aftermath of the accident.

 Key point: It is now the case that rescuers will not receive more favourable treatment by the courts when they bring claims involving psychiatric injuries.

Psychiatric injuries caused by damage to the pursuer's property

Two cases suggest that a pursuer may be able to sue the defender for psychiatric injuries suffered where the defender's negligence has caused damage to the pursuer's property.

 Attia v British Gas PLC (1987) the pursuer developed psychiatric injuries as a result of witnessing her home being burned down. This incident had been caused by the defender's negligence.
Held: the pursuer was entitled to compensation for the injuries that she had suffered.

 Clark v Scottish Power PLC (1994) employees of the defender had forced their way into the pursuer's home unjustifiably in order to switch off the power supply. The pursuer developed psychiatric injuries caused by the unexpected and sudden shock that she received when she was confronted by the damage caused by the defender's actions.
Held: the pursuer was entitled to damages from the defender in respect of her psychiatric injuries.

 Key point: A pursuer may be able to sue the defender for psychiatric injuries suffered where the defender's negligence has caused damage to the pursuer's property.

An employer's liability for psychiatric injuries

An employer owes a duty to his employees not only to take reasonable care for their physical, but also their mental well-being. In modern times, more stressful working environments and practices have led to a dramatic increase in the number of employees suffering from psychiatric injuries. An employer will usually start off from the understanding that the employee should be able to handle the normal pressures of the job unless he has knowledge that the employee has a particular problem or weakness that makes it much more likely that this person is more susceptible to the risk of developing psychiatric injuries as a result of a stressful working environment. Clearly, it is easier for an employee to put into place safety measures in the workplace that protect an employee's physical well-being. Reducing the risk of psychiatric injuries to employees caused by work-related stress is much more of a challenge for employers. Very often, employers can only take what an employee tells them about their emotional and mental health at face value. To go further, would be perhaps a breach of the employee's right to privacy.

In **Walker v Northumberland County Council (1995)** the pursuer worked in a particularly stressful social work post for the Council. He had already suffered a breakdown due to overwork and a lack of support from his employers. His employer gave assurances that safeguards would be put in place upon his return from sick leave in order to reduce the risks of stress. The pursuer returned to work, but suffered a second breakdown because the Council had failed to take reasonable care to prevent him suffering from psychiatric injuries. The pursuer brought a claim for damages against the Council.

Held: by the House of Lords that the pursuer should be treated as a primary victim who was entitled to claim damages as a result of the Council's negligence. The Council had returned him to his previous (stressful) post and it was, therefore, reasonably foreseeable that if the pursuer was exposed to these stressful conditions it was likely that this would cause him to suffer psychiatric injury. If an employee is regarded as a secondary victim, he must satisfy the tests laid down in **White and Others v Chief Constable of South Yorkshire Police (1998)** which was discussed above.

The English Court of Appeal in its recent decision **Hatton v Sutherland (2002)** stressed that the key question to be asked in situations where an employee raised an action for damages for work-related psychiatric injuries was whether the harm suffered by the pursuer was reasonably foreseeable. The pursuer had to prove that he had suffered an injury to his health which is quite different from occupational stress and this injury had been caused by stress at work and not other factors that could affect the pursuer's health. Very importantly, the Court of Appeal stated that it was wrong to assume that some jobs are more dangerous than others. All jobs should be judged according to the same test.

Hatton involved four claims in total against different employers: Mrs Hatton and Mr Barber were teachers in public sector secondary schools, Mrs Jones was an administrative assistant at a local authority training centre and Mr Bishop was a raw materials operative in a factory. All four pursuers won their cases in the County Court. However, the Court of Appeal dismissed three of the employees' claims and only narrowly approved the Mrs Jones' claim.

It will still be very important for employers to show that they take reasonable care to prevent their employees from developing psychiatric injuries, especially if the employer is aware that the employee is particularly vulnerable in this regard. The approach taken by the Court of Appeal in **Hatton** has recently been affirmed by the House of Lords in **Barber v Somerset County Council (2004)**. However, employers should be mindful of stress suffered by employees and they should regularly update their knowledge of the effects of stress in the workplace.

Key point: The most important question to ask in situations where an employee raised an action for damages for work-related psychiatric injuries is whether the harm suffered by the pursuer was reasonably foreseeable.

Defences to a negligence action

The two most common defences that are used by the defender in an action of delict are:

1 Contributory negligence

2 *Volenti non fit injuria* (to one who is willing a wrongful act cannot be done)

Contributory negligence

This defence is used where the defender is claiming that the pursuer failed to take reasonable care for his safety. In other words, the defender is claiming that the pursuer was partly to blame for his own injury. The aim of this defence is to, hopefully, reduce the amount of damages awarded against the defender to reflect the pursuer's responsibility for the damage or injury sustained.

The Law Reform (Contributory Negligence) Act 1945 states that 'if a person (the pursuer) is injured, partly because of his own fault and partly due to the fault of another (the defender), damages will be reduced to the extent that the court thinks fit, having regard to the pursuer's share in the responsibility for the harm.'

 Hanlon *v* Cuthbertson (1981) this involved a claim by a female passenger in a taxi who was injured as a result of an accident and the taxi driver's negligence. The taxi driver argued contributory negligence because she was not wearing a seat belt which would otherwise have protected her in the accident.

Held: that as a result of contributory negligence, the pursuer should have her damages reduced by ten per cent. Despite this reduction, she was still awarded compensation of £14,584 plus interest.

Volenti non fit injuria

The main point of this defence is that the pursuer has, with full knowledge of the facts, voluntarily assumed and accepted the risk of injury and, in this way, has absolved the defender of the consequences of the defender's breach of duty. The defender still owes a duty of care but the chain of causation has been broken by the pursuer voluntarily undertaking the risk.

 ICI *v* Shatwell (1965) the pursuer and his brother were explosives experts who, contrary to instructions issued by their employer, agreed to test their detonators before returning to a safety shelter. There was an explosion and one man was injured while his brother was killed. It was held that the employer could successfully plead *volenti* as the pursuer and his brother had agreed to run the risk of injury by not returning to the safety shelter.

Besides contributory negligence and *volenti non fit injuria*, there are several other defences which are available to the defender.

Prescription and limitation

In terms of the Prescription and Limitation (Scotland) Act 1973, most delictual claims must be brought within five years of damage being suffered. Personal injury claims must usually be lodged within three years.

Compliance with statutory authority

Authority to do something which would otherwise be actionable can be conferred by statute. This is the only defence which can be used when the defender is accused of committing behaviour which amounts to a nuisance.

 Lord Advocate *v* North British Railways (1894) waste which was being disposed of under statutory authority was left near an army barracks. Compliance with the statute could been achieved by disposing of the waste not at the army barracks, but at another, more suitable location. As a result, North British Railways could not use the defence against the accusation that it was causing nuisance.

The Consumer Protection Act 1987 also provides the defence of compliance with a statutory provision which the defender can use in order to escape liability for dangerous products.

Necessity

This may not be a terribly effective defence when used by the defender to escape liability for negligence, but may excuse a deliberate act on his part, for example, he acted in order to prevent an accident from occurring.

Damnum fatale

The defender could not have prevented an accident from occurring because it was completely unforeseeable. The incident which led to the harm being suffered by the pursuer amounts to an Act of God, for example, a tidal wave engulfing part of the City of Glasgow. In **Caledonian Railway Co *v* Greenock Corporation (1917)** the defender's argument that freakishly heavy rainfall in Greenock, but not for the rest of Scotland, should be considered as an act of God failed to impress the House of Lords and the defender was found liable for causing damage to the pursuer's property.

Criminality

The pursuer will be unable to claim damages if he and the defender were involved in criminal activity. In **Pitts *v* Hunt (1990)** the pursuer was injured while he was a passenger on a motorcycle being driven by the defender. The defender was not covered by insurance and he had been drinking. The pursuer was perfectly aware of these facts, but he still encouraged the defender to break the law by driving the motorcycle. The English Court of Appeal refused to award damages to the pursuer.

 Furthermore, in **Ashton *v* Turner (1981)** the pursuer and the defender had been involved in a plan to break into a house. The defender was to drive the getaway car, but he drove the car dangerously and the pursuer was injured as a result. The pursuer sued the defender for damages. The court refused to award damages to the pursuer because he had been involved in a criminal activity when he had suffered the injury caused by the defender's dangerous driving.

The Sovereign

Any delictual action commenced against Her Majesty Queen Elizabeth II would fail. The Queen enjoys personal immunity from suit meaning that such a court action would be incompetent.

Foreign Heads of State and Ambassadors and their diplomatic staff

Foreign Heads of State and members of their households generally enjoy immunity from suit and any delictual action commenced against them in the Scottish courts would be incompetent. Ambassadors and members of diplomatic staff present in the United Kingdom will also enjoy immunity, but in a more limited sense. The wrongful act must have occurred in connection with the carrying out of their diplomatic duties by the Ambassador and his staff.

 Key point: The most common defences that are used by the defender in an action of delict are contributory negligence, *volenti non fit injuria*, prescription and limitation, compliance with statutory authority, necessity, *damnum fatale* and criminality.

Landownership

A landowner may be entitled to exercise a broad range of rights in relation to his property thus allowing him to enjoy it to the fullest extent. A landowner is not entitled, however, to do whatever he wishes on his property and he should always display sensitivity towards his neighbours. A landowner who carries on dangerous activities on his property, or who subjected his neighbours to behaviour that could be classified as a nuisance, should made be aware of the serious penalties that may be imposed upon him. This will be especially the case if his conduct causes loss or injury to an innocent third party.

Restrictions imposed on land

A landowner's rights may be restricted in the following ways:

◆ by statute
◆ by common law and
◆ by agreement or by contract.

However, we are, of course, primarily concerned with the law of delict in relation to landownership.

We will first examine the liability of landowners for the escape of dangerous things from their property which cause loss or injury to neighbours. We will then consider the liability of a landowner or an occupier of property for loss or injury suffered by third parties who have entered the property in question.

The escape of dangerous things from property

It has been stated that Scots law takes a completely different approach from England as regards the burden of liability imposed on a landowner in relation to loss or injury caused by non-natural use of property. In England, the landowner's liability is said to be strict in relation to the escape of dangerous things from his property. English legal doctrine in this area stems from the decision of the House of Lords in **Rylands *v* Fletcher (1868)**. In several important Scottish decisions, such as **Kerr *v* Earl of Orkney (1857)** and **Caledonian Railway Company *v* Greenock Corporation (1917)**, there is a clear willingness on the part of Scottish courts to impose strict liability on the landowner who uses his property in a dangerous fashion. It should be emphasised that the burden of strict liability is confined to a small number of situations and is the exception rather than the rule in Scotland. Scottish judges have a distinct tendency to become almost apoplectic with rage in relation to any suggestion that a **Rylands v Fletcher** liability exists in Scotland. Lord Fraser of Tullybelton, in **RHM Bakeries (Scotland) Ltd v Strathclyde Regional Council (1985)**, was particularly opposed to any extension of the general rule of strict liability in **Rylands** becoming part of the law of Scotland.

Activities by a landowner that are considered to fall into the category of non-natural use of property by a landowner would include any of the following:

◆ Toxic chemicals used in industrial processes contaminating the environment
◆ The escape of fire from the premises
◆ Water accumulated in a dam which later bursts
◆ The escape of armaments or explosives stored on the property

It should go without saying that all of the above examples can expose a landowner's neighbours to terrible dangers. It is important to note that a landowner may bring something on to his property that is perfectly safe if proper precautions are taken. The issue of danger occurs (and so too, inevitably, the question of delictual liability) when the thing in question escapes from the property and causes loss or injury to a neighbour.

 Rylands v Fletcher (1868) the defender was a mill owner who had instructed independent contractors to build a dam on his property. The dam would be used to supply the defender's mill with water. While the dam was being built, the contractors discovered old mine shafts and passageways on the defender's property which extended into the mine of a neighbouring property owner. The contractors chose not to block up the passageways and shafts. The dam was filled with water and it burst into the neighbour's property via the old mine works causing substantial damage.

Held: by the House of Lords that a property owner who brings something onto his land for his own purposes, and the thing in question is likely to cause harm if it escapes, does so at his own peril and he will be responsible for any harm caused as a natural consequence of the thing's escape. In other words, the defender was strictly liable for the harm caused to his neighbour's property.

The House of Lords has considered the escape of dangerous things from land in the more recent case of **Cambridge Water v Eastern Counties Leather (1994)**. This case involved the escape of dangerous chemicals from the defender's property over a fairly lengthy period of time. The House of Lords held that the pursuer's claim should fail because the damage suffered was too remote. The really interesting aspect of this decision is that Lord Goff emphasised the fact that storage of chemicals on property (even if it is used for industrial purposes) is a classic case of a non-natural use of property. The defender will receive short shrift from the courts if he attempts to justify his non-natural use of the property by pointing to the benefits that the community receives – in this case, the employment opportunities afforded to the local community.

 Key point: Scots law often reflects the English rule which stipulates that a landowner is strictly liable for all damage caused by the escape of dangerous things as a consequence of his non-natural use of the property, for example, fire escaping, water accumulated in a dam which later bursts and stored explosives which later explode unintentionally. However, Scottish judges have made clear that the rule in **Rylands v Fletcher** is very much against Scottish legal practice.

Dangerous and harmful acts committed on the property of a landowner

What if dangerous or harmful acts were carried out on the property of an owner or an occupier by a third party with the result that neighbours suffer loss or injury? What if the harm or damage was reasonably foreseeable?

In what way might the Scottish courts impose liability on a landowner who abandons his property or fails to secure it properly thus affording an opportunity to third parties to enter the property and, while present there, carry out a range of dangerous or harmful activities? Situations involving vandals, squatters, trespassers or housebreakers who use property in a way that not only threatens the immediate interests of the landowner, but also the safety and security of his neighbours spring immediately to mind.

 The House of Lords clarified many of these issues in **Smith v Littlewoods; Maloco v Littlewoods (1987)**. Trespassers had entered an abandoned cinema owned by the defenders. The defenders were intending to clear the land in order to build a supermarket. The trespassers were using the premises to light fires amongst other things. One such fire got out of control and spread to a neighbouring building causing substantial damage.

Held: by the House of Lords that the defenders were not liable for the consequences of the dangerous activities carried out on their premises by the unauthorised third parties. The defenders were able to demonstrate that they had been unaware that their property constituted a danger to their neighbours i.e. that it had become a fire hazard. If the defenders had possessed knowledge that trespassers were in the habit of lighting fires, they would have owed a duty to take reasonable care in order to prevent the trespassers from entering the property and behaving in a dangerous manner that clearly threatened the interests of neighbouring owners and occupiers.

The consequences of Smith v Littlewoods; Maloco v Littlewoods (1987)

What does the above decision of their Lordships actually mean? What are its consequences for landowners and their neighbours?

Their Lordships stated that an owner or occupier of property owed important responsibilities to neighbouring owners or occupiers of properties.

The relevant standard imposed on the property owner is a duty to take reasonable care of his property so that his neighbours do not suffer physical injury or experience damage to their property. The House of Lords limited the extent of liability of an owner or occupier for physical injuries or damage caused to neighbours as a result of the dangerous or harmful activities of unauthorised third parties while on the property. A duty of care may be imposed on an owner or an occupier of property if it was highly probable (*not* reasonably foreseeable) that negligence on his part might provide an opportunity to a third party to cause physical injury or damage to a neighbouring owner or occupier of property.

An owner or occupier will not be liable to his neighbours for the consequences of the dangerous or harmful activities of unauthorised third parties merely because such consequences are reasonably foreseeable. If, for example, a person leaves the door of his flat unlocked and a thief enters the premises to gain access to the adjoining property, the owner of the flat is not under a duty of care to take reasonable care to prevent this situation. The owner or occupier of the flat will have to seek a remedy against the thief. The situation may have a radically different outcome, however, if the owner of the flat was well aware that a high number of burglaries had taken place in the area recently. However, as we shall from an examination of **Canmore Housing Association v Bairnfather (t/a B R Autos) [2004]** (below), the fact that the risk of harm must be highly probable can represent a significant obstacle to a pursuer's claim.

The decision reached by the House of Lords in **Smith v Littlewoods; Maloco v Littlewoods (1987)** sits very awkwardly with the decision of the Inner House of the Court of Session in **Squires v Perth and Kinross District Council (1986)** and it must be respectfully submitted (with the benefit of hindsight) that the earlier case was wrongly decided. In this case, the pursuer owned a jewellery business which had been successfully burgled by a thief. Apparently, the thief was able to gain access to the jeweller's premises because contractors for the District Council, who happened to be carrying out building work on a flat situated above the shop, had failed to take proper security precautions to prevent any unauthorised parties from gaining access to the flat. The Inner House allowed the pursuer to succeed in the action for damages against the building contractors.

The Court of Session recently had to reconsider the impact of **Smith v Littlewoods; Maloco v Littlewoods in Canmore Housing Association v Bairnfather (t/a B R Autos) [2004]**. The case involved a dispute between a Housing Association (Canmore) and a garage (owned by Bruce Bairnsfather t/a B R Autos). Bairnsfather was in the habit of leaving a variety of derelict and unroadworthy vehicles situated in a lane of which he was the owner. He claimed that the vehicles were used by him as a source of spare parts in his business. The lane bordered a block of flats owned by Canmore and both parties used the lane to gain access to their respective properties. The vehicles were placed nose to tail against one another and their presence often hindered access to Canmore's property. Canmore made an allegation that the vehicles were an eyesore, a danger to children, an invitation to vandals to come on to the property, constituted a nuisance and, furthermore, that they represented a potential risk to neighbouring property. Nuisance is harmful conduct or behaviour which is not a one-off event, but rather an ongoing series of incidents which harm a neighbour's enjoyment of his property.

One of the abandoned vehicles had been set on fire by vandals and Canmore's property had sustained damage in the region of £3,000. Canmore was so fearful that vandals might attempt to set fire to the other vehicles in the lane, that it had refused to allow 22 potential tenants to move in to the block of flats. Canmore was also concerned it might be denied fire insurance if the alleged nuisance was allowed to continue. Bairnsfather had attempted to defuse the situation by offering to remove one of the vehicles and by clearing up the rubbish which had accumulated around the remaining vehicles. This offer did nothing to pacify Canmore which brought a petition for an interdict on the basis that it was highly probable that the continuing presence of the vehicles would cause further acts of vandalism. It was accepted by Bairnsfather that risk of an event which would cause damage might be enough to prove nuisance on his part. Lord Brodie weighed up the risks represented by the presence of the vehicles: they could be potentially attractive to vandals because of their derelict condition, they could be potentially a fire hazard as they were filled with rubbish of a flammable nature and, within the immediate vicinity of the lane, there was a piece of waste ground where vandals were known to gather

Held: by the Court of Session that Canmore's petition for interdict should be dismissed. Taking all the elements together, it was not highly probable that there was a real risk of further fires threatening Canmore's property. Lord Brodie made the following statement:

'*. . . even having regard to the additional circumstances which favour the petitioners' [Canmore] contention that I should find there to be a material risk of fire damage to their property due to vandals setting the respondent's vehicles on fire, I am not persuaded, on the basis of one incident, that the necessary degree of risk has been established. On what has been put before me, therefore, I do not find the respondent's use of his property has been shown to be,* prima facie, *a nuisance.*'

In other words, following the test laid down in **Maloco v Littlewoods (1987)**, it was not highly probable that there was a real risk of fire damage to Canmore's property.

Tenant's liability

An occupier of property, for example, a tenant will often become liable to the owner for any loss or damage caused to the property as a result of his acts or omissions (whether deliberate or otherwise). Usually, but not always, an occupier of property will have a contractual relationship with the owner of the property and this agreement will specifically address the issue of liability for any damage caused. Where there is no contractual relationship, the occupier of property owes a duty care to the owner to behave in a way that does not cause loss or injury during the period of his occupation.

 Fry's Metals v Durastic Ltd (1991) the defenders were found liable for failure to ensure that a burglar alarm continued to operate properly. The defenders argued that their responsibility for the property had come to an end after their tenancy agreement with the pursuer had expired. However, the court said that it was an extremely significant fact that the defenders had failed to return the only set of keys to the property to the pursuer. Consequently, the defenders were liable for damage caused to the property by vandals who had broken into the pursuer's property. The likelihood of such an event occurring was made highly probable due to the fact that the defenders had failed to take adequate steps to ensure that the property was effectively protected by a functioning burglar alarm.

 Key point: A duty of care may be imposed on an owner or an occupier of property if it was highly probable (not reasonably foreseeable) that these individuals' negligence might allow a third party to cause real harm to a neighbouring owner or occupier of property.

Occupier's liability

An owner or occupier of property may well become liable if the derelict state of the property causes injury, loss or damage to another person or his property. The main piece of legislation in this area is the Occupiers' Liability (Scotland) Act 1960 which establishes the rule that the occupier of property must take reasonable care to minimise the risks that any visitors to the property (whether invited or not) might encounter. The term occupier is given a broad definition in terms of Section 1(1) of the Act of 1960 and means any person or corporate body in actual possession, physical control or occupation of the premises. The occupier of premises is not necessarily the owner of the premises. Premises could be any fixed or moveable structure and could include aircraft or ships.

In **Telfer v Glasgow District Council (1974)** it was held that the occupier was the person who could control or exclude others from entering the premises. In the case of **Fry's Metals v Durastic Ltd (1991)** examined above, the tenant of the property in question would be the occupier under the 1960 Act because he had retained the only set of keys and, therefore, controlled legitimate access to the building. Not even the landlord could gain access to the building while the tenant had the keys in his possession.

To stand any chance of success in such delictual actions, the pursuer must prove that the defender (i.e. the occupier) was at fault.

We can see an example of this test of reasonable care in relation to occupiers in **Glasgow Corporation v Taylor (1922)** where the Corporation had failed to put up fences or warning signs around the bush from which poisonous berries were growing. A very young child died as a result of eating the berries. The court stated that the Corporation as occupiers were liable for the child's death. It had failed in its duty to take reasonable care.

 In the House of Lords decision of **McGlone v British Railways Board (1966)**, a 12-year old boy climbed up an electricity transformer which was the property of British Railways Board and which was situated on its land. The boy had sustained an electric shock and, consequently, he had suffered severe burns. The Board had placed high fencing around the transformer on three sides. Access to the transformer could still, therefore, be gained by unauthorised individuals who simply entered by the unfenced side. The Board had also put up a danger sign in an attempt to deter members of the public from going anywhere near the transformer. The House of Lords felt that the Board had taken reasonable measures to implement its duty of care. All the circumstances were examined when reaching this decision such as the existence of high fencing, the danger sign and the age of the boy. A 12-year old boy should have been fully aware that he was taking part in a dangerous activity by climbing the transformer. After all, the strong element of danger probably explained his desire to climb the transformer in the first place.

 Titchener v British Railways Board (1984) the pursuer, a 15-year old girl, was hit by a train while she was attempting to cross a busy railway line in the company of her boyfriend. The couple were using railway property as a shortcut. The girl was perfectly aware of the dangers involved in taking such a shortcut and she was normally in the habit of taking the precaution of looking in both directions when crossing the line. In the couple's haste to get to the other side, they threw caution to the wind and did not bother to take this most basic precaution. Tragically, the girl's boyfriend was killed as a result of the accident. In her claim, the girl argued that the Board had been negligent as a result of its failure to repair holes in the railway fence – she alleged that the Board was fully aware of the dilapidated condition of the fence. The girl, however, was forced to make a fairly damning admission that she had pulled down a section of fencing in order to make the task of entering the Board's property that much easier.

Held: by the House of Lords that the existence of a duty of care owed by the occupier (the Board) hinged on the circumstances of the incident, the age and the intelligence of the particular person who entered the premises. In this case, the Board did not owe the girl a duty of care when the facts of her claim were scrutinised. Quite simply, the girl was of an age and possessed of an ordinary degree of intelligence where it should have been obvious that she was endangering her safety.

It will, of course, be appreciated that in both **McGlone** and **Titchener**, the pursuers failed precisely because they were aware or should have been aware that their activities were dangerous. British Railways Board was able to escape liability by relying on the defence of *volenti non fit injuria* i.e. a pursuer who knowingly and recklessly exposes himself to danger will not have a claim should he suffer injury. The outcome in both cases would have been very different if both pursuers had been young children who were unaware of the dangers of entering the Board's property. Clearly, the Board would have failed to exhibit the necessary level of care had this been the case.

 Key point: In terms of the Occupiers' Liability (Scotland) Act 1960, a pursuer must demonstrate that the occupier has failed to take reasonable care to ensure that a person entering his premises will not suffer injury or damage by reason of any danger due to the state of the premises or of anything done or omitted to be done on them.

The *actio de effusis dejectis* and the *actio de positis vel suspensis*

It has been (unsuccessfully) argued that an owner or an occupier of property could be strictly liable where something was poured or thrown out of a building (the *actio de effusis dejectis*) causing harm to the victim.

Similarly, where something was placed on the building or attached to the building fell, causing harm to the victim (the *actio de positis vel suspensis*) it has been argued (again unsuccessfully) that the owner or the occupier would be under strict liability.

It has even been suggested that these delicts are not a proper part of Scots law. Bankton, one of the Institutional Writers, argued, however, that Scots law had adopted these two actions from Roman law (*Institute* 1.4.31 and 32). Baron Hume, another Institutional Writer discussed both actions in his *Lectures* Vol. 3, Chapter 16. Hume, however, spoke about these actions in terms of negligence and fault as opposed to examples of strict liability. The position has now been clarified somewhat by the Court of Session's decision in **McDyer v Celtic Football and Athletic Company Ltd and Others (3 March 2000)**.

The facts of the case were as follows:

The Law of Delict

McDyer, the pursuer, was attending the opening ceremony of the European Special Olympics at Celtic Park in Glasgow on 21 July 1990. The pursuer and his family made their way to the West Terrace of the ground and sat with other spectators on a perimeter wall surrounding the park. While the pursuer was sitting on the wall, a block of wood fell and landed on his hand causing him to suffer injury. The wood had been used as a temporary measure to secure a banner which was hanging from the stadium canopy. The day was calm and a securely attached piece of wood was unlikely to have been dislodged in any case. Furthermore, the stadium canopy was not accessible to the public. The pursuer sued Celtic Football Club (the occupiers of the stadium), European Summer Special Olympic Games 1990 (Strathclyde) Limited (which had control of the stadium had the time of the incident) and Zurich Insurance.

In addition to Celtic Football Club's potential liability under Section 2 of the Occupiers' Liability (Scotland) Act 1960 and *res ipsa loquiter* (the facts speak for themselves), the pursuer also alleged that Celtic Football Club was

'strictly liable in terms of the actio de positis vel suspensis *for causing or allowing a piece of timber to be placed or suspended from the said stadium canopy where it could fall upon the pursuer who was in a part of the stadium where the public were likely to pass or congregate.'*

Their Lordships examined the influence of Roman law on Scots law and pointed out that many of the older cases supposedly involving the *actio de positis vel suspensis* were really concerned with the liability of occupiers and owners of buildings for injury and damage caused to those outside the premises, whether in the streets or in open spaces or on neighbouring properties. The issue as the Court of Session saw it could be dealt with in terms of the Occupiers' Liability (Scotland) Act 1960. It will be remembered, of course, that the occupier has to demonstrate he has taken reasonable care to ensure that a person entering his premises will not suffer injury or damage by reason of any danger due to the state of the premises or of anything done or omitted to be done on them. The pursuer's claim based on the *actio de positis vel suspensis* implying strict liability was, therefore, largely irrelevant and unnecessary. The Court of Session acknowledged that in Scotland, generally speaking, there can be no liability without fault (or *culpa*).

The Court of Session's reasoning in **McDyer** largely confirms the approach taken in two previous Sheriff Court decisions in which reliance on the Roman legal principles was defeated:

Gray v Dunlop (1954) the pursuer's son was passing a hostel run for homeless people when an unnamed individual poured a pot of urine from one of the upper floors of the building. The contents landed on the young boy and, consequently, his father (the pursuer) brought an action against the occupier of the building. The pursuer's claim proceeded on the basis that an occupier should be strictly liable for anything poured or thrown out of the property which resulted in injury to anyone in the vicinity. The pursuer's claim was based on the *actio de effusis dejectis*.

Held: by the Sheriff that the pursuer had failed to prove that the occupier (the defender) was at fault. In Scotland, generally speaking, there can be no liability without fault. The pursuer's argument that the defender's liability should be strict was dismissed.

 MacColl v Hoo (1983) high winds dislodged a slate from the defender's roof. The slate landed on the pursuer's car causing damage. The pursuer raised a claim against the defender basing the action on the *actio de positis vel suspensis*. The pursuer argued that the defender should be held strictly liable for any objects that were attached to his property which came loose and caused damage to property or injury to persons.

Held: by the Sheriff that the pursuer had failed to prove that the defender was at fault and that the claim must be dismissed. The argument that the pursuer's claim should be allowed to succeed on the basis of strict liability failed.

 Key point: A property occupier or owner will not be strictly liable for any object or thing that is poured out or thrown or falls from his premises – the pursuer will have to show that the owner did not take reasonable care to prevent loss or injury.

Delicts traditionally associated with landownership

The law of Scotland regards a landowner as owning his property 'from the heavens to the centre of the earth' (*a coelo usque ad centrum*). This means that the landowner's property rights extend to the skies (i.e. the airspace) above the land and the earth below. This important principle of landownership, however, can always be limited by law or by agreement or by the nature of the property i.e. a tenement building or block of flats where the owners of flats in the lower storeys will not benefit from the application of this principle. It is not an absolute right and Section 76 of the Civil Aviation Act 1982, for example, continues to allow the passage of aircraft over property. Furthermore, in **Farley v Skinner [2001]**, a decision of the House of Lords, Lord Steyn noted that:

*'Noise from aircraft is exempted from the statutory nuisance system and in general no action lies in common law nuisance by reason only of the flight of aircraft over a property (**see Section 6(1): Civil Aviation Act 1982**)'*

 The case of **Brown v Lee Constructions Ltd (1977)** provides an extremely interesting example of how this principle operates in practice. The pursuer, a house owner, objected to the intrusive behaviour of a construction firm in relation to his property. The defender, a construction company, was involved in a building project on neighbouring land and, as part of the its activities, the defender's crane operator was in the habit of sweeping the crane over the pursuer's property. The pursuer raised an action to obtain an interdict in order to prevent what was effectively an act of trespass by the defender.

Held: that the defender, by allowing the crane to sweep over the pursuer's property was committing an act of trespass i.e. committing an act of intrusion – albeit of a temporary nature. The court granted an interdict to the pursuer in order to prevent the defender from continuing to commit the act of trespass in the future.

Key point: An owner of property is said, subject to certain restrictions, to own the land from the heavens to the centre of the earth.

Trespass

This is an issue which will concern many landowners. Trespass is defined as a temporary intrusion upon land or property. A landowner's primary remedy will amount to the right to have trespassers ejected from his land. However, the means used in the ejection of an individual from the property should be reasonable. The courts would not treat a landowner sympathetically if he was shown to have used force to eject a person from his property.

The most common way that the Scottish courts will deal with an act of trespass is to grant an interdict or court order against the defender which prevents him from repeating the temporary intrusion on the pursuer's property. If the trespass is of a more serious nature i.e. where the defender's intrusive behaviour has caused loss or injury, the landowner always has the option of pursuing a claim for damages.

 The Scottish courts are not in the habit of granting the remedy of interdict where an incident of trespass is of a truly trivial nature. In **Winans v Macrae (1885)**, the court felt that the pursuer could have solved the problem of an alleged incident of trespass without having to approach it and request that the remedy of interdict be granted. The trespasser in question was the defender's lamb (kept as a pet) which was in the habit of straying on to the pursuer's land and eating the occasional blade of grass. Needless to say, the lamb did not cause any damage to the pursuer's property and, if the pursuer really found the animal's presence on his property so objectionable, he was perfectly at liberty to build a fence which would have kept the animal out.

In Scotland, an act of trespass is generally viewed as a breach of civil law. It is possible, however, for a trespasser to commit a crime in terms of the Trespass (Scotland) Act 1865. This will occur where a trespasser enters property with the deliberate intention of dispossessing the true owner and this state of affairs lasts for an unspecified period of time. Such a criminal offence will tend to be committed mainly by squatters.

In terms of the civil law, squatters should always be aware that they may fall foul of the delictual remedy of violent profits whereby the Scottish courts will award the dispossessed owner of property the greatest profits that he potentially could have made had it not been for the fact that he was prevented from occupying and using it. In addition, the owner may be entitled to claim damages for any loss or damage caused as a result of the illegal occupation of the property.

 Key point: Trespass is a temporary intrusion upon a person's land and the customary judicial remedy is that of interdict. Compensation may be payable by the trespasser if this causes damage to the property.

Statutory restrictions

Over the years, many statutes and secondary legislation have prevented or limited the uses to which a landowner can make in relation his property. Examples of statutes that impose a wide range of restrictions upon a landowner include:

- Housing (Scotland) Acts 1987, 1988 and 2001
- Water Act 1989
- Environmental Protection Act 1990
- Crofters (Scotland) Act 1993
- Town and Country Planning (Scotland) Act 1997
- Abolition of Feudal Tenure (Scotland) Act 2000
- Water Industry (Scotland) Act 2002
- Agricultural Holdings (Scotland) Act 2003
- Salmon and Freshwater Fisheries (Consolidation) Act 2003
- Title Conditions (Scotland) Act 2003

Common Law Restrictions imposed on a landowner

This area of law is primarily concerned with the 'law of the neighbourhood'. Very simply, a landowner is not permitted to use his property in a way that causes harm to his neighbours or their property (*sic utere tuo ut alienum non laedas*). This area of the law is very much part of the law of delict. A delict is a civil wrong causing loss or damage to another person. A landowner's liability for harmful conduct can arise under two headings:

- Nuisance and
- Spiteful use of property rights.

 Key point: A landowner must use his property in a reasonable and responsible manner so that he does no harm to his neighbours.

Nuisance

As has previously been stated, a landowner must behave in a considerate fashion towards his neighbours. A landowner who uses his property in a manner that causes harm or interference to a neighbour's property may find that the neighbour decides to take legal action against him on the grounds that his inconsiderate behaviour should be regarded as a nuisance. It is important to state from the outset that the courts will make a finding of nuisance against a landowner if the harmful behaviour is part of a regular and ongoing pattern. The neighbour who, once in a blue moon, plays music a little too loudly during the early hours of the morning will not generally fall foul of the laws regulating nuisance behaviour. Examples of nuisance include unacceptable levels of noise, neighbour's animals (especially dogs) which foul communal areas or cause damage to property, illegal dumping of rubbish or toxic chemicals/substances, carrying on commercial or industrial activities in a residential area and anti-social behaviour generally. Harmful occurrences which are caused by nature are not usually regarded as a nuisance.

Remedies for nuisance behaviour and limitation of actions

The remedies of damages and/or interdict (a court order that prevents the defender from repeating the harmful behaviour) are available to the neighbour of a landowner who is causing a nuisance.

In terms of the Prescription and Limitation (Scotland) Act 1973, a pursuer may lose the right to raise an action if he has consented to or tolerated a neighbour's nuisance activities for over twenty years (the negative prescription period). A pursuer who belatedly decides to complain after twenty years have passed will be regarded as having acquiesced (i.e. given in) to the nuisance. Twenty years, after all, is more than an adequate period of time in which to raise a complaint. However, should someone new move to the neighbourhood and rightly raise objections to the nuisance, the person causing the nuisance cannot rely on the fact that previous or existing neighbours fell foul of the negative prescription period. The new neighbour will have every right to take legal action against the individual causing the nuisance.

If the remedy of interdict is sought by the pursuer, there is no need to prove or imply fault on the part of the defender. The defender's liability is said to be strict. If the nuisance has caused loss or damage to the property and the pursuer is seeking compensation he must prove fault on the part of the defender.

Judicial attitudes towards nuisance actions

A particularly interesting example of nuisance arose in **Webster v Lord Advocate (1984)**. Miss Webster had purchased a flat within the vicinity of Edinburgh Castle. Miss Webster's enjoyment of her property, however, was spoiled by preparations for the annual Edinburgh Military Tattoo. The Tattoo was (and still is) a cultural and social event of international importance in the life of the City of Edinburgh. Deafening levels of noise were caused by workmen who were involved in the construction of a grandstand for spectators of the Tattoo. The grandstand was being raised on the Castle Esplanade and, consequently, was very close to Miss Webster's flat.

Miss Webster objected to the level of noise caused by the construction of the grandstand and, consequently, she raised an action against the organisers of the Tattoo claiming that their activities in preparation for the event should be regarded as a nuisance. The court found itself agreeing with Miss Webster that the noise caused by the preparations was a nuisance. The defender's argument that Miss Webster could reduce the level of noise suffered by her by shutting her windows or by installing double-glazing did not impress the court. Miss Webster stated, not unreasonably, that: 'One of the nice things about summer is that you are able to open your windows.'

Clearly, the court was faced with the conflicting interests in this case – Miss Webster's completely reasonable expectation that she be allowed to enjoy her property, and the fact that the Tattoo played a very important role in relation to Edinburgh's tourist industry. Lord Stott was only too aware of this when he remarked: 'I was left in no doubt that the Tattoo is a spectacle appreciated by the public and a valuable publicity and commercial asset to the city.'

The noise generated from the construction of the grandstand was a nuisance that no reasonable person should have to tolerate. Miss Webster was being prevented from enjoying her property to the fullest extent. Significantly, however, the court was not saying that the Tattoo should be banned, but the preparations for this important event in the cultural life of the City of Edinburgh could be achieved without an unacceptable level of noise being caused. The authorities responsible for the organisation of the Tattoo would have to be much more considerate of the rights of those people who lived within the vicinity of the Castle Esplanade and who would be directly affected by the noise.

Miller v Jackson (1977) the pursuers moved into a house which was located next to a cricket ground. It was very common for a large number of cricket balls to be hit into the pursuers' garden. This was such a common event that the pursuers applied for an interdict in order to stop the cricket club from holding any further games. The cricket club stated that the pursuers had known about the existence of the cricket ground before they had moved into their house. The pursuers, therefore, had come to the nuisance of their own free will.

Held: by the English Court of Appeal that the cricket club's attempt to argue that the pursuers had come to the nuisance of their own free will must fail. However, the cricket ground went on to win the case using a different argument. The point is well made by this decision that, an attempt to justify the continuation of a nuisance activity, will not meet a sympathetic response if the defender argues that he was there first and is, therefore, justified in acting in a harmful way.

 In the House of Lords decision **RHM Bakeries (Scotland) Ltd v Strathclyde Regional Council (1985)**, it was held that a pursuer will only be successful in a claim for damages in relation to a harm caused by nuisance if he can successfully demonstrate that the nuisance was caused as a result of the defender's acts or omissions. In other words, the pursuer must prove that the defender was at fault. In this case, a bakery was flooded owing to the collapse of a sewer. The flooding caused damage to food and packaging materials which were stored in the bakery. The responsibility for maintaining the sewer lay with the Regional Council. The pursuer's action was dismissed by the House of Lords because it failed to prove that the defender (the Regional Council) had been negligent as regards its responsibility for maintaining the sewer.

The RHM Bakeries case appeared to depart from the reasoning of the House of Lords in **Caledonian Railway Company v Greenock Corporation (1917)**. However, the House of Lords was at pains to stress that the legal issues in **Caledonian Railway Company** were quite different. The defenders, in the earlier House of Lords' decision, were strictly liable because they had deliberately diverted the natural direction of a stream. The **RHM Bakeries** case, on the other hand, was not concerned with damage caused by unnatural use of property and the issue centred around whether the defender had failed to take reasonable care to maintain the sewer.

 The judicial reasoning underpinning the **RHM Bakeries** decision was followed in **Argyll and Clyde Health Board v Strathclyde Regional Council (1988)**. The pursuer sought compensation for flood damage caused to a field that it owned. The flood damage had occurred when a water-pipe owned by the defender burst. The water-pipe in question was buried below the surface of the field.

Held: the pursuer's action for damages was dismissed because it had failed to prove that the defender's negligence had caused the water-pipe to burst. The claim might have been treated more sympathetically if the pursuer had been able to show that the damage to the property had been caused by a failure on the part of the defender to inspect and maintain the pipe on a regular basis.

 Hunter v Canary Wharf Ltd and London Docklands Development Corporation [1997] is one of the most recent and high profile actions dealing with nuisance to come before the House of Lords. In this case, hundreds of residents of an area in London sued for damages in relation to the huge amounts of dust generated from construction activity at the massive Canary Wharf site and the interference that the construction work caused to television signals. The House of Lords essentially stated that dust was a feature of urban life and that the builders could not have known that the construction work would affect television signals. All the claims for damages were dismissed. Furthermore, their Lordships stated that someone bringing a claim for damages in a nuisance action must have an interest in the land. All the pursuers in this case lacked an interest in the land and, therefore, they did not have the right to bring an action. This case also considered the issue of a defence to nuisance on the grounds of compliance with statutory authority. The Canary Wharf project had received fast-track planning permission by virtue of statutory regulations which had established the London Docklands Development Agency, the body created for the purpose of regenerating that particular area of the City. Their Lordships, however, rejected the argument that Parliament had conferred immunity on certain buildings in relation to actions for nuisance.

For a recent consideration of the approach by the Court of Session to alleged nuisance activities see **Canmore Housing Association v Bairnsfather (t/a BR Autos) [2004]** (above).

 Key point: Nuisance is harmful conduct or behaviour which is not a one-off event, but rather an ongoing series of incidents which harm a neighbour's enjoyment of his property.

Possible defences to a nuisance action

An individual causing a nuisance cannot make use the following arguments as defences if he is responsible for causing a nuisance. They will usually end in failure for the defender.

◆ A neighbour should not have purchased the property if he had known of the existence of the nuisance (see **Miller v Jackson (1977)** and **Webster v Lord Advocate (1984)**)
◆ The nuisance benefits the public in some way (see **Webster v Lord Advocate (1984)**)
◆ The complainer has contributed to the nuisance
◆ The nuisance is merely the net result of the owner's ordinary use of his property

Statutory authority

A defender will really only be able to justify a nuisance if he can prove that the nuisance occurred as a result of his compliance with statutory authority (see **Hunter v Canary Wharf Ltd and London Docklands Development Corporation Ltd [1997]** above).

 Lord Advocate v North British Railways (1894) waste which was being disposed of under statutory authority was deposited close to an army barracks. The aim of this particular statute could have been complied with by the defender disposing of the waste at another more suitable location.

Accordingly, the court was not impressed by the railway company's attempt to use this defence.

 Allen v Gulf Oil Refining (1981) local residents attempted to bring an action alleging nuisance against the operators of an oil refinery. The operators' defence was that the nuisance was a natural result of running the refinery and they had a statutory right to do so. The particular Act had given the operators the right to purchase compulsorily the land on which the refinery was to be built, but it did not appear to give the operators immunity from being sued in a nuisance action by the local residents.

Held: by the House of Lords that a power could be implied into the Act which prevented the operators from being sued in a nuisance action for the way in which they ran the refinery.

Whether an activity will be classed as a nuisance will very much depend on the location of the property. Activities which may be tolerated in the countryside may well meet condemnation in an urban or residential area.

 Key point: The only competent defence to a nuisance action is for the defender to show that the action complained of has been authorised by statute.

Aemulationem vicini or spiteful use of property rights

This delict reinforces the fact that a landowner will have to act in a responsible and reasonable way when he exercises his property rights in relation to his neighbours. *Aemulationem vicini* deals with situations where a landowner has certain, legally recognised property rights but he chooses to exercise these rights in a completely unjustified way with the deliberate intention of causing distress or inconvenience to a neighbour. The landowner's reason for behaving in this fashion is usually motivated by a sense of spite or malice towards his neighbours. In order for a pursuer to have any chance of success with this type of action, he will have to show that the landowner has used his legitimate rights in a way that is malicious. The spiteful behaviour is intended to prevent the neighbour making full use of his own property rights. A pursuer would be quite justified in raising a claim of *aemulationem vicini* in relation to spiteful behaviour that has occurred just once. There is no need for the pursuer to demonstrate that the behaviour complained of is part of an ongoing series of occurrences. The pursuer is entitled to ask the courts to grant an interdict and a claim for damages may also be competent.

An example of *aemulationem vicini* arose in **Campbell v Muir (1908)**. In this case, the defender conducted himself in a totally malicious fashion whereby he brought his boat as close to the river bank as possible in an attempt to stop anglers who were situated on the bank from casting out their fishing lines into the river. The defender was perfectly entitled to exercise his right to fish from the river using his boat, but he was not permitted to do this in a manner that blatantly interfered with the rights of other anglers. The defender's actions were motivated by spite and the court granted an interdict to stop this behaviour from reoccurring.

The House of Lords has stated in **Bradford v Pickles [1895]** that *aemulationem vicini* was not a concept recognised by the law of England. This statement stands somewhat at odds with some English decisions (**Christie v Davey (1893)** and **Hollywood Silver Fox Farm Ltd v Emmett (1936)**) which were most certainly concerned with spiteful use of property rights (or malice as the English would say). In **Bradford v Pickles**, Lord Watson, the Scottish Lord of Appeal in Ordinary, stated:

'No use of property, which would be legal if due to a proper motive, can become illegal because it is prompted by a motive which is improper or even malicious.'

Lord Watson's statement has been challenged by some leading Scottish lawyers and academics. Professor Joseph Thomson has argued that Lord Watson's confident assertion flew in the face of accepted Scottish legal practice. Lord Watson's statement of Scots law seems to have had little influence on the outcome of the decisions in **Campbell v Muir (1908)** and in **More v Boyle (1967)** (a later decision of the Sheriff Court). In any case, it should be remembered that, strictly speaking, Lord Watson was speaking *obiter* and his remarks did not form part of the *ratio decidendi* of the actual judgement in **Bradford v Pickles**.

Lord Brodie briefly addressed the issue of spiteful use of property rights and its application to Scots law in **Canmore Housing Association v Bairnsfather (t/a BR Autos) [2004] (above)**. His Lordship did concede that there was general acceptance that Lord Watson's *obiter* statement in **Bradford v Pickles** 'is far too widely stated,' but he refused to be drawn any further. Somewhat regrettably, an opportunity to clarify the law relating to *aemulationem vicini* was lost.

 Key point: Merely because a landowner has property rights does not mean that he can exercise them in a deliberately spiteful fashion which causes loss or injury to other property owners.

Agreements imposing restrictions on land use

A property owner drew up an agreement with a neighbour which imposed conditions or burdens upon the land. This agreement may prevent the landowner from using his property in a particular way or it may grant the neighbour certain (real) rights over the property. A servitude is an example of a burden imposed on land e.g. a right to use a footpath across someone's land.

An important issue for us to think about is that these agreements often survive changes in ownership of the property. They are said to run with the land and these agreements will legally bind past, present and future owners of the property. Landowners can have many restrictions removed from property by appealing to the Lands Tribunal for Scotland (**see Chapter 1**). However, many of the outdated feudal conditions imposed on land will be abolished when the Abolition of Feudal Tenure (Scotland) Act 2000 is finally brought into force in November 2004. The feudal system of landownership should not be viewed in entirely negative terms. Some feudal charters were useful in that they prevented landowners from carrying on certain types of activities that would be classified as nuisance. Many of these burdens contained in the old feudal charters may actually be preserved under the new system of land ownership which will operate from November 2004 onwards and which will be recognised by the Title Conditions (Scotland) Act 2003.

 Key point: Landowners can agree not to carry on activities which would be regarded as causing a nuisance, but these agreements will often survive changes of ownership of the land.

Interference with the natural course of a river or burn or non-natural use of water

Very often, rivers or burns will flow through a landowner's property. A landowner will have to be particularly sensitive to the rights of third parties where such a river or burn is concerned, especially if the water flows out of his property and into neighbouring properties. A landowner most certainly would not be allowed to alter or change the course of a water-channel (a river or burn) for irrigation and manufacturing purposes if this action interfered with the rights of his neighbours. These neighbours may also rely on the water from the river or burn in question for their own legitimate purposes. A landowner will be allowed to divert the course of a burn or a stream as long as this does not reduce the flow of water to his neighbours downriver. Diverting the course of a river or a burn landowner is, after all, interfering with the natural order of things and the dangers of flooding and pollution should always be uppermost in the mind of the landowner. The important question that the landowner should ask is: how will these activities affect my neighbours? A landowner will clearly incur delictual liability if his activities cause loss or damage to his neighbours, but he might like also to recall the provisions of the Water Act 1989 which make it an criminal offence for an individual to pollute a river or a burn.

In situations where a landowner takes it upon himself to alter or divert the course of a stream, the Scottish courts impose the burden of strict liability. This means that, where another landowner who has suffered loss or injury as a result of the defender's interference with the natural course of the stream or river, he will not be inconvenienced by the small matter of having to prove fault. This area of delict is commonly referred to as non-natural use of water. The dangers for a landowner when he decides to alter or interfere with the course of streams or rivers are all too obvious as **Kerr v Earl of Orkney (1857)** and **Caledonian Railway Company v Greenock Corporation (1917)** demonstrate.

 In **Kerr v Earl of Orkney (1857)**, the defender went ahead with plans to construct a dam on his property which had the effect of reducing the flow of water to his downstream neighbours. Four months later, after several days of heavy rain, the dam burst and a torrent of water was released which swept downstream and completely destroyed the pursuer's property. The pursuer's argument centred around the fact that the defender's decision to build the dam had interfered with the natural flow of the burn which created the conditions which led, ultimately, to the destruction of his property (his mill and houses were completely swept away by the torrent). The defender attempted to escape liability by claiming that the unfortunate incident was an act of God (*damnum fatale*). This defence, the only possible one that the defender could plead, did not find favour with the court. The defender was strictly liable for his actions in relation to diverting the natural flow of the burn for the purpose of building the dam. If the defender had not interfered with nature in the first place, the horrific damage to the pursuer's property would not have occurred.

When the defender puts forward a defence of *damnum fatale*, he is effectively arguing that an event has occurred which was not reasonably foreseeable and that no amount of precautions or safety measures put in place by a reasonable person would have prevented the harm from occurring. A huge tidal wave engulfing the City of Aberdeen might properly be regarded as an act of God or an example of *damnum fatale*, but heavy rainfall in Scotland is very unlikely to qualify for admission to the league of truly catastrophic disasters outwith human control and foresight.

Caledonian Railway Company *v* Greenock Corporation (1917)

Greenock Corporation diverted the course of a burn in order to fill a paddling pool. Later, heavy rainfall occurred which was unusual for Greenock at the time, but not for the rest of Scotland which habitually experienced very heavy rainfall. Subsequently, the paddling pool could not cope with the excess water and, as a result, it overflowed causing flood damage to the pursuer's property. The House of Lords awarded damages to the pursuer on the basis that Greenock Corporation should be held strictly liable for its decision to interfere with the course of the burn to create the paddling pool. This decision follows **Kerr** and emphasises the fact that a landowner will act at his peril if he alters or diverts the course of a water-channel.

The House of Lords, in a number of modern cases, has reaffirmed the burden of strict liability as illustrated by **Kerr** and **Caledonian Railway Company**. In **RHM Bakeries (Scotland) Ltd *v* Strathclyde Regional Council (1985)**, the House of Lords was at pains to point out that a landowner who diverts the course of a stream which causes damage to another person's property will continue to be held strictly liable.

Key point: In such cases where the individual diverts the course of a stream or a river, he will find himself strictly liable for his actions i.e. another landowner who has suffered loss as a result of the individual's actions has no need to prove fault.

Strict liability

So far in relation to the defender's liability for wrongful acts which cause harm, negligence has to be proved by the pursuer and this can be difficult to establish in many cases. The defender must owe a duty of care to the pursuer and, furthermore, it must be shown that he has failed to take reasonable care. In many cases, the defender is able to escape liability where he can satisfy the court that he has taken reasonable care.

Strict liability is different because there is no defence available to the defender to claim that he had taken all reasonable care to prevent the harm. Where there is strict liability, reasonable care is not enough. In other words, the pursuer is not under an obligation to prove negligence by the defender and this puts the pursuer in an immediately stronger position.

Strict liability as laid down by statute covers two important areas:

◆ Liability for animals
◆ Product liability

Key point: In situations where the defender is said to be strictly liable, the pursuer does not have to prove fault and it will do the defender no good if he claims that he took reasonable care to avoid causing loss or injury to the pursuer.

Liability for animals

This area is now governed by the Animals (Scotland) Act 1987. Section 1 of the 1987 Act states that:

'if an animal belongs to a species whose members generally are, by virtue of their physical attributes or habits, likely (unless controlled or restrained) to injure severely or kill persons or animals, or damage property to a material extent, the keeper of the animal is (strictly) liable for any injury or damage caused by the animal and directly referable to these physical attributes or habits.'

This means that if you are the owner of any animal that is covered by Section 1 of the Act and the animal causes injury or death to other persons or animals then you will be strictly liable for the harm caused. Liability cannot be escaped by showing that you took reasonable care and negligence does not have to be shown by the pursuer. Strict liability means that you must have taken effective precautions to stop the injury occurring in the first instance.

 Burton *v* Moorhead (1881) an extremely aggressive dog attacked the pursuer and injured him. The keeper of the animal tried to defend himself by stating that a strong chain was used for restraining purposes and that this chain normally did the trick. Unfortunately, the keeper's defence that he thought the chain was more than adequate to restrain the dog was simply not good enough. The keeper was fully aware of the dog's nature and, with this knowledge, he should have taken special precautions (not reasonable care) to make sure that the dog was prevented from harming passers-by.

 Behrens *v* Bertram Mills Circus (1957) the pursuer, a circus performer was injured by a circus elephant and he sued the circus. The circus claimed that the animal was extremely well trained, but the court felt that the circus should be judged according to the burden of strict liability. The circus should have taken special precautions to prevent the elephant from causing harm. The fact that the animal had not previously injured anyone was not enough to allow the circus to escape liability to the pursuer.

According to Section 5 of the Animals (Scotland) Act 1987, the keeper of the animal is deemed to be the person who:

◆ Is the owner

or

◆ Has possession of the animal at the time

or

◆ Has actual care or control of a child under 16 who is the owner or has possession of the animal

The keeper of an animal will remain strictly liable for injuries or damage caused by an animal for which he has responsibility, even where it has managed to escape from his custody or in situations where has abandoned it. A third party who finds such an animal and takes it into his custody will not become liable for it. However, if this third party adopted the animal as his own, then the burden of strict liability would now apply to him.

Defences available to the owner are the following:

◆ If the injury or damage was due wholly to the fault of the pursuer, for example, where the pursuer goaded a docile animal which then attacked the pursuer in defence

◆ Where the pursuer has voluntarily accepted the risk i.e. *volenti non fit injuria*

 Key point: A keeper of an animal will be strictly liable for any loss or injury that the animal has caused to the pursuer's person or property.

Product liability

The Sale of Goods Act 1979 (as amended) incorporates implied terms into a contract of sale to protect the buyer. In particular, Section 14 of the Act provides remedies to the buyer where the goods in question are dangerous and their use results in personal injury or property damage being suffered by the buyer. This piece of legislation is, however, designed only to protect the buyer of goods i.e. someone who has a contractual relationship with the seller. In **Donoghue v Stevenson (1932)** it was Mrs Donoghue's friend who had bought the defective product from Mr Minchella, the Paisley café owner. As a result, Mrs Donoghue had to sue the manufacturer of the ginger beer bottle that contained the decomposing snail because she did not have a contract with the seller and, furthermore, the seller could not be expected to open every sealed bottle of ginger beer in order to make sure that they were completely safe. It will also be recalled that bottles were not made of clear glass or clear plastic which might have assisted the seller in an examination to ensure that the products were safe.

In other situations, for example, where the product was given as a gift or if the pursuer was a bystander who was injured by the product, there would be no legal remedy under the Sale of Goods Act 1979 (as amended). There are a number of legal options that are available to someone who has suffered damage to property or a personal injury as a result of using a dangerous product or coming into contact with such a product. We are already well aware of the existence of the standard test for negligence as laid down in **Donoghue v Stevenson (1932)**. This case established the rule that a manufacturer owes a duty of care to anyone who may use his products or come into close contact with these products. Alternatively, however, a pursuer who has suffered harm as a result of a dangerous product can now make use of Part 1 of the Consumer Protection Act 1987. Unlike the test for negligence in **Donoghue v Stevenson (1932)**, the Consumer Protection Act 1987 imposes a burden of strict liability on the producer of the goods.

The Consumer Protection Act 1987

This Act brought into force the European Community Directive on Product Liability (Directive 85/374/EEC). Part 1 of the Act establishes a regime of strict liability in relation to defective products which cause damage to other property and/or injuries to people who were injured as a result of using the product or coming into close contact with the product. Strict liability, it is important to remember, means that the pursuer does not have to prove fault. In other words, strict liability automatically presumes that the defect in the product must be the fault of the producer of the goods – there is no other reasonable explanation for the defect. The producer must come up with a credible explanation to show why he is not to blame for the injuries or loss that the pursuer has suffered. Part 1 of the Act provides a civil remedy for those individuals who have suffered injury, loss or damage caused by a defective product. Part 1 of the Act is, therefore, not concerned with criminal liability in relation to the supply of defective and dangerous products.

A pursuer will be prevented from raising an action under the Act if the defective product was supplied before 1 March 1988. Furthermore, a producer cannot be held liable after ten years have passed since the date of supply of the product and any claims involving claims of personal injury or death must be brought within a three-year period. Under Section 7 of the Act, a producer cannot exclude or limit his liability for defective goods by means of exclusion or limitation clauses.

Parts 2 and 3 of the Act deal with criminal offences and are outwith the scope of this chapter. The Act is admittedly complicated as it operates within both the civil and the criminal law.

Key point: Part 1 of the Consumer Protection Act 1987 establishes a regime of strict liability where goods that are dangerous cause loss or injury to the pursuer.

The weakness of the common law on product liability

It should be remembered that the general rule in Scotland where delictual liability is concerned that the pursuer will fail to win his case if he cannot prove that the defender was at fault. The common law which governs product liability cases is no exception to this rule. **Evans v Triplex Safety Glass Co Ltd (1936)** is often used to demonstrate why Part 1 of the Consumer Protection Act 1987 is an improvement on the legal principle which established a manufacturer's liability for dangerous products as laid down in **Donoghue v Stevenson (1932)**. Although most product liability cases will now be brought under the Consumer Protection Act 1987, some cases will still continue to be brought under **Donoghue** and it is important to appreciate that the liability of a defender under the common law and under statute are quite different. The facts of **Evans** are as follows:

A windscreen was fitted to a car. The windscreen later shattered and it showered the driver and the passengers of the car with glass causing them to suffer injuries. The pursuer brought a claim against the manufacturer for supplying a defective and dangerous product that had caused him to suffer injury.

Held: the pursuer's claim failed because he could not prove that the manufacturer was to blame for supplying a defective product. The windscreen might have been defective and dangerous, but the way in which the windscreen was installed may have made it a dangerous product. The pursuer could not prove with certainty which of these two possibilities was the more likely explanation.

However, the English decision of **Carroll v Fearon (1999)** now makes it clear that the pursuer in negligence action does not have to pinpoint exactly which part of the manufacturing process caused the dangerous defect in the product. In this case, a car crash resulted in the death of a young girl, a woman lost her sight and six others were injured or harmed in a variety of ways. The cause of the crash was faulty tyres manufactured by Dunlop and the evidence presented at the trial very strongly suggested that Dunlop's manufacturing process had caused the defect. It also emerged at the trial that Dunlop was aware of these defects because there had been other accidents involving Dunlop tyres. The company, however, decided not to go public about these defects. If Dunlop had publicised the defects, the tyres could have been recalled thus preventing more accidents from happening in the future. The trial judge found that Dunlop had been negligent, but Dunlop decided to appeal on the grounds that the judge had not been able to specify where precisely in the manufacturing process Dunlop had been negligent.

Held: by the English Court of Appeal that it was not necessary for the pursuers to pinpoint where exactly in the manufacturing process the defender had been negligent. The pursuers had already presented very strong evidence to show that the tyres were defective and that Dunlop was only too well aware of this.

 Key point: The common law rules concerning product liability put the pursuer at a disadvantage because it had to be proved that the manufacturer had been fault by supplying a dangerous product that caused loss or injury to the pursuer.

What types of products are covered by the Act?

We first of all have to ask ourselves the question what is a product? This question is addressed in section 1. A product includes any goods (including components and raw materials) as well as gas, water and electricity. This definition would, of course, cover most consumer goods i.e. goods supplied for private use from a business seller/supplier. Heritable property i.e. land and buildings would not be covered by the Act, but the items used to construct buildings would be covered – so building contractors will fall within the scope of the Act. Agricultural produce is also covered by the Act. It used to be the case that agricultural produce had to have undergone some sort of an industrial process in order for Part 1 of the Act to apply. Agricultural produce is 'any produce of the soil, of stockfarming or fisheries'.

 Key point: Part 1 of the Consumer Protection Act 1987 states that a product includes any goods (including components and raw materials) as well as gas, water and electricity.

To whom does the Act apply?

The Act really applies to the producer of the defective and dangerous goods. We have to ask ourselves, however, who exactly is the producer? Section 2 of the Act provides us with some helpful answers. The producer can be any one of the following people:

◆ The manufacturer
◆ The abstracter of the product, for example, quarrying or mining activities
◆ The processor of the product (who must have altered the product's essential features)

- ◆ An own-brander (where someone else manufactures the product but another individual puts his own label on the product)
- ◆ The individual who imported the product into the European Union

Who will be regarded as a supplier of goods?

A supplier in the chain of supply could also find himself being sued by the pursuer under the Act. It is essential that a supplier responds as honestly as he can to any enquiries that the pursuer makes regarding the identity of the producer. The pursuer's efforts to identify the producer may not be successful and he will have no option but to rely on the supplier's assistance. If the supplier is unwilling to provide this information, the pursuer will suffer considerable inconvenience which may actually result in him being prevented from pursuing his claim against the producer. The pursuer must address a query to the supplier within a reasonable time and the supplier must respond to the pursuer with the information concerning the producer's identity within a reasonable time. A supplier includes any individual who supplies goods to the pursuer. Section 45 states that the act of supplying goods will include such activities as selling, hiring, lending or supplying them under a hire purchase contract. Furthermore, the goods need not be exchanged for money. Goods supplied as a prize would be covered by the Act.

 Key point: Part 1 of the Consumer Protection Act applies to the following individuals – the manufacturer, the abstracter of the product, the processor of the product, an own-brander and an individual who imported the product into the European Union.

What do we mean when we talk about defective and dangerous goods?

We are really concerned with the product's safety. It must be a dangerous product capable of causing damage to the pursuer's property or capable of causing the pursuer to suffer some sort of personal injury. The fact that the product is not working properly will not give a pursuer the right to raise an action against the defender. Many products are defective without being dangerous in any way. Section 3 deals with this issue and the standard of safety will depend on what individuals 'generally are entitled to expect'. The design of the product, the reasons why it was placed on the market, any warnings or instructions provided and when the product was supplied will all be issues which must be taken into account. To protect himself, a producer should take special precautions in order to reduce any danger that the product might cause. People, amateur DIY enthusiasts, teenagers and children especially, have a tendency to misuse products.

 Key point: A dangerous product is one that is capable of causing damage to the pursuer's property or capable of causing the pursuer to suffer some sort of personal injury – the fact that the product is not working properly will not give a pursuer the right to raise an action against the defender

In terms of damages, what will the pursuer be entitled to claim?

Section 5 addresses the question of damages that the pursuer is entitled to claim from the defender. The Act covers damage which includes death, personal injury or any loss or damage to any property. Liability cannot arise in situations of pure economic loss. When we talk about damage caused by defective products, we have to bear in mind the following issues:

- The Act only covers damage to private and not business property.

- The Act only applies to claims valued at over £275. The limit of £275 does not apply to cases involving death and personal injuries.

- The producer is not liable for damage caused to the defective product itself or any of the product's component parts. In such situations, the pursuer will have to continue to bring an action under the Sale of Goods Act 1979 or the law of delict. The defective product or component must cause injury to persons or damage to other property before the producer will be liable under the Act.

 Key point: Damages will be awarded for loss or injury caused by dangerous products, but economic loss is not recoverable.

Does the Consumer Protection Act give the producer any defences?

Section 4 provides the producer with several defences which he may use to try and escape liability for dangerous products. A pursuer will be fail in his action in the following circumstances:

- The defect was as a result of the defender complying with a statutory provision which relates to the product.

- The producer did not supply the product at any time to another person, for example, this would cover stolen products or products which the producer only intended for his personal use.

- The product's supply was not made in the course of business or for profit.

- The defect did not exist in the product at the time when it was supplied. This would cover wear and tear or tampering.

- The 'development risks' defence which allows the defender to escape liability because scientific or technical knowledge would not be able to pinpoint defects in the product at the time that it was supplied. In order to escape liability, the defender will have to show that no other producer of the goods could have discovered dangers lurking in the product. Manufacturers of mobile phones will no doubt be relieved to discover that they can rely on this defence if ten years from now scientists do manage to prove that these products cause cancer. The development risks defence is the only exception to the standard of strict liability in the Act. This defence is the statutory equivalent of Lord Denning's statement in **Roe v Ministry of Health (1954)** that 'we must not look at the 1947 accident with 1954 spectacles'.

- Contributory negligence i.e. the defect was partly caused by the producer's negligence and partly by the actions of the claimant. Accordingly, the amount of the pursuer's damages may be reduced by the court.

- *Volenti non fit injuria* i.e. the pursuer knowingly and recklessly continued to use the product in a dangerous fashion despite the apparent risks in such a course of action. This is a complete defence and the pursuer will receive no damages.

The defences available to a producer amount to the following:

◆ The product is not covered by the Act. As we have already seen, Section 1 provides a list of products that are covered by the Act.

◆ The pursuer cannot prove or identify that the defender is the producer or supplier of the product. Section 2 provides a list of individuals who can be regarded as the producer of the goods

◆ The defect in the product is not covered by section 3. In other words, the product has not caused the pursuer to suffer property damage or personal injury.

◆ The damage is not covered by Section 5. This would cover situations where the product is causes the pursuer to suffer pure economic loss only.

◆ The defect in the product did not cause the damage.

 Key point: Although a defender is said to be strictly liable in relation to dangerous products, there are a number of defences that he can plead in order to escape liability, for example, contributory negligence, *volenti no fit injuria* and the development risks defence.

Summary

● The law of delict is concerned with the defender's wrongful behaviour.

● Wrongful behaviour can have both criminal and civil consequences, but the law of delict is only concerned with the civil consequences of a wrongful act or omission.

● Delict is a very different area of law from contractual obligations. With contracts, the parties enter the agreement of their own free will – they are not forced to contract with one another. The law of delict is not about personal choice – we all owe a duty of care to other people and we are expected to comply with this duty.

● Delicts which are committed unintentionally by the defender resulting in loss, injury or damage to the pursuer are the most common type of civil wrong. In these situations, the defender is said to have been negligent or careless.

● Damages in a delictual action are awarded for personal injuries (whether physical or psychiatric) and for damage to property.

● Where the pursuer has suffered financial or pure economic loss as a result of the defender's negligent actions, the courts are much more reluctant to grant compensation.

● The courts will sometimes award damages for pure economic loss, but there must be evidence to show that the parties had a special relationship with one another.

- The leading case for negligence claims is **Donoghue v Stevenson (1932)**.

- The rule in **Donoghue v Stevenson** is that you must take reasonable care to avoid acts or omissions which you can reasonably foresee would be likely to injure your neighbour.

- The standard of care which is expected of the defender is one of reasonable care. Reasonable care is the standard of care expected of the 'hypothetical' reasonable man or woman who is a person of ordinary care and prudence and who is neither overcautious nor overconfident.

- Harmful conduct may be intentional, for example, assault or fraud.

- The civil remedies that are available to the injured party in a delictual are reparation and interdict.

- The general rule in Scotland is that there can be no delictual liability without fault. Quite simply, this means that the pursuer must prove, on the balance of probabilities that the defender's actions caused him to suffer loss, injury or damage.

- In certain situations, the defender's liability is said to be strict. In other words, the law automatically presumes that the defender is to blame for the harm caused to the pursuer.

- The most common defences that are used by the defender in an action of delict are:

    a) Contributory negligence

    b) *Volenti non fit injuria* (to one who is willing a wrongful act cannot be done)

    c) Prescription and limitation

    d) Compliance with statutory authority

    e) Necessity

    f) *Damnum fatale*

    g) Criminality

Short answer questions, exam standard essay style questions and case-studies.

1 The starting point for a pursuer in a negligence action is that he will have to prove that the defender owed him a duty care and that the defender's subsequent actions have breached that duty of care causing him to suffer loss or injury.

What is a duty of care?

2 a) Aggie, Mahmoud, Tom and Paul are neighbours who live in a shared property which has a communal back garden. There appears to be a problem with the property's water and sewerage system which has caused the back garden to be flooded on a number of occasions. The four property owners hold a meeting to discuss the best way of tackling the problem. Paul is friendly with a plumber and he suggests that they call the plumber in to carry out some basic exploratory work in order to trace the source of the problem. The other three think that Paul's suggestion is an excellent one and they tell him to go ahead and contact the plumber. The following week, Harry, the plumber, comes along to look at the water and sewerage system. Harry is under strict instructions from Paul to carry out a survey, but he is not authorised to dig up the garden. Harry carries out the survey and informs Paul that the local water company will have to be informed as the water and sewerage system appears to be in a serious state of disrepair. A week later, Paul receives a letter from Aggie's solicitor informing him that Aggie intends to sue him for £10,000 in an ordinary action at the local Sheriff Court. Apparently, Aggie is claiming that she broke her ankle when she fell into a twenty-two foot trench in the back garden. Aggie states that Paul and Harry dug this trench during the survey. Furthermore, Paul and Harry were negligent in that they did nothing to warn people about the existence of the trench.

What will Aggie have to prove in order to win her case?

b) Following on from the above incident involving Aggie, Paul and Harry, consider the following issues:

i) Paul and Harry deny digging a trench. Paul was away in London on business the day that the trench was allegedly dug and George claims that he merely carried out a survey.

ii) Paul's solicitor has a witness, Phil a window cleaner, who states that no trench was ever dug. Phil is a willing witness and he has absolutely nothing to gain by coming forward and offering to give evidence on Paul and Harry's behalf.

iii) Aggie produces one witness to back up her story, but under cross-examination by Paul's solicitor, she is forced to admit that she only saw Harry carrying out a survey in the back garden.

iv) During her evidence, Aggie begins to change her story and speak about a hole rather than a trench.

In the light of the above information, assess Aggie's chances of success at the trial.

3 a) In certain situations, a defender will be able to escape delictual liability by proving that he took all reasonable care to avoid causing loss or harm to the pursuer.

What is meant by reasonable care?

b) Graham is a keen golfer. One day when he was out on the course he was hit in the face by a golf ball. Due to this accident, Graham lost the sight in one eye. He successfully sued Lorne who hit the golf ball which caused the injury. Lorne is now claiming that the golf club should also take part of the blame for Graham's injuries. Lorne is arguing that the golf club should have put up a fence or a screen to protect golfers at the first hole from being hit by golfers teeing off at the second hole. The golf club did put up a sign which asked golfers on the second hole not to tee off until those golfers at the first tee had already done so, but this rule is hardly ever obeyed in practice. The golf club claims that it consulted an expert who advised them not to erect a fence or a screen between these two holes as it would do nothing to prevent the likelihood of accidents. Furthermore, over a million rounds of golf have been played on the course and only one accident at that particular spot has occurred (and it was by no means a serious accident).

Do you think that the golf club has taken reasonable care to prevent accidents from occurring?

4 A group of teenage boys who are currently serving sentences in a young offenders institution are taken on an adventure holiday. They are staying at a centre near Loch Lomond which caters towards the rehabilitation of young offenders. None of the boys is considered a threat to members of the public. On the last evening of the holiday, the staff who have accompanied the boys are so pleased with the success of the holiday that they decide to leave the boys unsupervised and head for a celebratory drink in the local pub. The boys are soon bored with nothing to do. Seeing an opportunity to liven things up, one of the older boys persuades some of the younger members of the group that it would be a good idea to go for a drive as it is a lovely summer's evening. In any case, they will all be back before the pub's closing time and no one will miss them for a few hours. They decide to borrow the centre's minibus and they decide to go on a tour up the western side of the Loch. None of the boys is a qualified driver. On the way up the road, the boy driving the minibus is forced off the road in order to avoid a sheep that was blocking the way. Although no one was injured in the accident, the minibus is a complete write-off and a farmer's wall has been extensively damaged. As a result, the farmer's sheep managed to escape from the field. It is only later that the farmer discovers that some of his lambs have drowned in the loch.

Evaluate the above situation.

5 **a)** As a general rule, the Scottish courts do not award damages to a pursuer in situations where the defender's behaviour causes the pursuer to suffer pure economic loss.

Evaluate this statement.

b) McBurney Leisure Services PLC has just entered a contract with builders who have been hired to build a new, luxury hotel. Each bathroom in the hotel will be fully tiled using only the best materials. In order to complete this task, the builders have recommended that McBurney use a particular firm of specialist subcontractors with which the builders have had extensive dealings. McBurney relied upon this recommendation and allowed the builders to use the subcontractors. After the completion of the bathrooms, however, it was discovered that many of the tiles had not been properly secured to the walls. The tiles in no way pose a danger to guests and staff, but this is a luxury hotel and the guests are likely to be unimpressed by the poor quality of the decor in their bathrooms. McBurney has had to spend a lot of money in order to repair the defective tiling. McBurney now wishes to take action against the builders claiming that it was negligent when it recommended the specialist subcontractors.

Should the builders be liable in negligence to McBurney for recommending the subcontractors?

6 Write short notes on the following matters:
a) The *causa causans* and the *causa sine qua non*
b) A *novus actus interveniens*.

5 **a)** In Scots law, who will have primary responsibility for animals that cause damage to property or cause harm or injury to other animals or humans?

b) Jan is driving her car along the promenade at Ayr Beach. Drivers are expected to observe a 20-mile-an-hour speed limit on this promenade because the road is next to a large grassy area where lots of children play. Jan is a very careful and experienced driver and she is observing the speed limit. Suddenly, Jan has to brake very hard in order to avoid a dog that has run out into the middle of the road. Unfortunately, Jan is unable to stop her car from hitting the dog. The dog is badly injured, but it will survive the accident if it receives immediate medical attention from a vet. The collision has also caused several hundred pounds worth of damage to Jan's car. It turns out that a 15-year-old boy (the owner's son) had responsibility for the dog. The boy had the dog on a leash but he was busy having a conversation on his mobile phone when the dog broke free and ran out into the path of Jan's car. This fact does not prevent the dog's owner from sending Jan a solicitor's letter demanding payment of the vet's bill. Jan is understandably enraged about this turn of events. After all, she took the boy with the injured dog straight to the vet in order that the animal would receive prompt medical treatment.

What is the legal position?

6 When a pursuer raises a delictual action in the Scottish courts, he must always be able to demonstrate that his loss or injuries were caused by the fault of the defender in order for his claim to have any chance of success.

Assess the accuracy of this statement.

7 **a)** The Occupiers' Liability (Scotland) Act 1960 uses the term 'occupier' rather than the owner of a property.

What is the difference legally between an occupier and an owner?

b) Examine the following notice carefully:

WARNING NOTICE

DEMOLITION OF DANGEROUS STRUCTURE IN PROGRESS.

UNDER NO CIRCUMSTANCES SHOULD MEMBERS OF THE PUBLIC ATTEMPT TO ENTER THESE PREMISES WITHOUT THE EXPRESS PERMISSION OF LYNCH DEMOLITION SERVICES LTD.

MEMBERS OF THE PUBLIC RUN THE RISK OF SERIOUS INJURY OR EVEN DEATH IF THEY ENTER THE PREMISES UNACCOMPANIED BY KEY SITE PERSONNEL.

VISITORS SHOULD REPORT TO DESMOND LYNCH, SITE MANAGER, IMMEDIATELY UPON ARRIVAL.

LYNCH DEMOLITION SERVICES LTD, 190 WEST REGENT STREET, GLASGOW G2 1PR, T: 0141-242 0999

Lynch Demolition Services Ltd is currently in the process of demolishing a dangerous structure. As the job is a matter of urgency, the demolition team has not had time to put proper fencing around the site which would ensure that trespassers are kept out and other curious members of the public are kept at a safe distance. However, the demolition team has placed the above notice at a numerous points around the site and it has hired the services of a security firm to provide security guards who work a nine to five shift, Monday to Friday. Patrick Lynch, a Director of the demolition company, felt that it was unnecessary to retain the services of the security firm at the weekends. This decision was all part of a cost-cutting exercise. On Sunday afternoon, Desmond Lynch, the site manager and a Director of the company, receives some bad news from one of his foremen. It would seem that a four-year-old child has managed to gain access to the site and, while there, was badly injured as a result of part of a wall falling on him. The child's parents are threatening to sue Lynch Demolition Services Ltd.

Advise Lynch Demolition Services.

8 a) What are the main defences to a delictual action in Scotland?

b) Michael was visiting Paisley Zoo when he accidentally dropped his mobile phone into the lions' enclosure. The phone is very expensive and Michael is desperate to retrieve it. He looks about to see if any of the keepers are around, but he does not see anyone. Michael is a very impatient person and the only lion that appears to be in the cage is sound asleep. Michael decides to take a chance and he climbs over the wall and drops into the enclosure. He quickly picks up the phone and heads back to the wall without disturbing the lion. At that moment, however, his phone begins to ring (it is a very loud ring tone) and the lion awakens. It sees Michael standing below the wall and promptly gives chase. Five minutes later, Michael is dragged from the enclosure by the keepers, more dead than alive, after having received a savaging from a very angry lion that was awakened from a sound sleep. He is very lucky, a member of the public alerted the keepers and one of them managed to shoot the lion with a fast-acting tranquilliser dart. On his way to the ambulance, a delirious Michael was heard to mumble that the Zoo would be hearing from his lawyers.

Assuming that Michael survives his experience, would he be advised to raise an action against the Zoo?

9 a) Part 1 of the Consumer Protection Act 1987 vastly improves the level of protection enjoyed by consumers in relation to the supply of dangerous products.

Discuss the above statement.

b) Lynne is a frequent mobile phone user (she spends some three or four hours per day on the phone). Recently, Lynne has been experiencing frequent dizzy spells and she has noticed that she is suffering from especially severe headaches. After an examination by a specialist at the hospital, Lynne is informed that she has a brain tumour. Luckily, the specialist informs Lynne that the tumour has been detected at a very early stage and the cancer is treatable. Lynne is absolutely convinced that the tumour has been caused by her exposure to the radiation being transmitted from her mobile phone. She now wishes to sue the mobile phone manufacturer.

Does Lynne have a claim against the manufacturer in terms of the Consumer Protection Act 1987 or the common law?

10 a) In certain situations, the defender's negligence will be the only obvious explanation for the loss or injury suffered by the pursuer.

Explain the phrase *res ipsa loquiter* and use examples from previously decided cases to illustrate your answer.

b) Brian went in to use the toilets at his local supermarket before he began his weekly shopping. The toilet floors were very slippery because one of the supermarket's employees had just finished cleaning them. Thinking that the supermarket was quiet, the employee decided to nip up to the staff room for an unofficial cigarette break. The employee did not think it was worth putting up signs to warn customers that the toilet floor was dangerous. It was during the employee's absence that Brian came in to use the toilets. He slipped and fell heavily breaking his arm in the process. He was totally unaware that the floor was slippery and he did not see any warning signs.

How strong a claim does Brian have against the supermarket?

11 a) The decisions of the House of Lords in both **Alcock and Others v Chief Constable of the Yorkshire Police (1992)** and **White and Others v Chief Constable of the South Yorkshire Police (1998)** have clarified the law of delict in relation to claims involving nervous shock or psychiatric injury.

Explain the guidelines in relation to cases involving psychiatric injuries as laid down by the House of Lords in **Alcock** and **White**.

b) Pamela was driving along the motorway when she fell asleep at the wheel of her car. She collided with a school bus and both vehicles skidded out of control before stopping in such a position that three lanes of the motorway were completely blocked off. As a result of this accident, the driver and several school children were killed. Many of the school children were also seriously injured in the accident. Pamela's legs were broken as a result of the crash and she was not able to escape from the wreckage of her car. To make matters worse, visibility was dreadful that day and ten cars were not able to stop in time to avoid the wreckage of the first accident and a multiple pile-up occurred on the motorway. The emergency services are called out and have to deal with a truly horrific road accident. The accident also receives extensive media coverage and images of the crash are

shown on the lunchtime, evening and late television news bulletins. The school is also named on these television programmes. Quite apart from the physical injuries that the victims have suffered in the accident, many are now claiming that they have gone on to experience psychiatric injury. Many relatives of the dead and injured have developed psychiatric illnesses which they claim were caused by the accident. Finally, several police officers, paramedics and fire personnel are bringing a legal action on the grounds that, since the accident, they have gone on to suffer from a variety of psychiatric conditions.

Using the legal principles laid down by the House of Lords in relation to claims involving psychiatric injury advise the pursuers.

c) Consider the following situation:

Tracy has just been released from the psychiatric unit of the local hospital. Tracy suffers terribly from a nervous condition for which she has to take medication in order to control it. Her home is situated not far from the motorway and she heard the crash involving Pamela and the school bus. Immediately afterwards, Tracy heard the sound of more cars being involved in a crash. Being in possession of a very curious nature, Tracy rushed to the side of the motorway and saw the immediate aftermath of the accident. She is absolutely horrified and she promptly suffers nervous shock. When Tracy regains consciousness, she realises that she has been admitted to the acute ward of the psychiatric unit. Tracy now wishes to sue the person who caused the accident on the motorway.

What are the chances of Tracy's claim succeeding?

12 Write explanatory notes on the following topics:
a) Trespass
b) Nuisance
c) Spiteful use of property rights
d) The *actio de effusis dejectis* and the *actio de positis vel suspensis*
e) Non-natural use of water

CHAPTER
4

THE SALE OF GOODS AND AN INTRODUCTION TO CONSUMER CREDIT

Introduction

This chapter looks at the Sales of Goods Act 1979 (as amended) and also considers consumer credit agreements and the main provisions of the Consumer Credit Act 1974. Consumer credit agreements are closely associated with sale of goods contracts because buyers will often insist that the seller permit them to purchase goods on credit.

This chapter covers the following areas:

- Introduction to the Sale of Goods Act 1979 (as amended)
- Classification of goods
- Transfer of title
- Implied terms in consumer law
- Delivery of goods
- Breach of contract
- The Consumer Credit Act 1974 (as amended)

Introduction to the Sale of Goods Act 1979 (as amended)

The rules which govern sale of goods transactions are contained in the Sale of Goods Act 1979 (as amended). The original Act of 1893 codified many of the common law provisions regulating contracts for the sale of goods. The Act contains detailed rules governing contracts for the sale of goods. The Act applies to those contracts formed after 1 January 1894. Despite amendments, it can be argued that Sir MacKenzie Chalmers, who was responsible for drafting the original Act of 1893, would have little difficulty in recognising many of the major provisions of the modern Sale of Goods Act. This is why that many of the cases used in this Chapter were decided by the courts before the introduction of the current version of the Sale of Goods Act. In other words, the rules relating to sale of goods transactions have survived in a remarkably consistent fashion over a long period of time.

 Key point: The rules which govern sale of goods transactions are contained in the Sale of Goods Act 1979 (as amended).

A genuine sale

Section 2 of the Sale of Goods Act 1979 defines a contract for the sale of goods as one where the seller transfers or agrees to transfer the property (ownership) of the goods for a money consideration called the price.

The provisions of the Act only apply to transactions that operate by way of a sale of goods contract. The Act does not apply to arrangements which operate by way of a mortgage, pledge, charge or other security arrangement (Section 62(4)). A security arrangement, for example, a mortgage arrangement is where a debtor grants security over an item of his property to a creditor in exchange for a loan. Under such an arrangement, the creditor hands over a sum of money to the debtor who, in turn, hands over his property. To the casual observer, this may look like a sale. However, the arrangement is merely a device whereby the creditor is protecting himself by insisting upon possession of the debtor's goods. Should the debtor fail to repay the loan, the creditor will refuse to hand over the goods and, in this way, he has managed to cut his losses to some extent. Sometimes, however, for reasons best known to the parties, it is not always simple to decide whether a transaction is a genuine sale and, therefore, covered by the 1979 Act, or some sort of security transaction which is outside the scope of the Act. This area of the law has often caused confusion for the Scottish courts (see **Aluminium Industrie Vaassen B V *v* Romalpa Aluminium Ltd (1976)** and **Armour and Another *v* Thyssen Edelstahlwerke AG (1990)**).

Furthermore, the courts have not always consistently distinguished between a contract for the sale of goods and a contract for services. Services would be classed as 'incorporeal moveable property' in terms of Scots law and would, therefore, fall outside the definition of goods under the Sale of Goods Act. Unfortunately, the courts have not always been consistent when it comes to being able to distinguish between a genuine sale of goods which is covered by the provisions of the Act and a contract for services which is outwith scope of the Act.

 Robinson *v* Graves (1935) the parties had entered into a contract for the purpose of painting a portrait.

Held: by the English Court of Appeal that this contract was not a sale of goods, but rather a contract for the provision of work (services) and materials.

 However, in **Philip Head & Sons *v* Showfronts Ltd (1970)** the parties into entered into a contract for the supply and the fitting of a carpet.

Held: this was a contract for a sale of goods.

This definition would seem to insist that in order to become the owner of the goods, the buyer must pay cash (or a cheque etc) for them. This would seem to rule out transactions where the parties exchange goods and no money changes hands. However, contracts which work as part exchanges of goods will be covered by the Act because the buyer makes a cash payment, for example, the buyer trades in his old car when he goes to buy a newer model from a dealership. It would seem that as long as some money is exchanged the conditions laid down in Section 2 are met.

 Key point: A sale of goods is where the buyer pays money to the seller or his agent in order to acquire ownership of the goods and the transaction does

not operate by way of a mortgage, charge, pledge or other similar
arrangement.

Corporeal, moveable goods

According to Section 61(1), the Act only applies to a particular class of goods – all
corporeal, moveable property with the exception of money.

Moveable goods are all goods which are by their very nature able to be physically
transferred from seller to buyer in a contract of sale. Corporeal means that the
goods are tangible (they have a physical shape). Thus, corporeal moveable property
covers all goods which are tangible and can be moved, for example, a chair, a table,
a stereo system, a video and a television – the list is endless.

The major types of property which are not covered by the Act include heritable
property, money and incorporeal moveable property. Incorporeal property would
include shares in a company, patents, trade marks and copyrights. Furthermore, the
Act does not apply to the contracts for the sale of services.

 Key point: The Act applies to corporeal, moveable goods i.e. goods that have
a physical shape and which can be moved from seller to buyer.

Rules about capacity, formality, the price and stipulations as to time

Many rules of contract are recognised by the Act in relation to capacity, formality,
the price and stipulations as to time. A number of significant examples are briefly
discussed below.

The parties to a contract must have contractual capacity (Section 3), but there is
no need for a sale of goods contract to be in writing (Section 4).

Sections 8 and 9 deal with the important issue of the price that is to be paid by
the buyer for the goods in question. Section 8 makes it clear that a sale will only
really be a sale if the buyer exchanges a money consideration called the price for the
goods. According to Section 8, the parties can leave the price to be fixed by the
contract or by reference to a method laid down by the contract. Alternatively, the
parties may have had previous dealings that can be referred to in order to calculate
the price. If the contract is silent on the issue of the price or there have been no
previous dealings between the parties, the buyer must pay a reasonable price for the
goods and what is reasonable will depend on the facts of each situation.

Section 9 does allow the parties to fix a price by appointing a third party to carry
out a valuation of the goods. If such a valuation cannot or is not carried out, the
contract is rendered voidable. If one of the parties to the contract of sale prevented
the valuation from being carried out, the innocent party could bring an action for
damages.

Section 10 makes it clear that, unless the parties agree differently, statements
about time in relation to the sale of goods transaction are not to be regarded as a
material term of the contract. In order to determine whether a contractual term
about time is material, the content of the contract and the intentions of the parties
will have to be examined. Late delivery of goods by the seller, for example, will not
necessarily mean that the buyer has the right to treat the contract as cancelled. The
most appropriate remedy for the seller's breach may be to lodge an action for

damages. Additionally, Section 59 states that where references are made to a reasonable time, the question of what is a reasonable time is a question of fact.

 Shaw, Macfarlane & Co v Waddell & Sons (1890) there was an express stipulation in the contract that the goods should be delivered at Grangemouth for shipment by the buyer's vessel L'Avenir between April 12 and 16. The buyer failed to honour this contractual term which was considered to be a material part of the agreement and the sellers were, therefore, justified in cancelling (rescinding) the contract.

 Key point: Stipulations as to time in the contract of sale are not necessarily material terms of the contract.

Property in the goods

Quite simply, property in the goods means that the person has now become the owner of the goods. An owner of goods is said to have real rights in the property or goods. By real rights we are talking about an exercise of power i.e. the owner of the goods can effectively say to the world at large 'get your hands off my property'. The owner can do anything he likes with the goods as long as he does not break the law.

It is worth remembering that it is not necessary to have possession of the goods to be the owner of the property. Ownership and possession are not the same thing. If I lend you my mobile phone for the day, you have possession of the item but I will still remain the owner. An agent and an employee will often have possession of their principal's or employer's property in the course of their duties, but they are most certainly not the owners of these items – the principal or the employer will continue to exercise ownership civil possession of the property through them.

We should, therefore, not place too much reliance on the old saying that possession is nine-tenths of the law. Even delivery of moveable goods in a contract of sale is not definite proof of the transfer of property from seller to buyer. Transfer of ownership of the goods can occur before or after delivery has taken place.

The general rule is that the parties to a contract will decide when property in the goods is transferred from seller to buyer. The parties to a contract of sale are said to have freedom of contract in the sense that they decide what arrangements best suit themselves. It is important to appreciate that the Sale of Goods Act 1979 provides a set of very detailed rules which govern the transfer of ownership, but at the end of the day, the parties are often free to use these rules or reject them entirely.

 Key point: Someone who has property in the goods or who has good title to them is regarded as having rights of ownership.

The importance of identifying when ownership is transferred

The main rules dealing with the transfer of ownership of corporeal moveable goods are contained in sections 16 to 19 of the Act. Determining when ownership will be transferred is important for a variety of reasons:

1   If the seller has not yet passed property in the goods, the buyer only has personal rights (i.e. the right to sue) in relation to the seller and this means that the seller can still exercise his rights of ownership over the goods.

2 If the seller has remained the owner of the goods, theoretically he can sell the goods to another buyer and this second buyer can gain good title to the goods.

3 The owner of the goods will have to suffer the risk of loss, damage or theft in relation to the property.

4 If the seller of the goods has not yet transferred ownership and becomes insolvent after the buyer has paid for the property, the buyer will not have a right to demand the goods. In this situation, the buyer will have to attempt to reclaim his money – which as an unsecured creditor may be a very remote possibility.

5 If the seller of the goods has transferred ownership and the buyer becomes insolvent before he has paid for the property, the seller no longer has ownership rights over the goods. In this situation, the seller is not in a position to demand any goods that he has delivered to the buyer. The seller will have to place a claim for payment of the goods – which as an unsecured creditor may well be an unsuccessful course of action.

6 The owner of goods is said to have real rights in the property which means that he has the power to determine who will use the goods, how the goods will be used and what they will be used for. Ownership is, therefore, an exercise of power. If a person is not the owner of the goods, they merely have personal rights in relation to the goods which usually amounts to the right to raise a claim for damages as a part of a breach of contract claim. Personal rights may give the party the right to sue, but this will not him the right to own or control the goods.

 Key point: Ownership is important because it is the owner of goods who will be able to exercise control over them (real rights) but, on the downside, the owner will have to suffer the risk of loss, damage or theft in respect of the goods.

The passing of ownership

The point at which ownership passes to the buyer depends on whether the contract is said to be a sale or an agreement to sell.

Section 2(4) states that if the property in the goods is transferred from the seller to the buyer the contract is called a sale.

So, upon the conclusion of a sale, ownership usually passes to the buyer immediately because the goods are identified and agreed upon. Imagine a situation where the buyer selects a particular shirt from the shelves and tries the item on for size, comfort and style. Once he has satisfied with the shirt, the buyer then makes an offer to buy the item which the seller accepts. The buyer now has a contract of sale with the seller and, more importantly, he has become the new owner of the shirt.

Section 2(5) states that if the transfer of property in the goods is to take place at a future time or upon the fulfilment of some condition, the contract is called an agreement to sell.

Therefore, in an agreement to sell, the passing of ownership is postponed until some time in the future, either by the mutual consent of the parties or after the fulfilment of some condition. What if the goods you have ordered have yet to be manufactured or acquired by the seller – a three-piece leather suite. Does the buyer wish to become the owner of the furniture before it is even made? In this situation, it is only when the suite has been manufactured and the buyer informed of this that ownership passes to the buyer. The agreement to sell has now become a sale regardless of whether the suite has been delivered or paid for.

 Key point: The point at which ownership passes to the buyer depends on whether the contract is said to be a sale or an agreement to sell.

Classification of goods

In deciding whether ownership of goods has been transferred from seller to buyer, Section 5 of the Act distinguishes between certain types of goods.

Existing goods are owned or possessed by the seller and can be specific or unascertained.

- Specific goods can be identified at the time of the contracting, for example, the painting entitled 'The Mona Lisa' by the artist Leonardo da Vinci. In this case, ownership usually passes immediately.

- Unascertained goods cannot be identified because they are part of a larger quantity, for example, 30 tonnes of cotton in a storeroom containing 100 tonnes of cotton. In this case, there can only be an agreement to sell.

Future goods are yet to be acquired or manufactured by the seller, for example, handmade jewellery. In this case, there can only be an agreement to sell. Ownership cannot pass until the goods are manufactured or acquired and the seller has notified the buyer of this fact.

 Key point: Existing goods are owned or possessed by the seller and future goods are goods that will have to be acquired or manufactured by the seller.

Specific goods and generic goods

Section 61(1) of the 1979 Act describes specific goods as goods identified or agreed upon when the contract of sale is formed. Specific goods include an undivided share, specified as a fraction or a percentage of goods that have been identified and agreed upon by the seller and the buyer.

Generic goods, on the other hand, can be obtained from a variety of sources. The buyer will often merely state that he wishes to purchase a particular quantity of these goods and he has absolutely no interest in the seller's source of supply. It has been remarked that generic goods can never really perish or be destroyed because the seller can easily replace them. Consequently, contracts involving generic goods which have perished or which have been destroyed cannot be made void, unlike contracts involving specific goods (see Sections 6 and 7).

Critically, section 17 of the Act states that in a contract for the sale of specific or ascertained goods, ownership passes when the buyer and the seller intend that it should pass. In this situation, the courts will examine the intentions and the conduct of the parties carefully. Usually but not always, in a contract for ascertained goods, ownership will be transferred as soon as the contract is formed i.e. offer +

acceptance. The seller, for instance, may choose to delay the passing of property until he has been paid for the goods (this very issue will be examined later).

An example of specific goods can be seen in the following situation:

An individual wishes to purchase a leather jacket from a retailer. She chooses the product in question from a display and makes an offer for it at the cashpoint which is accepted by the sales assistant (offer + acceptance = contract: see **Pharmaceutical Society of Great Britain v Boots Cash Chemists (1953)**). The leather jacket is an example of ascertained goods because it is that very jacket with which the customer will be leaving the store and not a similar item picked out by the sales assistant or ordered for the customer from the retailer's warehouse.

 Key point: Specific goods are the very goods that the buyer will physically receive from the seller – not a copy or a similar item.

Unascertained goods

The Sale of Goods Act does not define unascertained goods. These are goods which are not identified and agreed upon at the time when the contract was formed.

The customer has selected a widescreen television that she wishes to purchase. She approaches the cashpoint and makes an offer to buy the goods which the sales assistant accepts. However, the customer does not yet have a contract of sale with the seller. The sales assistant informs the customer that the store will have to contact its warehouse and arrange delivery of the product to the customer. Ownership of the television set has not yet passed to the customer and it will not do so until such time as the seller singles out the very item and puts the goods in a deliverable state and informs the buyer of this fact. Section 61(5) states that goods will be in a deliverable state when they are in such a state that the buyer under the contract would be bound to take delivery of them.

 Key point: Unascertained goods are goods that form part of a larger quantity held by the seller and the buyer cannot single out the goods that he will receive – the seller will have to do this and place the goods in a deliverable state.

There are two types of unascertained goods, those which:

◆ Form an unsevered (undivided) portion of a particular quantity of goods such as 20 tons of cotton taken from 100 tons of cotton lying in the hold of a ship named 'Peerless'

◆ Are generic goods i.e. a quantity of goods which can be acquired almost anywhere such as 1000 tons of cane sugar. The buyer is not the slightest bit interested where the seller will get his supplies.

Section 16 states that where unascertained goods are concerned, there can only be an agreement to sell and property will not pass to the buyer until the goods become ascertained i.e. until they become unconditionally appropriated to the contract by the seller. This will usually occur when the seller puts the goods in a deliverable state and informs the buyer of this development. Goods in a deliverable state means that the buyer must accept the goods.

The harsh reality of the rule in section 16 can be seen in **Hayman & Son v McLintock (1907)**.

The **Hayman** case concerned a contract for the sale of unascertained goods which fell into the first category above (i.e. a portion of a larger quantity of goods). McNairn, a flour merchant, sold and was paid for some sacks of flour. The merchant's flour was stored in a warehouse owned by Hayman. McNairn sent word to Hayman that two buyers had purchased 100 and 250 sacks of flour respectively. Hayman let the buyers know that he had the sacks at his warehouse and that he was awaiting their orders. In his records, Hayman kept a note of the number of sacks to which the buyers were entitled. However, he did nothing to separate these sacks from the other sacks belonging to the merchant. He did not even put the buyers' names on the sacks.

McNairn became bankrupt and a trustee in bankruptcy was appointed to seize all the merchant's property in order to sell it to pay his debts. The trustee, however, attempted to seize all the merchant's sacks in the warehouse. The buyers, understandably, objected to this course of action. The trustee in bankruptcy was held by the court to be entitled to keep all the sacks and use them to pay off the merchant's debts. The goods were unascertained, therefore, property in them could not pass to the buyer. Nothing had been done to make the goods ascertained, for example, by labelling them and thereby ensuring the transfer of ownership from seller to buyer.

Key point: In contract involving unascertained goods, there can only be an agreement to sell – ownership will not pass to the buyer until the goods become ascertained.

The Sale of Goods (Amendment) Act 1995

The effects of the Hayman case have been reduced with the introduction of the Sale of Goods (Amendment) Act 1995. This legislation addresses the question of unascertained goods which form part of an identifiable bulk and undivided shares in goods. The 1995 Act only applies to contracts formed on or after 19 September 1995. The 1995 Act inserts a new Section 20A into the Sale of Goods Act 1979.

Now, on payment of either some or all of the price, property in goods which form an undivided share in an identified bulk will immediately pass to the buyer. This means that the buyer becomes a common owner of bulk goods. This would cover a situation where the buyer has contracted to buy 30 sacks of flour and the goods in question are still lying in a warehouse. In other words, no attempt has yet been made to separate the buyer's property from all the other sacks of flour in the warehouse.

As a result of Section 20A, the Hayman case would be decided differently. The buyers would have become the owners in common of the bulk when the warehouse owner communicated to the buyers that he was holding the sacks for them. The buyers' claims would, therefore, rank ahead of that of the trustee in bankruptcy.

The parties to the contract, however, can still agree to opt out of this new provision. Such a term in the contract would have the effect of retaining the Hayman rule.

Key point: It is now possible to become the owner in common of bulk goods (unascertained goods) in situations where they form an undivided portion of particular goods, for example, 500 bottles of New Zealand cabernet sauvignon forming part of a quantity of 10,000 identical bottles in Smith's warehouse.

Future goods

Future goods are goods that the seller must either manufacture or acquire from a third party. There can only be an agreement to sell and ownership of the goods will not pass to the buyer until the seller manufactures the goods or obtains them from a third party and the buyer is given notice of this fact. An example of future goods can be seen in the following case:

 Stark's Trustees v Stark (1948) an uncle had left instructions in his will that his nephew was to inherit any motor car that the uncle possessed upon the event of his death. When the uncle died, he had a car on order but it had not yet been supplied to him. The nephew failed in his action to be given possession of the car because the goods were held to be future goods. Ownership of the car had never passed to the uncle and, therefore, it did not form part of his estate.

 Key point: Future goods are goods that do not yet exist when the contract is formed and the seller must acquire or manufacture them and, therefore, there can only be an agreement to sell.

Transfer of the title in goods

Property in the goods can only pass and the title be transferred if the goods are ascertained. If the goods are unascertained, the property in them passes to the buyer only when they become ascertained (see **Hayman v McLintock (1907)** above). Section 17 of the Sale of Goods Act 1979 states that the property in specific or ascertained goods passes when the parties intend that it should pass. This may be expressly stated in the contract, but if it is not, the intention will have to be implied.

 Re Blyth Shipbuilding & Dry Docks Co Ltd (1926) involved a shipbuilding contract i.e. a contract for future goods. The parties had agreed that the buyer would make payment by instalments. However, a term of the contract was that, on payment of the first instalment, ownership of the uncompleted ship would pass to the buyer. Normally, of course, ownership would not have passed to the buyer until the ship's completion and the ship was in a deliverable condition and the seller had given the buyer notice of this.

As we shall see in the Romalpa cases (see **Aluminium Industrie Vaassen BV v Romalpa Aluminium Ltd (1976)** and **Armour and Another v Thyssen Edelstahlwerke AG (1990)**), the parties are quite free to decide at what point ownership of the goods will pass from buyer to seller.

 Key point: Generally, ownership of the goods will pass from the seller to the buyer when they are ascertained, but the parties to the contract are always free to decide when ownership will be transferred.

Identifying the parties' intentions

Section 18 of the Sale of Goods Act 1979 provides five rules from which the parties' intentions can be presumed.

Rule 1

Where there is an unconditional order for the sale of specific goods in a deliverable state, the property in the goods passes when the contract is made and it is immaterial that the time of payment or delivery is postponed.

 We see how this rule operates by looking at the case of **Tarling _v_ Baxter (1827)**. The facts were as follows: the contract involved the sale of a haystack. The contract was formed on 6 January, the price was to be paid on 4 February and the haystack was to be removed on 1 May. The haystack, however, was burned down in a fire on 20 January. As a result of the formation of the contract, ownership of the haystack had been transferred to the buyer. The buyer not the seller, therefore, had to suffer the loss.

Rule 2

Where there is a contract for the sale of specific goods and the seller is bound to do something to put them into a deliverable state, ownership will not pass until this is done and the buyer has notice.

The case of **Underwood _v_ Burgh Castle Brick & Cement Syndicate (1922)** provides a demonstration of Rule 2:

 The sellers agreed to sell a condensing machine to the buyers. At the time the contract was made, the engine was at the seller's premises and was fixed to a bed of concrete by bolts. It was, therefore, necessary to detach the machine before it could be delivered. The machine was damaged whilst preparing it for dispatch and, when delivered, the buyers refused to accept it. The sellers naturally argued that the property in the goods had passed to the buyers when the contract was made – the buyers must accept the machine.

Held: that the property in the goods had not passed to the buyers because the goods were not in a deliverable state.

Rule 3

Where the contract is for the sale of goods in a deliverable state, but the seller is bound to weigh, measure or test, or do anything else to calculate the price, the property in the goods does not pass until this is done and the buyer has notice.

 Nanka-Bruce _v_ Commonwealth Trust Ltd (1926) involved a contract to sell a consignment of cocoa at an agreed price for a certain weight. The parties were unsure about the total weight of the cocoa. The buyer was going to resell the cocoa to another individual and it was agreed that this party would weigh the cocoa and this would allow the price to be calculated. The Privy Council decided that because, technically, the seller would not be weighing the cocoa, Rule 3 did not apply and ownership of the goods would pass to the buyer either under Rule 1 or 2.

Rule 4

Where the goods are delivered to the buyer on approval or a sale or return basis, the property in the goods passes to the buyer when the buyer does one of the following:

- Signifies his acceptance
- Adopts the goods as his own (by using them)
- Retains them without giving notice of rejection (in this situation, property passes after a reasonable time has expired or after the time stated in the contract)

 Kirkham v Attenborough (1897) the seller had provided the buyer with jewellery on a sale or return basis. The buyer, however, used the jewellery as a security for a debt that he owed to a third party. The seller attempted to reclaim the goods arguing that they were still his property.

Held: the seller's claim failed because the buyer had done something inconsistent with the seller's ownership. He had used the goods as security for a debt and he, therefore, no longer had control over the goods so that he was unable to return them to the seller when this was demanded.

 Elphick v Barnes (1880) the seller supplied a horse to the buyer on an eight-day trial. The horse subsequently became ill on the third day and died. The horse's death was the fault of neither party. However, the question arose as to who owned the horse.

Held: this was a sale on approval and, therefore, property in the goods remained with the seller who would have to bear the loss.

Rule 5

Where there is a contract for the sale of unascertained or future goods by description, ownership is transferred to the buyer when such goods, complying with the contractual description, are unconditionally appropriated to the contract in a deliverable state. Appropriation of the goods may be achieved either by the seller with the buyer's consent, or by the buyer with the seller's consent. Such consent may be express or implied, and may be given either before or after appropriation.

 Wardars v Norwood (1968) the sale of 600 frozen kidneys was a contract of sale of unascertained goods. At the time the contract was made, the buyers could not specify which 600 items they would receive from the other thousands of kidneys which made up the seller's stock. The sellers sent the buyers a delivery note for 600 kidneys which the buyers gave to a firm of carriers in order to have the goods delivered. The carriers, acting as the buyers' agents, picked up the goods and received a receipt with them. Unfortunately, the carriers forgot to switch on the refrigeration system in the truck and, as a result, the kidneys perished.

The vital question was: whose property were the kidneys?

Held: that the property in the goods belonged to the buyers and the sellers would have to be paid for the kidneys. The buyers would have to sue the carriers for their negligence. The act of handing over the goods by the sellers to the carriers was legally the same thing as handing the goods to the buyers personally.

This has the effect of making the formula of ascertainment by exhaustion part of the Sale of Goods Act 1979. This means in certain situations where the buyer's goods form part of a larger consignment, it may be possible to identify them eventually when other individuals have removed their goods from the consignment.

In other words, there can be no doubt that the remaining goods belong to the buyer, for example, an individual has contracted to buy 200 barrels of beer which form part of a larger consignment of 2000 barrels at the seller's warehouse. All the other buyers have long since taken possession of their barrels of beer leaving only 200 barrels. These must belong to the buyer.

Rule 5 is an addition to the Sale of Goods Act 1979 and was introduced as a result of the Sale of Goods (Amendment) Act 1995.

 Key point: Section 18 contains five rules that the courts can use to determine when ownership of the goods was transferred to the buyer from the seller, but these rules are subject to the terms of the parties' contracts which will often take priority.

The issue of risk (loss or damage) to the goods

One crucial issue that we have already considered is that of risk. The issue of risk relates to any harm or damage caused to the goods and, more importantly, who will have to bear the loss should this happen i.e. the buyer or the seller.

 We can see how risk operates in the following case. In **Philip Head & Sons v Showfronts Ltd (1970)** the sellers agreed to supply and to fit carpets in various rooms in an office block. A carpet for one of the largest rooms had to be made from several lengths of material that would be stitched together by the sellers. It would take six men to lift this carpet. The carpet was put together and left in the room on the Friday afternoon – although it was not fitted, the intention being to do so after the weekend. Some time during the weekend, the carpet was stolen. The question then arose as to who was to bear the risk – the seller or the buyer?

Held: this was a contract for the sale of unascertained goods to be put into a deliverable state by the sellers. Unfortunately, the sellers had not yet put the goods into a deliverable state. Had the sellers laid the carpet the property in the goods would have passed from them to the buyers. The carpet remained the sellers' property and, consequently, they would have to bear the loss caused by the theft.

Sometimes the terms of the contract will determine whether the buyer or the seller has to bear the risk in respect of the goods.

 Leigh and Sillavan Ltd *v* Aliakmon Shipping Co Ltd (the *Aliakmon*) (1986) Leigh and Sillivan had entered into a contract with a Korean seller for the purchase of a consignment of steel coils. The goods were to be shipped from Korea to England on the defenders' vessel, the *Aliakmon*. The contract of sale stipulated that the buyers were responsible for the risk to the goods. This was despite the fact that the buyers would not become the legal owners until the goods had been paid for. The goods were damaged while on board the *Aliakmon* due to the defenders' negligence. The buyers sued the defenders for damages caused by the their negligence.

Held: by the House of Lords that the buyers had not yet become the owners of the goods, despite the fact that they were responsible for the risk. The buyers' only possible claim was for damages for economic loss and the defenders owed them no duty of care in this respect.

 Key point: Risk refers to loss, damage or theft in respect of the goods and it is usually the owner (subject to the contractual terms) who will have to bear the risk in situations where the goods are lost, damaged or stolen.

Situations where the goods perish

Sections 6 and 7 of the Sale of Goods Act address situations where the goods are said to have perished and, in this way, they are closely related to the issue of risk. These provisions relate to specific goods – not generic goods which are considered not to be capable of perishing or being destroyed.

Section 6 states that where there is a contract for the sale of specific goods, and the goods have perished at the time that the contract was formed, such a contract will be declared void.

 Couturier v Hastie (1856) Hastie had placed a cargo of corn on a ship sailing from Greece. The documents of title were forwarded to London agents in order that the corn might be sold. The London agents employed Couturier to find someone to sell the goods to – which he duly did. Unknown to the parties, the cargo had overheated aboard the ship and had been landed at the nearest port and sold, so that when Couturier entered the contract the corn did not really exist.

Held: by House of Lords that the contract was void because the cargo (ascertained goods) did not exist when the contract of sale was formed.

 Barrow, Lane & Ballard Ltd v Phillip Phillips & Co Ltd (1929) the buyer entered a contract with the sellers for the sale of a specific lot of goods which consisted of 700 bags of Chinese ground nuts still in their shells. The lot was stored in the warehouse of a wharf company. Both the sellers and the buyer were completely ignorant of the fact that 109 bags had been stolen before the contract had been formed. Some 150 bags were delivered to the buyer after the original theft had taken place, but after this initial delivery, the remaining bags were also stolen.

Held: Section 6 applied since the original theft had caused the specific lot of 700 bags to perish. It was said that to force the buyer to accept delivery of the smaller quantity would be to make him accept something that he had not contracted to take would be an injustice.

Section 7 applies to situations where the seller and the buyer have an agreement to sell specific goods and the goods subsequently perish before the risk passes to the buyer. In such situations, the contract would be regarded as voidable.

 Key point: Sections 6 and 7 of the Act apply to specific goods – not generic goods.

The Sale and Supply of Goods to Consumers Regulations 2002

The Regulations introduce a new rule which governs the operation of risk. It will now make a difference whether the transaction is classified as a consumer contract or a non-consumer (i.e. business) contract.

Where business contracts are concerned, Section 20 of the Sale of Goods Act 1979 states that, unless the parties agree differently, the owner of the goods will have to bear the risk of any loss or damage to the property. The general rule is that risk passes with ownership. The seller will have to bear the risk to the goods until he transfers the ownership in them to the buyer. Transfer of ownership will usually (but not always) occur when a sale is formed between buyer and seller. Obviously, in an agreement to sell, ownership will not pass to the buyer until a later date or on the completion of some condition.

However, in certain situations the rule in Section 20 could be made redundant. In a non-consumer contract if delivery of the goods was delayed and, as a result, they were damaged lost or stolen, the party responsible for the delay (the seller or the buyer) would have to bear responsibility for the loss. So, if the seller failed to deliver the goods on time to the buyer and after this the goods were damaged, lost or stolen, the seller would have to bear responsibility for this even if the buyer was now the owner and, therefore, potentially the one who has to bear the risk.

The new Regulations mean that Section 20 deals differently with consumer contracts. It will now be the case that risk will not pass to a consumer buyer until the goods are delivered by the seller to him. The seller could hand the goods to the buyer personally or to the buyer's agent. Once these conditions have been met, the buyer will be responsible for the goods.

Interestingly, both parties owe one another a common law duty as custodians to take care of each other's property. If the goods were lost or damaged as a result of one party's negligence or carelessness, the owner may very well consider raising a delictual action for breach of a duty of care.

 Key point: In a consumer sale, but not a business or non-consumer sale, risk will not pass to the buyer until such time as the goods are delivered by the seller to him.

Title

Section 12 provides the rules which govern a seller's title to the goods or his right to sell them. In terms of Section 12(1), the seller must have the right to sell the goods at the time of the actual sale or, if the contract is an agreement to sell, he will have the right to sell the goods at the time when the property is to pass to the buyer. Problems usually arise in this area when the buyer later discovers that the seller has supplied him with stolen goods. Alternatively, the buyer's use of the goods may infringe a copyright or a trade mark.

Section 12(2)(a) also imposes a duty on the seller that the goods will continue to remain free from any undisclosed encumbrances after the sale has taken place. Encumbrances are anything that would interfere with the buyer's property rights in the goods. For example, an encumbrance would occur if the seller fails to disclose that he is only a part-owner of the goods and, that consequently, the buyer will only be entitled to a part-share in the goods. Furthermore, Section 12(2)(b) states that the buyer has the right to enjoy quiet possession of the goods and any disturbance of this right by third parties will mean that a potential claim lies against the seller.

Section 12(3) addresses situations where the seller can only give the buyer a limited title to the goods. If such a situation applies to the sale of goods, the seller is duty bound to inform the buyer that he only enjoys limited rights in the property and, therefore, it will be entirely the buyer's choice if he wishes to proceed with the sale. However, at least the buyer will have made an informed choice.

The main protection that Section 12 gives to a buyer is that the seller is promising that he has the right to sell the goods to the buyer. So, if the goods were stolen, then the seller would be in breach of the duty imposed by this Section and the buyer would be entitled to reclaim the whole of the purchase price from the seller.

 Rowland *v* Divall [1923] In April 1922, Divall bought an 'Albert' motor car from a man who had stolen it from the true owner. One month later, Divall sold the car to a dealer named Rowland for £334. Rowland repainted the car and sold it to a Colonel Railsden for £400. In September, the police seized the car from Railsden.

Held: by the English Court of Appeal that the car had to be returned to its true owner. Railsden brought a successful action to recover the price of £400 that he had paid to Rowland. Rowland, in turn, successfully sued Divall for £334. Poor Divall, however, was not so fortunate. As he had purchased the car from the person who had originally committed the theft, he would have to have brought a claim against this person. Thieves, by their very nature, tend not to hang around waiting to be caught and they have a nasty habit of vanishing into thin air. Rowland, the pursuer in this case, had contracted for the ownership of the car and not just the right to possess it. A fairer result might have been for the court to reduce the amount of money awarded to Rowland because he had enjoyed the use of the car.

 McDonald *v* Provan (of Scotland Street) Ltd (1960) the buyer was unfortunate enough to purchase a vehicle from the dealers which was later found to consist of two different Ford cars that had been welded together. One half of the car turned out to have been part of a stolen vehicle. The buyer was informed of this fact some three months after the sale when Police officers turned up to confiscate the whole car on the grounds that it partly consisted of stolen property. The buyer raised an action under Section 12 of the Sale of Goods Act 1893 on the grounds that the seller did not have the right to sell the goods at the time of sale as they partly consisted of stolen property.

Held: by the Outer House of the Court of Session that the sellers would be liable under Section 12 if the buyer could prove the facts.

 Key point: In terms of Section 12(1), the seller is promising that he has the right to sell the goods to the buyer.

Another important protection for the buyer contained in Section 12(2)(b) is that he has the right to enjoy quiet possession of the goods after the sale has taken place. Effectively, the seller promises that no third party can dispute the buyer's right to own the goods or disturb his enjoyment of them. This implied term can, however, operate very harshly against seller who has acted in good faith.

Microbeads AC _v_ Vinhurst Road Markings Ltd [1975] the buyer had purchased road-marking machines from Vinhurst. Some two years after this sale had taken place, a third party became the patent owner in relation to the machines. The net effect of this development was that if the buyer continued to use the machines this would represent an infringement of the third party's patent rights. The third party had made it clear to the buyer that an action for damages would follow if the machines continued to be used. The buyer was understandably furious and refused to pay the seller for the machines. The seller raised an action against the buyers for payment. As a defence, the buyers claimed that the seller had committed various breaches of Section 12. The alleged breaches amounted to the following: that, at the time of the sale, the seller did not have the right to sell the goods (**Section 12(1)**) and that the buyer's right to enjoy quiet possession of the goods had been disturbed (**Section 12(2)(b)**)

Held: by the English Court of Appeal that the buyer's quiet possession of the goods had indeed been disturbed after the sale had taken place. The seller was in breach of Section 12(2)(b) in this regard and the buyer was entitled to claim damages. However, the buyer was not entitled to claim damages under Section 12(1) on the grounds that when the sale had taken place, the seller had the right to sell the goods. There was nothing defective about the seller's title when the sale originally took place. At that point, the third party was not yet the patent owner and there was no way that seller could have predicted that the buyer's quiet possession would have been disturbed at some point in the future.

McDonald _v_ Provan (of Scotland Street) Ltd (1960) it was held by the Court of Session that the buyers would have a potential claim under Section 12(2)(b) if the facts of the case could be proved. It will be recalled that Police officers confiscated a car which the buyer had purchased from the sellers on the grounds that it partly consisted of stolen property. This might be construed as interference with the buyer's right of quiet possession.

Niblett Ltd _v_ Confectioners' Materials Co Ltd [1921] The defenders sold 3,000 cases of condensed milk to the pursuers. About 1,000 of these cases had labels with the name 'Nissly' attached to them. The Nestlé Company raised objections saying that this name infringed its trade mark. The use of the name 'Nissly' was an unauthorised attempt to trade on the goodwill of Nestlé which, understandably, may have created confusion in the minds of consumers. The pursuers accepted this claim by Nestlé and agreed to stop using the labels. Unfortunately, by removing the labels, the goods lost some of their value.

Held: by the English Court of Appeal that, at the time of the sale, the sellers had no right to sell the goods as this could only be achieved by infringing a third party's trade mark rights. Lord Justice Atkin also stated that the sellers had committed a breach of Section 12(2) because the buyer had not enjoyed quiet possession of the goods.

Key point: Section 12(2(b) guarantees that the buyer has the right to enjoy quiet possession of the goods.

However, as Section 12(3) recognises, there will be situations where the buyer purchases goods where his rights of ownership will be limited in some way. Provided that the seller honestly alerts the buyer to these limitations, the seller will be entirely in the clear. Such a situation may arise where the seller is a landlord and seizes goods from a tenant who has failed to pay the rent. The seller would have to point out to the buyer the precise circumstances relating to the goods. It may be that the tenant was not the owner of the goods e.g. he bought a stereo on hire purchase and the true owner (the retailer or the finance company i.e. the creditor) may appear at a later date to attempt to reclaim his property from the buyer.

 Key point: Section 12(3) does recognise situations where the buyer will gain only a limited title to the goods, but the seller would have to make this abundantly clear to the buyer.

 Beale v Taylor [1967] The defender advertised a second hand car for sale in a newspaper. The car was described as a 1961 Triumph Herald 1200 and the seller was acting in good faith when he applied this description to the goods. In response to the advert, the pursuer went to view the vehicle. During his examination, the pursuer saw a metal badge on the rear of the car with the figures 1200. The pursuer decided to go ahead and buy the car. However, it was later discovered that only rear of the car was 1961 Triumph Herald 1200. The front of the vehicle was actually a Triumph Herald 948 which someone had welded to the rear. The welding was unsatisfactory and, consequently, the car was dangerous and completely unroadworthy.

Held: The pursuer's claim for damages, based on Section 13 of the Sale of Goods Act 1979 was successful. The pursuer had relied upon the description contained in the advert and on the metal badge on the rear of the car. The sale was one of description and it made no difference that the buyer had actually seen and examined the vehicle before entering the contract of sale with the seller.

 Harlingdon v Hull Fine Art Ltd [1990] Hull, an art dealer, was asked to sell two paintings described as being painted by Gabriele Münter, a German Expressionist artist. Hull was completely ignorant of the work of the German Expressionists and he contacted Harlingdon, also art dealers, who possessed expert knowledge of this particular School. Hull stated to Harlingdon that he believed that the two paintings were by Münter, but he admitted to Harlingdon that he could not be certain of this because he was not an expert in this field. Harlingdon sent one of its experts, named Runkel, to conduct an inspection of the paintings. On the strength of this examination, Runkel bought one of the paintings on behalf of Harlingdon paying £6,000 for the privilege. It later emerged that this painting was a forgery and its actual value was probably only between £50 and £100. Harlingdon raised an action against Hull for breach of description in terms of Section 13.

Held: by the English Court of Appeal that the action against Hull should be dismissed. Harlingdon had not relied totally on Hull's description of the painting. They had taken steps to verify the authenticity of the painting by subjecting it to an expert examination (one of their own experts no less) and his decision to purchase the goods was based very much on the strength of his own judgement. The description had not, therefore, influenced Harlingdon to enter the contract with Hull for the painting.

 In **Cavendish-Woodhouse v Manley (1984)** a seller was able to demonstrate that the buyer was not entitled to claim that the description of the goods was a term of the contract of sale. A seller will be entitled to claim that the duty in Section 13 does not apply when certain phrases are applied to the goods, for example, 'sold as seen' or 'bought as seen'. Such phrases, however, will not protect the seller when he has breached the requirements of fitness and satisfactory quality in terms of Section 14 of the Sale of Goods Act 1979 because these phrases do not operate as general exclusion clauses. The effect of these phrases indicate is that they indicate to the buyer that the seller does not regard the transaction as a sale by description.

In both **Ashington Piggeries** and **Border Harvesters**, the pursuers claimed that the sellers had committed a breach of description in terms of Section 13. In fact, in both cases, the sellers had supplied goods that were either not fit for their purpose or did not comply with the required standard of quality. The sellers had, therefore, committed breaches of Section 14.

 Ashington Piggeries, foodstuff, which had been specially prepared, was supplied for mink that the buyer was breeding. Both the seller and the buyer were completely ignorant of the fact that a small quantity of the goods contained a chemical which would cause serious harm and even death if consumed by the mink. Apparently, the mink had a much lower tolerance to the chemical contained in the food preservative in comparison with other animals. The goods supplied under the contract were neither fit for their purpose nor did they meet the expected standard of quality. The seller had, therefore, committed a breach of Section 14 rather than Section 13 of the Sale of Goods Act 1893 (as it then was).

 Border Harvesters, the contract was for agricultural machinery, but its performance was unsatisfactory. Again, the sellers had committed a breach of the Sale of Goods Act 1979 in connection with the implied term relating to quality in Section 14 and not a breach of description relating to Section 13. As can be seen in both cases, the buyers' claims that there was a breach of description failed. Both buyers had received the item that they had contracted for so there was no breach of description. The goods were either unsatisfactory or unfit for their purpose and this raised a completely different legal issue which is addressed by Section 14, not Section 13.

 Nichol v Godt (1854) the buyer had entered a written contract with the seller to purchase 33 tonnes of what was described by the seller as 'foreign refined rape oil'. The seller had permitted the buyer to examine a sample of the goods. After the bulk of the goods had been delivered, the buyer discovered that they were a mixture of rape and hemp oil. As it turned out, the sample which the seller had allowed the buyer to examine was also a mixture of rape and hemp oil.

Held: the seller had committed a breach of description despite the fact that the buyer had examined the sample and, furthermore, that the bulk corresponded to this sample. The seller had applied a description to the goods which the buyer had relied on. The buyer thought that he was purchasing foreign refined rape oil not the mixture of rape and hemp oil which had been delivered to him. The bulk goods were clearly an inferior product in all respects. It will be recalled that the buyer in **Beale *v* Taylor [1967]** (above) had also examined the goods, but this did not prevent the transaction from being a sale by description.

Quality and fitness of the goods

Section 14 is the implied term in the contract of sale of which most sellers are likely to fall foul. A seller of goods may breach Section 14 in a number of ways. The buyer may bring a claim against the seller if the goods supplied are not of satisfactory quality or they were not fit for the buyer's purposes.

The protection extended to buyers by Section 14 will only apply if the seller is selling the goods in the course of his business. Therefore, a buyer purchasing goods from a private seller will not be protected by Section 14. Consequently, in private sales, the general rule is best summed up by referring to the old Latin expression *caveat emptor* – let the buyer beware. In other words, the law does not exist to protect a buyer in a private sale from the consequences of making a bad bargain as a result of his own stupidity or his failure to ask the seller important questions about the condition or the suitability of the goods.

 Key point: There are two heads of liability in Section 14: the goods may not meet the requirement of satisfactory quality or they are not fit for their purpose.

Who will be covered by Section 14?

Realistically speaking, only manufacturers, wholesalers, retailers and dealers in new or second hand goods will be caught out by the implied conditions contained in Section 14. Furthermore, a business seller will not be able to escape the provisions of Section 14 by claiming that he does not usually supply or deal in such goods. Therefore, if the buyer ordered a particular brand of goods from a business seller who previously had never sold these, he would have a claim against the seller under Section 14 if the goods were not fit for their purpose or defective in some way. The seller's protests that the goods supplied were not in the normal course of his business would cut little ice with the courts.

 Stevenson *v* Rogers [1999] the English Court of Appeal considered the meaning of the phrase 'a seller selling goods in the course of a business' in Section 14. The seller, a fisherman who had been in the business for than 20 years, put his trawler, *Jelle*, on the market because he was replacing it with a brand new vessel. *Jelle* turned out not to comply with the requirement of satisfactory quality and the buyer sued in terms of Section 14(2) of the Sale of Goods Act 1979. The seller argued that Section 14(2) did not apply to this case because it was a private sale. He was not in the business of selling second hand trawlers. The Court of Appeal disagreed stating that this sale was closely connected with the seller's commercial activities and should, therefore, be treated as a business sale which was governed by Section 14(2). The buyer had a right to challenge the seller in terms of Section 14 as it appeared that there had been a breach of the requirement of satisfactory quality.

Key point: Section 14 has the effect of ensuring that in all sales of goods, with the exception of private sales, that the goods supplied must comply with the requirements of satisfactory quality and fitness for purpose.

The two heads of liability in Section 14: satisfactory quality and fitness for purpose

It is absolutely vital that the two heads of liability in Section 14 are distinguished. Goods will fail to comply with the implied term of satisfactory quality (**Section 14(2)**) if they suffered from some sort of manufacturing defect or because they were faulty to a greater or lesser degree. To put it another way, if the seller had supplied a similar or identical product in perfect working order there would have been no cause for complaint from the buyer. In stark contrast, goods may not be fit for their purpose because of their design or mode of construction (**Section 14(3)**). By no stretch of the imagination could the goods be regarded as defective or faulty in any way – they are simply unsuitable for the buyer's intended purpose. If the seller attempted to repair or to modify such a product this would a totally inappropriate response to the buyer's problem. The goods are in perfect working order, but to all intents and purposes they are of absolutely no practical use to the buyer. A racing bicycle, for example, is not fit for the purpose of off-road racing – only a mountain bike in such circumstances would be adequate. Clearly, if the seller supplied the buyer with a racing bicycle in place of a mountain bike, the item would not be not fit for its purpose.

Baldry v Marshall [1925] is a particularly instructive case in that it goes a long way to dispel the confusion which often surrounds the two heads of liability in Section 14 i.e. satisfactory quality and fitness for purpose respectively. The facts of **Baldry** are as follows:

The pursuer owned a Talbot racing car. He made enquiries about the possibility of exchanging the Talbot for a touring car as a result of pressure from his wife who had bluntly informed her husband that she did not wish be driven about in a racing car. The pursuer contacted the defenders by letter requesting details of a model of car known as a Bugatti, for which they were agents and suppliers. The pursuer did not know anything about this type of vehicle, but he made quite clear to the defenders that he was relying on their skill and expertise when he stated that he required a car that was suitable and comfortable for the purpose of touring. The pursuer was, therefore, quite clearly communicating to the defenders that he required a particular type of car for a very specific purpose. In response to the pursuer's stated requirements, the defenders made a recommendation that he should purchase a Bugatti. Relying on this recommendation from the defenders, the pursuer decided to purchase the Bugatti. Admittedly, the pursuer had inspected the chassis of a Bugatti at the invitation of the defenders before he had entered the contract. Critically, the pursuer had not seen a completed vehicle. When the car was delivered to the pursuer, it was quite obvious that the defenders had supplied him with a racing car, not a vehicle suitable for touring as he had explicitly stipulated. The pursuer raised a claim to recover the purchase price of £1,000 on the grounds that the defenders had supplied him with a car that was not fit for its purpose.

Held: by the English Court of Appeal that the pursuer had clearly relied on the defenders' skill and expertise when he had entered into a contract with them to supply him with a suitable car. The pursuer had made known the particular purpose for which the goods were required. This reliance by the pursuer on the seller's skill and expertise could not be said to be in any way unreasonable because the defenders' business involved the sale of motor cars. The Bugatti, of course, was in perfect working order and the issue of whether it complied with the standard of quality that a buyer was entitled to expect was completely irrelevant in this case. The defenders had committed a breach of Section 14(1) of the Sale of Goods Act 1893 (now Section 14(3) of the 1979 Act) when they supplied the pursuer with an unsuitable vehicle.

 Key point: Goods which are not of satisfactory quality are defective in some way whereas goods which are not fit for purpose are in perfect working order but they are totally unsuitable for a specific purpose or requirement that the buyer has made known either expressly or impliedly to the seller.

Satisfactory quality

Section 14(2) of the Sale of Goods Act 1979 expressly states that a seller selling goods in the course of business will be under a duty to ensure that the goods are of 'satisfactory quality'.

Section 1 of the Sale and Supply of Goods Act 1994 changed the standard of quality which a buyer has a right to expect in terms of Section 14 of the Sale of Goods Act 1979. Prior to the Act of 1994, the standard of quality that the buyer could expect was that of *merchantable quality*. This was often a problematic concept. Goods that were slightly defective did not always mean that the seller had failed to comply with the requirement of merchantable quality. The concept of merchantable quality, therefore, could be a difficult one to understand, especially for consumers, and it has to be said that the courts did not always apply it consistently. In **Millars of Falkirk *v* Turpie [1976]** – perhaps one of the best known Scottish cases dealing with the problematic nature of merchantable quality – it was held that a new car which suffered from a minor defect could be easily remedied and, consequently, the seller had not failed to supply goods of merchantable quality (the power steering had a slight oil leak). Since the introduction of the reforms to the Sale of Goods Act 1979, it is highly likely that **Millars of Falkirk** would be decided in the buyer's favour. It is still permissible to use the older cases, which were decided prior to the reforms introduced by the Sale and Supply of Goods Act 1994, by bearing in mind that the older requirement of merchantable quality roughly corresponds to the current requirement that the goods are of satisfactory quality.

 Key point: In terms of Section 14(2) of the Sale of Goods Act 1979, when a seller sells goods in the course of business, the buyer is entitled to receive goods which are of satisfactory quality.

According to Section 14(2A), goods are of satisfactory quality if they meet the standard that a *reasonable person* would regard as satisfactory, taking account of any description of the goods, the price (if relevant) and all the other relevant circumstances. A point worth noting in relation to the operation of Section 14(2A), and one that will be discussed further in connection with partially defective goods and minor defects, is that satisfactory quality critically depends on the expectations of a reasonable person. The reference to a reasonable person in Section 14(2A) goes some way to providing sellers with protection from buyers who have impossibly high standards that can never be satisfied.

Section 14(2B) contains a list of five examples of quality that buyers can use to help them decide whether the goods supplied by the seller are in any way unsatisfactory:

- fitness for all the purposes for which goods of the kind in question are commonly supplied
- appearance and finish
- freedom from minor defects
- safety and
- durability.

 Key point: Section 14(2B) of the Sale of Goods Act 1979 lists five possible aspects of quality: fitness for purpose, appearance and finish, freedom from minor defects, safety and durability.

If a buyer felt that the seller had failed to provide goods which did not live up to just one of these aspects of quality, then the buyer would have a potential claim under Section 14(2). Buyers do not have to demonstrate that the seller has failed to meet all five aspects of quality in order to have a claim. Clearly, such a situation would only apply to the most dangerous, useless and unsatisfactory goods, as can be seen in the following case:

 Grant _v_ Australian Knitting Mills Ltd [1936] The buyer purchased a pair of long woollen underpants. The manufacturer had failed to remove sulphite, a dangerous chemical, used in the manufacture of the goods. The buyer wore the underwear next to his skin for a few days, when he broke out in a rash which spread over his body. The buyer was taken into hospital and, in fact, very nearly died as a result of his condition. The buyer raised a claim against the seller under the South Australian Sale of Goods Act 1895 which used the same terminology (i.e. merchantable quality and fitness for purpose) as the United Kingdom Sale of Goods legislation.

Held: by the Privy Council that the goods were not of merchantable quality in the sense that they were not fit for their purpose, that they were defective in the sense that they had not been properly finished and, most seriously of all, they were very clearly dangerous.

Obviously, if a case like **Grant** came before the Scottish courts today, the seller would continue to fall far short of the duty in Section 14(2) that goods supplied should be of satisfactory quality. If we use the five aspects of quality in Section 14(2B) and apply them to the facts of **Grant**, the goods were clearly not fit for their common purpose, their finish was unsatisfactory, they were unsafe and they were not durable (i.e. they suffered from a latent defect). The underwear would, therefore, fail to comply with four of the five aspects of quality outlined in Section 14(2B).

Unreasonable reliance by the buyer on the requirement of satisfactory quality

The seller's duty to supply goods to the buyer that are of satisfactory quality has its limits as Section 14(2C) makes abundantly clear. According to Section 14(2C), buyers will lose the statutory protection contained in Section 14(2) in the following circumstances:

- Defects which were specifically drawn to the buyer's attention before the contract of sale was concluded.

- Where the buyer examines the goods before the contract is made and this examination ought to have revealed defects.

- In a sale by sample, the buyer may lose his right to claim that the goods are not of satisfactory quality if a reasonable examination of the sample by him ought to have revealed any defects.

More generally, the buyer's claim that he was sold goods that were not of satisfactory quality will meet with little success in the following circumstances:

- Deterioration in the goods due to wear and tear caused by the buyer's use
- Misuse or accidental damage caused to the goods by the buyer and
- Where the buyer simply takes a dislike to the goods.

 Key point: Section 14(2C) lists a number of situations where the buyer will not be permitted to rely on the presumption that the goods supplied to him meet the requirement of satisfactory quality.

Does the buyer have to examine the goods?

The buyer is not under a duty to examine the goods before the contract is made. If, however, he chooses to examine the goods he will not be permitted to bring a claim under Section 14(2) if he fails to notice obvious defects e.g. the climate control system in a car only works on an intermittent basis during a test drive.

What about defects specifically drawn to the buyer's attention by the seller?

It is possible for the buyer to lose his right to bring a claim under Section 14(2) in situations where the seller has specifically drawn defects in the goods to the buyer's attention as can be seen in the following case:

 Bartlett v Sidney Marcus Ltd [1965] the buyer purchased a second hand car from the seller, a car dealer. The car had a defective clutch, but the seller alerted the buyer to this fact before the contract of sale was concluded. The seller reduced the price to be paid by the buyer to take account of the defective state of the car. The problem with the clutch turned out to be much more serious and more costly to repair than the buyer had anticipated. The buyer attempted to reject the car on the ground that it did not comply with the standard of quality that he was entitled to expect.

Held: the buyer's claim must fail because the seller had been at pains to alert him to the fact that the clutch was defective

 Key point: The buyer does not have to examine the goods in order to gain the protection of Section 14, but obvious defects should be noticed and he will have no claim in relation to defects specifically drawn to his attention by the seller.

Factors which may be used to determine whether goods are of satisfactory quality

It should be recalled that Section 14(2A) states that the certain factors should be taken into account when determining whether the goods meet the requirement of satisfactory quality that a reasonable person is entitled to expect. These factors, which may or may not be relevant, are:

- Any description applied to the goods by the seller
- The price paid by the buyer
- All other relevant circumstances.

We will now examine each of these factors in turn and their relationship to satisfactory quality.

How did the seller describe the goods?

Descriptions that the seller attaches to goods may very well have an impact on the buyer's perceptions as to their quality. Several years ago, one Glasgow fashion retailer had prominent notices displayed in the store that alerted customers to the fact that the clothes had been exposed to high levels of smoke which had been the direct result of a fire in a neighbouring building. These notices explained why the goods were being sold much more cheaply than usual. Therefore, any buyer who purchased clothing from this retail outlet would not have been able to bring a complaint under Section 14(2) on the grounds that the goods suffered from smoke damage. Similarly, in situations where the seller applies descriptions to the goods such as 'Seconds', 'Slightly soiled goods', or 'Second hand goods', the buyer would be completely unreasonable if he expected very high standards of quality. As previously discussed in relation to Section 13, the decision in **Cavendish-Woodhouse v Manley (1984)** demonstrates that phrases such as 'bought as seen' or 'sold as seen' simply indicate that the buyer has actually seen the goods and this is all that such a phrase means. An attempt by the seller to claim that he had successfully excluded or limited his liability in relation to the implied term of quality by using these phrases would almost certainly be bound to fail.

 Key point: The buyer will not be able to claim a breach of satisfactory quality where descriptions of the goods used by the seller clearly convey that the goods are not of satisfactory quality, for example, seconds or smoke-damaged goods.

What price did the buyer pay for the goods?

If the buyer intends to resell the goods after he has purchased them from the seller, he may find that the price he is able to get is less than the original price that he paid. In terms of Section 14(2A), it will be a question of fact for the courts to decide whether differences in the original price and the resale price indicate that the goods were not of satisfactory quality when they were originally supplied by the seller. If the goods are not defective it is highly unlikely that the difference in price could be used by the buyer to sustain a claim against the seller that the goods supplied were somehow of unsatisfactory quality. After all, it is no shock to learn that some goods lose value very quickly e.g. brand new cars can start to lose value as soon as they are driven away from the dealership! However, the buyer's suspicions may be aroused if the difference in purchase and resale price is substantial. The following case is an interesting example of a situation where the buyer claimed that a difference between the original price and the resale price clearly indicated that when the seller had supplied the goods they did not meet the required standard of quality.

BS Brown & Son Ltd v Craiks Ltd [1970] Brown bought a quantity of cloth from Craiks. The cloth was for making dresses, but Brown failed to tell Craiks, who thought the cloth was for industrial use. The price paid was higher than the normal price for industrial cloth, but not to the extent that this should have excited the buyer's suspicions. The cloth was unsuitable for dresses and Brown cancelled the contract and claimed damages. Both parties were left with substantial quantities of cloth but Craiks managed to sell some of its stock at a lower (but not a catastrophic) price. Perhaps fatally for Brown, he had not relied on the seller's expertise and an action on these grounds was, therefore, not competent. Brown was left with no option but to sue for damages under Section 14(2) claiming that the goods supplied were not of merchantable quality.

Held: by the House of Lords that Brown's claim that the seller had supplied goods that were not of merchantable quality (thus committing a breach of Section 14(2)) should be dismissed. The cloth was perfectly adequate for industrial purposes and it had not been difficult to find third parties who were perfectly willing to purchase the goods, albeit at a slightly lower price than the original price paid for the goods. The slight difference between the purchase and resale prices was not conclusive evidence that the goods had failed to meet the requirement of merchantable quality when they were originally supplied to Brown. It should be borne in mind that, if there is a significant difference between the original price and the resale value, it is always open to the buyer to lead evidence that the goods were not of satisfactory quality.

 Key point: A sharp or significant drop in the price of goods, especially in situations where the buyer intends to make subsequent sale shortly after his purchase, may indicate that the goods were not of satisfactory quality.

All other relevant circumstances

The description applied to the goods by the seller, and the price paid by the buyer for the goods, can obviously help to determine whether there has been a breach of quality in terms of Section 14(2). Other relevant circumstances that may assist a buyer to prove that the goods were not of satisfactory quality might include the following:

◆ Partially defective goods
◆ A lack of durability
◆ Manufacturer's guarantees supplied with the goods.

What if the buyer is supplied with goods that are partly defective?

When part of the goods is unsatisfactory, a buyer's position would seem to depend on the extent to which the goods are defective. However, even minor defects in the goods can represent a material breach of contract and the fact that only some of the goods are affected may be an argument that is unlikely to impress the buyer. It will also be recalled that since the reforms introduced by the Sale and Supply of Goods Act 1994, it is now much easier for a buyer to reject goods that are partially defective or where they suffer from minor defects. When address the issue of partially defective goods, it is always wise to bear in mind that the requirement of satisfactory quality is judged according to the standards of a reasonable person. Buyers who are overly fussy or those hard-to-please individuals may have a difficult task persuading a court that the goods were not of satisfactory quality.

 Jackson v Rotax Motor and Cycle Co [1910] the pursuers had sold a large quantity of car horns to the defenders. A particular consignment of goods was rejected by the defenders who stated that they did not meet the standard of merchantable (now satisfactory) quality that they were entitled to expect. Over half the goods were dented and scratched because the pursuers had not properly packed them when they were making them ready for delivery to the defenders. The pursuers offered to repair the defective car horns, but the defenders considered this offer to be totally unacceptable.

Held: by the English Court of Appeal that the buyers were entitled to reject the whole consignment on the grounds that the goods supplied were not of merchantable quality.

In **Jackson**, the fact that half the consignment was defective seemed to exert a particularly strong influence on the reasoning of the Court of Appeal. The situation outlined above does not represent a slight breach of the standard of satisfactory quality and the case would still be decided emphatically in the buyer's favour, even with the seller's right to offer to repair the goods for the buyer (**see now the provisions of the Sale and Supply of Goods to Consumers Regulations 2002**). No reasonable person would have accepted goods in the type of condition that were supplied to the pursuers in **Jackson**. Undoubtedly, the Court of Appeal was quite correct in its treatment of this case – the goods were simply not of merchantable quality.

 Key point: When part of the goods is unsatisfactory, a buyer's position would seem to depend on how much of the consignment is defective.

Duration of satisfactory quality

Before the introduction of the Sale and Supply of Goods to Consumers Regulations 2002, the law was very unclear as to the length of time during which goods must meet the standard of satisfactory quality. Admittedly, Section 14(2B) of the Sale of Goods explicitly stated that the durability of the goods was an important aspect of satisfactory quality. What the Sale of Goods Act most certainly did not attempt, however, was to state the length of time that goods should comply with the requirement of satisfactory quality. Disputes between the seller and the buyer involving the issue of durability would turn on their own facts. In any case, the seller is liable for any defects which were not obvious to the buyer when the goods were originally supplied and which may emerge to cause the buyer problems at some point in the future. As we have seen in **Grant v Australian Knitting Mills Ltd [1936]**, the buyer could not have been aware when he purchased the underwear that they contained a latent defect i.e. an excess of the chemical sulphite which should have been removed as part of the manufacturing process. It was only some time after the goods had been delivered and used by the buyer that their unsatisfactory nature became all too apparent.

As a result of Section 48A(3) of the Sale of Goods Act (a provision introduced the Sale and Supply of Goods to Consumers Regulations 2002), there will now be a strong presumption operating against the seller that, if the goods suffer from or develop defects within six months of delivery to the buyer, then they will probably have failed to meet the requirement of satisfactory quality. The seller is, of course, perfectly at liberty to challenge this presumption. It should be appreciated, however, that the new Regulations do not confer upon buyers a general right to wait six months after the goods have been delivered before deciding whether or not to bring an action against the seller for supplying unsatisfactory goods. The buyer is still under a duty to take reasonably swift steps to bring a claim against the seller when he discovers that the goods are not of satisfactory quality. The six month time period laid down by the Regulations merely recognises that some defects (particularly those of a latent nature) may take longer to appear. A seller who attempts to limit drastically the period of time in which defective goods can be returned by the buyer (e.g. *'Faulty or defective goods must be returned within 28 days of purchase'*) will not be treated sympathetically under the Regulations. Generally speaking, buyers must accept that the goods will not always meet the requirement of satisfactory quality as time marches on – deterioration of the goods through normal use, accidental damage and even misuse by the buyer ensure that the goods will not always remain free from defects for long. In such circumstances, the seller is not responsible for the fact that the goods no longer comply with the requirement of satisfactory quality.

 Key point: In situations, where goods become defective within six months of delivery to the buyer, there will be a strong presumption operating against the seller that, when originally supplied to the buyer, the goods were not of satisfactory quality.

 Mash and Murrell *v* Joseph I Emmanuel [1961], [1962] provides an interesting example regarding the issue of durability in relation to perishable goods. The goods (potatoes) were loaded aboard the *SS Ionian* in Cyprus for transport to the buyer in England. When the ship arrived at its destination in Liverpool, it was discovered that the goods had become rotten. In this case, two facts were important:

1   The potatoes were in good condition when placed aboard the vessel before it departed from the Port of Limassol in Cyprus.

2   The ship had not been seriously delayed during its voyage from Cyprus to Liverpool.

Held: by Diplock J at first instance that the sellers were liable in terms of Section 14(2). The sellers should have taken reasonable precautions to ensure that perishable goods, such as potatoes, reach their destination so that they comply with the statutory requirement of quality. The length of the voyage and the nature of the goods did not reduce the duty imposed by Section 14(2) upon the sellers. These were factors that the seller was only too aware of and which had to be taken into consideration. On appeal to the English Court of Appeal, the sellers were able to demonstrate that the potatoes perished owing to a combination of excessive heat (not entirely unexpected in the Mediterranean) which was made far worse by a lack of ventilation in the hold of the vessel. Simply put, it was not the fault of the sellers that the goods had perished while in transit. Although the decision of Diplock J in favour of the buyers was reversed on the facts in the Court of Appeal, his statement of the law regarding the sellers' duty in relation to perishable goods continues to be correct.

 Key point: Buyers are entitled to presume that the goods will continue to comply with the requirement of satisfactory quality for a reasonable time after they have been supplied by the seller.

Manufacturer's guarantees

Manufacturing guarantees may also give an indication as to the length of time that a buyer can reasonably expect the goods to meet the appropriate standard of quality. If, for example, a television broke down in the first 5 months following its purchase, when it was guaranteed for three years, this might be a strong indication that the product contained a major defect. Regulation 15 of the Sale and Supply of Goods to Consumers Regulations 2002 states that a manufacturer's guarantee is directly enforceable against both the manufacturer and any person who uses the guarantee in connection with goods that are for sale to a consumer. Sellers will have to be extremely careful in these circumstances as they often use guarantees to market the goods to potential buyers. Buyers may well be swayed by the seller placing a great deal of emphasis on the manufacture's guarantee and this may encourage them to purchase the goods. All guarantees must be in intelligible English and they must be made available in writing to consumers, if so requested, within a reasonable time. The provisions in the Regulations relating to guarantees can be found in Sections 14(2D), (2E) and (2F) of the Sale of Goods Act 1979.

 Key point: A guarantee is now directly enforceable against the person who issued it and against any other person who uses it as part of his marketing operations to sell goods.

How helpful is the requirement of satisfactory quality?

In theory, the reforms introduced by the Sale and Supply of Goods Act 1994 make it much easier for buyers to reject goods even when the defect is not particularly serious e.g. the occasional leaking of oil from a car's power steering system. In such situations, buyers should be able to rescind the contract and receive a refund from the seller. In addition, the buyer may also be entitled to claim damages where appropriate. This important reform affecting the standard of quality, which clearly favours the buyer, has meant that the seller has had to raise his game in order to ensure that he supplies goods which meet the standard of satisfactory quality.

The modern statutory requirement of satisfactory quality is a much easier concept to understand than the older requirement of merchantable quality. It will, of course, remain fatal to any claim brought by the buyer if he fails to take reasonably swift steps to cancel the contract upon the discovery of a defect in relation to the goods. However, the changes introduced by the Sale and Supply of Goods Act provide protection to buyers in one important respect. They will only be deemed to have accepted the goods when they have had a reasonable opportunity to satisfy themselves that the article in question conforms to the contract. The question of what is a reasonable opportunity will, of course, be a factual one for the courts to decide.

Key point: In theory, the requirement of satisfactory quality makes it much easier for a buyer to reject defective goods than was previously the case.

Fitness for purpose

Section 14(3) is concerned with a situation where the buyer relies expressly or impliedly on the seller's expert knowledge in relation to the goods. Where the seller sells goods in the course of a business and the buyer makes known to the seller any *particular purpose* for which the goods are being bought, there is an implied condition that the goods supplied under the contract are reasonably fit for that purpose whether or not that is one of the usual purposes for which those goods are commonly supplied. Section 14(3) would not apply if it was obvious from the circumstances of the contract that the buyer had chosen not to rely, or that it was unreasonable for the buyer to rely on the skill or judgement of the seller. In certain situations, the buyer may be more of an expert than the seller or the buyer will have given the seller very specific instructions concerning the type of goods that are to be supplied under the contract of sale.

There is no need for the buyer to spell out to the seller the particular purpose for which the goods are bought when they have, in the ordinary way of things, only one particular purpose e.g. a hot water bottle or a pair of woollen underpants. If ordinary goods in everyday use are required for a particular or unusual purpose this must be made known to the seller if the buyer is to have any chance of bringing a successful claim under Section 14(3) at some point in the future.

 Key point: Where the seller sells goods in the course of a business and the buyer makes known to the seller any particular purpose for which the goods are being bought, there is an implied condition that the goods supplied under the contract are reasonably fit for that purpose.

 Preist *v* Last [1903] An india rubber hot-water bottle burst open severely scalding the pursuer's wife in the process. The pursuer wife was suffering from cramp and she been had advised to apply a hot water bottle to those areas of her body that were particularly painful in order to ease her discomfort. The pursuer had asked the chemist if the hot water bottle could be filled with boiling water. The chemist told him only to use hot water to fill the bottle. The pursuer followed this advice, but unfortunately the bottle was not fit for its purpose (in terms of the old Section 14(1) of the Sale of Goods Act 1893) and the bottle burst open causing the pursuer's wife to sustain serious injuries when she was scalded by the hot water. The chemist was liable for the injuries caused.

 Griffiths *v* Peter Conway Ltd [1939] The pursuer bought a Harris tweed coat from the seller which had been made to order in accordance with the buyer's specific instructions. Unfortunately, the garment's material inflamed the pursuer's skin and, consequently, she developed serious dermatitis. The pursuer brought a claim for damages alleging that the goods were not fit for their purpose in terms of Section 14(1) of the Sale of Goods Act 1893 (now Section 14(3)).

Held: The pursuer failed in her claim under Section 14(1) because she had not taken steps to inform the seller that she was highly allergic to a material like Harris tweed. A very important aspect of this case was that the seller had acted in accordance with the buyer's instructions and, at no time, had the seller's skill and expertise been relied on by the buyer. Furthermore, the buyer's discomfort was a direct cause of her unusually sensitive skin and not a failure by the seller to supply goods that were fit for their purpose.

 Key point: If ordinary goods in everyday use are required for a particular or unusual purpose this must be made known to the seller if the buyer is to have any chance of bringing a successful claim under Section 14(3) at some point in the future.

Relying on the seller's skill and expertise

It is now a good question as to what extent buyers will rely on the seller's alleged skill and expertise in relation to the fitness of the goods for a particular purpose. Many retail outlets stock brand goods and, arguably, it is the manufacturer's reputation that will be a major influence on whether the buyer decides to enter the contract of sale. Volkswagen cars, for example, are considered to be very reliable products and have an excellent reputation. Will the buyer then be relying on the seller's skill and expertise when he purchases a Volkswagen car?

Clearly, however, there are many situations where the buyer will be relying on the expert knowledge of the seller. Basically, this means that the buyer expects the seller to select his stock with the necessary degree of care. The buyer, in turn, must show that he has made known the particular purpose for which the goods are being bought. Reliance will then be presumed and it will be up to the seller to show that this was not the case or that the buyer had unreasonable expectations.

Grant *v* Australian Knitting Mills Ltd [1936] the buyer was held to have relied on the seller's skill and judgement in the sense that there was an implied duty imposed upon the seller that he will take reasonable care when selecting goods to be sold in his shop, retail outlet or as part of his general business activity The goods (long woollen underpants) were not fit for their purpose and, as previously discussed, they were not of merchantable (now satisfactory) quality.

The difference in treatment of the buyers in both **Grant *v* Australian Knitting Mills Ltd and Griffiths *v* Peter Conway Ltd** can be explained by the fact that the buyer in Grant had perfectly normal skin and his injuries were caused by the seller supplying goods that were not fit for their purpose.

Situations where the buyer's reliance on the seller's skill and expertise will be unreasonable

 Slater *v* Finning Ltd [1997] the House of Lords decided that the buyers had not relied on the seller's skill and expertise. The sale involved the supply of a replacement camshaft that was to be fitted to a marine diesel engine. The camshaft was known to operate perfectly in many types of engines. Unfortunately, when it was fitted to the buyer's engine it caused a huge amount of noise and it was prone to a great deal of wear and tear. These problems, however, appeared to be caused by the design of the boat to which the engine was fitted. The buyer had failed to inform the seller that the boat had an unusual feature which made that particular camshaft unfit for the buyer's purposes. The seller had not committed a breach of Section 14(3) when the goods were supplied to the buyer.

Wren v Holt [1903] The defender held the tenancy of a public house. The pub was tied to a brewery and the defender was obliged to sell a particular type of beer supplied by the brewery. The pursuer was a regular customer and knew that the pub was a tied house, and that only one type of beer was sold. The pursuer became ill and it was proved that he had suffered arsenic poisoning as a result of the beer that he had consumed. The pursuer sued the defender.

Held: that there was no claim under Section 14(1) of the 1893 Act because the pursuer could not be said to have relied upon the defender's skill and judgement when it came to the selection of the stock, because the defender was bound to supply these products. However, Section 14(2) of the Act applied and since the beer was not of merchantable (satisfactory) quality, the pursuer was entitled to compensation.

 B S Brown & Sons Ltd *v* Craiks Ltd [1970] the buyers brought a claim against the sellers for breach of Section 14(1) of the Sale of Goods Act 1893 on the grounds that the sellers had supplied goods that were not fit for their purpose. The buyers failed to communicate to the sellers that the goods were required to make dresses. The sellers supplied cloth that was perfectly suitable for a variety of industrial uses.

Held: by the House of Lords that it was totally unreasonable for the buyers to insist that they had relied on the sellers' skill and expertise in terms of Section 14(1).

 Key point: The buyer must demonstrate that he relied on the seller's skill and expertise and that it was reasonable for him to so in order to be protected by Section 14(3).

Quality and fitness for purpose: an unfortunate overlap?

We have already noted that there is a distinction between the two heads of liability in Section 14: quality and fitness for purpose (**see Baldry v Marshall [1925]**). This distinction, however, is perhaps not quite as clear as it should be and there is certainly a relationship between the two heads of liability. The phrase fitness for purpose appears in both Section 14(2B) and Section 14(3). It would be a mistake to assume that the phrase, as it appears in both sub-sections, has the same meaning. In terms of Section 14(2B), fitness for purpose appears as an aspect of satisfactory quality. In relation to the requirement of satisfactory quality, fitness for all the purposes that goods of that type are commonly supplied refers to the common or general purpose of the goods. In clear contrast, the phrase fitness for purpose as it appears in Section 14(3) refers to situations where the goods are supplied for a very specific or particular purpose. Furthermore, Section 14(3) operates on the basis that the buyer has expressly or impliedly communicated the purpose for which he requires the goods and the seller is aware of this purpose. It is very unfortunate that Parliament, by introducing the modern standard of satisfactory quality, which goes a long way in greatly improving the law, has confused matters by using similar phrases which mean different things depending upon which sub-section is relevant.

Fitness for purpose distinguished?

A useful way of distinguishing between fitness for purpose in Section 14(2B) and Section 14(3) is to examine the decision of the House of Lords in **Slater *v* Finning**

Ltd [1997]. It should be recalled that the camshaft supplied for use in the buyer's engine was of satisfactory quality in the sense that it was perfectly fit for all its common purposes (or general uses) in terms of Section 14(2B). The camshaft was not fit for a specific purpose i.e. it was not suitable for use in the buyers' boat because a peculiarity of this vessel. However, the buyer failed to bring a successful claim against the seller on the grounds that the goods were not fit for their purpose in terms of Section 14(3). The reason for the failure of the buyer's action was the fact that the vessel suffered from a peculiarity of movement that was never communicated to the sellers.

A useful distinction can also be made here by applying the facts of **Griffiths v Peter Conway Ltd [1939]** to the modern Sale of Goods Act. Had the buyer taken steps to communicate to the seller the fact that she had hyper-sensitive skin, the seller would have been duty bound to supply a Harris Tweed coat that was fit for its purpose i.e. a garment that would not cause the buyer to develop dermatitis. In other words, the goods would be able to cope with any of the buyer's special needs or peculiarities. The buyer in **Griffiths**, of course, failed to alert the seller that she had hyper-sensitive skin condition. On the other hand, the coat was fit for all of its common purposes and would, therefore, comply quite easily with the modern requirement of satisfactory quality. It should be appreciated that most buyers who purchased such a coat would have experienced no problems and the item in question would have been perfectly suitable.

Does Section 14 apply to sale or discounted goods?

Where ordinary consumers are concerned, there appears to be something of an urban legend which suggests that buyers are not entitled to raise complaints with the seller in connection with the requirements of quality and fitness if the goods were purchased in the course of a sale or where the goods were discounted. Section 14 undoubtedly applies to situations where the goods are sold in a sale. Very often, the whole point of the seller holding the sale in the first place is in order to clear unwanted or out of season stock. It will hopefully be appreciated that there is nothing wrong with these sale goods and they should fully comply with the requirements of fitness for purpose and satisfactory quality. In any case, the seller will continue to be able to escape liability in a sale for defects which were drawn to the buyer's attention or defects which should have been obvious to a buyer who has carried out a reasonable examination of the goods before the contract was formed. Furthermore, the seller can also escape if he is able to prove that the buyer did not rely on his skill or expertise when the goods were sold during the sale. Should a seller even attempt to exclude the possibility of refunds in relation to sale goods this would be unlawful and such a disreputable practice is treated as automatically void in terms of the Consumer Transactions (Restrictions on Statements) Order 1976.

 Key point: Sale goods will be covered by Section 14, unless the seller makes it clear that the reduction in price relates to the fact that the goods are not of satisfactory quality or they are not fit for their purpose.

Packaging, instructions and other items supplied with the goods

The implied terms in Section 14 covering fitness and satisfactory quality also apply to any additional items supplied with the goods as part of the contract of sale – even if such items are returnable to the seller e.g. a glass bottle. Such items might include packaging, boxes, bottles, containers, batteries, tools and instructions detailing the various uses of the product. All these items must satisfy the requirements of fitness and quality.

 Geddling *v* Marsh [1920] The defenders were manufacturers of mineral water and they supplied these products to the pursuer who ran a small general store. The bottles were returned to the store when the mineral water had been drunk by the consumers. One of the bottles was defective, and while the pursuer was packing it away in a crate, it shattered and she sustained injuries as a result.

Held: that even though the bottles were returnable, they were supplied in connection a contract of sale and, therefore, Section 14(3) of the Sale of Goods Act applied. The court was of the opinion that, although the bottles had been supplied to the pursuer on a loan basis, the manufacturers were still subject to the implied term that items such as bottles must meet the requirement of fitness for purpose. Consequently, the defenders were liable in damages to the pursuer for the injuries that she had suffered.

 Wormell *v* RHM Agriculture (East) Ltd [1987] The English Court of Appeal was at pains to point out that instructions supplied with goods must meet the requirements of Section 14 of the Sale of Goods Act 1979. If instructions were supplied to the buyer that were either wrong or seriously confusing, this could mean that the buyer has a potential claim under Section 14(2) (satisfactory quality) and/or Section 14(3) (fitness for purpose). Happily for the seller in this case, the Court of Appeal held that the instructions complied with the requirements of Section 14 and the buyer's argument that the instructions supplied with the goods were completely inadequate was dismissed.

 Key point: Packaging and instructions supplied with the goods must also meet the standards of fitness and satisfactory quality as required by Section 14.

Goods in their natural state

If the sale involves goods which are still in their natural state i.e. they have not undergone some sort of manufacturing process, the buyer is still entitled to presume the goods meet the requirement of satisfactory quality in relation to Section 14(2) and he can rely on the seller's skill and expertise in selecting such items in terms of Section 14(3). Producers and sellers of organic food products will have, therefore, have to be particularly careful.

An extremely good example that goods in their natural state must comply with the requirement of fitness for purpose in Section 14(3) of the Sale of Goods Act 1979 can be seen in the following case:

 Frost *v* Aylesbury Dairy Co Ltd [1905] The pursuer was able to demonstrate that it was not unreasonable for him to rely on the seller's skill and expertise. The defenders had sold milk to the pursuer, but the milk had become contaminated with an extremely virulent germ that was the cause of the death of the pursuer's wife from typhoid fever. Despite the fact that the goods had not undergone a manufacturing process, the seller had a duty to select his stock with the necessary level of skill and care and it was not unreasonable for the buyer to rely on the presumption that the goods were fit for their purpose.

Held: by the English Court of Appeal that the sellers must have been aware that the milk had been purchased for a particular purpose which the buyer had no need to communicate to the seller i.e. the goods were to be drunk by someone. The defenders were in breach of Section 14(1) of the Sale of Goods Act 1893 for failing to supply goods that were fit for their purpose. It should be noted that the seller's liability in this case was deemed to be strict.

 Key point: A seller will be strictly liable for any breaches of the implied terms regarding quality or fitness in terms of Section 14 which have occurred in relation to the supply of goods in their natural state.

Second hand goods

It would obviously be unrealistic for buyers to presume that second hand goods comply with extremely high standards of quality or that they are fit for their purpose. Merely, however, because goods are second hand does not mean that the seller can escape liability for breaches of Section 14 in relation to the issues of quality and fitness for purpose. The buyer will be entitled to presume that the seller has demonstrated the necessary level of skill and care demanded by Section 14 of the Sale of Goods Act when it comes to selecting items of his stock.

 Crowther v Shannon Motor Company [1975] The pursuer had purchased an eight year old Jaguar car which had 85,000 miles on the odometer from the defenders. He claimed that he had relied on the skill and judgement of the defenders when selecting the vehicle for purchase. For a period of three weeks after purchasing the car, the pursuer's total mileage was approximately in the region of 2,000 miles. However, problems with the car began to occur and, soon afterwards, the engine seized up meaning that it had to be completely replaced. During evidence at the trial, given by the previous owner of the car, it emerged that the defenders were fully aware that the engine was not fit for its purpose.

Held: the defenders had committed a breach Section 14(1) of the Sale of Goods Act 1893 by supplying a vehicle to the pursuer that was not fit for its purpose. The buyer had quite clearly relied on the seller's recommendation and he had the right to expect that the seller's selected items of their stock with the necessary degree of skill and care. It made no difference whether the goods were second hand or not. It will also be appreciated that the car was not of merchantable quality in terms of Section 14(2) of the Sale of Goods Act 1893.

As a result of the introduction of the Sale and Supply of Goods to Consumers Regulations 2002, the buyer in the above case would now have an even stronger claim. The Regulations provide that if defects in goods emerge or they are not fit for their purpose within six months of the date of the contract of sale, there is a strong presumption in the buyer's favour that the seller has committed a breach of Section 14(2) and (3) of the Sale of Goods Act 1979.

Key point: The implied terms in Section 14 relating to quality and the fitness also apply to second hand goods sold by the seller in the course of business.

Trade customs and practices

Section 14(4) provides that an implied term relating to quality or fitness for a particular purpose may be incorporated into a contract by sale by reference to particular trade customs or practices. Certain trades and professions have their own rules or customs which permit a court to imply certain terms concerning fitness and quality into the agreement.

Using an agent to sell goods

If a private seller uses an agent to sell the goods, it is absolutely vital that the agent takes all necessary steps to alert potential buyers to the seller's status. The statutory protection afforded by Section 14 to a buyer will only apply if the seller is selling in the course of business. However, if the agent of a private seller fails to communicate the seller's status to the buyer, the seller may be liable under Section 14(5) if the goods do not comply with the requirements of quality and fitness in Section 14(2) and 14(3) respectively.

As the following case demonstrates, an auctioneer acting for a private seller will have take to special care to publicise the status of his principal:

 Boyter v Thomson (1995) an auctioneer, failed to alert potential buyers to the fact that the principal, the owner of a cabin cruiser, was selling the goods in his capacity as a private seller. The buyer later discovered that the vessel was unfit for its purpose (it was unseaworthy) and he sued the seller. The seller argued that Section 14 did not apply to him because he had not been selling the goods in the course of business. The buyer, in turn, argued that Section 14(5) applied since at no time had the auctioneer alerted him to the seller's private status.

Held: by the House of Lords that Section 14(5) applied and the buyer was entitled to damages for breach of the implied term as to fitness. The seller became liable to the buyer under Section 14 when the agent failed to communicate the information about his private status. It would, of course, be an option for the seller to sue the auctioneer for breach of his duty of care.

 Key point: Private sellers who use agents to sell the goods will have to be careful that they are not caught out by provisions of the Sale of Goods Act.

Strict liability

The seller is liable for all breaches of the implied terms in Section 14 even though he is merely marketing the goods as a wholesaler or a retailer. This means that the seller is also liable for any defects that were not apparent when the goods were originally sold, but which later emerge within six months of the goods being supplied to the buyer (**Sale and Supply of Goods to Consumers Regulations 2002**). The seller cannot use the fact that the goods have a manufacturing defect in order to escape his liability to the buyer. The buyer's contract is with the seller and it is irrelevant to the buyer whether the defect has been caused by a manufacturing fault or not. All the buyer is concerned with is that the seller has supplied him with faulty goods. In this way, the seller's liability is said to be strict in the sense that the buyer does not have to prove fault or blame on the seller's part. A seller can in turn sue the manufacturer for supplying him with defective goods if the buyer has successfully sued him for defects in the goods. In **Grant v Australian Knitting Mills Ltd [1936]**, the retailer was strictly liable to Grant for the sale of dangerous and defective goods which caused injury. Clearly, the injuries were caused as a direct result of the manufacturer's negligence i.e. the failure to remove the dangerous chemical from the underwear. However, the buyer had a contract of sale with the retailer and it was the retailer who remained strictly liable for the defective goods and for the buyer's injuries. The retailer would, of course, have a contractual claim for damages against the manufacturer.

It is important to appreciate that the seller is not just potentially liable to the buyer for the price of the goods. The buyer may have suffered a personal injury (as in **Grant v Australian Knitting Mills Ltd [1936]**) or his property may have been damaged as a result of using the defective goods. The seller will, therefore, have to compensate the buyer for any injuries suffered or any damage caused as a result of using the goods.

The seller's liability is also said to be strict if he breaches any of the other implied terms in relation to Sections 12, 13 and 15. In these situations, the buyer does not need to prove fault on the seller's part.

 Key point: When strict liability applies, the seller is responsible for all defects in the goods even though he may not be the manufacturer of the goods and he will do him no good if he states to the buyer that he is not responsible for the defects.

The seller's liability in respect of injuries to third parties

It is important for the seller to be aware of the following situation. Should he sell goods to the buyer which cause injury to third parties or damage to the property of these individuals as a direct consequence of the buyer using the goods, he must compensate a buyer who has been successfully sued by a third party. The seller, however, will escape liability if the buyer has continued to use the goods in the full knowledge that they have become defective and dangerous.

 Lambert v Lewis [1981] a trailer that was being towed behind a Land Rover owned by Lewis broke loose from the vehicle and crashed into a car coming in the opposite direction. Two of the occupants of the second vehicle (a father and son) were killed in the accident and the remaining two passengers (the mother and daughter) were badly injured. It later emerged that the trailer had been defective i.e. its towing hitch had been badly designed so that it was only a matter of time before the trailer broke free from any car to which it had been attached. The survivors of the accident brought an action for damages against Lewis who in turn claimed that the seller of the trailer should be liable for breach of the implied terms in Section 14 (i.e. the goods were not fit for their purpose nor were they of merchantable (satisfactory) quality).

Held: by the House of Lords that the victims' claims against Lewis should be allowed to succeed. However, the claim by Lewis against the retailer was rejected because he had been fully aware for some time that the trailer was defective and, indeed, dangerous. It is important to realise that if a buyer continues to use goods that he has become fully aware are dangerous, his claim for a compensation payment from the seller will be rejected.

Retention of title/ownership

Section 19 of the Sale of Goods Act 1979 permits the seller to retain title or ownership of the goods. Sometimes, the seller will have delivered the goods to the buyer, but he will be anxious to ensure that, although he has surrendered possession of the goods to the buyer, he continues to be the owner of the goods. The seller can insert a term in the contract which means that the goods continue to be owned by him despite the fact that the buyer has possession of the goods. Such a contractual arrangement may occur in situations where the seller has a very real fear that the buyer could become insolvent. If the seller has transferred ownership of the goods and the buyer becomes insolvent, the goods could be used as assets to pay off the buyer's creditors. Obviously, this is something that the seller will want to avoid as much as possible. One way of doing this is to delay the transfer of ownership of the goods until such time as the buyer can pay for the goods or until such time as the buyer as paid all debts that he owes to the seller. The buyer can, by all means, have possession of the goods, but he is not the owner. This arrangement means that, should the buyer become insolvent before paying for the goods, the seller can reclaim possession of his property. More significantly, the goods cannot be used to pay off the buyer's creditors.

If the buyer pays for the goods or pays all debts to the seller, then ownership of the goods will pass to him and the seller will quite happily surrender any of his rights over the goods to the buyer. Contractual arrangements whereby the seller retains title or ownership of the goods until the buyer fulfils some condition are often referred to as Romalpa clauses. Romalpa clauses are so named after the decision of the English Court of Appeal in 1976 that first permitted their use (at least in England and Wales). As we shall see, the Scottish courts had serious problems with Romalpa clauses and it was not until 1990 that Scots law and English law were brought into line with respect to this type of contractual term.

 Key point: Ownership of the goods will pass to the buyer when he complies with some condition laid down by the seller.

The English Court of Appeal decision which first permitted the use of Romalpa clauses was **Aluminium Industrie Vaassen B.V. *v* Romalpa Aluminium Ltd [1976]**.

 The contract involved the sale of aluminium foil. The seller was a Dutch company (**Aluminium Industrie Vaassen**) and the buyer was an English company (**Romalpa Aluminium Ltd**). The seller's standard terms of sale governed the contract of sale. Critically, one of the standard terms addressed the issue of the transfer of ownership of the aluminium foil from seller to buyer. According to this term, ownership would pass to the buyer when it had paid all debts owed to the seller. Until such time as the buyer had paid all debts to the seller, there were a number of conditions with which it had to comply:

1   The goods had to be labelled to indicate to third parties dealing with the buyer that they remained the property of the seller.

2   The buyer was free to sell the goods to third parties, but the proceeds from such sales were to be paid into a seperate bank account by the buyer and held on trust for the seller.

3   If any of these third parties had yet to pay the buyer for the aluminium foil, the Dutch seller could exercise its right to pursue these individuals for payment. This right, of course, effectively meant that the Dutch seller could step into the English buyer's shoes and prevent it from receiving payment from third parties.

4   Finally, the standard term imposed a duty on the buyer to the effect that any products which it manufactured using the aluminium foil and remained in its possession were to be treated as a guarantee for full payment of all monies owed to the seller.

A dispute arose concerning the legality of the standard term when the buyer went into receivership as a result of insolvency. The receiver put forward the argument that the aluminium foil and any proceeds of the sale of these goods to third parties should be regarded as assets of the buyer. If the receiver's argument was correct, these assets could be used to pay off the buyer's debts to its various creditors. The seller strongly objected to the receiver's argument claiming that, although possession of the goods had been transferred to the buyer, this did not mean that any rights of ownership had automatically transferred to the buyer. The standard term that the seller relied on stated that ownership of the goods would pass to the buyer when all debts owed to the seller had been paid. The buyer still owed debts to the seller and, therefore, under the terms of the contract of sale, ownership remained with the seller.

Held: by the English Court of Appeal that the seller had retained ownership of the goods and the receiver had no right to treat them as the property of the buyer which could be used to pay debts to creditors. The seller was entitled to reclaim possession of any foil that was still stored at the buyer's premises and it had the right to pursue third parties who had purchased the foil from the buyer. This meant that the receiver was barred from pursuing those third parties who still owed money to the buyer in relation to sub-sales of the foil. Furthermore, the receiver had to turn over any money to the seller that had been obtained from sub-sales of the foil by the buyer to third parties.

 Key point: The decision by the English Court of Appeal in Aluminium Industrie Vaassen B.V. v Romalpa Aluminium Ltd [1976] permitted the seller to give possession of the goods to the buyer, but not ownership. Ownership would pass when the buyer had paid for the goods and settled all other debts owing to the seller.

The Scottish approach to Romalpa clauses

In Scotland, there has been a huge amount of argument concerning the validity of such contractual clauses. The Scottish Courts appeared to tolerate clauses which allowed a seller to withhold the transfer of title to goods until he had been paid for that particular transaction only. These clauses were referred to as price-only retention clauses.

More powerful clauses, known as all-sums retention clauses, which allowed the seller to delay the passing of ownership until the buyer paid over all monies owed to the seller – regardless of whether they were part of one particular transaction or not – were unenforceable in Scotland. In three Scottish decisions: **Clark Taylor & Co. Ltd v Quality Site Development (Edinburgh) Ltd 1981, Emerald Stainless Steel Ltd v South Side Distribution Ltd 1982** and **Deutz Engines v Terex Ltd 1984**, it was held that Romalpa clauses were attempting to create a security situation without the need for the creditor to possess the goods. This situation was totally contrary to Scottish practice. In Scotland, therefore, the use of Romalpa clauses was forbidden. Lord Ross, who was particularly hostile towards Romalpa clauses, took the view, wrongly it has to be said and with the benefit of hindsight, that such arrangements were not really sales at all and, therefore, were not covered by the Sale of Goods Act (**Section 62(4)**). This view of Lord Ross ignored the fact that the seller had every intention of transferring the property in the goods to the buyer *at some time in the future to be decided by the parties*. Lord Ross's hostility towards such contractual terms also ignored the fact that the buyer had never owned the goods – the seller remained the owner of the goods until such time as the buyer paid all debts owed to the seller. In a security situation, the debtor who pledges goods must actually own the property – he cannot pledge goods as security that belong to someone else. The fact that the seller had surrendered possession of the goods to the buyer did not mean that he had also surrendered his rights of ownership.

 Key point: The Scottish courts, for many years, chose not to follow the English court of Appeal's decision in Aluminium Industrie Vaassen B.V. v Romalpa Aluminium Ltd [1976].

We can see the position that the Scottish courts adopted in relation to Romalpa clauses by examining the following example:

A wishes to borrow money from B. B wishes to minimise the risk which is involved in lending money to A. In order to lessen this exposure to risk, B demands that A pledges some item of moveable property in order to secure the loan. A writes a letter to B, which states that if he is unable to repay the loan, B can take the Van Gogh painting that he owns. This letter, however, does not create a valid security situation in Scotland. In order for B to have security which he can enforce, A would have had to hand the painting over physically to B. Therefore, under Scots law, there can be no security without possession.

There was one exception (to the former rule) in Scots law: a registered company may create a security over its corporeal moveable and heritable property (i.e. its assets) by way of a floating charge. This would allow a creditor to have security over the company's assets without having possession of them.

 Key point: The traditional Scottish legal approach to security situations is that there can be no effective security without possession.

Armour and Another v Thyssen Edelstahlwerke AG (1990)

This was the view held by the Scottish courts concerning Romalpa clauses until November 1990. In the important decision of **Armour and Another v Thyssen Edelstahlwerke AG**, however, the House of Lords ruled that Romalpa clauses were valid under Scots law.

The facts of the Armour case were as follows:

 A German company, Thyssen, had entered into a series of contracts with a Scottish manufacturing company, Carron Co. Ltd., which was based at Falkirk. The contracts involved the sale of steel strip by the Germans to the Scots. A dispute arose between the Germans and the Scots because Carron had been declared bankrupt. The heart of the dispute concerned the ownership of £71,769 worth of steel supplied by Thyssen to Carron. Thyssen put forward the argument that the contracts of sale were governed by its own "General Conditions of Delivery and Payment". These conditions contained a very important term to the effect that all goods delivered by Thyssen were to be regarded as its property until all debts owed by Carron to the Germans had been paid. Basically, the Germans were arguing that, although they had given Carron possession of the goods, this did not mean that they had surrendered any rights of ownership in relation to the goods.

The two receivers who had been appointed by some of Carron's creditors took a completely different view and claimed that the property in the goods had passed to the buyers. They saw the steel as a valuable asset which could be used to pay off Carron's debts. The receivers conveniently ignored the fact that the German company had not yet received any payment for the steel. Thyssen claimed, referring to the terms of its contract with Carron, that the steel clearly remained its property. The receivers, on the other hand, continued to argue that property in the goods had passed to the buyers.

When the case was heard by the Court of Session it followed the line of reasoning laid down in the earlier Scottish cases of **Clark Taylor & Co. Ltd *v* Quality Site Development (Edinburgh) Ltd 1981, Emerald Stainless Steel Ltd *v* South Side Distribution Ltd 1982** and **Deutz Engines *v* Terex Ltd 1984**. The term in Thyssen's "General Conditions of Delivery and Payment" should be viewed as a Romalpa clause and, therefore, had no legal force in Scotland. The sellers had transferred ownership of the steel to the buyers and this meant that the receivers were entitled to use these goods as an asset to pay of the buyer's debts. The sellers appealed against this judgement to the House of Lords.

The House of Lords completely disagreed with the judgement of the Court of Session which had favoured the receivers. The House of Lords explained the operation of a Romalpa clause. Under a Romalpa clause, the seller remains the owner of the goods until the buyer either pays for them or pays all debts that he may owe to the seller whether connected to this particular transaction or not. The seller had intended to transfer ownership of the goods the buyer, but only upon the fulfilment of certain conditions which may or may not occur. The transfer of ownership in this particular situation hinged upon the buyer's ability to pay for the goods until all debts owed by it to the German sellers had been paid. If the buyer could not pay these debts, then quite simply it would not become the owner of the goods. To create a security over the property, the debtor must be the owner of any goods that he is pledging. The problem with the reasoning of the Court of Session was that Carron had never owned the steel strip because Thyssen, although surrendering possession of the goods, had never allowed the Scottish company to acquire title to the goods.

Key point: The law relating to Romalpa clauses would now appear to be in harmony in both Scotland and England.

The limits of Romalpa clauses

The usefulness of Romalpa clauses should not be overestimated. The seller will lose the protection of such a clause if the goods are sold by the buyer to third parties who then convert them into other products by making them undergo some form of manufacturing process.

 Borden (UK) Ltd v Scottish Timber Products Ltd [1981] The sellers sold resin to the buyers. The contract contained an express term which stated that ownership of the goods would not pass to the buyers until all debts owed to the sellers by the buyers had been paid. The resin was used in an industrial process to make chipboard. This was an irreversible process meaning that the resin was effectively destroyed to make a completely new product. The sellers were owed £300,000 by the buyers, but the buyers became insolvent and the receivers were called in. The sellers attempted to claim rights of ownership over the chipboard and a share of the profits made as a result of its sale.

Held: the resin had effectively ceased to exist when it became part of the new product and, therefore, the sellers could not be owners of a product that no longer existed.

 Key point: Although Romalpa clauses can offer the seller valuable protection, they will not be effective where the character of the goods undergoes some drastic change or where the goods are destroyed in order to make other products, for example, a quantity of hops is converted into beer.

Exceptions to the nemo dat quod non habet *rule*

The *nemo dat quod non habet rule* is only a general rule. Like most general rules in the law, however, there are a number of exceptions under both the common law and statute which might mean that someone who is not the true owner of the goods can pass good title to a third party. The practical effect of this is that the third party will often become the lawful owner of the goods despite the original owner's protests.

The main exceptions to the general rule will occur in the following situations:

The doctrine of personal bar

This will arise in situations where an owner has put the seller in possession of the goods (the seller may be the owner's agent or employee) and the act of giving possession in relation to the property creates the strong impression in the mind of a buyer that the seller had fully intended a sale to go ahead. In such circumstances, Section 21(1): Sale of Goods Act 1979 actively prevents the owner from attempting to claim that the property in the goods has not passed to the buyer. In other words, the circumstances of the transaction prevent or personally bar the seller from claiming that a transfer of ownership to the buyer has not taken place. As we shall see in Chapter 5, which discusses the law of Agency, any third party dealing with the seller's agent may be entitled to claim that they had every right to assume that the sale was authorised by the seller. Why else would the seller have given the goods to the agent?

Sales under a voidable title

It is important to remember that a sale under a *voidable* title means that the contract is flawed in some way to a greater or less extent. The practical effect of a voidable contract in a sale of goods transaction is that the seller can exercise a right to have the agreement cancelled. Such a right of cancellation or rescission must, however, be exercised rapidly by the seller. Very often, an attempt to cancel the contract will be worthless with the result that the property in the goods can be transferred to third parties by the buyer. When a contract is merely voidable, the legal position is starkly different from cases such as **Morrisson v Robertson (1908) (discussed in Chapter 2)** where the contract is void (i.e. there never was a contract) from the very beginning owing to the buyer's fraud. In situations where a contract is said to be *voidable*, there is a legally enforceable agreement from the outset, but certain circumstances permit the seller to cancel the contract. In circumstances where the contract is said to be voidable, Section 23: Sale of Goods Act 1979 permits the seller to exercise his option to have the contract cancelled (i.e. made void). Sellers of goods, as we shall see, will have to be especially wary in these types of situations as the following case demonstrates only too well:

 Lewis v Averay (1972) Lewis, a student, was the owner of a car that he wished to sell. He entered into a contract of sale for the car with a buyer who wanted to pay for the goods by cheque. Lewis would much have preferred to receive cash in return for the car and he was not keen to hand over the vehicle to the buyer. The buyer then claimed to be none other than the famous British actor, Richard Greene. Greene had achieved fame playing a variety of swashbuckling roles in films and television during the 1950s. He became particularly well known for his portrayal on British television as Robin Hood). This individual bore a very strong resemblance to Richard Greene and, as proof of his identity, he presented a Pinewood Studio ID card to Lewis. On the basis of this evidence, Lewis permitted the buyer to take possession of the car in return for the cheque. Unfortunately, this story does not have a happy ending and, when Lewis cashed the cheque, the bank in question refused honour it. Lewis discovered rather belatedly that he was the victim of a fraudster. Sadly, his buyer was clearly an imposter. Lewis then took steps to recover possession of the goods, but the car had been very swiftly sold by the fraudster to an innocent third party, Averay.

Held: by the English Court of Appeal that the fraudster had managed to pass good title to Averay. Unfortunately, Lewis would have to raise an action against the fraudster to recover the price of the car – provided of course that he could find him, which he never did.

It is important to distinguish the abve decision in **Lewis** from **Morrisson v Robertson 1908** to which it bears superficial resemblances. However, it will be remembered that the decision reached in **Morrisson** was quite different. In Lewis, the identity of the fraudster was never a central issue regarding the formation of the contract. The identity of the buyer only became an important issue when the matter of payment for the car arose. Until methods of payment were discussed by the parties, Lewis could not have cared who the buyer was – he would have entered into a contract of sale with anyone willing to pay the price for the car. In **Morrisson**, the formation of the contract hinged on the identity of the buyer (albeit a false identity) and this factor clearly influenced the seller from the very beginning as to whether he should enter an agreement. The decision reached by the Court of Appeal in **Lewis** follows a line of cases where the identity of the buyer was not regarded as a material term of the contract (see **Kings Norton v Edridge Merret (1897), Phillips v Brooks [1919]; and Macleod v Kerr 1965 in Chapter 2**).

Mercantile Agents

Section 61(1) of the Sale of Goods Act 1979 continues to recognise the right of a category of agents known as mercantile agents to pass title to goods. Agents such as auctioneers, del credere agents, factors, brokers, commercial agents and warehousemen are regarded as mercantile agents. The rights of mercantile agents in this area were originally recognised by the Factors Act 1889 and the Factors (Scotland) Act 1890. Mercantile agents operate by possessing the goods of their principal i.e. the seller and this possession has been fully consented to by the seller. The mercantile agent will then enter into a contract with a third party, on his principal's behalf, for the sale of the goods. Such a sale must have taken place in the ordinary course of the mercantile agent's business and the buyer must not be aware of any problems with the agent's authority. Clearly, the very fact that the agent possesses the goods with his principal's consent would tend to allay any fears that a third party might have regarding the issue of a lack of authority on the part of the agent. It is important not to confuse an agent known as a factor in Scotland who acts as an estate manager because this type of agent is not a mercantile agent.

Pawnbrokers

Very often, a person will have to borrow money. In order to raise the sum required, this individual may approach someone who runs a pawn-broking business. A pawn-broking business operates on a simple principle: the pawnbroker will lend money on the understanding that the debtor pledges some item of property as security for the loan. The debtor is given a certain period of time in which to pay back the loan whereupon he can redeem his property. If, however, the debtor does not return within the specified period to pay back the loan, the pawnbroker is legally entitled to sell the goods to a third party. The third party who purchases goods from a pawnbroker will acquire good title to the property in question.

The seller remains in possession of the goods after the sale

As we should now be aware, it is perfectly possible for someone to be the owner of goods without necessarily having possession of them. Section 24 of the Sale of Goods Act 1979 comes into operation in circumstances where the seller remains the possessor of the goods, but the buyer has become the legal owner of the property. Before the buyer can acquire possession of the goods, however, the seller mistakenly sells the goods to an innocent third party. The Sale of Goods Act chooses to resolve this problem by deciding the question of ownership in favour of the innocent third party i.e. the second buyer. The only solution open to the first buyer is to sue the seller for damages for breach of contract.

The buyer is in possession of the goods with the seller's consent

According to Section 25 of the Sale of Goods Act 1979, a buyer who has entered into a sale or an agreement to sell and who obtains possession of the goods or documents of title to the goods *with the seller's agreement* can transfer good title in the property to an innocent third party. The buyer can enter into the sale with the innocent party personally or he may have appointed a mercantile agent to act for him in this second transaction or sub-sale. This innocent third party will be unaware of any lack of title to the goods on the buyer's part (i.e. he will have acted in good faith and will be unaware of the terms of the contract between the seller and the buyer). Consequently, the innocent third party will become the legal owner of the goods. Section 25 provides useful protection to an innocent third party especially in situations where the buyer's insolvency becomes an issue. Provided that the innocent third party is able to satisfy the conditions laid down in Section 25, it would seem that he will be able to defeat any claims that the seller may advance to repossess the goods under a retention of title clause.

 Archivent Sales & Development Ltd *v* Strathclyde Regional Council 1985 demonstrates such a situation where ownership of the goods became a very important issue on the event of the buyer's insolvency. In Archivent, it should be understood that the first buyer had been given possession of the goods with the seller's full consent. According to the terms of the contract, however, ownership of the goods had not yet transferred to the first buyer when the sale was concluded. Archivent had entered into a contract of sale for building materials with R Ltd, a firm of building contractors. Archivent had insisted that an enforceable price only retention of title clause should form part of its contract with R Ltd. It should be recalled that such clause operates to delay the transfer of ownership from seller to buyer until such time as the buyer pays in full for the goods *in relation to that particular transaction only*. This type of clause is not as powerful as a Romalpa clause.

Before the goods had been delivered, R Ltd entered into a further contract with Strathclyde Regional Council (a sub-sale with a third party). This second contract or sub-sale involved a building project for which R Ltd was one of the contractors and the building materials acquired from Archivent were going to be used for this work. Under this second contract, R Ltd and the Regional Council agreed that the Council would become the owners of the materials when they were delivered to the building site. The Council was completely unaware of any problems or restrictions relating to R Ltd's title to the goods. The Council had no reason to be suspicious that R Ltd may have lacked title to the goods since Archivent delivered them to R Ltd at the Council's building site. R Ltd later went into liquidation and a dispute between Archivent and the Council concerning the ownership of the building materials inevitably occurred. Archivent, not surprisingly, attempted to rely on the retention of title clause which formed part of the original contract of sale with R Ltd. The Regional Council, on the other hand, argued that it had become the owner of the goods by virtue of fulfilling the conditions laid down by Section 25 of the 1979 Act.

Held: by the Court of Session that R Ltd had come into possession of the goods with the full agreement of Archivent, the seller. The Regional Council had been unaware of any defect in R Ltd's title and had it had acted completely in good faith when it entered the sub-sale to purchase the building materials. By virtue of Section 25, the Council had acquired ownership of the goods.

Key point: The Sale of Goods Act recognises a number of exceptions to the rule in Section 12 which means that the buyer could acquire good title to goods even where the seller's title is defective in some way.

Sale by sample

Section 15(1) states that a contract of sale is a contract of sale by sample where there is a term in the contract, express or implied, to that effect. The mere fact that the seller provides a sample to the buyer is not enough. There must be an express provision in the contract to that effect, or there must be evidence that the parties intended the sale to be by sample.

There are three implied conditions in a sale by sample:

◆ That the bulk will correspond with the sample in quality (Section 15(2)(a))

◆ The buyer shall have a reasonable opportunity of comparing the bulk with the sample (Section 15(2)(b))

◆ That the goods will be free from any defect, making their quality unsatisfactory, which would not be apparent on reasonable examination of the sample (Section 15(2)(c))

The buyer will not have accepted the goods until he has had an opportunity to compare the bulk with the sample, and will be able, therefore, to reject the goods, even though they have been delivered, if the bulk does not correspond with the sample.

The seller is entitled to assume that the buyer will examine the sample. This means that the buyer will lose any protection guaranteed by the implied condition of satisfactory quality if the defect could have been discovered by reasonable examination of the sample. This will be the case whether or not there has in fact been an examination of the sample. A reasonable examination for the purpose of a sale by sample is the type of examination which is usually carried out in the trade concerned.

 Key point: The mere fact that the seller provides a sample is not enough for the transaction to be regarded as sale by sample – there must be clear evidence that the parties intended the transaction to operate in this way.

 Steels & Busks Ltd *v* Bleecker Bik & Co Ltd (1956) the buyers purchased five tons of pale, crepe rubber 'quality as previously delivered'. This phrase was understood to mean that the transaction was intended to be a sale by sample, the sample being the goods previously delivered. The goods were intended to be used in the manufacture of corsets, but unlike the previous deliveries the goods contained an invisible chemical which stained the corset fabric.

Held: the sample corresponded with the bulk in quality in terms of any visual examination and the goods were of merchantable (satisfactory) quality in that the stains could be easily washed out or neutralised. There was no breach of the implied term.

 This is in contrast to **Ruben *v* Faire (1949)** where the buyers had seen a sample of the goods which consisted of soft rubber. The bulk goods, however, were crinkly, but the sellers claimed that this problem could easily be solved by heating the goods to make them soft in order to comply with the sample that had been presented to the buyers. When the sample was compared with the bulk goods it was obvious, after a visual inspection, that the sample and the bulk did not correspond with one another.

Held: this was a breach of the implied term in Section 15.

 Key point: In a sale by sample, the actual goods must correspond with the sample in quality, the buyer must have a reasonable chance to compare the sample and the goods and the goods must not have any defects that would not have been apparent when the sample was first examined.

Exclusion or limitation of the implied terms

In theory, the seller could attempt to attempt to exclude these duties (Section 55). As was previously discussed in Chapter 2, the introduction of the Unfair Contract Terms Act 1977 and the Unfair Terms in Consumer Contracts Regulations 1999 has meant that a seller's ability to use such clauses has been considerably weakened. Section 20 of the Unfair Contract Terms Act states that the seller cannot attempt to exclude his liability for breaches of Section 12 in either a consumer or a non-consumer sale. Such an attempt by the seller would be automatically void. Breaches of Sections 13, 14 and 15 of the Sale of Goods Act will also be governed by Section 20 of the Unfair Contract Terms Act 1977. However, Section 17 of the Unfair Contract Terms Act classifies sales as either a consumer transaction or a non-consumer transaction. Any attempt by a seller to exclude or limit his liability in relation to Sections 13, 14 and 15 will be automatically void in terms of Section 20 of the Unfair Contract Terms Act. A seller in a non-consumer sale may be able to exclude or limit his liability in terms of Sections 13, 14 and 15 if he can show that this attempt is reasonable. Furthermore, Section 61(5A) of the Sale of Goods Act 1979 firmly places the burden of proof on the seller to show that the buyer is not acting as a consumer. The additional rights granted to consumers under the Sale and Supply of Goods to Consumers Regulations similarly cannot be excluded by the seller. It should be recalled from the discussion in Chapter 2, that the Unfair Contract Terms Act does not prevent a business seller from excluding or limiting his liability in a consumer transaction. The implied terms are sacred, of course, but the seller may be able to try his luck with some of the less important terms of the contract and this may be viewed as not an entirely unreasonable attempt. In terms of the test of reasonableness, useful guidelines are to be found in Section 24 and Schedule 2 of the Unfair Contract Terms Act (see Chapter 2 for a fuller discussion).

As for the Unfair Terms in Consumer Contracts Regulations 1999, any standard term in consumer contract for the sale of goods (whether written or verbal) can be subjected to a test of fairness. Many, blatantly unfair terms will fall foul of the Regulations. Schedule 3 of the Regulations, it will be recalled, provides 17 examples of clauses that may be regarded as unfair.

An example of an unreasonable clause in a non-consumer contract can be seen in the following case:

 Knight Machinery (Holdings) Ltd *v* Rennie (1995) the contract of sale imposed a term whereby the buyer of a printing machine had to give a

tten notice of rejection of the goods within seven days of delivery. The
stallation of the machine took several days and any defects would probably
ot be discovered by the buyer until a considerable period of time had
passed. The clause limiting liability was completely unreasonable.

ecision of the House of Lords in **Smith v Eric S Bush (1990)** and the
sion of the English Court of Appeal in **St Albans City and District Council v
ernational Computers Ltd (1996)** are both interesting examples of the
icial approach to the test of reasonableness under the Unfair Contract Terms Act
977. Both cases were reviewed in Chapter 2.

 Key point: There is a far greater chance that the implied terms could be
excluded by the seller in a contract of sale, but this is subject to the Unfair
Contract Terms Act 1977. Consumers, on the other hand, are very well
protected in terms of the 1977 Act and the Unfair Terms in Consumer
Contract Regulations 1999.

Delivery of corporeal moveable goods

The Sale of Goods Act 1979 provides a set of rules (Sections 27 to 37) which govern
delivery of the goods. According to Section 61(1) delivery is defined as the
voluntary transfer of possession from one person to another. Goods, therefore, are
considered to be delivered if the seller delivers them physically to the buyer or his
agent. In many situations, symbolic delivery of the goods will be enough, for
example, where the seller hands over the only set of keys to the buyer granting him
access to the warehouse where the goods are stored. Where bulk goods owned
commonly are concerned (Sections 20A and 20B) delivery can occur when the
goods are appropriated to the contract with the result that the ownership transfers
from seller to buyer.

It is worth emphasising that the delivery of the goods does not mean that the
seller has necessarily transferred the ownership of the goods to the buyer (see
Aluminium Industrie Vaassen BV v Romalpa Aluminium Ltd (1976) and
Armour and Another v Thyssen Edelstahlwerke AG 1990). Delivery is about
the transfer of possession as Section 61(1) makes abundantly clear.

 Key point: Delivery is the voluntary transfer of possession of the goods to the
buyer by the seller.

We shall now examine the rules relating to delivery in turn.

Section 27

The seller is under a duty to deliver the goods and the buyer has a duty to accept
the goods and to pay for them, in accordance with the contract.

Section 28

Unless otherwise agreed by the parties, the seller does not have to deliver the goods
unless the buyer is ready to pay for them. On the other hand, the buyer does not
have to pay for the goods until the seller is willing to deliver them.

Section 29

Some general rules concerning delivery are provided by this section:

1   The contract may indicate if the seller is to send the goods to the buyer or whether the buyer will have to pick the goods up. If the contract does not address the issue of delivery, the place of delivery is taken to be the seller's place of business, if he has one, and if not, the seller's residence.

In a sale of specific goods and both parties know that the goods are located in another location, then this location will be the place of delivery.

Where goods are held by a third party, there can be no delivery until this individual acknowledges to the buyer that he is holding the goods on the buyer's behalf.

2   Where the contract stipulates that the seller must deliver the goods to the buyer but no time period for this has been agreed by the parties, delivery must take place within a reasonable time. Delivery must take place at a reasonable hour of the day.

3   Unless the parties agree otherwise, the seller must bear the cost of putting the goods into a deliverable state.

Section 30

This section deals with situations where a quantity of goods delivered is wrong. If fewer goods are delivered, the buyer may reject the goods only if the shortfall is material (i.e. a serious breach of contract). The buyer could choose to accept the smaller amount of goods, but he must pay for this at the contract rate.

 Robertson v Stewart (1928) shipbreakers sold to Stewart the wreck of the SS Sheila and all the property that had been salvaged from her by them. Stewart claimed that he was entitled to cancel the contract for material breach on the ground that the shipbreakers had not delivered all the subjects sold but had disposed of some property salvaged by sale or donation to others.

Held: the buyer was entitled to rescind the contract with the seller and was not forced to accept the seller's proposals for a reduction in the price.

Where a larger quantity of goods is delivered, the buyer may accept the amount and pay for the contract amount and reject the remainder. The buyer could accept all the goods if he so wishes, but he must pay for the extra goods. The buyer can only reject the whole of the goods if the surplus is a material breach of contract.

 Shipton, Anderson & Co v Weil Bros & Co (1912) the seller contracted to deliver 4950 tons of wheat. He actually delivered 55 pounds too much, an excess in the goods representing an extra 20 pence in value. The contract between the parties was worth in the region of £40,000.

Held: the excess for which the buyer was not being charged was so slight that it was of no effect.

Section 31

Unless the parties agree otherwise, the buyer should not have to accept delivery of the goods by instalments.

The parties may agree that delivery of the goods can be made by instalments and each instalment will be paid for separately. However, a situation may arise where either the seller makes defective deliveries or the buyer refuses to accept or pay for one or more consignments of the goods. Depending on the circumstances, the breach of contract by either party may amount to a complete rejection of the contract. Alternatively, the contract may still be viable and any claim that a party has would be for damages.

 Maple Flock Co Ltd *v* Universal Furniture Products (Wembley) Ltd (1934) Maple had agreed to sell to Universal 100 tons of a particular product to be delivered in three loads per week as required. The weekly deliveries would be separately paid for. Eighteen loads had been delivered by the sellers each one weighing 1½ tons. The buyers, however, wrote to the sellers informing them that they wished to cancel the contract on the grounds that the sixteenth load was unsatisfactory.

Held: a single breach of contract did not justify the cancellation of the contract, the buyers' remedy was to seek damages.

Section 32

This covers delivery of goods to a carrier.

This Section has been altered by the Sale and Supply of Goods to Consumers Regulations 2002. A distinction will now be made between a consumer buyer and a buyer who purchases goods in relation to his trade, business or profession. We will deal first with the law as it stands for business buyers.

If the contract states that the seller must deliver the goods to the buyer, delivery to a carrier by the seller will discharge this duty. A seller must enter a contract of carriage on terms which are beneficial/reasonable to the buyer. In these circumstances, the seller should have regard to the type of goods and all the circumstances when he enters a contract with the carrier. If the seller does not take reasonable care and the goods are damaged in carriage, the buyer may reject the goods and sue the seller for damages.

 Young *v* Hobson & Partner (1949) the seller arranged a contract with the carrier where the goods were at the 'owner's risk'. The seller could have arranged a contract where the goods were at the carrier's risk at no extra cost to the buyer. The goods were damaged in transit.

Held: the buyer could reject the goods because the seller was in breach of his duty to make the best possible contract with the carrier.

If the buyer is a consumer, delivery of the goods to a carrier by the seller is not to be regarded as delivery to the buyer. This will be the case where the seller is authorised or required to send the goods to the buyer. However, if the buyer arranges for the seller to deliver goods to a carrier who is acting as his agent, this will mean that the goods have been delivered to the buyer. After all, by appointing a carrier to act as his agent, the buyer is sending this person to uplift the goods on his behalf.

Section 33

Goods delivered to a distant place. If the seller agrees to deliver goods at his own risk, the risk of damage to or destruction of the goods remains with the seller until delivery is accomplished. This is regardless of whether ownership has passed to the buyer. Crucially, however, the buyer must accept any deterioration in the goods which normally occurs in the course of transit.

Section 34

Unless otherwise agreed the buyer must accept goods which are delivered and which conform to the contract. If the buyer has not yet had an opportunity to examine the goods which have been delivered, he is considered not to have accepted them until he has had a reasonable chance to examine them. The buyer, of course, will wish to examine the goods in order to ensure that they comply with the contract.

Section 35

The buyer is considered to have accepted the goods:

♦ When he communicates his acceptance to the seller.

♦ When he does anything in relation to the goods which is inconsistent with the seller still being the owner (for example, by using them).

♦ When he has held on to the goods and he has not informed the seller that he intends to reject them. The buyer must inform the seller within a reasonable time that he intends to reject the goods. After the passage of a reasonable time, the buyer loses his right to cancel the contract.

 Mechans Ltd _v_ Highland Marine Charters Ltd (1964) the buyers agreed to purchase two steel water buses, the Lomond Lass and the Lomond Princess, from the sellers. The buses were delivered and, after inspection by Ministry of Transport inspectors as provided for in the contract, acceptance certificates were signed by the buyers. After the buses had been used for a few weeks, the buyers took steps to reject them on the grounds of major defects.

Held: that the buyers had expressly accepted the goods and were, therefore, no longer entitled to reject the goods.

Section 35A

The buyer may reject the goods owing to a breach of contract on the part of the seller which affects some or all of the goods. In this situation, the buyer will have the right of partial rejection. The buyer may even accept some of the goods i.e. those which are not affected by the breach and reject the remainder.

Section 36

Unless the parties agree otherwise, if the buyer rightfully refuses to accept goods which have been delivered, he is not obliged to return them to the seller. All the buyer must do is inform the seller about his refusal to accept the goods.

Section 37

If the buyer wrongfully neglects or refuses to take delivery of the goods, he will be liable in damages to the seller.

Shaw, Macfarlane & Co v Waddell & Sons (1890) the buyers had entered into a contract to purchase a cargo of coal at a fixed price per ton. There was an express stipulation in the contract that the goods should be delivered at Grangemouth for shipment by the buyer's vessel L'Avenir between April 12 and 16. At the time when the contract was made, a strike by Welsh miners was threatening and the price of Scottish coal was rising rapidly. The L'Avenir sailed late from Belgium and did not arrive at her destination until April 19. The cargo could not be loaded on board the ship until April 23. This delay meant that the sellers were caused great inconvenience because their railway sidings had become completely blocked by the wagons containing the coal intended for the L'Avenir. The sellers rescinded the contract.

Held: the time of delivery was of a material term of the contract, so the sellers were justified in rescinding the contract, and so the buyers were not entitled to damages for the sellers' failure to implement the contract.

 Key point: The rules governing delivery of goods are contained in Sections 27 to 37 of the Sale of Goods Act 1979.

Breach of contract

We are already familiar with the main remedies for breach of contract which form part of the common law of contract from our discussions on the subject in Chapter 2.

The Act provides the buyer and the seller with a number of remedies should they find themselves victims of a breach of contract by the other party.

The seller's remedies

The remedies that a seller can take action under can be divided into two groups and are outlined in Section 38:

◆ Personal remedies i.e. suing the buyer for the price of the goods and/or raising a claim for damages against the buyer.

◆ Remedies against the goods i.e. lien, stoppage in transit and resale.

The seller will wish to rely on these remedies usually when the buyer refuses to pay or cannot pay for the goods. Section 39 states that a seller is to be regarded as an unpaid seller in the following circumstances:

◆ If the whole price of the goods has not been paid or tendered by the buyer.

◆ If the buyer chooses to pay for the goods by cheque, for example, this is to be regarded as a conditional payment.

◆ If the buyer's cheque bounced, then the seller would not have been paid.

◆ If the buyer pays by credit or charge card and there are problems with this payment, then this is the responsibility of the card issuer and not the buyer. The seller would have to raise an action against the card issuer.

Key point: The seller's personal remedies in the event of a breach of contract consist of suing the buyer for the price of the goods and/or raising a claim for damages against the buyer. Additionally, the seller has remedies against the goods consisting of lien, stoppage in transit and resale.

Section 49 – an action for the price

The seller would be able to pursue the buyer for the price of the goods in either of the following circumstances:

◆ The buyer, having now become the owner of the goods, has wrongfully refused or neglected to pay for them as demanded by the contract.

◆ If the contract states that the price was to be paid by the buyer on a certain date and the buyer has wrongfully neglected or refused to do this. It will not matter whether the goods have been delivered or whether ownership of the goods has passed from seller to buyer.

In Scotland, there is nothing to prevent the seller from seeking interest on the price from the date of delivery or from the date of payment.

Section 50 – Damages for non-acceptance

In any of the situations outlined in Section 49 above where the buyer has committed a breach of contract, the seller is entitled to pursue a claim for damages against him.

Usually, the courts presume that the seller will attempt to find another buyer for the goods from the moment that the first buyer breached the contract. In other words, the seller is expected to minimise his losses (see **Gunter & Co v Lauritzen (1894)** in Chapter 2). The courts will calculate the amount of damages by comparing the difference between the contract price and the market price on the date that the buyer was bound to accept the goods. It may be that substantial losses could be suffered by the seller. Alternatively, the market price may have risen and the seller will suffer no real losses and, in that case, the court may merely award nominal damages. The seller will also have to demonstrate to the court that the loss suffered by him is not too remote (see **Hadley v Baxendale (1854)** in Chapter 2).

If the seller fails to take immediate action to find a replacement buyer, he will have to bear the consequences of this decision. He may be fortunate in that a buyer may be willing to pay a higher price for the goods. However, the price may have fallen dramatically causing the seller to make substantial losses. This is a risk that the seller will have to bear. Generally, if the seller does not suffer a loss as a result of the buyer's breach of contract, he will be awarded nominal damages only.

 Key point: A seller will be able to seek damages against the buyer, but he must minimise his loss and the loss claimed must not be too remote.

Sections 39 to 43 – Lien

A right of retention allows the unpaid seller to withhold possession of the goods from the buyer until the price is paid. A right of retention will arise where the buyer has become the owner of the goods but where he still does not enjoy possession of them.

An unpaid seller will have a right of lien where the buyer has not yet become the owner of the goods and where the seller has still not delivered them to him.

The rights of retention or lien are useful remedies for depriving the buyer of the use of his property. Very often the exercise of these rights by the seller will be enough to bring the buyer to his senses and offer payment for the goods to the seller.

 Key point: A right of retention is a very effective remedy in that it allows the unpaid seller to withhold possession of the goods from the buyer until the price is paid.

These rights are only useful where the seller lawfully has possession of the goods. If the seller surrenders possession of the goods then he effectively has given up his right of retention or lien. The seller cannot keep possession if he has given it up.

The seller will be able to use his rights of retention and lien in the following situations:

◆ The seller has not granted the buyer a period of credit in order to pay for the goods.
◆ The goods were sold on credit, but the time for repayment of the credit has expired.
◆ The buyer's insolvency.

Section 44 – Stoppage in transit

An unpaid seller can prevent delivery of the goods to the buyer as long as the goods are in the possession of an independent carrier. An independent carrier is an individual who is not an agent of the buyer. Delivery of the goods to the buyer's agent would, legally, just be the same as handing over possession of the goods to the buyer himself. It is important to note that this right can only be used by the seller in the event of the buyer's insolvency.

 Key point: Stoppage in transit of the goods is only effective in the event of the buyer's insolvency and as long as the goods have not been handed over to the buyer's agent for delivery.

Section 45 defines the duration of transit. Transit will usually begin when the goods are forwarded to a carrier for delivery to the buyer. Transit is regarded as having ended if any of the following apply:

◆ The buyer obtained possession of the goods before delivery.

◆ The goods arrive at their destination and the carrier informs the buyer that he is holding the goods for him.

◆ The goods are delivered to a ship chartered by the buyer and the ship's captain is the buyer's agent.

◆ The carrier has wrongfully refused to deliver the goods to the buyer.

◆ Part delivery of the goods has been made to the buyer and under the contract this indicates an agreement by the seller to give up possession of all of the goods.

Transit will not have ended:

◆ If the goods are rejected by the buyer and the carrier still possesses them. This is even the case if the seller refuses to take the goods back.

◆ If the goods are delivered to a ship's captain who commands a ship which has not been chartered by the buyer and the goods are on this vessel.

◆ Where part delivery of the goods has been made to the buyer, the remainder of the goods may be stopped in transit.

In terms of Section 46, the seller will issue orders to the carrier to the effect that the goods must be returned to him or he will take possession of the goods personally.

 Key point: The seller can only exercise his right of stoppage if the goods are deemed to be in transit and nothing has been done that gives the buyer possession of them.

Section 48 – Resale

Where the unpaid seller has used his right of lien or has exercised his right to stop the goods in transit, the right to resell the goods may be an attractive option. The right of resale can be used in situations where the goods are perishable (such as foodstuffs). The seller will have informed the buyer that he intends to resell the goods to someone else if the buyer fails to make payment for the goods within a reasonable time.

Alternatively, the contract of sale may contain an express term allowing the seller to resell the goods in these circumstances. If the seller enjoys such a power under the contract, he can sell the goods to alternative buyers and give them good title to the property. If the seller makes a larger profit then he is entitled to this. The only duty imposed on the seller in these circumstances is where the buyer has already made a part payment for the goods and the seller will have to refund this. However, if a refund to the buyer resulted in the seller suffering a loss, the return of the part payment would not be necessary.

There is always the possibility that the seller could make a loss if he chooses to resell the goods to another buyer. An action for damages against the original buyer is, therefore, a viable possibility.

In addition to his right of resale under Section 48, the seller will be able to resell the goods if the buyer has informed the seller that he intends to withdraw from the contract without justification and the seller has accepted this situation.

 Key point: The seller's right of resale can only be exercised by him if the goods are of a perishable nature.

The buyer's remedies

The buyer has three main remedies:

◆ Rejection of the goods
◆ Damages
◆ Specific implement

Section 15B – Rejection of the goods

This remedy will only be available to the buyer if the seller has committed a material breach of contract i.e. a breach of one of the implied terms in sections 12, 13, 14 and 15. If the buyer chooses to reject the goods, he will be able to claim back part or all of the price that he may have paid. Additionally, he may also sue the seller for damages.

Section 51 – Damages for non-delivery

The buyer has a right to sue for damages in situations where the seller wrongfully refuses or neglects to deliver the goods. The buyer may or may not go out and immediately seek a replacement supplier for the goods. If the buyer delays finding replacement goods, he will have to bear the consequences of this decision; he may be fortunate and the price of the goods has gone down in value. However, the price may have risen steeply causing the buyer to pay out more than the original contract price. This is a risk that the buyer will have to consider. Generally, if the buyer does not suffer a loss as a result of the seller's breach of contract, he will be awarded nominal damages only. The amount of damages (as already discussed in relation to the seller's remedies) is subject to the buyer mitigating or minimising his loss and being able to show the court that the loss is not too remote.

Section 52 – Specific implement

It will be remembered from the law of contract that a court can force the party who has broken the contract to carry out his duties under the agreement. In a contract of sale, this would mean that the seller is ordered to deliver the goods. However, this is a very limited remedy and will only be available if the goods are specific or ascertained. Furthermore, the goods must have a unique value, for example, a valuable painting or an antique.

Section 53A – The amount of the buyer's damages

This provision addresses the issue of the amount of damages payable to the buyer as a result of the seller's breach of contract. This amount will be decided by reference to the losses suffered by the buyer which are reasonably foreseeable and are a direct result of the seller's breach. Additionally, if the seller delivers goods to the buyer which are not of the quality required under the contract, the buyer may retain the goods. The amount of damages would be the difference in value of the goods at the time of delivery to the buyer and the value that they would have had if the goods had complied with the contract.

 Key point: The buyer has three main remedies in respect of the seller's breach of contract – specific implement, damages and rejection of the goods.

Additional remedies

Additional remedies of the consumer buyer are:

◆ Repair
◆ Replacement
◆ Reduction
◆ Rescission

If the seller supplies goods which breach Section 13 (sale by description) or Section 14 (implied terms about quality or fitness), then the goods do not conform to the contract of sale.

Under the Sale and Supply of Goods to Consumers Regulations, new provisions are introduced to the Sale of Goods Act 1979 in the shape of Sections 48A to 48D. The aim of these new Sections is to give consumers more remedies in situations where the goods do not conform to the contract at the time when the buyer becomes the owner of the goods.

Goods which do not conform to the contract of sale within six months of the date of delivery to the consumer will be presumed not to have been in conformity with the contract at the time of delivery (Section 48A(3).

In certain circumstances, the buyer may ask the seller to repair the goods or replace them (Section 48B). The seller will be under a duty to give effect to the buyer's wishes within a reasonable time. The seller must not cause significant inconvenience to the buyer and the seller has responsibility for paying any necessary costs which arise as a result of the buyer's choice of remedy (labour, material or postage). However, the buyer's rights are limited in the sense that it may be impossible for the seller to provide the buyer with his preferred remedy. Furthermore, the buyer's choice of remedy may either place the seller under a completely unreasonable burden or it may be simply more appropriate for the seller to give the buyer a reduction in the price of the goods (Section 48C) or, as a last resort, cancellation of the contract (rescission) may be the only reasonable solution (Section 48C). Although the Regulations use the language of consumer choice, the seller will still have a great deal of say as to whether the goods are repaired or replaced.

If the seller fails to comply with the buyer's wishes within a reasonable time, the buyer will, in any case, be able to demand a reduction in price or rescission of the contract. The courts have power under the Regulations to award an appropriate remedy to a consumer – although it may not be the one originally requested.

However, the remedy of rescission must still be exercised speedily in Scotland and the new Regulations most certainly do not give a consumer a six-month period in which to make up his mind whether to accept or reject the goods. The Regulations also establish a very peculiar legal position. The Regulations give the consumer a right of rescission in respect of the contract, but the seller may be able to side-step this by repairing or replacing the goods. However, many consumers may not realise that the Sale of Goods Act continues to give them a right of rescission which is completely independent of the new Regulations. Consumers who are aware of their legal rights will be able to push for rescission of the contract despite the Regulations.

 Key point: The Sale and Supply of Goods to Consumers Regulations 2002 give consumers additional remedies of repair, replacement, reduction and rescission in situations where the seller breaches Sections 13 and 15.

The Consumer Credit Act 1974 (as amended)

The credit industry has seen a dramatic expansion since the 1960s onwards in the United Kingdom. There are many new financial products being introduced every month. It is true to say that large numbers of people would not even consider entering a contract of sale for goods and/or services if the supplier was either unwilling to give them credit or allow them to use credit. If, for example, you were thinking about buying a new television from a store and the assistant informed you that the store did not accept credit cards it is highly likely that you would decide to go and shop elsewhere at an outlet where your card was accepted. Similarly, many consumers will often frequent retail outlets where generous credit terms are available, for example, 12-months interest-free credit on any leather suite purchased. Furthermore, retailers are well aware of this growing sophistication on the part of shoppers. Suppliers of goods and services advertise the fact that credit is available in order to tempt consumers to enter into contracts with them. The credit industry provides a valuable service because how many of us would be in a position to purchase the goods and services at the drop of a hat? The reality is that for a vast majority of people a range of goods and services would be out of their reach – perhaps even permanently – if it were not for the availability of credit.

Credit clearly makes the world go round, but it is an industry where strict controls must be applied. For all those individuals who use credit wisely there are many more who incur serious levels of debt which means they face a variety of legal and social problems. The Consumer Credit Act 1974 (as amended) was largely a result of the recommendations of the Crowther Committee. In 1968, the Committee, under the chairmanship of Lord Crowther, had been given a remit by the Labour Government of Harold Wilson to investigate the possibility of introducing a new and unified regulatory system for the consumer credit industry in the United Kingdom. The Committee also had as one of its aims the need to protect ordinary consumers who very often found themselves being taken advantage of by unscrupulous creditors. The poor were often particularly vulnerable and many of these individuals found themselves in the clutches of illegal moneylenders with no realistic hope of paying off the debts that they had run up.

The 1974 Act swept away the old fragmented system of controls on the consumer credit industry. One of the major disadvantages of the law before 1974 was that there were several pieces of legislation which contained different rules governing different areas of the industry. This made the law very confusing for ordinary consumers. There were four major pieces of legislation before 1974:

- Pawnbrokers Acts 1872 and 1960
- Moneylenders Act 1900
- Hire Purchase (Scotland) Act 1965

It was hoped that, by introducing a single, unified regulatory system for the industry, widespread abuses would be stamped out. One of the most distinctive features of the 1974 Act is the fact that those businesses or individuals wishing to provide credit facilities to members of the public must be in possession of a licence. Failure to obtain a licence means the imposition of a number of civil and criminal penalties. As we shall see, licences are not just given to anyone.

It should also be noted that the 1974 Act established a licensing system which covers all activities related to the provision of credit.

 Key point: The Consumer Credit Act 1974 had the effect of establishing a single, unified regulatory system and the linchpin of the Act would be the requirement that credit providers must be licensed.

The annual percentage rate

The Consumer Credit Act 1974 also makes it easier for debtors to compare rates of interest that different creditors charge for providing credit. All creditors must use a standard measure for calculating the interest that they will charge debtors on the sum that they have borrowed. This standard measure is known as the Annual Percentage Rate or the APR. A creditor who charges 9.9 per cent APR on credit card loans for the next six months is a more attractive option that another creditor who charges 17.4 per cent APR for the same period. In this way, the APR can be used by debtors to identify loans with a lower rate of interest payable on them. Previously, creditors could use very different methods to calculate the interest payable on credit and this, obviously, put the debtor at an immediate disadvantage who very often had little idea of how the interest had been calculated and even less of an idea how to make comparisons between different lenders.

The Credit (Total Charge for Credit) Regulations 1980 (as amended) will be used to determine the amount of the total charge for credit (TCC) and specify how to calculate the APR, which takes into account many of the additional charges that are required to be paid by the debtor. The Regulations also provide guidance in respect of the relevant APR to be paid when a debtor makes early payment of the sums due under a credit agreement.

 Key point: The Annual Percentage Rate allows debtors to make valid comparisons between the different rates of interest charged by creditors.

A regulated consumer credit agreement

Section 8 of the 1974 Act lays down a definition of a regulated consumer credit agreement i.e. one to which the rules contained in the Act will apply. Such an agreement is a personal credit agreement by which the creditor provides the debtor with credit not exceeding £25,000. The limit of £25,000 can be reduced or increased by a statutory instrument.

According to Section 9, the provision of credit would include a cash loan or any other financial arrangement, for instance, a period of time given to the debtor in order to make payment such as a six-months interest-free period on goods purchased.

If the credit is granted to a debtor who is a company, a limited partnership or a limited liability partnership, the transaction will not be regarded as a consumer credit agreement falling within the provisions of the Act. However, a partnership is not a corporate body and, therefore, a loan of less than £25,000 advanced to it could be a regulated consumer credit agreement.

 Key point: A regulated consumer credit agreement must not exceed £25,000 in value.

What is consumer credit?

A consumer credit agreement is a contract and, according to Section 189 of the Act, there are two parties to this type of agreement:

◆ The creditor is the person supplying the finance
◆ The debtor is the person who borrows the money

The 1974 Act contains rules which apply to two types of credit agreements. These agreements are:

- Consumer credit agreements
- Consumer hire agreements

A *consumer hire agreement* is where goods are hired to an individual. The agreement is not a hire purchase agreement in that the hirer is not given an option to purchase the goods at the end of the agreement. A consumer hire agreement usually lasts for more than three months and the hirer will not have to make payments which exceed £25,000.

In a *hire purchase agreement*, the hirer of the goods has an expectation that ownership of the goods will pass to him when he either pays the final instalment of the credit loan or makes a final nominal payment for the goods.

 Key point: The Consumer Credit Act covers two types of credit agreement – consumer credit agreements and consumer hire agreements.

A consumer credit agreement can be further classified in the following ways:

Running account credit where the debtor can borrow money up to an agreed limit. This category would cover bank overdrafts, credit cards and store cards (Section 11).

Fixed-term credit where the sum borrowed by the debtor is fixed at the beginning of the agreement. This category includes bank loans and hire purchase agreements (Section 11).

Restricted use credit where the sum borrowed by the debtor is for an agreed purpose, for example, a car loan from a bank. This category includes bank loans and hire purchase.

Unrestricted use credit where the debtor is completely free to spend the credit provided on whatever he wishes. This category would include credit cards, store cards and bank overdrafts.

Small agreements are fixed sum credit or running account credit agreements where the value of the credit advanced to the debtor is less than £50 (Section 17). Small agreements tend to be exempt from many of the rules contained in the Act.

Debtor-creditor agreements where the debtor simply borrows money from the creditor. The creditor is not involved in any further transaction which the debtor may enter with a supplier of goods. The creditor lends the money to the debtor and this credit will be used to pay for the goods from the supplier. This is the traditional type of credit agreement and would cover such activities as bank loans.

Debtor-creditor-supplier agreements where the creditor and the supplier of goods may be the same person or where the supplier has links to a creditor who will provide credit to the supplier's customers (the debtors). This is a very common arrangement where car dealerships are concerned in that customers will buy a car from the dealer and then be offered credit to pay for their purchase through a finance house or a bank associated with the dealer (Section 12).

 Key point: Consumer credit agreements can also be classified in the following ways – running account credit, fixed-term credit, restricted use credit, unrestricted use, small agreements, debtor-creditor agreements and debtor-creditor-supplier agreements.

In terms of Section 56, the supplier in a debtor-creditor-supplier agreement is the agent of the finance house or the bank. This is not the legal position, however, where the contract is a consumer hire agreement. When the debtor deals with the supplier during the discussions leading up to his purchase of the goods, the supplier is acting as an agent for the finance house or bank. This kind of arrangement benefits all three parties. The debtor is given access to a source of credit; the supplier can be confident of selling more goods because he is in a position to offer credit to potential customers and the finance house/bank gets someone else (the supplier) to drum up custom on its behalf.

Debtor-creditor-supplier agreements are relevant in the following situations:

1 Credit sale

2 Credit cards

3 Conditional sale

4 Hire purchase

5 Loans

Loans and credit cards are not always necessarily examples of debtor-creditor-supplier agreements. A loan made by a bank to one of its customers is unlikely to be an example of such an arrangement because the bank is only providing credit and it is not the slightest bit interested where the customer buys the goods. The bank does not have an arrangement with the supplier of goods. However, a company that supplies fitted kitchens may make a loan to a customer so that the customer can have the work carried out. This would be an example of a loan being a debtor-creditor-supplier agreement. The use of credit cards by debtors might also be an example of a debtor-creditor-supplier agreement. If the debtor is not under a duty to pay off the credit owed in one payment, but can make a series of repayments then this will be a debtor-creditor-supplier agreement.

Debtor-creditor-supplier agreements, however, have certain legal consequences for the finance house or bank. Section 75 of the Act allows a debtor to sue either the creditor or the supplier in the above arrangement for a breach of contract committed by the supplier. Section 75 makes the creditor and supplier jointly and severally liable to the debtor for any misrepresentations or breaches of contract committed by the supplier. If the supplier, for example, provides a car which is not of satisfactory quality under Section 14 of the Sale of Goods Act 1979, the debtor could sue either the supplier or the creditor. This may be an attractive option because the supplier may have become insolvent, the debtor may have bought the goods from a foreign supplier, the supplier may be refusing to accept responsibility or the supplier may be difficult to trace.

It should be noted that the cash price of the item purchased by the debtor must be over £100 but must not exceed £30,000.

 Key point: In a debtor-creditor-supplier agreement, the creditor and supplier are jointly and severally liable to the debtor for any misrepresentations or breaches of contract committed by the supplier.

Credit sales, hire purchase and conditional sales

Credit sales involve arrangements whereby the debtor is allowed to use a credit card or a store card in order to finance the purchase of goods or services. Alternatively, the debtor may be given an interest free period in which to pay for the goods (for example, a six, nine or 18-months interest-free credit period). It should be noted that such interest-free arrangements are probably debtor-creditor-supplier transactions where the supplier of goods (the store) has an agreement with a creditor, usually some sort of finance company or a bank, which allows customers to buy goods on credit. It is, therefore, the creditor who is providing the finance to the customer in order that he can purchase the goods.

Generally speaking, in situations where the credit sale involves the purchase of goods, the debtor becomes the owner of the goods when the transaction is classified as a sale (see Section 2(4) Sale of Goods Act 1979).

In hire purchase and conditional sales, the debtor will not become the owner of goods until he has paid the creditor all the instalments owed under the agreement. There are also differences between these two types of agreement.

In a hire purchase transaction, the debtor agrees to hire the goods and he must make regular payments to the creditor. The debtor will be given an option to purchase the goods only when he has paid all instalments due to the creditor under the agreement or the agreement may state that the debtor must make an additional payment for the right to become the owner. Hire purchase can never involve the purchase of land.

 Key point: At the beginning of the hire purchase agreement (which cannot involve the purchase of land), the debtor merely agrees to rent or hire the goods and acquiring ownership of them is not an issue at this point.

In a conditional sale, the debtor agrees to purchase the goods from the beginning. Ownership of the goods will not pass to the debtor until he has paid all instalments owed to the creditor. Unlike hire purchase, a conditional sale agreement can be used to buy land.

 Key point: In conditional sale agreements (which can involve the purchase of land), the debtor does agree to become the owner of the goods at the beginning of the contract, but this will not occur until all money due under the contract has been paid.

Exempt agreements

Some agreements are not governed by the rules contained in the 1974 Act. Exempt agreements, however, do not escape sections 137 to 140 of the Act which deal with agreements that are considered to be extortionate. A list of exempt agreements is set out below.

 Key point: Merely because an agreement is exempt in respect of the Consumer Credit Act does not mean that it cannot fall foul of the provisions relating to extortionate credit agreements.

Fixed sum debtor-creditor-supplier agreements
The credit borrowed must be repaid within one year and must not exceed four instalments.

Low cost debtor-creditor agreements

This is an agreement where the cost of the credit does not exceed a predetermined rate of interest or a rate of interest that is one per cent above the highest of lenders' base rates in the 28 days leading up to the formation of the contract.

Debtor-creditor-supplier agreements

The purpose of the agreement is to enable the debtor to purchase land and the credit must be repaid in no more than four instalments.

Hire of a gas, electricity or water meter

Where the owner of the meter is a gas, electricity or water company and the meter is used to monitor the supply of gas, electricity or water under a relevant agreement for these types of services.

Credit to be used in relation to international trade transactions

The credit will be provided in connection with an international trade contract i.e. where the parties to the contract are based in different states, for example, the United Kingdom and the United States.

Running account debtor-creditor-supplier agreement

Each periodical account (of the whole amount of the credit then outstanding) will be paid in a single payment.

House purchase or mortgage loans

These will be provided by a local authority or a named bank, building society or insurance company.

 Key point: Not every consumer credit agreement will be covered by the Act and the concept of exempt agreements is recognised by the legislation.

The Office of Fair Trading

The Consumer Credit Act 1974 originally gave authority to a Director-General of Fair Trading assisted by the Office of Fair Trading to oversee the regulation of the consumer credit industry in the United Kingdom. The post of Director-General of Trading had been established by the Fair Trading Act 1973. However, the introduction of the Enterprise Act 2002 has resulted in the Office of Fair Trading being given legal status as a corporate body. The post of Director-General of Fair Trading has been abolished.

The new body is headed by an individual simply known as the Chairman who also acts as the Chief Executive. A separate Chief Executive will be appointed in 2005. The Chairman is appointed by the Secretary of State at the Department of Trade and Industry and is aided in his tasks by a Board of six members. The Chairman, Chief Executive and the Board are appointed for a period of office not exceeding five years.

The Office of Fair Trading has a major role to play in promoting free and fair competition amongst businesses and consumer protection. It will continue to be the major enforcement body in the United Kingdom for the law relating to consumer credit.

Local authorities and their Trading Standards Departments will also have a role to play as enforcement bodies under the Consumer Credit Act 1974. These bodies will often assist the Office of Fair Trading to carry out investigations of those businesses and individuals suspected of breaking the rules under the Act. If a breach of the Act results in a criminal offence, the local procurator fiscal will commence criminal proceedings against the accused.

Officials of the various enforcement bodies can gain access to premises for the purposes of examining goods and documentation related to credit business activities. These items may even be seized by enforcement officers and used in evidence in later civil or criminal proceedings. Often, the enforcement officers may be refused entry to premises in which they wish to carry out an investigation. If this is the case, it will be necessary to obtain a search warrant from a Sheriff, stipendiary magistrate or a Justice of the Peace. It is a criminal offence to hinder or to prevent an enforcement officer from carrying out his duties.

 Key point: The Office of Fair Trading is the body that enforces the provisions of the Consumer Credit Act 1974.

The licensing system

The Office of Fair Trading has primary responsibility for the granting of credit licences under the 1974 Act. Any individual or business wishing to provide credit facilities must obtain a licence. The licensing system is the main way in which the Office of Fair Trading regulates the credit industry. Activities for which a licence is required include:

1 Consumer credit

2 Consumer hire

3 Credit brokerage

4 Debt adjusting and debt counselling

5 Debt collecting

6 Credit reference agencies

Activities 3, 4, 5 and 6 are classed as ancillary credit businesses. Failure to obtain a licence when carrying out any of these ancillary credit activities is regarded as unlicensed trading. Creditors will have to be particularly careful that they do not carry out any activities which are forbidden by their licences or which fall outside the scope of their licences.

It is possible for a business to give credit to customers if this is regarded as an occasional transaction. Sometimes, businesses will give particularly good customers credit in order to pay for goods or services. As long as this does not happen very often, the business will not need a licence from the Office of Fair Trading. However, businesses will have to be particularly careful here because if giving credit to various customers becomes a common practice, they may very well be breaking the law if they fail to get a licence. The moral of the story is that if granting credit to customers becomes more frequent, it is better to apply for a licence.

 Key point: In order to carry on a consumer credit business in the United Kingdom it is necessary to obtain a licence from the Office of Fair Trading.

Failure to obtain a licence has certain consequences:

1 It will be a criminal offence to provide credit without a licence (Section 39).

2 The unlicensed trader may be unable to enforce a regulated agreement against the debtor (Section 40).

3 An ancillary credit agreement will be unenforceable if the creditor had failed to obtain a licence when it was made (Section 148).

4 A regulated credit agreement will be unenforceable, if the credit broker who set it up did not possess a licence (Section 149).

However, a creditor who has broken the rules in relation to the licensing requirements of the Act can always apply to the Office of Fair Trading for what is known as a validating order. A validating order allows the creditor to enforce agreements which would otherwise fall foul of the licensing requirements in the Act.

 Key point: Failure to obtain a licence by a provider of consumer credit will invite serious criminal and civil penalties, although the initial failure can always be cured by the issuing of a validating order by the Office of Fair Trading.

Types of consumer credit licence

Section 22 states that there are two types of licence which can be granted by the Office of Fair Trading:

- ◆ Standard
- ◆ Group

Standard licences are granted to individuals for a period of five years. The standard licence is personal and cannot be transferred by the licence holder to any other individual. This would mean that if the licence holder sold his credit business, the new owner would have to apply for a licence on his own merits and such an application may or may not be granted by the Office of Fair Trading. The Office of Fair Trading will only grant licences to those individuals who are considered to be fit and proper persons. Those persons who have previously broken the rules contained in the Consumer Credit Act 1974 need not apply for a licence.

If the applicant has breached equality laws such as the Sex Discrimination Act 1975, the Race Relations Act 1976 or the Disability Discrimination Act 1995, a licence will not be issued. It is worth pointing out that the scope of discrimination legislation has widened considerably since the Consumer Credit Act was first introduced (see Chapter 7). Criminal convictions for violence and dishonesty are likely to result in the applicant being refused a licence. If the applicant has been involved in any undesirable business practices, for example, he has been disqualified as a company director under the Company Directors (Disqualification) Act 1986, a licence will not be issued.

It is not merely the individuals who control credit businesses who are scrutinised, but also their employees, associates and agents who will have to meet the requirement that they be fit and proper persons.

A group licence, on the other hand, is issued to professional associations and organisations, for example, the Law Society of Scotland or the Association of

Chartered Certified Accountants. These professional bodies apply for authorisation on behalf of their members. This means that the individual members of an organisation do not have to apply for a licence personally. The professional body is, of course, responsible for policing the conduct of its members and it can remove the right of its members to conduct a credit business. A group licence is not issued for any particular time period.

However, merely because a licence has been issued is not the end of the story for the applicant. All licence holders must ensure that they conduct their businesses properly. Any undesirable conduct on their part could mean that the Office of Fair Trading may decide to suspend or, even more seriously, withdraw the licence.

 Key point: There are two types of licence, group and standard licences, and the holders must be fit and proper persons.

The Office of Fair Trading maintains a register of those who hold a credit licence and Section 35 allows members of the public to inspect the register and take copies of entries or obtain official copies of entries. Interested individuals who wish to make use of the register will be required to pay an administrative fee for the privilege.

Section 36 imposes a duty on a standard licence holder to inform the Office of Fair Trading of particular changes which affect the credit business within a period of 21 days. A business would have to inform the Office of Fair Trading if there were changes in personnel to the company's officers or changes affecting the membership of partners in a firm. If the changes in a partnership meant that a firm had a new name, the licence would no longer have any legal effect.

Under Section 37, the following events will cause a licence to become null and void:

◆ If the licence holder dies
◆ If the licence holder goes bankrupt and has his estate seized by creditors
◆ If the licence holder becomes mentally incapacitated

If the applicant is refused a licence by the Office of Fair Trading, the reasons for this decision must be set out in writing. It will then be up to the applicant as to whether he wishes to challenge such a decision. An appeal against the decision to refuse to grant a licence by the Office of Fair Trading should be addressed to the Secretary of State at the Department of Trade and Industry. If the Secretary of State agrees with the decision of the Office of Fair Trading, the applicant could always appeal against the Secretary of State's decision on a point of a law to the Court of Session. In the Court of Session, the judges will scrutinise the grounds upon which the application for a licence was refused. Any earlier decisions by the Office of Fair Trading and the Secretary of State could be overturned.

Decisions by the Office of Fair Trading to suspend or withdraw a licence can be challenged by following the procedure outlined above.

 Key point: The Office of Fair Trading maintains a register of licence holders and it is up to these individuals to inform the Office of Fair Trading in relation to any changes that affect their licence.

Advertising

There are strict controls imposed on businesses which advertise credit facilities to members of the general public. Under Section 44 of the Act, the Secretary of State has the power to make Regulations in relation to credit advertising activities. Clearly, the ways in which credit are presented to members of the public could be a very influential reason for their decision to enter a credit agreement. It is, therefore, of vital importance that debtors are given the correct information by advertisers.

Section 46 of the Act states that it is an offence for an advertisements to be false or misleading in a material respect.

The duty imposed on creditors in Section 46 is fleshed out by the Consumer Credit (Advertising) Regulations 1989 (as amended). The 1989 Regulations cover advertising in any form and this would include print, radio, television, film, video, DVD, notices, goods, circular letters or price lists. Any attempt to advertise credit will fall within the reach of the Regulations. Basically, the main aim of the Regulations is to provide potential debtors with enough information to weigh up the true costs of borrowing credit. If credit is to be secured on the debtor's home, the creditor is under a legal duty to inform the debtor that his home may be at risk if repayments are not made.

The Regulations provide strict guidelines as to how an advertisement is to be presented (its *form*) and what sort of information will appear in it (its *content*). Advertisements should be easily understood by debtors. In all advertisements, the creditor's name and business address must be shown together.

The Regulations apply to the following types of agreements:

- ◆ Consumer credit
- ◆ Consumer hire
- ◆ Credit brokerage

Credit brokerage is a common practice whereby businesses such as car dealerships introduce customers to institutions such as banks who will provide the customer with credit to pay for goods and services.

It is worth noting that some agreements which would otherwise be exempt under the Act, may fall within the scope of the Regulations. Furthermore, a creditor who is offering to lend a sum over £25,000 which is to be secured on land, will be covered by the Regulations.

 Key point: It is an offence for an advertisement to be false or misleading in a material respect.

There are three types of regulated advertisement:

- ◆ Simple
- ◆ Intermediate
- ◆ Full

A *simple advertisement* is a tool by which creditors can publicise their existence to interested members of the public. Such an advertising tool is not designed to provide detailed information. Simple credit advertisements tend to provide details of the creditor's name, address, phone number, a logo and the creditor's main occupation.

Intermediate advertisements are more detailed than simple advertisements. The creditor will be able to use more information in these types of advertisements, but always subject to the requirement that written quotations will be provided to interested members of the public on request. Some information is compulsory, but with other types of information the creditor will have a choice whether or not to include them in the advertisement.

Full advertisements will force a creditor to provide extremely detailed information about the type of credit being offered. Again, written quotations must be provided on request to interested members of the public.

In intermediate and full advertisements, there will be a requirement that the Annual Percentage Rate (APR) is prominently displayed. The APR is the flat rate of interest for the year and this allows debtors to compare the interest rates being offered by a range of different creditors. Clearly, an APR of 9.9 per cent is more favourable than a rate of 12.9 per cent.

According to Sections 44 and 167 of the Act, a breach of the rules contained in the Regulations is a criminal offence. However, misleading advertisements which influence a debtor will not necessarily cause any agreement formed to become invalid. Anyone who produced the misleading advertisement may also have committed a criminal offence under Section 47 of the Act.

 Key point: There are three types of advertisements regulated by the Advertising Regulations – simple, intermediate and full.

Quotations

Since 10 March 1997, creditors are given discretion as to how they respond to requests for a written quotations. Previously, under the Consumer Credit (Quotations) Regulations 1989, there were strict rules for providing a written quotation to a member of the public. These 1989 Regulations no longer have legal force and it would seem that the main duty that a creditor has is to ensure that a quote is not misleading. If the creditor issues a misleading quote, he could fall foul of Part 3 of the Consumer Protection Act 1987 which makes it a criminal offence to provide a misleading price indication.

 Key point: Creditors must ensure that any quotations that they provide to potential customers are not misleading and, if this is the case, a creditor could commit a criminal offence in terms of Part 3 of the Consumer Protection Act 1987.

Other criminal offences under the Act

A creditor can commit several potential criminal offences under the Act:

1 Door-to-door selling which is also known as canvassing off trade premises was a particular abuse that the Act was determined to stamp out. This practice was often used by unscrupulous creditors to persuade poorer debtors to take out loans which they would have to pay back at extremely high (extortionate) rates of interest. To approach potential debtors in this way is now an offence under Section 49(1) of the Act.

2 Distributing circulars to young persons (i.e. 16 and 17-year-olds) and to children (i.e. those under 16 years of age) with the purpose of inviting them to apply for credit or to obtain goods on hire is an offence in terms of Section 50.

3 Forwarding credit tokens, for example, store cards and credit cards, other than a renewal one, which are unsolicited by the debtor i.e. the debtor does not request these is an offence according to Section 51.

 Key point: Creditors can commit a number of criminal offences in terms of the Consumer Credit Act – canvassing off trade premises, distributing circulars to young persons and children and forwarding unauthorised credit tokens.

Documentation requirements under the Act

The Consumer Credit Act 1974 insists that all the main terms of a regulated credit agreement must be in writing, otherwise the creditor will only be able to enforce the agreement with a court order. In this way, the Act provides debtors with an important protection because all their rights and duties under an agreement will be contained in a document and the creditor will have to provide the individual debtor with a copy of this agreement. Furthermore, there are strict rules governing the style and the content of the agreement.

 Key point: A consumer credit agreement must be in writing otherwise it will be unenforceable by the creditor unless a court order is issued.

The content of the agreement

The Consumer Credit (Agreements) Regulations 1983, which were introduced as a result of Section 60 of the Act, lay down certain rules that govern the content of a regulated agreement. The agreement must include the following:

◆ The amount of credit that the debtor has borrowed or the credit limit
◆ The amount of each repayment by the debtor and the times when these are to be made
◆ The total charge for the credit
◆ The annual percentage rate (APR)
◆ Details of any security that the debtor has had to provide to the creditor
◆ The debtor's rights in relation to cancellation of the agreement, termination of the agreement and repossession of the goods

 Key point: The content of the consumer credit agreement is very strictly regulated and the creditor must ensure that certain information is included.

The form of the agreement

Section 61 of the Act imposes a duty on the creditor to make sue that the agreement presented to the debtor is legible and, additionally, that all the main terms are contained in it. The Consumer Credit (Agreements) Regulations 1983 make it compulsory for the agreement to have a heading which describes what type of agreement it is that the creditor and the debtor have entered into, for example, 'This is a Consumer Credit Agreement regulated by the Consumer Credit Act 1974'. The 1983 Regulations also make it compulsory for the creditor to outline the protections available to the debtor and such information must be presented to the debtor in the appropriate way. The agreement must have a signature box where both the creditor and the debtor will be able to sign the agreement.

An agreement will only be considered to form a binding contract between the parties when both of them sign it. The agreement will then be known as an executed agreement. The debtor must be given a copy of the agreement when his signature forms the contract (Section 62). If the debtor has signed the agreement, but the creditor has not yet done so, there is no binding agreement. In these circumstances, the creditor must provide the debtor with a copy of the unexecuted agreement and then a second copy within seven days of the agreement being signed by the creditor (Section 63).

 Key point: an agreement will be enforceable when it has been executed i.e. signed by both parties.

Failure to comply with any of the documentation rules will mean that an agreement can only be enforced by a court order (Section 65). The courts may not always grant an enforcement order where the agreement is improperly executed. A court, for example, may well decide not to enforce an agreement if it is a cancellable one and the creditor has failed to notify the debtor of his right to cancel the agreement.

Sometimes the creditor will demand that the debtor provide some sort of security or collateral for the loan, for example, an item of the debtor's property, such as shares in a company. In other words, the debtor could lose ownership of this item pledged as security if he fails to repay the loan to the creditor. The beauty of this arrangement for the creditor is that he will be able to cut his losses if the debtor either refuses to pay the loan completely or only pays back part of it. At the very least, the creditor will be able to put his hands on something of value belonging to the debtor.

However, the creditor will not be able to enforce the security against the debtor if the documentation requirements listed above are not complied with. According to Section 105, the creditor must get a court order to enforce the security and, ultimately, the court has the final say as to whether it will allow the creditor to enforce the security (Section 127).

 Key point: Failure to comply with the documentation rules set down by the Act will mean that a creditor will have real difficulty enforcing the agreement and this may affect any security that he has been granted by the debtor.

The debtor's cancellation rights

As should be apparent from the study of contract law, it is usually the case that once a legally enforceable agreement has been formed both parties are now committed to it and for one of them to break the contract would give the other party the right to sue. Under the Consumer Credit Act 1974, however, it is possible for the debtor, in certain situations, to withdraw from the credit agreement without being sued by the creditor for breach of contract. The debtor's right to cancel an agreement was deliberately introduced in order to clamp down on the disreputable practice of door-to-door salesmen pressurising people to enter credit agreements which they did not want or could not afford.

Under Section 67, a debtor will have the right to cancel a credit agreement if two conditions are met:

♦ If you, the debtor, entered into face-to-face discussions with the creditor or the creditor's agents with the aim of entering a credit agreement.

♦ The signing of the credit agreement by both parties did not take place on the creditor's business premises.

If a debtor signed a credit agreement in his own home after discussions with the creditor's agent, then the debtor can take advantage of what is known as a 'cooling-off period'. This period gives the debtor time to decide whether he wishes to cancel the agreement or not.

It does not matter whether the face-to-face discussions with the creditor took place at the creditor's place of business or in the debtor's home, but in order to have the right to cancel, the debtor must not have signed the agreement on the creditor's business premises. This 'cooling-off period' runs for five days from when the debtor receives his second copy of the agreement.

If the agreement can be cancelled, there must be a notice next to the signature box on the form which tells the debtor that he has a right to cancel. The creditor must tell the debtor how and when he can cancel the contract.

The reason a debtor signing an agreement at home was given the right to cancel was because it was considered much harder to get a determined sales agent of the creditor out of the debtor's home. Debtors were often placed under tremendous pressure by a determined sales agent to sign an agreement and many people found it hard to ask the agent to leave without appearing rude or aggressive. This situation can be contrasted with signing an agreement on the creditor's business premises where it is much easier for the debtor to walk out if he dislikes the terms of the agreement or if he is just having second thoughts about it.

A debtor, therefore, will not have a right to cancel the agreement if he signed the agreement on the creditor's premises.

An important consideration for the debtor is that any cancellation notice which he intends to send to the creditor must be in writing. The debtor will have to make sure that this cancellation notice reaches the creditor before the five-day 'cooling-off period' is over.

 Key point: A debtor will have the right to cancel a consumer credit agreement if he has held face-to-face discussions with the creditor or his agent and the debtor did not sign the agreement on the creditor's trade premises.

Termination of consumer credit agreements

Consumer credit agreements like most contracts come to an end sooner rather than later. They can end in a number of ways:

Default by the debtor

One of the most common ways in which the agreement can be brought to an end is where the debtor breaks the agreement. If the agreement is broken by the debtor this is often referred to as the debtor defaulting on the agreement.

If the debtor defaults on the agreement, the creditor, under the terms of Section 87, must serve a default notice on the debtor. Without serving this default notice, the creditor is not entitled to use any of the following remedies for breach of contract:

1   To end the agreement

2   To demand early repayment of any money owed by the debtor under the agreement

3   To recover possession of any goods that the debtor holds

4   To behave as if any of the debtor's rights under the agreement have been suspended, limited or even terminated

5   To enforce any security

It should be noted that the terms of the credit agreement will often state what action the creditor will be able to take against the debtor if he defaults. Only some of the options listed in 1 to 5 may be available to the creditor. The agreement will, therefore, determine what the creditor can and cannot do. The important thing to remember is that any of the actions open to the creditor under the agreement will be useless if a default notice was not served on the debtor.

If the creditor wishes to sue for payments that the debtor has fallen behind with, he is entitled to so without having to serve a default notice. Furthermore, credit card companies often prevent debtors from using a card if the credit limit has been reached and default notices are not required for this type of action.

Under Section 88, the default notice must contain the following information:

- ◆ It must inform the debtor in what way he has broken the agreement
- ◆ Whether it is possible for the debtor to take action to resolve the situation and what this action is
- ◆ If the breach cannot be resolved, the creditor must state the amount which the debtor must pay in compensation
- ◆ The date by which the action to resolve the breach must be taken or the date by which compensation must be paid

The debtor will be given at least seven days by the creditor to resolve the breach or pay compensation. If the debtor takes steps to comply with the default notice, Section 89 states that the breach of the agreement cannot be referred to by the creditor in the future. It will be as if the breach of the agreement committed by the debtor never occurred.

 Key point: In order for the creditor to take any action against a debtor, a default notice must first be served on the debtor.

The debtor, however, may not comply with the creditor's default notice. There are still options available to the debtor in that he could apply to the court for a time order under Section 129. In these kinds of situations, the court can either allow the creditor to use one of the remedies under the agreement or the debtor can be given the protection of a time order.

A time order basically gives the debtor more time to pay the money owed to the creditor under the agreement. Obviously, the court will have to look at the debtor's financial circumstances and the likelihood of his being able to pay back the money before a time order was granted.

Section 131 does potentially provide the creditor with some peace of mind. The creditor can apply to court for what is called a protection order. This order effectively means that the court can restrict or prohibit the use of the creditor's property which the debtor currently has in his possession. These orders are very useful while the creditor is awaiting the outcome of the court's decision mainly in relation to disputes that centre around the debtor's alleged default.

 Key point: Service of a default notice by the creditor does not mean that the debtor is forced to comply with this – the debtor can always apply to court for a time order or a protection order.

Termination clauses

This type of contractual term is commonly found in hire purchase and conditional sale agreements and is relevant when the debtor defaults on the contract. Such a clause means that, theoretically, a debtor will be forced to return the goods to the creditor. The debtor will not become the owner of the goods. The debtor is not entitled to the return of any payments that he has already made under the agreement and will also have to pay any arrears. There is even the possibility that the goods may be damaged or may have lost value during the time that they were in the debtor's possession and the creditor may receive compensation to reflect this. Finally, the debtor will have to pay any interest charges due under the agreement, but this must not exceed the APR payable under the agreement.

 Key point: Termination clauses are commonly found in hire purchase and conditional sale agreements and will become effective upon the event of the debtor's default meaning that the debtor will have to return the goods to the creditor.

Accelerated payments clauses

An agreement may contain an accelerated payments clause. The clause comes into operation when the debtor defaults on the agreement. The debtor will have to pay all of the instalments due under the agreement even if these were to be made some time in the distant future i.e. months and years from now. The immediate effect of such a clause is that the debtor will become the owner of the goods if the agreement is hire purchase or a conditional sale. In all other types of credit agreement, the debtor is entitled to keep the goods. The debtor may be charged interest on any payments that he has fallen into arrears with, but the interest rate will not exceed the APR payable under the agreement. The debtor may even be entitled to a rebate of charges for the early payment of the loan.

There is always the situation that the debtor could face severe financial difficulties if he was forced to make all payments under the agreement immediately to the creditor. This may be a very real pressure that the debtor could face if he has fallen into arrears of payment. The debtor could, therefore, ask the court to make a time order under Section 129 which gives him extra time to make the repayments to the debtor.

 Key point: Accelerated payments clauses become effective when the debtor defaults on the agreement meaning that all sums due under the contract become payable to the creditor, but the debtor will either become the owner of the goods or will be able to retain possession of them.

Protected goods

Under Sections 90 and 91 of the Act, a creditor may be prevented, however, from repossessing the goods from the debtor until he gets a court order permitting him to do this. Sections 90 and 91 only apply to hire purchase and conditional sale agreements. In hire purchase agreements and conditional sales, the creditor remains the owner of the goods until the debtor has paid all of the instalments owed. Goods are considered to be protected if the debtor has both:

- defaulted
- paid at least one-third of the total price payable under the agreement

If the creditor went ahead and seized the goods without the debtor's permission, the debtor would be entitled to get back all the payments that he made under the hire purchase agreement or conditional sale.

In Scotland, a creditor would have to get an order from the court allowing him to repossess goods no matter what type of agreement the creditor and the debtor had entered into.

 Key point: If the goods are designated protected goods, a creditor will not be able to repossess them without the permission of the court.

Termination

Not all credit agreements will come to an end because the debtor has defaulted. Both the creditor and the debtor may wish to end the agreement for other reasons.

Under hire purchase and conditional sale agreements, the debtor is given a statutory right to terminate the agreement under Section 99. This allows the debtor to end the agreement at any time before the final payment is made to the creditor. The debtor must inform the creditor of his decision to end the agreement. Ending the agreement in this way has certain consequences in that the debtor:

- Must return the goods
- Will not be entitled to the return of any payments that he has already made
- Must still pay any arrears owed
- May have to pay a further sum so that he will have paid in total one half of the price payable under the agreement

Section 94 allows the debtor to make early repayment and for him to receive a rebate of credit charges.

Section 98 states that a creditor may end an agreement if he gives the debtor at least seven days' notice of this intention as long as the debtor has not defaulted in any way.

 Key point: Credit agreements can come to an end by the mutual agreement of the parties.

Extortionate credit agreements

Under Sections 137 to 140, a court may examine the terms of a credit agreement in order to establish whether it operates fairly between the parties and to ensure that it is not an extortionate agreement.

An agreement may be considered extortionate if the debtor is forced to make grossly exorbitant payments under the agreement to the creditor. The term grossly exorbitant means that the agreement would fall foul of the ordinary principles of fair dealing. In other words, a reasonable or fair-minded person would consider the agreement to be completely unbalanced in that it blatantly favoured the creditor's interests.

Usually, a credit agreement will be examined in this way when the debtor makes an application to the court. The court will look at the following factors:

- ◆ Current interest rates at the time when the bargain was made.

- ◆ The personal circumstances of the debtor including his age, experience and health.

- ◆ The level of financial pressure that the debtor was experiencing when he entered the agreement.

- ◆ The level of risk that the creditor was accepting and his relationship with the debtor.

- ◆ Any other material facts or circumstances.

 Key point: A court may find that a credit agreement is extortionate if the contractual terms force the debtor to make grossly exorbitant payments under the agreement to the creditor.

Credit reference agencies

It is no secret that creditors will want to look hard at the previous credit records of potential customers before making a decision as to whether or not to provide them with finance. One of the ways in which a creditor can obtain this information is by approaching a credit reference agency. Section 145 defines a credit reference agency as a person who carries on a business with the purpose of providing other persons with information about a particular individual's financial status. Credit reference agencies will, therefore, collect this information with the express purpose of supplying it to creditors.

The result of this particular activity is that creditors may refuse to supply finance to those individuals who have a bad history of making repayments or failing to repay money under previous credit agreements. If debtors have a poor credit history they are effectively blacklisted and this means that they will find it very hard to secure credit at all or on favourable terms in the future.

Unfortunately, a lot of information that the credit reference agency holds on various debtors may be inaccurate and completely misleading. It would not be the first time that debtors with impeccable credit records were wrongly listed as having a poor or atrocious credit history. It is vital, therefore, that the agency's records are kept as accurate as possible.

 Key point: A credit reference agency is an organisation that provides information to creditors about the individual credit histories of a debtor and once the creditor has studied this information he will decide whether or not to lend credit to the debtor.

Debtors, whether they have been wrongly blacklisted or not, have certain rights:

1 The creditor will have to provide the debtor with details of the credit reference agency which he used in order to make a decision.

2 After making a written request, the debtor has a right to obtain a copy of his file from the agency within seven days.

3 The debtor has a right to demand that any wrong or inaccurate information that the agency holds on file is corrected within 28 days.

The debtor's right to a copy of his file held by the agency is guaranteed by Section 158 and a failure to comply is a criminal offence. If the debtor is dissatisfied with the agency's response, he can apply to the Office of Fair Trading which will take the appropriate action on his behalf.

 Key point: Credit reference agencies will have to be particularly careful that the information that they hold is in no way misleading or inaccurate and debtors will have the right of access to their files and can force the agency to correct any mistakes.

Summary

- The Sale of Goods Act 1979 establishes rules that govern the transfer of ownership of corporeal, moveable goods from seller to buyer.

- The Sale of Goods Act 1979 imposes certain implied duties upon a seller of goods with which he must comply.

- The implied terms (Sections 12 to 15) cover the following issues – the seller's title or his right to sell the goods, the way in which the goods are described, the quality and the fitness of the goods and those situations where the goods are sold using a sample.

- A material breach of contract in Scotland would include breaches of Sections 13, 14 and 15.

- The Sale and Supply of Goods to Consumers Regulations 2002, which came into force on 31 March 2003, make important changes to the Sale of Goods Act 1979. The new Regulations provide consumer buyers with additional remedies – repair, replacement, reduction and rescission.

- Since the introduction of the Unfair Contract Terms Act 1977 and the Unfair Terms in Consumer Contracts Regulations 1999, a seller's ability to use exclusion and limitation clauses in order to avoid the implied duties of the Sale of Goods Act has been considerably weakened. However, consumer buyers, as opposed to business buyers, will continue to enjoy much greater protection in relation to the use of exclusion and limitation clauses.

- The Sale of Goods Act 1979 also lays down important rules that govern the delivery of corporeal, moveable property (Sections 27 to 37).

- The Act provides the buyer and the seller with a number of remedies should they find themselves victims of a breach of contract by the other party.

- The Consumer Credit Act 1974 applies to regulated credit agreements that do not exceed £25,000 in value.

- One of the most distinctive features of the 1974 Act is the fact that those businesses or individuals wishing to provide credit facilities to members of the public must be in obtain possession of a licence and failure to do so could mean the imposition of a number of civil and criminal penalties.

- The 1974 Act contains rules which apply to two types of credit agreements. These agreements are consumer credit agreements and consumer hire agreements.

- A consumer credit agreement is a contract consisting of a debtor (the borrower) and a creditor (the lender).

- The Consumer Credit Act 1974 originally gave authority to a Director-General of Fair Trading assisted by the Office of Fair Trading to oversee the regulation of the consumer credit industry in the United Kingdom.

- The introduction of the Enterprise Act 2002 has resulted in the Office of Fair Trading being given legal status as a corporate body and the post of Director-General of Fair Trading has been abolished.

- The Office of Fair Trading has primary responsibility for the granting of credit licences under the 1974 Act.

- Under the 1974 Act, there are strict controls imposed on businesses which advertise credit facilities to members of the general public.

- Strict guidelines regulate how an advertisement is to be presented (its *form*), what sort of information will appear in it (its *content*) and that they should be easily understood by members of the public.

- According to the 1974 Act, all consumer credit agreements must be in writing.

- The 1974 Act imposes a duty on the creditor to make sue that the agreement presented to the debtor for signing is legible and, additionally, all the main terms must be contained in it.

- Failure by the creditor to comply with any of the rules regulating the content and appearance of a regulated agreement will mean that it can only be enforced by a court order against the debtor.

- Under the 1974 Act, a debtor will have the right to cancel a credit agreement if two conditions are met – if you, the debtor, entered into face-to-face discussions with the creditor or the creditor's agents with the aim of entering a credit agreement; and the signing of the credit agreement by both parties did not take place on the creditor's business premises.

- Under the 1974 Act, a court may examine the terms of a credit agreement in order to establish whether it operates fairly between the parties and to ensure that it is not an extortionate agreement.

- Creditors often use credit reference agencies in order to discover whether someone is creditworthy before giving that person a loan or some other from of credit.

- Credit reference agencies must ensure that the information that they hold in relation to actual debtors and potential debtors is up to date and accurate.

Test your knowledge

Short answer questions, exam standard essay style questions and case-studies.

1 a) What do we mean by a sale of goods?

b) Explain the following terms:

 i) A sale

 ii) An agreement to sell

 iii) Specific goods

 iv) Unascertained goods

 v) Future goods

c) What kinds of goods have the various individuals purchased in the situations described below and does a sale or an agreement to sell exist?

 i) Sarah has had her offer accepted to buy a second hand Volkswagen Polo (registration number: FA52 DKY; colour black) from Harold Marks Automobiles.

 ii) Fred owns the local licensed grocer and he has just placed an order with the local wholesaler for 1000 bottles and cans of beer (lager and ale), 200 bottles of white wine, 150 bottles of red wine, 75 bottles of whisky, 60 bottles of vodka and 50 bottles of gin. To complicate matters, these goods are supplied by a variety of brewers, distillers, vineyards and manufacturers. It is normal practice for the wholesaler to confirm two days after Fred has placed his order that the goods are ready for delivery.

 iii) Alan and Caroline have recently become engaged to be married. To mark the special occasion, Alan has asked the jeweler to supply an engagement ring according to his own design. The jeweler is quite happy to accommodate Alan, but it will take six weeks to make the ring.

2 a) In a contract of sale, a buyer may be able to acquire ownership rights to property in situations:

 • Where the seller lacked the authority to sell the goods

 • Where the seller was not the true owner of the goods

Explain the above statement.

b) Laura is a student at Granton College of Further and Higher Education. Financially, she is finding it very tough as a full-time student. Although Laura has part-time employment and she has taken out the full student loan, this is not enough to make ends meet. Laura's parents gave her an expensive mobile phone for her Christmas present and she decides to take it along to the local pawnbrokers to see whether she can use it to secure a cash advance. The pawnbroker gives Laura £60 for the phone. She is also given a ticket which states that she has 30 days in which to repay the loan otherwise she will lose the right to reclaim her goods.

What action can the pawnbrokers take if Laura fails to reclaim her property within the 30-day period?

3 a) It is important to remember that the Sale of Goods Act 1979 (as amended) applies to contracts of sale involving the transfer of ownership of corporeal, moveable goods.

Define corporeal, moveable goods and provide ten examples of this type of property.

b) Derek has sold a house to Marina. A dispute has arisen in relation to the property because Derek is arguing that, under the contract, he has the right to remove an ornamental shrub from the front garden, but Marina is refusing to allow Derek to do this. Marina claims that the ornamental shrub is rightfully her property. In any case, removing the shrub would cause it to suffer irreparable damage.

Will Marina or Derek be entitled to raise an action under the Sale of Goods Act 1979 (as amended) in order to resolve this dispute?

4 a) What are the implied terms in a sale of goods transaction?

b) Consider the following transactions:

 i) Kevin wishes to purchase a new leather jacket. He has a bit of money to spend and he decides to have the jacket specially made. Kevin goes to a local gents clothing store which has an excellent reputation for producing leather jackets made especially to the customer's order. Kevin is shown several styles of jacket. He particularly likes one style of jacket. All that remains is for him to choose the colour and the texture of the finished article from a range of leather samples shown to him by the sales assistant. Kevin decides to select a sample which is camel in colour and made from nubuck leather. The jacket will cost Kevin £400 and he makes it very clear to the assistant that he wants to get everything just right. He is particularly anxious that the sample shown to him accurately represents the colour and the texture of the finished article. The sales assistant is very quick to lay these anxieties to rest. A week later, Kevin receives a phone call from the gents store informing him that the jacket is ready to be picked up. When Kevin see the jacket, he is acutely aware that it is the wrong colour (it is a brown jacket, but it is a much darker brown than camel) and the appearance and texture of the jacket consists of glazed leather rather than the nubuck leather that he had anticipated.

ii) Tariq bought a brand new turbo diesel car at a cost of £16,000 from a reputable car dealer. Two weeks after the delivery of the car and with less than 200 miles on the odometer, the car experiences a catastrophic engine failure. This incident occurred when Tariq was driving along a road where the national speed limit of 60 miles per hour applied. He was not able to bring the vehicle under control quickly enough and it spun off the road ending up in a ditch. The car was extensively damaged and Tariq suffered severe whiplash and minor cuts and bruises. The car dealer is refusing to admit liability for the fault in the engine claiming that Tariq will have to take the matter up with the vehicle's manufacturer.

iii) Foundation Menswear has just received its new range of shirts for Spring/Summer. The contract stated that each box of clothing supplied would each contain 30 short-sleeved shirts. When the boxes are all opened, they each contain 25 shirts. This packaging method makes no difference whatsoever to the number of shirts supplied. However, when the plastic wrapping is removed, it becomes evident that a large number of the shirts have long-sleeves.

With reference to the Sale of Goods Act 1979 (as amended), how would you decide the three cases above?

5 **a)** Section 14(2) of the Sale of Goods Act 1979 (as amended) states that the seller must supply the buyer with goods which meet the standard of satisfactory quality and Section 14(3) of the Act stipulates that the seller must supply the buyer with goods which are fit for their purpose.

What is the difference between satisfactory quality and fitness for purpose?

b) Tartan Touring Services Ltd is a company which organises touring holidays throughout the UK and to far-flung destinations throughout Europe. Tartan needs to replace seven buses which form part of the company fleet. To this end, Tartan has entered into a contract with Cameron Coachbuilders Ltd for the construction of seven buses. Tartan told Cameron that the buses should be suitable for long-distance travel and should have luxury seating. When the vehicles are delivered, Tartan discovers that they do not have toilets, entertainment systems (TV, DVD and video) and the buses are not sufficiently robust or comfortable enough for touring purposes. These vehicles would be more suitable for traveling short journeys around the local bus routes in Edinburgh and Glasgow.

Where does Tartan Touring Services stand legally?

6 **a)** The Sale and Supply of Goods to Consumers Regulations 2002 came into force on 31 March 2003 and they introduce important changes to the existing sale of goods legislation of the United Kingdom.

Would you agree that consumers are much better protected with the introduction of the Sale and Supply of Goods to Consumers Regulations 2002?

b) Ethsham bought a brand new LCD television from SHOCKZ, a well-known electrical retailer. The television was very expensive and Ethsham was unsure whether he wanted to spend such a large amount money on this item. The sales assistant was very keen to sell the television to Ethsham and he pointed out that the goods were covered by a three-year manufacturer's guarantee. Some four months later, however, the television broke down and Ethsham took it back to SHOCKZ. Ethsham demanded a refund, but the store informs him that the situation is not that simple. The store can either replace or repair the goods, but it does not have to refund the purchase price of the goods. Furthermore, the store cannot be held responsible for the manufacturer's guarantee which was issued independently. Ethsham is very confused and now seeks your advice.

Advise Ethsham.

7 **a)** Any attempt by a seller to exclude or limit his liability to a buyer in a sale of goods transaction will be automatically void.

Assess the accuracy of this statement.

b) Entertainment Services Ltd, an international supplier of DVDs, CDs, videos and books, has entered into a contract of sale with Specialist Software Solutions plc for the purchase and installation of a cutting edge software package. The software package would allow Entertainment Services to set up a database which would keep track of its distribution and supply operations. Customers would be automatically billed when a transaction was completed and this would stop the Entertainment Services from wasting a great deal of time going through the paper records and sending out a paper invoice to customers. As an alternative, customers would receive an invoice via e-mail. However, the software package contained some sort of error and a lot of important customer information was wiped from the database. This information included details of customers who had still not paid for goods. This meant that Entertainment Services could not account for a valuable source of revenue. Entertainment Services is now suing Specialist Software Solutions for substantial damages for the losses it has suffered. Specialist Software Solutions is attempting to rely on a clause in the contract of sale which reduces its liability to a sum of £10,000.

Will Specialist Software Solutions be able to enforce the contractual term against Entertainment Services?

8 **a)** Risk passes with property.

Is this statement true in light of the recent changes made to sale of goods transactions by the Sale and Supply of Goods to Consumers Regulations 2002?

b) i) Smith Solicitors have selected two new leather sofas from Luxury Leather Ltd to be used in their client waiting room. The goods in question were sale items and were the last two items in stock of that particular line of furniture. Luxury Leather had promised to deliver the sofas first thing on Monday morning, but on Sunday evening Luxury Leather was broken into by thieves and the sofas were stolen.

Who will be responsible for the risk to the goods in the above situation?

ii) Consider the following scenario:

What if Euan and Lynne had entered into a contract to purchase the two sofas from Luxury Leather for their sitting room which has just been redecorated and the sofas had been stolen from the storeroom. Luxury Leather had promised the couple that it would deliver the goods on Thursday.

What would have been the legal position in this situation?

9 Examine the following situations carefully:

a) Jasminder went shopping for some new clothes on Saturday morning. She is really pleased with her purchases having bought a couple of pairs of jeans and a pair of leather boots from her favourite designer store. Just as she is leaving the store to head back to her car, Jasminder runs into an old friend, Sadia, and they spend the next 20 minutes talking. When Jasminder eventually reaches the car park, she realises that she has left her bag containing all her new clothes in the store. She must have put the bag down while she was deep in conversation with Sadia. In a complete panic, Jasminder heads back into the store to see whether she can find the bag. Unfortunately, after searching everywhere with the help of the staff it becomes obvious that the bag is nowhere to be seen.

b) Steve has just entered into a contract with Reddie Motors for the purchase of a luxury second hand car. Before the contract was formed, Steve stated that he wanted Reddie to make a number of adjustments to the car:

1 Alloy wheels were to be fitted
2 The car was to be fitted with a multi-changer CD player
3 The glass in the car windows were to be tinted.

Reddie Motors have informed Steve that these modifications to the car will be carried out on Saturday and that he can pick the vehicle up on Monday morning. On Friday afternoon, the car was damaged when one of Reddie's employees was moving it into the workshop.

c) FreshFields Supermarket has agreed to purchase Farmer Giles' entire crop of potatoes which he just harvested. However, a term of the contract stipulates that Farmer Giles will have to weigh the potatoes in order to calculate the price to be paid by FreshFields. Before Farmer Giles can weigh the potatoes, he discovers that the some of the potatoes have been infected by blight.

d) Norma ordered an expensive new dress from the catalogue because she needed something to wear at Janice's wedding. The catalogue operates a policy whereby customers must return goods that they have no intention of keeping within a two-week period. The dress has now been in Norma's possession for three weeks and, furthermore, she wore the dress to the wedding where Ellen accidentally spilled a glass of wine over the dress and the stain is so bad that it cannot be removed.

e) Sweeney's Slaughterhouse has agreed to sell Bill, a butcher, 50 frozen lamb carcasses. Sweeney's Slaughterhouse is a huge business concern supplying meat to butchers all over Central Scotland. At any one time, it has hundreds of animal carcasses in stock. Bill sent two of his employees, Andy and Jamal, to pick up the goods. One of Sweeney's foremen had arranged for Andy and Jamal to uplift the goods from loading bay 9 of the slaughterhouse. When Andy and Jamal arrived at Sweeney's, the last crate is being piled up ready for them to put into their refrigerated lorry and all Jamal had to do was sign the invoice for the goods. It was nearly lunchtime and Andy suggested that he and Jamal should go over to the local café and have a quick bite to eat. Jamal was a bit dubious at first, but Andy said that they would be no more than half an hour at most and, in any case, there were plenty of people about the loading bay who would keep an eye out for the goods. When Andy and Jamal returned from lunch, the goods had been stolen.

Who is the owner of the goods in each of the five situations described above?

10 **a)** Romalpa clauses and other retention of title clauses can provide a seller of goods with valuable protection where there is a real danger that the buyer may become insolvent and will, therefore, become unable to pay the seller. These types of contractual terms, however, have their limitations and there may be situations where the seller's attempt to rely upon them will be utterly doomed to failure.

How effective are Romalpa and other retention of title clauses and are they worth the paper that they are written on?

b) Stuart owns the local timber merchants. On Friday, he was approached by Wylie Homes, which is currently building a new housing estate, and it wishes to purchase a large consignment of timber from him. Stuart has had previous dealings with Wylie, but lately he has become somewhat wary of doing business with the builder. Stuart has heard rumours that the builder has serious financial problems and, furthermore, Stuart is still owed a substantial amount of money from previous transactions. The proposed contract represents a very valuable piece of business that Stuart can ill afford to turn down. Stuart decides to supply the goods to Wylie but he insists that an all sums retention of title clause is inserted into the contract. Several months later, Stuart receives information that Wylie has become insolvent and he attempts to enforce the all sums retention of title clause.

Since the contract was formed, only a very small part of the timber that Stuart supplied is in its original state. Most of it has been used by Wylie to build the houses on the new estate.

What are the chances of Stuart being able to enforce the all sums retention of title clause?

11 **a)** What is the definition of delivery in terms of the Sale of Goods Act 1979 (as amended) and in what part of the Act would you find the rules relating to delivery?
b) What is the appropriate section of the Sale of Goods Act 1979 (as amended) in relation to each of the scenarios described below:
   i) The contract states that the seller must deliver the goods to the buyer, but there is nothing in the agreement which lays down a time period for delivery of the goods.
   ii) The seller has delivered a larger quantity of goods than the amount stated in the contract.
   iii) The seller is proposing to deliver the goods by instalments, but the buyer is totally opposed to this arrangement.
   iv) The seller has handed the goods over to a carrier in order to carry out delivery.
   v) The goods have been delivered to the buyer, but he has not yet had a reasonable opportunity to examine them.
   vi) The buyer has rightfully refused to accept the goods, but the seller is demanding that the buyer return the goods.
   vii) The buyer has wrongfully refused to take delivery of the goods from the seller.
   viii) The seller has breached the contract and the buyer wishes to exercise his right of partial rejection in relation to some of the goods.
   ix) The buyer has accepted the goods.
   x) Where the seller agrees to deliver the goods to a distant place.

12 When one of the parties commits a breach of contract, the innocent party will have access to a number of remedies.

Describe the remedies available for breach of contract to **a)** the buyer and **b)** the seller.

13 Write explanatory notes on the following topics:
a) The difference between a sale or security situation
b) Frustrated contracts
c) Calculating the price in sale of goods contracts
d) Capacity to enter into contracts
e) Stipulations as to time in a contract of sale

14 Morag has been running a shop which specialises in the sale of work by local artists. When Morag first started the business, she generally refused to give credit to customers. Very occasionally, she would make an exception and extend credit to close friends. As her business has grown, Morag finds that customers expect to be given six months credit (at the very least) when they make a purchase from her shop. Morag has had to move with the times and credit sales now represent the majority of her sales. However, Morag is now very concerned because one of her friends has told her that she has been breaking the law for some time. Morag does not possess the necessary legal documents which would permit her to provide credit facilities to her customers.

Is Morag's friend correct and, if so, what steps will she have to take in order to comply with the law?

15 Sheila and her husband are interested in having a conservatory built. The couple had received a telephone call from a company that specialises in building conservatories and they decided to allow a salesperson to come to their house to explain the various options which would be available to them. One Monday evening, the agent arrived at the couple's house at 7 p.m. and did not leave until 11 p.m. Against their better judgement, the couple decided to sign the contract allowing the company to build the conservatory. Sheila and her husband would have liked more time to think about things, but the salesperson was very persuasive and very determined to close the deal. The couple would now like to withdraw from the agreement, but they are bound in contract to the company aren't they?

Can Sheila and her husband cancel the consumer credit contract?

16 The Consumer Credit Act 1974 gives powers to a court permitting it to examine the terms of a credit agreement in order to establish whether it operates fairly between the parties and to ensure that it is not an extortionate agreement.

What is an extortionate credit agreement?

17 The Bank of the Firth of Clyde has been running a series of advertisements. The advertisements give the impression that if anyone applies for a loan with the Bank they will automatically be granted one. Asif applied for a loan, but was turned down on the grounds that he has been unemployed for six months. The advertisements did not say that loans were dependent upon an applicant's employment status.

Should the Bank have taken greater care when it used the above advertisement?

18 One of the most common ways in which a credit agreement can be brought to an end is where the debtor breaks that agreement. If the agreement is broken by the debtor this is often referred to as the debtor defaulting on the agreement.

What steps can the creditor take when the debtor breaches the credit agreement?

19 Write short, explanatory notes on the following:
a) Running account credit
b) Fixed term credit
c) Restricted use credit
d) Unrestricted use credit
e) Debtor-creditor agreements
f) Debtor-creditor-supplier agreements

20 Some agreements are not governed by the rules contained in the Consumer Credit Act 1974. Exempt agreements, however, do not escape sections 137 to 140 of the Act which deal with agreements that are considered to be extortionate.

What agreements are exempt from the provisions of the Consumer Credit Act 1974?

CHAPTER
5

THE LAW OF BUSINESS ORGANISATIONS

Introduction

Many people talk about running a business. What many people will fail to realise is that there are a variety of business organisations which the law recognises, for example, sole traders, partnerships, limited partnerships, limited liability partnerships, private limited companies, public limited companies and unlimited companies. An important thing to appreciate from any study of the law of business organisations is that there are different rules that apply to different types of businesses. This chapter will take a look at some of these rules.

> ### This chapter covers the following areas:
>
> - The law of agency -
> - Business organisations -

The law agency

Introduction

Partners in a firm, members of a limited liability partnership and directors of a company are all considered to be agents or legal representatives of their respective business organisations. It is vital to possess a basic understanding of the rules that regulate the conduct of the various types of agent who are involved in running business organisations. It is a simple statement of fact that few businesses could survive without relying on the services of agents, therefore, an introduction to the law of agency is necessary.

Agents

An agent is the legal representative of someone called the principal. The principal authorises the agent to act on his behalf in dealings with third parties. The agent, therefore, negotiates and enters contractual agreements on behalf of the principal with third parties. When the third party deals with the agent it is as if he is dealing directly with the principal. The agent, of course, expects to receive some sort of reward from the principal for negotiating contracts with third parties for the benefit of the principal. Such a reward could be in the form of a commission, a salary, a customary rate or at least something of value. To put it bluntly, an agent does not provide his services to the principal out of the goodness of his heart. The principal and the agent have a commercial relationship. As will be appreciated later, the expectation of being paid or rewarded is one of the most important characteristics of an agent.

 Key point: An agent is the legal representative of someone called the principal. The principal authorises the agent to act on his behalf in dealings with third parties. The agent, therefore, negotiates and enters contractual agreements on behalf of the principal with third parties.

An example of how an agent will represent his principal in dealings with a third party can be seen where someone wishes to sell a house. The seller (the principal) hires a solicitor (the agent) to deal with a potential buyer (the third party) of the house. Hopefully, the solicitor can set up a contractual agreement between the seller and the buyer.

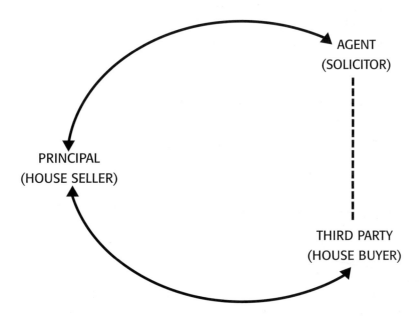

It should be noted that any contract which the agent negotiates is between the principal and the third party. As long as the agent sticks closely to his instructions and does nothing wrong, he will have no further interest in the contract which he has managed to negotiate between the principal and the third party. This means that, if the principal or the third party breaks the agreement, the agent cannot be sued by either party. The role of the agent is merely to represent the principal in order to conclude contracts with third parties. Once this has been achieved, the agent fades into the background and plays no further part in any of the dealings between the principal and the third party.

 Key point: The agent is not a party to the contract agreed between the principal and the third party.

The importance of agents

Why appoint an agent in the first place? There are two reasons why the principal would wish to appoint an agent to represent him. First, it will not be physically possible for the principal to carry out every task which is necessary for the successful running of a business. There are only so many hours in the day and there are only so many tasks that even the most gifted person can get through in a day. Sometimes you just have to delegate tasks to another person in order to complete them. Second, an agent will often be appointed by the principal because he will have special skills or experience of which the principal wishes to take advantage. When it comes to selling a house, for example, many ordinary people would not even know how to go about this and would have even less knowledge of the legal rules that have to be complied with in order to complete the transaction successfully. It is no wonder in such a situation that they would choose to appoint a solicitor to act for them.

 Key point: Agents are often employed or hired as it is physically impossible for the principal to carry out every activity that relates to his business personally and the agent may have special skills or expertise from which the principal can benefit.

Agents crop up in many different areas of commercial life. A list of agents can be seen below:

- Solicitors
- Architects
- Accountants
- Auctioneers
- Commercial agents
- Partners in a firm
- Members of a limited liability partnership
- Company directors
- Managers
- Sales assistants
- Factors
- Stockbrokers
- Captain of a ship or an aircraft

 Key point: Agents are encountered in many different areas of commercial life.

Employees or independent contractors

An agent can either be an employee or an independent contractor. An agent who is an employee will carry out services for the principal under a contract *of* service, whereas an independent contractor carries out services for the principal under a contract *for* services. It may be useful to think of a contract of service as an employment contract and, by way of a comparison, a contract for services involves a situation where the agent will hire out his services on an as required basis to the principal. A solicitor may serve as a useful example. If a solicitor works permanently for the legal services department of a local council, he will be an agent *and* an employee of the council. If, however, a solicitor is a partner in a private law firm and hires out his services to private clients as and when they require his advice and assistance, he will be acting as an agent, but he is an independent contractor and not an employee of his private clients.

Not all employees, of course, can call themselves agents of their employer. It should be remembered that the most important function of an agent is to bind his principal into contracts with third parties. Many employees will simply not have the power to do this. It is highly unlikely that someone who works on a factory production line and has absolutely no dealings with third parties would be in a position to describe himself as his employer's agent.

 Key point: Agents can either be employees of the principal or independent contractors for services.

Mandatory and agent

An agent expects to receive some sort of reward for performing services for the principal. In Scotland, a person can act for someone very much like an agent, but this type of representative would not expect to receive a reward. Sometimes this type of relationship is referred to as gratuitous agency or unpaid agency. It is more properly called mandate and the person who acts in this way is known as a mandatory. Although acting on an unpaid basis, a mandatory will still owe a duty of care to the person for whom he is acting. This means that a mandatory will not be able to use the fact that he was acting unpaid as a defence to a claim of negligence. The following two cases provide interesting examples of the duty of care expected of a mandatory.

 Copland v Brogan (1916) a school teacher had asked a carriage driver to go to a bank in a nearby town in order to cash three cheques at the bank. The carriage driver had carried out various tasks for the school teacher in the past. The carriage driver was not expecting to be paid for carrying out this favour. However, after cashing the cheques at the bank, the carriage driver lost the school teacher's money. There was no question of dishonesty on the carriage driver's part. The school teacher sued on the grounds of the carriage driver's negligence. The carriage driver's defence was, that as he was acting on an unpaid basis, he could not be sued for negligence.

Held: by the Inner House of the Court of Session that a mandatory must take the same sort of care that would be expected of him in the management of his own affairs. Had the proceeds from the cheques belonged to the mandatory, it is likely that he would have made sure that they were kept safe. This he had failed to do and he had not taken reasonable care of the school teacher's property.

 Chaudhry v Prabhakar (1989) Chaudhry had recently passed her driving test and she asked a friend, Prabhakar, to advise her in relation to buying a second-hand car. Chaudhry made it clear to Prabhakar that she did not want to buy a car that had been involved in an accident. Prabhakar found a car for Chaudhry, but the car had a dent in its bonnet. Prabhakar noticed the dent, but he did not make any enquiries as to whether or not the car had been involved in an accident. Chaudhry specifically asked Prabhakar if the car had been involved in an accident and he replied that it had not. Relying on Prabhakar's statement, Chaudhry bought the car from the seller. Later, the car turned out to be unroadworthy as result of the accident. Chaudhry sued Prabhakar for negligence.

Held: the English Court of Appeal decided that Prabhakar had been negligent when he told Chaudhry that the car had not been involved in an accident in response to her very specific question. It made no difference that Prabhakar had acted for Chaudhry without payment. He should have exercised the type of care that would have been expected if he had been looking after his own interests. He had failed to take reasonable care and, therefore, he was liable.

 Key point: A mandatary or gratuitous agent does not expect to be paid by the principal for his services, but he must take reasonable care in the way that he performs his duties.

Del credere agents

A *del credere* agent is an agent who introduces third parties to his principal and, critically, he promises to indemnify or compensate the principal if the contract does not go as planned and the principal suffers losses as a result.

 Couturier v Hastie (1856) Hastie had placed a cargo of corn on a ship sailing from Greece. The documents of title were forwarded to London agents in order that the corn might be sold. The London agents employed Couturier to find someone to sell the goods to – which he duly did. Unknown to the parties, the cargo had overheated aboard the ship and had been landed at the nearest port and sold, so that when Couturier entered the contract the corn did not really exist. The buyer later cancelled the contract and Couturier was sued by Hastie on the grounds that he was a *del credere* agent.

Held: the claim against Couturier failed on an important technicality because the contract was based on the understanding that the goods were actually in existence when Couturier contracted to sell them to the third party.

 Key point: A *del credere* agent is an agent who introduces third parties to his principal and, critically, he promises to indemnify or compensate if the third party fails to honour the contract causing the principal to suffer loss as a result.

General and special agents

General agents act for the principal in connection with all of his interests in a particular line of business. One example of a general agent is a solicitor. General agents can possess both actual and ostensible authority.

Special agents, on the other hand, have extremely limited authority. They usually act for the principal in one type of transaction only. An example of a special agent would be an estate agent. Special agents possess actual authority only.

 Morrison v Statter (1885) Calder, the head shepherd on Statter's farm, bought sheep from Morrison without having received explicit instructions from Statter. Morrison attempted to obtain payment from Statter for the sheep, but Statter refused claiming that he had never authorised Calder to act in this way.

Held: Calder had no actual authority to bind Statter in this way. There had been no previous dealings between Morrison and Statter which might have led Morrison to believe that this type of transaction was within Calder's ostensible or apparent authority. Morrison knew that Statter had not given Calder authority to purchase the sheep.

 The Ocean Frost (1986) the third party was well aware that the agent, who held a senior position with the principal, had no general authority to enter into a particular contract on the principal's behalf. Both the English Court of Appeal and the House of Lords stated that the third party knowing full well that the agent had no authority to act could not rely on the agent's statement that he did have the necessary authority to bind his principal in contract with the third party.

 Key point: General agents act for the principal in connection with all of his interests in a particular line of business whereas special agents have extremely limited authority.

The capacity of the principal and the agent

Clearly, it is important that the law recognises the ability of the principal and the agent to enter into the agency agreement. Factors such as the mental incapacity of one of the parties, intoxication as a result of alcohol or drugs, or one of the parties being declared an enemy alien in times of war may undermine the agency agreement. Interestingly, however, it would appear that an agent lacking capacity will not undermine any agreement that he may have negotiated between the principal and the third party. However, the position would be very different if the principal lacked capacity. The principal cannot use an agent to get round the problem of his lack of contractual capacity if the law would prevent him from entering a contract with the third party personally. A young person under the age of 16, for example, will not be able to use an agent in this way to enter contracts which he would otherwise be prevented from entering.

An agent must also be acting for a principal who actually exists and who is recognised by the courts as being able to take on rights and duties under a contract. It is not possible to act as an agent for someone who has not yet been born or for someone who has since died.

 Tinnevelly Sugar Refining Co v Mirrlees, Watson & Yaryan Co Ltd (1894) Darley & Butler claimed to be acting on behalf of a company called Tinnevelly. They entered into a contract with Mirrlees to purchase new machinery for Tinnevelly. Unfortunately, at the time Darley & Butler entered the contract with Mirrlees, Tinnevelly did not exist. It had not yet been registered as a company and, therefore, it was not recognised as a legal person capable of being a party to a contractual agreement. The new machinery later broke down and Tinnevelly sued Mirrlees for breach of contract.

Held: Tinnevelly was not a party to the contract with Mirrlees because Darley & Butler could not have been acting as agents for a principal that did not yet exist. When the original contract had been entered into (11 July 1890), Tinnevelly did not exist as a person in the eyes of the law. In fact, Tinnevelly only became a legal person on 29 July 1890 a number of weeks after the contract of sale had been entered into. It is not possible to act as an agent for a non-existent principal. In other words, the law must recognise the existence of the person who is supposedly the agent's principal.

 Key point: An agent cannot represent a non-existent principal.

The creation of an agency relationship

The relationship between the principal and the agent is based on the law of contract. In the diagram below, two contracts exist. The primary and most important contract is the one between the principal and the agent. The secondary contract is between the principal and the third party.

There are five ways in which an agency relationship can be created:

1   By express contract

2   Implied by the conduct of the parties or by law

3   By holding out

4   By ratification

5   By necessity

 Key point: The agency relationship can be created in the following ways – express contract, implied by the conduct of the parties or by law, holding out, ratification and necessity.

Express agency

The contract between principal and agent can either be of a verbal nature or it can be in writing. This is known as an express contract. A written agreement is obviously a more desirable option because if the parties have gone about things properly it will spell out clearly the agent's powers and duties. There is no legal requirement to have a written agency agreement, but generally speaking, courts tend to prefer dealing with documents because in the event of a dispute the rights and the duties of both parties are much easier to identify. Partners in a firm may well choose to have a written deed of partnership which names each partner and lays out very clearly the rights and duties of each partner. Similarly, members of a Limited Liability Partnership may also choose to draw up a members' agreement which will name each member and determine the extent of the members' ability to bind the business into contracts with third parties.

Key point: An agent can be appointed expressly by way of a written contract or a verbal agreement.

Implied agency

Agency can be implied by law or by the actions and conduct of the parties. By law under Section 5 of the Partnership Act 1890, every partner is an agent of the firm and an agent of his fellow partners for the purpose of the business of the partnership. Furthermore, according to Section 6 of the Limited Liability Partnerships Act 2000, every member of such a business organisation is to be regarded as an agent. Very often, a person's occupation or job will indicate that they are entitled to be regarded as an agent. The director of an incorporated company is impliedly an agent for the company in all the matters usually entrusted to directors. It can also be implied that a pub manager who contracts on behalf of the pub owner with third-party suppliers of goods and services as part of his job is acting as an agent.

 Key point: Sometimes the law recognises that an individual who holds a particular position is to be regarded as an agent or, alternatively, it can be implied that someone is an agent because of the position that he holds.

Agency by holding out

Such a situation arises when the principal's actions allow or encourage third parties to believe that a person is acting as an agent on the principal's behalf. Problems will occur later when the principal tries to deny that he encouraged the third party to believe that someone was acting as his agent. However, if the third party can show that he relied on the principal's representations, the principal will be liable to the third party for any agreement that the agent has negotiated. The principal may have made statements to the effect that someone is to be regarded as his agent.

 Hayman *v* American Cotton Oil Co (1907) the American Cotton Oil Company had made statements in several newspaper advertisements and in letters to prospective customers that McNairn & Co, a Glasgow firm, were acting as its agent. Ferguson Shaw & Sons, a third party, bought a quantity of goods from McNairn and paid for them before delivery. McNairn became insolvent and its creditors attempted to claim the goods that Ferguson Shaw & Sons had bought. Ferguson Shaw & Sons then turned to the American Cotton Oil Company demanding that it honour the contract that McNairn had negotiated on its behalf. The American Cotton Oil Company now attempted to deny, conveniently, that McNairn had ever been its agent. Ferguson Shaw & Sons pointed out that they had always believed that McNairn was the American Cotton Oil Company's agent. The newspaper advertisements and the letters to potential customers had led to an understandable belief that McNairn was the agent of the American Cotton Oil Company.

Held: the American Cotton Oil Company by placing advertisements and sending out letters to potential customers had given the impression to third parties dealing with McNairn that the Glasgow firm was its agent.

 Key point: Agency by holding out occurs when the principal's words or actions encourage a third party to believe that another individual is his agent.

Agency by ratification

This occurs when an agent does something which he has not been authorised to do by the principal. The principal however, chooses to ratify or approve the unauthorised actions of the agent. In other words, by ratifying the agent's unauthorised actions, the principal is prepared to forgive the fact that the agent has committed a breach of the agency agreement. It is not necessary for a relationship to have existed between the agent and the principal when the unauthorised actions occurred, but, usually there is some kind of existing contractual relationship. In order for the principal to be able to ratify an unauthorised transaction, a number of conditions must be satisfied:

◆ The agent must disclose all material facts surrounding the contract so that the principal is fully aware of all liabilities that he is taking on.

◆ The principal must ratify the contract within a reasonable time.

◆ The principal must have existed at the time the contract was entered into.

◆ The principal must have the power and capacity to ratify the act otherwise the contract will be void.

◆ The agent must act with an identifiable principal in mind and not contracting on his own with the hope that he will find someone who will later ratify the contract. It is important that the third party knows that the agent *is* acting as an agent and does not believe the agent to be in business on his own account.

◆ The principal will not be in a position to ratify any contract that is illegal.

 Keighley Maxsted & Co v Durant (1901) Roberts was an agent authorised to buy wheat at a certain price. Roberts made a contract with Durant for wheat at a higher price than the price his principal had originally authorised. Furthermore, Roberts made the contract in his own name without mentioning to the third party that he was acting for his principal, Keighley. Keighley originally agreed to ratify the contract which Roberts and Durant had entered into, but when Keighley failed to take delivery of the wheat at a later date, Durant sued for damages.

Held: the House of Lords stated that Roberts had not told Durant that he was working for Keighley and, as a result, Durant was not entitled to sue them on the contract.

 Kelner v Baxter (1866) the pursuer, Kelner, sold a quantity of wine to Baxter who claimed to be acting as an agent of a hotel company which had not been registered. This meant that the company did not yet exist in the eyes of the law and, therefore, was not capable of having rights and duties which would be recognised by the courts. The wine had been used, but Kelner had not been paid.

Held: Baxter was personally liable to Kelner for payment since a principal who does not exist at the time the contract was made cannot later ratify it.

 Key point: The process of ratification allows a principal to approve the actions of an agent who, strictly speaking, has gone beyond the limits of his authority.

Agency by necessity

In the event of an emergency, a person is deemed by law to have the authority to act as agent for another party. However, it must be impossible for the person acting as agent of necessity to contact the principal. Before the use of modern communications such as faxes, telephones, ship-to-shore radios and e-mail, this type of agency was extremely useful, but it is now highly unlikely that a principal would be unable to be contacted in an emergency situation. In saying that, however, this type of agency should not be written off completely and it may still have its uses. As long as the agent of necessity acts in good faith to protect the interests of the principal, he will not be held liable for any losses which his actions may have caused the principal.

 Couturier v Hastie (1856) the cargo had overheated aboard the ship and was beginning to rot. In order to prevent the cargo from being written off completely, it had been landed at the nearest port and sold. The captain of the ship was acting as an agent of necessity in an emergency situation in order to prevent further losses to his principal. It will be understood that in the 1850s when this case occurred, the captain was stuck on board a ship in the middle of the Mediterranean Sea. He did not have modern communications available to him in order to contact the principal for further instructions and he had to make a swift decision about the cargo.

 Great Northern Railway v Swaffield (1874) a horse was being transported to Swaffield who failed to collect it at the railway station. There was no accommodation at the station and the Railway company arranged for the horse to be put in a livery stable for the night. It was held that the Railway was entitled to claim reimbursement of the expenses involved because it had acted as an agent of necessity in an emergency situation where the principal could not be contacted and his instructions as regards the welfare of the horse established.

In order to be able to show that someone acted as an agent of necessity, it is necessary to prove that the principal could not be contacted.

 Springer v Great Western Railway (1921) Springer was the owner of tomatoes delayed in a railway strike. The railway company's traffic agent sold the tomatoes locally as he believed they would not have made it to Covent Garden in a saleable condition. Springer argued that if the agent had contacted him he could have transported them by road and still got the same high price.

Held: the claim that the railway's traffic agent had acted as agent of necessity should fail because the principal could have been contacted.

 Key point: In the event of an emergency, a person is deemed by law to have the authority to act as agent for another party.

Duties of an agent

The relationship between an agent and his principal is known as a fiduciary relationship i.e. a relationship of trust. At all times, the agent is expected to act in the best interests of the principal. This means that the principal's interests must come first. The agent must ensure that there are no conflicts of interest. As with all contracts, the agent will enjoy the protection of certain rights, but the agreement also imposes certain duties which are owed to the principal.

 Key point: The relationship between an agent and his principal is known as a fiduciary relationship i.e. a relationship of trust and the agent must place the principal's interests above his own.

An express contract (whether existing as a written or verbal agreement) between the principal and the agent will usually set out the agent's duties and it is the primary obligation of the agent to carry out these duties. If, however, there is no express contract, there are certain basic duties implied by law. The law imposes five key duties:

- To obey the instructions of the principal
- To exercise skill and care
- To act in person
- To keep proper accounts
- To act in good faith

To obey the instructions of the principal

The agent must carry out all lawful and reasonable instructions given to him by the principal. Where the agent fails to fulfil his principal's instructions he will be personally liable to the principal.

 Gilmour v Clark (1853) Gilmour gave instructions to Clark, a carrier, to take goods to the docks and put them on a ship called the Earl of Zetland. Clark put them on a ship called The Magnet instead – the ship sank and the goods were lost.
Held: Clark had to compensate Gilmour for the loss of the goods as a result of his failure to follow his instructions properly.

In situations where the principal has failed to give the agent proper instructions he must make use of his professional judgement in order to act in the best interests of the principal. Where the principal's instructions are ambiguous or vague, the agent will not be liable if he fails to interpret them properly. Very often, the agent will have been given only general instructions and, therefore, he should try to act in accordance with the rules of his trade or profession. A solicitor, for example, will often refuse to continue to act for a client if that client has either failed to provide proper instructions or the instructions which have been received are so vague as to be effectively meaningless.

It is extremely important for the agent to follow instructions from the principal because failure to do so will mean that he loses his right to claim payment. Furthermore, by not following the principal's orders, the agent may go far beyond his authority and this will mean that he may be personally liable to the third party.

 Key point: The agent must obey the instructions of the principal and, in the absence of such, he must use his professional judgement to safeguard the principal's interests.

To exercise skill and care

If the agent is a member of a profession or a trade, certain standards may be expected of him. Should the agent fail to meet the standards expected of a reasonably competent member of his trade or profession, he may be liable in negligence to his principal. As we have seen, even a mandatary or a gratuitous agent has to take reasonable care when acting on someone's behalf in dealings with third parties (see **Copland v Brogan (1916)** and **Chaudhry v Prabhakar (1989)**). Obviously, when the agent belongs to a particular profession or trade, the principal will have selected this person because there he has the perfectly reasonable belief that the agent will have the necessary level of skill and care to complete transactions on the principal's behalf.

 Key point: The agent must exercise the skill and care that would be expected of a reasonably competent member of his profession.

To act in person

The general rule in agency is that the agent must act personally. This general rule can be expressed in the following way: *delegatus non potest delegare* which basically means that an agent cannot delegate.

There are, however, exceptions to the general rule and an agent will be allowed to delegate certain tasks to another party if the principal has authorised such an occurrence or if trade practice and custom permit. If an agent has authority to delegate some of his powers, the principal will have to pay for the sub-agent's services because the law regards the principal and the sub-agent as having formed a contract.

 Black v Cornelius (1879) Cornelius employed Deas as his architect. Cornelius was planning to construct buildings on a site in Edinburgh. Deas, therefore, had authority as Cornelius' agent to draw up plans for the construction project. Deas hired Black, a surveyor, to take some measurements in order to complete the plans. The buildings were never built, but Black claimed that he was entitled to be paid for his services from Cornelius who had refused to make payment on the grounds that Deas had not been given authority by him to hire Black.

Held: Cornelius was liable to pay Black because there was a well-established custom amongst architects that they were permitted to make use of the services of a surveyor.

 Key point: Generally, an a agent must not delegate his functions to another individual.

To keep proper accounts

An agent must keep proper accounts to which his principal is entitled to have access. The agent will be handling the principal's money and it is clearly important that the principal knows how the agent is dealing with it. The agent will be personally liable to the principal for any shortfall in money even if there is no dishonesty on the agent's part.

Tyler *v* Logan (1904) Tyler owned a number of shops which specialised in selling boots. Tyler had appointed Logan as a branch manager of one of his shops in Dundee. At a stocktaking carried out by Tyler, it was discovered there was a shortfall of about £62 at the Dundee branch. No one could explain this loss and Logan was not suspected of any dishonesty or negligence. Tyler, however, brought an action against Logan for the payment of the missing amount of money.

Held: Logan had to pay Tyler the missing £62.

If the agent acts for several principals, he must ensure that he keeps proper and separate accounts for each of his clients. Many trades and professions will have their own rules which affect client accounts. The Law Society of Scotland which regulates the conduct of solicitors has very strict rules about how client accounts should be kept and solicitors who fall foul of these rules can find themselves in very serious trouble.

 Key point: The agent must keep proper accounts and allow the principal access to these as and when required.

To act in good faith

Agency is a fiduciary relationship and this means that the agent must show that he can be trusted by the principal and he must do this by always acting in good faith. The agent must not allow his personal interests and those of his principal to conflict with one another. It is often the case that a dishonest agent will be able to profit personally from the agency because of his position or because third parties may offer him a benefit or bribe if the agent introduces them to his principal. It is worth emphasising that an agent who sees the opportunity to make a fast buck or take advantage of some benefit which comes his way will not have the principal's best interests at heart. The agent may view these benefits as perks of the job, but such behaviour could result in disastrous consequences for the principal. The agent may not have properly scrutinised the deal proposed by the third party and this could cause the principal some serious losses in the future.

Conflict of interests

There does not need to be an actual conflict between the agent's and the principal's interests. It is very often enough for there to be a potential conflict. If the agent sees an opportunity to make a profit, the principal should always be informed of this. It will then be completely up to the principal whether or not to allow the agent to receive the benefit. It is often forgotten that the only reason that the agent is in a position to receive a benefit is because the principal appointed him in the first place.

The extent of the agent's fiduciary duty is limited to how it affects the agency agreement. It is still entirely possible for an agent to promote his own interests when he is not acting for the principal. The agent may even act for a number of different principals. If a principal wished to prevent his agent from pursuing his own interests outside the agency agreement or from working on behalf of other principals, there would have to be an express term in the agency agreement to this end. Such a condition could never be implied into all agency agreements. However, such a restraint of trade might be declared illegal if it was in any way excessive or anti-competitive.

McPherson's Trustees _v_ Watt (1877) Watt, a solicitor acting for the trustees, had to sell four houses for them but he arranged to sell them to his brother, on the understanding that the brother would then sell two of the houses to Watt for half the purchase price. The 'contract' was formed but the trustees discovered the secret contract and raised an action to stop it going ahead.

Held: by the House of Lords that the contract for the sale of the houses that Watt and his brother had negotiated was cancelled. A solicitor, as a law agent, has a duty to act in good faith and there must be no conflict between the principal's interests and those of the agent.

 Lothian _v_ Jenolite Ltd (1969) Jenolite Ltd, an English company, entered into an agreement with Lothian, under which Lothian was instructed to sell some of Jenolite's products in Scotland and receive a commission on sales. The contract was to last for four years from July 1964, but in November 1965, Jenolite ended the agency agreement. Lothian claimed damages for breach of contract. Jenolite claimed that the reason that the agreement had been ended in this way was because Lothian had bought and resold a rival business's products. It was claimed by Jenolite that Lothian had even ordered his staff to sell the rival business's products in preference to Jenolite's products. Jenolite considered this to be a material breach of contract.

Held: there was no implied condition in the agency agreement which meant that Lothian had to have secured Jenolite's permission in order to sell the products of a business rival.

The agent must not divulge any confidential information in relation to the principal's business that he obtains in the course of his agency.

 Liverpool Victoria Legal Friendly Society _v_ Houston (1900) as an agent of the insurance company, Houston had access to lists of customers and their details. Houston was later dismissed by the insurance company whereupon he decided to pass these customer details to another insurance company which was competing against his former principal.

Held: the details of customers were strictly confidential and by divulging them to business rivals of his former principal, Houston was in breach of his fiduciary duty. Furthermore, Houston would have to compensate his former principal for the loss of any custom that his breach of duty had caused.

 Key point: The agent must not allow his personal interests and those of his principal to conflict with one another – the agent's interests must take second place to the principal's.

Secret profits

The agent must not accept bribes from the third party or keep the benefit of any transaction to himself which he knows would result in him breaching his fiduciary duty to his principal. In such cases, the principal could sue the agent in order to recover the bribe or the benefit that the agent had gained.

 Islamic Republic of Iran Shipping Lines _v_ Denby (1987) a solicitor accepted a sum of $200,000 from a third party in order to settle a legal dispute which the solicitor's client had brought against the third party.

Held: the sum of $200,000 was quite simply a bribe and the solicitor had to pay this to his client.

 Attorney-General for Hong Kong v Reid (1994) Reid had been the acting Director of Public Prosecutions in Hong Kong. He accepted bribes in order to prevent the prosecution of a number of criminals.

Held: the Privy Council stated that Reid, as an agent of the British Crown, had to account for all the bribes that he had accepted. Consequently, the British Crown could recover all these sums.

There are a number of serious consequences which arise as a result of an agent making a secret profit:

◆ The agent has committed a material breach of the agency agreement and the principal is, therefore entitled to terminate the contract with immediate effect.

◆ The agent cannot claim payment for that particular transaction.

◆ The agent can be sued by the principal with the intention of recovering the secret profit that the agent has made.

◆ The third party may find that the principal refuses to honour the contract that the agent negotiated.

◆ The third party himself may be sued by the principal if he bribed or encouraged the agent to breach his fiduciary duty to the principal.

◆ If the third party refuses to pay the bribe or the commission to the agent, the agent cannot take legal action against the third party because their agreement is illegal and, therefore, unenforceable.

◆ Bribery is a criminal offence in terms of the Prevention of Corruption Acts 1906 and 1916.

 Key point: An agent who makes secret profits on his own account will be in breach of his fiduciary duty to the principal and, if discovered, will have to face the potentially criminal and civil consequences of his actions.

Rights of an agent

The agent enjoys the following rights in relation to his principal under the agency agreement:

◆ Right to receive payment
◆ Right to be indemnified by the principal
◆ Right of lien over the principal's property

Right to receive payment

The agent is entitled to be paid for the performance of services on behalf of the principal. The agent is not performing these services on a charitable basis or because he is acting from feelings of goodwill towards the principal. Quite simply, the agent expects some sort of reward for his efforts.

Payment can take the form of a salary, a commission or some other kind of material benefit. Normally, the contract should address the amount that the agent is entitled to receive from the principal. If the contract is silent on this matter, certain trades and professions may have a customary rate which determines what amount the agent will receive. If, for example, a solicitor is carrying out work for a client who receives Legal Aid, the solicitor will receive payment from the Scottish Legal Aid Board up to an agreed limit. If there is no customary rate, the agent is entitled to be paid on a *quantum meruit* basis which literally means that he will be paid at reasonable rate. What is a reasonable rate will clearly be determined according to the circumstances of each case.

As long as the agent carries out his instructions from the principal faithfully and competently, he will have a right to receive his reward even if the final contract causes the principal to suffer loss. The agent should in no way suffer for the principal's stupidity in authorising a bad bargain with the third party. The agent will have the right to receive payment for his services even if the principal fails to take advantage of the agent's work or if he fails to go ahead and implement the contract formed with the third party.

 Dudley *v* Barnet (1937) the agent had been given the task of finding a suitable tenant for premises that belonged to the principal. The principal declined to follow the agent's suggestion and accepted an offer from another third party. The principal refused to pay the agent justifying this behaviour on the grounds that as he had not benefited from the agent's advice, the agent was not entitled to be paid. The agent sued for payment.

Held: the principal had to pay the commission owed to the agent.

 Kennedy *v* Glass (1890) Glass had a business dealing in old building material and machinery. Kennedy, an architect, was in the habit of introducing third parties to Glass and often these individuals entered into contracts with Glass. For introducing these third parties to Glass, Kennedy received a commission. Kennedy was, therefore, clearly acting as an agent for Glass. In 1883, Kennedy introduced Glass to a company which was interested in selling machinery to Glass. Glass eventually formed a contract to buy this machinery, but later he withdrew from this contract. Kennedy claimed to receive £250 as commission for carrying out services on behalf of Glass in relation to this contract. Glass claimed that the commission owed to Kennedy was more in the region £50 which was only payable if the contract between Glass and the third party was completed.

Held: there was clear evidence to show that Kennedy had been acting as an agent for Glass throughout the negotiations between Glass and the third party. Kennedy had put in a lot of time and effort on behalf of Glass in order to complete the contract. Kennedy, therefore, had the right to receive commission from Glass. Kennedy was not, however, a professional agent and, therefore, he received a reasonable rate of commission of £50.

 Key point: An important feature of agency is that an agent is entitled to be paid for his services i.e. agency is onerous not gratuitous.

Right to be indemnified

The agent has the right to be relieved of any liabilities or expenses that he has incurred as a result of acting properly on the principal's behalf.

Stevenson & Sons v Duncan (1842) the principal refused to honour the contract that the agent had completed with the third party for the benefit of the principal. The agent had acted within his authority and had behaved correctly at all times. The third party sued the agent for damages for breach of warranty of authority. In turn, the agent sued the principal for the damages that he had to pay to the third party.

Hold: the agent was entitled to be indemnified or compensated for the losses that he experienced as a result of the principal's failure to honour the agreement with the third party.

 Drummond v Cairns (1852) Drummond instructed Cairns, a stockbroker, to buy 100 shares in the East India Railway Company. The price was 20/6d per share, and the settlement day, when the shares had to be paid for, was May 28. Cairns duly notified Drummond that the transaction had been completed succesfully. When the settling day arrived, Drummond refused to pay the price owed for the shares. On June 10, Cairns was forced to sell the shares at 9/4d each which meant that he made substantial osses.

Held: Drummond was liable to compensate Cairns for the difference between the two share prices.

 Key point: The agent is entitled to be indemnified in respect of any expenses properly incurred by him in the course of his duties.

Right of lien

The right of lien is a remedy that the agent can use when the principal is in breach of the agency agreement. Perhaps the principal has failed to pay or indemnify the agent under the agreement. In such cases, the agent is entitled to retain possession of the principal's property or money that he holds in trust for the principal. An agent would not have the right, however, to help himself to the agent's property in order to have goods over which the lien can be exercised. The agent must, therefore, have the goods in his possession when the principal breaches the agreement in some way. Furthermore, the agent owes the principal a duty of care and this means that the property must be looked after. The agent does not, however, have the right to sell the principal's goods. Lien merely allows the principal to prevent the principal from getting access to his property.

A solicitor, for example, may refuse to hand over the principal's documents that he holds in his possession because the principal is either unwilling or is slow to pay his legal bill. Using the right of lien, can often encourage the principal to honour his side of the agency agreement.

 Sibbald v Gibson (1852) Sibbald was a corn factor in Leith. They employed Gibson & Co who were Glasgow corn merchants as their agents. Gibson bought a large amount of oats. The goods were stored by the agents at their premises so that they could be delivered to the principal's customers. A dispute arose between Sibbald and Gibson which involved the amount of commission that the agent was to receive. Some time later, the principal forwarded goods to the agents who were under instructions to find third parties to sell these to. The agent duly sold the goods to third parties on the principal's behalf. However, the agents decided to hold back the amount of commission that was owed to them for the previous transaction.

Held: the agents were within their rights to withhold the commission that was due to them from earlier dealings.

 Key point: Where the principal is in breach of the agency contract, the agent is entitled to exercise his right of lien which allows him to retain possession of property or money that he holds in trust for the principal.

Authority of an agent

An agent can have two types of authority:

◆ Actual
◆ Ostensible

Actual authority of an agent

This is the true extent of the authority that the principal gives to an agent. The principal can give the agent this type of authority expressly or impliedly. Express, actual authority will be contained in either a written document or in verbal instructions that the principal issues to the agent.

Express, actual authority

 Ireland *v* Livingston (1872) the principal had contacted the agent asking him to buy and ship 500 tons of sugar. The principal gave the agent a certain amount of leeway by stating that he would accept 50 tons over or above the 500 tons of sugar. The principal's main aim was to get the sugar at a suitable price. The agent shipped 400 tons of sugar in one ship and fully intended to ship the remaining goods in another ship to the principal. The principal refused to accept the 400 tons and wrote to the agent telling him not to bother shipping the remaining goods to him.

Held: by the House of Lords that the principal was bound to accept the goods because the agent had acted within his express, actual authority. The principal had issued a confusing order to the agent that was capable of more than one meaning. The agent had carried out his orders in good faith. With access to modern communications, it is now likely that an agent, even at the other end of the world, would be expected to contact the principal in order to clarify any confusing instructions that the principal has issued.

If a situation arises where the agent acts outwith his actual authority, but the principal does not discipline the agent for what would almost certainly be seen as a serious breach of the agency agreement, then any third parties dealing with the agent would be entitled to assume that the agent was acting within his actual authority. Where the principal appears to approve or endorse the actions of an agent acting outwith his actual authority, this is known as ratification.

Implied, actual authority

Implied, actual authority will arise where the agent holds a particular position and it is implied by law or by the behaviour of the principal and the agent that this kind of agent would have actual authority to bind the principal into contracts with third parties.

According to Section 5 of the Partnership Act 1890, a partner in a firm is considered to be an agent of the firm and his fellow partners. A partner will, therefore, have implied, actual authority to bind the firm and his fellow partners in respect of contracts negotiated and entered into with third parties in the usual course of the firm's business.

Similarly, Section 6 of the Limited Liability Partnership Act 2000 gives similar authority to members of this type of corporate body.

 Hely-Hutchinson *v* Brayhead Ltd (1968) the chairman of Brayhead Ltd was acting as the company's managing director. He was doing so, even though he had not been officially appointed to this position. He entered into various transactions on behalf of the company, as a managing director would do.

Held: by the English Court of Appeal that Brayhead were bound to honour the resulting contracts, because, although the chairman had no express, actual authority, the company had implied that he had the authority, by allowing him to act as the managing director and these would normally be transactions that such a person would carry out on behalf of his principal.

In Brayhead, Lord Denning MR made the following comments about authority:

'. . . *(authority) is express when it is given by express words, such as when a board of directors passes a resolution which authorises two of their number to sign cheques. It is implied when it is inferred from the conduct of the parties and the circumstances of the case, such as when the board of directors appoint one of their number to be managing director. They therefore impliedly authorise him to do all such things as fall within the scope of that office. . . .'*

 Key point: The true extent of the agent's powers to act for the principal is referred to as actual authority which can be express or implied.

Ostensible authority

Ostensible authority is the authority which a third party believes the agent possesses. Ostensible authority is not true authority, it is fictitious and exists only in the mind of the third party. The principal, however, has encouraged the third party to believe that the agent has the necessary authority. The third party must show that the principal's statements or behaviour encouraged him to believe that the agent had the necessary authority. A third party's claim that he believed that the agent had ostensible authority purely because the agent told him that he had been given authority by his principal will not be accepted by the courts. The false impression of authority must have been created by the principal's actions.

 Reckitt *v* Barnet & Company (1929) an agent who had the authority to write cheques for the company, paid a private debt using money in his principal's account.

Held: the principal was entitled to recover his money from the third party, as they should have suspected that the agent did not have the authority to write company cheques in order to pay a private debt. This is the type of transaction that the third party should have questioned because it should have been immediately obvious that the principal was unlikely to allow his bank account to be used by the agent in this way.

The third party must also show that he had no reason to suspect that the agent may, in fact, have had his authority limited or withdrawn by the principal. If an agent acts beyond his actual authority, but within his ostensible authority then the principal will have to honour the contract that has been formed with the third party. The principal will be bound in contract to the third party because it will have been the principal himself who will have encouraged the third party to believe that the agent has authority to act in a particular way. However, the principal can still sue the agent for breaching the agency agreement.

The creation of ostensible authority

The third party may have been encouraged by the principal to believe that the agent had authority to act in a particular way for the following reasons:

1   The agent's authority has been changed or limited in some way. Stupidly, however, the principal fails to tell third parties of this very important change and so third parties understandably continue to believe that the agent still has the same powers.

2   The agent did not have authority to act in a particular way when he entered a contract with the third party. The principal, however, decides to ratify or approve the contract and this leads the third party to assume that this type of contract is well within the agent's powers. Again, the principal will have failed to take steps to notify the third party of the true extent of the agent's authority.

3   The agent has had implied authority in the past, for example, he may be a partner in a firm or a director of a company. Third parties dealing with these types of agents would have been entitled to assume that they possessed certain powers or had authority to enter into contracts of a particular kind. However, these individuals may have had their authority limited or withdrawn by their principals, but this fact has not been publicised to third parties.

It is vitally important that the principal communicates any change in the agent's authority to third parties. If the principal does notify third parties about the true extent of the agent's authority then he will not be held accountable for any of the agent's unauthorised actions.

If there are circumstances which should have caused the third party to suspect that the agent was acting outwith his authority, but the third party still goes ahead with the contract then the principal will not be legally bound. The third party's remedy is to sue the agent for what is known as breach of warranty of authority.

Examples of ostensible authority

 Freeman & Lockyer _v_ Buckhurst Park Properties (Mangal) Ltd (1964) Buckhurst, a company, had been set up to purchase and resell a large estate. Although the company had proper procedures for appointing a managing director, the board of directors allowed one of its members to act as the managing director without him being formally appointed as such. This director entered into various contracts with third parties on the company's behalf. On one occasion, this director appointed a firm of architects who were going to carry out all sorts of work for the company. After the work had been completed, the architects, naturally, asked to be paid by the company. Clearly, this director had no actual authority of the express or of the implied variety as he had never been formally appointed as the company's managing director.

Held: the English Court of Appeal stated that the director in question did not have actual authority to act on the company's behalf when he entered the contracts with the architects. He was, however, acting within his ostensible authority and the architects had good reason to believe that he had the necessary authority to bind the company.

 Watteau *v* Fenwick (1893) a pub manager was forbidden to purchase cigars on credit. Despite this restriction imposed on him by his principal, the pub manager went ahead and bought cigars from a travelling salesman who happened to visit the pub looking for business opportunities. The salesman had no reason to be suspicious about any aspect of the contract and, furthermore, the pub owner had failed to inform third parties dealing with the pub manager that there was a limit on his authority. The only people who knew about the limitation of authority were the pub owner and the pub manager.

Held: The pub owner was bound by the contract that his manager had made with the salesman since this was within the usual authority given to pub managers.

 International Sponge Importers *v* Watt & Sons (1911) International Sponge Importers had a travelling salesman called Cohen. Cohen visited customers who placed orders with him for the company's products. Cohen carried some of the company's products with him that he was allowed to sell to customers. The company had stated to Cohen that he should only accept payment from customers by cheque which must be made payable to the company. In the past, Watt & Sons had paid the company by giving Cohen cheques that had been made out to him personally and not to the company. The company had never once objected to this practice by Watt & Sons. A legal dispute later arose, however, because Watt & Sons had paid Cohen in cash which he stole and he then conveniently disappeared. The company tried to sue Watt & Sons for the payment.

Held: by the House of Lords that Watt & Sons were not required to pay the company the stolen money. It was the duty of International Sponge Importers to inform third parties like Watt & Sons of the true extent of Cohen's authority i.e. that he had no right to accept cheques that were made out to him personally. By failing to do this, International Sponge Importers had helped to create the impression that any method of payment was acceptable to the principal.

 Barry, Ostlere & Shepherd Ltd *v* Edinburgh Cork Importing Co (1909) a third party had negotiated with an agent, the manager of cork merchants, to buy goods and to have them delivered. The agent failed to deliver the goods and the third party had to find goods from an alternative supplier at a higher price. The third party sued the agent's principal for damages claiming that it had failed to honour the contract negotiated on its behalf by the agent. The principal argued that the agent had not been given authority to enter into a contract with the third party.

Held: a contract had been formed between the third party and the principal since the third party had every right to assume that, because of the agent's position as a manager in the principal's company, entering into a contract for these goods was well within his authority.

 Key point: Ostensible authority is the authority which a third party (wrongly) assumes that an agent possesses and it is the actions of the principal that creates this false impression in the third party's mind. Therefore, the principal will be bound in contract to the third party.

Liability when agents act outwith actual and ostensible authority

If an agent acts outwith both his actual and ostensible authority then he will bring personal liability upon himself. There will be no contract between the principal and the third party, but the third party can sue the agent for breach of warranty of authority.

 Anderson *v* Croall & Sons (1903) an auctioneer had been given instructions to sell the winning horse at a race meeting. The auctioneer, however, carelessly sold the horse that had come in second at the race. The horse's owner had no intention of selling it. The horse had to be returned to its true owner.

Held: the auctioneer was liable in damages to the third party who had bought the horse for acting completely outwith his authority.

 Key point: When the agent acts outwith his authority and the third party is fully aware of this fact, the principal will not be bound into contract with the third party.

Summary of an agent's authority

Actual authority (Real authority)	Principal is bound into contract with third Party. (Agent incurs no liability.)
Ostensible authority (Presumed, fictitious authority)	Principal is bound into contract with third Party. The third Party genuinely believes the agent has authority and has no reason to be suspicious. (Agent is liable to principal for breach of agency agreement.)
Agent has no authority	Principal is not bound in contract to third Party. The third Party cannot claim that he believed the agent had actual or ostensible authority. The agent can be sued by third Party for breach of warranty of authority.

A disclosed and undisclosed principal

Where the third party is aware of the existence of the agent's principal, such a person is referred to as a disclosed principal. It does not matter whether the third party can name the principal personally.

The Santa Carina (1977) the defenders were agents who acted as brokers on the Baltic Exchange. The defenders had telephoned the pursuers, also brokers on the Baltic Exchange, and asked them to supply bunkers to the ship called the *Santa Carina*. The bunkers were supplied to the ship, but the defenders' principal failed to pay the pursuers. The pursuers sued the defenders for breach of contract. The defenders claimed that they were acting as agents and although they had not disclosed the name of their principal the pursuers were perfectly aware of this situation.

Held: the English Court of Appeal stated that the principal was a disclosed principal and in this situation the defenders should have sued the principal.

However, there may be situations where the third party is completely unaware that the agent is, in fact, acting for a principal. In such a case, the principal would be described as an undisclosed principal.

It is important to determine whether the agent is acting for a disclosed or an undisclosed principal. Generally, an agent who acts for a disclosed principal plays no further part in proceedings when an agreement is eventually completed between the principal and the third party. Should a dispute arise in relation to the agreement, the agent – as long as he acted properly – will not be liable to the third party for the principal's failure to honour the agreement.

The position is more complicated where the agent has not revealed to the third party that he is acting for a principal. Should the principal fail to honour the agreement, the third party will, naturally enough, sue the agent. At this moment, the agent may then reveal the fact that he was acting as an a agent. It will be up to the third party whether he wishes to sue the principal or the agent for breach of contract. Once the third party makes this choice, such a decision will be final.

It is usually a sensible precaution on the agent's part to indicate to third parties that he is acting as an agent in order to avoid any potential liability in the future. It is widely understood that the abbreviation pp (*per pro*) at the end of a letter indicates that the signatory is acting as an agent and not acting in his personal capacity:

Yours sincerely
Alistair B Wylie
pp The Business Law Consultancy

Therefore, Alistair B Wylie is clearly indicating to anyone who receives this letter that he has signed the letter in his capacity as an agent of The Business Law Consultancy.

 Stewart v Shannessy (1900) Shannessy acted as an agent for two companies that sold bicycles. He decided to employ Stewart to act as a representative of one of the companies. Stewart's appointment and his terms and conditions of employment were confirmed in a letter that Shannessy sent him. Shannessy's letter was written on company headed notepaper, but when Shannessy signed the letter it seemed to suggest that *he* was employing Stewart and not the company. The letter contained indication that Shannessy was, in fact, acting for the company in his capacity as an agent. Stewart received all of his instructions from Shannessy, all payments from Shannessy and was dismissed by Shannessy. Stewart then sued Shannessy for arrears of pay that he claimed that he was still owed.

Held: Shannessy was personally liable to Stewart since he had signed the letter and had not given any indication that he was acting as an agent for the company.

 Key point: Very often it may not be obvious to a third party whether the agent is acting as an agent when the identity of the principal is undisclosed.

The Commercial Agents (Council Directive) Regulations 1993

The Commercial Agents (Council Directive) Regulations 1993 give effect to the EEC Directive 86/653 on self-employed commercial agents. The Regulations came into force on 1 January 1994 and were slightly amended in 1998. Commercial agency contracts created or amended after 1994 will be primarily affected by these rules. The Regulations are unusual because, unlike the common law rules, they single out a particular group of agents for protection. Furthermore, the Regulations emphasise the fact that a commercial agency agreement is almost a partnership of equals where the principal and the agent should cooperate with one another in order to benefit from the relationship.

The overall purpose of the European Council Directive was not only to achieve harmonisation of the legal relationship between commercial agents and principals throughout the European Union but also to deal with the insecurity that commercial agents experienced especially when principals decided to terminate the agreement. It might take many years of hard work on the agent's part to turn a profit. If the principal then ended agreement the commercial agent would lose his livelihood with very little to show for all of his efforts. The principal, on the other hand, will often continue to profit from the agent's efforts on his behalf.

 Key point: The Commercial Agency Regulations are unusual because, unlike the common law rules of agency, they single out a particular group of agents for protection.

Commercial agents

Regulation 2(1) states that a commercial agent is a self-employed intermediary who has continuing authority to negotiate the sale or the purchase of goods on behalf of the principal or to negotiate and conclude the sale or purchase of goods on behalf of or in the name of the principal.

As we have seen, the agency relationship at common law lists the rights and the duties of both the agent and the principal. The Regulations very much build on this situation and Part II lists the duties of both parties.

 King *v* T Tunnock Ltd (2000) the agents were father and son who had entered into a verbal agreement with Tunnock that ran for many years. The contract stated that the father and son were to act as Tunnock's agents in order to sell its cakes and biscuits. The agents sold Tunnock's products only and were paid commission on the products that they sold. The agents had no freedom to fix the prices of the products as Tunnock determined this. All monies received from customers were made payable to Tunnock. The agents were even provided with a van for their business activities which Tunnock maintained. The agents were also required to wear Tunnock's uniforms. However, despite the close relationship with the principal, the agents were self-employed. According to Sheriff Reeves, who decided the case at first instance, the definition of a commercial agent in Regulation 2(1) was an exact description of the activities of the agents in this case.

 Key point: A commercial agent is a self-employed intermediary who has continuing authority to negotiate the sale or the purchase of goods on behalf of the principal or to negotiate and conclude the sale or purchase of goods on behalf of or in the name of the principal.

The scope of the Regulations

The 1994 Regulations, however, only apply to a very small number of agents, so their impact will be limited. They only apply to commercial agents who trade in goods. The Regulations do not cover the following types of agents:

◆ Commercial agents who provide services
◆ Commercial agents working on commodity exchanges in the commodity market
◆ Unpaid or gratuitous agents
◆ Persons who act as commercial agents but this is regarded as a secondary activity and not part of their main business

The Regulations will also not apply to agreements where the parties have decided that their agency agreement will be governed by the law of another European member state. However, since the decision of **Ingmar GB Ltd v Eaton Leonard Technologies Inc (2001)**, the Regulations will apply even if the parties have attempted to exclude them by stating in their agreement that the agreement is governed by the law of a state which is *not* a member of the European Union.

 In **Ingmar**, an English agent carried on business activities in the United Kingdom on behalf of a Californian principal. Both the agent and principal had agreed that the contract was to be governed by Californian law. This would have appeared to exclude the Regulations. However, the English Court of Appeal referred the matter to the European Court of Justice which made it clear that the Regulations applied to situations even where the parties themselves had chosen the law by which they wished to be bound.

The Regulations do not apply to Northern Ireland.

 Key point: The Regulations apply to a very small group of agents only.

The agent's duties (Regulation 3)

◆ The agent must protect the principal's interests by acting dutifully and in good faith at all times.

◆ The agent must make proper efforts to negotiate and, where appropriate, conclude the transactions that he has responsibility for.

◆ The agent must provide the principal with all the information that he has at his disposal.

◆ The agent must obey all reasonable instructions given to him by the principal.

The principal's duties (Regulation 4)

◆ The principal must pay or remunerate the agent for carrying out his duties under the agency agreement.

◆ The principal must reimburse the agent for any expenses that the agent has incurred in the line of duty.

◆ The principal must provide the agent with the necessary documents and the necessary information relating to the goods in order for the agent to carry out his duties.

◆ The principal must tell the agent within a reasonable time whether he intends to honour or refuse to honour the contract that the agent has set up with a third party.

◆ The principal must inform the agent within a reasonable time of any breach of the contract with the third party that the principal is responsible for.

According to Regulation 5(1), the rights and duties contained in Regulations 3 and 4 are not negotiable and both parties are bound by them whether they like them or not.

 Key point: The Regulations outline the agent's duties and the principal's duties in Regulations 3 and 4 respectively.

The agent's right to be paid or to be remunerated (Regulations 6 to 12)

Part III of the Regulations deal with the issue of the agent's right to be paid or remunerated.

The agent has a right to receive payment for carrying out his duties under the agency agreement even where the parties have failed to address the issue directly. If there is no term about payment in the agency agreement, the agent is entitled to be paid at the customary rate which agents of his type and background would normally or customarily receive. If there is no customary or normal practice that exists to help the principal decide how much the agent should be paid, then the agent should be paid a reasonable remuneration. What is a reasonable rate of remuneration or pay will, obviously, depend on the circumstances.

The agent has a right to receive commission and this commission will become payable when the agent concludes a contract with a third party on the principal's behalf.

An important right that an agent will enjoy under the Regulations is where he has acted as the principal's sole agent in relation to a specific geographical area or a specific group of customers. Even after the agency agreement has ended, the agent will continue to be entitled to receive commission from the principal. This is only fair because the principal may continue to enjoy the fruits of the agent's work for a long time after the agency agreement has ended. It is worth bearing in mind that, very often, it is the efforts of a determined and successful agent which will ensure that the principal enjoys a loyal customer base or strong business links in a particular area.

As a result of Regulation 10, there are strict time limits for the payment of commission. Commission will, therefore, become payable to the agent from the time that the agreement between the principal and the third party should have come into force. However, should the agreement fail to come into effect and this is through no fault of the principal, the agent is not entitled to receive commission. In fact, if any commission has been paid to the agent in these circumstances, the agent will have to return his part payment to the principal.

Regulation 12 now means that the agent has a right to receive a statement from the principal detailing the amount of commission owed to him. This statement must be received by the agent no later than the last day of the month following the quarter in which the commission was earned. The statement must give a breakdown detailing how the amount of the commission was arrived at and the agent will be able to demand information from the principal which allows him to check the principal's calculations.

 Key point: Regulations 6 to 12 deal with the agent's right to be paid by the principal.

The termination of the commercial agency agreement (Regulations 14 to 16)

Like all contracts, a commercial agency agreement will come to an end sooner rather than later and the rules which apply to this event will be found mainly in Part IV of the Regulations.

Regulation 13 establishes beyond any doubt that either party has the right to request a signed copy of the agency agreement which lays out the main terms of the commercial agency agreement. The terms of the agreement will, of course, address how the commercial agency will come to an end. It should be noted that the parties are not allowed to opt out of this requirement to provide a signed copy of the agreement.

Regulation 14 applies to contracts that are to last for a fixed period of time, for example, five years. In many situations, the parties will continue to keep the agreement running without feeling the need to renegotiate the terms. In cases like this, the parties will continue to have the same rights and duties as before, the only major difference being that the agreement is now considered to last for an indefinite period of time.

Regulation 15 establishes compulsory minimum notice periods which the parties have to obey if they wish to end the agreement. The basic periods of notice are as follows:

◆ One month's notice during the first year of the agreement
◆ Two months' notice during the second year of the agreement
◆ Three months' notice during the third year or any subsequent year of the agreement

All notice periods end on the last day of the month, unless the parties have agreed a different arrangement. The parties to the commercial agency agreement are, of course, free to negotiate longer notice periods if they so wish. They are just prevented from shortening the minimum notice periods as outlined above. If the agreement was originally to last for a fixed term but has since become one of an indefinite duration, the minimum notice periods also apply.

However, Regulation 16 makes it perfectly clear that both parties can end the agency agreement immediately where one of the parties has failed to carry out all or part of his duties under the contract. The contract can also be ended in exceptional circumstances.

 Key point: Regulation 15 establishes compulsory minimum notice periods which the parties have to obey if they wish to end the agreement.

The Agent's right to an indemnity or compensation (Regulations 17 to 19)

The Agent's right to an indemnity or compensation is a completely new development in both Scottish and English law. This right reflects the fact that the principal benefits from the agent's efforts to build up a customer base. If the principal ends the agreement, the agent is the party who tends to suffer financially from this decision. The principal, on the other hand, will often continue to enjoy the fruits of the agent's labours for a very long time to come. It is important to stress that the agent has a right to receive compensation, not a windfall.

It is important to distinguish between the agent's right to compensation and his right to an indemnity because they are not the same thing. Lord MacFadyen in **Hardie Polymer Ltd *v* Polymerland Ltd (2001)** stated that:

'Compensation and indemnity are distinct concepts. It is not surprising that there are elements of similarity between them, since they are alternative ways of making provision for the same situation, namely the termination of the agency contract.'

Usually, according to Regulation 17(2), the agent shall be entitled to be compensated rather than indemnified, unless the commercial agency agreement specifies that he is entitled to receive an indemnity.

 Key point: Under the Regulations, compensation and indemnity are two different rights.

In **King *v* T Tunnock Ltd (2000)** the Court of Session made a distinction between compensation and indemnity:

'on any view indemnity and compensation, as set out by both Directive and Regulations, have different features . . . The agent is entitled to compensation for damage he suffers as a result of the termination of his relationship with the principal. The word "suffers" is in the present tense, which suggests that the point of time defining damage is the termination of the agency. Moreover, what is compensated is "the termination of his relations with his principal". The emphasis is not on his future loss but on the impact of the severance of his agency relationship with the principal. An agency generally has commercial value.'

According to Regulation 17, therefore, the agent will be entitled to be compensated by the principal where he has suffered loss as a result of the principal terminating the commercial agency agreement.

In the English High Court decision **Moore *v* Piretta PT Ltd (1998)** Deputy Judge John Mitting QC described the agent's claim to an indemnity in the following terms:

'The purpose of the indemnity seems to me to be to award a share of the goodwill built up by the efforts of the agent to him on the termination of the agency. Otherwise the whole benefit of that goodwill will remain with his former principal.'

Deputy Judge Mitting QC then went to say that according to Regulation 17, there are three stages involved in assessing an agent's right to an indemnity:

◆ Where the agent has increased the number of the principal's customers or where the agent has dramatically increased the amount of the principal's business with existing customers.

◆ The payment of the indemnity must be fair and equitable taking into account all of the circumstances surrounding the agreement. The commission lost by the commercial agent on the business carried out with such customers will be a factor to which the court will have to pay particular attention.

◆ The calculation of the indemnity itself, but this is subject to limits provided for in Regulation 17(4).

 Key point: An agent will be entitled to be compensated by the principal where he has suffered loss as a result of the principal terminating his agency agreement and he will be entitled to an indemnity where he has increased the number of the principal's customers or where he has dramatically increased the amount of the principal's business with existing customers.

The amount of the indemnity

In terms of Regulation 17(4), the amount of the indemnity awarded to the agent shall not be greater than a figure equivalent to an indemnity for one year calculated from the commercial agent's average annual remuneration over the previous five years and, if the contract goes back less than five years, the indemnity shall be calculated on the average for the period in question.

It is important to note that the payment of an indemnity does not prevent the agent from seeking compensation or damages from the principal.

Commercial agency case law

In **Moore v Piretta PT Ltd (1998)** it was said that the aim of Regulation 17 was to give British commercial agents the same rights and duties in relation to remuneration as was the case in France and Germany. Regulation 17 was held to apply to the whole of an agency agreement even if the agreement had come into force before the Regulations.

 In **Moore**, the pursuer had acted as an agent for the defender under an unbroken series of contracts commencing in 1988. The last agency agreement had been in force in 1994. Although most of the agency agreements had been entered into before the Regulations came into force, the agent was still entitled to claim an indemnity from the principal which covered the period from 1988 to 1994. Significantly, of the 40 customers whom the principal had dealings with, only six or seven of these had not been acquired by the agent. Therefore, the agent was directly responsible for the success of the principal's business.

Regulation 17(6) states that the agent shall be entitled to compensation for damages that he has suffered as a result of the principal ending the commercial agency agreement. Regulation 17(7) strongly suggests that the agent will have suffered loss or damage in one or both of the following situations:

- Loss of future commission by the agent
- The agent has been unable to recover any expenses which he properly incurred on the principal's behalf

The agent's claim for compensation should be lodged, however, within one year of the end of the agreement. If the agent's death has caused the agreement to end, then the agent's estate will not be prevented from pursuing the principal for any compensation or expenses owed.

The agent must receive a fair amount. In **King v T Tunnock Ltd (2000)** the Inner House of the Court of Session unanimously decided that the sum paid to an agent on termination of the agreement should be based on two years' gross commission.

However, in **Ingmar GB Ltd v Eaton Leonard Technologies Inc (2001)** (see below), Mr Justice Morland in the English High Court stated that the Court of Session in **King** had laid down guidelines, not binding rules of law. The English judge preferred to calculate compensation by looking at three years' gross commission in order to determine the level of compensation payable to the agent. It should be noted that the courts have been given a great deal of freedom to decide what is a fair amount in each case.

 Graham Page v Combined Shipping and Trading Co Ltd (1997) the pursuer had been appointed as a commercial agent on a fixed-term basis by the defender. The defender's South African parent company had ended all business links with the defender not long after the agent had been appointed. The pursuers treated this turn of events as a repudiation of the agency contract. The pursuer decided to freeze the defender's goods which had a value of £300,000 on the grounds that they were entitled to compensation under Regulation 17(6). The defender argued that he was not obliged to use the services of the pursuer for every transaction in order to sell his goods. The defender argued that, in this situation, the pursuer would have made a profit of precisely zero and, therefore, no compensation was payable.

Held: The English Court of Appeal overturned the decision of the lower court. The pursuer had an arguable case that this claim for compensation owed by the principal in terms of Regulation 17(6) might well be successful. The central issue in the case was the amount of commission that the pursuer would have earned if the contract had continued to be performed in the normal manner intended by both parties during its fixed-term period.

 Duffen v FRABO SpA (2000) it was held that the agent's right to claim damages for loss of future commission because the principal had ended the agreement was very much dependent on whether the agent could prove that the principal was still reaping the benefits of his efforts. In this case, the agent failed to secure new customers for the principal during the agency agreement and his attempts to retain those existing customers of the principal were extremely unsuccessful. His claim for compensation under the Regulations was, therefore unsuccessful. However, owing to the express provisions of his contract, the agent was still entitled to claim some compensation from the principal.

 Hardie Polymer Ltd *v* Polymerland Ltd (2001) the meaning of Article 10 of the commercial agency agreement was in doubt as to whether the agent was entitled to compensation or an indemnity. Much of the confusion in this case stemmed around the fact that the parties had failed to use clear language when the agreement was originally drawn up. Admittedly, the heading of Article 10 – 'Compensation after Termination' was not helpful to the principal's claim that the agent was only entitled to an indemnity and not compensation in the sum of £120,000 as claimed. Lord MacFadyen in the Court of Session took the view, however, that despite this heading, all that Article 10 of the agreement entitled the agent to claim was an indemnity for the termination of the agreement. The agreement, therefore, prevented the agent from claiming compensation. Lord MacFadyen expressly approved the remarks of Deputy Judge Mitting QC in **Piretta**:

'I agree with the view expressed by the Deputy Judge . . . that the purpose of indemnity . . . is to award to the agent a share of the goodwill built up by his efforts. That being so, the use of the phrase "the goodwill payment" in article 10.2 [of the commercial agency agreement] *is in my view confirmation that the parties did indeed intend to elect for indemnity.'*

 Ingmar GB Ltd *v* Eaton Leonard Technologies Inc (2001) the principals were the manufacturers of sophisticated products including specialist equipment costing up to and beyond £100,000 designed for a limited but high quality market in the aircraft and automotive industries. An agent selling such products had to have engineering training and experience and expert knowledge of the qualities and performance of the principals' products so as to be able to sell them to the limited potential customer base which would also be expert and knowledgeable.

Held: that the pursuer had the right to receive compensation of £183,600 under Regulation 17.

The loss of a right to claim compensation or an indemnity

Regulation 18 describes certain situations where the agent will forfeit any rights to compensation or an indemnity under Regulation 17:

◆ Where the principal ends the agency agreement because the agent has committed a repudiatory breach of the agreement.

◆ If the agent ended the agreement, he may not be entitled to receive compensation unless the reason involved the agent's age, infirmity or illness.

◆ If the agent transfers or assigns his rights and duties under the agreement with the principal's consent.

A repudiatory breach by the agent would cover extremely serious breaches of the agency agreement, for example, where the agent has made secret profits on his own behalf or where the agent has pursued his own interests at the expense of the principal's.

It will, of course, be appreciated that the agent will be allowed to terminate the agreement if the principal behaves in a totally unreasonable way by, for example, committing a material breach of the contract.

According to Regulation 19, the rules about compensation and indemnity may not be excluded or limited by contract.

 Key point: Regulation 18 outlines situations where an agent will lose the right to claim compensation or an indemnity from the principal.

Restraint of trade or restrictive covenants (Regulation 20)

It will often be the case that the principal will want to protect his business interests by limiting the agent's ability to work for a competitor after the agency agreement has ended. The agent will have had access to all sorts of sensitive information about the principal's business, for example, customer lists, designs, products, business development plans and marketing strategies. Obviously, the principal will not want to see a business rival benefiting from this information to which the agent has been given access as a result of the agency agreement. Therefore, can the principal prevent the agent from taking up new employment with a new principal and, if so, for how long?

Regulation 20 provides the answers to these important questions. First, in order for a restraint of trade clause to be valid, it must be in writing and it must cover the group of customers and goods to which the agent's work was connected. Second, the maximum amount of time that such clause can last for is two years after the end of the agency agreement.

 Key point: A restraint of trade clause in an agency agreement must be in writing, must cover the agent's customers or goods and cannot last longer than two years after the agency has ended.

Termination of the agency relationship

The agency relationship, like any contract, can be terminated in a number of different ways by:

♦ Mutual agreement
♦ The principal withdrawing the agent's authority
♦ The agent withdrawing from the relationship
♦ Insolvency of the principal
♦ Death or insanity
♦ The expiry of a fixed term contract

Mutual agreement

This will occur when the parties have both agreed that the agency agreement will end on a particular date or after the completion of a particular transaction by the agent.

 Galbraith & Moorhead v The Arethusa Ship Co Ltd (1896) Galbraith offered to buy £500 worth of shares in The Arethusa Ship Company on the basis that they were appointed sole chartering brokers. The offer was accepted by Arethusa and an agency relationship between the company and Galbraith lasted for several years. Arethusa later experienced a change of management which attempted to end the arrangement as it currently stood with Galbraith. The company no longer wished Galbraith to act as its sole agent. Galbraith brought an action against Arethusa claiming £600 in damages for breach of contract.

Held: the agency agreement, in the particular circumstances of this case, could not be ended simply by the decision of one of the parties.

Withdrawal of the agent's authority

The agent is the principal's representative and has been given authority to bind the principal into contracts with third parties. If the principal decides to withdraw the agent's powers or authority, then quite simply, the agent can no longer carry out his tasks. In these circumstances, the relationship between the principal and the agent is as good as over.

The agent's withdrawal

The agent may withdraw from the agency agreement at any time as long as it is not in the middle of a transaction. If the agent failed to complete a transaction this may cause loss to the principal.

The principal's insolvency or the ending of the principal's business

The agency agreement may also come to an end if the business of the principal is coming to an end or if the principal is declared insolvent. The principal may no longer wish to carry on a particular business or he may be forced to end his operations in a particular line of business. This would, of course, mean that the agent may no longer have a role to play as the principal's representative in a particular business activity.

 Patmore & Co *v* Cannon & Co Ltd (1892) Patmore & Co, warehousemen, agents and merchants of Glasgow and Leith, agreed with Cannon to act as Cannon's agent in Scotland for sales of goods manufactured by Cannon for a fixed period of five years from October 1891. In January 1892 Cannon communicated to Patmore, its intention to give up its fancy leather trade.

Held: Patmore was unsuccessful in its claim for damages for breach of contract. Cannon should not be forced to carry on a business against its will for five years or for any other period of time in order to keep Patmore in work as an agent.

The death of the principal or the agent

The death of either party has the effect of ending an agency relationship. There may be rare occasions, however, when an agent will not be aware of the principal's death and contracts with third parties may have been entered into after this event. Before the invention of modern communications, it may have been difficult to contact an agent to inform him of the principal's death and much of the case law in this area is quite old. In situations where the agent is unaware of the principal's death, the contract with a third party will be enforceable against the principal's estate and the agent is in no way personally liable.

 Campbell v Anderson (1829) the agent believed that his principal was alive when he negotiated the contract on the principal's behalf. It was only after the contract had been entered into with the third party that the agent heard the news that his principal was dead and, as a result, the agency agreement was at an end.

Held: the principal's estate was bound to honour the agreement with the third party and the agent was not personally liable to the third party.

Expiry of a fixed contract

Both the principal and the agent may have negotiated an agency agreement which is to last for a fixed period of time, for example, two years. Once the period of time has passed, the agency relationship comes to an end.

 Brenan v Campbells Trustees (1898) Brenan was employed in 1890 as a factor by the Trustees, the appointment to last for four years. Brenan claimed that he was entitled to six months' notice and sued for six months' pay.

Held: Brenan was not entitled to notice as he was well aware that his contract was of a fixed period of four years.

 Key point: The agency relationship can be terminated in a number of different ways – mutual agreement, principal withdrawing the agent's authority, the agent withdrawing from the relationship, principal's bankruptcy, death or insanity or the expiry of a fixed term contract.

Business organisations

To say that someone runs a business is to make a very vague statement. What kind of business does that person run? This is an important question because there are different rules which govern the creation of the various types of businesses that Scots law recognises. If, for example, someone wished to set up *business* as a sole trader, there are not that many legal rules covering this type of business. A sole trader does not even have to register the fact that he has set up a business. On the other hand, however, someone who wished to set up a *company* would have to be aware of the many different legal requirements that they would have to satisfy before they were allowed to do this. A new company must be registered with the Registrar of Companies and its directors must ensure that all sorts of information about the company's business activities are available to interested members of the public.

 Key point: In order to set up a business, certain legal requirements will have to be followed whereas in other situations there may be no rules about setting up a business.

Another important factor in setting up a business is the kind of liability that those individuals who are responsible for running it will face should the business fail. Some businesses like sole traders and partnerships operate under unlimited liability. This means that a sole trader or partners in a firm could lose everything if the business

393

collapses. Alternatively, other businesses like limited liability partnerships and corporate bodies enjoy limited liability. Should the business fail, the members will only be liable for business debts up to a limit which they have already agreed amongst themselves. Clearly, this type of arrangement is much better than being chased by the creditors of the business for your last penny.

Key point: The extent of a person's liability for business debts will often determine the type of business to be set up.

There are a number of different business organisations which exist under Scots Law:

- Sole trader
- Partnerships
- Limited partnerships
- Limited liability partnerships
- Corporate bodies

We will examine each of these in turn.

Sole traders

A sole trader is the simplest form of business organisation recognised by Scots law. In many respects, the law regards someone operating as a sole trader as a self-employed person. There are no legal requirements imposed on a person who wishes to operate as a sole trader except for the submission of income tax returns to the Inland Revenue and the disclosure requirements of the Business Names Act 1985. In law, no difference is made between the sole trader and his business; they are indistinguishable.

A sole trader will have total control over his business and will not have to take into account the opinions of any shareholders, members or partners. However, should the business fail, the sole trader is said to have unlimited liability for any debts or obligations owed to third parties. In practical terms, this means that a sole trader can be pursued through the courts for his last penny – in other words he could lose everything. Additionally, a sole trader may find it difficult to fund an expansion of the business because he cannot offer shares to other parties in order to raise funds. If he wished to do this, he would lose the control that he has over the business. Furthermore, he would be forced to change the nature of his business operation by converting it into a partnership or a corporate body.

 Key point: A sole trader is the simplest form of business organisation recognised by Scots law.

Partnership

A partnership is special type of business organisation which is often referred to as a firm. The name under which the partners collectively carry on business is referred to as the 'firm name'. The partners can, within limits, choose whatever name they want. However, the firm name will be subject to disclosure requirements of the Business Names Act 1985 if the partnership uses a name other than the surnames of each partner. A partnership calling itself The Business Law Consultancy will have to disclose the fact that its two partners are Alistair B Wylie and Seán J Crossan and the location of the firm's principal place of business. The official stationery of The Business Law Consultancy should contain these details so as to provide important information about the firm to third parties. These details should also be displayed in a prominent place to which customers will have access at the firm's business premises. If the partners fail to comply with these rules, they will commit a criminal offence. A partnership must not, for example, use a firm name which suggests government or local authority connections. Other important restrictions in relation to the firm's name are that a partnership must not use 'limited', 'public limited company' or 'limited liability partnership' as the last words of its name.

 Key point: A partnership is often referred to as a firm.

The main features of partnership

A partnership agreement is a contractual relationship. According to Section 1 of the Partnership Act 1890, a partnership is 'the relation which exists between persons carrying on a business with a view of profit'. The Partnership Act 1890 does not provide details as to how a partnership is formed, but it is quite obvious that the partners have entered into a contract with one another for the purpose of setting up the business.

Two or more individuals up to a maximum of 20 people can come together to form a partnership. There must be at least two members of a partnership in order to set up the business. According to Section 716 of the Companies Act 1985, the maximum number of partners permitted by law is 20. In practice, however, many partnerships have been given an exemption by the Secretary of State at the Department of Trade and Industry which allows them to have more than 20 partners. The Secretary of State has wide powers of discretion to grant exemptions to various partnerships who wish to have more than 20 partners.

The main purpose of the partnership is to make a profit. Partnership is a business which has been set up with a view to making a profit. According to Section 45 of the Partnership Act 1890, a business can include every trade, occupation or profession. The definition in Section 45 would, therefore, prevent charities and clubs of a social or religious nature from being classed as partnerships. Clearly, these types of organisation are not set up to make profits for the members.

The members of the partnership contribute money, time or skills as a contribution towards the success of the business.

Generally speaking all the partners are agents of the business and of each other which means that they can, therefore, bind the partnership into contracts with third parties. Section 5 of the Partnership Act 1890 states quite clearly that every partner is to be regarded as an agent of the firm and of his fellow partners. This means that, if any partner enters into a contract with a third party which is in the partnership's usual line of business, the partner will bind the firm into a contract with the third party.

 Key point: A partnership is a business where two or more individuals have entered into a contract in order to make a profit and the members will contribute finance and/or time and skills to achieve this goal.

The separate personality of the firm

Section 4 of the Partnership Act 1890 states that a firm is to be regarded as a legally distinct person from the partners who are numbered amongst its members. This means that a partnership is capable of entering into contracts with third parties in its own right. Although a firm can own moveable property in its own right, any heritable property that it owns i.e. land or buildings must be held in trust for the firm usually by a named partner or a group of the partners. The firm can also raise a legal action in its own name and it can be sued by a third party in the event of a legal dispute occurring.

 Key point: In Scots law, subject to several limitations, a firm is legally distinct from its partners.

Liability of the partners

Creditors of the firm must first sue the business for any debts that are owed, but if a firm lacks assets or funds to meet the payment of the debt, the creditors are entitled to raise an action against individual partners or the partners as a group. In this way, the partners are to be regarded as jointly and severally liable for the firm's debts. Normally, partners operate under the burden of unlimited liability which, practically speaking, will mean that every partner can be pursued to his last penny by the firm's creditors. In theory, a partner in a failed business could be forced to use all of his personal assets to pay off the debts of the firm. Should any partner have to pay a debt, he has the right to demand that his fellow partners compensate him. So, if there are five partners in a firm and they are all equally liable for the firm's debts, they must each pay one-fifth towards the debt owed to the creditors. The partnership agreement, however, may state that different partners are expected to pay different levels of contributions towards partnership debts. The assumption that the Partnership Act makes about the partners contributing equally towards the firm's debts cannot always be taken for granted.

 Key point: Creditors must first sue the firm for any business debts owed and, after having exhausted this source, the partners who are said to be jointly and severally liable.

The vicarious liability of the firm

Sections 10, 11 and 12 of the Partnership Act impose the burden of vicarious liability on the firm for any delicts or negligent acts which are committed by the partners. This means that the firm will be liable to a third party if a partner injures the third party or if damage is caused to the third party's property while the partner is acting in the course of the firm's business. It is important to stress that the firm will not be liable where one partner causes loss or injury to a fellow partner while acting in the course of the partnership business. In such a situation, the injured partner would have to sue the partner who had committed the wrongful act in his personal capacity.

 Key point: A firm can be responsible to third parties for the negligent actions of the partners which cause loss or injury.

Partnership by holding out

It will be remembered from the study of agency, that a principal can create an agency relationship by holding out someone as an agent. This means that the actions or words of the principal can give third parties the impression that someone is acting as his agent. Third parties will often take the principal's words or actions at face value and deal with an individual as the principal's agent. The principal can then find himself being bound into contracts with third parties due to the actions of 'his agent'. Section 14 of the Partnership Act addresses situations where an individual could become liable for the debts and wrongful acts of the firm by holding himself out to be a partner or where the firm itself has held him out to be a partner. If an individual claims to be a partner in a firm or where he allows third parties to believe that he is a partner, such a person will be liable to any creditor who has loaned the firm money on the strength of these claims. Clearly, the individual who has allowed himself to be represented as a partner is not really a member of the firm, but the important point to consider here is that third parties believe that he is a partner. If the partnership has led third parties dealing with the firm to believe that someone is a partner, the partnership will be liable for any debts incurred or wrongful acts committed by the false partner. If the third party is aware that an individual's claims to be a partner in a firm are false, there is no liability.

 Key point: If the firm encourages third parties to believe (wrongly) that an individual is a partner, the firm will be liable for the debts or wrongful acts of the false partner.

The liability of an incoming partner for debts or wrongful acts

Under Section 17 of the Partnership Act, new partners joining the firm will not be responsible for any partnership debts or wrongful acts committed by the business that were run up or occurred before their involvement in the firm. Similarly, a partner who has left the firm will cease to have any responsibility for business liabilities after his departure. A former partner in order to escape liability will have to publicise his departure from the firm in the *Edinburgh Gazette* and this is regarded as giving proper notice to third parties of his changed role in relation to the business. It is worth pointing out that former partners continue to be liable for business debts or for wrongful acts committed by the partnership which occurred during their involvement with the firm.

 Key point: A notice in the *Edinburgh Gazette* informs outsiders and third parties that a partner has left the firm and that he has no further responsibility for debts incurred by the firm after the publication of this notice.

The relationship between the partners in a firm

Partnership is a contract *uberrimae fidei* – a relationship of the utmost good faith. The partners have a special relationship with one another and, as a result, they are expected to be completely honest and above board in their dealings. In other words, they owe fiduciary duties towards one another because they are regarded as being in a relationship of trust. Partners must not do anything which undermines the firm, for example, by competing against it by running another business. A partner must not make secret profits at the expense of his fellow partners (see **Pillans Brothers v Pillans (1908)** in Chapter 2).

The Partnership Act 1890 spells out the fiduciary duties of a partner in the following ways:

1   Every partner must keep proper accounts when handling and receiving partnership funds on behalf of his fellow partners. A partner is also under a duty to inform his fellow partners about any matter which may affect the firm (Section 28).

2   Every partner must inform his fellow partners of any profit made or benefit received as a result of his position as a partner or as a result of using the firm's property or assets (Section 29).

3   Any partner who competes against the firm by running another business without having been given permission by his fellow partners will have to hand over all profits made in the course of the competing business to the firm (Section 30).

 Key point: Partnership is a contract *uberrimae fidei* i.e. of the utmost good faith.

The creation of a partnership

When a partnership is set up, the members do not have to comply with any formal legal requirements. In other words, unlike companies, limited partnerships and limited liability partnerships, a partnership does not have to be registered with the Registrar of Companies. The contract of partnership can be a verbal agreement, a written agreement or it can even be implied from the behaviour of the members. Obviously, a written agreement between the partners which clearly sets out their rights and duties will make good business sense because it will give the courts something to work with in the event of a dispute. If the partners have failed to put anything in writing, the courts can use the rules contained in the Partnership Act 1890 to resolve any problems or disputes that the partners may currently be experiencing in relation to one another. It should be stressed from the beginning, however, that the Partnership Act 1890 only provides guidelines which the partners are free to ignore if they so wish. In theory, the partners are largely left to run their business as they see fit. If the partners have chosen to depart from any of the rules contained in the Partnership Act 1890, the courts will have to respect this decision.

 Key point: There are no formal legal requirements for setting up a partnership, but the 1890 Partnership Act can be used by the courts to resolve issues in the event of a dispute if the partners have failed to provide a partnership agreement.

The rights of the partners

Section 24 of the Partnership Act 1890 provides some important guidelines which illustrate the rights and duties of each partner in the firm (unless the partners have come to a different agreement among themselves):

◆   All partners can expect to share equally in the profits that a partnership makes. On the other hand, of course, all partners are expected to contribute equally towards any losses that the firm may suffer.

- All partners are expected to share equally the partnership funds or capital.

- All partners have the right to be relieved of any liabilities or expenses that they have incurred as a result of acting properly in the course of the partnership business.

- All partners who have advanced money to the partnership over and above their agreed contribution to partnership funds are entitled to receive interest on the money loaned at the rate of 5 per cent per annum from the date on which the loan was made.

- All partners have the right to participate in the running of the partnership.

- All partners are entitled to receive a share of the profits and this means that individual partners are not entitled to be paid for participating in the business.

- All the partners must first agree before any new partner can join the partnership.

- The partners can reach a decision by majority vote. However, any changes to the nature of the partnership agreement must be agreed by all of the partners.

- The partnership books are to be kept at the partnership's head office where all the partners are entitled to have access to them so that they can be consulted at any time.

 Key point: Section 24 of the Partnership Act lists the rights and duties of a partner in the absence of any agreement to the contrary.

Section 25 of the Partnership Act 1890 prevents a majority of partners from expelling a fellow partner from the firm, unless this power is part of the contract of partnership. If such a power of expulsion exists, the partners who wish to make use of it must be seen to be acting in good faith.

It must be emphasised again that the above rules governing the rights and duties of the partners in a firm are merely guidelines which the members of a partnership are free to exclude if they so wish. Many partnerships will be run along very different lines from the model that is described in Section 24 of the Partnership Act 1890.

Determining the existence of a partnership

The question as to whether or not a partnership exists may arise either between the alleged partners or between the alleged partners and a third party. According to section 2 of the Partnership Act 1890 if an individual is entitled to a share of the profits of the business, this may be used in evidence to prove that he is a partner in a firm. It is obviously open to the individual concerned to dispute this allegation made by a third party.

The Partnership Act 1890 provides rules for determining whether a partnership does or does not exist. These are a re-enactment of rules originally contained in 'Bovill's Act', which was passed in 1865 to regulate the liabilities of persons sharing profits.

The first rule is that owning property jointly or in common does not of itself create a partnership, even where profits from its use are shared.

 Sharpe v Carswell (1910) Sharpe had a small shareholding in respect of the ownership of a schooner named *Dolphin*. He was also employed as the master of this vessel receiving a fixed salary for his services. Sharpe was involved in an accident which had occurred, within the course of his employment, on board the vessel and he suffered serious injuries which later caused his death. His widow attempted to claim compensation for his death in terms of the Workmen's Compensation Act 1906. The Act operated a scheme whereby victims of industrial accidents who were classified as 'workmen' received compensation in respect of injury and death. The vital question here was whether Sharpe's shareholding in the vessel meant that he was a partner in the business and not a workman (i.e. an employee of the venture). If Sharpe had been a partner in the business his widow would be disqualified from claiming compensation for his death in terms of the Act.

Held: the fact that Sharpe had owned some shares in the vessel did not mean that he ought to be classified as a partner in the business. His widow was, therefore, entitled to receive compensation under the Act in respect of his work-related death.

 Davis *v* Davis (1894) a father left his two sons his business and a number of freehold houses. Both sons had equal shares as tenants in common in the freehold property. The sons let one of the houses and used the rent obtained to enlarge the workshops attached to the remaining two houses. The sons continued to carry on the business. They each drew out from it a weekly sum, but no accounts were kept. The proceeds from rent for the third house were divided between them.

Held: the sons were carrying on a partnership in relation to the business, but not in relation to the freehold houses.

The second rule is that the sharing of gross returns does not of itself create a partnership. It does not matter whether the persons sharing the returns have or have not a joint or common right or interest in any property from which the returns are derived. This rule can be seen in the case of **Cox *v* Coulson (1916)**.

 The defender, Coulson, was the manager of a theatre and he had entered into an agreement with a Mr Mill to provide the use of the theatre, pay for the lighting and promotional materials for plays. He was to receive 60 per cent of the gross takings, whilst Mr Mill was to secure the services and pay for a theatrical company. Mr Mill was also to provide the scenery and he had the right to receive the remaining 40 per cent of the takings. The pursuer was injured by a shot fired by an actor during the performance of a play at the theatre. The pursuer claimed that the defender was liable on the ground that he was a partner of Mr Mill.

Held: by the English Court of Appeal that the defender could not be made liable because he was not a partner, for by Section 2(2) of the Partnership Act 1890 the sharing of gross returns did not by itself create a partnership.

The third rule relates to the sharing of profits, as opposed to gross returns. The word 'profits' means net profits, i.e. the amount remaining after the expenses of the business have been deducted from the gross returns.

It will be remembered that Section 2 of the Partnership Act 1890 states that, if a person receives a share of the profits of a business, this will strongly suggest that such an individual is a partner in the business. However, the sharing of profits is by no means conclusive proof that someone is a partner in a business. Before the case of **Cox v Hickman (1860)**, the sharing of profits was regarded as conclusive evidence of a partnership. However, this case changed the common law and it established the rule that parties may share profits without necessarily being partners.

In accordance with the decision in **Cox v Hickman**, the Partnership Act describes certain situations where the sharing of profits does not of itself make the recipient a partner in the business. These situations are as follows:

- ◆ If a person is owed a debt by the partnership and this debt is paid by instalments from partnership profits.

- ◆ Where an individual is an employee of the partnership and his wages are paid from partnership profits.

- ◆ A deceased partner's widow or child who receives a pension or an annuity from partnership funds.

- ◆ Where money is loaned to a person engaged in a business where the contract states that the lender is to receive a rate of interest varying with the profits or is to receive a share of the profits, the lender is not a partner in the business. However, so close is the relationship to partnership in this instance that the contract must be in writing and signed by or on behalf of all the parties to it. Otherwise the lender would be held to be a partner.

- ◆ A person who has sold the goodwill of a business and receives as payment a portion of the profits or a pension or annuity from partnership profits is not a partner.

 Key point: A person who is entitled to a share of the profits of a business may be a partner unless he can bring evidence to defeat this presumption.

Termination of a partnership

According to provisions contained in Sections 32 to 35 of the Partnership Act 1890, a partnership may be dissolved in the following ways:

End of fixed period

If a partnership was created for a fixed period of time, the business comes to an end when this period expires. The members of a firm may set up a business which is to operate for, say, ten years (Section 32). Once this ten-year period has passed, the business is at an end. However, there is nothing to stop the partners continuing in business together after the expiry of the ten-year period if they are so minded. This would be known as partnership at will or tacit relocation and the firm will continue to trade for the indefinite future.

Goal accomplished

If the firm was set up to achieve a particular goal, it will come to an end when this purpose is accomplished (Section 32).

 Winsor v Schroeder (1979) Schroeder and Winsor contributed equal amounts of money in order to buy a house, modernise it and then sell it on at a profit – the profit to be divided equally between the partners.

401

Held: the partnership would come to an end when the land was sold and the profit, if any, was divided between Winsor and Schroeder.

Notice given

One of the partners could give notice to the other members that he wishes the firm to cease trading. So long as a partnership has not been formed for a particular period of time or for a particular purpose, it can be dissolved by notice given by any partner. The notice must be in writing if the partnership agreement is in the form of a deed. If not, then a partner can notify the other members verbally of his desire to dissolve the business. This notice will take effect when all partners have knowledge of it. No particular period of notice is required.

 Peyton *v* Mindham (1972) it was held that a court could and would declare a dissolution notice to be ineffective if it was given in bad faith as where A and B dissolve a partnership with C by notice, in order to exclude C from sharing in valuable, future contracts. Dissolution by notice may be prevented by the provisions of the partnership agreement.

 Moss *v* Elphick (1910) the partnership agreement stated that dissolution could only occur if all the partners were in agreement (Section 32).

Death of a partner

The death of a partner dissolves the firm. The share of the partner who has died goes to his personal representatives who are usually appointed by his will. They have the rights of a partner in a dissolution. Partnership agreements usually provide that the firm shall continue after the death of a partner so that the dissolution is only a technical one. A deceased partner's share is paid out to his personal representatives, although partnership agreements do sometimes provide for repayment of capital by instalments, or by annuities, for example, to a spouse or any other dependant (Section 33).

Bankruptcy of partner

The personal bankruptcy of a partner also dissolves the firm. The partnership agreement usually provides that the business shall continue to operate with the participation of the solvent partners. This means that the dissolution is, again, only a technical one, and the bankrupt partner's share is paid out to his trustee in bankruptcy. The partnership agreement must address the possibility of a member's bankruptcy occurring in the future so that the firm can continue to operate in these circumstances. It is no use agreeing to continue to keep the business running after the bankruptcy of one of the partners has occurred, if this eventuality is not covered by the partnership agreement (Section 33).

Illegality

If the operation of the partnership becomes illegal, the business will be dissolved. An instance of dissolution by illegality occurred in **Stevenson & Sons Ltd *v* AG für Cartonnagen Industrie (1918)** where the English company, Stevenson, was in partnership with a German company as a sole agent to sell the German company's goods. This would obviously involve trading with enemy aliens in wartime and the partnership was, therefore, dissolved on the grounds of illegality (Section 34).

Private debt

If a partner's share in the partnership comes under the control of a creditor to whom the partner owes a private debt, the remaining solvent partners of the firm can exercise an option to dissolve the business (Section 33). The Partnership Act 1890 does not indicate whether this can be done by a single partner, or by a majority of the partners or whether such a decision would have to be unanimous. A private creditor of a partner who has been to court and obtained a court order to enforce the debt can force the other partners to sell the firm's assets to pay a private debt. However, in terms of Section 23 the other partners can pay off the creditor and take over the charge, which they can then enforce gradually against the indebted partner. For example, they could take a small share of his profits as payment of the debt.

Order for dissolution

A partner may apply to the courts so that an order for the dissolution of the partnership can be issued (Section 35). Such an order will be granted in the following situations:

1   A partner suffers from some mental disorder or insanity.

2   A partner suffers from some permanent incapacity.

3   A partner conducts himself in a way that is harmful to the continued operation of the business.

4   A partner persistently commits a breach of the partnership agreement or conducts himself in a way that it would be unreasonable to expect the other partners to continue working with him.

5   Where the business can only be carried on at a loss.

6   Where the court thinks that it would be just and equitable that the partnership should be dissolved.

After the dissolution of the firm, the authority of each partner to bind the firm will continue for as long as necessary in order to complete those transactions with third parties which were entered into before the partners decided to dissolve the business. It will also be necessary for the partners to continue to have authority to deal with matters which are related to the termination of the partnership agreement. However, the partners are most definitely prevented from drumming up new business on behalf of the firm.

The partners will usually manage to dissolve the business themselves without having to rely on outside help. There may be situations, however, where the intervention of the courts will be necessary to achieve the termination of the partnership agreement. Under Section 39, partnership property and assets must first be used to pay off the firm's debts and liabilities. If anything is left after the debts and liabilities of the firm have been paid off, any partner who has loaned the firm money is entitled to be repaid. Next, the partners will effectively be repaid their contribution towards the firm's capital. If anything remains of the firm's capital or assets after this, then the partners share what is left according to the rules by which they share profits.

Rescission

A partnership can also come to an end where the contract is rescinded. Rescission involves the setting aside of the contract usually on the grounds of misrepresentation or fraud.

 In **Ferguson v Wilson (1904)** a partnership agreement was rescinded on the grounds of innocent misrepresentation. Wilson, an engineer in Aberdeen, had advertised for a partner. Ferguson replied to the advertisement and, during the contractual negotiations that followed, Wilson innocently misrepresented the profitability of his business. On the basis of these figures, Ferguson agreed to enter a partnership with Wilson.

Held: Ferguson was entitled to rescind or cancel the partnership agreement owing to the fact of Wilson's innocent misrepresentation.

 Key point: The rules concerning termination of partnership are contained in Sections 32 to 35 of the Partnership Act 1890.

The Scottish and English Law Commissions' Joint Report on Partnership Law

On 18 November 2003, the Scottish and English Law Commissions (Scot Law Com No 192 and Law Com No 283) published a Joint Report on Partnership Law.

The Commissions wish to see the introduction of a new Partnership Act to replace the existing 1890 Act. If these proposals were formally adopted by the Westminster Parliament, it would mean that, for the first time, the law in relation to partnership in Scotland, England and Wales would largely be the same. Partnerships in England and Wales would become legal entities as is already the case in Scotland in order to reflect commercial reality. Partnerships would, therefore, be able to enter contracts and hold property in their own right. Partners would still be personally responsible for obligations of the firm and they would continue to stand in a fiduciary relationship to one another. This means that partners will still have to labour under the burden of unlimited liability.

The current restriction on partnerships being limited to a mere 20 members would be removed. Perhaps one of the most significant changes that the proposed new law would make is that partnerships would not automatically be wound up when there is a change of partner as is presently the case. Where partnerships, which are solvent, are going to be wound up, the Report proposes that, in both jurisdictions, the law allows the partners to decide by majority vote how this will be achieved. Currently, the courts in England and Wales or a judicial factor become involved when a partnership is wound up. Insolvent partnerships could be wound up under the Insolvency Act 1986.

 Key point: In November 2003, the Scottish and English Law Commissions published a joint report on partnership which proposed having the same general rules governing this type of business in Scotland and England and Wales.

Limited partnerships

This type of business is governed by the Limited Partnerships Act 1907. Unlike a traditional partnership, this type of business must be registered with the Registrar of

Companies in Edinburgh. The following information must be supplied to the Registrar:

- The name of the limited partnership.
- A brief description of the type of business that it carries on.
- The location of its main office.
- The full names of each of the partners.
- A statement, if appropriate, of how long the partnership is to last and the date upon which the business began.
- A statement that the partnership is limited and who the limited partners are.
- The amount of each limited partner's contribution to the business.

The Act allows at least one general partner and one limited partner to form a business. However, there must always be at least one general partner at any time. The limited partner is effectively a silent or a sleeping partner and plays no part in the day-to-day running of the business. In an ordinary partnership, all the partners operate under the burden of unlimited liability where they will all be responsible for the firm's debts. This is not the case in a limited partnership, where the limited partner will lose only the amount of money that he advanced to the firm. If the limited partner becomes involved in the daily management of the business, his liability for business debts or delicts which were the responsibility of the business would become unlimited. Limited partners see their role as that of an investor wishing to make a profit. They do not want to be bogged down with the responsibilities of management. The 1907 Act makes it quite clear that a majority of the general partners will decide the aims and the policies of the business. A limited partner will not even be able to oppose the introduction of a new general partner if the existing general partners have made up their minds on this matter.

Even the death, lunacy or bankruptcy of a limited partner will not mean that the partnership has to be ended as with an ordinary firm. It will be the general partners who will decide when the business is to be ended. The major disadvantage of being a limited partner is that it will not be possible for such a person to withdraw his investment while the partnership is still trading. The general partners may allow a limited partner to transfer or assign his investment in the business to a third party, the public must be notified by the placing of an advertisement to this effect in the *Edinburgh Gazette*. These types of businesses tend to be encountered rarely because private limited companies are seen as a more popular means of investing money.

The relationship between the general partners is governed by the Partnership Act 1890 and the associated case law in mostly the same way as would be found in an ordinary firm.

Key point: A limited partnership allows the firm to have silent or limited partners who take no part in the day-to-day running of the firm's business and, furthermore, these individuals enjoy limited liability. However, limited partnerships must register with the Registrar of Companies.

Limited liability partnerships

The Limited Liability Partnership Act 2000 came into force on 6 April 2001. The Act introduces a new type of business vehicle in addition to companies, traditional partnerships, limited partnerships and sole traders.

According to Section 1 of the Act, a limited liability partnership or LLP is a corporate body which has completely separate legal personality from that of its members. Section 1 also makes it very clear that the law of partnership does not apply to LLPs.

A business trading as a limited liability partnership will be immediately recognisable by the use of the initials LLP after its name

It was originally thought that LLPs would be attractive business organisations for existing professional partnerships such as law firms, surveyors and accountants. In many situations, though they are exceptions, such businesses have faced difficulties in trying to run limited companies because of the rules laid down by their professional associations. The major advantage of setting up an LLP for existing partnerships is that the members can limit their liability. In a traditional-style partnership, it will be remembered that should the business fail and run up huge debts, the members will face the burden of unlimited liability. This effectively means that creditors of the partnership can and will pursue the members to their last penny. The partner's personal assets, for example, a home, savings, a car and other valuables will be eyed up by creditors.

 Key point: Limited liability partnerships (LLPs) are corporate bodies and the members can limit their liability in respect of the business's creditors.

People involved in setting up new businesses may also wish to form LLPs. Previously, the individuals involved in this type of venture would have probably chosen to run the business as a limited company. Existing limited companies, however, are prevented from re-registering as LLPs.

The creation of limited liability partnerships

Section 2 of the Act contains the rules for establishing an LLP:

- The LLP must have at least two members who have signed an incorporation document.
- The founding members of the LLP must register this incorporation document and other necessary documentation with the Registrar of Companies.
- A fee of £95 is also payable by the proposed members of the LLP to the Registrar.

If an LLP operates with just one member for more than six months, the business loses the protection of limited liability and the remaining member will have complete responsibility for any business debts or liabilitites.

The incorporation document

An incorporation document must contain the following details:

- The name of the limited liability partnership.

- The country in which the registered office of the limited liability partnership is to be situated i.e. England and Wales, in Wales or in Scotland.

- The address of that registered office.

- The name and address of each of the persons who are to be members of the limited liability partnership on its incorporation.

- Details of those persons who are to be designated members or details of every person who from time to time will be a member of the limited liability partnership and who is to be a designated member.

If a person deliberately makes a false statement to the Registrar in the incorporation document, he commits a criminal offence.

In terms of Section 3, when the Registrar is satisfied that all legal requirements have been complied with, he will then issue a certificate of incorporation which allows the new business to begin trading. The certificate of incorporation is conclusive proof that the members of the LLP have complied with all the necessary legal requirements.

 Key point: An LLP must be registered with the Registrar of Companies who will issue a certificate of incorporation signifying that the business has complied with all necessary legal requirements.

The members of an LLP

It is very important that those people who are involved in running an LLP should not be called partners. The proper term for these individuals is members.

Section 4 states that the first members of the LLP are those individuals whose names appear on the incorporation document which is delivered to the Registrar. At least two members must be 'designated members' and their names must be given to the Registrar as such. Designated members have additional responsibilities in comparison to the general members of an LLP. The designated members will be responsible for administrative and filing duties which would normally be carried out by a director or a company secretary in a company. Some of the tasks that a designated member is responsible for include the following:

- Signing the annual accounts
- Filing the annual accounts and annual returns with Companies House
- In the event of insolvency proceedings, providing any statement setting out the affairs of the business i.e. assets, debts and liabilities

There is nothing to stop a person becoming a member of the business at a later date either with the agreement of the existing members or under the terms of a membership agreement (if one exists). A person may no longer be regarded as a member as long as this is with the agreement of the other members or in accordance with the membership agreement (again if one exists). The death of a member (if the LLP was not thereby dissolved) means that membership of the business will come to an end. Generally speaking, members are not regarded as employees of the business.

 Key point: The designated members of an LLP have additional responsibilities that would normally be carried out by a director or a company secretary in a company.

A membership agreement

Corporate bodies must register a memorandum and articles of association with the Registrar and these documents provide important information about the way in which the business is run. Although there is no legal requirement for LLP members to commit anything to paper, Section 5 of the Act makes it clear that it would be a very sensible practice for the LLP members to draw up a detailed members' agreement (currently known as a partnership agreement). This agreement would deal with all the important issues that the business will face, for example:

- The authority of the members to bind the LLP
- Each member's financial contribution to the LLP
- Shares of profits and losses
- The circumstances in which the LLP agreement will come to an end
- The appointment of new members
- Special classes of members with different rights and duties
- The expulsion of existing members
- How disputes between the members are to be resolved
- Whether changes to the members' agreement are to be made unanimously or by majority

 Key point: There is no legal requirement for the members of an LLP to have a written agreement, but it will be sensible to have one in order to determine how the business is to be run.

The authority and liability of LLP members (Sections 6 and 7)

According to Section 6, the members of an LLP are to be regarded as the agents of the business. However, an LLP will not be bound in contract to a third party by the actions of one of its members if the member in question lacked authority to act on behalf of the business and the third party dealing the LLP member in question is fully aware that the member lacks authority. Where the third party does not know or believe a person to be a member of the LLP, the business will not be bound in contract to the third party.

If an individual ceases to be an LLP member, this fact must be communicated to third parties dealing with the business and, additionally, there is a legal requirement to inform the Registrar of Companies. Failure to inform third parties dealing with the business that someone is no longer an LLP member means that the former member will continue to be regarded as being involved in the business.

An LLP is classed as a completely separate legal entity from its members. In a partnership, the partners are jointly and severally liable for the firm's debts and any delicts committed by the partners in the course of partnership business. Members of an LLP are not jointly liable for contracts entered into by the LLP and they are not jointly and severally liable for any delicts committed by the LLP. However, members will be liable for their own acts of negligence or wrong-doing in a very similar way to company directors. It would be a sensible precaution for members to take out professional liability insurance which would offer them protection if a third party decided to bring an action against one of them.

The main benefit of an LLP in relation to a traditional partnership is that the members of the LLP enjoy limited liability if something goes wrong with the business, in much the same way as shareholders in a company do. It will often, however, continue to be the usual practice where anyone who lends money to the LLP, for example, a bank will demand personal guarantees from the members, as is the current practice when dealing with shareholders in a company.

Section 7 describes a number of situations where an individual will lose the right to be involved in the affairs of the LLP as a member. Such individuals would include:

- Those persons who have left the LLP
- Those members who have died
- Those members who have become insolvent or who have had their estate sequestrated by creditors
- Those members who have granted a trust deed for the benefit of their creditors
- Those members who have transferred all or part of their share in the business to provide security for a debt

However, these individuals may be entitled to continue to receive a share of any profits that the business makes. It is important to stress that they are prevented from being involved in the day-to-day running of the business. Furthermore, the representatives, creditors, trustees in bankruptcy of individuals, trustees under a trust deed for the creditors or assignees of those members or ex-members of an LLP who are affected by Section 7 are forbidden to interfere in the management of the business.

 Key point: Every member of an LLP is to be regarded as an agent of the business and of the his fellow members and each member has a right to participate in the running of the LLP.

Changes in the membership of an LLP (Section 9)

Any changes in the membership of an LLP must be notified to the Registrar of Companies within 14 days. When there is any change in the name or residential address of a member, notice of this fact must be given to the registrar within 28 days. The Registrar does not require notice where individuals either become or cease to be designated members of the LLP. Failure to comply with these notice requirements is a criminal offence.

Taxation and National Insurance (Sections 10 to 13)

Where business owners have wanted to limit their personal liability in the past, they have normally set up companies and any profits made by those companies are subject to corporation tax. Dividends paid by the companies can then be taken as income of the shareholders. LLPs are taxed quite differently in that any profits are treated as the personal income of the members as if they had run their business as a partnership. There are no such things as shares in an LLP as would be the case with a company.

LLPs are required to produce and publish financial accounts which contain a level of detail equivalent to a similar sized limited company and they will have to submit accounts and an annual return to the Registrar of Companies each year. This legal requirement is far stricter than the rules which apply to traditional style partnerships.

Existing partnerships which wish to convert to an LLP will not necessarily be negatively affected in relation to their tax burden. This is likely to be the case provided there are no changes in membership or in the way in which the partnership operates. Obviously, the members of an existing partnership would be advised to seek advice on taxation matters before making any final decision to convert their business into an LLP.

Key point: LLPs will have to publish financial accounts containing the same sorts of detail as a similarly sized limited company and these accounts and an annual return will have to be submitted to the Registrar of Companies.

Corporate bodies

The vast amount of corporate bodies or companies are business organisations where the members have agreed to limit their liability to an agreed amount of money. This money will either a) have already been paid to the company or b) will be paid to the creditors of the company should the business fail. Most limited companies are limited by shares, although on some occasions the company may be limited by guarantee. Even more rarely, the members of a company may be under the burden of unlimited liability as in sole trader businesses and partnerships. Limited companies may be either private or public in nature. The main legal provisions relating to limited companies are to be found in the Companies Act 1985 to which further changes were made by the Companies Act 1989. It is possible for some companies to be founded by earlier legislation such as the Companies Act 1948. In other cases, companies or corporate bodies were founded by Royal Charter, for example, the University of Strathclyde in 1964, or even by Papal Bull, for example, the University of Glasgow in 1452. In modern times, however, the most common way of forming a company will be to meet the requirements of the Companies Act 1985. A company is the most complicated type of business organisation recognised by Scots law. Unlike sole traders or partnerships, certain legal requirements have to be met before a company can be formed. The main legal requirement consists of registering the company with the Registrar of Companies. Until the new business has been registered, it is not regarded as a person recognised by law and, therefore, it cannot enter into contracts with third parties.

 Key point: A modern company is a business which has been incorporated in terms of the Companies Act 1985 and has been registered with the Registrar of Companies.

Limited liability

The term 'limited' relates to the fact that the members of the company enjoy 'limited liability' status. This means that a member's individual liability is confined solely to the amount unpaid, if any, on their shareholding in the business. If, for example, a member has agreed to purchase £30,000 worth of shares in a company, should the company fail the creditors can only pursue the individual member for any money that he still owes for the shares. So, if the member still owed £15,000 for his shares he would have to pay this sum over to the company's creditors. Once this sum has been paid, however, the member cannot be held liable for any more of the company's debts – he has met all his obligations. If, on the other hand, the member has paid for all of his shares his liability is at an end and he cannot be forced to pay out over and above the sum that he agreed to pay for his shares. In companies limited by guarantee, the members agree to be liable to the company's creditors for an agreed sum should the business fail. Companies limited by guarantee are run as private companies. Clearly, no member of a company will want to have to pay money to the business's creditors, but limited liability is a very effective way by which the members can protect themselves. With unlimited liability, it will be remembered that the members of a business can be pursued to their last penny – in other words, they can lose everything. Companies where the members are under the burden of unlimited liability can only be set up as private companies. The members of a public company are spared the worry of unlimited liability. The huge advantage of limited liability is that it allows members of a company to at least reduce their losses to an agreed sum.

 Key point: Generally speaking, subject to a few exceptions, members of a company enjoy limited liability.

The separate legal personality of companies

All limited companies, whether private or public, must be registered under the Companies Act. This means that the company becomes an independent legal person in its own right, legally separate from its members and officers, a person recognised by the law, a person capable of having rights and taking on duties which the courts will recognise and enforce.

When a company with limited liability becomes a separate legal person this process is referred to as 'the veil of incorporation'.

It is worth remembering that separate corporate personality means that:

♦ The company can raise legal actions in its own right and be the subject of legal actions against it.
♦ The company has legal capacity and becomes a party to the contracts which it enters into.
♦ The company can exercise ownership over its property.
♦ The company continues to exist despite changes in its membership.
♦ The company's members enjoy limited liability.

The concept of separate corporate personality was forcefully recognised in the following case:

 Salomon v Salomon & Co Ltd (1897) Salomon owned a boot business which he sold to a company which he had formed, called Salomon & Co Ltd. There were seven members in the business: his wife, daughter and four sons who took one share each and Salomon himself who took 20,000 shares. The price paid by the company to Salomon was £30,000 but instead of giving him cash, the business gave him 20,000 fully paid £1 shares and £10,000 in secured debentures i.e. he lent the company £10,000. As a result of strikes within the boot trade, the company was wound up. The assets of the business amounted to just £6000 out of which £10,000 was owed to Salomon and £7000 to unsecured creditors. The unsecured creditors claimed that as Salomon & Co Ltd and Salomon were really the same person, he could not owe money to himself and that they should be paid their £7000 first.

Held: the House of Lords stated that Salomon was entitled to the £6000 and the unsecured creditors got nothing. The reason for this decision was that the company was to be regarded as a completely separate person in the eyes of the law from its members and its officers. The House of Lords thought it a completely irrelevant argument that Salomon was the leading shareholder in the company and that he could effectively control the destiny of the business.

The Salomon decision has been followed in other court cases described below:

 MacAura v Northern Assurance Co Ltd (1925) MacAura controlled a company where he was the majority shareholder. He was the owner of a forest and he decided to transfer ownership of this property to his company. MacAura had insured the forest against possible damage or loss, but when the company became its owner MacAura failed to transfer responsibility for insuring the property to the company. Unfortunately for MacAura, the forest later burned down and he tried to enforce the insurance policy. However, the insurance company argued that MacAura was no longer the owner of the forest and that he did not have an insurable interest. The person who did have an insurable interest in the forest and who should have protected it against loss or damage was the company, its new owner.

Held: although MacAura remained the majority shareholder in the company he had transferred ownership of the forest to the company. Therefore, the company should have insured the forest. It had not and the insurance company did not have to pay out. MacAura and the company were completely separate persons in the eyes of the law and should be treated as such.

 Lee v Lee's Air Farming Ltd (1961) Lee had set up a company where he was the owner of all but one of the shares. Lee was the company's only director and he had appointed himself as the company's chief pilot. Tragically, Lee was killed in an air accident while on company business and his wife later sued the company for compensation for his death.

Held: Mrs Lee was entitled to compensation from the company. Again, Lee and the company were to be regarded as completely separate people in the eyes of the law. One person (Lee) an employee of another person (the company) had been killed in the course of his employment and under current rules his widow was entitled to receive compensation from the company.

 Key point: A company is treated as a completely separate legal person in relation to its members.

The Salomon rule will be ignored in the following situations:

1   In a public company, there must be at least two members. If, for a period of more than six months, the company operates with a single member this individual becomes personally responsible for all debts of the business.

2   If a company was set up so that the members can carry out an illegal activity, they will not be allowed to benefit from the Salomon rule.

3   In times of war, a company that is controlled by citizens of an enemy state will not be allowed to continue trading for the duration of hostilities. Normally, the law is not interested in the nationalities of individual members, but in times of war this becomes a very important issue.

4   Company officers, for example directors and company secretaries, will have to be especially careful when signing cheques in their personal capacity and where

third parties will not be aware that they are doing so on behalf of the company. Additionally, the company officer can make an error when he writes the name of the company on a cheque that will be given to the third party. In both situations, the company officer will be personally responsible to the third party if the company does not meet the debt that the cheque represents.

 Key point: The concept of separate corporate personality will sometimes be ignored and this is known as 'lifting the veil of incorporation'.

The main characteristics of private and public limited companies

The main characteristics of a private limited company are:

1 Company name must end in 'limited' or 'ltd'.

2 The articles of association of a private limited company may provide for a right of pre-emption so that when a member wishes to sell or to transfer ownership of his shares he must first offer them to existing members.

3 There is no minimum capital requirement.

4 The shares in a private limited company cannot be traded or listed on the stock exchange.

5 Only one director is required.

6 In terms of the Companies (Single Member Private Limited Companies) Regulations 1992, a private company limited by shares or by guarantee need only have one member.

7 There is no upper age limit for directors.

8 Audited accounts must be produced within ten months of the year end.

9 Trading can start as soon as a Certificate of Incorporation is obtained.

The main characteristics of a public limited company are:

1 The company name must end in 'public limited company' or 'plc'.

2 Members must be free to transfer their shares as they please.

3 A public company must have minimum issued share capital of at least £50,000.

4 Shares can be listed on the stock exchange and can be traded.

5 There must be at least two directors.

6 There must be at least two members.

7 Directors must retire when they reach the age of 70.

8 Audited accounts must be produced within seven months of the year end.

9 After incorporation, trading cannot begin until a 'trading certificate' is issued by the Registrar of Companies upon satisfaction of the nominal value of share capital. This trading certificate is referred to as a section 117 certificate after the relevant section of the Companies Act 1985.

Key point: Limited companies and public limited companies have different characteristics.

Certificate of incorporation

The certificate of incorporation is issued by the Registrar of Companies at Companies House. This proves that the company has met the statutory requirements and the date on the certificate indicates the point at which the company became a corporate body with separate legal personality.

There are several documents that must be given to the Registrar of Companies before the certificate of incorporation can be issued:

◆ The Memorandum of Association
◆ The Articles of Association
◆ The names and particulars of the directors and the company secretary along with the address of the registered office of the company

The Memorandum of Association

This document defines the company's activities and powers. The Companies (Tables A to F) Regulations 1985 provide model memoranda of association. In other words, members of the company do not have to go to the expense and trouble of drawing up a memorandum because the 1985 Regulations already provide completed examples ready for immediate use. The members would simply select the most appropriate table depending on the type of company, for example, a public limited company or a company limited by guarantee. In Table A, the memorandum of association is suitable for a public limited company and a private company.

There are five main clauses contained in the memorandum:

Clause 1 – The name clause
Any name can be chosen for the business as long as the last word is 'limited', 'ltd' or 'plc'. A register of names is maintained by the Registrar of Companies at Companies House and names must comply with the Business Names Act 1985.

 Exxon v Exxon Insurance Consultants (1982) an insurance company attempted to use the name Exxon. The Standard Oil Company which traded under the internationally recognised name of Exxon objected to this because it would suggest to many people that the insurance company was connected to Standard Oil when this was not the case. The oil company raised a successful legal action which prevented the insurance company from using the name Exxon.

Clause 2 – The registered office clause
Every company must have a registered office as soon as it commences trading or within 14 days of its incorporation, whichever is earlier. The memo must state whether the registered office is in Scotland or England.

Clause 3 – The objects clause
This defines the purposes for which the company is incorporated. Prior to the Companies Act 1989, if a company was engaged in any activities or contracts not covered by the objects clause then these contracts were considered *ultra vires* i.e.

outwith the powers of the company and could not be enforced by either the third party or the company. The *ultra vires* rule was originally established to protect potential and existing members of a company. Companies were forced to list all of their business activities and they were not allowed to become involved in any business transaction which was not on the list. This meant that members could control the directors and prevent them from entering into contracts which might be regarded as risky in some way. More basically, all the members knew exactly what line of business the company was in and as long as the company confined itself to these activities everyone in theory was happy. Since the 1989 Act, companies are now allowed to state that its objects are to carry on a business as a 'general commercial company' meaning that it can be involved in any trade or business whatsoever. This means that *ultra vires* has become an internal matter for most companies. Directors and officers of the company may still be sued in their personal capacity if they carry out any act or enter into any transaction which strictly speaking would be forbidden by the company's objects clause. Third parties, however, dealing with the company need not worry that the contract is in any way unauthorised. Such a contract can be enforced against the company by the third party and now the third party cannot use the *ultra vires* rule to escape a contract with the company. (See **Ashbury Railway Carriage and Iron Co. v Riche 1875**) in Chapter 2.)

Clause 4 – The limitation of liability clause

This is a statement to confirm that the liability of the members is limited.

Clause 5 – The capital clause

This states the amount of nominal or authorised share capital and its division into shares of a fixed amount.

Clause 6 – The association clause

This clause perhaps states the obvious in that the members or shareholders of a company make an official declaration that they wish to form a corporate body.

 Key point: The Memorandum of Association defines the company's activities and powers.

The Articles of Association

The Articles of Association regulate the internal management of the company such as the appointment and removal of directors. Companies do not have to go to the expense of hiring a company lawyer to draw up Articles of Association. The Companies Act 1985 provides model sets of Articles of Association for companies. A private company limited by shares might wish to adopt Table B and a public company limited by shares could always make use of Table F. Table C provides articles of association which are suitable for a company limited by guarantee provided it does not have share capital.

The main clauses in the Articles of Association are:

- The process by which changes can be made to the Articles of Association
- Rules about share capital and changes which affect shareholders' rights
- Alteration of share capital
- Notice of general meetings and procedure at these meetings

- Voting powers of members
- Number, remuneration, qualifications, duties, rotation and removal of directors
- Appointment of directors
- Use of company seal
- Declaration and payment of dividends
- Keeping of accounts and audit
- Borrowing powers

 Key point: The Articles of Association regulate the internal management of the company.

The legal effect of the Memorandum of Association and the Articles of Association

According to Section 14 of the Companies Act 1985, the Memorandum of Association and the Articles of Association are together to be regarded as forming a binding contract between the members themselves and between the members and the company.

Section 14 has, therefore, a number of consequences for members of a company:

1   If a member feels that one of his membership rights that he enjoys under the Memorandum and the Articles has been ignored or abused by the company, he can raise a legal action against the company and force it to recognise these rights.

 Wood v Odessa Waterworks Co (1889) the Articles stated that all dividends payable to shareholders of the company must be paid in cash. The company tried to get round this rule by passing a resolution which would have prevented the shareholders from receiving the dividend in cash.
    Held: the shareholders were entitled to use the Articles to force the company to pay the dividend in cash.

2   On the other hand, however, the company can raise a legal action against members of the company who breach the rules regulating membership as laid out in the Memorandum and the Articles.

 Hickman v Kent or Romney Marsh Sheep Breeders' Association (1915) a member took his dispute with the company to the courts. Under the rules contained in the Articles, the members had all agreed to resolve any dispute with the company under an internal arbitration procedure.
    Held: the court action was halted and the member was forced to use the internal arbitration procedure to resolve his dispute with the company.

3   The members can sue one another for breach of the Memorandum and the Articles.

 Rayfield v Hands (1960) company members were obliged under the Articles to offer their shares to the directors if they wished to sell or transfer ownership of their shares. The directors were supposed to give members wishing to sell their shares a fair price for them. However, this rule in the Articles meant that members were prevented from selling their shares to outsiders. The directors refused to buy the member's shares thus making it impossible for him to leave the company. He raised a legal action against the directors.

Held: as a result of the Articles, the directors had no choice but to buy the shares from the member at a fair price determined by the court.

4   The rights given to members under the Memorandum and the Articles cannot be enforced by non-members or where the member is effectively acting as an outsider.

 Eley *v* Positive Life Assurance Co Ltd (1876) the Articles appointed Eley as the company's solicitor. He took up this position and he bought shares in the company. Some time later, the company decided to dispense with his services as solicitor. Eley claimed that his rights as a member had been abused as a result of his dismissal.

Held: Eley's dismissal did not affect his rights as a member of the company. He would continue to enjoy his rights and any benefits which membership of the company involved. The contract of employment between Eley and the company was in no way connected to his role as a member of the company.

 Key point: Section 14 of the Companies Act 1985 provides that the Memorandum of Association and the Articles of Association form a binding contract between the company and its members and between the members themselves.

Promoters of companies

Someone or a group of people will often be required to set up a company and comply with all the necessary registration procedures. Practical steps will have to be taken by such an individual or individuals such as buying or leasing property in order to have premises for a registered office, entering into contracts with third parties in order to buy or lease equipment that will be used by the new company or entering into contracts of employment with prospective employees of the new business. Clearly, it would not make good business sense to wait until all the legal requirements of the registration process had been complied with before attending to these important matters. The sooner everything is in place, the sooner the new business can begin to trade and, hopefully, begin to make profits for its members.

A person who takes care of these matters before the company is formed is referred to as a promoter. In **Twycross *v* Grant (1877)**, a promoter was defined as someone who undertakes to form a company with reference to a given project, and to set it going, and who takes the necessary steps to accomplish that purpose. A promoter of the company is not an agent of the company. In **Tinnevelly Sugar Refining Co *v* Mirrlees, Watson & Yaryan Co Ltd (1894)** Darley & Butler claimed to be acting on behalf of a company called Tinnevelly. Tinnevelly, however, did not exist when Darley & Butler entered into the contract for machinery supposedly on its behalf. Therefore, Tinnevelly was not a party to the contract with Mirrlees because Darley & Butler could not have been acting as agents for a principal that did not yet exist. Darley & Butler had the right to sue Mirrlees, but Tinnevelly had no such right.

Section 36(4) of the Companies Act 1985 makes the legal position of promoters very clear. They are not to be regarded as agents of a non-existent company. As a promoter is not an agent of the new company, he has no right to be paid for his services. In reality, many promoters are likely to be directors or members of the new company and, therefore, they have an interest in setting the company up. In any case, the new board of directors may have powers in the Articles of Association to pay the promoter or reimburse him for his expenses.

The downside of being a promoter is that they are personally responsible for any contracts that they enter into with third parties. The company cannot sue or be sued in relation to contracts that were formed before it was registered. This is a dangerous situation for the promoter because it means that the company need not reimburse him for any expenses which result from entering into contracts with third parties. A promoter is regarded as having a fiduciary relationship with the as yet non-existent company. This means that the promoter cannot use his position to make a profit unless the directors or members of the new company are aware of this and are comfortable with this situation. This means that a promoter will have to account for everything that he has done in his role. It is not beyond the realms of possibility that the new board of directors or members might sue a promoter to regain any secret profit that he has made from his activities.

A promoter can always try to escape personal liability for contracts with third parties by insisting that third parties agree not to sue him in the event that the company fails to honour the contract once it has been registered. Alternatively, a promoter may insist that the contracts will only take effect when the new company is legally recognised and that such a contract will be between the new company and the third party.

 Key point: A promoter is someone who undertakes to form a company with reference to a given project, and to set it going, and who takes the necessary steps to accomplish that purpose, but he is not an agent of the company.

Summary

- No business organisation, no matter its shape or size, can operate without the assistance of agents.

- An agent is the legal representative of someone called the principal and the principal authorises the agent to act on his behalf in dealings with third parties.

- The agent, therefore, negotiates and enters contractual agreements on behalf of the principal with third parties. When the third party deals with the agent it is as if he is dealing directly with the principal.

- The agent is not a party to the contract between the principal and the third party – he merely makes this business transaction occur.

- An agent is appointed in the first place because it is either physically impossible for the principal to carry out all the tasks demanded by his business or he possesses skills and expertise to carry out a particular job.

- The agency relationship is a contractual agreement.

- Both the principal and the agent have rights as well as duties under the agreement.

- One of the most important features of agency is that an agent expects to be paid for carrying out tasks on the principal's behalf.

- The agency relationship can be created in a number of ways – by express contract, implied by the conduct of the parties or by law, by holding out, by ratification or by necessity.

- Agency is a fiduciary relationship and this means that the agent must show that he can be trusted by the principal and he must do this by always acting in good faith.

- The agent's ability to bind his principal into a contract with a third party depends on the extent of his authority.

- There are two types of authority that an agent can possess – actual or ostensible.

- Actual authority is the authority which the agent really possesses whether expressly or impliedly. If he stays within his actual authority, the agent will bind the principal into a contract with the third party.

- Ostensible authority is the authority which a third party mistakenly assumes that the agent possesses. This mistaken belief is caused by the principal and, because of this, the third party will be able to enforce the contract against the him.

- Where the agent has no authority and the third party either knows this or should be aware of this, the principal will not be bound in contract.

- The Commercial Agents (Council Directive) Regulations 1993 are unusual because, unlike the common law rules, they single out a particular group of agents for protection and codify the rights and duties of the parties.

- The agency relationship, like any contract, can be terminated in a number of different ways. This can be done by mutual agreement, the principal withdrawing the agent's authority, the agent withdrawing from the relationship, the bankruptcy of the principal, the death or insanity or the expiry of a fixed term contract.

- Scots law recognises a variety of business organisations, for example, sole traders, partnerships, limited partnerships, limited liability partnerships, private limited companies, public limited companies and unlimited companies.

- It is very important to be able to differentiate between types of business because they are all governed by different rules.

- Another important factor in setting up a business is the kind of liability that those individuals who are responsible for running it will face should the business fail.

- Some businesses like sole traders and partnerships operate under unlimited liability. This means that a sole trader or partners in a firm could lose everything if the business collapses.

- Alternatively, other businesses like limited liability partnerships and corporate bodies enjoy limited liability. Should the business fail, the members will only be liable for business debts up to a limit which they have already agreed amongst themselves.

- Some types of business organisation are relatively informal, for example, sole traders and partnerships can be set up immediately – there are no formal requirements.

- Other types of business organisations, however, do have to be registered, for example, companies, limited liability partnerships and limited partnerships.

- Some businesses have a completely separate legal personality from that of their members, for example, partnerships, companies, limited liability partnerships and limited partnerships.

Test your knowledge

Short answer questions, exam standard essay-style questions and case-studies.

1 a) Describe the various ways in which an agency relationship can be established.

Examine both case studies carefully:

b) i) Katrina has written to several of her customers informing them that Beverley is acting as her agent. Katrina also publicises this information about Beverley in a number of newspaper adverts. Jocelyn entered into a contract with Beverley in order to purchase some goods. Jocelyn had always believed that Beverley was acting as Katrina's agent. Before the goods were delivered to Jocelyn, Beverley is declared bankrupt and her creditors seize all the goods that are currently stored in her warehouse. Jocelyn now turns to Katrina and demands that she honour the contract. Katrina is now denying that she ever appointed Beverley to act for her.

ii) Jonathan appointed Robert to act as his agent in relation to the purchase of a house. The owners of the house are also selling an adjoining piece of land, but Jonathan has not given Robert any instructions to purchase this land. However, Robert goes ahead in any case and purchases both the house and the land. When informed about this turn of events by the seller's agent, Jonathan makes the following statement: 'He is my agent after all and I'll just have to accept everything that he has done on my behalf.' Jonathan later attempts to withdraw from the sale involving the land.

Using previously decided cases and principles from the law of agency, advise the parties in each of the case studies outlined above.

2 a) The agency relationship is characterised by its contractual nature and, accordingly, both the principal and the agent have rights as well as duties.

Outline the rights and duties of the principal and the agent.

b) Mitchell owns a business which specialises in finding suitable tenants for residential properties in Glasgow and Edinburgh. One client has approached Mitchell and asked him to find a tenant to occupy her flat in Glasgow's West End. This client is being sent on a work placement by her employers to Canada and she will be out of the country for the next nine months. Mitchell has found a tenant for the property and the lease has been duly signed. A week later, however, Mitchell receives a telephone call from his client informing him that her work placement in Canada has fallen through and, consequently, she no longer wishes to lease the property out for the agreed nine-month period. Mitchell has to inform the tenant of this decision by his client and the tenant promptly sues Mitchell for breach of contract. To add insult to injury, Mitchell's client is now refusing to pay him for his efforts on her behalf.

What advice would you give Mitchell?

3 a) What is the difference between an agent's actual and ostensible authority?

b) Pamela, Laura and Lindsey-Anne are members of a partnership. According to the partnership agreement, Pamela and Laura have the authority to sign cheques on the firm's behalf. One day, Lindsey-Anne is purchasing a new computer and she uses a partnership cheque to pay for the goods. The firm does a great deal of business with the computer store and its manager is well aware that Lindsey-Anne is a partner in the firm. The bank later dishonours the cheque and the store sues the firm for payment.

What is the legal position?

4 a) What is the difference between an agent and a mandatary?

b) Michelle has just passed her driving test and she is looking for a suitably reliable second-hand car. Michelle does not feel confident enough to select a car without first consulting a more experienced driver. Michelle has a friend, Joe, who although not a qualified car mechanic does have some knowledge about cars. Joe is prepared to accompany her around various motor dealers and give her the benefit of his advice. After going round various dealerships, Michelle has seen a car that she really likes. Joe is also of the opinion that the vehicle is just right for Michelle and he encourages her to purchase it. Joe did notice that one of the car's doors had been repaired, but he did not think that this was an issue worth raising with the dealer. In fact,

Michelle specifically asked Joe whether he thought that the car had been ever been involved in an accident to which he replied no. Michelle went ahead and bought the car. Some weeks later, the car broke down and it turned out that the car was completely unroadworthy because it had been previously involved in a serious accident.

What can Michelle do?

5 a) The relationship of agency is said to be a fiduciary relationship.

Explain the concept of a fiduciary relationship and what are the consequences for the agent if he does anything to undermine this relationship?

b) Bob is a buyer for Jazz Clothing which runs a highly successful chain of gents clothing shops. Recently, Bob entered into contracts with a clothing manufacturer that Jazz has dealt with on numerous occasions. This manufacturer gave Jazz a ten per cent discount on all clothing purchased by Bob. Bob has not informed Jazz about these discounts and, with the aid of an accomplice in the finance office, he has managed to forge the invoices from the manufacturer. Bob now fully intends to keep the discounts given by the manufacturer to Jazz. Bob is also in the habit of accepting bribes from other clothes manufacturers who are keen to enter contracts with Jazz. Many of the products supplied by these manufacturers do not meet the highest standards of quality that customers of Jazz have come to expect and, recently, Jazz has experienced less than healthy sales figures. The Chief Executive decides to hold an investigation and Bob's misdeeds are uncovered in the process.

What are the legal consequences of Bob's actions?

6 Rapid changes in communications and technology have meant that agency of necessity is a concept that is no longer relevant in the modern world.

Do you agree with this statement?

7 a) In terms of Regulations 3 and 4 of the Commercial Agency Regulations 1993, describe the duties of an agent and his principal.

b) Lesley-Anne is a commercial agent for a Californian company which specialises in the production of sophisticated software packages. Lesley-Anne has customers in France, Germany, Italy and Spain. The principal's software packages are designed for a limited but high quality market in the banking and financial services sector. An agent selling such products must have the proper training, experience and expert knowledge of the qualities and performance of the principals' products so as to be able to sell them to potential customers. Lesley-Anne has acted for her principal for the last seven years. Over the last three years, her activities have resulted in profits of £20 million pounds. The commercial agency agreement states that Lesley-Anne is entitled to receive five per cent commission on all sales directly achieved as a result of her efforts. Lesley-Anne has managed to secure a number of new customers for her principal and, furthermore, she has increased the volume of business with the principal's existing customers. Recently, however, it has become obvious that the principal has decided to terminate the agency agreement. Lesley-Anne, therefore, seeks your advice in connection with the following matters:

i) Is the principal legally obliged to give her any notice if he decides to terminate the agreement?
ii) Will she be entitled to receive some sort of indemnity or compensation package from the principal which takes into account the fact that the she managed to increase the volume of business with existing customers and, furthermore, the new customers that she managed to acquire?
iii) What if the principal insists on enforcing the restrictive covenant in the agency agreement that prevents Lesley-Anne from accepting work with any business rival for a period of five years?
iv) What if the principal attempts to rely on a term in the agreement that states that Californian law will govern the contract and not Scots law?

Explain to Lesley-Anne where she stands legally.

8 Write brief notes on the following topics:
a) General and special agents
b) Disclosed and undisclosed principals
c) *Del credere* agents
d) independent contractors and employees

9 Describe the ways in which an agency relationship can be terminated.

10 To say that someone runs or is involved in a business in some way is not a particularly precise statement as Scots law recognises the existence of a variety of different business organisations.

What are the main the main types of business organisations recognised by Scots law?

11 Cameron, Howard and Iain have decided to form a partnership trading under the name of the League of Highland Gentlemen. They have recently purchased a hotel in the Highlands and they intend to offer guests traditional Highland hospitality and outdoor pursuits (hunting, shooting and fishing). The three partners are in complete ignorance of the legal requirements for setting up this kind of business. They do not wish to leave anything important out of their partnership agreement. Fortunately, Cameron, Howard and Iain are in agreement about the most important aspects of the business. Each of the three will have to contribute the same amount of capital to the firm's account. Furthermore, they have agreed that each partner will take part in the day-to-day running of the firm's affairs. They are all agreed that the death or insanity of a member of the firm would not necessarily mean that the partnership should be dissolved. They also have stated that the firm should continue to trade if one of the partners chooses to leave. Finally, all three partners are agreed that the business should run for an initial period of five years on the condition that the agreement will be reviewed at the end of this period.

Cameron, Howard and Iain have appointed you as the firm's solicitor and they wish your guidance in respect of the following issues:
a) the personal liability of each partner to the firm's creditors should the business run up debts or should it fail completely;
b) the ability of each partner to bind the firm into contracts with third parties;
c) the introduction of new partners to the firm;
d) the ability of the partners to participate in other business ventures;
e) the firm's liability for delicts committed by one of the partners;
f) the termination of the partnership agreement; and
g) the way in which the partners make decisions.

Advise Cameron, Howard and Iain.

12 Eileen, John and Barry are members of a partnership. They wish to secure an injection of capital to expand the business. They are not keen, however, to admit another partner to the firm as they are perfectly happy with the current set-up. They are perfectly aware that, unlike a company limited by shares, their investment opportunities are somewhat restricted. Barry is vaguely aware that the law permits a partnership to have silent or sleeping partners, but he is unsure what this actually means in practice.

What are silent or sleeping partners and how does this arrangement work in practice?

13 On 6 April 2001, the Limited Liability Partnerships Act 2000 came into force in the United Kingdom.

As a result of this legislation, a new type of corporate body is recognised by Scots law.

What is a limited liability partnership and what would be the point of setting one up?

14 Aaron is engaged in the promotion of a new company (to be incorporated on 31 December) and he seeks your advice in relation to a number of issues, namely, his legal status, his rights and his duties as a promoter.

What advice would you give Aaron?

15 The concept of separate corporate personality is a very important legal rule, but situations will arise when the courts are prepared to ignore it.

Outline the situations where a court will refuse to recognise the separate legal personality of a company.

16 **a)** What does the Companies Act 1985 have to say about the legal relationship between the various company members *and* the relationship between the members and the company itself?

b) Look at the following situations carefully:

i) Stephanie is a large shareholder in a newly formed company. The company's Articles of Association appointed Stephanie to the first Board of Directors. Stephanie, however, does not attend regularly Board meetings regularly and a majority of her fellow Directors decide to remove her from her position as a Director. Stephanie decides to sue the company.

ii) Emma is a member of a plc. The company has recently updated its previous paper records containing all shareholder details to a computerised system. During the data transfer, the company's employees wrongly entered details about the extent of Emma's shareholding. The effect of this mistake is that Emma is credited with a much smaller shareholding than is actually the case. Emma is not best pleased about this and, with a group of her fellow disgruntled shareholders who are also affected by this error, they lodge a class action at the Court of Session. However, there is a provision in the company's Articles of Association which states that all disputes between members and the company must be referred to independent arbitration.

iii) Gillian is a shareholder in a small, privately owned family company. Recently, she has not been getting on with her two uncles, who are the other shareholders in the company. Gillian now wishes to sell her shareholding in the company and move on. She is prevented, however, from selling her shares to an outsider by reason of the company's Articles of Association. The Articles state that, if a member wishes to leave the company, he or she must offer the shares to the existing shareholders who will then give the seller a fair price for the shares. Gillian's uncles are refusing to purchase her shares and things have become so unpleasant that she is at a loss what to do next.

iv) Fiona is the Chief Executive of what has been a very successful company. Over the years, shareholders in the company have been paid regular dividends. This year, however, Fiona will have to address the shareholders at the company's Annual General Meeting and inform them that they will be receiving debentures as an alternative to the payment of dividends. The company has made some bad financial decisions and it is necessary to take drastic steps to get the business back on even keel – even if this means upsetting the shareholders. Predictably, the shareholders are furious about this decision and they decide to take legal action against the company.

Advise the parties.

17 **a)** List and describe the six main clauses that form part of a company's Memorandum of Association.

b) Donna is the Chief Executive and a member of the Board of Directors of a company called Ashbury Engineering Services

plc. The company specialises in building hulls to be used in the construction of on-off passenger and car ferries. One of Ashbury's major customers, Tartan Transport Ltd, is a ferry operator which runs services between the various Hebridean Islands. Tartan Transport has approached Ashbury with a request to build four new ferries. Ashbury has never built a complete ferry before and the company's objects clause would appear to rule out this particular activity, but this is a very valuable project. Donna persuades her fellow Directors, despite a few reservations on their part, to enter into a contract with Tartan Transport. Problems begin to emerge for Ashbury when it turns out the design of the ferries is substandard. Tartan Transport has raised an action for substantial damages against Ashbury because one of the ferries sank off the island of Lewis during its maiden voyage and it was only a miracle that no one was killed. Donna and her fellow Directors now attempt to avoid their liability to Tartan Transport by relying on Ashbury's objects clause.

Answer the following questions:
i) Will Ashbury be able to escape its liability to Tartan Transport?
ii) What are the consequences for Donna and her fellow Directors?

18 What are the major differences between a company with the word 'limited' after its name and a company with the words 'public limited company' in its title?

CHAPTER 6

INTRODUCTION TO THE LAW OF EMPLOYMENT PART 1

Introduction

During the nineteenth century, the terms and conditions which made up the contract of employment were almost wholly determined by negotiations carried out between the employer and the employee. In theory, therefore, it was up to the parties to the agreement to decide which terms and conditions would form part and parcel of the contract. Very often, employment contracts were not even in writing and it is still a common misconception that such contracts have to be in writing and witnessed. Historically, the employer was often in the stronger position and he could dictate the terms of the employment contract to the employee. It was for this reason that the employment relationship was often characterised in terms of master and servant.

> ### This chapter will cover the following areas:
> - The contract of employment -
> - Dismissal -

The contract of employment

From the beginning of the twentieth century, the terms of the contract of employment became increasingly subject to parliamentary intervention and employers now have to be aware of the effects of such major pieces of legislation as the:

- Equal Pay Act 1970
- Health and Safety at Work Act 1974
- Sex Discrimination Act 1975
- Race Relations Act 1976
- Disability Discrimination Act 1995
- National Minimum Wage Act 1998
- Working Time Regulations 1998
- Employment Relations Act 1999
- Employment Act 2002

The European Union is also a very important source of contractual terms and conditions. As we shall see in Chapter 7, some of the Articles of the Treaty of Rome

(Article 141) and Directives (the Equal Treatment Directive 76/207/EEC) have been used to imply terms relating to equal pay directly into the employee's contract. Admittedly, European Union law will be mostly implemented by the Westminster Parliament, but nonetheless an employer will have to be aware of the numerous, ongoing developments in employment policy at the European level.

The contract of employment can also be influenced by the following sources:

- The common law rights and duties of the parties
- Collective agreements
- The written statement of terms and particulars of employment issued by the employer
- Handbooks, codes of practice and other documents issued by the employer

 Key point: During the twentieth century, it became increasingly common for the Westminster parliament to pass legislation that had a direct influence on the main terms and conditions of the employment contract, although statute law is not the only source of the rules that govern the employment relationship.

The importance of the contract of employment

Section 230(5) of the Employment Rights Act 1996 defines the terms 'employee' and 'contract of employment' in the following ways:

- 'Employee' means an individual who has entered into or works under (or, where the employment has ceased, worked under) a contract of employment

- 'Contract of employment' means a contract of service or apprenticeship, whether express or implied, and (if it is express) whether oral or in writing

If you are an employee i.e. you have a contract of service you are theoretically in a much better position than someone who has a contract for services i.e. an independent contractor. This is an absolutely critical distinction in UK employment law and one that we shall return to time and time again in this particular area.

Why should this distinction matter?

If you are an employee the law gives you greater protection and more benefits that you would not receive if you were merely an independent contractor for services. The rights that an employee is entitled to claim can be highly significant:

- Statutory protection against unfair dismissal (as long as they can show that they have the appropriate length of service or meet certain requirements)
- Entitlement to compensation if they are made redundant if certain conditions are met
- A statutory right to a minimum period of notice of termination of their employment contracts
- Rights to maternity pay and leave
- Rights to paid paternity
- The right to time-off for public duties

- ◆ The right to statutory sick pay
- ◆ Access to important social security and welfare benefits

 Key point: An individual who has a contract of service (i.e. is an employee) will enjoy greater employment rights than someone who has a contract for services (i.e. is an independent contractor).

It is worth emphasising that those individuals who work as independent contractors (under a contract for service) are highly unlikely to receive any of these benefits. So, it follows that if a particular contract comes to an end, an independent contractor, for example, will not be entitled to a redundancy payment. However, employers should be aware that other classes of people in the workforce, known by the catch-all term 'worker', have been given rights under a variety of statutes. Workers, therefore, benefit from and are protected by provisions in the major anti-discrimination laws such as the Sex Discrimination Act 1975 and in more recent legislation such as the Working Time Regulations 1998, the Part-time Workers Regulations 2000, the Employment Equality (Sexual Orientation) Regulations 2003 and the Employment Equality (Religion or Belief) Regulations 2003.

Workers can be but are not necessarily employees and the term will include a person who undertakes to perform personally any work or services for another party to the contract. Some lawyers have gone as far as to argue that the traditional distinction between employees and independent contractors is becomingly increasingly irrelevant. This is an oversimplification and many of the key employment rights recognised by United Kingdom employment law are really only available to employees. However, it is not always easy to distinguish between employees and independent contractors and employers will have to tread particularly carefully in this area.

 Key point: The concept of a worker does not merely include those individuals who would be traditionally regarded as employees – it also covers individuals who would normally be classified as independent contractors for services.

Distinguishing between employees and independent contractors

With some difficulty is the probably the most honest answer! The legal system has developed a number of different tests in an attempt to determine whether someone works under a contract of service or a contract for services. However, the British courts have not always applied these tests in a way that makes sense to the lay person and even lawyers.

The control test

In the nineteenth century, it was relatively easy to determine whether someone was an employee. The courts had developed what was known as the 'control test'. If the employer could effectively control what tasks a worker did and how s/he carried them out, then it was highly likely that the worker in question was an employee/servant (see **Mersey Docks and Harbour Board *v* Coggins & Griffith (Liverpool) Ltd (1947)**). The control test was a relatively effective device for societies that were not particularly advanced economically or technologically.

Imagine nowadays an employer dictating how a job is to be carried out to a highly skilled and educated computer software engineer. Clearly the control test will largely be redundant for many modern workers.

There were also other problems with the control test. For instance, what if you have a situation where a worker is sent by his/her employer to work at another location which the employer has no control over? Who is responsible for the worker? The legal position is that the employer continues to be responsible for the worker despite the fact that the worker is no longer on the employer's premises.

The economic reality test

In response to the obvious limitations of the control test, the courts developed what was to become known as the 'economic reality test'. This test is more concerned with the overall reality of the working relationship rather than merely being swayed by labels. Just because someone states that a contract is one of service does not mean that this is in fact the case. It has often been said that a judge knows a contract of employment when he sees one. Many different factors will be taken into account by a judge in determining whether someone is an employee or an independent contractor. The following factors will be given due consideration by the courts to determine what kind of working relationship exists:

- ◆ How much control does the employer exercise over the worker?
- ◆ Does the worker provide his/her own equipment or does the employer provide this?
- ◆ Can the worker take the important decision of hiring additional workers to assist him/her in the completion of the task?
- ◆ Will the worker be exposed to some degree of personal financial risk if s/he agrees to undertake the task on behalf of the employer?
- ◆ Will the worker be able to make a personal profit from the work undertaken?
- ◆ What label have the parties attached to the relationship (although this in itself is rarely conclusive)?
- ◆ Does the employer deduct income tax and national insurance contributions from the worker's salary?
- ◆ Is the worker duty-bound to accept work as and when the employer makes it available?
- ◆ What if the parties have genuinely attempted to change the status of their relationship?

This area of the law is fraught with difficulties and can be extremely confusing. Often the courts will come to completely different conclusions about the status of a relationship in what appears to be very similar circumstances. An example of the economic reality test in action can be seen below:

 Ready Mixed Concrete (South East) Ltd *v* Minister of Pensions (1968) the dispute centred around the payment of national insurance contributions. Employers must pay national contributions in respect of their employees, but the issue in this case was whether or not an individual could be said to be an employee or an independent contractor.

A cement lorry driver carried out work for Ready Mixed Concrete. The contract between the driver and the company stated that the driver had self-employed status. The contract also imposed a duty on the driver to provide a vehicle for his work (he did so by means of a hire purchase agreement whereby the company provided the finance in order for him to purchase the vehicle). The vehicle had to be painted in the company's colours and the driver had to wear a company uniform and to drive the vehicle on company business for the maximum number of hours that the law permitted. The driver had to follow orders from the company – in this respect as if he was acting as an employee of the company. The driver also received a payment for his services which was calculated on the basis of each mile that he drove in his vehicle. The contract did permit the driver, however, to employ another driver when he was ill, when he was on holiday and when he was not driving on company business.

Held: the driver was an independent contractor for services. The really compelling fact that determined the court's decision was that the driver was allowed to employ someone else to drive the vehicle in his absence. Such a power of appointment is not generally exercised by employees. The court attempted to lay down useful guidelines which could be used to decide whether an individual was an employee or an independent contractor. It is likely that someone will be an employee if the following three conditions are met:

1   He agrees to supply work and skills to an employer in return for payment.

2   He agrees to be subject to the employer's control (either expressly or impliedly).

3   The agreement between the parties must be a contract of employment.

An individual is less likely to be an employee in the following circumstances:

1   He is expected to pay for his own materials and to provide his own equipment in order to complete a job.

2   An individual who is permitted to hire his own staff to help out in a job.

3   An individual who is responsible for his own tax and national insurance arrangements.

The organisation or integration test

Another test that has been used by the courts is to ask the question whether a worker is part of the employer's organisation (i.e. he is fully integrated) or whether he is in 'business on his own account'. In order to meet the requirement of being in 'business on his own account', a worker will have to show, amongst other things, that he provided his own equipment, is exposed to financial risk, has hired his own staff, undertakes managerial and administrative jobs, has built up a client base and has a range of fees that he will charge clients for his services. Although this test can be very useful, it does not replace either the control test or the economic reality test.

 Hall _v_ Lorimer (1992) there was a tax dispute surrounding the employment status of the defender who worked as a freelance television technician. If the defender was classified as an employee for taxation purposes, he would be liable to pay more to the Inland Revenue. In order to prove that the defender was an employee, the Inland Revenue relied on the control test by arguing that this particular individual had to follow the orders of the television companies for whom he worked.

Held: by the Court of Appeal that the defender was not in business on his own account and should, therefore, be regarded as an employee. The mere fact that someone carries out a job where a higher level of skill or technical expertise is required does not mean that he should automatically be regarded as an independent contractor for services. The Court of Appeal also made the point that the labels used by the parties to a contract will not always be decisive.

 Key point: The courts have developed a number of different tests in an attempt to determine whether someone works under a contract of service or a contract for services, for example, the control test, the economic reality test and the organisation test.

Casual and atypical workers

One area of the law that causes particular difficulty for employers are contracts involving the use of casual and atypical workers. Casual and atypical workers are being increasingly used by employers and one of the main concerns here is whether these individuals should be given the benefit of employment rights. Usually, the employment status of such workers is resolved by asking a relatively simple question i.e. when the employer offers such an individual work is s/he bound to carry out the work for the employer? If the answer is in the positive, then the worker is likely to be an employee and not an independent contractor for services.

In more recent times, the courts have also tended to stress the importance of a mutuality of obligation between an employer and employee. In other words, the employee is under a duty to accept work when the employer requires his services.

 Carmichael *v* National Power plc (2000) two women, Carmichael and Leese, were employed by National Power for the purpose of taking visitors on a guided tour around a power station. National Power made it quite clear that the work was on a casual basis and the women would be employed as and when their services were required. There was no fixed pattern of working hours and the women could be called upon at any time during the day to come into work in order to conduct the guided tours for National Power. When they were first appointed, both women were more than happy to be employed on a casual basis. They did receive some training in how to conduct the tours and they were expected to wear a uniform when working and to follow National Power's first aid policy. Problems arose, however, when both women claimed that National Power was in breach of its obligation to provide them with a written statement of terms and particulars of employment as required under Section 1 of the Employment Rights Act 1996. It should be remembered that only individuals who have a contract of service (employees) are entitled to receive a written statement from the employer. National Power denied that both women were employees. One of the compelling arguments that the House of Lords considered was that Carmichael and Leese were not obliged to accept work when it was offered to them. On quite a number of occasions, both had turned down offers of work because they were either unavailable or simply not interested. There was never any question of National Power taking disciplinary action against the women on these occasions when they failed to turn up to work. There was no mutuality of obligation between the parties.

Held: by the House of Lords that the parties had never intended to create a contract of employment. Carmichael and Leese both performed work for National Power under a contract for services. They were, therefore, not entitled to a written statement as they were not employees of National Power.

The point has been well made in **McMeechan *v* Secretary State for Employment (1997)** that the label placed on a relationship between the parties is not always decisive. After analysing the content of the contract at the centre of the case, the English Court of Appeal came to the view that its title 'Conditions of Service' (Temporary Self-Employed Workers) was not a true reflection of the nature of the contractual relationship. Upon closer examination, it became apparent that, despite the label, this agreement was not a contract for services at all, it ought to be regarded as an employment contract.

 Key point: Casual or atypical workers can be problematic category when it comes to distinguishing between those individuals who have a contract of service and those who have a contract for services.

Vicarious liability

Vicarious liability can arise where there is a contract of service meaning that the employer may be vicariously liable for the delicts or negligence of an employee. This means that the employee can be liable for harm that he did not directly cause. An employer can only be liable for the negligent acts of an employee not an independent contractor. Vicarious liability of the employer is another area where it is very important to distinguish between an employee and an independent contractor.

For an employer to be vicariously liable, the harm must have been caused by the employee while within the scope of his employment. The courts will often look to see whether or not the employee was acting within the scope of his employment and this can be a difficult point to establish.

Generally, if the employee was acting for the purpose, protection or enhancement of the employer's business and was not using his employer's time for his own purposes then the employer would be held vicariously liable if the employee committed a delict.

Furthermore, an employer may be vicariously liable for the acts of an employee even if the employee:

◆ Did what he was employed to do but carrried out these functions in a negligent or unauthorised way
◆ Was negligent whilst doing something he was not authorised to do
◆ Committed the act outwith working hours
◆ Commits an assault in the course of the employment but only with a contract of service

Century Insurance Co v Northern Ireland Transport Board (1942) the driver of a petrol tanker negligently discarded a lighted match that he had used to light a cigarette. This act was carried out while he was standing in a petrol station just as the petrol from the tanker was being unloaded. The match landed on flammable material and this caused a fire to start which spread to the tanker. The driver attempted to drive the burning vehicle from the petrol station into the street. Unfortunately, the vehicle exploded causing damage to other vehicles and houses in the street. The driver's employers attempted to make their losses by claiming their insurance policy, but the insurers argued that the driver was not actually working at the time when his negligence caused the accident. It was agreed that the driver had struck the match for his own purposes. The driver, however, had been standing by while the petrol was being unloaded from his vehicle and, during this process, he was not actually being called upon to drive. Therefore, the insurers stated he was not within the scope of his employment.

Held: by the House of Lords that the driver was within the scope of his employment and, consequently, his employers were vicariously liable for his actions. The driver was expected to supervise the unloading of his vehicle and this meant that he was still acting within his employment. The insurers had to pay out to the driver's employers. The Lord Chancellor made a very strong statement to the effect that 'they also serve who only stand and wait.' This statement can be taken to mean that there will be periods in any job where the individual employee may not actually be working strictly speaking, but he will still be considered to be within the scope of his employment. In this particular case, the employee may not have been driving, but he was still supposed to be acting in his own employers' interests.

Conway v George Wimpey & Co (1951) a driver, against the express orders of his employer, gave a lift to an individual who was not a fellow employee. An accident occurred and the passenger was injured as a result of this. The passenger sued the employer for damages.

Held: the employer was not vicariously liable to the victim because the driver could not be said to be promoting his employer's interests by giving this individual a lift. The employer was not benefiting from the driver's decision to give a lift to a third party.

Rose v Plenty (1976) the employers had a very clear policy whereby children were not allowed to travel on milk floats. One of the milkmen, in clear defiance of this policy, allowed a young boy to travel on his milk float in order to help him with his rounds. Due to the milkman's negligent driving, the boy was injured.

Held: this case differed from **Conway v George Wimpey & Co** in that the employers were benefiting from the assistance that the victim had provided to the milkman. There was no question that the milkman was doing anything other than acting within his employment.

Williams v Hemphill (1966) a lorry driver had been instructed by his employer to pick up a group of Boys Brigade members who were camping at Benderloch near Oban. The driver was supposed to take the boys directly back to Glasgow. He was persuaded by some of the boys, however, to make a detour on the way home to Glasgow. The boys wanted him to stop at a camp for Girl Guides. An accident occurred due to the driver's negligence and some of the boys were injured. The father of one of the boys who had not asked the driver to make the detour raised an action on the grounds of the driver's negligence.

Held: by the House of Lords that the driver, although acting in defiance of his orders, was still within the scope of his employment and, consequently, his employer was vicariously liable for his negligent actions. The House of Lords chose not to answer the question of what would have happened if the parents of the boys who had asked the driver to make the detour had tried to sue the employer.

 Key point: Vicarious liability means that an employer can be liable to third parties for the negligent acts that were committed by one of his employees, as long as the act complained of was committed within the scope of employment.

Joint and several liability

If an employer falls foul of vicarious liability, he can sue the employee who committed the delict and, in this way, he may be able to get back some or all of the damages that he has had to pay out to the victim. Vicarious liability means that an employer and an employee are both jointly and severally liable for the negligent acts or omissions of the employee that result in harm being caused to third parties. The negligence of the employee may also provide the employer with a good reason to dismiss him summarily on the ground of gross misconduct.

 Lister *v* Romford Ice and Cold Storage (1957) a lorry driver drove his vehicle negligently and injured his father who was also a fellow employee. The father sued his employer on the grounds of vicarious liability and was awarded damages. These damages were paid to the father by the employer's insurers. At the insistence of the insurers, the employer then sued the lorry driver for failing to drive safely (an implied term of his employment contract).

Held: by the House of Lords that the employer was entitled to regain the damages from the lorry driver that it had paid to his father.

In practice, insurers tend not to insist that the employer use **Lister** in order to sue negligent employees. **Lister** has been criticised because employers find it much easier to obtain insurance to cover themselves against the negligent acts or omissions of their employees.

 Key point: When vicarious liability is established, both the employer and the employee will be jointly and severally liable to the innocent third party.

Independent contractors (or employment *pro hac vice*)

Vicarious liability only becomes an issue when a contract of service exists. Generally speaking, individuals are not responsible for the negligent actions of an independent contractor (an individual acting under a contract for services).

Mersey Docks and Harbour Board *v* **Coggins & Griffith (Liverpool) Ltd (1947)** A, a mobile crane driver, was employed by B who sent him out to do a job for C. The contract between B and C contained a term which stated that A was to be regarded as C's employee for the duration of the job. Despite this contractual term, B, however, would continue to pay A's wages and had the power to dismiss him. A was negligent whilst operating the crane and someone was injured. The question then arose as to which party – either B or C – should be sued by the victim of A's negligence?

Held: by the House of Lords that B was to be regarded as A's employer. At no time could C be regarded as having control over A's activities. It was quite clear from the evidence, that A would have resented and resisted any attempt by C to tell him how to do his job.

The House of Lords laid down three rules to resolve similar issues that might arise in future cases:

1   The reality behind the contractual terms agreed between two potential employers will have to be investigated. These terms should not necessarily be taken at face value.

2   The permanent employer will usually be presumed to bear responsibility for any of his employee's negligent acts, unless he can show that this should not be the case.

3   In situations where employees are hired out, it will often be presumed that the hirer is the employer. If a skilled employee brings equipment to the job, the situation becomes more complex because the hirer may not be in a position to dictate how the job should be carried out. In other words, the employee will enjoy considerable freedom from interference and he will basically decide how the job is to be carried out. A hirer can become vicariously liable if it was proved that he told the employee how to carry out the job.

The hirer will, however, become responsible for the activities of an independent contractor if he is aware that this individual is not a reasonably competent member of his trade or profession. In other words, it is likely that the contractor will act negligently.

 Key point: Usually, employers are not liable to third parties for the negligent actions of an independent contractor.

The nature of the contract of employment

Generally speaking, in Scotland, employment contracts do not have to be in written form and witnessed. It is quite legitimate to have an employment contract which is completely verbal in nature. Employment contracts may even be implied from the behaviour of the parties i.e. it is perfectly obvious to all and sundry that an employment relationship exists between two individuals. However, it is probably advisable to have some written proof concerning employment contracts as this can be used to determine the extent of the rights and the duties of the parties to the agreement in the event of a dispute.

The ordinary rules about offer and acceptance which govern the law of contract which were discussed in Chapter 2 are particularly relevant in this area of the law.

However, under Section 1 of the Employment Rights Act 1996, employees must be issued with a written statement of the terms and particulars of their contract of employment. It should be noted that this statement is not the contract of employment. Merely, it provides general information about the nature of the relationship and the extent of the main provisions of the agreement. Such a statement must be issued to the employee within two months of the start of the employment contract. If the employer does not give the employee a copy of a written statement of terms and particulars, the employee can take him to an Employment Tribunal for the purpose of forcing him to issue such a statement. However, this is generally an unusual course of action on the part of the employee.

Under Section 38 of the Employment Act 2002, an employer who neglects to issue an employee with a written statement may be ordered by an Employment Tribunal to pay an employee up to four weeks' wages in respect of any failure to issue the statement. Any employee who is dismissed by the employer because he requested a written statement will have the right to claim unfair dismissal regardless of the length of service he has with the employer. Any such dismissal will be regarded as automatically unfair.

 Key point: An employment contract does not have to be in writing, but the employer must issue an employee with a written statement of the main terms and conditions of employment within two months of the commencement of his employment.

Terms and conditions of employment

The terms and conditions of employment should contain the following:

1 The employer's name

2 The employee's name

3 The date of commencement of employment and the period of any continuous employment

4 Wages/salary details

5 Details of working hours

6 Holiday entitlement/pay and entitlement to accrued holiday pay upon termination of the employment contract

7 Entitlement to sick pay

8 Pensionable service

9 Notice requirements

10 Job title or brief description of the job

11 Whether the job is permanent or for a fixed-term duration

12 The location(s) of the employee's place of work

13 Collective agreements and how they affect the employment contract

14 If the employee has to work outside the UK for more than a month, the length of such time, the currency in which wages are to be paid, details of any additional payments and benefits and terms about return to the UK

15 Details of the employer's disciplinary code or reference to a document containing the code to which the employee can readily access

As you can see, the written statement covers a wide range of issues. To reiterate, such a statement must be provided to the employee within two months of the commencement of employment. The statement may be given to the employee by instalments, but a complete statement must be in the employee's possession within the two month deadline.

If the employer and the employee decide to alter any terms and conditions of employment, a new written statement must be issued no later than one month after the changes have been introduced.

The legal status of the written statement

The written statement is not a contract of employment. However, there is nothing to stop the employer and the employee adopting the terms of the statement as the contract of employment. When the employer issues the employee with the statement and asks the employee to sign his copy and return it to the personnel department, the employee can make it clear that he is simply acknowledging receipt of the statement. This would indicate to the employer and to an Employment Tribunal, in the event of a future dispute, that the employee has not accepted some or all of the terms contained in the written statement. It will then be for the Employment Tribunal to determine what terms and conditions are part of the employment contract.

 Key point: The statement of terms and conditions of employment should not be regarded as the employment contract or a substitute for it.

Collective agreements

Sometimes, employers will prefer to have a situation where terms and conditions of employment can be negotiated collectively with a large number of employees rather than by individual negotiations. Such arrangements are known as 'collective agreements'.

This arrangement allows groups of workers to be employed on identical or fairly similar terms and conditions of employment. Such agreements are usually found in workplaces where there is a recognised trade union which can negotiate with the employer.

It is important to realise that such agreements do not bind the employer and the trade union. It is important to stress that the trade union is not acting as an agent of the employees and, therefore, any agreement negotiated by the trade union with the employer is not legally enforceable against either the employer or the employees. If these agreements are to be enforceable, they must be made part of the employees' contracts of employment. This means that when changes are made to employees' contracts as a result of negotiations under the collective agreement, they will be automatically incorporated into the employees' contracts.

It is probably advisable for the employer to include an express provision in a contract of employment which mentions the collective agreement and the results of any negotiations concluded under such an agreement i.e. the fact that changes to contracts of employment automatically take effect upon the successful conclusion of negotiations between the employer and the trade union.

 City of Edinburgh Council *v* Brown (1999) IRLR 208 the Council decided, without consultation, to change its regrading policy. Brown argued that this change of Council policy was in breach of the collective agreement negotiated by his trade union and the Council. Furthermore, Brown argued this agreement was part of his employment contract having been directly incorporated into the contract.

Held: by the Employment Appeal Tribunal that the collective agreement, which covered issues such as the regrading of posts within the Council, could not be changed unilaterally by the employer as it had been directly incorporated into the employees' contracts. The employees had to agree to this change in their terms and conditions of employment – something that they were unwilling to allow. The Employment Appeal Tribunal also made the point that there are no special rules governing the incorporation of collective agreements into employment contracts.

Similarly in **John Anderson *v* Pringle of Scotland (1998) IRLR 64**, the employer could not depart from its redundancy policy which formed part of a collective agreement that had been incorporated into the employees' contracts.

 Key point: In order for collective agreements to be enforceable, they must be incorporated into the employee's contract of employment.

Handbooks, codes of conduct and other documents

When a new employee is appointed to a post within the organisation, the employer may issue a handbook or other documents which govern such matters as dress codes, equal opportunities policy, disciplinary codes and internal grievance procedures. These handbooks, codes or documents are often referred to by informal names such as 'the blue book' or 'the red book'. If the employer wishes these extra-contractual sources to be binding on the employee, there should be a term in the employment contract which expressly incorporates them into the employment contract.

Freedom of contract?

It may now be said that true freedom of contract hardly exists at all as far as the employer is concerned. This doctrine is based on the idea that the parties are free to choose the terms and conditions which will be contained in the final version of the employment contract. The idea of freedom of contract also presupposes that genuine negotiations have taken place between the parties. It is debatable whether many employees ever really enjoyed the notion (let alone the practice) of freedom of contract. In any case, parliament has intervened in so many ways that the employer has lost the right to dictate some of the most important terms of the contract.

The Working Time Regulations 1998 guarantee all workers (there are exceptions) the right not to be forced to work more than 48 hours per week. The Regulations also force the employer to give workers regular breaks and they also regulate the amount of hours that the worker can be forced to work in any one day. There is special protection for younger workers regarding breaks and the maximum daily hours that they are permitted to work.

The National Minimum Wage Act 1998 now means that workers must receive a basic hourly wage depending on their age. Workers aged between 18 and 21 years or below will receive £3.80 per hour (the development rate, rising to £4.10 from 1 October 2004). Workers aged over 22 years will receive £4.50 per hour, rising to £4.85 from 1 October 2004. Workers aged 22 years who are in the first six months of a new job with a new employer and receiving accredited training can be paid the development rate. The scheme does not apply to those workers who are under 18 years of age.

Female workers who give birth to a child are entitled to take 26 weeks' paid maternity leave. This entitlement applies to all female employees who wish to take maternity leave regardless of their length of service. This period of leave is referred to as ordinary maternity leave. Female workers with more than one year's continuous service are entitled to take another 26 weeks' maternity leave on an unpaid basis. This period of further leave is referred to as additional maternity leave. The employer cannot penalise a female worker who takes maternity leave by refusing to allow her to return to work when the period of leave is at an end and the employer cannot treat a female employee less favourably for exercising her statutory maternity rights. The law in this area is complicated because it is contained in several different pieces of legislation:

- The Employment Rights Act 1996
- The Employment Relations Act 1999
- The Maternity and Parental Leave etc. Regulations
- The Maternity and Parental Leave (Amendment) Regulations 2001
- The Maternity and Parental Leave (Amendment) Regulations 2002
- The Employment Act 2002

New paternity rules have come into force since 6 April 2003. New fathers who qualify under the rules of the scheme are now entitled to take two weeks' paid paternity leave. The rules are, again, complicated and are contained in several pieces of legislation:

- The Employment Rights Act 1996
- The Employment Act 2002
- The Paternity and Adoption Leave Regulations 2002
- The Statutory Adoption Pay and the Statutory Paternity Pay (General) Regulations 2002

There are also statutory rights giving parents who adopt children an entitlement to paid leave and there are also general statutory rights to time off for dependents.

 Key point: As a result of parliamentary intervention, the doctrine of freedom of contract has become increasingly irrelevant.

The rights and duties of the parties to a contract of employment

As with any contract of employment, the parties have rights, but they also have duties. One party's duties should, of course, be viewed as the other party's rights under the contract. We will begin by looking at the employer's duties under the contract of employment. These include:

- To pay wages
- To provide work
- To indemnify his employees
- To treat employees with trust and respect
- To take reasonable care for the safety of employees

The employer's duty to pay wages and to provide work

In return for performing his duties under the employment contract, the employee is entitled to be paid by the employer. It is highly debatable whether the employer has a duty to provide work for the employee. Implying a general duty that the employer must provide work would cause all sorts of practical and economic difficulties. In **Turner v Sawdon & Co (1901)** it was stated that an employer is under a duty to pay wages in return for the employee's services. The employee, however, will be in no position to complain in situations where the employer pays wages, but does not provide any work for the employee to carry out.

This point was re-emphasised in **Collier v Sunday Referee Publishing Co Ltd (1940)** with the remark that 'provided I pay my cook her wages regularly, she cannot complain if I take any or all of my meals out'.

Failure by the employer to pay the agreed wages is a material breach of the contract of employment. The Employment Rights Act 1996 states that the employer must not make any unauthorised deductions from the wages of any worker employed by him or receive any payments unless:

- The deduction is authorised by a statutory provision, for example, PAYE
- The deduction is authorised in the employee's contract, for example, pensions contributions
- The worker has agreed to the deduction in writing in advance

 Key point: The employer may have a duty to pay wages, but it is doubtful whether the employer has a duty to provide work.

The employer's duty to indemnify his employees

An employer will have a duty to indemnify or compensate an employee who has incurred expenses while properly carrying out his duties under the employment contract.

The employer's duty to treat his employees with trust and respect

This is a duty which has taken on more importance in recent years. If the employer fails to treat an employee with trust and respect and this may lead to the complete breakdown of the employment relationship. In such a situation, an employee may feel that he can no longer remain in employment and the only option is to resign. An employee who is forced to resign in such circumstances may be able to argue that he was constructively dismissed by the employer's conduct and this would give rise to a claim for unfair dismissal.

 TSB Bank PLC v Harris (2000) IRLR 157 Harris was employed by TSB. She was looking for new employment with another employer and she put down on her application form that TSB were her current employers. TSB informed Harris' prospective employers that a large number of customers had made complaints about her conduct. The prospective employers naturally refused to go further with Harris' application. Significantly, TSB had completely failed to bring these complaints to the attention of Harris. Harris later discovered that she had been the subject of customer complaints and this had led to her failing to secure new employment. Harris, of course, had been denied the right of natural justice to defend herself against these customer complaints. Given the present circumstances, Harris felt that her employer had lost all trust and confidence in her. In response, Harris, therefore, resigned and brought a claim of constructive dismissal against her employer.

Held: by the Employment Tribunal and the Employment Appeal Tribunal that the employer had failed in its duty to demonstrate trust and confidence in Harris as an employee. Harris had been constructively dismissed and, even more damaging from Harris' point of view, the employer's conduct had made it impossible or very difficult for her to pursue a career in the financial services industry where personal integrity is vitally important.

An employer who breaches the duty of trust and confidence by running his business in a corrupt and dishonest manner and this conduct later destroys or seriously damages an employee's future career prospects may have to pay stigma damages to the employee.

 Malik v BCCI SA (1997) IRLR 462 the House of Lords awarded stigma damages to an employee who found it impossible to secure employment because the bank (BCCI) that he had previously worked for had become internationally notorious for its corrupt and dishonest business practices.

Generally, the employer owes a duty of care not to damage the employee's future career prospects.

 Spring v Guardian Royal Assurance PLC (1994) Guardian Royal Assurance provided a negligent reference for an ex-employee to his new employer. The reference claimed that the ex-employee had been in the habit of behaving fraudulently while in the course of his employment. The ex-employee failed to secure the post with the new employer. However, the reference was negligent – the ex-employee had been incompetent, but not fraudulent. The ex-employee sued Guardian Royal for breach of its duty of care.

Held: by the House of Lords that Guardian Royal owed the pursuer a duty of care and it was foreseeable that he would suffer harm as a result of the negligent reference.

The importance of the employer providing an honest, but accurate and fair reference for the employee as part of the duty of trust and confidence was re-emphasised by the English Court of Appeal in **Bartholomew v London Borough of Hackney (1999) IRLR 246**.

 Key point: A failure by the employer to treat an employee with trust and confidence may lead to the complete breakdown of the employment relationship.

To take reasonable care for the safety of employees

The employer's contractual duties as regards the safety of employees were spelled out in the following decision by the House of Lords:

 Wilson's and Clyde Coal Ltd v English (1938) English had been employed as a miner. He was injured as a result of an accident at work. An action was raised against the employer for the injuries sustained by English. The employer attempted to avoid liability for the injuries by blaming it on the negligence of one of his normally competent mining managers.

Held: by the House of Lords that an employer owed an employee a personal duty of care. In this situation, the employer had failed to take reasonable care for the safety of the employee and, therefore, it was liable for his injuries.

As a result of **Wilson's and Clyde Coal Ltd v English (1938)**, the House of Lords imposed three common law duties on the employer in respect of his employees. These include:

- The appointment of reasonably competent fellow employees
- The provision of safe equipment and materials
- To put in place reasonably safe working systems

A fourth common law duty was later added to the previous three:

- The provision of a reasonably safe place of work

Competent fellow employees

An employee must act in responsible manner at all times to ensure that he does not place his colleagues in a position where they would suffer harm as a result of his actions or failure to act properly. The negligent and dangerous behaviour of such an employee must cause a fellow employee to suffer harm and must be reasonably foreseeable in order to make the employer liable in delict. Two interesting examples from case law are described below:

 Smith v Crossley Brothers (1951) two apprentice motor mechanics seriously injured a fellow apprentice because they subjected him to a bizarre and demeaning initiation ritual. The two employees in question had forcibly inserted a piece of hose-pipe into the victim's rectum. Pressurised air was then pumped through the hose-pipe causing serious injury to the victim. The victim sued his employer for breach of his duty in subjecting him to the dangerous actions of his employees.

Held: the employer escaped liability because the actions of the two apprentices were not reasonably foreseeable. Such an initiation ritual had never occurred before in that particular workplace. There was no way that the employer could have taken reasonable care to protect fellow employees from a danger that could not have been foreseen.

Waters _v_ Commissioner of Police for the Metropolis (2000) Waters, a female police constable, had accused a male colleague of subjecting her to a sexual assault. The alleged assault had taken place outside working hours. The police force had conducted an enquiry into Waters' allegations, but there was not enough evidence to prove that she had been sexually assaulted. Consequently, no further action was taken against her male colleague. Waters then claimed that she had been victimised by her colleagues for making the allegation in the first place. She believed that this victimisation had caused her to suffer psychiatric injuries.

Held: by the House of Lords that her delictual claim against her employer should be allowed to proceed. An employer may be in breach of his personal duty of care if either he knew that fellow employees were behaving in such a way as to cause the employee in question to suffer physical or psychiatric injury or if it was reasonably foreseeable that such actions would cause harm and that he failed to put reasonable safeguards to prevent the employee suffering harm.

Adequate equipment and materials

 Paris _v_ Stepney Borough Council (1951) the employer was aware that the employee was blind in one eye, but safety goggles were not provided to protect the sight in the other eye. The employee was involved in a workplace accident and lost the sight in his remaining good eye.

Held: the employer had failed to take reasonable care for the safety of this employee by providing adequate equipment. The House of Lords that the employer had been negligent in that it had fallen far short of the standard of reasonable care which would be expected of a reasonable employer.

 Bux _v_ Slough Metals (1973) the pursuer worked in a foundry and, whilst at work, he was splashed with molten metal and was made blind in one of his eyes. The employer had a statutory duty to provide the pursuer with safety goggles and had done so.

Held: the common law duty of providing adequate went much further than the statutory duty. The common law imposed a duty upon the employer to encourage or even enforce the use of safety equipment. The employer had failed to take reasonable steps to do this and was, therefore, liable.

Safe working systems

An employer must take reasonable care to ensure that the work is properly and safely organised, that adequate numbers of workers are on site to carry out the job and that there are competent supervisors and managers in place to oversee the workers, especially if the work involves inexperienced and new employees.

 Walker _v_ Northumberland County Council (1995) the pursuer worked in a particularly stressful social work post for the Council. As a result of the Council's failure to provide proper safeguards, the pursuer had developed a psychiatric injury.

The pursuer was eventually dismissed by the Council on the grounds of his poor health. The pursuer's injury was reasonably foreseeable as the Council knew that the he was vulnerable and had not taken proper steps to protect him.

Withers v Perry Chain (1961) the employee had, in the past, suffered from dermatitis. The dermatitis was appeared to be triggered when the employee came into contact with grease. In order to reduce the risk of her suffering from this condition in the future, the employer gave her work where she would not come into contact with grease. Despite this, the employee developed dermatitis again. The employee sued her employer on the ground that a duty of care was owed to her to eliminate or reduce all risks to her health.

Held: the English Court of Appeal stated that the employer had put in place a reasonably safe system of working for this particular employee which was aimed at protecting her health.

A safe place of work

An employer must take reasonable care to provide a safe working environment, but this does not mean that he has to ensure that employees are protected from all possible risks.

 Latimer v AEC (1952) an employee who had been injured at work when he slipped and fell on the factory floor which had been heavily flooded. The employer had taken great care to put down sawdust on the floor to minimise the risk of accidents. The employee argued that the factory should have been shut down until the water was cleared.

Held: the House of Lords stated that closing the factory would be a solution that was out of proportion to the actual risks involved of continuing to work there.

 Key point: In terms of the duty to take care for the safety of employees, an employer must provide adequate plant and equipment, competent fellow employees and supervisors, safe systems of working and a safe place of work.

Defences

An employer may use two defences if a delictual claim is brought by an employee that he is in breach of one of his common law duties:

◆ Contributory negligence
◆ *Volenti non fit injuria* (those who wish an injury cannot be injured)

These defences were, of course, discussed in some detail in Chapter 3.

Health and Safety at Work Act 1974

It is worth noting that the employer's common duties which aim to protect the health and safety of employees establishes a regime of civil liability. In other words, should the employer breach these duties, he will most likely face a civil action by the injured employee who will be attempting to recover compensation.

The Health and Safety at Work Act 1974, on the other hand, makes an employer criminally liable if he fails to take reasonably practicable steps to protect the health and safety of his employees. An employer will, therefore, face criminal penalties in a criminal court for breaches of the Act. This means that an employer could face both a criminal action and a civil action for damages where he has neglected to obey the criminal law and the common law regulating the employees' health and safety.

The Health and Safety Executive and Commission are primarily charged with the enforcement of health and safety. Given the very small numbers of Health and Safety inspectors in relation to the huge number of workplaces in the United Kingdom, the Health and Safety Inspectorate cannot give every employer a clean bill of health. The Act, therefore, places a duty on employers and employees to cooperate fully with one another to promote health and safety within the workplace. Usually, a workplace will establish a health and safety committee, which will include trade union or employee representatives, with the express purpose of advising the employer on what steps or procedures are reasonably practicable to ensure that the health and safety of employees and visitors to the workplace is protected.

The Health and Safety at Work Act 1974 is a parent Act from which the appropriate British government minister is authorised to bring secondary legislation into force in order to make the Act work. Much of the law relating to health and safety is not actually contained in the original Act itself, but in a vast array of Regulations that it has spawned.

 Key point: The Health and Safety at Work Act 1974 imposes criminal penalties on an employer who fails to take reasonably practicable steps to ensure the health and safety of his employees.

The employee's duties

The common law duties of an employee are:

- To provide personal service
- To provide loyal service
- There must be no inconsistency with the duty of fidelity
- The employee must not make secret profits
- Act with honesty and integrity
- Do not disclose confidential information
- To obey lawful and reasonable orders
- To take reasonable care in the exercise of your employment

The employee's duty to provide personal service

An important characteristic of the employment relationship is that the employer expects the employee to carry out his job personally. It is not usually acceptable for an employee to delegate some of his functions under the employment contract to a third party. This was one of the reasons why the Court of Appeal in **Ready Mixed Concrete (South East) Ltd *v* Minister of Pensions (1968)** stated that the contract was one for services because the driver could appoint a substitute to cover for him when he wished to take time off from driving.

The employee's duty to provide loyal service

An employee is expected to serve his employer loyally which means that he must not do anything that would harm his employer's business by carrying out work for business rivals. Even work that the employee carries out in his own time may actually interfere with the employer's interests – especially if these activities could be viewed as harming the employer's business. The employee should not divulge any trade secrets or business secrets to his employer's rivals that he has acquired in the course of his employment.

 Forster & Sons Ltd *v* Suggett (1918) the defender, an ex-employee of the pursuers, had learnt secret production methods during the course of his employment. The defender had agreed that, for five years after his employment with the pursuers ended, he would not compete against them by setting up a rival business in the United Kingdom. In breach of his contract, the defender set up a business in direct competition against his ex-employer.

Held: the pursuers were entitled to enforce this perfectly reasonable contractual restraint in order to protect important business secrets.

In order to safeguard his business secrets, an employer should really insist that an express restrictive covenant be included in the employment contract. Such a restrictive covenant must, of course, be reasonable.

According to **Briggs *v* Oates (1991)** if a contract containing an employee restraint is repudiated by the employer, all contractual duties no longer have legal force and the restraint is completely worthless. In situations where an employer's conduct, for example, bullying or harassment results in an employee treating himself as constructively dismissed, the contract can no longer be enforced against the employee. The decision in **Briggs** will not apply if the employee resigns and is not dismissed.

 Faccenda Chicken Ltd *v* Fowler (1986) Fowler worked as a sales manager for Faccenda for seven years. During his employment, he was responsible for establishing operations where the company sent out vans containing its products with the purpose of approaching and selling these products directly to local retailers and suppliers. Later on, Fowler left his employment and set up his own business which was directly in competition with that of his ex-employer. A number of his fellow employees joined his business in order to work for him. All Fowler's fellow employees had in-depth knowledge of their ex-employer's business operations. Fowler's ex-employer was unsuccessful in its attempt to sue him for damages.

Held: by the English Court of Appeal a former employee will be entitled to use information in his new job if this information does not fall into the category of trade or business secrets. Very significantly, however, the Court of Appeal stated that the outcome of the case would have been different if the ex-employer had been able to prove that the employees had deliberately written down the information to use in their future employment. This would have been a clear breach of an employee's duty of confidentiality.

 Robb *v* Green (1895) the employee in question wrote down the names of his employer's customers before he left his employment. It was his intention to approach these individuals personally, after his employment had ended, in order to persuade them to use the services of the business that he had since set up and which was now competing directly against his that of his ex-employer.

Held: the employee was prevented from approaching his ex-employer's customers in order to poach them for his own business.

Key point: An employer will be able to use a restrictive covenant in an employment contract in order to protect genuine trade secrets to which the employee has gained access.

The employee's duty to obey lawful and reasonable orders

An employee is under a duty to obey any lawful and reasonable orders that an employer may issue to him. Clearly orders to commit crimes or that would endanger safety should not be followed.

Ottoman Bank v Chakarian (1930) Chakarian, who worked for the Ottoman Bank in Greece, was ordered to relocate to Istanbul in Turkey. Chakarian was not willing to go to Istanbul because he was an Armenian and the Turkish authorities had already sentenced him to death. Chakarian had no doubt that this was a sentence that the Turks would only be too happy to carry out if he ever set foot in Turkey again. He refused to obey his employer's order to relocate his employment to Turkey.

Held: by the Privy Council that the Ottoman Bank's order to Chakarian was unreasonable. He was entitled to refuse to obey the order given the extreme circumstances that his life would be placed in if he went to Turkey.

The following case is in complete contrast to **Chakarian** and also involved an Armenian employee:

Bouzourou v Ottoman Bank (1930) the employee was an Armenian Christian who was ordered to work at a bank branch in Turkey. The employee was only too aware of the Turkish Government's aggressive attitude towards his race and religion and he refused to obey his employer's order.

Held: the employee had wrongfully refused to obey a lawful and reasonable order from his employer. It will, of course, be appreciated that the employee in this case did not face a death sentence, unlike the employee in the previous case.

Morrish v Henleys (Folkestone) Ltd (1973) 2 All ER 137 an employee was ordered by his employer to falsify the business accounts in order to aid and abet a tax fraud. He refused to carry out this order and was subsequently dismissed.

Held: the employee's refusal to carry out what was an illegal order was reasonable and, therefore, not in breach of his contract. He had been wrongfully dismissed by his employer.

See also **Macari v Celtic Football and Athletic Company Ltd (1999)** the facts of which are discussed in Chapter 2.

Key point: The employee is obliged to follow the employer's lawful and reasonable orders.

The employee's duty to act with honesty and integrity

An employee must not attempt to cheat his employer or to behave in a dishonest fashion towards his employer.

Reading v Attorney-General (1951) AC 507 Reading was a British Army Sergeant who was based in Egypt. The smugglers had paid Reading substantial bribes to accompany their lorries to certain destinations. The smugglers had calculated quite correctly that the presence of a uniformed British Army Sergeant in their lorries would prevent the vehicles being searched by the police for illegal cargos. Eventually, Reading's illegal activities were discovered and he was arrested by the Military Police, but not before he had been paid almost £20,000 by the smugglers for his services. This huge sum of money was confiscated by the British authorities. Reading later attempted to recover this money.

Held: by the House of Lords that Reading had behaved in a totally dishonest fashion and that he had used his position as a servant of the Crown to obtain an unauthorised benefit. He failed to recover the confiscated sum.

An employee must act in good faith and must cooperate with his employer. However, employees do not owe fiduciary duties to their employers. If this were the case, employees would be labouring under an extremely heavy burden.

 Nottingham University v Fishel (2000) IRLR 471 Dr Fishel was employed by a University clinic that specialised in invitro-fertilisation (IVF) techniques. In addition to his work for the clinic, Fishel also performed a large amount of private work overseas in the area of IVF. He was also in the habit of sending the clinic's junior staff abroad to perform private work in order to gain valuable experience. Fishel's employment with the University was later terminated and it sought compensation for the work that he had carried out privately. The University claimed that this private work had been unauthorised and was, therefore, in breach of his employment contract.

Held: by Elias J in the English High Court that although Fishel had failed to gain prior approval for his private work, he was not in breach of any fiduciary duty to the University. The private clients would not have come to the United Kingdom for treatment, so the University had suffered no financial loss. Furthermore, the clinic may have benefited from Fishel's experience gained during his private work. However, Fishel had broken his contract by not seeking permission to continue his private work and, as a result, the University was entitled to damages for breach of contract.

 Key point: The employee must act with integrity and do nothing which undermines the interests of his employer.

The employee's duty of care

There is an implied duty that the employee will take reasonable care in the discharge of his duties. Breach of the duty of care may arise in situations where the employer is held liable to an innocent third party for the negligent actions of his employee. The employer (or more likely his insurance company) can always exercise the right to sue the employee for breach of his duty of care. Insurance companies appear to have an informal agreement that they will not pursue the employee for breach of his duty should they have to pay out to his employer under an insurance policy. This has meant in practice, that these types of cases tend to be few and far between, but not unheard of.

447

Lister *v* Romford Ice and Cold Storage (1957) at the insistence of the insurers, the employer sued his employee, a lorry driver, for failing to drive safely (an implied term of his employment contract) and causing a fellow employee to suffer a personal injury as a result of the negligent driving.

 Janata Bank *v* Ahmed (1981) IRLR 457 Ahmed was employed as bank manager. His employer sued him for damages for overdrafts that he had negligently authorised in respect of certain customers. Unfortunately, Ahmed had failed to investigate whether these customers were in a financial position to pay back the overdrafts. They were not and the debts owed to the bank amounted to a considerable sum.

Held: by the English Court of Appeal that Ahmed was liable in damages (£34,640) to his employers for the losses caused by his negligence.

Key point: The employee owes his employer a duty of care when he carries out his functions under his employment contract.

Termination of the contract of employment

The contract of employment can be terminated like any other contractual agreement. It is normal practice for the contract to state the required notice period which binds both employer and employee. In the absence of such a contractual term, the common law states that either of the parties must give a reasonable amount of notice to the other party of their wish to terminate the contract. What is a reasonable amount of notice will clearly differ from situation to situation.

Statutory minimum notice periods

Section 86 of the Employment Rights Act 1996, however, lays down statutory minimum periods of notice. These statutory minimum periods of notice, which affect employees who have been continuously employed for four weeks or more, are detailed below:

- One week's notice is required to be given to those individuals who have been employed for more than four weeks but under one year
- If the employee has between one and 12 years' continuous service he is entitled to a week's notice for every year of service
- If an employee has more than 12 years' continuous employment, the maximum notice period is 12 weeks

It is important to note that these are statutory minimum periods of notice and that contracts of employment may actually lay down a requirement for longer periods of notice.

Material breach of contract

A contract of employment can also be terminated in situations where one of the parties commits a material breach of contract.

 Gannon and Others *v* J C Firth Ltd (1976) 18 employees who walked off the job in order to take part in strike action committed a breach of their contracts by failing to provide their employer with services. The striking employees had also committed another breach of contract by failing to turn off a high pressure steam system. As a result of this failure, severe damage was caused to the employer's factory.

Held: by the Employment Appeal Tribunal that the 18 employees had automatically terminated their contracts by reason of them committing a material breach.

At common law, an employer can terminate the contract of employment summarily i.e. without giving notice, but legislation regulating unfair dismissal and redundancy make this a less useful right for the employer to exercise. Summary dismissal has been held to be an appropriate course of action where the employee has been found guilty of misconduct or wilful disobedience.

 Blyth *v* The Scottish Liberal Club (1983) an employee deliberately disobeyed his employer's instructions to attend certain meetings.

Held: that the employer was entitled to dismiss the employee summarily i.e. without notice on the grounds of his disobedience.

Termination by mutual agreement

A termination of contract can also occur where both parties agree either to end the agreement or that it will end on the occurrence or non-occurrence of some specified event. If there is genuine agreement between the parties that the contract should be ended, there is no dismissal of the employee at either common law or in terms of statute.

 Brown *v* Knowsley Borough Council (1986) Brown was employed as a temporary lecturer. Her contract came to an end because the course that she was teaching on did not receive further funding. The contract of employment contained a term which stated that 'the appointment will last only as long as sufficient funds are provided either by the Manpower Services Commission or by other firms/sponsors to fund it.' Brown brought an action against her employer claiming that she had been dismissed.

Held: by the Employment Appeal Tribunal that Brown had not been dismissed. Her contract had terminated on the failure of her employer to secure new funding for the course on which she was employed. Brown knew that her continued employment depended on securing additional funding and she had accepted the employment on these terms. Therefore, the failure to secure the funding resulted in mutual termination of the contract.

Frustration

Further performance of a contract may be frustrated i.e. the contract becomes impossible to perform or further performance becomes radically different from the agreement that was originally contemplated by the parties (**Lord Radcliffe: Davis Contractors Ltd *v* Fareham UDC (1956)**). The Employment Appeal Tribunal sitting in England has stated that frustration of contract in employment cases means that the employee loses his entitlement either to notice or to a payment in lieu of notice (**G F Sharp & Co Ltd *v* McMillan (1998)**).

In situations, where the employee's sickness may result in the contract of employment being frustrated, certain guidelines were laid down in **Marshall *v***

Harland & Wolff (1972) Sir John Donaldson asked whether the employee's inability to work was of such a nature that further performance of his duty to provide services to the employer would either be impossible or radically different from that originally contemplated by the parties. Factors such as the employee's entitlement to sick pay, the likelihood of the relationship surviving the period of absence, the nature of the employment, the nature of the employee's ill-health and the employee's past employment with the employer should all closely examined before deciding whether the contract is indeed frustrated. All of these factors are related and should be taken into account, but there may be other factors to consider in different situations.

Performance of the contract

It may be the case that the employment contract will end upon completion of some task and it is this event that is said to terminate the agreement.

By operation of law

The contract may terminate automatically by operation of law without the intervention of either the employer or the employee. Such a situation may arise where the employer is compulsorily wound up under the insolvency legislation.

Fixed-term contracts

If a fixed-term contract is not renewed, the employer is regarded as having dismissed the employee and the employee may thus claim that the employer acted unfairly in not renewing the contract. If the employer attempts to dismiss an employee during the performance of a fixed-term contract, there is a very strong argument that the employee will be able to claim payment for the remainder of the period of the contract.

 Key point: Like all contracts, an employment contract can be terminated in a variety of ways – by giving notice, mutual agreement, material breach, frustration, completion of a task, operation of law and the expiry of a fixed-term contract.

Redundancy

Section 139(1) of the Employment Rights Act 1996 states that dismissal on the grounds of redundancy will occur if:

1   The employer has ceased or intends to cease carrying on the business

or

2   The requirements for employees to carry out work of a particular kind or to carry it out at the place in which they are employed have ceased or diminished

An employer can always manage redundancies by offering suitable, alternative employment to the affected individuals or the employment contract may contain a mobility clause which allows the employer to relocate employees to an alternative workplace.

If the employer makes an offer of suitable, alternative employment or the employment contract contains a mobility clause, an employee who either refuses the new post or refuses to move to a new work location may find that the refusal deprives him of the right to claim a redundancy payment.

When an employer is intending to terminate an employee's contract by reason of redundancy, he has a duty to consult with the appropriate representatives of the individuals who are affected by this decision (Section 188: Trade Union and Labour Relations (Consolidation) Act 1992).

Section 188 makes it very clear that an employer who fails to consult with the representatives of the affected employees could find himself taken before an Employment Tribunal by the appropriate representatives. This action could result in the Tribunal ordering the employer to pay compensation (a protective award) to the affected employees where it is proved that the employer failed to carry out proper consultation procedures.

Appropriate representatives of the affected employees will either be officials of a recognised and independent trade union or representatives whom the affected employees have elected for this purpose. Employers are under a duty to consult with representatives in situations where 20 or more redundancies will take effect at the one establishment within a 90-day period. Consultations must be commenced within good time and certain guidelines must be followed:

1   If at least 20 but less than 100 employees are to be affected by the redundancy situation within 90 days or less, the employer should begin consultations with their representatives at least 30 days before the first dismissal becomes effective.

2   If over 100 employees are to be made redundant within 90 days or less, consultation must take place 90 days before the first proposed dismissal.

If the above situations apply, an employer must notify the Secretary of State by putting his redundancy proposals in writing. The same time periods as outlined above must be observed and a failure to notify the Secretary of State at all or within the relevant time will mean that the employer has committed a criminal offence (Section 193: Trade Union and Labour Relations (Consolidation) Act 1992).

Employees who have two years' continuous service with the employer are entitled to statutory redundancy pay which is calculated according to the same rules for basic awards in unfair dismissal claims. The maximum award that could be made under this scheme is £8,100 (20 years × 1½ × £270). Some employers may, however, operate a contractual redundancy payments scheme which is much more generous than the statutory scheme.

As will be discussed later in the chapter, an employer can use redundancy as a reason to justify the employee's dismissal. However, there will be situations where certain employees are selected for redundancy in circumstances where the employer will face accusations of unfair dismissal.

 Key point: An employee whose contract is terminated by reason of redundancy may be entitled to a statutory redundancy payment if he has two years' continuous service with his employer.

Dismissal

A dismissal of the employee by the employer will result in the termination of the contract of employment. It is important to ask what kind of dismissal terminated the contract – fair, wrongful, unfair or constructive dismissal. It is important to distinguish between these types of dismissal because there are different legal rights available to the dismissed employee. We have to be quite clear that there was, in fact, a dismissal and not a resignation by the employee or mutual agreement between the employer and the employee to terminate the contract.

The statutory definitions of dismissal

Section 95 of the Employment Rights Act 1996 states that an employee shall be treated as dismissed by his employer if, and only if:

◆ The employer terminates the contract of employment with or without notice
◆ The employee terminates the contract of employment with or without notice because of the employer's conduct (this is known as constructive dismissal)
◆ The employee is on a fixed-term contract which expires without being renewed by the employer

Section 136(1) of the Employment Rights Act 1996 contains an identical definition of dismissal in respect of situations where the dismissal is on the grounds of the employee's redundancy.

It must be appreciated that protection against unfair dismissal covers those individuals who have a contract of employment with their employer. In any claim for unfair dismissal, an Employment Tribunal must discover what was the employer's main reason for dismissing the employee *and* whether this reason actually justifies the dismissal. Section 94 of the Employment Rights Act 1996 makes it clear that an employee has the right not to be unfairly dismissed.

Wrongful dismissal

Wrongful dismissal arises in situations where an employer dismisses the employee in breach of his contract. In order to claim that he has been wrongfully dismissed, the employee does not have to show that he has had continuous service with his employer for at least one year. Employees with under a year's continuous service can also claim wrongful dismissal. Claims for wrongful dismissal should be lodged with the Office of Employment Tribunals within three months (less one day) of the date of the employee's dismissal. So, if the employee was dismissed on 10 February, a claim should be lodged by 9 May at the very latest. Time limits are very strictly adhered to and failure to submit the claim by the appropriate date will cause it to be time-barred.

When making an application to an Employment Tribunal, wrongful dismissal is referred to as 'breach of contract'. A note of caution, however, should be sounded. If the employee decides to pursue a wrongful dismissal claim, the employer can counter-claim for any losses caused by the employee's conduct. So, for example, an employee who broke a computer screen accidentally may find themselves being sued by the employer for compensation because he decided to pursue a wrongful dismissal claim against the employer.

The employer could dismiss an employee wrongfully by failing to give either the contractually agreed period of notice or the minimum period of notice laid down by Section 86 of the Employment Rights Act 1996. Very often, an employer will include a term in the contract which permits him to pay the dismissed employee a payment in lieu of notice. This payment is regarded as compensation to the employee for breach of his contract. In such situations, the employer will not force the employee to work either his contractual or statutory notice period. Wrongful dismissal may also arise where the employer breaches or ignores the disciplinary procedure, which must be followed under the terms of the employment contract, and dismisses the employee with unseemly haste.

 Morran *v* Glasgow Council of Tenants (1998) the employer dismissed Morran, but it failed to give him the necessary contractual notice period of four weeks to which he was entitled. The employer also failed to make a payment to Morran in lieu of the contractual notice period. Morran argued that, had he been allowed to work his contractual notice period of four weeks, he would have had enough continuous service to claim unfair dismissal against his employer. Morran raised an action for damages against the employer for wrongful dismissal and for the loss of his right to claim unfair dismissal.

Held: Morran was entitled to claim damages for wrongful dismissal. He was, however, not entitled to claim damages for the loss of his right to claim unfair dismissal. The point was well made that the employer had an option under the contract of employment to terminate the contract and make a compensatory payment to Morran which would effectively have freed him from the duty to work his contractual notice period of four weeks. Morran did not have a right to work his notice period – this arrangement was very much at the employer's discretion. The net effect of this contractual term would have been that Morran was still four weeks short of the necessary qualifying period required in order to claim protection against unfair dismissal. He had not lost his right to claim unfair dismissal because he never had this right in the first place.

It may, of course, be the case that an employer dismisses an employee in strict accordance with the terms of the contract of employment, for example, the employee receives his proper contractual notice period or receives a payment in lieu of this entitlement. In these circumstances, it would be premature to assume that the dismissal was fair. Employees with over a year's continuous service can challenge the decision on the grounds that it was unfair in terms of the Employment Rights Act 1996. Furthermore, there may be other employees who belong to protected categories, for example, dismissals for pregnancy and childbirth-related reasons who will have the right to claim unfair dismissal.

 Key point: Wrongful dismissal occurs in situations where the employee is dismissed in a manner that breaches the terms of his contract.

Remedies for wrongful dismissal

The main remedy that an employee who has been wrongfully dismissed may claim would be that of damages. The remedy of damages ensures that the employee will receive compensation from his employer which will usually be measured by reference to the wages that he would have earned had he been allowed to work his period of notice. The remedy of specific implement is not generally available to a dismissed employee. Specific implement, of course, is where the court forces the party who has breached the contract to perform his duties which he has failed to carry out properly. In an employment situation, this would mean that the employer would be forced to take back the dismissed employee. In Scotland, an employment contract is a contract which is highly dependent on the personalities of the contracting parties and the promotion of goodwill between them. It is, therefore, not appropriate for the courts to force the parties together where personal relationships have broken down completely with the result that there is little or no goodwill between them. So damages will be the preferred remedy for breach of an employment contract. Admittedly, Scottish courts have allowed interim relief (by way of interdict) in wrongful dismissal cases whereby the dismissal is effectively frozen until the contractual notice period has passed (**John Anderson v Pringle of Scotland (1998) IRLR 64**). It should be noted that the granting of interim relief will not prevent the employer from dismissing the employee eventually. The interim relief merely forces the employer to comply with the employment contract for a temporary period which could be very short. So, in **John Anderson v Pringle**, all the employee could do was force the employer to follow the contractual redundancy procedure that ultimately led to his dismissal.

Section 236 of the Trade Union and Labour Relations (Consolidation) Act 1992 reinforces the common law rule that no court shall issue an order for specific implement or an interdict which effectively forces both parties to continue to perform the employment contract.

Unfair dismissal

Generally, an employee who has less than one year's continuous employment cannot lodge a claim for unfair dismissal with the Office of Employment Tribunals (Section 92: Employment Rights Act 1996). Furthermore, people over the age of 65 are, generally speaking, not entitled to bring unfair dismissal claims. There are, however, many exceptions to these qualifications. As we shall see, dismissals on the grounds of the employee's sex, race, disability, sexual orientation and religious beliefs will be regarded as automatically unfair. Dismissals for health and safety reasons or the fact that the employee is a whistleblower will also be treated as automatically unfair. Unfair dismissal should be seen as a dismissal which contravenes statute and Section 94(1) of the Employment Rights Acts 1996 which states that an employee has the right not to be unfairly dismissed. If the employee qualifies for protection against unfair dismissal he can request that the employer provide a written reason for the dismissal. Failure by an employer to issue a written response would be highly suspect and an Employment Tribunal would be entitled to imply that the employer had not acted fairly when he dismissed the employee.

As with claims for wrongful dismissal, an application to the Office of Employment Tribunals alleging unfair dismissal should be lodged within three months (less one day) of the date of the original dismissal. Very often in unfair dismissal cases, the affected employee will submit an appeal against the employer's decision to dismiss. It is often mistakenly assumed that the three-month time limit for submitting an Employment Tribunal application begins to run from the date when the employer's decision in respect of the appeal is communicated to the employee. To reiterate, it is the date of the original decision to dismiss that matters, not any later decision which forms part of the appeals process. An employee aged 65 or over will not be able to claim unfair dismissal.

Key point: Unfair dismissal is a dismissal which is contrary to statute.

The employer's pre-dismissal procedures

The employer's pre-dismissal procedures will now come under greater scrutiny as a result of the decision of the House of Lords in **Polkey v A E Dayton Services Ltd (1987)**. Polkey had been made redundant by his employer without warning. He argued that this was breach of the employer's pre-dismissal procedures. His employer countered this argument by stating that he would have been made redundant in any case whether or not the pre-dismissal procedure had been followed. In other words, Polkey's dismissal on the grounds of redundancy was inevitable. The House of Lords stressed that an Employment Tribunal must take into consideration all the circumstances as to whether the employer has acted reasonably or not as the case may be by failing to follow procedure. It is no longer enough for the employer to rely on the fact that consultation with the employee is pointless because a dismissal will happen in any case. A pre-dismissal procedure which the employer fails to apply in a reasonable manner could lead a Tribunal to find that the employee has been dismissed unfairly. A tribunal must examine what the actions the employer took leading up to the dismissal and not what actions he might have taken.

Polkey is a very important case because the House of Lords overruled the decision of the Employment Appeal Tribunal in **British Labour Pump v Byrne (1979)**. **Byrne** was often used by employers to justify flaws in their disciplinary procedures especially if such a procedure led to the dismissal of the employee. In effect, an employer could argue that the employee's dismissal was inevitable and that the employee's fate would have been exactly the same even if the procedure had been followed to the letter.

Granting a right of appeal to an employee who is threatened with dismissal on the grounds of misconduct was confirmed in the case of **West Midlands Co-operative Society v Tipton (1986)**.

 In this case, the employee was prevented from exercising his right of appeal against dismissal where such a right was guaranteed under the employer's disciplinary code. The House of Lords was of the opinion that such a refusal to allow an employee to appeal could make a dismissal unreasonable and, therefore, unfair. An employer can often rescue himself from having committed earlier defects in the way that he applies the disciplinary procedure by ensuring that the employee is given full access to an impartial appeal hearing.

Section 10 of the Employment Relations Act 1999 states that a worker has the right to be accompanied by a companion to disciplinary or grievance hearings. This companion can be a trade union official who is employed by the union or who has experience of attending grievance and disciplinary hearing or someone who received training in this respect. Alternatively, the worker could request that a colleague accompany him to the disciplinary or grievance meeting.

Where public sector employees are concerned, employers will have to be very careful that disciplinary procedures are applied in way that does not breach a person's right to a fair hearing guaranteed by Article 6 of the European Convention on Human Rights. The European Convention was, of course, implemented into Scots law by way of the Scotland Act 1998 and the Human Rights Act 1998. In any case, the Employment Act 2002 will force all employers to adopt internal disciplinary and dispute resolution procedures by 10 October 2004 which must meet certain basic standards. A failure to follow these procedures by the employer will almost certainly result in an Employment Tribunal deciding that the dismissal was unfair.

Automatically unfair dismissals

In a variety of situations, a dismissal by the employer will be automatically unfair and the employee does not need to have one year's continuous service in order to lodge a claim with the Office of Employment Tribunals.

Dismissal on the grounds of pregnancy (Section 99: ERA 1996)

It will be automatically unfair, in terms of Section 99 of the Employment Rights Act 1996, to dismiss a woman from employment because she is pregnant, for a reason connected with her pregnancy or childbirth or for enforcing her rights under statutory maternity provisions. There is no need for a woman to have one year's continuous service with her employer in order to be protected under Section 99.

 O'Neill *v* Governors of St Thomas More (1996) IRLR 27 O'Neill was employed as a school teacher at a Roman Catholic school. She began a sexual relationship with a Roman Catholic priest and, subsequently, she discovered that she was pregnant. The Board of Governors decided to dismiss O'Neill on the grounds that she had failed to meet the strict moral standards expected of a teacher in a Roman Catholic school. O'Neill lodged a claim for unfair dismissal and sex discrimination on the grounds of her pregnancy.

Held: by the Employment Appeal Tribunal that the dismissal was automatically unfair. The Governors' argument that O'Neill had been dismissed due to the circumstances of her pregnancy (i.e. that her conduct amounted to immorality) rather than the pregnancy itself was rejected by the Employment Appeal Tribunal.

Dismissal on the grounds of race (Section 4: Race Relations Act 1976)

If an employer dismisses an employee on the grounds of his colour, nationality, racial, ethnic or national origin such a dismissal would be automatically unfair. The dismissal would also be an example of direct discrimination.

Dismissal on the grounds of disability (Section 4: Disability Discrimination Act 1995)

If an employer dismisses an employee on the grounds of his disability such a dismissal would be automatically unfair. The dismissal would also be an example of less favourable treatment.

Health and safety dismissals (Section 100: ERA 1996)

 Hynes *v* D E Bliss (Builders) ET Case No 12874/96 on a number of occasions, Hynes, a carpenter, had expressed fears about the safety of scaffolding used by the employers. Hynes eventually threatened to report his employer to the health and safety authorities unless something concrete was done to tackle the concerns that he had raised. The employer's response was to do nothing. In reaction to the employer's response, Hynes decided to resign from his employment and claim constructive dismissal.

Held: Hynes was entitled to claim constructive dismissal under Section 100 of the Employment Rights Act 1996. The employer owed a duty to the employees to provide a reasonably safe system of work and by failing to do this it had committed a material breach of contract. Hynes had, therefore, been dismissed on health and safety grounds.

 Harvest Press Ltd *v* McCaffrey (1999) IRLR 778 McCaffrey was employed by the company to work the night shift with one other fellow employee. He had reason to make a complaint about his fellow employee's behaviour to the company management. Unfortunately, for McCaffrey, his fellow employee discovered who made the complaint against him. From then on, McCaffrey was subjected to abuse by his colleague. This abuse was extremely threatening and McCaffrey, fearing for his safety, left his place of employment one night after experiencing a particularly abusive exchange from his colleague. McCaffrey told his employer that he would return to work if his colleague was moved to another post within the organisation. The employer refused to do this and took the attitude that McCaffrey had actually resigned from his post. McCaffrey then claimed that he had been constructively dismissed.

Held: by the Employment Appeal Tribunal that McCaffrey had been constructively dismissed in terms of Section 100(d) of the Employment Rights Act 1996. Section 100(d) permits an employee to leave his workplace if to stay there would place him in risk of danger. Risks to an employee's health and safety could also include dangers caused by an employee's colleagues.

Dismissal for refusal to work on a Sunday (Section 101: ERA 1996)

In terms of Section 101 of the Employment Rights Act 1996, some workers, known as protected workers, have the right to refuse to work on a Sunday. If such a refusal results in their dismissal by an employer, the employee will have the right to claim unfair dismissal. The employee does not have to have a year's continuous service before they are entitled to the protection of Section 101. Generally speaking, employees who were not required to work on Sundays before the Sunday trading laws were liberalised are entitled to refuse to work on a Sunday. Employees who commenced employment after the newer, more liberal laws can give their employers three months written notice of their intention to opt out of Sunday work. After this notice period has expired, they cannot be forced to work on a Sunday.

Trustees of occupational pension funds (Section 102: ERA 1996)

A trustee of an occupational pension fund who is dismissed by his employer because he has carried out or proposes to carry out some task connected with his role will be regarded as having been unfairly dismissed.

Employee representatives (Section 103: ERA 1996)

According to Section 103 of the Employment Rights Act 1996, an employee who is classified as an employee representative or a candidate for such a position and who is dismissed by the employer because they have either carried out or propose to carry out the activities of such a representative will be regarded as having been unfairly dismissed. An employee representative will either be a member of a recognised and independent trade union or someone who has been elected to such a position by his fellow employees. These dismissals will either be connected to redundancies that the employer is proposing to make or to the transfer of an undertaking.

Whistle-blowing (Section 103A: ERA 1996)

The Public Interest Disclosure Act 1998 inserts a new provision, Section 103A, into the Employment Rights Act 1996.

The 1998 Act came into force on 2 July 1999 and gives employees additional protection against unfair dismissal by their employer. Since 1999, approximately 1200 cases involving the Act have arisen. The primary aim of the 1998 Act is to encourage employees to go public about their employer's criminal or fraudulent practices, for example, tax evasion, social security fraud or breaches of health and safety legislation. The Act also covers civil offences where the employer's conduct amounts to negligence or breach of contract where this could potentially cause harm or injury. As long as the employee (the whistle-blower) makes the disclosure in good faith, he will have the right to take a claim to an Employment Tribunal if he subsequently suffers victimisation or harassment by his employer. The conduct complained of may have occurred either here in the United Kingdom or abroad. It is not necessary for an employee to have one year's continuous service in order to claim the protection of the 1998 Act in situations where the employer has decided to punish the disclosure by dismissing the employee.

Where the employee experiences victimisation as a result of making a disclosure under the 1998 Act, he can lodge a claim with the Office of Employment Tribunals. Awards will be uncapped and based on the losses suffered. Furthermore, where an employee is dismissed, he may apply for an interim order to keep his job. An employer cannot rely on confidentiality clauses within the employee's contract where this would have the effect of preventing a disclosure under the Act.

In addition to employees, the Act also applies to trainees, agency staff, contractors, homeworkers, trainees and every professional in the NHS. Certain groups of people are not covered by theAct such as the genuinely self-employed, volunteers, the intelligence services, the army or police officers.

In the first instance, many employees will choose to address their concerns about malpractice in the organisation to a senior manager or representative of the employer. Many organisations will have an internal procedure for dealing with complaints by whistle-blowers. However, the existence of such a procedure is no guarantee that the employee's complaint or disclosure will be handled correctly.

In some situations, an employee may choose to make a disclosure to a prescribed regulator. In Scotland, some of the following bodies are recognised as prescribed regulators for the purposes of the 1998 Act:

- Accounts Commission for Scotland
- Audit Scotland
- Crown Office
- Customs and Excise

- ◆ Health and Safety Executive
- ◆ Inland Revenue
- ◆ Scottish Criminal Cases Review Commission
- ◆ Scottish Environment Protection Agency
- ◆ The Scottish Ministers
- ◆ Scottish Information Commissioner
- ◆ Scottish Social Services Council
- ◆ Secretary for Trade and Industry
- ◆ Standards Commission for Scotland and the Chief Investigating Officer
- ◆ Water Industry Commissioner for Scotland

In extreme cases, a failure by the employer to deal properly with a disclosure may result in the employee being forced to go outside the organisation by making a public disclosure to the media, the police, Members of the Westminster and Scottish Parliaments and non-prescribed regulators. A public disclosure will be permissible if it meets the following conditions:

- ◆ The disclosure has not been made for personal gain.
- ◆ The individual employee had a reasonable belief that he would suffer victimisation if he raised the matter internally or with a prescribed regulator.
- ◆ The individual employee had a reasonable belief that his employer would attempt to conceal malpractice and there was no prescribed regulator.
- ◆ The individual employee had already raised the matter internally or with a prescribed regulator.

In assessing how reasonably the person who made the disclosure has acted, an Employment Tribunal will wish to know to whom the disclosure was made, how serious were the concerns being raised by the disclosure, has the employer's conduct caused third parties to be exposed to danger, and has the disclosure breached a duty of confidence the employer owed a third party. If the disclosure was addressed to an employer or a prescribed regulator, the reasonableness of their response will be very important. Employment Tribunals will often examine an employer's internal whistle-blowing procedure (assuming, of course, that one exists) in order to assess if the employee's concerns or complaints were dealt with properly.

 Miklaszewicz *v* Stolt Offshore (2002) IRLR 344 Miklaszewicz had been dismissed in 1993 by Stolt Offshore after he had reported the company to the Inland Revenue for questionable taxation practices. Consequently, the company had been fined £3 million by the Inland Revenue. Miklaszewicz then obtained another job in the oil industry. In 1999 his current employers were taken over by Stolt Offshore. In 2000, Stolt Offshore made Miklaszewicz redundant and Miklaszewicz sued, claiming dismissal in breach of Public Interest Disclosure Act 1998 which had come into force in 1999.

Held: by the Employment Tribunal that Miklaszewicz's disclosure had been made before the Act came into force it could not, therefore, be regarded as a protected disclosure. On appeal, however, the Employment Appeal Tribunal overturned this decision because the important factor to consider was when the employee had suffered a detriment and not when he had made the original disclosure. Stolt Offshore continued to argue that the date of the disclosure was the crucial issue and appealed to the Court of

Session. The Court of Session dismissed Stolt's appeal, stating that what the legislation affected was the dismissal, rather than the disclosure.

Dismissal on the grounds of sexual orientation (Employment Equality (Sexual Orientation Regulations) 2003)

In terms of Regulation 6 of the Employment Equality Regulations, it is unlawful for an employer to dismiss an employee by reason of their sexual orientation.

Dismissal on the grounds of religion or belief (Regulation 6: Employment Equality (Religion or Belief Regulations) 2003)

As with a person's sexual orientation, it will be unlawful for an employer to dismiss someone by reason of their religion or belief.

Dismissal for asserting a statutory right (Section 104: ERA 1996)

 Mennell v Newell & Wright (Transport Contractors) Ltd (1997) IRLR 519 Mennell was employed as an HGV driver by Newell & Wright. The company wanted the employee to sign a contract which would have given it the right to make deductions from his wages when his contract ended in order to pay for training that it had provided. It was made quite clear to Mennell that he would be sacked if he continued to refuse the sign the contract. Mennell continued to refuse to sign the new contract. Mennell was eventually dismissed because of this refusal. Mennell lodged an unfair dismissal claim against his employer. At the Employment Tribunal, Mennell's action failed because he had not actually suffered unauthorised deductions from wages. His employer had only issued a potential threat that it intended to make unauthorised deductions from wages. It had not actually carried out this threat. Mennell appealed to the Employment Appeal Tribunal.

Held: by the Employment Appeal Tribunal that there was no requirement placed upon the employee to show that there had been an actual breach of one of his statutory rights. As long as the employee could demonstrate that he honestly believed that one of his statutory rights had been infringed and that his complaint had led to him being unfairly dismissed, a claim was competent. The case eventually went as far as the English Court of Appeal. However, on the facts of the case Mennell failed to win his claim because he had failed to make an allegation that there had been an infringement of his statutory rights under Section 13 of the Employment Rights Act 1996. He could not say with any certainty where, when and to whom he had made the allegation of unauthorised deductions from wages. He had merely refused to sign the contract until the employer removed the contractual term that he found offensive.

Dismissals while the employee is taking part in industrial action (Section 16 & Schedule 5: Employment Relations Act 1999)

An employer cannot dismiss employees who are taking part in lawful, balloted industrial action for the first eight weeks of such action. This protection is absolute as long as the employee does not commit a further unlawful act over and above his initial breach of contract (i.e. by going on strike). A dismissal, regardless of the employee's age or length of service, will be automatically unfair as long as it is connected to the industrial action. This statutory protection could be extended beyond the first eight weeks if the employer has not taken reasonable steps to end the dispute.

After the initial period of eight weeks has ended, the employer cannot be selective as to which employees he decides to dismiss. All those employees engaged in the industrial action must be dismissed no matter what their motives for taking part might have been. If the employer decides to dismiss the employees who took part in industrial action, he cannot take back any of the dismissed employees for a period of at least three months.

If employees are taking part in unofficial industrial action, they will have no protection against dismissal. It is important to note that the employees who have been dismissed must be involved in unofficial action on the date of their dismissal. However, the employer cannot dismiss employees who have returned to work after taking part in an unofficial strike. A dismissal in those circumstances would not prevent these employees from lodging a claim for unfair dismissal with the Office of Employment Tribunals.

Dismissal on the grounds of trade union activity (Section 152: Trade Union and Labour Relations (Consolidation) Act 1992)

Dismissal for trade union membership and activity where the trade union is independent of the employer (i.e. not a staff association controlled by the employer), or a dismissal in connection with a refusal to join a trade union or a particular trade union whether it is independent or not will be regarded as unfair. Participation in trade union activities must take place at an appropriate time i.e. in the employee's own time or at time to which the employer has given his consent.

 O'Donovan v Central College of Commerce ET case No 103652/2002
O'Donovan was employed as a lecturer at the College where he also acted as the Branch Secretary of the Educational Institute of Scotland (Scotland's largest teaching union). O'Donovan was accused of the bullying and harassment of a support staff member who happened to be a member of the College's Board of Management. O'Donovan had put a question to this support staff member about possible lecturing staff redundancies in the event of a proposed restructuring exercise by College management. The support staff member had taken exception to this question and had made a formal complaint to the College's Principal. The College Principal, who had a very difficult relationship with O'Donovan owing to the latter's effectiveness as a trade union official, saw an opportunity to get rid of him. O'Donovan was accused of gross misconduct on very flimsy evidence. The College's disciplinary procedures were not followed correctly and O'Donovan was later dismissed. The College denied that O'Donovan had been dismissed on the grounds of trade union activity.

Held: by the Employment Tribunal that no reasonable employer would have concluded that O'Donovan's behaviour towards his colleague could have been interpreted as bullying or harassment. No rational person would have come to the conclusion that there had been gross misconduct on O'Donovan's part. In the absence of any other reasonable explanation, the Tribunal found that O'Donovan had been unfairly dismissed, in terms of Section 152 of the

Trade Union and Labour Relations (Consolidation) Act 1992, for reason of his trade union activities.

Transfer of an undertaking (TUPE Regulations 1981 (as amended))

The European Community Acquired Rights Directive of 1977 applies in situations where one employer is taken over (or transferred to) by another employer. The Directive ensures that when employees have been transferred to the new employer they will continue to enjoy the same contractual conditions that they had with their previous employer. The Directive states that the new employer will have to respect these contractual terms for a minimum of one year after the transfer has taken place. Unfortunately, this part of the Directive has never been implemented into United Kingdom law. The main provisions of the Directive were, however, brought into force as a result of the Transfer of Undertakings (Protection of Employment) Regulations 1981. Regulation 8(1) states that a dismissal of an employee that occurs either before or after a transfer will be automatically unfair if the reason for the dismissal was the transfer or a reason connected with it. It was previously the practice of many employers to dismiss the workforce either shortly before or after a transfer of a business had taken place and then offer the employees new terms and conditions of employment which were worse than those that they had previously enjoyed.

The Acquired Rights Directive 1977 and the 1981 Regulations apply in situations where a business (i.e. an undertaking) is taken over by another business. Furthermore, when a service is privatised or put out to contract, the Directive and the Regulations will also apply. The Directive and the Regulations will not apply to situations where a business is taken over by someone buying up shares. Admittedly, transfers of undertakings can be a very difficult area of law to understand.

The European Court of Justice in **Allen v Amalgamated Construction (2000)** stated that a relevant transfer is:

'a change in the nature or legal person responsible for carrying on the business who by virtue of this acquires the obligations of an employer vis-à-vis employees of the undertaking, regardless of whether or not ownership is transferred.'

The European Court of Justice in **Allen** also stated that an entity or an undertaking is:

'an organised grouping of persons or assets facilitating the exercise of an economic activity which pursues a specific object.'

An undertaking could be, therefore, be identified by reference to its employees or workers, its management, the way in which it is organised, its operating procedures and its assets. An undertaking must be stable, identifiable and not confined to the performance of just one contract.

 Litster v Forth Dry Dock and Engineering Co Ltd (1990) Forth Dry Dock went into receivership in September 1983. A company was formed in order to acquire the business of the dry dock. The transfer of the business to the new company was to take place at 4.30 p.m. on 6 February 1984. At 3.30 p.m. on that day, Forth Dry Dock dismissed the entire workforce with immediate effect. Within 48 hours, the new company began to recruit a similarly sized workforce, but at a lower rate of pay. Only three of the former dry dock workers obtained work with the new company. Litster, one of the employees who had failed to gain new employment with the new owner of the dock, lodged a claim for unfair dismissal in connection with a transfer of an undertaking.

Held: by the Industrial Tribunal found that Litster had been unfairly dismissed and that the Transfer of Undertakings (Protection of Employment) Regulations 1981 applied to his situation. Accordingly, the transferee, the new company had to pay him compensation. However, the Court of Session disagreed stating that even one hour before the transfer was long enough for the Forth Dry Dock to claim that the worker was not employed immediately before the transfer. Litster appealed to the House of Lords. Here, the Court of Session's decision was overturned. The TUPE Regulations 1981 had to be interpreted on such a way as to give effect to the United Kingdom's duties under the Acquired Rights Directive 1977. The House of Lords effectively inserted new wording into the Regulations to cover instances of unfair dismissal. Litster could pursue an action for damages against the transferee because he would have been employed immediately before the transfer had he not been unfairly dismissed.

Regulation 8(2) states that paragraph (1) will not apply if the reason for the dismissal is an economic, technical or organisational reason involving changes in the workforce of either the transferor or transferee. If the employer can show that he has dismissed an employee for an economic, technical or organisational reason, the dismissal will not be classed as automatically unfair.

In **Katsikas v Konstantidis C132/91 (1993) IRLR 179** the European Court of Justice ruled that an employee could not be transferred to the employment of a new employer against his will. If such an employee does object to his employment being transferred, the transfer effectively terminates his employment, but he will not be able to claim that he has been unfairly dismissed.

Dismissal in connection with spent convictions in relation to Section 4(3)(b) of the Rehabilitation of Offenders Act 1974

If the employee has previously been convicted of a criminal offence, he will, for certain periods of time laid down by the Rehabilitation of Offenders Act 1974, have to declare his conviction when applying for employment. However, there will come a point when many convictions are regarded as spent i.e. the individual will no longer have to declare them. If the employer decides to dismiss an employee for reason of a spent conviction, then the dismissal will be regarded as automatically unfair.

Other automatically unfair dismissals

An employee will be regarded as having been unfairly dismissed where he attempts to assert his rights to the national minimum wage (Section 104A:ERA 1996) and where he asserts his right to a tax credit (Section 104B:ERA 1996).

 Key point: When a dismissal is regarded as automatically unfair, an employee does not have to show that he or she has one year's continuous service with the employer in order to lodge a claim for unfair dismissal.

Constructive dismissal

Section 95(1)(c) of the Employment Rights Act 1996 recognises the concept of constructive dismissal. The employee's right to claim constructive dismissal arises in situations where the employer's conduct is to be regarded as a material breach of the employment contract and the employee is left with no alternative but to resign. However, the employee's resignation is not treated as the act which terminates the contract, rather it is the employer's conduct. The employer's conduct must be so serious in order to justify the employee's decision to resign. When an employee claims that he has been constructively dismissed, he is claiming that he was unfairly dismissed. The right of constructive dismissal would arise in situations where the employer made unauthorised deductions from wages, where the employer refused to follow the proper disciplinary or grievance procedures or where the employee was ordered to use equipment that was clearly dangerous.

 Sharp *v* Western Excavating Ltd (1978) Sharp's contract of employment entitled him to claim time off in lieu if he worked overtime for his employer. Sharp played cards as part of a team and he wished to take some time off from work in order to play in a particular game. His request for time off was refused because the company had a lot of work on and could not spare him from his duties. Undeterred by his employer's refusal, Sharp decided to take the time off in any case. As a result of this conduct, the company's foreman decided to dismiss Sharp. He then appealed to the employer's Internal Disciplinary Board which overturned the dismissal and, in its place, he received a five-day suspension without pay. Sharp found himself short of funds and asked his employer for an advance on his accrued holiday pay. This request was refused by the employer. Sharp then asked his employer to lend him a sum of £40 which the employer again refused to advance. Sharp then decided to resign from his employment in order to force his employer to pay his accrued holiday pay. He also claimed that his employer had behaved unreasonably and that he had no option but to treat himself as having been constructively dismissed.

Held: by the English Court of Appeal that the employer's treatment of Sharp had been reasonable throughout and he could not treat himself as constructively dismissed. The employer's conduct could in no way be described as a repudiation of the contract which would have allowed Sharp to consider himself as having been constructively dismissed. In a very important passage from the Court of Appeal's judgement, Lord Denning laid down the essential conditions for constructive dismissal:

'An employee is entitled to treat himself as constructively dismissed if the employer is guilty of conduct which is a significant breach going to the root of the contract of employment, or which shows that the employer no longer intends to be bound by one or more of the essential terms of the contract, then the employee is entitled to treat himself as discharged from any further performance. If he does so, then he terminates the contract by reason of the employer's conduct. He is then constructively dismissed. The employee is then entitled in those circumstances to leave at that instant without giving any notice at all or, alternatively, he may give notice and say that he is leaving at

the end of the notice. But the conduct in either case must be sufficiently serious to entitle him to leave at once. . . . . the employee must make up his mind soon after the conduct of which he complains. If he continues for any length of time without leaving, he will be treated as having elected to affirm the contract and he will lose his right to treat himself as discharged.'

 Sinclair *v* Fritz Companies (1999) EAT/904/99 Carole Sinclair received an invitation to go for lunch with her supervisors. During lunch, it became evident that this was not a purely social occasion as the supervisors began to discuss the possibility of imposing a disciplinary penalty on Sinclair. Sinclair had received absolutely no warning that the possibility of disciplinary action being taken against her would be discussed during lunch. Consequently, Sinclair felt that her trust and confidence in her employer had completely broken down and she resigned from her employment claiming that she had been constructively dismissed.

Held: by the Employment Appeal Tribunal that Sinclair's claim for constructive dismissal should succeed.

 Key point: An employee is entitled to treat himself as constructively dismissed if the employer is guilty of conduct which is a significant breach going to the root of the contract of employment, or which shows that the employer no longer intends to be bound by one or more of the essential terms of the contract.

Remedies for unfair dismissal

Sections 111 to 132 of the Employment Rights Act 1996 contain much of the detail relating to remedies for unfair dismissal.

An Employment Tribunal, on finding that an employee has been dismissed unfairly, may issue an order addressed to the employer to the effect that the employee is to be re-employed. The problem with issuing these orders is that the Employment Tribunal cannot force the employer to re-employ the dismissed employee. This is because of the nature of employment contracts which depend, of course, on the personalities of the parties and a level of goodwill continuing to exist between these individuals. At common law and at statute, a court will not force an employer to take back a dismissed employee if re-employment means that the relationship between employer and employee was going to be characterised by conflict.

Many employers will choose not to comply with an order to re-employ the dismissed individual and will be quite happy to pay the increased compensation which follows as a result of this decision on their part. Section 117(4)(a) of the Employment Rights Act 1996 allows the employer to argue that it is not practical to re-employ the dismissed employee. An employer may wish to use this provision in situations where a considerable length of time has passed between the dismissal and the Employment Tribunal's decision. Very often, the employer will have appointed a new employee to take the dismissed employee's place and this individual may well have acquired employment rights i.e. protection against unfair dismissal so the employer cannot dismiss this person without risking further legal problems. Additionally, the dismissed employee's job may since have disappeared as a result of a reorganisation of the employer's business or because the post has become redundant.

The two orders that an Employment Tribunal can issue requesting that the employee be re-employed are:

1   Reinstatement orders

2   Re-engagement orders

Reinstatement order

This requires the employer to give the employee back the job that he previously held and to treat him as if the dismissal had never occurred. The employee is entitled to any benefits that he would have received, but for the termination of his contract. This would include pay rises or salary increments or any other benefits, for example, concessionary rail travel (Section 114(1) Employment Rights Act 1996).

Re-engagement order

This requires the employer to engage the employee on comparable employment to that from which he was dismissed or to be offered suitable, alternative employment. The Employment Tribunal will decide the terms upon which the employee is to be re-engaged. It should be noted that this type of Order differs from a Reinstatement Order in that the employee is not being given back his old job (Section 115(1) Employment Rights Act 1996).

Compensation

In most situations, an Employment Tribunal will award compensation to the dismissed employee. Compensation consists of two parts:

1   The basic award

2   The compensatory award

The basic award

The basic award is calculated according to the following formula:

- The employee is entitled to one and a half weeks' pay for each year of service including and above the age of 41
- The employee is entitled to one week's pay for each year of service when the employee was aged between 22 and 40 inclusive
- The employee is entitled to half a week's pay for each year of service between the age 18 and 21 inclusive

However, this formula is subject to two further conditions:

- The maximum weekly wage that can be claimed is £270 – anything above this figure cannot be included in the calculation of the basic award
- The employee will only receive compensation for a maximum of 20 years' service – anything above 20 years will not be counted

In order to calculate the basic award, the employee should start with the effective date of the dismissal and count backwards. The following example can be quite useful:

Helen Smith, age 55, was employed continuously for a period of 30 years until dismissed on 12 December 2003. Helen received weekly wages of £250 at the time of her dismissal. To calculate her basic award Helen would count backwards from 12 December up to a maximum of 20 years. Therefore, ten years of her employment would not count towards the final total for the basic award and she could only claim £250 for her weekly wage not the maximum of £270. So, Helen has worked for 15 years between the ages of 55 and 41: (1½ × £250) = £375 × 15 = £5625. Helen has also worked for five years between the ages of 40 and 36: (1 × £250) = £250 × 5 = £1250. If the totals are added together (£5625 + £1250), Helen's basic award comes to £6875.

The basic award that the employee receives could be reduced for a number of reasons:

- Where the employee's conduct has contributed to the dismissal.
- Where the employer gave the employee a redundancy payment or ex-gratia payment.
- Where the employee has unreasonably refused an offer of reinstatement from the employer.
- Where the employee is aged 64, the award will be reduced by 1/12 for each whole month that has passed from his last birthday to the estimated retirement date (of 65).

The compensatory award

The compensatory award for unfair dismissal from 1 February 2004 is subject to a limit of £55,000. The award will cover immediate loss of wages, future loss, loss of pension rights and loss of statutory protection. The maximum award may be much greater in health safety dismissals, whistle-blowing cases and cases involving discrimination.

 Key point: An Employment Tribunal can issue Orders for Reinstatement or Re-engagement or, more commonly, an award of compensation will be made consisting of a basic award and a compensatory award.

Compensation for injury to feelings

In the House of Lords' decision **Johnson v Unisys Ltd [2001]**, Lord Hoffman suggested (in a remark which was *obiter* i.e. did not form part of the court's decision) that compensation can include an element for injury to the feelings of the dismissed employee. This, however, goes against the rule established in the much older case of **Norton Tool Co Ltd v Tewson [1972]**. In **Norton**, Sir John Donaldson was at pains to point out that compensation for dismissal only includes financial loss - not injury to feelings. These types of awards are, of course, available in discrimination cases. Strictly speaking, Lord Hoffman's remark about compensation for injury to feelings was not binding and did not overrule Sir John Donaldson's position in **Norton**. Lord Steyn, who was sitting as part of the same panel of judges that included Lord Hoffman in **Johnson**, did point out that, as the issue of mental stress and anxiety was not raised as part of the original action, it would be wrong for the House of Lords to comment.

However, since **Johnson v Unisys Ltd [2001]**, there has been a potentially significant development in this area of unfair dismissal law. It would now appear that compensation for injury to feelings caused by the *manner of the dismissal* may now be awarded (as per Lord Hoffman's obiter remark in **Johnson v Unisys Ltd**

[2001]). In February 2004, the English Court of Appeal in **Dunnachie v Kingston upon Hull City Council** stated that an award for unfair dismissal could also include injury to feelings. The English Court of Appeal overruled the Employment Appeal Tribunal's verdict in **Dunnachie** and is a major blow to the conventional wisdom that injury to feelings could not be included in an award for unfair dismissal as stated in **Norton**. Obviously, the House of Lords will now have to settle this matter in order to restore clarity to the law in this area.

 Key point: Compensation in unfair dismissal cases could now potentially include an element for injury caused to feelings by the manner of the dismissal.

Interim relief

In several situations, the Employment Tribunal can issue an interim order which means that the dismissed employee's contract will continue to have legal force until the outcome of the case is decided. An interim order can also be used to prevent the employee from being dismissed until the Employment Tribunal has made its decision. The employee, therefore, will continue to enjoy the benefits of his employment contract while his claim for unfair dismissal is being heard and ultimately decided upon. An interim order will only be granted in trade union dismissals, health and safety dismissals and dismissals where the employee has made a protected disclosure.

 Key point: An interim order can be very useful because it can prevent an employer from dismissing an employee until such time as the Employment Tribunal has made its decision.

Fair dismissal

Some dismissals by the employer will be automatically fair:

- On the grounds of national security
- During a strike or a lock-out

Section 98(2) of the Employment Rights Act 1996 details the reasons which an employer may rely upon to demonstrate that the dismissal was fair. The following reasons for dismissal are, therefore, potentially fair:

- Capability and qualifications of the employee for performing the work he was employed to do
- Sickness
- Conduct of the employee within and outwith employment
- Redundancy
- To avoid contravening statute
- Any other substantial reason

 Key point: Where an employee is claiming unfair dismissal, the employer may be able to counter this by relying on one of the potentially fair reasons for dismissal i.e. capability and qualifications, conduct, redundancy, contravention of statute or any other substantial reason.

Capability and qualifications

With respect to qualifications an employer may insist that, in order to be given employment, the employee must possess any relevant degree, diploma or other academic, technical or professional qualifications.

An employee may be said to lack qualifications if the employer states that he is required to pass any test after starting work which he then fails. In order to make this requirement legally binding upon the employee, there must be a term in the contract of employment which imposes a duty on the employee to gain the relevant qualifications.

Lack of qualifications

 Blackman v Post Office (1974) ICR 151 NIRC Blackman was appointed to the position of a post and telegraph officer. Blackman was appointed to the post on the strict understanding that he had to pass an aptitude test after he had he successfully completed his probationary period. Blackman failed the test three times (his third attempt was a very narrow fail). There had been no complaints about the quality of Blackman's work.

Held: the dismissal was fair because he had failed to secure the necessary qualification that his employer had made a condition of his continuing employment.

 Tayside Regional Council v McIntosh (1982) IRLR 272 McIntosh was employed by the Regional Council as a motor mechanic. When the post was originally advertised, the Council had made it perfectly clear to all applicants that the successful candidate had to possess a clear, current driving licence. A potential problem later arose for the Council in that there was no term in McIntosh's contract that stated that he had to possess a clear, current driving licence. McIntosh had been disqualified from driving and the Council had dismissed him.

Held: by the Employment Appeal Tribunal that McIntosh's failure to retain a clear, current driving licence was a breach of a material and continuing condition of his employment with the Council.

Usually, the employer will have to include a term in the contract of employment stating that an employee's continued employment depends on him securing a particular qualification, for example, a welder's certificate or a teaching qualification. Obviously, failure to secure such a qualification will give the employer the option of dismissing the employee fairly.

However, there will be situations where the employer has failed to include such a term in the employee's contract. An argument open to the employer would be to state that his requirements have changed since the employee was first appointed and that he can no longer be kept fully employed. The employer must act reasonably in applying a unilateral change to the employee's contract.

 Rooney v Davies Engineering Ltd (1979) ET Case No 14518/79 Rooney had passed the company's test and had successfully completed his probationary period. However, the company experienced a sharp decline in a particular area of work that Rooney was involved in. In fact, 90 to 95 per cent of the company's work was then carried out for one customer in particular.

This customer demanded that those of the company's workers who were engaged in producing his goods had to possess a particular welding qualification. Rooney did not possess this qualification. He had, in fact, sat the test to obtain the qualification on three occasions and each attempt had ended in failure. The Company had warned Rooney of the potentially serious consequences of such a failure in respect of his continuing job security. After his third failure, Rooney was dismissed by the company because it did not have enough work to keep him fully employed. The customer had refused to allow the company to give Rooney a fourth opportunity to gain the necessary qualification.

Held: by the Employment Tribunal that the dismissal was fair because there had been a change in the employer's requirements and Rooney was fully aware of the consequences of a failure to gain the necessary qualification.

Incapability

Lord Denning MR in **Taylor *v* Alidair (1978)** stated:

'Whenever a man is dismissed for incapacity or incompetence it is sufficient that the employer honestly believes on reasonable grounds that the man is incapable or incompetent. It is not necessary for the employer to prove that he is in fact incapable or incompetent.'

A reasonable employer is in the best position to decide whether an employee is not up to the job on the ground of incapability. It is not the place of the Employment Tribunal to overrule the decision of a reasonable employer in this matter.

 Taylor *v* Alidair (1978), an airline pilot had landed the plane in a grossly negligent way that clearly endangered life and limb. The employer was quite clearly justified when it decided to dismiss this particular employee.

 Clark *v* Airflow Streamlines PLC (1983) the employee was an experienced motor mechanic who had failed to carry out a job on a customer's car properly. Due to his negligence, the engine seized and the rear wheels locked while the customer was driving the vehicle. The employee was dismissed.

Held: the Employment Tribunal was influenced by the fact that the customer's safety could have been endangered and there was also the issue of the employer's good reputation being damaged by the employee's negligence. The dismissal was, therefore, regarded as fair.

 Steelprint Ltd *v* Haynes (1995) the company had introduced a new computer system. This meant that the employee's duties changed considerably. Her post had previously entailed proofreading. Her new duties meant that she was expected to input data into the new computer system. She was not able to carry out these duties to the standard required by the company. The employee had not received any training to help her cope with her new duties nor had she been offered alternative employment with the company that would have better suited her abilities. Nonetheless, the company decided to dismiss her for reason of incapability.

Held: by the Employment Appeal Tribunal that the dismissal was unfair. The lack of training and the failure to provide other opportunities was not the act of a reasonable employer.

Sickness

It is important that an employer investigate the background to the employee's sickness as fully as possible.

Smith *v* Post Office ET Case No 7707/95 the Employment Tribunal found that it was highly unlikely that the employee in question who was suffering from clinical depression would be able to achieve a satisfactory level of attendance at his work in the future. The dismissal of the employee on the grounds of his ill-health was considered to be fair.

The Employment Appeal Tribunal stated in **Spencer *v* Paragon Wallpapers Ltd (1977)** that Tribunals must look at all the circumstances before weighing up the economic needs of the employer and the need to treat the sick employee decently. The question that should be asked is 'how long the employer must be kept waiting for the employee to return to work?'

Employment Tribunals, however, tend to take a more lenient approach where an employer has dismissed an employee for a series of short-term and unconnected absences from work which are usually justified on the grounds of illness. An Employment Tribunal will often be swayed by the hardship caused to smaller employers by these periodic absences.

International Sports Co Ltd *v* Thomson (1980) in the last 18 months of employment leading to Thomson's dismissal, her absences from work reached a total of 25 per cent. All these absences could be explained by reference to medical certificates that Thomson had submitted. All of the illnesses were unconnected and there was no way that they could be independently verified by sending Thomson to a doctor for a medical examination. The employer, therefore, chose not to obtain a medical report before dismissing her. Thomson had been warned about her poor attendance on four previous occasions by the employer.

Held: by the Employment Appeal Tribunal that this dismissal was on the grounds of misconduct rather than the employee's sickness record and was, therefore, fair.

Rolls-Royce *v* Walpole (1980) Walpole had just managed to achieve an attendance record at work of approximately 50 per cent during the last three years of his employment. The employer had warned Walpole about his failure to attend work and it had even sent him for counselling to identify the reasons behind his absences two years before he was dismissed. The employer, however, failed to obtain medical evidence before he decided to dismiss Walpole.

Held: by the Employment Appeal Tribunal that the dismissal was fair.

Even if the employee's absence from work is covered by a sick note, this should not be considered as conclusive proof that the employee is medically unfit for work.

Hutchinson v Enfield Rolling Mills Ltd (1981) Hutchinson had
submitted a sick note to cover his absence from work due to sciatica. He was
later seen attending a trade union demonstration in Brighton during the
period that the sick note covered. The employer did not follow any procedure
and Hutchinson was dismissed.

> *Held*: the dismissal was fair.

In **East Lindsey District Council v Daubney (1977) ICR 566** the Employment
Appeal Tribunal stated that before an employee decides to dismiss an employee on
the grounds of ill-health, proper consultation must have taken place. Proper
consultation will consist of the following factors:

- The employer must hold discussions with the employee at the outset of the
  illness and these should continue throughout the course of the illness. The
  employee should be alerted when his dismissal is a serious option.

- There should be personal contact between the employer and the employee.

- The employee should be asked for his opinion regarding his medical condition by
  the employer.

- The employer should consider alternative employment for the employee within
  the organisation.

In **Taylorplan Catering (Scotland) Ltd v McInally (1980)** the Employment
Appeal Tribunal again stressed the importance of the employer holding
consultations with a sick employee. Such a consultation exercise means that the
employer's need to have the employee present at work can be weighed against the
employee's need to be given time to regain his health and fitness which makes his
return to work possible.

This area is now more complicated as a result of the Disability Discrimination Act
1995. When dealing with an employee who is absent from work due to ill-health, a
reasonable employer should take steps to establish whether the individual in
question is suffering from a disability. A disability will affect not only the individual's
ability to perform his job, but also his ability to perform normal day-to-day activities.
If this is the case, the employer will have to make reasonable adjustments in terms
of Section 6 of the Disability Discrimination Act 1995 to the employee's working
conditions in order to aid his return to work.

 Key point: When the employer decides to dismiss an employee on the
grounds of his sickness record, he will have to tread carefully in order to avoid
potential charges of disability discrimination.

Misconduct

This is a potentially fair reason that the employer can use to justify the employee's
dismissal. However, dismissal for a single act of misconduct will normally be
considered to be fair in cases of gross misconduct only. In many workplaces, the
employer will have a disciplinary code. Where there are 20 or more employees, such
a disciplinary code should form part of the written statement that each employee
should receive within two months of commencing their employment.

Disciplinary codes should be well publicised and consistently applied. Consistent application of the disciplinary code does not mean, however, that the employer will achieve the same result in every situation. Sometimes a warning, whether written or verbal, may be a more appropriate method of disciplining an employee who has been found guilty of misconduct. Alternatively, more serious penalties such as demotion or dismissal may be considered to be the correct approach in dealing with the employee's misconduct. This range of options available to an employer in cases involving the employee's misconduct is known as the band of reasonable responses. A reasonable employer should be allowed to select the most appropriate punishment.

Dismissal is the harshest punishment that can be imposed on the employee for behaviour that the employer considers to be gross misconduct. If the employer has acted reasonably in making the decision to dismiss the employee, an Employment Tribunal has no right to overturn this by stating that it would have imposed a more lenient punishment. The Tribunal must accept a reasonable employer's decision (**Iceland Frozen Foods Ltd *v* Jones (1983) ICR 17**).

A recent example of an employer failing to follow consistent disciplinary procedures is illustrated by the following case:

Rankin *v* Compaq Computers ET Case No S 103023/2002 three computer plant workers were dismissed by the employer for sending and/or receiving e-mail messages with a sexual content. The three employees claimed that they were treated more harshly in that, previously, other workers had committed equivalent and, in some case, worse offences. The three went on to claim that the practice of sending offensive e-mails via the employer's network was widespread. Evidence was shown that at least 100 employees were investigated for alleged abuse of the network, but in many cases no further action was taken by the employer. In fact, one of the managers, who was supposed to monitor the network and prevent such abuses from occurring, was an active participant in these activities. The manager was not dismissed and the employer chose not to pursue disciplinary action against this individual.

Held: by the Employment Tribunal that the three employees who had been dismissed knew that their behaviour was inappropriate and furtive. The Tribunal found that the employer had failed to apply the disciplinary procedures consistently and that the three dismissals were unfair. Two of the workers received a year's salary in compensation, whereas the third employee was entitled to receive nine months' salary.

In **L B Harrow *v* Cunningham (1996)** the Employment Appeal Tribunal stated that factors such as an employee's record might justify an employer punishing different employees in different ways.

In **British Home Stores Ltd *v* Burchell (1980) ICR 303** it was held that the employer does not have to prove beyond a reasonable doubt that the employee is guilty of misconduct. If the employer can show that, after a reasonable investigation has been carried out, he reasonably believes the employee to be guilty of misconduct, the dismissal will be fair.

If more than one employee is suspected of misconduct and it is not possible for the employer to discover who is in the wrong, the employer may be justified in dismissing all those employees who fall under suspicion.

Monie *v* Coral Racing Ltd (1981) ICR 109, the employer suspected several employees of having committed theft by breaking into the company safe during the course of their employment. After an investigation by the employer, it was still not possible to identify beyond a reasonable doubt which of the two employees was to blame. However, of the two employees suspected, one of them had to have committed the crime. Both employees were, therefore, dismissed.

Held: by the English Court of Appeal that the dismissals were fair.

Key point: In misconduct dismissals, the employer will have to show that he acted reasonably.

Misconduct committed outside working hours

It is often mistakenly assumed that if the employee commits an act of misconduct outside working hours, the employer cannot dismiss him. It is open to the employer to argue that his public reputation will suffer as a result of the employee's misconduct or that there are health and safety concerns that would arise. Many Employment Tribunal decisions have explicitly recognised that there is a clear relationship between the act of misconduct committed outside working hours and the interests of the employer. In this respect, it could be argued that employees are still acting within the scope of their employment when they committed an act which is considered to be one of misconduct. The consumption of alcohol and drug-taking after hours have landed many an employee in hot water with their employers.

McLean *v* McLane Ltd EAT 682/96 McLean was employed as a fork-lift driver. He had been convicted of being drunk and disorderly and of being in possession of cannabis. His employer read about his convictions in a newspaper. There was no suggestion and no evidence that McLean had ever performed his duties under the influence of alcohol or drugs. The employer decided to dismiss McLean on the grounds of misconduct.

Held: the Employment Appeal Tribunal ruled that the dismissal was fair as the employer was entitled to have real concerns about the consequences if McLean had come to work in an intoxicated state.

H B Raylor *v* McArdle EAT 573/84 McArdle was seen on a building site where he worked in an extremely drunken state. Admittedly, McArdle was off duty at the time when the incident took place. McArdle's employer, however, decided to treat his drunkenness as misconduct and he was dismissed.

Held: the dismissal was considered to be fair because the employer was protecting its reputation.

Pay *v* Lancashire Probation Service (2003) EAT/1224/02/LA Mr Pay was employed as a Probation Officer with specific responsibility for sex offenders. Outside working hours, Pay performed a type of circus act as a fire-eater and, to this end, he was a member of a troupe of performers known as House of Roissy which changed its name latterly to Roissy Workshops. Pay's extra-curricular activities were not especially controversial and he had even performed his act for the benefit of the public at a Probation Service Open Day. Problems began to emerge, however, when the local Police received an anonymous complaint concerning Pay's circus act. It was alleged that he had performed in a variety of public fetish clubs where he had been in the company of semi-naked female performers and where there had been a strong emphasis on sado-masochism. The Police forwarded these complaints to one of Pay's managers in the Probation Service. At first, Pay was suspended and later, following a disciplinary committee hearing, he was dismissed from employment. Pay's appeal against this dismissal was unsuccessful. Pay then lodged a claim with the Office of Employment Tribunals alleging unfair dismissal and, in addition, a breach of his human rights had occurred in respect of Article 8 (the right to private and family life) and Article 10 (the right to freedom of expression) of the European Convention on Human Rights.

Held: by the Employment Tribunal at first instance that Pay had not been unfairly dismissed in terms of the Employment Rights Act 1996 and that, furthermore, his human rights had not been breached. Pay's outside activities were clearly inappropriate when his position with the Probation Service was taken into consideration and his special area of responsibility (for sex offenders). His employers were justified in dismissing him in terms of Section 98(1) of the Employment Rights Act 1996 for some other substantial reason. Pay appealed to the Employment Appeal Tribunal who upheld the decision of the Employment Tribunal.

Misuse of drugs and alcohol

Employment Tribunals have tended to take a much tougher approach to the issue of drug abuse by employees. The use of drugs is illegal in terms of the Misuse of Drugs Act 1971 and employers can also find themselves being convicted of a crime if they have knowledge that drugs have been consumed on the premises.

 Key point: Many Employment Tribunal decisions have explicitly recognised that there is a clear relationship between the act of misconduct committed outside working hours and the interests of the employer.

Dismissal in order to avoid contravening statute

In certain situations, the continued employment of the employee will cause the employer to breach a statute. Such situations are particularly common in relation to health and safety issues or where the employee holds a position as a driver and he has received a ban in terms of the road traffic legislation.

 Yarrow v QIS Ltd ET Case No. 1270/79 Yarrow was employed as a radiographer whose continued employment was covered by the Ionisation Radiation (Sealed Sources) Regulations of 1969. The Regulations made it illegal for an employer to continue to employee an individual who had developed a number of specified diseases. Yarrow developed psoriasis – a disease which the Regulations listed – and, as a result, the employer decided to dismiss him. The employer had thought about suspending Yarrow, but the trouble with psoriasis is that it is a disease that cannot be cured – it can only be controlled. There was no real likelihood that Yarrow would be able to return to his work and, therefore, he was regarded as being permanently unfit for work.

Held: there was no alternative work that Yarrow could have performed for the employer. The employer had been correct to dismiss Yarrow as to continue to have employed him would have meant breaking the Regulations.

 Appleyard *v* F M Smith (Hull) Ltd (1972) Appleyard was employed as a driver and maintenance fitter who was banned from driving for a period of 12 months. The employer decided to dismiss him when it learned about his driving ban. A condition of the contract of employment was that employees had to hold a current driving licence. As part of the job, Appleyard had to carry tools and spare parts which the employer argued could not be carried on public transport. Furthermore, Appleyard's colleagues could not be expected to drive him out to jobs. There was very little point in continuing to employ Appleyard if all he was doing was hanging about the workshop while his colleagues were forced to take on his duties.

Held: the dismissal was fair on the grounds of a statutory ban. The Employment Tribunal did make the point that a larger employer may have been a position to offer Appleyard alternative employment, but in the present case where there were only three employees in the department this was not possible.

Dismissal on the grounds of redundancy

Section 139(1) of the Employment Rights Act 1996 states that dismissal on the grounds of redundancy will occur if:

1   The employer has ceased or intends to cease carrying on the business

or

2   The requirements for employees to carry out work of a particular kind or to carry it out at the place in which they are employed have ceased or diminished

It is important to determine whether an employee has been dismissed on the grounds of redundancy or if the employee and the employer have both agreed to bring the contract to an end. Obviously, if both parties have agreed to a mutual termination of the contract of employment, no dismissal on the grounds of redundancy can be said to have taken place. It is vitally important to establish, therefore, who was responsible for bringing the employment to an end. If the employer was responsible, then potentially the employee has a claim for a redundancy payment and, if the procedures were not properly carried out, the employee may have a further claim for unfair dismissal.

 Caledonian Mining Ltd *v* Bassett & Steel (1987) a number of the company's employees were faced with the prospect of redundancy. The company, which was part of a group, had given assurances to the affected employees that it would attempt to find them suitable alternative employment with an associated employer. Bassett and Steel received an offer of new employment from the National Coal Board. Both employees resigned from their employment with the company in order to take up the offer of new employment. Both Bassett and Steel later attempted to claim a redundancy payment from their former employer. Their old employer was disputing the fact that both men had been dismissed and argued that they had resigned from their employment in order to take up new employment with the National Coal Board. Therefore, both men were not entitled to a redundancy payment.

Held: by the Employment Appeal Tribunal that the employer's proposal to make these employees redundant had in effect terminated the contract. Bassett and Steel were entitled to receive a redundancy payment from their former employer.

 Murray *v* Foyle Meats Ltd (1999) Murray had been employed in an abattoir as a meat plant operative. Murray's duties under his contract of employment were mainly concerned with working on the slaughter line. However, his contract did allow his employer to move him to other jobs within the abattoir and, from time to time, this had happened. Some of Murray's colleagues, who did not work on the slaughter line, had a similar term in their contracts that allowed the employer to move them to different jobs as and when required. The employer later experienced a fall in business and it was proposed that Murray and a group of his colleagues who worked on the slaughter line should be made redundant. The employer argued that there was now less demand for a particular type of work carried out by a particular group of employees to which Murray belonged. Murray argued that his dismissal was unfair by claiming that the employer had been wrong to select only those employees who worked on the slaughter line for redundancy. Those employees who could be asked to work on the slaughter line, but who usually did not, should also have been included in the redundancy pool. The employer had, therefore, unfairly selected Murray for redundancy.

Held: by the House of Lords that the requirements of the business for employees to work on the slaughter line had decreased and this state of affairs had led to Murray's dismissal on the grounds of redundancy. The fact that other employees were employed on similar conditions to Murray was not a relevant factor. The employer's dismissal of Murray had been carried out fairly. Murray's dismissal had been *attributable* (the key word in Section 139(1)(b) of the Employment Rights Act 1996) to the fact that the employer's requirement for a particular type of work had decreased.

Dismissal on the grounds of redundancy will be automatically unfair if the employee was selected for redundancy in relation to any of the following:

1 Participation in trade union activities (Section 153: Trade Union and Labour Relations (Consolidation) Act 1992).

2 Pregnancy or for a reason connected with it (Section 99: Employment Rights Act 1996).

3 Making a protected disclosure in terms of the Public Interest Disclosure Act 1998 (Section 103A: Employment Rights Act 1996).

4 Raising or taking action on the grounds of health and safety (Section 100: Employment Rights Act 1996).

5 Involvement in activities related to his role as a trustee of an occupational pension scheme (Section 102: Employment Rights Act 1996).

6 Assertion of the right not to be forced to work on a Sunday because he was classified as a protected worker or a betting shop worker or because he has given an opting out notice to the employer (Section 101: Employment Rights Act 1996).

7 Assertion of certain statutory rights (Section 104: Employment Rights Act 1996).

8 Acting as an employee representative during consultations in relation to proposed redundancies or during the transfer of an undertaking (Section 103: Employment Rights Act 1996; and Regulations 10 and 11: Transfer of Undertakings (Protection of Employment) 1981).

 Key point: In order to show that the dismissal is on the grounds of redundancy, it is important that the termination of the contract meets the statutory definition of redundancy in Section 139(1) of the Employment Rights Act 1996.

Dismissal for some other substantial reason

Section 98(1)(b) of the Employment Rights Act 1996 gives an employer the opportunity to argue that an employee has been dismissed for some other substantial reason. This is a potentially a very broad category, but it should be viewed as dealing only with a very small number of situations that are not covered by the other four named categories in Section 98(2) of the 1996 Act.

The employer must show that the substantial reason used to justify the employee's dismissal was potentially a fair one. Once this has been established, the employer must convince the Employment Tribunal that its actions leading to the dismissal of the employee have been reasonable. The substantial reason for dismissal must not be trivial or frivolous. The category of some other substantial reason has been used to justify dismissal in the following situations:

◆ Where the employer wishes to reorganise the business and it becomes necessary to change the terms and conditions of employment in respect of the employees.

◆ Where the employer tries to prevent the employee from divulging business secrets to competitors or where the employee is attempting to establish a rival business of his own.

◆ Where the employer has come under pressure from a customer who has threatened to break off business relations unless a particular employee is dismissed.

◆ Where a fixed-term contract has expired.

◆ Where a transfer of an undertaking has taken place and economic, technical or organisational reasons make it necessary to dismiss the employee.

 Hollister *v* National Farmers' Union (1979) Hollister was employed as an official by the NFU. The NFU wished to reorganise its activities and this meant that Hollister would be forced to accept new conditions of employment. Hollister had no intention of accepting the new contract and he made these feelings adequately clear to his employer. The employer was unimpressed and informed Hollister that, if he did not agree to the new contract, it would have no alternative but to dismiss him. Hollister continued to refuse to accept the new contract and the employer made good its threat to dismiss him.

Held: by the English Court of Appeal that the NFU had an urgent need to reorganise its activities. The only way in which this could be done was to end the contracts which employees like Hollister currently enjoyed and offer new contracts with reasonable terms and conditions in their place. Hollister had unreasonably refused to accept this situation and, therefore, his dismissal was fair for some other substantial reason.

 Abey *v* R & E Holdings (Yorkshire) Ltd t/a Quick Pass School of Motoring ET Case No 14985/82 Abey was employed as a receptionist by Quick Pass, a driving school. She had a long-running personal relationship with one of the driving instructors. This driving instructor later left the company's employment and set up his own business which was directly in competition with Quick Pass. Quick Pass saw a substantial decline in its business. Given that Abey's position gave her access to customers and confidential information, her employer took the decision to dismiss her because there was a genuine commercial risk to the business if she remained in employment. It was felt that she would in a position to provide a serious competitor of Quick Pass with all sorts of confidential information and no reasonable employer could tolerate this situation.

Held: the dismissal was fair on the grounds of some other substantial reason.

In **Simmons *v* S D Graphics Ltd EAT 548/79** the Employment Appeal Tribunal pointed out that in situations where two employees with a close personal relationship both have access to confidential information, it is for the Tribunal to examine the facts in order to determine whether or not the decision of one of their employers to dismiss one of these individuals was for some other substantial reason.

 Meikle *v* McPhail (Charleston Arms) (1983) IRLR 351 the previous employer (the transferor) who ran a public house had transferred the business to a new employer (the transferee). The new employer had to dismiss employees because he discovered that, by purchasing the business, he had financially over-extended himself. In order to remedy this situation, the new employer had to make cutbacks and this meant the loss of several jobs. Meikle claimed unfair dismissal in relation to the transfer of an undertaking.

Held: by the Employment Appeal Tribunal that Regulation 8(1) of the Transfer of Undertakings (Protection of Employment) Regulations 1981 states that a dismissal of an employee that occurs either before or after a transfer will be automatically unfair if the reason for the dismissal was the transfer or a reason connected with it. Regulation 8(2) states that paragraph (1) will not apply if the reason for the dismissal is an economic, technical or organisational reason involving changes in the workforce of either the transferor or transferee. If the employer can show that he has dismissed an employee for an economic, technical or organisational reason, the dismissal will not be classed as automatically unfair. In other words, the employer will able to rely on the defence of some other substantial reason for the dismissal, but he must show that the dismissal was reasonable. Meikle's dismissal was held to be fair for some other substantial reason because the new employer was now in financial difficulty as a result of buying the business and, therefore, cutbacks had to be made.

 Key point: Dismissal for some other substantial reason is not a broad category that allows the employer to dismiss an employee with impunity – it covers a limited number of situations that are not covered by the other four named categories in Section 98(2) of the Employment Rights Act 1996.

Summary

- During the nineteenth century, the terms and conditions which made up the contract of employment were almost wholly determined by negotiations carried out between the employer and the employee.

- From the beginning of the twentieth century, however, the terms of the contract of employment became increasingly subject to parliamentary intervention.

- The contract of employment can also be influenced by the following sources – the common law rights and duties of the parties, collective agreements, the written statement of terms and particulars of employment, handbooks, codes of practice and other documents issued by the employer.

- If you are an employee i.e. you have a contract of service you are theoretically in a much better position than someone who has a contract for services i.e. an independent contractor.

- This distinction matters because if you are an employee the law gives you greater protection and more benefits that you would not receive if you were merely an independent contractor for services.

- Admittedly, some pieces of legislation, for example, the Working Time Regulations 1998 protect the broader category of workers and not just employees.

- The courts have developed a number of different tests in an attempt to determine whether someone works under a contract of service or a contract for services, for example, the control test, the economic reality test and the organisation test.

- Vicarious liability can arise where there is a contract of service meaning that the employer may be vicariously liable for the delicts or negligence of an employee, but not those of independent contractors.

- In Scotland, employment contracts do not have to be in written form and witnessed and it is quite legitimate to have an employment contract which is completely verbal in nature or implied from the actions of the parties.

- Sources of the employment contract include legislation, the common law, collective agreements, written statement of terms and particulars and company handbooks and codes of practice.

- The employer's duties under the contract of employment include – the payment of wages, providing work, indemnifying employees, treating employees with trust and respect and to take reasonable care for the safety of employees.

- The Health and Safety at Work Act 1974 imposes criminal penalties on an employer who fails to take reasonably practicable steps to ensure the health and safety of his employees.

- The common law duties of an employee are to provide personal service, to provide loyal service, to obey lawful and reasonable orders and to take reasonable care in the exercise of the employment.

- The contract of employment can be terminated like any other contractual agreement, for example, material breach, mutual agreement, frustration, operation of law, completion of task and expiry of a fixed-term contract.

- Wrongful dismissal arises in situations where an employer dismisses the employee in breach of his contract.

- Unfair dismissal is a dismissal which is contrary to statute and usually the employee must have at least one year's continuous service with his employer to be able to claim protection under the Employment Rights Act 1996.

- An employee and not an independent contractor will enjoy protection against unfair dismissal.

- Where an employee is claiming unfair dismissal, the employer may be able to counter this by relying on one of the potentially fair reasons for dismissal i.e. capability and qualifications, conduct, redundancy, contravention of statute or any other substantial reason.

- In a variety of situations, a dismissal by the employer will be automatically unfair and the employee does not need to have one year's continuous service in order to lodge a claim with the Office of Employment Tribunals

- The employee's right to claim constructive dismissal arises in situations where the employer's conduct is to be regarded as a material breach of the employment contract and the employee is left with no alternative but to resign.

- When an employee claims that he has been constructively dismissed, he is claiming that he was unfairly dismissed.

- In relation to successful unfair dismissal claims, an Employment Tribunal can issue Orders for Reinstatement or Re-engagement or, more commonly, an award of compensation will be made consisting of a basic award and a compensatory award.

- Compensation in unfair dismissal cases can now include injury for hurt caused to feelings.

- An interim order can be very useful because it can prevent an employer from dismissing an employee until such time as the Employment Tribunal has made its decision.

Test your knowledge

1 **a)** What is the difference between a contract of service and a contract for services?

b) It has been said that a judge knows an employment contract when he or she sees one.

Explain this statement.

c) Leigh, Lloyd and Laurence are employed by the Metropolitan University of Aberdeen as guides in its Wilsonian Museum. The University made it quite clear that the work was on a casual basis and Leigh, Lloyd and Laurence would be employed as and when their services were required. There was no fixed pattern of working hours and the three individuals could be called upon at any time during the day to come into work in order to conduct the guided tours for the University. Lloyd, Leigh and Laurence are responsible for their own tax arrangements as the University does not deduct their tax at source. When they were first appointed to their present positions, all three were more than happy to be employed on a casual basis. On many occasions, all three turned down shifts at the Museum because it was not convenient. The University accepted this and, at no time, was the threat of disciplinary action raised for refusing to turn up to work. The three did receive some training in how to conduct the tours and they were expected to wear a uniform when working and they had received some instruction so that they could follow the University's first aid policy. In the last week, however, the University has informed Leigh, Lloyd and Laurence that it intends to terminate their contracts after the summer holiday has ended. All three have been working for the University for just over a year and are convinced that they will have the right to bring an unfair dismissal claim if the University goes ahead with its proposal to terminate their contracts.

What is the legal position?

2 **a)** There is no such thing as freedom of contract where the modern relationship between an employer and an employee is concerned.

Assess the accuracy of this statement.

b) Helen was offered a new job and she duly signed the contract. Her new employer had insisted that a number of terms be included in the contract of employment. Under the contract, Helen can be forced to work more than 48 hours per week, she will be paid less than the minimum wage and, should she become pregnant, she will not be entitled to take maternity leave or receive maternity pay.

Can the employer force Helen to accept these extremely poor terms of employment?

3 **a)** Examples of vicarious liability almost always arise in situations involving an employer and employee.

Explain the concept of vicarious liability.

b) Iain is employed as an electrician by Sparks Ltd. Sparks Ltd was awarded a contract by the local education authority to carry out extensive rewiring of the electrical circuits in one of the local schools. Iain was sent out by Sparks to complete this work. Unfortunately, Iain was not particularly careful when completing the job and, consequently, some of the teachers at the school have been the victims of particularly nasty electric shocks when they switched on their computers in the classrooms. The injuries were so serious that some of the victims were admitted to hospital and they will be absent from work for the foreseeable future. The victims, however, are unsure whether to sue the local authority or Sparks.

What course of action should the victims take?

4 **a)** What should the written statement of terms and conditions of employment contain?

b) What is the legal status of the written statement of terms and conditions of employment?

c) Jennifer, a student, works part-time as a waitress in a small, family-run restaurant. She has been employed in the restaurant for just over two months, but she has not been issued with any written contract or even a basic, written statement outlining the main terms of her employment. Jennifer has even approached the restaurant manager, Mark, and asked him to issue her with something in writing which she can keep for future reference. Mark replied that small businesses do not have to issue anything in writing to employees. Jennifer, however, is persistent and will not let the matter drop. A fortnight later, Mark asked to see Jennifer at the end of her shift. Mark told Jennifer that he had to let her go because the business had not been doing so well lately. Mark gave Jennifer a month's pay in lieu of her notice and he told her that she could be sure of a good reference. Jennifer knows that Mark is not being honest about the reason for her dismissal and she suspects that she was dismissed because she insisted on being issued with written terms and particulars of employment.

Where does Jennifer stand legally?

5 a) List the various sources of the contract of employment.

b) What is a collective agreement and in what way is it of benefit to both an employer and the employees?

c) United Scottish Airlines has witnessed a dramatic decline in business over the last year. It has now become obvious to the company's board of directors that the only way out of this crisis is to make redundancies amongst the cabin crew. Shirley, a stewardess, has been selected for redundancy by United Scottish Airlines. Shirley is extremely unhappy about this development because she feels that the company has ignored the collective agreement that contained a redundancy policy. This collective agreement, negotiated by the company and the employees' trade union, had been directly incorporated into Shirley's contract of employment. Under this redundancy policy, staff were allocated marks according to criteria such as educational qualifications, language skills, aptitude, work experience and length of service with the company. Those employees who scored the highest marks would retain their jobs, whereas those individuals with lower marks would be selected for redundancy. The company has now decided to use a single criterion to determine who will be made redundant. The company is now operating a redundancy policy of last in first out. Shirley is strongly of the opinion that United Scottish Airlines cannot simply change the terms of the collective agreement without consultation. Furthermore, Shirley's trade union did not agree to make any changes to the collective agreement.

Advise Shirley.

6 a) In a contract of employment, both the employer and the employee owe duties to one another.

Provide an outline of the main duties of the employer and the employee in an employment contract.

b) Examine the following situations carefully:

i) Samir worked for a very well-known firm of accountants. Some time ago, it became apparent that the partners in the firm were helping various criminals to launder money. The partners were all charged and convicted at the High Court of Justiciary in Edinburgh. The trials were widely covered by the newspapers and television. Consequently, the firm was dissolved and Samir found himself unemployed. Samir is a very honest person and he knew nothing of the illegal activities of his employers. He has found it very difficult to secure another job as an accountant because of his employment history. Samir is a young man who once had a very bright future in accountancy and he feels bitterly upset at the way things have turned out for him.

ii) William has his own firm of builders and, over the last few years, he has gathered together an excellent team of employees. During the winter months, work in the building trade tends to decrease significantly and many businesses have to lay off their workers. William, however, has always been in the habit of retaining his employees. It would be bad for the business if highly skilled and experienced members of the workforce were made redundant. These employees will continue to receive wages from William, but they will not necessarily be given any work to do until the Spring of the year when business picks up. Some employees have been complaining because they feel that William has a legal obligation to provide them with work.

iii) Shona is employed as a computer trainer by a training and education organisation. Part of Shona's job involves running computing courses for recovering drug addicts. These computing courses are held in local church and community halls as part of an outreach programme. Her employer has provided Shona with a van in order to transport the laptop computers to the various locations where each class is held. Usually 20 machines are required for each session. One day, when Shona was out at one of her classes, she received threats from some drug addicts, who were not members of her class, who wanted to steal the computers. Shona managed to get away without any of the equipment being stolen. Shona has reported this incident to her employer. She has asked her employer to improve security precautions at these classes. Her employer has refused to do anything and it informed Shona that she will have to continue to work alone at these classes. Shona is terrified that next time her personal safety could be seriously endangered.

iv) Norrie works as a barman in a pub in Stirling. His employer is determined to cut the costs involved in running the pub. Alcohol and tobacco products are considerably cheaper in countries such as France and Belgium in comparison to the United Kingdom. One day, Norrie's employer asks him to drive a truck to France and, while there, buy a large amount of alcohol and tobacco products which he is to bring back to the UK. Norrie can take two other members of staff so that if the Customs and Excise people stop the truck, he and his passengers can claim that their purchases are for personal use only and, therefore, the employer can avoid paying a substantial amount of duty. Norrie is deeply unhappy about this situation. His employer has told Norrie that if he does take the truck to France, he will be disobeying a lawful and reasonable order.

v) Gerry is a plumber who is employed by a large firm. Gerry feels that his employers could be paying him a much better salary in recognition of the amount of work that he does. Gerry is finding it very difficult to meet his mortgage repayments and he has a couple of bank loans to pay off. To make ends meet, Gerry approached some of his employer's customers and offered to do work for them at lower prices. Many of his employer's customers were very receptive to Gerry's proposal and took him up on his offer. The nature of Gerry's job means that he can work unsupervised and he fit these private jobs around his official work for his employer. Another bonus for Gerry was that he could use the tools, equipment and materials supplied by his employer to carry out jobs for his private clients. His employer is, of course, completely in the dark about Gerry's private clients. Eventually, Gerry is so successful in building up his private clients that he decides to quit his job and start up a business of his own which will be in direct competition with that of his former employer.

vi) David was employed as a driver by a florist. He was out delivering flowers when he decided to stop at a newsagents in order to buy a paper. When David drew up the van in front of the newsagents, he could see that the shop was empty. Thinking that he would not be in the shop for long, he left the keys in the ignition and he did not lock the van. When David came back out of the shop, the van had been stolen by some teenage joyriders. The van was later found abandoned and burnt out on a piece of waste ground and all the flowers which were in the van were completely destroyed in the fire.

With reference to the contract of employment, what is the legal position in relation to each of the scenarios described above?

7 a) Describe the ways in which a contract of employment can be terminated.

b) Hannah, a former solicitor, was sentenced to 18 months' imprisonment for embezzling money from her clients. Hannah had not been permitted to practise as a solicitor by the Law Society before her criminal trial, but she had managed to secure employment as an adviser to a local community group. Her employer has decided not to keep her job open for her during her prison sentence. The employer is arguing that the vacancy caused by Hannah's absence will have to be filled immediately and it would be totally unreasonable for Hannah to expect to walk back into her job 18 months down the line. The employer is also of the opinion that he does not have to give Hannah a period of notice or make her a payment in lieu of notice.

Do you think that Hannah's employer has behaved correctly?

8 a) What is the difference between wrongful dismissal and unfair dismissal?

b) Charlene has been dismissed by her employer. In terms of her contract, Charlene was entitled to receive four weeks' notice from her employer if he intended to terminate her employment. In fact, Charlene was given one hour to clear her desk and leave the premises. Her contract of employment also stated that the employer could make a payment in lieu of notice, but so far Charlene has not received a penny from her employer. Charlene's conduct during her employment has been absolutely impeccable and she is totally mystified at her employer's conduct. She has attempted to appeal against her employer's decision to terminate the contract, but she has been told that the decision has been made and will not be reversed.

What can Charlene do?

9 a) What is constructive dismissal and when are employees entitled to treat themselves as constructively dismissed by their employers?

b) Rose was employed as a sales assistant in a department store for a year and a half. She was subjected to bullying and harassment carried out by one of her supervisors. Rose took out a grievance against the supervisor and her employer promised to take appropriate action. In fact, the bullying got worse and Rose decided that she had had enough and resigned from her post.

Would Rose be entitled to bring a claim of constructive dismissal against her former employer?

10 In all of the situations described below, the employees have been dismissed from employment. Comment on the fairness of each dismissal.

a) Penny was the Branch Secretary of a trade union. She was very popular with her colleagues because she had successfully defended their terms and conditions of employment over many years. Penny was dismissed on the grounds of redundancy despite the fact that some of her colleagues with less experience and poorer qualifications retained their jobs. Penny is convinced that her employer's actions towards her are motivated by her trade union activities.

b) Colin was the Treasurer of his local golf club. He was convicted of stealing money from the cash register behind the club bar. Luckily for Colin, he received a fine and a suspended sentence because he had no previous criminal convictions. The criminal case, however, was widely reported in the local newspaper and Colin's employer decided to dismiss him from his employment. Colin had been a manager of a local building society.

c) Forth Council has decided to close some of the primary schools in the area because of falling numbers of pupils attending some of the schools. The Council has a redundancy procedure, agreed with the trade unions, which it has followed to the letter. Those individuals threatened with redundancy were offered suitable alternative employment where possible, but some redundancies were still unavoidable. Karen, a teacher with two years' teaching experience has been made redundant. She now wishes to challenge the fairness of her dismissal.

d) Monica worked for a butchers. She felt that her employer was not observing the appropriate food safety and hygiene rules.

Monica expressed her fears to the shop manager who promised to investigate matters. Several months later, it became obvious to Monica that her manager had no intention of following up the concerns that she had raised. Deciding that she had to take matters into her hands, Monica contacted the Council's Environmental Health Department and informed it of her fears. Monica's employer discovered that she had made the complaint to the Council and, consequently, she was dismissed from her employment.

e) Reza obtained employment as a trainee financial adviser. His contract stated that he would have to pass his financial planning certificate within three years of starting his employment. Reza has now been with his company for just over three years and he has not managed to obtain the appropriate qualification. He has attempted to pass his exams on the maximum number of opportunities permitted to him. His employer has now told him that it intends to terminate his contract.

f) The doctor has just confirmed that Susan is pregnant. She has informed her employer who has told her that he will have to dismiss her and employ someone in her place.

g) Arlene has a dreadful absence record. Every few weeks, she is absent from work due to ill health. There is no pattern to these illnesses and Arlene's employer asked her to attend a doctor's examination. The doctor can find nothing wrong with Arlene and her employer informs her that it will be monitoring her attendance at work for the foreseeable future. Several weeks later, Arlene sends in a sick-note from her doctor stating that she will be absent from work for the next eight weeks. Her employer has decided that enough is enough and informs Arlene that she is being dismissed from employment.

h) Ellie has been employed as a nurse in a psychiatric unit of a local hospital for the last six months. Some of the patients that Ellie has to work with can be dangerous and, on some shifts, not enough members of staff are present to supervise the patients adequately. On one occasion, a patient stabbed a nurse. Ellie, who is a health and safety representative, has consistently raised her concerns about the poor staffing levels in the psychiatric unit with the hospital management. Just before Ellie's temporary contract comes to an end, she is informed by one of the hospital managers that, regrettably, the hospital will have to let her go.

i) Sheelagh runs a business and many of her customers purchase goods on credit. The Consumer Credit Act 1974, of course, imposes a duty upon Sheelagh to apply for a licence from the Office of Fair Trading to be able to enter into consumer credit agreements with her customers. Recently some serious allegations about Sheelagh's her manager, Andrew, have come to her attention. It seems that in a previous job, Andrew had been successfully sued at the Employment Tribunal by individuals who claimed that he had discriminated against them on the grounds of their sex and race. Andrew is primarily responsible for deciding which customers are granted credit facilities by the business. Sheelagh's solicitor has informed her that by continuing to employ Andrew she may be endangering her credit licence because if the Office of Fair Trading hears about Andrew's previous history it will surely revoke the licence.

j) Workers at Boyle's factory have decided to go on strike for better pay and conditions as negotiations between the trade union and the management have completely broken down. The union has carried out the proper balloting procedure which the law demands, but two weeks into the strike the employer decides to dismiss Richard, Julie and Lorraine as they are considered to be the ringleaders behind this particular episode of industrial action.

k) Kevin is a senior manager with an IT company. He has just married Maureen, who is a director with a company which is a serious rival of his employer's. Upon his return to work from his honeymoon, Kevin is invited to a meeting by the Chief Executive of the company. The purpose of the meeting is to discuss Kevin's future employment with the company. The Chief Executive is extremely concerned that Kevin may divulge important business secrets to his wife. Unfortunately, his employer will now have to dispense with Kevin's services.

11 Describe the remedies that are available to a person who proves to an Employment Tribunal that he has been unfairly dismissed.

INTRODUCTION TO THE LAW OF EMPLOYMENT PART 2

Introduction

Over the last thirty years, the Westminster Parliament has introduced a large amount of equality legislation aimed at combating discrimination experienced by people in a variety of situations. This chapter, however, is primarily concerned with discrimination in employment. Employees will suffer discrimination if they can demonstrate that their employers subjected them to less favourable treatment by reason of their gender, race, disability, sexuality, religion or even employment status. It should be appreciated that British equality legislation covers a huge area and, in 2006, it will expand further to cover discrimination on the grounds of a person's age.

This chapter will cover the following areas:
* Sexual and racial discrimination *
* Equal pay *
* Disability discrimination *
* Part-time workers and fixed-term employees *
* Discrimination on the grounds of sexual orientation, religion or belief *
* The legal framework of employment law *

Discrimination in employment

British employment law now provides protection to a variety of individuals and groups of people who may suffer some form of discrimination. In the United Kingdom, discrimination is forbidden in the following circumstances:

* On the grounds of gender or sex (the Equal Pay Act 1970, the Sex Discrimination Act 1975 (as amended), Equal Pay Directive 75/117/EEC, the Equal Treatment Directive 76/207/EEC and the Sex Discrimination (Gender Reassignment) Regulations 1999).

* On the grounds of marital status (the Equal Pay Act 1970, the Sex Discrimination Act 1975 (as amended), Equal Pay Directive 75/117/EEC and the Equal Treatment Directive 76/207/EEC.

- On the grounds of colour, nationality, racial, ethnic or national origin (the Race Relations Act 1976 (as amended)).

- On the grounds of disability (the Disability Discrimination Act 1995).

- On the grounds of being a part-time worker (the Part-Time Workers (Prevention of Less Favourable Treatment) Regulations 2000).

- On the grounds of being a fixed-term worker (the Fixed-Term Employees (Prevention of Less Favourable Treatment) Regulations 2002).

- On the grounds of sexual orientation (the Employment Equality (Sexual Orientation) Regulations 2003).

- On the grounds of religious or philosophical beliefs (the Employment Equality (Religion or Belief) Regulations 2003).

In 2006, it will also become illegal to discriminate against someone because of that person's age. After a brief examination of the above list, it should now be obvious that protection from discrimination in the field of employment has expanded greatly since the 1970s onwards.

 Key point: The United Kingdom's discrimination legislation protects a wide variety of individuals and groups.

What do we mean by discrimination?

Put simply, an individual or a group of individuals will suffer less favourable treatment by reason of gender or sex, transsexuality, colour, nationality, racial, national or ethnic origin, disability, their sexual orientation, religious or philosophical beliefs or employment status. In other words, someone will suffer some sort of detriment or harm which is related to one of their personal characteristics, for example, his race or her employment status, for example, the fact that she is a part-time worker. Detriments can come in all shapes and sizes:

- Lack of promotion and training opportunities
- Different pay scales and conditions of employment
- Unfairness in the recruitment process
- Dismissal from employment
- Failure to receive the same contractual benefits as fellow employees
- Different retirement ages
- Different dress codes
- Unilateral changes to an employee's contract of employment
- Age requirements in relation to certain posts
- Harassment and victimisation
- Selecting certain individuals for redundancy first
- Refusal to allow more flexible working patterns

 Key point: Discrimination means that an individual or a group of individuals will suffer less favourable treatment by reason of gender or sex, transsexuality, colour, nationality, racial, ethnic or national origin, disability, sexual orientation, religious or philosophical beliefs or employment status and this difference in treatment cannot be objectively justified.

Sexual and racial discrimination

Sexual and racial discrimination are illegal in terms of the Sex Discrimination Act 1975 (as amended) and the Race Relations Act 1976 (as amended) respectively. Both pieces of legislation are very similar in that they use a common framework. However, the Race Relations Act has been amended twice since 2000 and very significant changes have been made to it. This is partly in response to the recommendations of the MacPherson Inquiry, published in 1999, in relation to the death of the black teenager, Stephen Lawrence, in 1993 and the European Race Directive (Council Directive 2000/43/EEC).

The Race Relations Act

The Race Relations Act 1976 outlaws racial discrimination in relation to terms of employment, trade union membership, education, the provision of goods and services, and in the disposal and management of housing and other premises. Section 4(2) provides that an employer may not commit an act of race discrimination in the same circumstances as outlined in Section 6 of the Sex Discrimination Act.

The Race Relations (Amendment) Act 2000 came into force on 2 April 2001 in England and Wales. The new Act came fully into force in Scotland on 30 November 2002. It strengthens and extends the scope of the Race Relations Act, but the new Act does not replace the 1976 Act. The amended Race Relations Act also imposes general duties on listed public authorities to promote racial equality. The general duty means that public authorities will have to eliminate unlawful discrimination and promote equality of opportunity and good race relations in carrying out their functions. The British government minister known as the Home Secretary can impose specific duties on listed public authorities (including non-devolved Scottish bodies) and Scottish Executive Ministers can impose specific duties on devolved bodies in order to meet the general duty.

The phrase 'public authority' can be interpreted very widely and will most obviously include bodies such as the national government departments, devolved government in Scotland and Wales and local authorities across the United Kingdom. However, bodies such as the National Health Service, the Police, housing associations, schools, universities and further education colleges could all be classified as 'public authorities' in terms of the Race Relations Act.

The Race Relations Act makes it unlawful for any public authority to discriminate in the carrying out of all its functions. The definition of 'function' will include any action that a public authority takes in the course of its duties, and will cover law enforcement activities which were not covered previously by the Act. Public authorities will now have to draft a race equality scheme. This is a statement of how a listed public authority plans to meet both its general and specific duties to promote equality under the amended Race Relations Act. A listed public authority is one that is named in schedule 1A to the Race Relations Act.

The Race Relations Act also makes it illegal for private and voluntary sector bodies to discriminate in the carrying out of any function which is classed as a 'public function'. If a local council contracts work out to a private company, for example, to provide social work and care services to the elderly, the private company will be covered by the Act. In terms of employment law, public authorities with more than 150 full-time employees must pay particular attention to the following:

- Grievance procedures
- Disciplinary procedures
- Performance appraisals
- Training
- Dismissals

Furthermore, all public authority employers must take particular care must be able to provide information as to the numbers of individuals from the various ethnic groups who are currently employed, who have applied for positions, who have been promoted within the organisation and who have received training. This information must be published every year.

The Race Relations Act applies to all employers no matter how small or large these organisations may be. The Act also applies to employment agencies.

On 19 July 2003, the Race Relations Act 1976 (Amendment) Regulations 2003 ('the Race Regulations') were introduced to take account of the important changes introduced by the European Race Directive which, amongst other things, affects the definition of indirect discrimination. Significantly, the amended Race Relations Act now applies to police forces. Chief Constables will now be responsible for acts of race discrimination carried out by officers of their police forces.

 Key point: The Race Relations Act 1976 outlaws race discrimination in relation to terms of employment, trade union membership, education, the provision of goods and services, and in the disposal and management of housing and other premises.

Selecting a comparator in race discrimination claims

Section 3 of the Race Relations Act demands that a complainant alleging race discrimination must be able to carry out a like with like comparison with someone who is of a different colour or nationality or who is a member of a group that has different racial, ethnic or national origins. If the complainant cannot identify such a comparator, his case will fall at the first hurdle. The complainant can compare himself to an actual or hypothetical comparator.

The Sex Discrimination Act

The Sex Discrimination Act 1975 outlaws sexual discrimination in relation to terms of employment, training, education, the provision of goods and services and the disposal of premises. Section 6 of the Act specifically applies to employment. An employer may commit an act of sex discrimination in the following circumstances:

- Making arrangements for the purpose of determining who should be offered employment, for example, discriminatory advertisements or sexist job titles.

- The terms on which employment is offered, for example, men enjoy more favourable treatment in respect of their conditions of employment in comparison with their female colleagues.

◆ A person is refused employment because of their sex or marital status.

◆ a person experiences discrimination or less favourable treatment in relation to opportunities for promotion, transfer or training or to other benefits, facilities or services by reason of his or her sex.

◆ A person is dismissed or experiences some other kind of detriment by reason of their sex.

Since November 1987, it is now unlawful, in terms of the Sex Discrimination Act 1986, for an employer to operate two different compulsory retirement ages – one for men and women. The European Court of Justice held that the practice of having different compulsory retirement ages where men retired at age 65 and women at age 60 was in breach of the Equal Treatment Directive (**Marshall South West Hants Area Health Authority (1986) IRLR 40**).

 Key point: The Sex Discrimination Act 1975 outlaws sexual discrimination in relation to terms of employment, training, education, the provision of goods and services and the disposal of premises.

Selecting a comparator in sex discrimination claims

Section 5 of the Sex Discrimination Act make it very clear that it is absolutely central to the success of a claim that the complainant can compare his or her allegedly less favourable treatment to an actual or hypothetical male/female comparator. If he or she cannot do this, the claim will fail. A woman claiming that she has suffered discrimination on the grounds of her sex must be able to carry out a like with like comparison. The woman's circumstances and those of her male comparator must be the same or they should not be materially different otherwise a meaningful comparison cannot be made. In cases where the alleged discrimination is connected to pregnancy, it is not necessary for a female complainant to identify an actual or hypothetical male comparator.

 Shamoon v Chief Constable of the Royal Ulster Constabulary (2003) ICR 337 the Royal Ulster Constabulary removed one of its female Chief Inspectors from certain staff appraisal duties which formed part of her post. There had been a number of complaints made about the way in which she had handled these appraisals. Two of her male colleagues (also senior officers) were not removed from these duties. Significantly, there had been no complaints made against these male officers concerning the way in which they operated procedures for staff appraisals. The female officer took lodged a claim with the Office of Employment Tribunals alleging unlawful sex discrimination.

Held: by the House of Lords that there was a genuine material factor which explained the difference in treatment. The male officers were not the subjects of complaints whereas the female officer was. Consequently, this justified the way that she had been treated. She could not compare herself to her male colleagues because their circumstances were materially different from her own. To have permitted her to make such a comparison would have been totally inappropriate i.e. she would not have been comparing like with like.

Key point: The Sex Discrimination and Race Relations Acts employ a common framework, but the race legislation has been strengthened to take account of the recommendations of the MacPherson Report and the provisions of the European Race Directive.

The burden of proof

Sex and race discrimination claims must be lodged with the Office of Employment Tribunals within three months (less one day) of the discriminatory act complained of.

Once a claim has been lodged before an Employment Tribunal, the difficult issue of proving that the employer discriminated against the employee on the grounds of sex or race comes very much to the forefront. Many employers who are guilty of sex and race discrimination are unlikely to admit this publicly and even privately they will try to justify to themselves the less favourable treatment to which they subjected an employee.

So, how do Employment Tribunals approach this problem? As a result of the Sex Discrimination (Indirect Discrimination & Burden of Proof) Regulations 2001 implemented the EU Burden of Proof Directive (Council Directive 97/80/EC) into United Kingdom law, things have become much easier for an employee. In sex discrimination claims, it will be for the employee to show the facts that prove less favourable treatment and if the employer is unable to come up with a satisfactory explanation which would disprove the complaint, the Tribunal *must* now decide in favour of the employee. Previously, an Employment Tribunal could infer discrimination where the employee presented evidence that she had been discriminated against and where the employer failed to provide a satisfactory explanation for his treatment of the employee (**King v Great Britain-China Centre (1991)**). However, according to the House of Lords, the Employment Tribunal was not forced to reach this finding of less favourable treatment (**Zafar v Glasgow City Council (1998)**).

 Key point: In sex discrimination claims, the European Burden of Proof Directive makes it easier for an employee to prove less favourable treatment.

In discrimination claims involving race, there are two standards to be applied. Where the employee is raising a discrimination claim on the grounds of his colour or nationality, the older standard of proof established in **King v Great Britain-China Centre (1991)** and **Zafar v Glasgow City Council (1998)** will apply. However, as a result of the Race Regulations, discrimination claims involving a person's race or ethnic or national origin, the new burden of proof that is used in sex discrimination claims will apply. There is not much to separate the two burdens of proof for race claims and, in practice, once an employee has presented evidence which shows discrimination on the employer's part and the employer has failed to provide a satisfactory explanation of his behaviour, Employment Tribunals may, in any case, draw the appropriate conclusion.

 Key point: In race discrimination claims, the burden of proof that is used will depend on whether the case concerns the person's colour or nationality *or* his racial, ethnic or national origin.

Less favourable treatment

In terms of both the Sex Discrimination Act and the Race Relations Act, the less favourable treatment suffered by the complainant must have occurred by reason of that person's sex or race. In **Law Society & others v Bahl (2003)**, the Employment Appeal Tribunal stated that the Law Society had treated Ms Bahl, its former Vice-President, unreasonably. Ms Bahl had brought a claim of race discrimination against the Law Society. Unlawful discrimination will always be an example of unreasonable treatment. However, merely because someone has been treated unreasonably does not mean that they have been discriminated against. Employment Tribunals will have to be careful and bear this in mind when dealing with cases where it is alleged that discrimination has taken place.

Sex and race discrimination questionnaires

The Sex Discrimination and Race Relations Acts permit a person making a complaint (the complainant) to serve a questionnaire on his or her employer. This is a process whereby the employee ask the employer to provide important information which should help establish whether there is a potential discrimination claim. The questionnaire and the responses can be used in evidence at an Employment Tribunal Hearing. It will be for the Employment Tribunal to decide whether discrimination has taken place. Employers are, therefore, encouraged to cooperate with such a questionnaire and any refusal to answer the questions on their part or if evasive responses are given, the Employment Tribunal may draw the appropriate conclusions and find that discrimination has indeed taken place.

The Equal Opportunities Commission and the Commission for Racial Equality

The Equal Opportunities Commission (EOC) was established by the Sex Discrimination Act 1975. Its primary role is to promote gender equality in the workplace, in education and in training. Recently, the EOC has been given greater responsibilities as a result of the introduction of the new equality laws in December 2003 which prohibit discrimination on the grounds of sexual orientation and religion or belief. The EOC monitors practices that could be a breach of the sex discrimination and equal pay laws. The EOC will often take legal action against organisations and employers who are deemed to have broken the equality legislation and this has resulted in some landmark legal decisions (see **R v Secretary of State for Employment *ex parte* Equal Opportunities Commission (1994)**). The EOC will often fund the legal fees of those individuals who wish to take sex discrimination claims to court, but would otherwise lack the means to do so. The EOC publishes reports and statistics and runs campaigns which highlight areas where there still exist substantial inequalities between men and women in respect of pay, terms and conditions of employment, employment opportunities, education and training. Employers can consult the EOC in order to obtain advice and assistance and, to this end, the EOC often publishes Codes of Practice in order to clarify the equality laws and to promote best practice in the workplace. The EOC has a Scottish Office in order to take account of the different legal system and education system in Scotland. The Equal Opportunities Commission is an independent, non-departmental public body, funded primarily by the government. Although independent from the government, it is responsible to the Equality Minister.

The Commission for Racial Equality (CRE) was established by the Race Relations Act 1976. Like the EOC, it is an independent, non-departmental public body, funded primarily by the government. Although independent of the government, it is responsible to the Equality Minister. The CRE performs very similar functions to the EOC in the field of racial equality. Both the EOC and the CRE have been given powers to conduct formal investigations where an allegation of sex or race discrimination has been made. These investigations can take place against a background of an allegation against a named individual (usually a business or an organisation) or an investigation into areas of general interest, for example, how many Black and Asian people are recruited into all of the United Kingdom's police forces. As part of their investigations, the EOC and CRE can order people and organisations to hand over documents or give evidence (although in order to exercise this power, the Secretary of State must have authorised this). If the EOC or the CRE finds that unlawful discrimination has occurred, they can issue a non-discrimination notice to the relevant parties forcing them to take steps in order to ensure that further acts of discrimination are prevented. The CRE can take legal action against parties who either fail or refuse to comply with such a notice. As a result of an investigation, the EOC and the CRE can make recommendations to any relevant bodies and it must produce a report which can be made public.

 Key point: The Equal Opportunities Commission and the Commission for Racial Equality are statutory bodies which have responsibility for policing the Sex Discrimination Act and the Race Relations Act respectively.

Positive discrimination

Generally speaking positive discrimination i.e. where an individual or a group are treated more favourably by an employer is not permitted. In **James v Eastleigh Borough Council (1990)** the House of Lords stated that although the Council was acting from motives of good faith, its policy in charging men entry to the swimming pool when women were admitted free was discriminatory. An employer can, however, under the Sex Discrimination and Race Relations Acts provide vocational training to existing employees of a particular sex, colour, nationality, race, ethnic or national origin on an extremely limited basis (SDA 1975: Sections 47 to 48 and RRA 1976: Sections 35 and 37 to 38)

It is, however, lawful for an employer to give preference to female candidates despite the fact that there is a suitably qualified male candidate. Such conduct by the employer is permitted where this forms part of an equality policy to try and do something about imbalances between men and women in the workplace (**Kalanke v Freie Hansestadt Bremen (1995)** and **Badeck and others (2000)**). The employer can claim, in terms of European law, that the positive discrimination is permitted by Article 2(4) of the Equal Treatment Directive which allows an employer to act to promote equal opportunity for men and women.

Exceptions to the Sex Discrimination and Race Relations Acts

The rules promoting sexual equality may not be applicable in the following situations:

◆ Employment Overseas – persons working wholly or mainly outside the UK are not covered by the Act.

◆ Police – male and female officers may be treated differently in relation to requirements relating to height, uniform and equipment. Female Police officers may receive special treatment in connection with pregnancy and childbirth.

◆ Prison Officers – different height requirements may be applied to male and female prison officers.

◆ Ministers of Religion – particular faiths and denominations may require that their ministers be of the one gender, for example, the Roman Catholic priesthood is an all male institution and its members are not allowed to marry or be married.

◆ Provisions relating to death or retirement.

◆ Pregnancy or childbirth – special treatment may be given to women in connection with pregnancy or childbirth.

The rules promoting racial equality may not be applicable in the following situations:

◆ Employment Overseas – persons working wholly or mainly outside the UK are not covered by the Act.

◆ Employment on board ships – if a person making a complaint of racial discrimination was recruited abroad.

◆ The United Kingdom's immigration laws and nationality quotas for Civil Service posts.

◆ Employment in private homes.

◆ Judicial acts and decisions, as are decisions of the Lord Advocate and the Crown Office not to prosecute in criminal cases.

 Key point: The Sex Discrimination and Race Relations Acts will not always apply to every situation and will be subject to a number of exceptions.

Forms of discrimination

In terms of the equality legislation, discrimination can take a number of forms:

◆ Direct discrimination
◆ Indirect discrimination
◆ Harassment
◆ Victimisation

This equality legislation does, however, explicitly recognise that in some situations it may actually be right and proper to discriminate against someone by reason of that person's gender or race or nationality. Employers will be able to rely on genuine occupational qualifications when they are recruiting potential employees or when they are considering employees for promotion or for training opportunities. In some situations, for example, the post of rape counsellor it would probably be inappropriate to employ a man. Many victims of this appalling crime would doubtless prefer to be counselled by a female professional. Therefore, it would be perfectly legitimate for an employer to hire a female applicant for the post of counsellor in preference to a male counterpart.

 Key point: The main types of less favourable treatment are direct discrimination, indirect discrimination and victimisation.

Direct discrimination

The concept of direct discrimination is found in Sections 1 (relating to women) and 2 (relating to men) of the Sex Discrimination Act and Section 1(1)(a) of the Race Relations Act centres around the concept that someone, for example, a woman or a member of an ethnic minority has suffered discrimination in relation to their employment if the employer treats them less favourably than he treats or would treat other persons. The reason for this less favourable treatment is related to the person's gender or their membership of a racial group. Very often, an employer will be accused of direct discrimination because he has consciously made a decision to discriminate against someone by reason of a person's gender or race.

The House of Lords stated in **James v Eastleigh Borough Council (1990) ICR 554** that the test that should be applied to cases of alleged direct discrimination is the 'but for' test. This test operates on the following principle: a person will have suffered direct discrimination if it can be demonstrated that a person would have been treated differently but for his or her sex or race. In **James**, men were forced to pay an entry fee for use of the Council's swimming pool whereas women were not forced to pay the entry fee. Mr James claimed that this was an example of direct sex discrimination because he would not have had to pay the entry fee, but for the fact that he was male. Interestingly, this case emphasises the fact that a man can use the Sex Discrimination Act to bring a claim of discrimination.

Direct discrimination will not be excused if an employer attempts to explain it by stating that he was motivated by good intentions. The less favourable treatment suffered by the employee will still be regarded as unlawful sex or race discrimination. So, in a situation where an employer refused to employ a woman because she would be the only female member of the team, his justification that he felt that the female employee would not be accepted by her male colleagues and that she may even have faced hostility cut little ice with the Employment Appeal Tribunal (**Greig v Community Industry (1979) ICR 356**). This was an example of direct sex discrimination.

 Key point: Employers will not be able to justify direct discrimination on the grounds of sex or race by stating that the actions were motivated by good intentions.

Employers are not permitted to discriminate against people on the grounds of their marital status (Section 3: Sex Discrimination Act). This means that a married person must not be less favourably treated in comparison to a single person of the same sex.

Dekker *v* Stichting Vormingscentrum voor Jonge Volwassen Plus (1991) was a Dutch case which came before the European Court of Justice. It was assumed to have clarified the law relating to sex discrimination claims where pregnancy is the issue. When Dekker went for a job interview, she informed the interviewing committee that she was pregnant. Dekker was undoubtedly the best candidate that the committee interviewed and, understandably, the committee selected her for appointment. Dekker's employers were less than happy about her pregnancy. They argued that it would be too expensive to pay her while she was on maternity leave and to pay the additional costs of hiring a replacement worker during this period. The employers refused to approve Dekker's appointment to the post.

Held: by the European Court of Justice that it is *always* direct discrimination to refuse to offer employment to a woman for reason of her pregnancy. The European Court of Justice made it clear that a pregnant woman does not have to compare herself to a man. The need for pregnant women to compare their situations with men was one of the major weaknesses of the Sex Discrimination Act as it was originally enacted. For the avoidance of doubt, men generally do not become pregnant and for a woman to look around for a pregnant man would be like looking for the proverbial needle in the haystack. A woman can also allege that she has suffered less favourable treatment which amounts to direct sex discrimination during the recruitment process when there are no male candidates for the job.

An employer will also commit an act of direct sex discrimination if a female employee is dismissed by reason of her pregnancy (see **O'Neill *v* Governors of St Thomas More (1996)**). The dismissal can also be challenged on the grounds that it is automatically unfair in terms of Section 99 of the Employment Rights Act 1996.

Dekker seems a fairly simple legal principle: employers must not discriminate against women on the grounds of their pregnancy. An interesting question arises as to the legal position where a woman is appointed to a fixed-term temporary post and a short time later she discovers that she is pregnant. It would obviously be impossible for the individual in question to perform her contractual duties as a result of her taking maternity leave. It would now appear that the European Court of Justice has dealt with the issue in the following case:

In **Webb *v* EMO Air Cargo (UK) Ltd (1992)** the dismissal of a pregnant woman, recruited for an indefinite period, could not be justified merely because she would be prevented on a temporary basis from performing her work. The fact that Webb had initially been employed to cover another employee's maternity leave was irrelevant. Further, it was stressed that there should be no question of comparing Webb's position to that of a man similarly incapable for medical or other reasons. Clearly, Webb would not have won her case had she been employed on a fixed-term, temporary contract. Lord Keith of Kinkel was obviously influenced by the possibility that a woman on a fixed-term contract who goes on maternity leave may not be able to fulfill her contractual duties to her employer. This would place the employer at a clear disadvantage. A female employee who enjoys all the benefits of an indefinite or permanent contract, on the other hand, will only be temporarily absent from work due to her pregnancy.

 Key point: A woman who is treated less favourably on the grounds of pregnancy or for pregnancy related reasons will have suffered direct sex discrimination.

Direct discrimination on the grounds of race, colour, nationality or membership of an ethnic group or racial group

Racial discrimination will arise when a person suffers less favourable treatment by reason of colour, race, nationality or ethnic or national origin. Discrimination on the grounds of religion is covered indirectly by the Race Relations Act 1976 in that the religion in question must be one of the identifying characteristics of a racial, national or ethnic group. Jews and Sikhs are covered by the Race Relations Act, but Roman Catholics, Protestants and Muslims are not protected specifically by the legislation. Roman Catholics, Protestants and Muslims are found in many different racial, national and ethnic groups, so these religions cannot be said to be identified with any one particular group. Jews and Sikhs, for example, belong to distinct ethnic and racial groups where their religion is just one example of a shared identity.

Section 3 of the Race Relations Act defines 'racial grounds' as meaning a person's colour, race, nationality or ethnic or national origins. In other words, a person's membership of a specific racial group can be determined by reference to the criteria laid down in Section 3 above.

 Mandla *v* Dowell Lee (1983) a private school refused to give a Sikh boy a place at the school because he would not stop wearing his turban or have his hair cut. Sikhs, of course, belong to a religious group and the turban and long hair are symbols for male Sikhs. Obviously, the boy had suffered direct discrimination on the grounds of his religion, but the Race Relations Act 1976 does not forbid religious discrimination.

The House of Lords had to consider whether Sikhs were part of a racial group for the purposes of Section 3. It was held that Sikhs were not just a religious group, they were also an ethnic group who enjoyed protection under the Act.

The term ethnic group has a much wider meaning than a racial group. It will be important to establish that the members of an ethnic group have a shared history and culture of which they are conscious and which sets them apart from other groups. Other important issues to consider are whether the group originates from the same geographical area or whether the members share a common ancestry. A common language may indicate membership of such a group, although it does not have to be peculiar to the members of this group. The group may also have a common literary tradition and religion. Finally, the group may, throughout its history, have experienced persecution and harsh treatment in its dealings with larger groups.

Under the above criteria, Jewish people have qualified as an ethnic group because being a Jew is not just about a person's religion it is also connected to notions of ethnic identity and national origin (**Seide *v* Gillette Industries Ltd (1980)**).

Certain racial groups who are predominantly Muslim in terms of their religion have been able to claim the protection of the Race Relations Act where indirect racial discrimination has been an issue. Generally, however, Muslims, like other religious groups, are not protected by the Act.

 J H Walker Ltd *v* Hussain & Ors (1996) IRLR 11 the Employment Appeal Tribunal found that the employer's change of shift patterns resulted in fewer Asian employees being able to comply with a requirement of the employer that they work a particular day. The day that the employer wished the employees to work just happened to coincide with one of the holiest days in the Muslim calendar (the Feast of Eid). Many Asian employees simply refused to turn up to work on that day and were issued with final written warnings. They later claimed that they had suffered indirect racial discrimination. The employees had been discriminated against indirectly not because they were Muslims, but because as Asians a smaller number of them could comply with the employer's demand that they work a particular day in comparison with non-Asian employees.

 Key point: Discrimination on the grounds of a person's religion is not generally covered by the Race Relations Act 1976.

The fact that religious discrimination is not covered by the Race Relations Act is no longer such a disadvantage with the introduction of the Employment Equality (Religion or Belief) Regulations 2003 on 2 December 2003. Interestingly, the provisions of the Race Relations Act were extended to combat religious discrimination in Northern Ireland, but not the rest of the UK. The new regulations are discussed in more detail later in the chapter.

 King *v* Great Britain-China Centre (1991) Ms King, who was ethnic Chinese, applied for a post with the Great Britain-China Centre. She had been born in China and was fluent in the Chinese languages. King believed that she was more than suitably qualified for the post, but she failed to gain an interview. The Industrial Tribunal noted that the Centre did not employ anyone from an ethnic Chinese background. Five ethnic Chinese candidates in total had applied for the post, but none had been interviewed.

Held: by the English Court of Appeal that the employer could offer no satisfactory explanation as to why King had not been given an interview for the position of Deputy Director of the Centre. King had suffered direct discrimination on the grounds of her race. In this case, the Employment Tribunal chose to make an inference (a presumption) that there had been discrimination on the grounds of race because King had presented strong evidence to support such a finding. Until recently, **King** was the standard burden of proof in race discrimination claims. It is still the appropriate test for claims involving a person's colour or nationality and it has been extended to disability discrimination claims (see **Rowden *v* Dutton Gregory (2002)**).

The cases of **Northern Joint Police Board *v* Power (1997)** and **BBC Scotland *v* Souster (2001)** demonstrate that the term 'racial group' can cover the Scots, English, Irish and Welsh people within the United Kingdom. It will be appreciated, of course, that the Scots, English, (Northern) Irish and Welsh share a common British nationality.

 Northern Joint Police Board *v* Power (1997) an applicant for the job of Chief Constable of the Northern Constabulary claimed that he had been discriminated against as he had been rejected for the post because he was English. There was no discrimination on the grounds of nationality because Scots and English people are British, but there could be direct discrimination on the grounds of a person's racial origins.

Held: that the Scots and the English, although sharing the same nationality, were to be regarded as distinct racial groups who were protected by the Race Relations Act.

Discriminatory adverts or job titles

Advertisements used in the recruitment process or the use of particular job titles in employment will be unlawful if they give the impression that a person from a particular gender or racial group will be given preferential treatment. If a public house placed an advertisement in the local paper stating that it required a barman, it would give a strong impression that women need not apply for the position as the employer obviously favours men over women. Such an advertisement would be unlawful. Similarly, glossy advertisements that give the impression of an all white workforce may deter people who belong to ethnic minorities from applying for a position with the organisation. However, a member of the public could not bring a claim under either the Sex Discrimination or Race Relations Acts in respect of a discriminatory advertisements or job title unless this person had actually applied for the job and had been refused employment on the grounds of sex or race. Generally speaking, either the Equal Opportunities Commission or the Commission for Racial Equality will take legal action against employers in respect of discriminatory advertisements or job titles, not disgruntled members of the public. It is, of course, always open to members of the public to complain to one of the Commissions about the discriminatory behaviour of employers.

 Key point: Employers will have to be particularly careful to avoid using discriminatory job titles or advertisements.

Segregation

An employer will commit unlawful direct race discrimination if he insists on segregating his workforce on grounds of colour nationality, racial, ethnic or national origin. An employer cannot have separate washroom facilities or recreational areas that are for the use of one race only. The workforce must be integrated. However, there have been situations where employees have chosen to segregate themselves without any involvement by the employer. In such a situation, the employer has not committed an unlawful act of race discrimination (**Pel *v* Modgill (1980)**).

Transferred discrimination

The Race Relations Act also makes transferred discrimination unlawful. An example of transferred racial discrimination can be seen in the following case:

Showboat Entertainment Centre Ltd *v* Owens (1984) an amusement arcade operated a policy whereby black youths were barred from entry. Owens, the arcade manager who was white, refused to implement this policy which amounted to direct racial discrimination against black people. Owens was dismissed from employment as a result of his principled stand against the policy.

Held; by the Employment Appeal Tribunal that Owens had suffered unlawful discrimination and, therefore, his dismissal from employment had been unfair.

Sexual orientation

The House of Lords has recently had to deal with the issue of whether discrimination on the grounds of a person's sexual orientation is covered by the Sex Discrimination Act.

 Macdonald *v* Advocate General for Scotland and **Pearce *v* Governing Body of Mayfield School (2003)** their Lordships held that discrimination on the grounds of a person's sexual orientation is not covered by the Sex Discrimination Act 1975. The Act makes it unlawful to discriminate against someone on the grounds of his or gender.

Macdonald was dismissed from the Royal Air Force because he was a homosexual. Pearce was suffered an ongoing campaign of harassment while employed as a teacher at Mayfield School, because she was a lesbian. Both Macdonald and Pearce claimed that this treatment was an example of direct sex discrimination (Section 1(1)(a) of the 1975 Act). Section 1(1)(a) states that a person discriminates against a woman if 'on the ground of her sex he treats her less favourably than he treats or would treat a man'. The definition also applies to cases where a man suffers sex discrimination (since 2001, Section 2 of the amended Sex Discrimination Act makes it explicit that the protection given to women also applies to men).

Macdonald claimed that but for the fact that he was man, he would not have been dismissed. He was dismissed because he was sexually attracted to men. A woman in a similar position to Macdonald i.e. one who was sexually attracted to men would not have been dismissed. Therefore, Macdonald claimed that he was less favourably treated than a woman in his position would have been, and he received this treatment because he was a man, that is, on the grounds of his sex. The House of Lords heard evidence that the investigating officer who interviewed Macdonald about his sexual preferences would have conducted the investigation in exactly the same way if the suspect had been a lesbian. Macdonald had chosen the wrong female comparator i.e. a heterosexual woman. He should have compared his treatment to that of a female colleague who was homosexual and this is where he ran into trouble. The policy that banned homosexuals from serving in the armed forces was obviously discriminatory, but it was 'gender neutral' in that it applied equally to men and women. Macdonald's appeal failed. He had been dismissed because of his sexual orientation, not because of his gender. Discrimination on the grounds of sexual orientation was not unlawful when this case first came to court.

Pearce's appeal took a slightly different approach. Pearce claimed that she had suffered sexual harassment – an example of direct discrimination. She was subjected to name calling by the pupils at the school where she taught because they knew that she was a lesbian. This was clearly an unpleasant experience for Pearce, but treatment of this sort is not necessarily an example of sexual harassment. Pearce would have to show that she experienced this discriminatory treatment because she was female i.e. on the grounds of her gender. Pearce accepted that the pupils would have pursued a similar campaign of harassment against a homosexual man. Pearce was abused by reason of her sexual orientation not her gender. Therefore, her appeal also failed.

Changes to the law

As a result of the Human Rights Act 1998, a person will enjoy substantial protection in relation to his or her sexual orientation. Article 8 of the European Convention on Human Rights establishes the places a duty on a public authority to have respect for a person's private life. Furthermore, Article 14 of the European Convention confers a right on individuals not to be subjected to discrimination. So, employers which are defined as a public authority will have to ensure that they do not discriminate against an employee on the grounds of sexual orientation. Interestingly, Macdonald attempted to argue that his rights had been infringed in terms of the Human Rights Act 1998, but this argument failed because the Act was not in force when he was dismissed from the Royal Air Force.

From 1 December 2003 it is now unlawful to discriminate against someone by reason of that person's sexual orientation. The Employment Equality (Sexual Orientation) Regulations 2003 now provide protection to employees like Macdonald and Pearce who suffer discrimination in employment by reason of their sexual orientation. In the their judgement, the House of Lords drew attention to the new equality law, but stated that its introduction would be too late for both Macdonald and Pearce. The new regulations are discussed in more detail later in the chapter.

 Key point: Discrimination on the grounds of a person's sexual orientation is not covered by the Sex Discrimination Act, but the Employment Equality (Sexual Orientation) Regulations 2003 now make it unlawful to discriminate on these grounds.

Transsexuals

The European Court of Justice in **P v S & Cornwall County Council (1996)** held that discriminatory treatment of transsexuals was a breach of the Equal Treatment Directive. The individual in question had been dismissed from employment because she undergone a gender reassignment operation.

As a result of the Sex Discrimination (Gender Reassignment) Regulations 1999, transsexuals are protected against direct discrimination under Section 2A of the Sex Discrimination Act 1975. This protection extends to those individuals who undergo 'a process which is undertaken under medical supervision for the purposes of a reassigning a person's sex by changing physiological or other characteristics of sex, and includes any part of such a process.' There will be no protection for those individuals where their performance in employment suffers as a result of side effects caused by the medical treatment.

The Gender Recognition Bill

In 2003, the Government introduced a Gender Recognition Bill, which is expected to become law sometime in 2004, will provide transsexual people with legal recognition in their acquired gender. Legal recognition will follow from the issuing of a full gender recognition certificate by a Gender Recognition Panel. The individual applying for such a certificate must be able to satisfy certain criteria. This will lead to further amendments of the Sex Discrimination Act 1975 limiting the use of genuine occupational requirements in relation to transsexuals which were introduced by the Sex Discrimination (Gender Reassignment) Regulations 1999.

 Key point: Transsexuals are now entitled to protection against discrimination under the Sex Discrimination Act.

Indirect discrimination

Indirect discrimination on the grounds of sex is unlawful in terms of Section 1(1)(b) and Section 2 of the Sex Discrimination Act 1975.

Indirect discrimination on the grounds of colour or nationality is unlawful in terms of Section 1(1)(b) of the Race Relations Act 1976.

As we shall see, the Race Regulations 2003 introduce a wider definition of indirect discrimination on the grounds of a person's racial, national or ethnic origin.

Indirect discrimination on the grounds of sex, colour or nationality, will occur when an employer:

◆ Applies to an individual a condition or requirement which the employer appears to apply equally to everyone; and

◆ The proportion of people from the affected person's group (based on sex, colour or nationality) that can comply is considerably smaller than the proportion of people not from that group who can comply with it; and

◆ The employer cannot justify the requirement or condition on gender neutral or non-racial grounds; and

◆ The requirement or condition is to the affected person's detriment, because he or she cannot comply with it.

At first glance, the condition or the requirement that the employer imposes on everyone looks completely harmless. However, upon a closer inspection, it becomes obvious that more men than women can comply in practice with the employer's condition or requirement or that more white people can comply with the requirement or condition than can people from an Afro-Caribbean background. It is not just the fact that fewer people from a particular gender group or individuals of a particular colour or nationality can comply in practice with the requirement, they suffer an adverse impact because of it i.e. they suffer less favourable treatment.

What if, for example, the employer imposed a requirement that all job applicants had to be at least six feet in height? Admittedly, there are many tall women, but realistically there are many more tall men than tall women who can comply with this requirement in practice. More women would, therefore, be prevented from applying for this job. In other words, women are denied employment opportunities because the employer has imposed a height restriction.

In situations where an employer imposes 'desirable' and 'essential' criteria in a job advertisement, they may be examples of indirect discrimination (**Falkirk Council v Whyte (1997)**). In **Briggs v NE Education and Library Board (1990)**, a requirement of the employer that the successful applicant for a job be able to work full time was an example of indirect discrimination because fewer female applicants could comply in practice with this condition than their male counterparts.

Very often, a detailed statistical analysis will be carried out in order to calculate, for example, how many women or how many people of a particular colour, nationality, race, ethnic or national origin can comply in practice with the requirement imposed by the employer. If fewer Sikhs, for example, can comply with the requirement, it may be that the employer has indirectly discriminated against them.

Examples of the ways in which claims of indirect discrimination are dealt with can be seen in the following cases:

 London Underground v Edwards (No 2) (1998) a female lone parent, was employed as a train operator by London Underground. The employer decided to change the shift patterns. Such a change applied across the board to all drivers, whether male or female. The female employee complained about the new shift patterns claiming that fewer women than men could comply with them in practice.

She stated that as women had child-rearing responsibilities, the new shift patterns would make it much more difficult to organise child-care arrangements. The new shift patterns, therefore, indirectly discriminated against women. The employer carried out a statistical analysis comparing the percentages of men who could comply with the new patterns in practice with the percentage of women who were able to do so. The employer had to compare like with like, so male drivers were compared to female drivers. The results were as follows:

2023 male employees – 100% of them were able to comply with the new arrangements.

21 female employees – 95.2% of them were able to comply with the new arrangements.

In fact, only the complainant amongst all her female colleagues was unable to comply with the new pattern. This was, however, not the point. In practice, fewer women than men were capable of complying with the employer's requirement. The Tribunal found that the complainant had suffered less favourable treatment as a result of the employer's indirect discrimination.

Held: by the English Court of Appeal that the Tribunal was entitled to establish that Edwards had suffered indirect discrimination on the grounds of sex. Admittedly, the percentage difference between the two groups was small, but the Court of Appeal did not feel that this was an important factor in this case.

An employer's change of shift patterns was also held to have be an example of indirect discrimination in **J H Walker Ltd v Hussain & Ors (1996) IRLR 11**.

Here, the Employment Appeal Tribunal found that the employer's change of shift patterns resulted in fewer Asian employees being able to comply with a requirement of the employer that they turn up for work on a particular day.

 In **Singh v Rowntree MacKintosh (1979) ICR 554** the employer imposed a requirement that male employees who were involved in the manufacture of products (sweets and chocolate) were not allowed to wear beards. This requirement indirectly discriminated against Sikh employees. It will be recalled that the Sikh religion insists that men wear their hair long and that they do not shave their beards.

Held: by the Employment Appeal Tribunal that such a condition, although it indirectly discriminated against Sikh employees, was justifiable on the grounds of hygiene in terms of Section 1(1)(b)(ii) of the Race Relations Act 1976. There is also a similar justification defence in terms of Section 1(1)(b)(ii) of the Sex Discrimination Act 1975.

 Key point: Employers will have to be particularly careful that they do not apply general conditions, requirements or criteria in relation to employees which may actually be examples of indirect discrimination.

A new definition of indirect discrimination

The Race Regulations 2003 provide a wider definition of indirect discrimination than arguably is the case under the Sex Discrimination Act 1975 and as was the case in terms of the Race Relations Act prior to 19 July 2003. However, it is important to note that the new rules in the Regulations regarding indirect discrimination apply only to a person's race or ethnic or national origin. Discrimination on the basis of an individual's colour or nationality will still be covered by the previous definition of indirect discrimination as laid down in Section 1(1)(b) of the Race Relations Act 1976. This means that are now two types of indirect discrimination in race discrimination cases.

According to Section 1A of the Race Relations Act, indirect discrimination will occur when an employer applies to another person:

◆ A provision, criterion or practice which the employer applies to everyone; and

◆ This provision, criterion or practice puts (or would put) people from the affected person's race or ethnic or national origin at a particular disadvantage; and

◆ The employer cannot show that the provision, criterion or practice is a proportionate means of achieving a legitimate aim

The words 'provision, criterion, or practice' have a broader meaning than the words 'requirement or condition' which still apply to claims brought under the Race Relations Act in respect of a person's colour or nationality. The new wording will, therefore, apply to an employer's informal as well as formal practices. Informal practices might include advertising posts or promotion opportunities by word of mouth as opposed to advertising these positions formally. It is hoped that this will mean that many more people will be placed in a position where claims of indirect discrimination may be brought against their employers.

There is another important difference between the older definition of indirect discrimination and the more modern approach. Previously, individuals making a complaint often had to base their claim on complex statistical evidence in order to show that people belonging to their particular group were placed at more of a disadvantage in comparison to another group of people.

 Key point: The new definition of indirect discrimination introduced by the Race Regulations 2003 will apply when a person alleges that he has suffered less favourable treatment by reason of his racial, national or ethnic origin.

Justification

In terms of Sections 1 of both the Sex Discrimination and Race Relations Acts, an employer will be permitted to discriminate on the grounds of sex or race in certain, appropriate circumstances. An employer can, therefore, justify discriminatory treatment by claiming that a candidate for a job, promotion, training or other benefit must be of a particular gender or be a member of a particular racial group.

Indirect discrimination on the grounds of hygiene has been justified in **Singh v Rowntree MacKintosh (1979) ICR 554,** where the employer did not allow male employees who were involved in producing confectionary to wear beards. This rule indirectly discriminated against Sikh employees, but it was justifiable on hygiene grounds.

Genuine Occupational Qualifications (Sex Discrimination)

Section 7 of the Sex Discrimination Act lists seven situations where the person's sex may be regarded as a genuine occupational qualification:

1   For physiological reasons (not physical strength or stamina). The employer requires a candidate to be a member of a particular sex, for example, a local college running an art course may require a male model to pose for still life classes. This genuine occupational requirement would also cover situations where directors required male actors to appear in dramatic performances or other forms of entertainment.

2   To preserve decency and privacy because the job is likely to involve physical contact with members of a particular sex in situations where the presence of someone of the opposite sex might cause embarrassment or personal discomfort. The post might involve coming into contact with people who are in a state of undress or where individuals are using sanitary facilities. Clearly this would cover situations where a woman applied for a job and that job involved working in a men's changing room at a sports centre or a swimming pool. The job involves the candidate working or living in a private home and this work entails a great deal of intimate contact with people of the opposite sex. This requirement would most obviously apply to nursing or care jobs.

3   The job requires that the candidate share sleeping accommodation with workers who are members of the same sex and the location of this accommodation makes it completely impracticable for the employer to provide separate sleeping accommodation and sanitary facilities for workers of the opposite sex. Furthermore, it would also be unreasonable to expect the employer to provide such accommodation and facilities for workers of the opposite sex.

4   The job is in a single sex institution, for example, a prison, a hospital, or other institution which provides its inmates with special care or supervision and it is reasonable that the job should be held by a person of a particular sex.

5   The holder of the job provides individuals with personal services aimed at promoting their welfare or educational services and where those services can be most effectively provided by a person of a particular sex. The best person for the post of a rape counsellor would probably be a female professional.

6   The job needs to be held by a person of a particular sex because performance of the employee's duties outside the United Kingdom will take place in a country whose laws or customs place considerable restrictions on the ability of a man or woman to carry out the job effectively. A company may refuse to appoint a woman to a senior position overseas if this job was based in Saudi Arabia where there are severe restrictions placed upon women generally.

7   The job is one of two to be held by a married couple.

Examples of attempts by employers to use sex as a genuine occupational qualification can be seen in the following cases:

 O'Connor v Kontiki Travel (1976) O'Connor, who was female, applied for a job as a coach driver on overseas tours. She was not given the job and the employer justified the refusal to hire her because she would have to drive through a number of Muslim countries where there restrictions placed on women which would effectively prevent her from carrying out her duties. On further investigation, it was discovered that the only Muslim country that the coach would be travelling through was Turkey. Although most Turks are Muslims, Turkey did not have particularly strict laws that prevented women from carrying out many jobs. In fact, Turkey was a liberal Muslim country and no objections would have been raised in relation to O'Connor being employed as a driver.

   Held: the employer could not justify O'Connor's treatment on the grounds that being male was a genuine occupational requirement. O'Connor had been treated less favourably on the grounds of her sex and, consequently, she had suffered direct discrimination. However, O'Connor ultimately lost her case because the employment in question would be performed totally outside the UK and the Sex Discrimination Act did not, therefore, apply.

 Wylie v Dee & Co (Menswear) Ltd (1978) IRLR 103 Wylie, who was female, applied for a job in a menswear shop. The employers refused to hire her because she was female. The employers attempted to justify this discriminatory treatment on the grounds that being male was a genuine occupational requirement for the job. Evidence was led by the employers to show that the post involved a degree of intimate physical contact with male customers. From time to time, employees were required to take the inside-leg measurements of male customers who might be less than comfortable having their measurements taken by a female member of staff.

   Held: by the Industrial Tribunal that the employers could not rely on a genuine occupational requirement to justify the refusal to employ Wylie. It was proved that the intimate physical contact with male customers did not occur on a regular basis and, furthermore, when male customers had to be measured in this way there were seven male employees who could take the measurements if so required. Wylie had suffered less favourable treatment as a result of her sex.

The Sex Discrimination (Gender Reassignment) Regulations 1999 also introduce additional genuine occupational qualifications which apply to transsexuals only. These are:

◆ The employment entails intimate body searches permitted by statute (Police and Customs officers).

◆ The employment is in a private home where there is social and physical contact with members of the household or where the employee gains knowledge of intimate details of house members' lives and distress may be caused if the employee is a transsexual.

◆ The employer has provided premises for the employee and it would be impractical for the employee to live elsewhere other than on these premises. Furthermore, it would offend decency and privacy if the employee was undergoing gender reassignment and it was not practical for the employer to provide separate facilities.

◆ The employee provides vulnerable individuals with personal services promoting their welfare.

Genuine Occupational Qualification (Race Discrimination)

Where the issue of race is concerned, there is less scope for an employer to justify discriminatory treatment. Section 5 of the Race Relations Act lists three very limited situations where the person's colour, nationality, race, ethnic or national origins may be regarded as a genuine occupational qualification:

1 Where a person of a particular race is required for authenticity to participate in a dramatic performance or other form of entertainment. Such a situation would apply to a director who casts a black actor as the Shakespearean character Othello in preference to a white colleague. For the avoidance of any confusion, Othello is black in William Shakespeare's play. This genuine occupational requirement would also apply where an artist's or photographic model is required for the production of a work of art or visual image where members of particular racial groups are needed for reasons of authenticity.

2 Where a person is required to serve food and drink to the public in a place where members of a particular racial group are required to promote authenticity. It does not matter whether this work is carried out on a paid basis or not. This genuine occupational requirement allows Indian and Chinese restaurants to employ Indian and Chinese waiting and bar staff in order to provide customers with an authentic experience. However, it does not cover situations where staff do not have contact with the public, for example, kitchen staff. Being ethnic Chinese is not a genuine occupational requirement for working as a chef in the kitchen of a Chinese restaurant.

3 The holder of the job provides individuals with personal services aimed at promoting their welfare and where those services can be most effectively provided by a person of that particular racial group.

Special Occupational Requirements (Race Discrimination)

Section 4A of the Race Relations Act introduces allows an employer to impose a genuine occupational requirement in respect of job applicants. Theoretically, this is much wider than the limited genuine occupational qualifications allowed by Section 5. It may be the case that certain jobs are best carried out by people belonging to particular race or who have particular ethnic or national origins. If this is indeed the case, an employer can legally discriminate in favour of certain races or people having certain ethnic backgrounds or national origins. However, an employer must show that imposing a genuine occupational requirement on the holder of a particular post is not disproportionate. Therefore, the employer must demonstrate that, having regard to the nature of the job or its context, it is best performed by a person who is a member of a particular race, ethnic or national group. Furthermore, by employing such a person the employer must be in a position to show that the benefits of discriminating in favour of particular applicants outweighs any disadvantages of such a policy.

Genuine occupational requirements do not apply to a job applicant's colour and nationality. An employer wishing to rely on a genuine occupational qualification in respect of an applicant's colour or nationality will have to continue to use the limited exceptions permitted by Section 5.

 Key point: Genuine occupational qualifications or special occupational requirements allow an employer to discriminate against certain individuals on the grounds of sex or race.

Sexual and racial harassment

To make offensive remarks of a sexually or racially motivated nature to a person will be regarded as direct sex or racial discrimination. Making discriminatory comments about a woman's body or racist comments in relation to a person's colour or race will amount to less favourable treatment. One sexually or racially motivated remark could amount to harassment. Employment Tribunals have been greatly assisted by the publication of a European Commission Code of Practice on Measures to Combat Sexual Harassment. In **Wadman v Carpenter Farrer Partnership (1993)** the Employment Appeal Tribunal stated that Tribunals should use the Code to decide when sexual harassment has taken place.

 Institu Cleaning Co Ltd v Heads (1995) IRLR 4 a male colleague had made a remark about the large breast size of a female colleague. This remark was unwelcome and the male colleague attempted to defend himself (unsuccessfully) by stating that he would not have made the remark if he had known it was going to cause offence.

Held: by the Employment Appeal Tribunal that this was a remark of a sexual nature that caused offence – it was totally unwanted and unsought – and, therefore, it was direct discrimination on the grounds of sex.

In **Reed and Bull Information Systems *v* Stedman (1999) IRLR 299** the Employment Appeal Tribunal laid down some guidelines as to what constitutes unwanted conduct in cases of sexual harassment. The test for sexual harassment is a subjective one in that it great stress will be placed on the feelings of the person who was subjected to the remark or the behaviour in question. Are the remarks or behviour unwelcome to the recipient and it is up to the recipient to decide what is welcome and what is offensive.

Obviously, racist remarks and racist behaviour should be treated completely differently in that they should not be tolerated at all. Racist remarks and behaviour will almost always be offensive in nature. The newly amended Race Relations Act now takes a much tougher approach to harassment. Section 3(A) states that harassment on the grounds of race or ethnic or national origin will be unlawful, if a person engages in unwanted conduct which has the purpose or effect of violating another person's dignity or creates an intimidating, hostile, offensive or disturbing environment. Section 3(A) makes it very clear that the perception or the opinion of the person claiming that they have suffered harassment will often be decisive in establishing that discrimination has occurred. Furthermore, Section 4(2A) states that it is unlawful for an employer to subject any employee or a person who has applied for employment to harassment on the grounds of race or ethnic or national origin.

 Key point: Harassment will occur when a person is subjected to unwanted conduct which has the purpose or effect of violating his or her dignity or creates an intimidating, hostile, offensive or disturbing environment.

It is not necessary for the person making the complaint to show that there has been a series of remarks. Similarly, direct discrimination will take place if an individual is subjected to a sustained campaign of sexual or racial harassment. It was wrongly thought by some commentators that women bringing claims of sexual harassment did not need to compare their treatment to that of a male comparator. It will be important to demonstrate that a woman would not have suffered sexual harassment but for the fact that she was female.

 Porcelli *v* Strathclyde Regional Council (1986) Mrs Porcelli was employed by the Regional Council as a school lab technician. She worked with two male colleagues with whom she had a very poor working relationship. Both of these male colleagues went out of their way to subject her to a sustained campaign of harassment and bullying in order to force her to seek a transfer to another job or to leave her job altogether. Mrs Porcelli's colleagues had destroyed her work, slammed doors in her face and thrown her personal possessions into the bin. This was quite obviously appalling treatment, but it was gender neutral in the sense that Mrs Porcelli's colleagues would have subjected a man that they disliked to similar treatment. However, her colleagues' behaviour took a much nastier turn when the harassment and bullying started to take on sexual overtones. Both men used obscene language when they either spoke to or about Mrs Porcelli. They often used to compare her body (unfavourably) with nude pictures of women that appeared in newspapers and magazines. Mrs Porcelli was also subjected to suggestive remarks of a sexual nature and, on occasion, the men had brushed their bodies against Mrs Porcelli's body.

Held: by the Inner House of the Court of Session, affirming the decision of the Employment Appeal Tribunal, that Mrs Porcelli's treatment was an example of direct sex discrimination. Mrs Porcelli's colleagues had subjected her to a campaign of bullying and harassment that had sexual overtones. They would not have subjected a male colleague to the same kind of treatment. Mrs Porcelli had experienced this kind of treatment precisely because she was female. Lord Grieve remarked that: the treatment should be viewed as a 'sexual sword' which 'had been unsheathed and used because the victim was a woman'.

 Pearce v Governing Body of Mayfield School (2003) Pearce's claim that she had suffered sexual harassment on the grounds that she was a lesbian failed because the employer was able to show that a male homosexual would also have been subjected to homophobic name calling by pupils at the school.

Held: by the House of Lords that although the treatment suffered by Pearce was extremely nasty, it was gender neutral. Pearce had suffered discrimination on the grounds of her sexual orientation, not her sex.

 Jones v Tower Boot (1997) a black employee was subjected to racist name calling over a period of time by a colleague. He was physically assaulted by his colleagues – his arm had been branded by a colleague who had attacked him with a hot screwdriver, metal bolts had been thrown at his head and his legs had been whipped.

Held: by the English Court of Appeal that this was harassment on the grounds of race and, therefore, direct discrimination. More significantly, the Court of Appeal stated that employers who failed to respond adequately in these situations to complaints were responsible for the racist bullying and harassment committed by other employees.

 Key point: A person may subject another person to harassment by making a single sexist or racist remark or indulging in behaviour of this nature just once.

Victimisation

Section 4 of the Sex Discrimination Act and Section 2 of the Race Relations Act provide an important range of safeguards and protection to individuals who have been involved in some way in sex and racial discrimination actions. Very often, the employer will subject an individual to less favourable treatment in the future because, at one time, they have had some involvement in a discrimination claim against the employer. It will be unlawful for an employer to victimise or harass such individuals in the following situations:

1   Where a person has brought an Employment Tribunal or a court action against the employer under the Equal Pay Act 1970, Sex Discrimination Act 1975 or the Race Relations Act 1976.

2   Where a person has given evidence in support of someone who has taken an Employment Tribunal or a court action under the above legislation.

3   Where a person has taken a legitimate course of action, for example, making a complaint against the employer in relation to the above legislation.

4   Where a person has made allegations against the employer that discrimination
has occurred which is unlawful in terms of the above legislation.

 Waters *v* Commissioner of Police for the Metropolis (2000) Waters, a
female police constable, had accused a male colleague of subjecting her to a
sexual assault. The alleged assault had taken place outside working hours.
The employee later claimed that she had suffered victimisation as a result of
making the complaint of sexual assault against her colleague.

Held: by the House of Lords that her delictual claim against her employer
should be allowed to proceed. An employer may be in breach of his personal
duty of care if either he knew that fellow employees were behaving in such a
way as to cause the employee in question to suffer physical or psychiatric
injury or if it was reasonably foreseeable that such actions would cause harm
and that he failed to put reasonable safeguards to prevent the employee
suffering harm.

The issue of whether victimisation can continue after the employment relationship
has ended has recently been decided by the House of Lords in a number of cases:

In **Relaxion Group plc *v* Rhys-Harper (FC)**; **D'Souza *v* London Borough of
Lambeth**; and **Jones *v* 3M Healthcare Limited and Others (2003) UKHL 33** all
the cases involved allegations of victimisation that had occurred after the employment
of the individuals in question had ended. Claims were brought under the Sex
Discrimination Act 1975, the Race Relations Act 1976 and the Disability Discrimination
Act 1995. Their Lordships thought it would be illogical and completely arbitrary to give
protection from victimisation up and until the contract of employment ended and,
after this point, the employee could expect no further protection from victimisation. It
was pointed out that an employee's duties towards his employer did not necessarily
cease when the contract came to an end. An employee may be subject to obligations
of confidentiality or restrictions on where he may work or for whom he may work. An
employer may be subject to obligations regarding pension rights or bonus payments.
The House of Lords used the following examples:

'. . . *the employee who asks for a reference before he retires from his
employment is protected but the employee who asks for a reference the day
after he left is not. It would mean that the employee who is dismissed with
notice and whose appeal is heard before his notice expires is protected against
discrimination in his recourse to the employer's appeal procedure, but the
employee who is dismissed summarily and without notice is not. It would
mean that retaliatory action taken by an employer before the contract of
employment ends is within the scope of the legislation, but retaliatory action
taken later, for instance, regarding bonus payments, is not.*'

Their Lordships concluded that it could not have been the intention of Parliament
when it brought the equality legislation into force to deny protection to former
employees who suffered victimisation after their employment had ended.

 Key point: It is important that those individuals who have been involved in
discrimination claims either as a complainant or as a witness should be
adequately protected against acts of victimisation by the employer during and
after their employment.

The Equal Pay Act 1970

The Equal Pay Act 1970 did not come into force until 29 December 1975. Significantly, the Sex Discrimination Act 1975 was given legal force on the same day and there has been a close relationship between both pieces of legislation ever since. However, the Sex Discrimination Act is designed to provide protection against discrimination on the grounds of a person's sex in connection with the areas of recruitment, promotion and dismissal. The Equal Pay Act, on the other hand, is primarily concerned with discrimination in respect of employment terms and conditions. The Equal Pay Act is also more limited in its scope in that it does not cover discrimination on the grounds of marital status and it does it appear to deal with indirect discrimination. It is important to understand that the Act is not a charter for establishing fair pay in the labour market generally. There will continue to be many sectors of the labour market where low pay and poor conditions will be the norm and this will affect men as well as women. The Equal Pay Act attempts to eliminate inequalities as regards conditions of employment between men and women working for the same or an associated employer. There are exceptions, but generally women are not allowed to compare themselves with male workers who are employed by a different employer.

The phrase 'equal pay' in the title of the Act can be highly misleading. The Act does not just attempt to address inequality between men and women in relation to their pay. It would be unlawful, in terms of the Act, for an employer to give male employees all sorts of contractual benefits and not to extend these to female employees. Such benefits could include free or discounted membership of a gym, free or discounted rail travel, air-mile vouchers, gift vouchers, free or discounted PCs and mobile phones, access to subsidised mortgages and bank loans. However, many of the cases that are brought under the Act will be primarily concerned with the gap between the sexes in respect of what they earn.

 Key point: The Equal Pay Act can be used to combat inequalities in the terms and conditions of employment offered to men and women.

Pay

Pay has been defined as the ordinary basic or minimum wage or salary and any other consideration, whether in cash or in kind, which the worker receives, either directly or indirectly, in respect of his employment from his employer.

The above definition does not just include a person's salary. It also applies to pensions, employers' contributions to pensions, concessionary travel, social security benefits, maternity pay, sick pay, paid leave, contractual and statutory redundancy pay, paid leave, overtime pay and compensation for unfair dismissal.

According to the Equal Opportunities Commission in December 2003, it remains a shocking fact that, nearly 30 years after the Equal Pay Act made it unlawful to pay women less than men for doing the same job, statistically women working full-time are likely to be paid 18 per cent less than their male counterparts.

The European Union dimension

Article 141 of the Treaty of Rome 1957 and the Equal Pay Directive 75/117/EEC place a duty on Member States to ensure that men and women should receive equal pay for equal work. Furthermore, the Equal Treatment Directive 76/207/EEC makes it unlawful for an employer to discriminate in relation to conditions of employment. Very often, European Union legislation has been used to promote equality in order to overcome the shortcomings of the Equal Pay Act 1970. Article 141 can be directly applied and relied upon by litigants in the British courts – it is said to have direct effect (**Defrenne *v* Sabena (No 2) (1976)**). This means that individuals bringing equal pay cases will not be defeated by any deficiencies in United Kingdom legislation or where the British parliament has failed to bring equal pay rules into force which it is obliged to do so under European law. Individuals bringing a claim under Article 141 will able to rely on the principle of the supremacy of European Union law i.e. where there is a conflict between European law and United Kingdom law, the European rules are followed.

The Equal Pay Directive

In **Commission of the European Communities *v* UK (1982)** the Equal Pay Directive declared that the principle of equal pay for men and women was to be taken to include equal pay for work of equal value. This enables a woman to seek the same pay as a man doing an entirely different job where the woman believes her work is of equal value to his. The European Commission did not believe that the Equal Pay Act 1970, as originally introduced, gave protection to women in this situation. Enforcement proceedings were brought against the UK and the Commission's complaint was upheld. As a result, the UK government introduced secondary legislation (the Equal Pay (Amendment) Regulations 1983) which introduced the concept of equal pay for work of equal value.

Although the Equal Pay Act applies to direct discrimination only, Article 141 of the Treaty of Rome has been used to eliminate measures that would be regarded as examples of indirect discrimination.

 Re Secretary of State for Employment *ex parte* Equal Opportunities Commission (1994) IRLR 176 the Employment Protection (Consolidation) Act 1978 contained a requirement that for an employee to be entitled to a statutory redundancy payment they had to work more than 16 hours per week. The employees in question worked less than eight hours per week.

Held: by the House of Lords that the Employment Protection (Consolidation) Act 1978 indirectly discriminated against women as fewer of them were able to comply in practice with the rules relating to entitlement to a redundancy payment. Many more men than women were employed in excess of 16 hours per week. Women tended to do more part-time work than men and they were less likely to meet the requirements of the 1978 Act.

 Key point: European Union law has often been used to overcome the shortcomings of the United Kingdom's equal pay legislation.

Identifying a comparator

Under Section 1 of the Equal Pay Act, women must be able to compare themselves to man in the same employment otherwise their claim for equal pay will fail. It is, therefore, very important that a female worker is able to identify a male comparator (Section 1(2) and (6)). Unlike the Sex Discrimination Act 1975, where a woman can compare herself to a hypothetical male comparator, comparators in equal pay claims must be named.

In most cases, the male comparator will work for the same employer as the woman or for an associated employer. A male comparator employed by an associated employer will have common terms and conditions of employment. A female employee of the National Health Service who works for one Trust could compare her pay to that of a male comparator who is employed by another Trust under common conditions of employment. The woman must be employed at an establishment within the United Kingdom.

However, in some recent decisions, the courts have allowed women to compare themselves to men who, traditionally, would not be regarded as being in the same employment.

 South Ayrshire Council v Morton (2001) IRLR 28 a female teacher employed by South Ayrshire Council was permitted to compare herself with a male teacher employed by Highland Council as part of her equal pay claim. The reason behind this decision appears to centre around the fact that the terms and conditions that teachers are employed under in Scotland are so similar that the profession can be regarded as a national service.

On 17 September 2002, the European Court of Justice gave its ruling in **Lawrence v Regent Office Care Ltd (Case No C-320/00)**. The case centred around the choice of 'comparator' in a situation where the woman claimed that she was paid less than a man doing work of equal value. Until recently it was thought that the comparator had to be working for the same employer or an associated employer as the woman making the claim. However, this condition has not been regarded as being essential in a number of cases where the woman has been able to prove that the relationship between two different employers is sufficiently close. The European Court of Justice has held that for the relationship to be sufficiently close in order for European Union equal treatment rules to apply it is essential that the differences in pay must 'be attributed to a single source'. A single source would be where a Parliament or legislature makes the rules which govern the employment relationship or where the terms and conditions of employment come from a collective agreement or a policy laid down by the management of a corporate group.

This requirement for a single source of terms and conditions of employment is strictly interpreted by Tribunals as is clearly demonstrated in the following case:

 Department of Environment Food and Rural Affairs (DEFRA) v Robertson and Others (2003) EAT/0273/DM Robertson and his co-applicants were employed as civil servants by DEFRA which is a UK Government Department. The six applicants brought a claim under the Equal Pay Act 1970. All six men sought to compare themselves with female civil servants working for the UK Department of Transport and the Regions (Central). On the face of it, every members of the UK civil service (as opposed to the devolved governments throughout the UK) is employed by the same employer and, theoretically, this meant the applicants should have faced little problem with their choice of comparators. However, there was no single source of terms and conditions of employment within the UK civil service because each Department was responsible for negotiating these with its own civil servants. Previously, the UK Treasury, as a central source, had set national terms and conditions of employment for the civil service, but this was now no longer the case.

Held: by the Employment Appeal Tribunal that the new arrangement meant that employment conditions varied significantly from department to department and the applicants were, therefore, not making a valid comparison when they selected their female colleagues in Department of Transport and the Regions (Central). The six applicants failed in their equal pay claim.

In **McCarthys Ltd *v* Smith (1979)** a woman discovered that she was being paid less as a manager than the man who held the post previously. The English Court of Appeal had held that the wording of the Equal Pay Act 1970 allowed comparisons only to be made with men employed at the same time as the woman. However, the European Court of Justice held that comparisons were not restricted to those individuals who were employed at the same time as the person seeking equal pay. The female applicant was entitled to compare herself with the man who had previously held her job.

Significantly, the Equal Pay Act does not prevent women from taking their employer to court in circumstances where a token man is employed on the same terms and conditions as they are (**Pickstone *v* Freemans PLC (1988)**). If this were allowed, the Equal Pay Act would be dealt a serious blow. As long as the women can demonstrate that they have been less favourably treated in comparison to a fellow male employee, they have the right to bring a claim.

 Key point: When bringing an equal pay claim, the Applicant must identify a suitable comparator who works for the same employer or an associated employer.

Grounds for a claim

Section 1 of the Equal Pay Act ensures that each contract of employment contains an equality clause which means that it will be implied that men and women in the same employment should receive equal pay for equal work. The Equal Pay Act 1970 is not about establishing fair pay for everyone. Claims can only be brought under the Act if a person of a particular sex can show that she does not receive equal pay for equal work in comparison to a male colleague and the reason for this difference is related to her sex.

Section 1 of the Act states that women have the right to equal treatment in pay where they are employed on:

◆ Like work with a man
◆ Work rated to equivalent to that of a man
◆ Work of equal value compared to that of man

Like work

This applies in situations where a woman is the same or broadly similar work to a man. There may indeed be differences between the work carried out by the man and the women, but these are so slight or have little practical importance.

Capper Pass v Lawton (1977) Lawton was employed as a cook in the kitchen from which prepared meals for the company directors and their guests. Lawton brought an equal pay action against her employer claiming that she was employed to perform like work in comparison with two male employees of the company. The two men, Brattan and Smith, were employed as assistant chefs in the kitchen which served food to the employees who worked in the company factory. Lawton worked alone and she prepared between ten and 20 meals a day approximately. Brattan and Smith, on the other hand, reported to a head chef, they had to prepare 350 meals per day in six sittings. Both men worked longer hours than Lawton.

Held: by the Employment Appeal Tribunal that although there were differences between the job that Lawton performed and the jobs performed by Brattan and Smith, it was work of a similar nature. The work was similar in that it required the employee to possess similar skills and expertise. Lawton was, therefore, employed to perform like work and she was entitled to equal pay.

Work rated as equivalent

Work rated as equivalent applies to situations where a job evaluation scheme is carried out. This category applies when a man and the woman are not be engaged in the same line of work. A woman who is employed as nursery nurse by a local council may be able to claim that she performs work rated as equivalent in comparison to a male clerical worker who receives a higher salary. Under the job evaluation scheme, both jobs must have an equal value in relation to the types of demands made upon a worker under such headings as effort, skill and decision-making. The jobs are broken down into their various functions and points will be awarded to each worker in relation to a function or heading. The scheme must be scrupulously fair in that it must be analytical and deploy objective (quantitative) criteria (**Eaton Ltd v Nuttall (1977)**). Furthermore, the study should have been carried out at the organisation where the employee and her comparator are employed. Should the female worker's job receive a different score from that of her male comparator, she will not be in a position to claim that her work should be rated as equivalent. Job evaluation schemes can always be challenged on the basis that the employer did not use objective criteria when comparing a woman's job with that of a male comparator.

Ryder and 113 Others v Warwickshire County Council and Others ET Case No 1301481/97 when a job evaluation study has been carried out, and the men's and the women's jobs had been rated as equivalent and the basic pay was the same, the employer had to justify why male staff received performance bonuses or other additional payments and female staff did not.

It is necessary to have regard to the full results of the job evaluation scheme, including the allocation of the claimant to the scale or grade at the end of the process:

In **Springboard Sunderland Trust v Robson (1992)** a job evaluation scheme was carried out and two jobs were analysed. The woman received 410 points and her male comparator 428 points. Under the rules of the scheme they were placed on the same grade, but the employers refused to pay the woman properly for the grade that she had been allocated.

Held: by the Employment Appeal Tribunal that the two jobs were rated as equivalent within the meaning of Section 1(5) of the Equal Pay Act 1970.

Work of equal value

A woman may be able to claim that her work is equal value to that of a male comparator in situations where a job evaluation scheme has not been carried out. Again, the man and the woman are not engaged in like work, but this procedure allows the woman to compare herself to a man who is engaged in a completely different type of work. It is perfectly possible for the work carried out by a cleaning lady to be compared to that of a male solicitor who work for the same or associated employer. An Employment Tribunal can determine whether a woman is engaged in work of equal value in comparison to a male worker and the services of an independent expert are no longer required as used to be the case. When deciding whether a woman is employed in work of equal value, the Employment Tribunal will look at the demands made on the workers under such headings as effort, skill and decision-making.

 Ms White and Others *v* Alstons (Colchester) Ltd (1987) female employees who were sewing machinists wished to compare themselves to male colleagues who were employed as upholsterers and who were paid a higher wage. The women claimed that they were engaged on work of equal value to their male colleagues.

Held: the women were engaged on work of equal value and they were awarded equal pay.

 Key point: The Equal Pay Act ensures that each contract of employment contains an equality clause which means that it will be implied that men and women in the same employment should receive equal pay for equal work.

A genuine material difference

Section 1(3) of the Equal Pay Act allows an employer to justify the difference in pay by claiming that it is related to a genuine material difference and is not based on the grounds of the person's sex.

 Glasgow City Council *v* Marshall (2000) eight instructors, seven women and one man, working in special schools within the former local government area of Strathclyde region brought a claim for equal pay. Their employer had been previously been Strathclyde Regional Council before the local government reorganisation in the 1990s. That was the position when the applicants lodged their claims. After the local government reorganisation of 1996, the instructors were employed by the Regional Council's statutory successors. The instructors claimed that they were employed in like work to teaching colleagues at the schools in which they were employed. The staff at special schools included teachers as well as instructors. Admittedly, the teachers were more highly paid than the instructors. The teachers all possessed a teaching qualification, which the instructors did not. Some of the instructors were qualified, but the minimum qualifications demanded of teachers were much higher than those asked of qualified instructors. The seven female instructors claimed that, although they did not possess formal teaching qualifications, they were employed on like work with male teachers working in the same special schools. The only male instructor claimed that he was engaged on like work with female teachers. The instructors claimed that, accordingly, they were entitled to the same pay as their respective male and female teacher comparators. The Employment Tribunal and the Employment Appeal Tribunal ruled in favour of the instructors – they were employed on like work in comparison to their teaching colleagues. The education authorities appealed to the Inner House of the Court of Session which found in their favour. The instructors appealed to the House of Lords.

Held: by the House of Lords that the difference in the pay between the instructors and their teaching colleagues had nothing to do with discrimination on the grounds of sex. There was a genuine material difference between instructors and teachers. Teachers had to be more highly qualified than instructors and this justified the difference in pay.

 Key point: Employers will be able to justify a difference in the terms and conditions of employment offered to men and women if this is due to a material difference and is not based on the grounds of a person's sex.

Time limits for equal pay claims and the burden of proof

In terms of Section 2(4) of the Equal Pay Act, a claim for equal pay must be lodged with the Office of Employment Tribunals either during a person's employment or within six months (less one day) of the termination of the employee's contract of employment.

According to Section 2(5), successful parties in an equal pay action were limited to claiming two years back pay from their employer which runs back from the date upon which legal proceedings were commenced. However, in **Levez v T H Jennings (Harlow Pools) Ltd (2000) ICR 58** the European Court of Justice has ruled that this two-year limit is unlawful in terms of Article 141 of the Treaty of Rome and the Equal Pay Directive 75/117/EEC. In **Levez**, the European Court of Justice allowed the successful party to claim six years' back pay.

The Equal Pay Act 1970 (Amendment) Regulations 2003 have now changed the law in this regard.

In an equal pay claim, the burden of proof is on the person making the complaint to the Employment Tribunal that have been discriminated against.

Equal pay questionnaires

From 6 April 2003, it is now possible for an employer to serve an equal pay questionnaire on the employer in terms of Section 7B of the Equal Pay Act 1970. Such a procedure should make the issues surrounding equal pay claims easier to understand and identify and reduce the delays which are often a feature of such cases. It is hoped that the use of questionnaires will also promote out of court settlements. By serving a questionnaire, it allows the employee to request important information from the employer which should help establish whether there is a potential equal pay claim. The questionnaire and the responses can be used in evidence at an Employment Tribunal hearing. It will be for the Employment Tribunal to decide whether discrimination has taken place. Employers are, therefore, encouraged to cooperate with such a questionnaire, but there may be some confidential information that they are entitled to withhold from the person bringing the complaint. If the employer fails or refuses to cooperate with the questionnaire procedure, this behaviour could be viewed very suspiciously by an Employment Tribunal where there is no justification on the employer's part.

The Disability Discrimination Act 1995

The Disability Discrimination Act 1995 aims to promote equality of opportunity for disabled people in the following areas:

- Employment
- The provision of goods and services
- Buying or renting land or property
- Education

The Act should also be read together with a Code of Practice and Guidance. The Secretary of State, under powers contained in Section 3 of the Act, issued a document called Guidance which was to be used when questions relating to the meaning of disability arose in discrimination cases. The Employment Appeal Tribunal has stated in **Goodwin v The Patent Office (1999)** that Employment Tribunals must apply the Guidance in relation to disability discrimination claims. Part II of the Act which relates specifically to employment and is accompanied by a Code of Practice that aims to introduce measures which will eliminate disability discrimination. The Code of Practice can be used as evidence in Employment Tribunal and other legal proceedings. Part III of the Act which deals with the rights of disabled people in respect of access to goods, facilities, services and premises should also be interpreted in line with the Code of Practice. These provisions were reinforced in 1999 when the Secretary of State for Education and Employment issued a Code of Practice regulating the conduct of trade associations in relation to disabled members and applicants.

Both the Codes of Practice and Guidance are, therefore, extremely useful resources in that they provide important clarification of the law in relation to many of the issues in this area.

The provisions of the Act currently apply to those employers who employ more than 15 employees. Smaller employers are, however, encouraged to take the Act into account and develop good employment practices. Some professions and occupations also fall outside the scope of the Act, for example, the police, prison officers, advocates and barristers in chambers and partners in a firm. Charities and employment outside the United Kingdom are not covered by the Act. There are also exceptions for national security.

The Act was amended by the Special Educational Needs and Disability Act 2001. This means that it will be unlawful for bodies responsible for the provision of education and other related services to discriminate against disabled students and disabled persons.

The Disability Rights Commission

The Act originally established a National Disability Council, but this has since been replaced by a Disability Rights Commission (the Disability Rights Commission Act 1999). The Commission has a very similar role to that of the Equal Opportunities Commission and the Commission for Racial Equality. Like both of these Commissions, the Disability Rights Commission has statutory powers to commence formal investigations against individuals and organisations and to issue them with non-discrimination notices. The Disability Rights Commission promotes disability equality by supporting disabled people who have embarked on legal action, by taking test cases to court or tribunal, issuing Codes of Practice, publishing research and running important campaigns that promote greater public awareness of disability issues. The Commission is a statutory body which is publicly funded, but which is independent of government. The Commission is, therefore, a very important source of information for employers regarding the rights of disabled employees.

 Key point: The Disability Rights Commission is a statutory body, with similar powers to the Equal Opportunities Commission and the Commission for Racial Equality, that polices the Disability Discrimination Act.

Definition of a disability

In terms of Section 1(1) of the Disability Discrimination Act 1995, a disability is defined as a physical or mental impairment which has a substantial and long-term adverse effect on someone's ability to carry out normal day-to-day activities.

This is an important definition because the disability can either be a physical, sensory or mental impairment. Previously, popular notions of a disabled person may have centred around a person in a wheelchair. The definition of a disabled person under the Act would, obviously, include such an individual, but people suffering from a medically recognised psychiatric illness would also be protected. The disability must also be substantial i.e. not trivial and have a long-term adverse effect on a person's ability to carry out normal day-to-day activities. Merely because someone is ill does not mean that he is disabled in terms of the Act. The illness could be short term and the person suffering from it could make a full recovery in a very short space of time. In any case, a disability will be regarded as long term if it has lasted or is expected to last for at least 12 months. Furthermore, the illness may have absolutely no effect on the person's ability to perform everyday tasks like being able to wash, prepare meals, clean the house and do shopping.

Some conditions are not regarded as a disability:

- An addiction involving drugs such as alcohol or nicotine
- HIV and AIDS
- A condition or a compulsion where a person lights fires, engages in acts of theft or commits acts of physical or sexual abuse against another person
- Exhibitionism and voyeurism
- Multiple sclerosis
- Cancer

 Key point: A disability is a physical, sensory or mental impairment which has a substantial and long-term adverse effect on the ability of a person to carry out day-to-day activities.

Definition of disability discrimination

Undoubtedly, disabled people face discrimination and prejudice in the area of employment. Section 5 of the Act defines discrimination in relation to employment. Disability discrimination, according to Section 5, can occur in two ways:

1   An employer, for a reason related to a person's disability, may treat that person less favourably than he treats or would treat a person in relation to whom that reason does not apply and the employer cannot show that this treatment is justified.

2   An employer may discriminate against a disabled person in situations where he is under a duty to make reasonable adjustments (Section 6), but he fails to do this and can offer no justification for this failure.

The first type of discrimination has very close similarities to the concept of direct discrimination which is encountered in cases involving sex and race discrimination. There is one crucial difference, however, where disability is concerned because the employer's less favourable treatment of a disabled employee can be justified. There is also a further type of discrimination which often arises in discrimination cases – victimisation (Section 55).

Section 4(1) of the Act details situations where discrimination against a disabled applicant will be unlawful:

- The arrangements that the employer puts in place to decide who should be offered employment.
- The terms on which a disabled person is offered employment.
- Where the employer refuses to offer employment to a disabled person.

Similarly, Section 4(2) details situations where it will be unlawful for an employer to discriminate against a disabled employee:

- The terms of employment that are granted to the disabled employee.
- The opportunities for promotion, training, transfer or any other benefit in relation to a disabled employee.
- Where the employer deliberately refused or deliberately failed to offer the disabled employee access and opportunities to promotion, training, transfer or any other benefit.
- Where the disabled person is dismissed or subjected to any other detriment on account of his disability.

Establishing less favourable treatment of disabled employees

It would be a mistake to assume that the concept of less favourable treatment under the Disability Discrimination Act operates in exactly the same way as cases involving sex and race discrimination. In sex discrimination cases, for example, the employee must compare the treatment that s/he suffered with the treatment experienced by a person of the opposite sex (race cases operate in a similar way). It is totally wrong to assume that the appropriate comparison to be made in disability discrimination cases is for the disabled person to compare themselves to a person who is either not disabled or who does suffer from the same disability that affects them. An Employment Tribunal must examine two issues:

1   Whether the reason for the less favourable treatment is related to the person's disability.

2   Whether the disabled person was treated less favourably in comparison with a person to whom this reason does not apply.

 Clarke v Novacold Ltd (1999) the employee had suffered an industrial injury which prevented him from attending his work. The employer decided to dismiss this employee because it believed that he would be prevented from returning to work for at least another year. The employee lodged a claim with the Office of Employment Tribunals claiming that he experienced disability discrimination as a result of his dismissal. The Employment Tribunal felt that the employer had treated the disabled employee in exactly the same way as a non-disabled employee and, therefore, there was no disability discrimination. The employee appealed against the Employment Tribunal's judgement.

Held: by the English Court of Appeal that, in sharp contrast to claims of sexual and racial discrimination, it was totally inappropriate to compare the treatment of a disabled employee to that of a non-disabled colleague. The dismissal was discriminatory because it was an example of less favourable treatment and it was completely unjustified because the employer had been unreasonable by failing to offer the employee alternative employment within the organisation that he could perform in spite of his disability.

Employers will, therefore, have to tread very carefully when dealing with an employee's absence from work due to sickness. If, however, an employee gives assurances to his employer that his health is not having an adverse effect on his ability to do the job, the employer may be able to rely on this to counter any claims of unfair dismissal.

 Portman v Bromley Hospitals NHS Trust EAT 1300/96 the employee had been absent from work for a long period. After her sick leave, the employee returned to work but her performance in her job was extremely poor. The employee claimed repeatedly, however, that her illness had nothing to do with her failure to cope with her job. The employer then gave her the choice of being demoted or being dismissed on the grounds of incompetent performance of her duties. The employee requested early retirement on the grounds of ill-health. She was examined by a doctor who diagnosed her as suffering from very serious depression and this meant that it was unlikely that she would ever be fit to work again. Her employer eventually dismissed her for incompetence, but the doctor's report was not brought to the attention of the appeal committee.

Held: the Employment Appeal Tribunal agreed with the Tribunal's decision that the employee had been fairly dismissed on the grounds of her incompetence. The employee had always stated that her inability to carry out her job had nothing to do with illness.

 Key point: A disabled person will have been discriminated against if the reason for the less favourable treatment is related his disability and a person to whom this reason does not apply would not have been treated less favourably.

Harassment

This is an issue which is taken very seriously under the other equality legislation of the United Kingdom. Sexual and racial harassment would be regarded as a detriment i.e. an example of the employee suffering less favourable treatment. Paragraph 6.22 of the Code of Practice states that the harassment of a disabled person will almost always amount to a detriment under the Disability Discrimination Act. The disabled must show that he has been subjected to harassment by his employer by reason of his disability.

 Verma v Herbie's Pizzas Ltd ET Case No 2701994/00 Verma suffered from profound deafness. He completely lacked the ability to lip-read and he was not capable of reading or writing in English. Verma claimed that he had been subjected to abusive treatment by his colleagues – something that his social worker confirmed.

Held: by the Employment Tribunal that Verma's disability prevented him from defending himself against the behaviour of his colleagues. The employer had taken no steps to put an end to the treatment that Verma had suffered. Verma's claim of harassment, therefore, succeeded.

Justification of less favourable treatment

Section 5(3) states that less favourable treatment of a disabled employee can only be justified if, but only if, the reason for the less favourable treatment is material to the circumstances of the particular case and substantial. It is for the employer to prove that the less favourable treatment was justified. When the employer relies on the justification defence, his reasons for doing so cannot be minor or trivial. The employer must demonstrate that he will face serious problems if he is not permitted to treat the employee less favourably on the grounds of disability.

Paragraph 6.21 of the Code of Practice gives a useful example of situations where the employer may be justified in treating a disabled employee less favourably. What if the employee, as a result of his disability, was prevented from performing the core duties of his contract and it was totally impracticable to transfer this individual to another post or it is simply not reasonable for the employer to make a transfer? In these situations, the employer may very well benefit from the defence that his treatment of the employee was justified.

 Mansoor v Guest & Chrimes Ltd ET Case No 2802060/97 Mansoor was a machinist who injured his back in a while he was at work in November 1995. As a result of the injury, he was unable to work and his employers wrote to him in March 1996 in order to find out when he would be able to return to work. Mansoor was unable to give an answer to this question. In June 1997, the employers decided to dismiss Mansoor. Mansoor raised an Employment Tribunal claim for disability discrimination.

Held: the Employment Tribunal dismissed Mansoor's claim on the ground that his employers had been justified in dismissing him. The Employment Tribunal drew on Paragraph 6.21 of the Code of Practice stating that Mansoor could no longer perform the main duties of his contract and it was not practicable for the employer to move him to another post within the organisation. Furthermore, Mansoor's inability to provide his employers with a date when he would be able to return to work gave them no option but to dismiss him.

 A *v* London Borough of Hounslow EAT 1155/98 the employee was a school laboratory technician who suffered from paranoid schizophrenia. He refused to medication to control his illness. The employer dismissed him on health and safety grounds because he was a risk to staff and pupils if a dangerous incident related to his illness occurred at work.

Held: by the Employment Appeal Tribunal that the dismissal was justified for material and substantial reasons.

 Callagan *v* Glasgow City Council (2001) Callagan was employed as a care worker at a residential children's home. Callagan was assaulted twice by children at the home and his sickness record went downhill rapidly. The employer attempted to speak with Callagan in order to find out what the position was with his health, when he could return to work and the options that were available to him. Callagan failed to attend any of the meetings that the employer had arranged. The employer eventually decided to dismiss Callagan. Callagan was suffering from a mixture of stress and depression which fell within the definition of a disability under the Act. When he was dismissed, Callagan was in no position to return to his work and the employer was none the wiser when this would be likely. Callagan had failed to discuss the option of part-time work – which the employer would have been happy to consider. It soon became apparent, however, that even part-time work was not a viable option for Callagan. The Employment Tribunal decided that the dismissal had been justified. Callagan appealed mainly on the ground that the employer should have offered him part-time work.

Held: by the Employment Appeal Tribunal that the reason for the dismissal was both material and substantial. The dismissal was, therefore, justified. The Employment Appeal Tribunal also felt that, on the facts of the case, the employer was not under a duty to offer Callagan part-time work.

 Key point: Less favourable treatment of a disabled employee can be justified if, but only if, the reason for the less favourable treatment is material to the circumstances of the particular case and substantial.

Failure of an employer to make reasonable adjustments

In terms of Section 6, an employee could experience discrimination where the employer either refuses or fails to make reasonable adjustments. Reasonable adjustments are measures which an employer will put in place in order to eliminate any physical features of the employer's premises or practices that would place a disabled person at a substantial (i.e. not trivial) disadvantage in comparison with a non-disabled person. When a disabled person brings a claim against an employer that he has failed to make reasonable adjustments, the Employment Tribunal must be satisfied that there is, in fact, a duty on the employer to make such adjustments. When such a duty has been established, the Employment Tribunal must then ask whether or not the employer has taken reasonable steps to put adjustments in place that will remove the substantial disadvantage in relation to the disabled person. The Employment Tribunal can make use of Section 6(3) to decide whether the employer has failed to implement his duty. The following factors are reasonable adjustments that an employer might put in place:

◆ Making adjustments to the employer's premises
◆ Transferring some of his duties to another person
◆ Giving him greater flexibility in his working hours
◆ Transferring him to suitable, alternative employment
◆ Changing his physical place of work
◆ Permitting him to have time off to attend medical treatment
◆ Providing him with training opportunities
◆ Modifying equipment for use by him
◆ Modifying instructions and training or reference manuals
◆ Modifying procedures for testing and assessment
◆ Providing an interpreter or a scribe
◆ Providing appropriate supervision

An employer may be able to argue that he is not under a duty to make reasonable adjustments if he either did not know or could not have been reasonably expected to know that an employee or a job applicant is disabled (Section 6(6)). However, this argument will fail if it can be implied that any of the employer's agents or employees had knowledge of the disability. From October 2004, the employer will have to take more active steps to discover whether any of his employees are, in fact, disabled and what reasonable adjustments can be put in place.

 Key point: Reasonable adjustments are measures or steps that an employer can take which should assist a disabled employee to carry out his job effectively.

Victimisation

Section 55 deals with the concept of victimisation. It will be unlawful to victimise either a disabled or a non-disabled employee in circumstances that are very similar to those laid down in sex and race discrimination complaints. As we have seen, victimisation can continue after the employment relationship has ended, for example, the employer's refusal to give a reference. The House of Lords decided that victimisation after a contract has ended is unlawful (see **Relaxion Group PLC v Rhys-Harper (FC); D'Souza v London Borough of Lambeth; Jones v 3M Healthcare Limited and Others (2003)**).

What the Act doesn't cover
Discriminatory advertisements
The Sex Discrimination and Race Relations Acts both contain rules that forbid the use by employers of discriminatory job advertisements. Strangely, the Disability Discrimination Act does not contain any rules that prohibit the use of discriminatory advertisements. It would, however, be very foolish on the part of employers to think that they can use such advertisements in respect of their recruitment activities and get away with this. In terms of Section 11, an Employment Tribunal would be entitled to take into account the impact of the advertisement if, for example, the employer refused to offer the disabled person employment or if it gave an indication that only a non-disabled person would be considered for the job. However, the

Disability Discrimination Act 1995 (Amendment) Regulations 2003 which come into force in October 2004 will change the law in this regard and punish employers who use discriminatory advertisements in recruitment.

Transferred discrimination

Unlike cases involving race, sexual orientation or religion or belief, the Disability Discrimination Act does not recognise the concept of transferred discrimination. Transferred discrimination would arise where a non-disabled person suffered less favourable treatment due to an association with disabled people. Such a non-disabled person could be a carer for a disabled person and might be refused employment or promotion. Furthermore, the employer does not have to make reasonable adjustments for those non-disabled persons who are associated or connected with a disabled person.

Lodging a disability claim and the burden of proof

An employee who believes that he has suffered less favourable treatment on the grounds of his disability must lodge a claim with the Office of Employment Tribunals within three months (less one day) of the discriminatory act complained of.

A decision of the Employment Tribunal – **Rowden v Dutton Gregory (2002)** – establishes a precedent that the rules governing the burden of proof in race discrimination claims (involving colour and nationality) should be used in disability claims. In **King v Great Britain – China Centre (1991)**, it will be remembered that once an employee brought evidence to demonstrate discrimination on the employer's part and the employer failed to offer a satisfactory response in return, the Employment Tribunal was entitled to infer that discrimination had taken place. This now appears to be the case for employees taking disability claims to Tribunal.

 Key point: In disability discrimination claims where there is strong evidence of less favourable treatment, the Tribunal is entitled to infer discrimination in the absence of any reasonable explanation by the employer.

Employer's liability for the discriminatory acts of employees

Section 58(1) states that anything done by anyone in the course of his employment shall be treated . . . as also done by his employer, whether it was done with the employer's knowledge or approval. The question which an Employment Tribunal must pose is whether the employee was acting in the course of his employment when he committed the discriminatory act against the disabled employee. This is a much wider concept than the one used in cases involving an employer's vicarious liability for the acts of employees. Section 58(5) does, however, protect an employer who has taken reasonably practicable steps to prevent the discriminatory acts of his employees.

The Disability Discrimination Act 1995 (Amendment) Regulations 2003

These new Regulations, if approved by Parliament, will come into force in October 2004. The Regulations will make fundamental changes to the way in which the Disability Discrimination Act 1995 currently operates. Firstly, the definition of disability will be extended to include those individuals suffering from HIV, cancer and multiple sclerosis. Many more individuals will, therefore, be protected as a result of the amended Disability Discrimination Act.

The provisions of the Act do not apply to employers with less than 15 employees, but the Regulations will abolish this exemption. A club with 25 or more members will also be covered by the newly amended Act and this will cover organisations such as political parties.

The Regulations will mean that certain professions or occupations which were not previously covered by the Act will also lose their exemption. These professions or occupations include advocates or barristers who operate from chambers, the police, prison officers and partners in a firm. The Regulations will also place greater responsibility on employers to discover who amongst the workplace suffers from a disability. Employers will be expected to take more active steps to promote equal opportunities for disabled people within the workplace. Generally speaking, employers who are classified as public authorities (a concept which should be familiar from the amended race equality legislation) will be under a duty to promote equality of opportunity for disabled people.

Transport will also come under the remit of the Disability Discrimination Act. This is a major step forward since, currently, it is only the transport infrastructure which is covered by the Act rather than the provision of transport services. Landlords and managers of premises will also have to make reasonable adjustments to policies, practices and procedures and to provide additional assistance and services, where reasonable, to enable a disabled person to rent a property. It is also important that these adjustments and the provision of additional assistance and service promote the disabled person's full use of the property.

Part-time workers and fixed-term employees

As we have seen, the United Kingdom equality legislation makes it unlawful for an employer to discriminate against workers on the grounds of sex, race, disability, sexual orientation and religion.

However, workers can also experience discrimination by reason of their employment status. It is now unlawful for an employer to discriminate against a worker by reason of his part-time status or because an employee is employed under a fixed-term contract. Therefore, an employer commits a potential discriminatory act if he advertises a post which stipulates that only full-time workers need apply. Unless the employer can objectively justify the less favourable treatment of part-time workers, he may leave himself open to a charge of part-time worker discrimination.

Part-time workers and fixed-term employees tend to be overwhelmingly female and the new rules can be seen, in part, as an extension of the sexual equality laws. The reason that women choose to work part time is in order to organise their family commitments. As for fixed-term employment, many women will be offered fixed-term employment rather than a permanent contract when they re-enter the workforce after having taken a break to have a family in the first place. However, men are also able to claim the various rights which the equality legislation sets out to protect. There are now two significant pieces of legislation which protect the rights of part-time workers and fixed-term employees:

1 Part-time Workers (Prevention of Less Favourable Treatment) Regulations 2000

2 Fixed-term Employees (Prevention of Less Favourable Treatment) Regulations 2002

Part-time Workers (Prevention of Less Favourable Treatment) Regulations 2000

The Regulations came into force on 1 July 2000 and were subsequently amended on 1 October 2002. They implement European Council Directive No 97.81 on part-time work. The aim of the Regulations is to ensure that part-time workers are not less favourably treated than comparable full-time workers, solely because they work part time, unless the treatment can be justified on objective grounds. Regulation 5 is very explicit that it will be an act of discrimination to treat a part-time worker less favourably than a comparable full-time worker. Part-time workers have often experienced less favourable treatment at the hands of their employers in respect of being denied access to employment, promotion and training opportunities. There can also be significant differences (in a negative sense) between the terms and conditions that full-time workers enjoy and those of part-time workers.

It is important to point out that part-time workers should receive the same benefits as a full-time comparable worker in the same employment on a *pro rata* basis. This would mean that if a full-time worker was paid a basic salary of £30,000 per year, working a 35-hour week, a part-timer working 17 and a half hours per week (i.e. half the hours worked by the full-timer) should be paid an annual salary of £15,000 according to the *pro rata* principle.

 Hendrickson Europe Ltd *v* Pipe EAT 0272/02 a part-time employee had been selected for redundancy by reason of the fact that she had a part-time contract.

Held: by the Employment Appeal Tribunal that this was an example of less favourable treatment on account of the employee's part-time status.

Justification of less favourable treatment

An employer will be able to justify less favourable treatment on objective grounds. Objective reasons for discrimination may be that the part-time worker has inferior qualifications or less experience than her full-time colleague and this explains the difference in treatment (see **Glasgow City Council *v* Marshall (2000)** – an equal pay case where a material factor was held to be genuine and, therefore, objectively justified).

 Key point: Workers who are treated less favourably by reason of their part-time status will now be able to take a discrimination claim to an Employment Tribunal.

Definition of a worker

From the title of the Regulations it can be deduced that part-time workers rather than just employees are protected. Regulation 1 defines a worker as someone who has:

◆ An employment contract

◆ Any other contract, whether express or implied, where she has agreed to perform personally any work or services for another party to the contract

Someone who performs work or services as part of her business for a client or a customer will fall outside the above definition of a worker and, therefore, is not covered by the Regulations.

The Regulations grant important rights to workers in two situations:

◆ Those workers who have previously held a full-time position and who now wish to change to part-time work (Regulation 3).

◆ Workers returning from a period of absence who previously held a full-time position but who now wish to change to a part-time work. This would cover workers returning from maternity leave (Regulation 4).

Workers in the above two situations may actually find that their part-time terms and conditions of employment are less favourable than their previous full-time employment. The Regulations come to these workers' assistance because they permit them to compare their current part-time contracts to their previous full-time contracts.

Identifying a comparator

In order to bring a claim of less favourable treatment against her employer, Regulation 2(4) makes it very clear that a part-time worker must demonstrate the following:

◆ She and her comparator are employed by the same employer under the same type of contract;

and

◆ She and her comparator are engaged in the same or broadly similar work.

Furthermore, as Regulation 2(4) makes abundantly clear, the full-time comparator must work or be based at the same establishment as the part-time worker. However, Regulation 2(4) recognises that situations may arise where there is no full-time worker working or based in the same workplace who satisfies the requirements listed above. This situation would obviously be fatal to the part-time worker's claim. In order to deal with this problem, the part-time worker is, therefore, permitted to compare himself with a full-time worker who is based at a different establishment and satisfies the two requirements laid down by Regulation 2(4).

Regulation 2(3) lists various types of contracts which are considered to be very different in nature:

1 Employees employed under a contract that is not a contract of apprenticeship.

2 Employees employed under a contract of apprenticeship.

3 Workers who are not employees.

4 Any other description of worker that it is reasonable for the employer to treat differently from other workers on the ground that workers of that description have a different type of contract.

A part-time worker cannot compare herself to any full-time comparator. It would not be the correct legal approach for a part-time worker employed under an apprenticeship contract to compare her situation to full-time worker who is employed on a contract which is not an apprenticeship contract. A part-time apprentice alleging less favourable treatment must compare her situation with a worker employed under a full-time apprenticeship contract.

 Matthews and Others v Kent and Medway Towns Fire Authority and Others (2003) 12,000 part-time firefighters brought a claim under the Part-time Workers Regulations 2000 alleging that they were being less favourably treated than full-time firefighters.

Held: by the Employment Appeal Tribunal that the part-timers were not employed under the same type of contract and nor could it be argued that they were employed in the same or broadly similar work.

 Key point: A part-time worker alleging less favourable treatment by the employer must compare himself with an appropriate comparator.

Bringing a claim and the burden of proof

A part-time worker can ask the employer to explain the difference in treatment. The employer has 21 days from the employee requesting an explanation to issue a written statement laying down the reasons for the difference in treatment between part-time and full-time workers (Regulation 6). It is open to the employer to deny that any discrimination has taken place. The employer's statement can be used in Employment Tribunal proceedings at a later date. If the employer fails to provide a statement on request or issues reasons for the treatment that could be considered evasive, it is up to the Employment Tribunal to draw its own conclusions. If the employee still wishes to take matters further, she is entitled to lodge an Employment Tribunal application within three months (less one day) of the conduct complained of (Regulation 8).

 Key point: A part-time worker is entitled to a written statement from his employer explaining any difference in treatment which should be issued within 21 days of the initial request for information.

Victimisation

Any part-time worker who makes a complaint or proceeds with an action under the Regulations has the right not to be victimised by the employer. Victimisation could take the form of dismissal or some other detriment, for example, harassment. If the employer dismisses a part-time worker for enforcing her rights under the Regulations, such a dismissal will be automatically unfair (Regulation 7). This protection is also extended to any other worker who agrees to be a witness or give evidence in respect of any complaint made against an employer under the Regulations.

An employer will be responsible for any breaches of the Regulations committed by an employee whether this act was done with or without the employer knowledge (Regulation 11).

Examples of case law dealing with part-time worker discrimination

 Clarke & Powell *v* Eley Kinoch Ltd (1982) the employer decided to make redundant 20 full-time male employees, 26 full-time female employees and all 60 of the part-time workers (all of whom were female). The company's policy was to make part-time staff redundant first, then to use the 'last in first out' principle in relation to all of the full-time workers. If the 'last in first out' principle had been applied to the whole workforce, Ms Clarke and Ms Powell would not have been made redundant.

Held: by the Employment Appeal Tribunal that the way in which the company had handled the procedures for redundancy was an example of indirect sex discrimination. The 'part-timers first' clause imposed a requirement or condition, which was to the detriment of the two women, and could not be objectively justified.

 Bilka-Kaufhaus *v* Weber Von Hartz (1986) part-time workers, who were employed by a German department store, were treated less favourably than their full-time colleagues in that they were not allowed to become members of the employer's occupational pension scheme. Some time later, the pension scheme was extended to part-timers as long as they had worked for at least 15 years out of a total of 20. Mrs Von Hartz did not receive a pension because she failed to meet this requirement. The European Court of Justice stated that this example of less favourable treatment could not be justified by the employer on objective grounds – there was no reason why part-timers could not be admitted to the pension scheme. Most of the part-time workers were, of course, female and the employer's refusal to admit them to the pension scheme amounted to indirect sex discrimination.

 Re Secretary of State for Employment *ex parte* Equal Opportunities Commission (1994) the Employment Protection (Consolidation) Act 1978 contained a requirement that for an employee to be entitled to a statutory redundancy payment had to work more than 16 hours per week. Those employees who worked less than eight hours per week had no rights in terms of protection from unfair dismissal. The employees in question worked less than eight hours per week.

Held: by the House of Lords that the Employment Protection (Consolidation) Act 1978 indirectly discriminated against women as fewer of them were able to comply in practice with the rules relating to entitlement to a redundancy payment and rights against unfair dismissal. Women tended to do more part-time work than men and they were less likely to meet the requirements of the 1978 Act. Since this decision, all workers regardless of whether they are employed on a full-time or part-time basis have the same rights in respect of unfair dismissal and redundancy.

It is worth noting that these decisions were made before the introduction of the Part-time Workers (Prevention of Less Favourable Treatment) 2000 and they depend on the application of the principle of indirect sex discrimination. The Regulations now simply make it unlawful for employers to discriminate against part-timers (sex discrimination may be an issue, it may not be), unless the difference in treatment can be objectively justified.

The Fixed-term Employees (Prevention of Less Favourable Treatment) Regulations 2002

These Regulations came into force on 10 October 2002. Employees on a fixed-term contract should not receive less favourable treatment than comparable employees on the grounds of their contractual status unless this treatment by the employer can be objectively justified. Fixed-term employees will often experience less favourable treatment in comparison to their permanent colleagues. For the purposes of the Regulations, a permanent employee is someone who is not on a fixed-term contract. Permanent employees will, therefore, enjoy contracts for an indefinite or an indeterminate period of time.

The aim of the Regulations is to regularise as much as possible the position of fixed-term employees within the organisation. To this end, employees who have less than three months' service with the employer will be entitled to receive statutory sick pay, payments as a result of medical suspension and guarantee payments. In terms of notice requirements, fixed-term employees must receive from the employer at least one month's notice of his intention to terminate the employment contract. On the other hand, the employee must provide the employer with a similar notice of period if it is her intention to terminate the contract.

The widespread practice of employers continuing to employ fixed-term employees on a series of rolling contracts will be curtailed as a result of the Regulations (Regulation 8). In the past, it has not been unusual to see some employees working on temporary contracts for seven or eight years at a time – sometimes even longer. The Regulations aim to tackle this practice. Employers will now be able to keep an employee on a fixed-term contract for a maximum of four years only, unless the further use of such a contract can be objectively justified. The main impact of the Regulations will be that anyone who has been employed on a fixed-term contract from 10 July 2002 will automatically become a permanent member of staff in July 2006, providing of course that the contract with the employer has continued to be renewed over that four-year period. After four years, the employee can request and is entitled to receive a statement from the employer to the effect that his contract is now of an indefinite or indeterminate duration (i.e. she has become a permanent worker) (Regulation 9). The employer is under a duty to issue such a statement within 21 days of receiving the employee's request.

 Key point: Employers will now be able to keep an employee on a fixed-term contract for a maximum of four years only, unless the further use of such a contract can be objectively justified.

Fixed-term employees are also given additional rights in respect of redundancy and dismissal (Regulation 10). From 1 October 2002, the employer will no longer be able to include a term in the employment contract which effectively prevents the employee having a remedy against the employer in the event of redundancy. Such a term, amounting to a redundancy waiver, will be automatically void. Fixed-term employees who have more than two years' continuous service and who are dismissed by reason of redundancy will be entitled to a statutory redundancy payment in common with their permanent colleagues.

Furthermore, if an employer terminates a contract for a specified task once the task has been completed or if the contract comes to an end upon the occurrence or non-occurrence of a specific event, the employee will have been dismissed if the employer fails to renew the contract. Assuming that the dismissed employee has more than one year's continuous service, she can ask the employer to provide her with written reasons setting out the justification for the dismissal. Ultimately, the dismissal could be regarded as unfair and the employee will have the option of lodging a claim with the Office of Employment Tribunals.

Definition of a fixed-term employee

A fixed-term employee is defined, in terms of the Regulations, as someone who is employed on a contract that will last for a specified period of time or whose employment will end when a specified task has been completed or when a specified event either occurs or does not occur (Regulation 1).

Less favourable treatment

Less favourable treatment of a fixed-term employee could take many forms (Regulation 3). Such individuals could be denied access to the employer's sick-pay scheme, denied access to the employer's pension scheme, the employer may fail to notify them about permanent vacancies within the organisation, and they may be denied access to employment, promotion or training opportunities generally. There may be discrimination if a fixed-term employee's terms and conditions of employment were less favourable in comparison to their permanent colleagues with whom they would wish to make a comparison. Fixed-term employees now have a right to receive information from the employer about permanent vacancies in the organisation.

 Key point: A fixed-term term employee should not be treated less favourably in comparison with a relevant permanent colleague.

Justification of less favourable treatment

An employer will only be able to justify less favourable treatment of a fixed-term employee on objective grounds (Regulation 4). An employer may be able to justify the less favourable treatment by bringing evidence which demonstrates that a permanent worker has better qualifications and/or more experience than the person bringing the complaint.

Identifying a comparator

If a fixed-term employee decides to make an allegation of discrimination against the employer, it is important that they are able to compare themselves to a permanent employee (Regulation 2). The fixed-term employee cannot choose any permanent colleague with whom to compare himself. The comparator must be employed by the same employer and do the same or broadly similar work (the influence of the Equal Pay Act 1970 can undoubtedly be felt here). The employee must show that she has similar skills, qualifications and experience to her comparator. Like must be compared with like as much as possible. If the employee cannot point to a comparator in his workplace, he can always search for another permanent employee to make a comparison, as long as this individual is employed by the same employer the only difference being that he is employed at another workplace.

Lodging a claim and the burden of proof

The employee has a right to ask the employer to respond to his allegation of discrimination. The employer should respond by issuing a written statement, within 21 days of the employee's original request, setting out the reasons for the treatment that the employee has experienced (Regulation 5). The employer is perfectly at liberty to take issue with the employee's perception that he has somehow been discriminated against by reason of his status as a fixed-term employee. If the employee is still not satisfied with the employer's written response, she is entitled to lodge an Employment Tribunal application within three months (less one day) of the conduct complained of (Regulation 7).

An individual who claims that they have been discriminated against by an employer on the grounds that he is a part-time worker or a fixed-term employee must bring evidence to support such a claim. Once evidence of discrimination has been established, it will be up to the employer to rebut this. If the employer is unable to do this, the Employment Tribunal is entitled to make a finding of less favourable treatment.

Victimisation

Regulation 6 makes it very clear that employees who make complaints against the employer or who give evidence on behalf of a discriminated colleague have the right not to be victimised by the employer in respect of unfair dismissal or other detriments.

Employer's liability for breaches committed by an employee

An employer will be responsible for any breaches of the Regulations committed by an employee whether this act was done with or without the employer knowledge (Regulation 12).

Discrimination on the grounds of sexual orientation, religion or belief

On 1 December 2003, owing to the introduction of the Employment Equality (Sexual Orientation) Regulations 2003, it became unlawful for an employer to discriminate against someone by reason of that person's sexual orientation.

Furthermore on 2 December 2003, in terms of the Employment Equality (Religion or Belief) Regulations 2003, it became unlawful for an employer to discriminate against someone on the grounds of religion or beliefs.

Both sets of Regulations, which implement the European Employment Directive (Council Directive 2000/78/EC), now provide protection to workers (not just employees, but also contract workers) who experience this kind of discrimination and harassment in the workplace. Employers and providers of vocational training are covered by both sets of Regulations. They cover all aspects of the employment relationship, including recruitment, pay, working conditions, training, promotion, dismissal and the provision of references. It does not matter whether the employer is a large or small organisation or whether it is in the public or private sector, the Regulations will apply. The police are also covered by the Regulations.

The Regulations apply to office holders appointed by the government and other office holders where they fall within the scope of the Directive (that is, if they are paid and are subject to some form of direction). This means that the regulations will cover clergy and judicial offices, for example, including magistrates and Employment Tribunal members. They do not cover people who hold elected office, or an office that cannot be regarded as a job, for example, a child's guardian.

 Key point: Both sets of Employment Equality Regulations 2003 now make it unlawful to discriminate against a person on the grounds of sexual orientation and religion or belief.

The Employment Equality (Sexual Orientation) Regulations 2003 make it unlawful for employers to deny lesbian, gay and bisexual people employment and training opportunities. Obviously, lesbian, gay and bisexual people will benefit the most from the new law, but heterosexuals will also have a right to bring a claim against employers who discriminate against them on the grounds of their sexual orientation.

The Regulations will protect people from discrimination on the grounds of their sexual orientation, whether they are orientated towards people of the same-sex, the opposite-sex or both sexes.

The Employment Equality (Religion or Belief) Regulations 2003 will for the first time, outlaw discrimination and harassment on grounds of religion or belief in large and small workplaces in England, Scotland and Wales, both in the private and public sectors.

According to the Regulations, a religion or belief is defined as being any religion, religious belief or similar philosophical belief. This does not include any philosophical or political belief unless it is similar to religious belief. Obviously, this definition would cover members of the Church of Scotland, the Roman Catholic Church, members of other Christian churches, Muslims, Jews, Hindus, Sikhs and Buddhists. It would not provide protection to someone with strong political beliefs, for example, a Marxist. Similarly, supporters of football clubs would not be protected by the Regulations.

It will be for the Employment Tribunals and other courts to decide whether a belief has the status of a religion and, therefore, whether it is covered by the Regulations. Adherents of the Jedi religion would probably not be protected under the Regulations.

It is worth remembering, if a comparison is being made, that the earlier gender and racial equality legislation was primarily designed to protect women and ethnic minorities, but men and the majority white British population were also protected by these anti-discrimination laws. There is no reason to prevent heterosexuals and members of majority religious groups from using the appropriate set of Regulations to bring a claim if they feel that they have suffered discrimination as a result of their sexual orientation or religious beliefs.

Transferred discrimination

Transferred discrimination will also be illegal under the Regulations (see **Showboat Entertainment Centre Ltd v Owens (1984)** for an example of transferred race discrimination). Transferred discrimination occurs where person experiences less favourable treatment because of the sexual orientation or religious beliefs of the people with whom they associate, for example, their family and friends.

Perceptions about a person's sexual orientation or religious beliefs

The law also covers situations where an employer perception of a person's sexual orientation or religious beliefs will result in the employer treating that person less favourably. An employer may believe, wrongly, that an employee is gay and subject that person to discrimination, for example, by refusing to promote him. The fact that the employee is heterosexual does not prevent him from bringing a claim against his employer for discrimination on the grounds of sexual orientation. Similarly, an employer may wrongly believe that an employee is a Roman Catholic and, as a result, refuse to employ that person.

 Key point: Both sets of Employment Equality Regulations 2003 make transferred discrimination and less favourable treatment arising from perceptions about a person's sexual orientation or religion unlawful.

Types of discrimination

The Employment Equality (Sexual Orientation) Regulations 2003 and the Employment Equality (Religion or Belief) Regulations 2003 take a common approach to the issue of discrimination:

Direct discrimination
Treating people less favourably than others because of religion, belief or sexual orientation (Regulation 3 of both Regulations).

Indirect discrimination
Applying a provision, criterion or practice which disadvantages people of a particular sexual orientation, religion or belief and which is not justified in objective terms (Regulation 3 of both Regulations).

Harassment
Unwanted conduct that violates people's dignity or creates an intimidating, hostile, degrading, humiliating or offensive environment (Regulation 4 of both Regulations).

Victimisation
Treating people less favourably because of action they have taken under or in connection with the new legislation – for example, made a formal complaint of discrimination or given evidence in an Employment Tribunal case (Regulation 5 of both Regulations).

The Regulations give protection to employees throughout the course of the employment relationship. Employees have the right not to be discriminated against during the recruitment process, in the workplace, on dismissal. In terms of Regulation 21 of both sets of Regulations, employees have the right not to be discriminated by way of victimisation in certain circumstances after the employment has ended (see **Relaxion Group plc v Rhys-Harper (FC)**; **D'Souza v London Borough of Lambeth**; **Jones v 3M Healthcare Limited and Others (2003)**).

 Key point: The Employment Equality Regulations 2003 make the following types of discrimination unlawful: direct discrimination, indirect discrimination, harassment and victimisation.

Genuine occupational requirements (Regulation 7 of both Regulations)

Regulation 7 of the Employment Equality (Sexual Orientation) Regulations states that an employer will be allowed to discriminate against people on the grounds of their sexual orientation where it is important that an applicant or an employee be of a particular sexual orientation. In situations such as these, a person's sexual orientation is a genuine and determining occupational requirement. The employer's insistence on applying such a requirement to an applicant or an employee must be proportionate (i.e. reasonable) in order to achieve a legitimate aim. The Arbitration, Conciliation and Advisory Service (ACAS) has used the example of a Gay Rights group (such as Stonewall) applying a genuine occupational requirement that its Chief Executive be a gay man or a lesbian or a bi-sexual in order for that person to enjoy credibility within the gay and bi-sexual community.

Regulation 7 of the Employment Equality (Religion or Belief) Regulations also allows organised religions, for example, the Church of Scotland or the Roman Catholic Church to apply genuine occupational requirements to employment where it is necessary to comply with religious doctrine, the nature of the post or the fact that by appointing a person who has a particular sexual orientation this may lead to conflict with a significant number of the religion's followers. Local authorities in Scotland will still be able to insist that being a practising Roman Catholic is a genuine occupational requirement for Head Teachers of Roman Catholic schools.

When applying genuine occupational requirements, both sets of Regulations state that the employer must either show that the individual to whom it is applied could not comply with the condition or the employer reasonably believed this to be the case.

 Key point: The Employment Equality Regulations 2003 permit employers, in limited situations, to discriminate against employees or applicants by reason of their sexual orientation or religion.

The burden of proof

Regulations 29 and 32 of the Employment Equality (Sexual Orientation) Regulations 2003 and of the Employment Equality (Religion or Belief) Regulations 2003 state that the burden of proof will be placed on the person bringing the complaint to show that he has suffered an act of discrimination on the grounds of his sexual orientation or religion or beliefs if the claim is brought before either the Employment Tribunal or the Sheriff Court. Once the Employment Tribunal or the Sheriff Court is satisfied from the circumstances of the case that an act of discrimination has taken place, the complaint must be upheld if the employer is unable to provide a satisfactory explanation for his conduct. This favours the employee and goes further than **King v Great Britain-China Centre (1991)** and **Zafar v Glasgow City Council (1998)** where Employment Tribunals and courts were permitted to infer discrimination, but they were not forced to make this finding.

Liability of employers

According to Regulation 22 of both the Employment Equality (Sexual Orientation) Regulations and the Employment Equality (Religion or Belief) Regulations, an employer will be liable for the discriminatory actions of any employee. Furthermore, Regulation 23 of both sets of Regulations makes it quite clear that it will be unlawful for any individual to aid someone to commit a discriminatory act.

A significant improvement?

Both sets of Regulations represent significant progress in the sense that many more people will now enjoy protection from discrimination, victimisation and harassment than was previously the case. It should be recalled that discrimination on the grounds of a person's sexual orientation was not unlawful in terms of the Sex Discrimination Act 1975 (see **Macdonald v Advocate General for Scotland and Pearce v Governing Body of Mayfield School (2003)**). Similarly, the Race Relations Act 1976 did not prevent individuals suffering discrimination by reason of their religious beliefs, except in very narrowly defined circumstances (see **Mandla v Dowall Lee (1983); Seide v Gillette Industries Ltd (1980) and J H Walker Ltd v Hussain & Others (1996)**). It is anticipated that the Regulations will now plug a very large and undesirable loop-hole in the United Kingdom's equality legislation.

The Regulations also use a wider definition of indirect discrimination which is very similar to that used in the amended Race Relations Act 1976. The words 'provision, criterion, or practice' have a broader meaning than the words 'requirement or condition' used in the older equality legislation from the 1970s. The new definition will apply to formal and informal practices of an employer where he imposes a provision, criterion or practice which disadvantages people of a particular sexual orientation or religion or belief. Furthermore, the more modern approach to indirect discrimination should mean that many more cases are brought before Employment Tribunals without having to rely on a complex statistical exercise in order to initiate them (see **London Underground v Edwards (No 2) (1998)**).

A single Equality Act?

The Liberal Democrat peer, Lord Lester of Herne Hill QC introduced a Private Member's Bill in the House of Lords on 14 January 2003 entitled the Draft Equality Bill. On 12 May 2003, the Bill had its First Reading in the House of Commons after successfully completing its passage through the House of Lords. If this Bill became law, it would bring together all of the discrimination laws in a single Equality Act. The proposed Act would deal with discrimination on the basis of a person's age, gender, gender reassignment, pregnancy, colour, race, nationality, ethnic or national origin, family status, marital status, sexual orientation and religion or belief within a single framework. It will now, of course, be appreciated that the current equality legislation is not easy to understand and does not always take a consistent approach. The Bill also aims to replace the three Commissions (EOC, CRE and DRC) which currently police the existing discrimination legislation with a single Commission that will also have responsibility for the enforcement of human rights.

The Equality Bill has been criticised by the Disability Rights Commission because it makes no provision for reasonable adjustments in post-16 education and it fails to address the issue of reasonable adjustments in relation to premises. The Commission is also concerned that the Bill ignores aspects of the Disability Rights Taskforce which submitted its report in 1999.

The aims of Lord Lester's Bill are to be welcomed, but in the absence of government support it has little chance of becoming law. The government has indicated its intention, however, to introduce a single Human Rights Commission to replace the EOC, the CRE and the DRC.

The legal framework of employment law

Many employment law cases, for example, dismissal, discrimination, working time disputes, paternity and maternity rights will be dealt with primarily by Employment Tribunals. There is, of course, a right of appeal from Employment Tribunals on a point of law to the Employment Appeal Tribunal with a possibility of further appeals to the Inner House of the Court of Session and, ultimately, the House of Lords.

Employment law claims can also be brought before the civil courts in Scotland, for example, the Sheriff Court and the Court of Session. The institutions of employment law will, of course, be familiar from the descriptions contained in Chapter 1.

Summary

- The United Kingdom's discrimination legislation makes it unlawful to treat a person less favourably on the basis of gender, marital status, gender reassignment, pregnancy, colour, race, nationality, ethnic or national origin, sexual orientation and religion or belief and employment status (part-time workers and fixed-term employees).

- Someone will suffer discrimination when he or she is treated less favourably or experience some sort of detriment or harm which is related to one of their personal characteristics, for example, race or sexual orientation and this treatment cannot be objectively justified.

- Detriments can come in all shapes and sizes – lack of promotion and training opportunities, different pay scales and conditions of employment, unfairness in the recruitment process, dismissal from employment, failure to receive the same contractual benefits as fellow employees, harassment and victimisation, selecting certain individuals for redundancy first and refusal to allow more flexible working patterns.

- Sexual and racial discrimination are illegal in terms of the Sex Discrimination Act 1975 (as amended) and the Race Relations Act 1976 (as amended) respectively.

- The Sex Discrimination Act 1975 outlaws sexual discrimination in relation to terms of employment, training, education, the provision of goods and services and the disposal of premises with Section 6 applying specifically to employment.

- In sex discrimination claims, it will be for the employee to show the facts that prove less favourable treatment and if the employer is unable to come up with a satisfactory explanation which would disprove the complaint, the Tribunal must now decide in favour of the employee.

- The Race Relations Act 1976 outlaws racial discrimination in relation to terms of employment, trade union membership, education, the provision of goods and services, and in the disposal and management of housing and other premises with Section 4(2) applying specifically to employment.

- The amended Race Relations Act also imposes general duties on listed public authorities to promote racial equality. The general duty means that public authorities will have to eliminate unlawful discrimination and promote equality of opportunity and good race relations in carrying out their functions.

- Where the employee is raising a discrimination claim on the grounds of his colour or nationality, an Employment Tribunal is entitled, but not compelled, to infer less favourable treatment by the employer.

- Where the employee is raising a discrimination claim on the grounds of his racial, ethnic or national origins, an Employment Tribunal is compelled to make a finding of less favourable treatment if the complainant brings strong evidence to demonstrate this and there is no reasonable explanation for this treatment from the employer.

- The Equal Opportunities Commission and the Commission for Racial Equality are statutory bodies which have responsibility for policing the Sex Discrimination Act and the Race Relations Act respectively.

- The types of less favourable treatment which the Sex Discrimination Act and the Race Relations Act regard as unlawful are direct discrimination, indirect discrimination, harassment and victimisation.

- Direct discrimination occurs when a person experiences less favourable treatment by reason of their sex or race.

- Employers will have to be particularly careful that they do not apply general conditions, requirements or criteria in relation to employees which may actually be examples of indirect discrimination.

- Harassment on the grounds of sex or race will occur when a person is subjected to unwanted conduct which has the purpose or effect of violating his or her dignity or creates an intimidating, hostile, offensive or disturbing environment.

- It is important that those individuals who have been involved in discrimination claims either as a complainant or as a witness should be adequately protected against acts of victimisation by the employer during and after their employment.

- The Race Relations Act uses two definitions of indirect indiscrimination – a narrower one when the less favourable treatment involves colour and nationality and a broader one where a person experiences less favourable treatment on the grounds of racial, national or ethnic origin.

- Discrimination on the grounds of a person's sexual orientation is not covered by the Sex Discrimination Act, but the Employment Equality (Sexual Orientation) Regulations 2003 now make it unlawful to discriminate on these grounds.

- Discrimination on the grounds of a person's religion or beliefs is not generally covered by the Race Relations Act, but the Employment Equality (Religion or Belief) Regulations 2003 now make it unlawful to discriminate on these grounds.

- As a result of the Sex Discrimination (Gender Reassignment) Regulations 1999, transsexuals are protected against direct discrimination under Section 2A of the Sex Discrimination Act 1975.

- Genuine occupational qualifications or special occupational requirements allow an employer to discriminate against certain individuals on the grounds of sex or race.

- The Equal Pay Act 1970 can be used to combat inequalities in the terms and conditions of employment offered to men and women and not just pay as its title misleadingly suggests.

- European Union law has often been used to overcome the shortcomings of the United Kingdom's equal pay legislation.

- The Equal Pay Act ensures that each contract of employment contains an equality clause which means that it will be implied that men and women in the same employment should receive equal pay for equal work.

- Employers will be able to justify a difference in the terms and conditions of employment offered to men and women if this is due to a material difference and is not based on the grounds of a person's sex.

- A disability is a physical, sensory or mental impairment which has a substantial and long-term adverse effect on the ability of a person to carry out day-to-day activities.

- A disabled person will have been discriminated against if the reason for the less favourable treatment is related to his disability and a person to whom this reason does not apply would not have been treated less favourably.

- The Disability Rights Commission is a statutory body, with similar powers to the Equal Opportunities Commission and the Commission for Racial Equality, which polices the Disability Discrimination Act.

- Reasonable adjustments are measures or steps that an employer can take which should assist a disabled employee to carry out his job effectively.

- Less favourable treatment of a disabled employee can only be justified if, but only if, the reason for the less favourable treatment is material to the circumstances of the particular case and substantial.

- In disability discrimination claims where there is strong evidence of less favourable treatment, the Tribunal is entitled to infer discrimination in the absence of any reasonable explanation by the employer.

- As a result of the Part-Time Workers Regulations 2000, workers who are treated less favourably by reason of their part-time status will now be able to take a discrimination claim to an Employment Tribunal.

- Under the Fixed-Term Employees (Prevention of Less Favourable Treatment) Regulations 2002, a fixed-term term employee should not be treated less favourably than a comparable, permanent colleague.

1 What types of discrimination in employment does United Kingdom legislation prohibit?

2 In terms of the United Kingdom's equality legislation, list five ways in which an employee or a job applicant can experience discriminatory or less favourable treatment.

3 **a)** With reference to sex and race equality legislation, what is meant by the terms direct and indirect discrimination?

b) Examine the following advertisement carefully:

WANTED

BARMAN REQUIRED FOR BUSY CITY CENTRE BAR AND RESTAURANT.

THIS IS A FULL-TIME POSITION AND THE SUCCESSFUL APPLICANT WILL BE EXPECTED TO WORK 4–5 NIGHTS PER WEEK.

IDEALLY, THIS POSITION WOULD SUIT A SINGLE PERSON.

INTERESTED?

PHONE JASON ON 07967 43210 FOR FURTHER DETAILS.

Comment on the legality of the above advertisement.

c) McTavish Biscuits Ltd is currently recruiting production line workers for its factory in Dalry in Ayrshire. Dalry is a small village and is in a predominantly rural part of Ayrshire. McTavish has stated that the following criteria for prospective employees is highly desirable:
i) A high degree of fluency in spoken and written English
ii) Possession of educational qualifications from British schools and colleges
iii) Preference will be given to residents of Dalry and its surrounding area
McTavish is also insisting that every applicant selected for interview must sit and pass an aptitude test. McTavish has placed advertisements in attempt to recruit delivery drivers for its operation. Jutinder Singh, who is a Sikh, applied for a job and received an application form from the company. The form states that McTavish requires all male drivers to be clean shaven and have neat and tidy haircuts.

Do you think that McTavish acted properly in relation to its recruitment procedures?

4 **a)** In what situations will an employee be subjected to harassment in the workplace?

b) Sharon is a young graduate who is working as a trainee marketing executive. One day, Sharon logs on to her computer where she discovers that Tony, her manager, has sent pornographic images via the e-mail system. A colleague later informs Sharon that Tony has also been spreading stories about Sharon's sexual history. Tony had asked Sharon out on a date, but Sharon had politely, but very firmly turned him down. Sharon feels extremely angry and upset about Tony's offensive behaviour. Tony claims that he is merely indulging in a bit of harmless flirting and, if he had known that his behaviour would cause offence, he would never have sent the e-mails in the first place.

What are the consequences of Tony's behaviour?

5 **a)** When would less favourable treatment of employee by an employer be regarded as victimisation?

b) Shamaila has just left her old job. She saw a job advertised in the local paper and she has decided to apply for this post. The application form requires a reference from her former employer. Unfortunately, Shamaila had to leave her former job under something of a cloud. Shamaila had been forced to take a race discrimination claim to an Employment Tribunal against her former employer – which she won. To say that her former employer was not pleased about this outcome would be something of an understatement. Nevertheless, Shamaila decides to ask for a reference, but her former employer tells her that she must be joking to expect to be given a reference after the grief that she gave him by taking a claim to an Employment Tribunal. As a result of Shamaila failing to secure a reference, her application for new employment is rejected.

What can Shamaila do?

6 a) Until the introduction of the Employment Equality (Sexual Orientation) Regulations 2003, employees who were gay, lesbian or bisexual were not adequately protected by United Kingdom equality laws.

Discuss the accuracy of this statement.

b) Terry has been openly gay for many years. He has applied for a senior managerial position in the company for which he presently works. Terry was not given the job and a more junior colleague was appointed to the position in his place. Terry was considered to be the front-runner for the job and all the senior managers are shocked that he failed to secure the appointment. In the past, however, the Chief Executive of the company, who chaired the selection and interview panel, has made no secret of his intolerance of gay and lesbian people. The Chief Executive, who has strong religious views, is on the record as having said that he regards homosexuality as a grave moral disorder.

Advise Terry.

7 a) In terms of the Sex Discrimination Act 1975 and the Race Relations Act 1976, what is a genuine occupational qualification?
b) Examine the following situations carefully and decide whether the employer is entitled to claim that he is relying upon a genuine occupational qualification:

i) Joanne, a theatre director, is recruiting cast members for her latest play, a modern version of William Shakespeare's Romeo and Juliet. Joanne is refusing to consider male actors for the part of Juliet. Conrad, a struggling young actor who desperately wanted to play Juliet, is convinced that Joanne's decision not to audition male actors for this part is an example of less favourable treatment on the grounds of sex.

ii) Amanda applied for a job as a labourer on a building site. Kenny, the site manager, refused to employ her because he thought that Amanda would not be strong enough to carry some of the heavy lifting tasks involved in this type of work. Kenny feels that men are physically stronger than women and are, therefore, better suited for work on a building site.

iii) Rick and Debbie are trained counsellors. They have both applied for employment with Greenhill Men's Voluntary Association, an organisation, which amongst other things, provides counselling and support services, to men who have been the victims of serious sexual assaults. The Association also provides advice on matters relating to men's sexual health. Rick's application for employment with the Association is successful, but Debbie is not so fortunate. She feels that she has been discriminated against by the Association.

iv) Zura is from the former Soviet Republic Georgia and he has been resident in the United Kingdom for the last five years. The Georgian Cultural Society has just opened an office in Glasgow and it is looking to fill the post of development officer. The Society provides a range of cultural, support and welfare services to Georgians who are living in Scotland. Zura applied for this job and was accepted for the position after completing a successful interview. The successful applicant had to be fluent in the Georgian language and had to possess an in-depth knowledge of Georgian culture. Sandra, who had applied for the job but was not given an interview, feels that there was clear favouritism shown to certain candidates during the recruitment process for the job. Sandra has always been interested in Georgia and its people. She did complete a beginner's course in Georgian while she was at University back in 1989. The course was very basic and mainly dealt with everyday phrases that tourists would find useful when visiting Georgia.

v) Angus applied for a job as a chef in Mumbai Sunset, an Indian restaurant in Dundee. He was very surprised to be rejected for this job because he has extensive experience as a chef in relation to the preparation and cooking of Indian food. The restaurant owner, however, is keen to promote an authentic Indian experience for diners and he has decided to employ Rajiv, who is an ethnic Indian, in preference to Angus.

vi) The police service is currently running an advertising campaign in order to attract more recruits from ethnic minorities. As part of the campaign, black and Asian models will appear on posters which are to be displayed in public places such as train and bus stations. These posters will also appear in national and local newspapers. Fraser, who is white, applied to be a model in the poster campaign, but he was turned down by the advertising agency which is running the recruitment campaign on behalf of the police service.

8 In cases involving race discrimination, what is the difference between a genuine occupational requirement and a special occupational requirement?

9 a) The Equal Pay Act 1970 inserts an equality clause into every contract of employment.

What is an equality clause?

b) Give five examples of situations where an employer may breach the Equal Pay Act 1970.

c) With reference to the Equal Pay Act 1970, explain the following terms:

  i) Like work
  ii) Work rated equivalent
  iii) Work of equal value

d) Five female primary head teachers, supported by their trade union, decided to lodge a claim with the Office of Employment Tribunals alleging discrimination on the grounds of sex. These individuals are claiming that the local council pays them less for doing the same job as two male head teachers of local secondary schools. A major part of the council's defence to this Employment Tribunal claim is that the two secondary head teachers have far greater responsibilities than their female colleagues and this is why they are paid a higher salary.

Does the council have much chance of success in putting forward this particular defence?

10 In sex, equal pay and race claims, an employee who suspects that he or she is the victim of discriminatory treatment is permitted to serve an equality questionnaire on his or her employer.

Will an employee's case before an Employment Tribunal be helped in any way by serving an equality questionnaire on the employer?

11 a) How does the Disability Discrimination Act 1995 define less favourable treatment of disabled person?

b) In terms of the Disability Discrimination Act 1995, an employee could experience discrimination where the employer either refuses or fails to make reasonable adjustments.

What are reasonable adjustments and list five of them?

c) Matthew is registered blind and he has a guide dog to make his life much easier. Without his guide dog, Matthew would lose much of his independence and he would lack the confidence to leave his home. One day when Matthew was in the local shopping mall, he was refused entry to a particular store on the grounds that the management had banned pets. Matthew tried to explain to the store's security guards that his dog was not a pet. The security guards were completely unimpressed and continued to refuse Matthew entry to the store. Matthew was completely humiliated by his experience because it occurred on a Saturday afternoon when the shopping mall is at its busiest.

In terms of the Disability Discrimination Act 1995, what action can Matthew take against the store?

d) Simon is a technician who is employed at a local school. Simon suffers from schizophrenia, but for some time, he has been refusing to take his medication. Without the help of drugs to control his condition, Simon can become extremely violent and he is a serious threat to those around him. His employers have tried everything possible to encourage Simon to take his medication, but without success. Simon's job brings him into daily contact with staff and pupils at the school and there have already been complaints about some of his outbursts which are becoming much more frequent. Simon's employers decide that they have no alternative but to dismiss him.

Are Simon's employers justified in dismissing him?

12 Kathy has just returned to work on a part-time basis after her maternity leave. Kathy's employer had informed her that the only way that her request to work part-time could be accommodated if she agrees to accept a lower salary grade. Kathy is in a dilemma because she wants work part-time in order to spend more time with her new baby.

Advise Kathy.

13 Angela is employed in a temporary capacity. Recently, Angela was absent from her work for a week due to ill health. Her employer has informed Angela that, under the terms of her contract, she is not entitled to receive sick pay. Angela thinks that this unfair because all her permanent colleagues are contractually entitled to sick pay.

Do you think that Angela has been unfairly treated by her employer?

14 a) The introduction of the Employment Equality (Religion or Belief) Regulations 2003 now means that it will be unlawful for an employer to treat an individual less favourably as a result of that person's religion or beliefs.

Is this statement entirely accurate?

b) Heather, who is an atheist, applied for the post of Head Teacher of a Roman Catholic Secondary School. She was not even given an interview for the post despite the fact that she is currently employed as a Depute Head

Teacher at a non-denominational school within the same local authority area. Heather feels that she has been unfairly treated. The local authority has stated that the Head Teacher of a Roman Catholic school must be a practising member of the Roman Catholic Church.

Do you agree with the local authority's point of view?

15 a) In order to win a discrimination case at an Employment Tribunal, an Applicant must satisfy the burden of proof. What is the necessary burden of proof in each of the following cases?

    i)   A sex discrimination claim

ii)   A race discrimination claim

iii)   An equal pay claim

iv)   A disability discrimination claim

v)   A part-time worker discrimination claim

vi)   A fixed-term employee discrimination claim

vii)   A discrimination claim involving sexual orientation

viii)   A discrimination claim involving religion or belief.

b) In each of the above discrimination claims, what are the relevant time-limits that an Applicant must observe in order to lodge a claim effectively with the Office of Employment Tribunals?

TABLE OF CASES

T

U

V

TABLE OF STATUTES

Table of Statutes

Table of Statutes

ANSWERS

Chapter 1

1 Statute law, judicial precedent, custom, institutional writers, European Union law, Canon law, Feudal law.

2 Common law can consist of customs and practice e.g. recognised rights of way or customs in trades, businesses and professions and previously decided case law.

3 An Act of Parliament is part of the written law of the country. It starts off life as a Bill (a draft law) and it has to pass through either the Westminster Parliament or the Scottish Parliament before receiving the Royal Assent before becoming law. Examples include the Consumer Credit Act 1974, the Sale of Good Act 1979, the Companies Act 1985, the Employment Rights Act 1996 and the Employment Act 2002.

4 A Bill must pass through the House of Commons and the House of Lords before receiving the Royal Assent which means that it becomes law. The main stages in the House of Commons are the First Reading, the Second Reading, the Committee Stage, the Report Stage and the Third Reading. A very similar procedure is followed in the House of Lords.

5 A government Bill is a draft law introduced into parliament by a government minister. It will apply to the public generally. A private member's Bill is sponsored by an individual member of parliament. It will not necessarily have the backing of the government and therefore is less likely to succeed. It also applies generally to the public.

6 There are 25 judges each from one of the member states who are assisted by eight Advocates General. The court sits in Luxembourg. A President of the court is elected from the twenty-five judges.

7 The Single European Act 1986 also established a Court of First Instance in order to ease the pressure in relation to the European Court of Justice's workload. The Court of First Instance deals primarily with issues such as agriculture, state subsidies, competition, commercial policy, regional policy, trademark law, transport and disputes between the European Union and its staff. The Court of First Instance has twenty-five judges each appointed from one of the member states.

8 The European Council or the Council of Ministers, the European Parliament, the European Commission, the European Court of Justice.

9 Primary legislation or law is contained in the original three Treaties – Paris 1951, Rome 1957 and Euratom 1957. These Treaties lay down broad goals which the member states will attempt to achieve. They can often be sketchy where details are concerned. However, it is possible to use Treaty Articles to enforce a variety of rights if the Article in question is sufficiently clear and precise. Other Treaties such as the Treaty on European Union 1992, the Treaty of Amsterdam 1997 and the Treaty of Nice 2000 have also added to the primary law of the European Union.

Article 249 of the Treaty of Rome 1957 lists the five sources of European law which are known as secondary legislation. The Treaties list broad aims or objectives, but they often do not provide the details. Secondary legislation is, therefore, necessary to flesh out the Treaties of the European Union. Secondary legislation includes:
- Regulations
- Directives
- Decisions
- Recommendations
- Opinions

10 As soon as Regulations are published in the Official Journal of the European Union, they are legally binding. They do not need to be implemented by the Westminster Parliament or the Scottish Parliament. They can be enforced in all the national courts. In this way, Regulations are said to be directly applicable and have direct effect.

In order to have legal force, the Westminster Parliament must pass legislation to make Directives effective. The Sale and Supply of Goods to Consumers Regulations 2002 began life as the European Directive 1999/44/EC on Certain Aspects of the Sale of Consumer Goods and Associated Guarantees. It was only when the Regulations were passed into law on 31 March 2003 that the Directive became effective. However, member states will have to obey a strict time period for implementing Directives because failure to introduce legislation could result in legal action being taken against the British Government.

Decisions include judgements of the European Court of Justice and the courts of the member states will have to obey these and follow them. The Council and the Commission can also issue Decisions but these are usually addressed to particular member states, individuals or bodies who will have to abide by them.

Recommendations and Opinions are generally held to have no binding force, but in **Grimaldi v Fonds des Maladies Professionelles (1990)** it was held that they may have some indirect legal effect. The European Court of Justice stated that domestic courts are bound to take Recommendations into consideration in order to decide disputes submitted to them, in particular where they are capable of clarifying the interpretation of other provisions of national or Community law.

11 Parliament was first known as the Assembly, but since 1962, it has been referred to as the European Parliament. Currently, the Parliament has 626 members, but the 1997 Treaty of Amsterdam set a limit of 700 members. The name parliament can be very misleading – it in no way resembles the Westminster parliament and it is often restricted in all sorts of ways. Additionally, it cannot pass laws in its own right, but a failure to consult Parliament might lead to any subsequent legislation being cancelled. The European Parliament sits in Strasbourg, France.

12 The European Commission is effectively the civil service of the European Union. The Commission employs a staff of over 21,000. The Commission has no formal power to make laws. It can propose new laws, but the Council and Parliament may have other ideas. The Commission's main task is to ensure that member states, business organisations and individuals follow the laws of the European Union. The Commission will not be slow in taking parties to a court if it considers that laws have been broken or ignored.

13 The Council is by far and away the most powerful institution as it represents the interests of the member states directly. Representatives of the government e.g. the Foreign Minister or Finance Minister of each member state sit on the Council. At the most important meetings of the Council (the European Council), the Heads of Government will take their places at the table to make the most important policy decisions.

14 The three main Scottish Civil Courts are the Sheriff Court, the Court of Session and the House of Lords.

15 The Sheriff Court is the most junior court in Scotland, the Court of Session is the next court and the House of Lords is the highest civil court in Scotland.

16 There are six Sheriffdoms – Glasgow and Strathkelvin, North Strathclyde, South Strathclyde, Dumfries and Galloway, Tayside, Central and Fife, Lothian and Borders and Grampian, Highland and Islands

17 Jurisdiction concerns the power of a court to hear and decide the outcome of a case.

18 The Small Claims procedure deals with cases which have a value of less than £750. It is supposedly an informal and streamlined judicial procedure which should encourage people to take cases to court. Litigants are expected to represent themselves and expenses are confined to a maximum of £75. The right of appeal is limited to points of law to the Sheriff Principal.

19 The Sheriff Court is organised under various procedures – Small Claims which deals with cases valued under £750; Summary Procedure which deals with cases valued between £750 and £1500; and Ordinary Procedure which deals with cases valued at over £1500. Geographically, the Sheriff Court is organised into six Sheriffdoms and 49 Sheriff Court districts.

20 The Court of Session is divided into an Outer House and an Inner House. The Outer House is primarily a trial court where one judge will sit to hear cases. The Inner House deals mostly with appeals and is subdivided into a First and Second Division with four members each although three will sit at any one time. There is also now an extra division which takes pressure off the other two. The Court is headed by the Lord President who is assisted by the Lord Justice Clerk.

21 A judge will arrive at his decision based on weighing up the balance of probabilities.

22 A civil court seeks to resolve disputes between private individuals and provide compensation for victims.

23 Pursuer and defender.

24 Litigants.

25 Sheriff Court – Sheriffs. Court of Session – Senators of the College of Justice. House of Lords – Lords of Appeal in Ordinary.

26 Sheriff Court – Solicitor. Court of Session – advocate and solicitor advocates. House of Lords – advocate and solicitor advocates. Technically, advocates and solicitor advocates can appear in all courts.

27 The First Minister and the Scottish Executive ensure the smooth administration of the Sheriff Court system.

28 Divorce – Sheriff Court or Court of Session. Tenor of a lost document – Court of Session. An appeal from a summary cause – Sheriff Principal or Inner House of the Court of Session.

29 It will probably be cheaper and quicker to have the case heard in the Sheriff Court.

30 John Willis – Outer House of the Court of Session – appeal to Inner House of Court of Session. Agnes Pratt – Small Claims Court – appeal to Sheriff Principal. Dougie Fisher – Sheriff Court Summary Procedure – appeal to Sheriff Principal and possibly Inner House of the Court of Session. Frank – Small Claims Court – appeal to Sheriff Principal. Jim – Court of Session – appeal to Inner House of the Court of Session and possibly the House of Lords.

31 District Court, Sheriff Court and High Court of Justiciary.

32 A crime is behaviour which the state regards as threatening the security of the community at large and people who indulge in criminal activities should be punished by imprisonment or fine.

33 The prosecution must prove that the accused is guilty beyond a reasonable doubt.

34 Summary – judge sits alone and decides the question of the accused's guilt or innocence and if the accused is found to be guilty the judge will decide the sentence. Solemn – the judge sits with a jury of 15. The jury will decide whether the accused is guilty or not. The judge will impose the appropriate punishment where the accused has been found guilty.

35 District Court – Justice of the Peace and a Stipendiary Magistrate. Sheriff Court – Sheriff. High Court of Justiciary – Lords/Ladies and Commissioners of Justiciary.

36 All criminal appeals go to the High Court sitting as an appeal court (Justiciary Roll Court for summary cases and Scottish Court of Criminal Appeal for solemn cases).

37 Justice of the Peace – £2500 fine and/or 60 days imprisonment. Stipendiary Magistrate – £5000 fine and/or three to six months' imprisonment.

38 Sheriff – £5000 fine and/or three to six months' imprisonment.

39 Unlimited powers of fine and imprisonment.

40 Procurator fiscal – District Court and Sheriff Court. Advocate Depute – Sheriff Solemn Court and High Court of Justiciary.

41 The Crown Office.

42 Guilty, not guilty and not proven.

43 The Lord Advocate, Solicitor General and Advocate Depute.

Chapter 2

1 A contract is undoubtedly an agreement, but, crucially, it is an agreement that the courts will enforce. In other words, should one of the parties fail to keep his side of the bargain, the innocent party can go to court and seek a remedy for breach of contract. The courts will not enforce other types of agreements such as gambling contracts, agreements binding in honour only, domestic agreements and social agreements. These types of agreements are not contracts see, for example, **Jones v Vernon's Pools (1938)**, **Robertson v Balfour (1938)**, **Spellman v Spellman (1961)** and **Ferguson v Littlewoods Pools Ltd (1997)**. The courts will not enforce agreements that are not contracts because they are considered to be unworthy of judicial time.

2 The advertisement by Wylie and Crossan Beauty Products should be viewed as an invitation to treat and not as an offer. The advertisement in this example is not as specific as the one in **Carlill v Carbolic Smokeball Co (1893)**. Admittedly, the advertisers do make some pretty strong claims but these may be regarded as trade puffs or advertising hype. It will be up to customers to go into a store that supplies the product and make an offer to purchase it – an offer which may or may not be accepted by the store. For the difference between an offer and an invitation to treat see **Harvey v Facey (1893)** and **Pharmaceutical Society of Great Britain v Boots Cash Chemists (1953)**.

3 a) *Consensus in idem* quite literally means a meeting of minds. In order for the parties to form a contract, the offer must mirror the acceptance. In other words, the parties must reach agreement on all the important aspects of the contract. If there are still areas of disagreement between the parties, they continue to be in a state of negotiation and no contract exists. For examples of failures to achieve agreement see **Harvey v Facey (1893)** and **Mathieson Gee (Ayrshire) Ltd v Quigley (1952)**.

   b) Sandeep and Balinder have failed to achieve *consensus in idem* (i.e. agreement) and, therefore, no contract exists. Their situation is very similar to **Mathieson Gee (Ayrshire) Ltd v Quigley (1952)** where the parties were at cross-purposes and had totally misunderstood one another. In this case, the court decided that no contract existed and it is likely that a court would arrive at a similar decision where Sandeep and Balinder are concerned.

4 Generally speaking, a valid acceptance must reach the offeror otherwise it cannot be said that a contract has been formed by the parties. It does

not take a great stretch of the imagination to realise that a message containing an acceptance by the offeree can be misdirected or even rendered unreadable when received by the offeror – especially if they are sent via fax or e-mail. Furthermore, telephones, especially mobiles, can be cut off and messages left on answering machines can be accidentally deleted. The responsibility will very often be on the offeree's shoulders to ensure that the acceptance was received and actually understood by the offeror (see **Entores Ltd v Miles Far Eastern Corpn (1955)** and **Brinkibon v Stahag Stahl (1982)**). It is not enough for the offeree to say that he has sent the message. The one exception to the rule that an acceptance must physically reach the offeror arises when the acceptance is sent via the Royal Mail in response to a postal offer (see **Adams v Lindsell (1818),** and **Jacobsen v Underwood (1894)**). Even if the acceptance is lost in the post, a valid contract is formed between the parties as soon as the acceptance is posted (see **Household Fire Insurance Co v Grant (1879)**). Acceptance must be communicated by a person generally authorised to do this. In **Powell v Lee (1908)**, a person who had no authority to communicate an acceptance sent an acceptance to the offeror, but the court concluded that there had not been a valid acceptance. Acceptance must also be a positive act – the offeree's silence cannot be regarded as acceptance (see **Felthouse v Bindley (1862)**).

5   Unfortunately, Suhail is bound into contract with McCannell Ltd and he will have to pay for the shares. Suhail's offer was accepted by McCannell Ltd as soon as it posted the letter of acceptance on 20 June and it makes absolutely no difference that Suhail failed to receive this letter. According to the postal rule, an acceptance is valid as soon as it is posted (see **Adams v Lindsell (1818), Jacobsen v Underwood (1894)** and **Household Fire Insurance Co v Grant (1879)**).

6   The problem with instantaneous communications is that an acceptance sent by fax or e-mail may not actually reach the offeror or it may reach the offeror in a totally different form from that intended by the offeree. These types of communications can be garbled or parts of the message can be lost in transmission. The responsibility is on Asma's shoulders to ensure that the acceptance was received and actually understood by Creative Designs (see **Entores Ltd v Miles Far Eastern Corpn (1955)** and **Brinkibon v Stahag Stahl (1982)**). Merely because Asma faxed her acceptance does not mean that she sent a valid acceptance. In this situation, Asma has failed to

form a contract with Creative Designs Ltd. The offeree should double-check that the message was received by the offeror and in the form intended.

7   What is a reasonable time for acceptance of an offer by the offeree depends on the situation at hand. Sometimes, the offeree will have weeks or even months to make up his mind whether or not to accept an offer. Often, the offeree will have to make up his mind rather more quickly, for example, in minutes, hours or even a matter of days. What is a reasonable time for acceptance of an offer will really be determined by the subject matter of the contract. If the subject matter of the proposed contract is subject to regular price fluctuations (i.e. commodities such as oil, precious metals, coffee) or the subject matter is of a perishable nature (e.g. agricultural products), it is likely that the offeree will have to make up his mind very quickly whether or not to accept the offer. Delay will often mean that the offeree loses an opportunity to accept the offer. However, to avoid disputes arising, a sensible offeror will often impose a time limit for acceptance of the offer. For examples of the approach taken by the courts to the question of what is a reasonable time see **Wylie and Lochhead v McElroy and Sons (1873)** and **Glasgow Steam Shipping Company v Watson (1873)**.

8   McCracken undoubtedly made Anne-Louise an offer, but she has responded by making him a completely new offer. The effect of this new offer or counteroffer from Anne-Louise means that she has rejected McCracken's original offer and he is absolutely entitled to go elsewhere and look for work. McCracken cannot be forced to work for Anne-Louise even if she is now willing to pay the original price of £15,000. McCracken and Anne-Louise never achieved agreement or *consensus in idem*, so there is no contract between them. For examples of counteroffers see **Wolf & Wolf v Forfar Potato Co Ltd (1984)**, and **Hyde v Wrench (1840)**.

9   a) In Scotland, a person who makes a promise can have it enforced against him by the beneficiary of that promise (see **Morton's Trustee v Aged Christian Friend Society of Scotland (1899)**, **Petrie v Earl of Airlie (1834)**, **Littlejohn v Hawden (1882)** and **Paterson (A & G) v Highland Railway Co (1927)**). In other words, the phrase 'my word is my bond' is particularly appropriate to describe this type of obligation. The beneficiary can sue the promisor in order to have the promise enforced. However, it is not possible for the promisor to sue the beneficiary in an attempt to force him to accept the benefits of the promise. Examples of unilateral promises include

offers of rewards, promises of gifts or donations and a promise to keep an offer open for a specified period of time. Generally speaking, unilateral promises should be in writing according to the rules laid down by the Requirements of Writing (Scotland) Act 1995 so that the beneficiary can enforce it against the promisor. However, unilateral promises made in the course of business do not need to be in written form in order to be enforceable. It is still possible to enforce an unwritten promise against the promisor if the beneficiary can prove that he has relied on the promise, the promisor knew of this and if the promise is not enforced the beneficiary will suffer real harm as a result. In England, unilateral promises are not enforceable unless the promisor draws up a formal deed. In any case, English law emphasises the importance of consideration whereby to receive a benefit a party must contribute something of value to the other party.

b) The dealings between Katy and Craig may have taken place in the course of business and, therefore, the promise to keep the offer open for ten days does not need to be in writing. However, if these were private dealings, the promise should have been in written form in order to be enforceable (Requirements of Writing (Scotland) Act 1995). An unwritten promise will not be fatal to Katy's claim if she can show that Craig knew that she was relying on the promise and that she would suffer real harm if he refused to stand by it. In either situation, Katy could sue Craig for any losses that she has suffered as a result of his breach of promise i.e. if she had had to buy a similar car at a more expensive price she could sue Craig for the difference between what he offered to sell his car and the car that she actually ended up buying. It should be noted that there isn't and never was a contract between Katy and Craig and, therefore, she is not entitled to get the car from him.

10 There is no contract between Gavin and the store because the display in the window was an invitation to treat and not an example of the store making an offer (see **Fisher v Bell (1961)**). Gavin has made an offer to the store to purchase the television for £200 which has been rejected (see **Pharmaceutical Society of Great Britain v Boots Cash Chemists (1953)**). Gavin could make a complaint in terms of a misleading price indication being made by the store under Part 3 of the Consumer Protection Act 1987. A misleading price indication is a criminal offence, but Gavin will still not get the television set for £200 – he will have to pay the £2000 that the shop is asking for.

11 Generally, gambling agreements are not enforceable by the courts because they are regarded as *sponsiones ludicrae*. This means that if a bookmaker, the national lottery or the pools company refuses to pay out winnings to some lucky gambler, the courts will refuse to enforce the gambling contract (see **Jones v Vernon's Pools (1938)**, **Robertson v Balfour (1938)** and **Ferguson v Littlewoods Pools Ltd** (1997)). These may be agreements, but they are not contracts and, therefore, not worthy of judicial time. However, rather strangely, agreements to share winnings between members of a gambling syndicate can be enforced by the courts. Annie and Netta's agreement is one such example of a contract that the courts would enforce. In other words, Netta will have to pay Annie the remaining £59,000 that she originally agreed to pay out (see **Robertson v Anderson (2002)**).

12 **a)** Many people believe that it is a legal requirement that all contracts must be in writing and witnessed. Under Scots Law, many contracts do not require formalities i.e. the need to have written terms and conditions. The majority of contracts will be verbal agreements or their existence can be proved by looking at the parties' behaviour or by implication (see **Carlill v Carbolic Smokeball Company (1893)** or **Thornton v Shoe Lane Parking (1971)**). The existence of contracts can be usually proved by any type of evidence (statements from parties' testimony and their witnesses). Some contracts, however do need to be in written form. In modern Scots law, contracts involving land and buildings (heritable property) are covered by the Requirements of Writing (Scotland) Act 1995. A contract for the sale of land has to be in writing and must contain all the terms expressly agreed by the parties and each of those terms must be set out in the written document. The Consumer Credit Act 1974 insists that all the main terms of a regulated credit agreement must be in writing, otherwise the creditor will only be able to enforce the agreement with a court order. Furthermore, the Bills of Exchange Act 1882 insists that all negotiable instruments, for example, a bank cheque or promissory note must be in written form.

b) Lisa and Suzanne have failed to provide a written agreement or document when the Requirements of Writing (Scotland) Act 1995 Act places a duty on them to do so. It might be thought that if the parties have a purely verbal contract involving heritable property, the courts would refuse to enforce it. However, this is not the case. Despite the fact that the 1995 Act states that all contracts involving heritable property should be in writing, there are situations where the courts will enforce unwritten contracts. A contract (and for that matter a unilateral promise) can be enforced where there have been 'significant actings'. Suzanne and Lisa should have put their contract in writing and it may be thought that this is the end of the matter. The contract involves land, should have been in writing but the parties failed to do this. Therefore, the contract is not enforceable. If one party attempted to withdraw from an informal contract involving heritable property on the grounds that there was nothing in writing, they might be in for something of a shock. It will not be possible to use the argument that as there is no written contract then the agreement can be cancelled if:

1 The other party has relied on the contract; and

2 Where the other party knew of their actions and agreed to them; and

3 Where the actions of the party wishing to honour the contract were material (not trivial) so that they would be prejudiced or severely disadvantaged if the other party pulled out.

It is highly likely that Lisa could enforce the contract against Suzanne despite the lack of a written contract.

c) The Contract (Scotland) Act 1997 clarified the law in relation to written contracts. It is now permissible for the parties to rely on additional external sources of information. These sources may consist of verbal statements or documentary evidence which can be used in court to flesh out additional express terms in relation to a written contract. Otherwise, the 1997 Act assumes that a written document will contain all the main terms of the agreement.

13 **a)** A person of full capacity is capable of taking on duties which the law recognises and will force them to comply with. Additionally, the law will recognise any rights that these individuals are entitled to and will enforce these rights on their behalf. Most natural legal persons i.e. human beings have full capacity. Certain groups, have no capacity or limits are placed on their ability to enter contracts:

- Young people under the age of 18
- Adults with incapacity
- Intoxicated persons
- Enemy aliens
- Young people and children

b) Young persons aged 16 and 17, such as Hugh, are regarded as having full legal capacity in much the same way as an adult would. However, the Age of Legal Capacity (Scotland) Act 1991 does explicitly recognise that this group of young people will perhaps require some protection. It should be

remembered that young people will have less experience of life and could be taken advantage of by unscrupulous older people like Simon. The courts will, therefore, cancel a contract that a young person has entered into if it can be shown that the agreement was harmful/prejudicial to the young person's interests. Potentially, Hugh's contract with Simon could made with a young person aged 16 or 17 could be declared voidable by the courts. Hugh would have to prove that no sensible/reasonable adult would have entered into the contract under the same circumstances; and the contract is likely to cause substantial prejudice/harm to the young person. Only the young person can use the protection that the 1991 Act provides. Other people (usually older persons) cannot use it to get out of the contract. Hugh must use this defence before he reaches the age of 21. Interestingly, Hugh may also lack contractual capacity because he was under the influence of drugs (see **Taylor v Provan (1864)** and he may be able to prove that he was in such a state of intoxication that he did not know what he was doing when he agreed to enter the contract with Simon).

c) The Adults With Incapacity (Scotland) Act 2000 allows a guardianship (formerly known as a *curator bonis*) to be declared where someone can act for a person who lacks capacity. The guardian may act for the incapable person in one transaction only, in a series of transactions or in relation to all the incapable person's affairs. The 2000 Act recognises various means by which a guardianship can be established.

14 A void contract means that a contract has never existed – despite what the parties may have said or done and despite what they may have believed. In this situation, neither party can acquire rights or duties because there is no contract. Void contracts arise in a variety of situations such as error in the substantials, contracts with the insane, contracts with children under the age of 16, contracts with enemy aliens and contracts that are illegal. In **Loudon v Elder's *Curator Bonis* (1923)**, the contract was void on the grounds of one of the party's insanity.

A voidable contract means that a contract did exist in the first place, but that it suffers from a flaw of some type and this gives one or both of the parties an option to have the agreement cancelled. Such an option to cancel the agreement must be exercised rapidly by one of the parties because any property that has changed hands under the original contract can be further transferred to third parties who acquire ownership rights (see **Lewis v Averay (1972)**). If the parties fail to take steps to cancel the contract, despite its flawed nature, a valid agreement continues to exist. Examples of voidable contracts arise where one of the parties has made a misrepresentation; facility and circumvention; where the parties have failed to put a contract in writing when the law requires this; failure to disclose all material facts; less serious examples of error; intoxication and undue influence.

15 **a)** As a general rule, the doctrine of illegality penalises those parties who create particular contracts that are regarded as illegal (sometimes referred to as *pacta illicita*). The greatest sanction that the court has is to refuse to enforce the agreement if its creation breaches the common law or statute. Such an agreement is void from its creation. This means that, in the event of a dispute, the parties will not have any rights or duties under the agreement – the courts will simply not recognise its validity. The general rule regarding illegal contracts is often expressed as *ex turpi causa non oritur actio* i.e. a party can have no right of action when the dispute involves an immoral or illegal situation. Examples of these types of agreement would be contracts that are either illegal at common law (see **Pearce v Brooks (1866)**) or those that have been declared illegal by statute (see **Bigos v Bousted (1951)**).

b) Henry cannot enforce his agreement with the contract killer because it is an agreement to commit a crime and is, therefore, illegal at common law. The agreement is completely void and Henry will not be able to get his money back from the contract killer. If he raises an action to recover the money, he risks exposing himself as an accessory to a crime. Examples of contracts being declared illegal and void in terms of common law include **Pearce v Brooks (1866)**, **Regazzoni v Sethia (1958)**, **Parkinson v College of Ambulance (1925)** and **Cantiere San Rocco SA v Clyde Shipbuilding and Engineering Co Ltd (1923)**.

16 Substantial error completely undermines any potential agreement. In such situations, the mistaken beliefs of the parties do not centre around trivial matters which can easily be resolved. Error in the substantials concerns one or more of the important aspects of the agreement (the identity of the contracting parties, the subject matter of the contract, the price or the nature of the contract). In situations where an agreement is affected by substantial error there can be no true *consensus in idem* or agreement. In fact, the actual contract is radically different from the one that the parties originally intended to create.

17 **a)** The price that one party expects to pay and the price that the other party expects to receive will, obviously, be a very important term of the contract. Any confusion surrounding the price will render the contract void. Admittedly, it is possible for the parties not to fix a price and still have a valid contract as long as some mutually agreed system or mechanism exists for determining the price. Here Ruaridh is in total disagreement with Gary about the price (see **Wilson v Marquis of Breadalbane (1859)**). The problem centres around the fact that the goods have now been used to make something else and they no longer exist. The court would, therefore, have to determine what was a reasonable price and Gary will have to pay this to Ruaridh.

b) This situation concerns error in relation to the identity of one of the contracting parties (see **Morrisson v Robertson (1908)**). The issue of mistaken identity must be fundamental to the formation of a contract. In order to convince a court that mistaken identity should render the agreement void, a person would have to demonstrate that he intended to enter into a contract with a particular person and no other. In this situation, Ruaridh clearly intended to enter into a contract with Campbell. He would, therefore, be entitled to reclaim the sheep from McDonald who would have to pursue O'Donnell in order to get his money back.

c) A mistaken belief as to how the contract will operate may completely undermine matters. Here, we have two different types of mortgages which operate in a fundamentally different way. There is no proper agreement and, therefore, no contract (see **Foster v Mackinnon (1869)**).

d) Such a situation is likely to arise where the parties are completely confused and mistaken as to the subject matter of the agreement. One party (the potential buyer) believes that a particular item is being offered for sale whereas the other party (the potential seller) believes that she has made an offer to sell a completely different item. Both parties are completely at cross-purposes. There can be no real agreement between them and, therefore, no contract (see **Raffles v Wichelhaus (1864)**).

18 **a)** A misrepresentation occurs when one party, during negotiations leading to the formation of a contract, makes a materially false statement of fact which has the effect of encouraging or inducing the other party to enter the agreement. It is usually after the contract has been formed that the party who relied on the statement will discover that it factually false. The innocent party must be able to prove that, if he had been aware that the statement was in fact false, he would never have entered the contract in the first place. In the course of making a misrepresentation, a party does not have to be aware that the statement was false. A misrepresentation is not necessarily a deceitful or dishonest statement. Since the decision of the House of Lords in **Hedley Byrne & Co Ltd v Heller & Partners Ltd (1963)**, three categories of misrepresentation are recognised by the Scottish Courts:

1 Innocent
2 Fraudulent
3 Negligent

With an innocent misrepresentation, the party who made the statement genuinely believes what he is saying to be the truth. There is no intention to deceive, but the statement is still factually incorrect and it may have encouraged another individual to enter the contract Fraudulent misrepresentation, on the other hand, is a deliberate attempt by the party making the statement to deceive another person and, therefore, influence the innocent party to enter the contract. The party who made the fraudulent statement is fully aware of the falseness of his statement. In other words, he is being consciously dishonest when he makes the misrepresentation to the other party. For comparisons between innocent and fraudulent misrepresentation see (see **Derry v Peek (1889)** and **Boyd & Forrest v Glasgow & South-Western Railway Company (1915)**) A negligent misrepresentation is very different from innocent and fraudulent misrepresentation. Someone who makes a negligent statement does not intend to deceive the other party but, at the same time, he cannot prove that he had reasonable grounds for believing the truth of his statement. In other words, he has made the statement recklessly without verifying its accuracy (see **Hedley Byrne & Co Ltd v Heller & Partners Ltd (1963)**).

b) The misrepresentation is clearly fraudulent in nature because it involves a deliberate attempt to deceive. Alasdair was clearly influenced by the false statement. The contract is potentially voidable and Alasdair has a variety of options:

1 Rescission or cancellation of the contract
2 Rescission or cancellation of the contract and an award of damages
3 Retention of the contract and an award of damages

19 a) In a small number of situations, the law demands that, during pre-contractual negotiations, a party must act with the utmost good faith (*uberrimae fidei*). The example of insurance contracts are often used to demonstrate how this

duty to act with the utmost good faith works in practice. The proposer (the person intending to take out the policy) is under a positive duty to bring all material facts to the insurer at the time of making the contract of insurance. If the proposer is in any doubt about the importance of a fact, for safety's sake and to protect his own position, he should bring it to the attention of the insurer. Failure to do so by the proposer may allow the insurer to treat the contract as voidable and refuse to pay out under the policy as the House of Lords made it quite clear in **Pan Atlantic Insurance v Pine Top Insurance (1994)** (see also **The Spathari (1925)**).

b) Fiduciary Relationships – a fiduciary relationship is a relationship of confidence that imposes a special duty of care on one or both of the parties. Examples of such relationships include those of solicitor/client, principal/agent, doctor/patient, parent/child and the partners in a firm. If a party owes a fiduciary duty to someone else this means that he must disclose all material facts to the other person (see **McPherson's Trustees v Watt (1877)**).

20 a) A restraint of trade clause or a restrictive covenant prevents or limits an employee from seeking employment with a new employer who happens to be a business rival of the employee's previous employer. The use of such agreements is an extensive practice to be found in a wide range of modern business contracts. They are most common in employment contracts, where the employer seeks to restrain the right of the employee to compete or work for a competitor once s/he has left the employer's business. They are commonly applied to managerial, marketing, scientific and professional staff. Such covenants are increasingly being used in franchising, distribution and supply agreements. Restraints of trade are anti-competitive rather than being strictly illegal and the effect of such contractual terms is that they are presumed to be void unless the party wishing to enforce such terms can show that they are, in fact, reasonable. The courts will examine a number of factors in order to determine whether such restraints or restrictions are reasonable:

1 The contract must be reasonable between the parties
2 It must be reasonable in terms of time and geography
3 It must be reasonable in the public interest
4 It must be reasonable in terms of trade practice and custom

If the court finds that the restraint is unreasonable, it will be declared void but, crucially, the court will not replace it with a more reasonable provision. This means that the person who wished to rely on the restraint will not have any protection.

b) Iain will probably not be entitled to take up the offer of new employment with one of his current employer's business rivals. Iain will undoubtedly have had access to all sorts of trade secrets and may have dealt with customers extensively. The restraint is not unreasonable and can probably be justified on the grounds that the employer has legitimate business interests that he needs to protect (see **Scottish Dairy Farmers Company (Glasgow) Ltd v McGhee (1933)**, **Home Counties Dairies v Skilton (1970)**, **Bluebell Apparel v Dickinson (1978)** and **C-MIST v Crute (2003)**).

c) An employer can always use an alternative approach to the problem of protecting trade secrets and business connections. Some employers, rather than including a restrictive covenant in the employment contract – which can always be challenged on the grounds that it is unreasonable, will insist that an employee has to give an extended period of notice if he wishes to terminate his employment. Eighteen month notice periods are not unknown in some trades and professions where the employee is in a very senior position within the organisation. This gives the employer time to prepare for the employee's departure by taking precautions to protect trade secrets or business connections. Furthermore, the current employer may actually state that it is not necessary for the employee to turn up for work – he may as well tend his garden (hence the phrase 'garden leave'). The beauty of these contractual notice periods is that the employee cannot work for any other employer who is competing against his current employer. Employees who are affected by these 'garden leave' clauses can challenge them by putting forward the argument that it is important that they are allowed to continue to work in their chosen profession in order to keep vital skills updated and current. In **William Hill Organisation Ltd v Tucker (1998)** the English Court of Appeal criticised the growing use by employers of garden-leave clauses in employment contracts. The Court was particularly concerned that this was little more than an attempt to get round the strict rules governing the use of restrictive covenants in employment contracts. It was felt that garden-leave clauses should be scrutinised carefully and, furthermore, the rules surrounding these types of clauses should be considerably tightened to prevent abuse by employers.

21 Susan has been the victim of undue influence. Undue influence renders the contract voidable so that it may be rescinded or cancelled. However, if rescission is being sought by Susan, there must be no delay in claiming relief after the influence has ceased to have an effect. Delay in claiming relief in these circumstances may bar the claim since delay is evidence of affirmation or agreement (see **Allcard v Skinner (1887)** and **Anderson v The Beacon Fellowship (1992)**).

22 The notice is certainly prominent enough and is an attempt by the store to exclude its liability. Before the Unfair Contract Terms Act 1977, it was possible for a person to exclude his liability for negligent performance and non-performance of the contract as long as he gave the other party adequate notice of the existence of an exclusion clause. The law before 1977 meant that it was possible for someone to exclude his liability for death and personal injury caused by his negligence or by failing to perform the contract. Under section 16 of the Unfair Contract Terms Act 1977, any clause where a party attempts to escape or limit his responsibility for having caused death or personal injury to another as a result of his actions will be automatically void. The clause cannot be relied upon and will not be enforced by the courts. Section 20 of the Unfair Contract Terms Act 1977 states that any attempt to exclude or limit the implied terms of the Sale of Goods Act in a consumer sale will be automatically void. In a non-consumer sale, Section 20 of the Unfair Contract Terms Act makes it clear that any attempt by a seller to limit his liability in terms of Section 12 of the Sale of Goods Act, will be automatically void. In a non-consumer sale, a seller may be able to exclude or limit his liability in relation to Sections 13 to 15 of the Sale of Goods Act, but Section 20 of the Unfair Contract Terms Act states that this will only be permitted if this is fair and reasonable. Furthermore such an attempt by the store to exclude its liability to consumers may be regarded an unfair term under the Unfair Terms in Consumer Contract Regulations 1999.

23 Exclusion and limitation clauses are governed by the common law, the Unfair Contract Terms Act 1977 and the Unfair Terms in Consumer Contract Regulations 1999. The law here is very complex. Basically, the common law allows a person to exclude his liability for negligent performance and non-performance of the contract as long as he gives the other party adequate notice of the existence of an exclusion clause. The law before 1977 meant that it was possible for someone to exclude his liability for death and personal injury caused by his negligence or by failing to perform the contract. The Unfair Contract Terms Act 1977 prevents some of the worst abuses that exclusion and limitation clauses encouraged such as excluding or limiting liability for death and personal injuries. The Act makes a clear distinction between consumer and non-consumer contracts (i.e. business agreements) which means that consumers are better protected than business parties. Many (but not all) unfair terms in consumer contracts will automatically be declared void by the 1977 Act. Otherwise, the test of fairness will be applied. The Unfair Terms in Consumer Contract Regulations 1999 only applies to consumer contracts and many clauses that are deemed to be unfair will be declared void.

24 In the Scots law of contract, there are four possible remedies available to a party who has suffered a breach of contract. These are:
- Damages
- Specific implement
- Retention and lien
- Rescission

25 **a)** This is a very limited remedy in the sense that it will only be granted to the pursuer if the court thinks that it is appropriate. Basically, the pursuer is asking the court to make an order (a decree) which will force the defender to carry out his contractual obligations. In a small claims action in the Sheriff Court, for example, a pursuer could ask the court to force a builder who has only half-completed a patio to finish the job. A recent example of the remedy of specific implement being granted to a pursuer by the Scottish courts can be seen in **John Anderson v Pringle of Scotland (1998)**. The remedy of specific implement will not be appropriate in the following circumstances:

- Where the court is of the opinion that an award of damages is a more than adequate remedy.

- Where the defender owes the pursuer money, the court will not grant specific implement because the appropriate action on the pursuer's part is to sue for damages. On a technical point, a decree of specific implement is a court order and failure to comply with it would mean that the defender was in contempt of court. This means that the defender would face imprisonment, but being sent to prison for a civil debt is no longer available to the courts in Scotland.

- Where the pursuer can obtain goods or services from a variety of alternative sources and there is no great inconvenience caused. If the pursuer had to pay a greater price than the contract price for these goods and services, he could sue the

defender in damages for the difference. It is only where the goods or services have some unique value that the courts will grant an order for specific implement.

- Where the grant of an order would cause injustice or harm to someone.

- Where the contract in question involves a high degree of personal contact e.g. an employer cannot be compelled by an Employment Tribunal to reinstate or re-engage an employee that has been dismissed. Even if the employee wins his unfair dismissal claim and the Employment Tribunal grants a Reinstatement Order, the employer cannot be forced to take him back.

- Where the defender is outwith the jurisdiction of the Scottish courts.

- Where the granting of an order would, in effect, be ordering the defender to do something which was impossible to carry out.

b) Chapelhill Housing Association should pursue an action for payment of money in the Sheriff Court under small claims procedure because a decree of specific implement cannot be granted in Scotland in relation to actions for the recovery of debt.

26 **a)** The injured party has a duty to mitigate or to minimise his loss i.e. he must take all reasonable steps to cut his losses. Thus, a seller whose goods are rejected must attempt to get the best price for them elsewhere and the buyer of the goods which are not delivered must attempt to buy as cheaply as possible elsewhere. Should the parties in both these situations fail to cut their losses, they cannot rely upon the courts to award them full damages in respect of their losses. However, a pursuer only has to show the courts that he has taken reasonable steps to cut his losses. Superhuman efforts on the part of the pursuer are unnecessary (see **Gunter & Co v Lauritzen (1894)**).

b) Remoteness of damage means that damages in a contract will not be recovered by the pursuer unless they are proved to be a direct and natural consequence of the defender's breach i.e. the losses caused to the pursuer occurred because of the defender's actions. If the losses have not occurred directly owing to the defender's fault, then it is likely that the defender, as a reasonable man, did not realise that such an outcome was likely to occur. Damage which does not arise naturally and which is not in the contemplation of a reasonable man can only be recovered if the defender was made aware of it and agreed to accept the risk of the loss (see **Hadley v Baxendale (1854)**).

27 **a)** The parties to an agreement may actually be far-sighted enough to insert a remedy into their contract which addresses the issue of the amount of damages payable should one of them break the contract. These damages are known as liquidated damages and sometimes such a clause is known as a penalty clause. The phrase penalty clause can be misleading because the courts will not enforce the provision for liquidate damages if the amount is not a genuine pre-estimate of loss. The courts, in other words, will not allow one party to punish the other – even if one of the parties is in breach. The courts will then award damages in the usual way i.e. by applying the tests of remoteness of damage and mitigation of loss.

b) The penalty clause is completely excessive and is not a genuine pre-estimate of loss (see **Cameron-Head v Cameron & Co (1919)** and **Clydebank Engineering & Shipbuilding Co v Yzquierdo y Castaneda (1904)**). The courts will award Davinder damages in the usual way i.e. by applying the tests of remoteness of damage and mitigation of loss. This means that Tommy will have to pay Davinder £2000 to £3000 in damages for breach of contract.

28 General damages are awarded to the pursuer when the loss he has suffered is a reasonably foreseeable and direct result of the defender's breach of contract. The amount of damages will ensure that the pursuer is placed in the position that he would have been had it not been for the defender's actions. General damages, therefore, compensate the pursuer for loss caused in the ordinary way of things. Special damages, on the other hand, are awarded to the pursuer when the defender's breach of contract causes abnormal loss or loss which was not reasonably foreseeable. In these situations, the pursuer will have to take steps to inform the defender that there are special circumstances that would cause him to suffer losses far in excess of what might ordinarily be the case. If the pursuer fails to inform the defender about these special circumstances, there can be no award of special damages (see **Hadley v Baxendale (1854)** and **Victoria Laundry v Newman Industries (1949)**).

29 A material breach of contract is such a serious breach that it goes to the very roots of the agreement and completely undermines the contract. This remedy will be sought by the pursuer when the defender has committed a material breach of contract. The practical effect of rescission is that the pursuer wishes the court to cancel the contract. Minor breaches of contract will rarely allow the pursuer to cancel the contract and very often the court will grant damages to the pursuer as an alternative. The parties to a contract could state, however, that certain breaches of the agreement will be regarded as material and this will allow the innocent party to apply to the courts for rescission (see **Shaw, Macfarlane & Co v Waddell & Sons (1890)** and Sections 15B(1)(b) and 15B(2)(a) of the Sale of Goods Act 1979 for examples of rescission).

30 There various ways in which a contract is discharged or terminated:
1 Performance and payment
2 Acceptilation and discharge
3 Delegation
4 Novation
5 Compensation
6 Confusion
7 Material breach of contract
8 Lapse of time – prescription, impossibility
9 Frustration
10 Illegality

Furthermore in contracts for personal services, such a contract is discharged by the death of the person who was to perform it. The incapacity of a person who is to perform a contract may discharge it. The purpose of the contract becomes impossible to perform or the purpose of the contract becomes illegal. A contract could also be discharged by breach.

Chapter 3

1 A delict can be defined as a situation where the defender voluntarily commits an act or fails to act when the law imposes a duty of care and this failure to implement the legally required standard care causes the pursuer to suffer a personal injury or loss or damage to his property. If, for example, a motorist hits a pedestrian while driving his car the question that would have to be asked is whether the motorist was paying due care and attention when the accident happened. If the road accident occurred as a direct result of the motorist's failure to drive carefully then the victim would have a potential claim in terms of the law of delict against the motorist. The motorist owed a duty of care to pedestrians and other road users but he has failed to meet the necessary standard when he caused the accident. Put simply, the accident can be blamed on the motorist's actions or his failure to act properly – it is the motorist's fault that the victim has been injured. It is worth stressing that the motorist cannot get into his car and decide that he is not going to drive safely today. He has no choice in the matter because the law expects him to show all necessary care when he gets behind the wheel. The motorist may, of course, also have to face criminal charges of dangerous driving, but this aspect of the incident need not concern us. Cases which illustrate the concept of a duty of care include **Donoghue v Stevenson (1932)** and **Bourhill v Young (1942)**. It is important to remember that a duty of care is not owed to everyone – only those individuals who are likely to be harmed by the defender's actions or failure to act are owed a duty of care.

2   a) Aggie will have to prove that Paul and Harry actually dug the trench in the first place. Assuming that a trench existed, she will then have to prove that Harry and Paul acted in a negligent way by not putting up appropriate warning signs and placing fencing around the trench in order to prevent people falling into it. In other words, Aggie will have to prove that Paul and Harry failed to implement a duty of care that they owed to her and their failure to implement the necessary level of care has caused her to suffer injury (see **Donoghue v Stevenson (1932)**, **Bourhill v Young (1942)** and **Haley v London Electricity Board (1965)**). Clearly, if Paul and Harry did dig the trench, they do not owe a duty of care to all the world, but only to those people who are likely to be harmed by their actions or failure to act.

b) i) Aggie must prove that Paul and Harry were responsible for digging the alleged trench. If she cannot prove this, her claim must necessarily fail. Aggie is alleging that Paul and Harry have been negligent and in these types of claims, it is for the pursuer (Aggie) to prove that the defenders (Paul and Harry) have not taken the appropriate level of care that the law expects. Liability in negligence claims is generally based on proving the defender's fault and if the pursuer cannot establish that the defender was at fault the claim will fail. However, Paul and Harry may be able to defeat a negligence claim by demonstrating that they both took reasonable care to avoid injury or harm being caused to another person (**see Bolton v Stone (1951)** and **Paris v Stepney Borough Council (1951)**).

ii) Assuming that Phil is a credible and honest witness, Aggie's case will be much weaker if the existence of the trench is in doubt.

iii) Aggie is really in trouble now because her witness has been forced to admit that he only saw Harry carrying out a survey in the garden and that he was not digging a trench. Aggie's argument that the trench existed has been considerably undermined.

iv) Aggie is quite simply not a credible witness. She cannot change her story now by stating that it was a hole that she fell into rather than a trench. Her testimony completely lacks consistency. She has been unable to establish that a trench was dug by Harry and Paul and, if she can't prove this, her whole case collapses. It is highly unlikely that Aggie will win her case.

3   a) If the pursuer can show that he is owed a duty of care, the defender can escape liability in many situations by demonstrating that he took the appropriate standard of care which the law expects of him in order to reduce the risk of loss or injury being suffered by the pursuer. The standard of care which is expected of the defender is one of reasonable care. Reasonable care is the standard of care expected of the 'hypothetical' reasonable man or woman who is a person of ordinary care and prudence and who is neither over-cautious nor over-confident. This is an objective test and is not based on the defender's personal characteristics. Very often, a reasonable person will foresee or predict that are particular individuals who are especially vulnerable in some way and this means that they may suffer a greater degree of harm if the defender fails to take reasonable care. For examples of the standard of reasonable care see the following cases: **Bolton v Stone (1951)**, **Paris v Stepney Borough Council (1951)**, **Bolam v Friern Barnet Hospital Management Committee (1957)**, **Bolitho v City & Hackney Health Authority (1997)** and **Mullin v Richards (1998)**).

b) Following the decision in **Bolton v Stone (1951)**, it is unlikely that Lorne will be able to sue the Golf Club successfully. The Club looks as if it has taken reasonable care to minimise the risk of accident to people using the course. Over a million rounds of golf have been played and only one accident has taken place at the spot in question. The accident was by no means serious. The Golf Club also took the precaution of bringing in a expert to provide advice on a range of safety measures that it might implement. The Club has taken its duty of care seriously and it has taken reasonable care to minimise the likelihood of injuries occurring.

4   The situation closely mirrors the case of **Home Office v Dorset Yacht Co Ltd (1970)**. The question which must be addressed is whether the chain of events which was set in motion and the end result (the damage to the farmer's property) was entirely foreseeable or predictable. The boys in question were young offenders who were not properly supervised. Admittedly, these boys were not considered to be a danger to the public, but it

is highly likely that, if they were left unsupervised, they would misbehave. Should we really be surprised that they decided to take a vehicle and go joyriding? Probably not. Is it likely that they lack the necessary driving skills? This also is probably the case. Should we really be surprised that the failure of the boys to control the vehicle properly has caused damage to someone's property? The staff who accompanied the boys on the holiday failed to implement their duty of care and, as a result of this, harm has been caused. (See also **Hughes v Lord Advocate (1963)**.)

5 a) It is important to stress that, generally speaking, the courts tend to award damages to a pursuer who has suffered some sort of harm in the shape of personal injuries (whether physical or psychiatric) or for damage to property which has been caused by the defender where the defender has been negligent. We have to be very clear when we talk about damage in terms of delictual liability. Where the pursuer has suffered financial or pure economic loss as a result of the defender's negligent actions, the courts are much more reluctant to grant compensation. For the correct judicial approach, see **Spartan Steel & Alloys Ltd v Martin & Co (Contractors) (1972)**. Defects in property will not be regarded as providing a pursuer with an opportunity to sue the defender for damages. The defects in the property must actually cause damage to other property or cause injuries to other people. However, the courts have not always been consistent on this point. In a number of situations, the pursuer has been able to show that he has a special relationship with the defender who made the negligent statement and that he relied upon the information supplied by the defender (see **Hedley Byrne & Co Ltd v Heller & Partners Ltd (1963)**). As a result of satisfying these conditions, the courts have awarded damages to the pursuer for pure economic loss caused by the defender's negligent statement.

b) Clearly, McBurney has suffered economic loss as a result of the subcontractor's negligence. The courts are, traditionally, reluctant to award damages to a pursuer who has suffered economic loss (see **Spartan Steel & Alloys Ltd v Martin & Co (Contractors) (1972)**). However, McBurney may be able to rely on the case of **Junior Books v Veitchi Co (1982)**. **Junior Books** appeared to suggest that a defender could be liable for causing pure economic loss if the pursuer relied on negligent advice supplied by the defender. It has been argued that courts will still continue to refuse to grant compensation where a negligent act committed by the defender causes pure economic

loss to the pursuer. If this reasoning is correct, it would make **Junior Books** much more closely related to the line of cases which started with **Hedley Byrne & Co Ltd v Heller & Partners Ltd (1963)**.

6 a) Where there is an alleged breach of a duty of care, the actual breach must be the *causa causans* (the direct cause) of the harm to the pursuer. This means that the pursuer must be able to show, on the balance of probabilities, that the defender's negligence caused him to suffer loss or injury. The defender will be able to escape liability if he can show that his negligence should be regarded as the *causa sine qua non*. This means that the defender may have behaved negligently, but his actions should not be regarded as the direct cause of the loss or injury suffered by the pursuer. The *causa sine qua non* should be seen as part of the background and not a primary cause of harm to the pursuer. As the following cases demonstrate, it is not always obvious whether the defender's actions caused the pursuer to suffer loss or injury (see **Barnett v Chelsea & Kensington Hospital (1969)**, **McGhee v National Coal Board (1972)**, **Kay's Tutor v Ayrshire & Arran Health Board (1987)**, **Wilsher v Essex Area Health Authority (1988)** and **Mount v Barker Austin (1998)**).

b) On certain occasions, the courts will have to consider situations where the defender has breached his duty of care, but after this event some new factor is introduced into the picture which can also cause harm to the pursuer. This new cause of loss or injury will not have been the defender's fault. The introduction of this new factor can have effect of breaking the chain of causation. This means that the defender will only be liable for the harm that he has caused and he will not be liable for any harm caused to the pursuer by the introduction of the new factor to the equation (see **Rouse v Squires (1973)**, **Reeves v Commissioner of Police for the Metropolis (1999)**, **MacFarlane v Tayside Health Board (1999)** and **Sabri-Tabrizi v Lothian Health Board (1999)**).

7 a) Section 1 of the Animals (Scotland) Act 1987 states that 'if an animal belongs to a species whose members generally are, by virtue of their physical attributes or habits, likely (unless controlled or restrained) to injure severely or kill persons or animals, or damage property to a material extent, the keeper of the animal is (strictly) liable for any injury or damage caused by the animal and directly referable to these physical attributes or habits.' The keeper of the animal is deemed to be the person who:

- Is the owner or;
- Has possession of the animal at the time or;
- Has actual care or control of a child under 16 who is the owner or has possession of the animal.

b) According to Section 1 of the Animals (Scotland) Act 1987 as outlined in **7a)** above, the keeper of the animal would be strictly liable to Jan for the damage caused to the car when the dog hit it. It will be no defence for the owner/keeper to say that a 15-year-old boy had responsibility for the dog. For examples of strict liability involving animals see **Burton v Moorhead (1881)** and **Behrens v Bertram Mills Circus (1957)**.

8 For a delictual liability to exist, there must be harm, loss or injury which is caused by fault on the part of the wrongdoer. The pursuer must establish that the wrongdoer was to blame for what happened. The fault is called *culpa* and, generally, there can be no liability without *culpa*. The general rule in Scotland is that there can be no delictual liability without fault. Quite simply, this means that the pursuer must prove, on the balance of probabilities that the defender's actions caused him to suffer loss, injury or damage. If the pursuer cannot prove to the court that the defender was responsible for his loss or injury, then the pursuer's case will collapse. Very often, all the defender has to show is that he has taken reasonable care to prevent the harm from occurring (see **Bolton v Stone (1951)** and **Paris v Stepney Borough Council (1951)** both discussed below) and if the court is satisfied that all reasonable precautions were taken, the defender will escape liability. Admittedly, there are situations where the pursuer does not have to show that the defender was to blame for the injuries or the losses caused. In certain situations, the defender's liability is said to be strict. In other words, the law automatically presumes that the defender is to blame for the harm caused to the pursuer. This means that the defender will have to bring evidence to show, on the balance of probablities, that he was not responsible for the injuries or losses caused to the pursuer. A defender will be strictly liable for injuries or losses caused to the pursuer for dangerous products (Part 1 of the Consumer Protection Act 1987), and animals that he is responsible for cause loss or injury to the pursuer (Animals (Scotland) Act 1987). Situations of strict liability favour the pursuer as the burden of proof is the defender to show that he is not liable for the harm that occurred.

9 **a)** An owner or occupier of property may well become liable if the derelict state of the property causes injury, loss or damage to another person or his property. The main piece of legislation in this area is the Occupiers' Liability (Scotland) Act 1960 which establishes the rule that the occupier of property must take reasonable care to minimise the risks that any visitors to the property (whether invited or not) might encounter. The term occupier is given a broad definition under the Act of 1960 and means any person or corporate body in actual possession, physical control or occupation of the premises (see **Telfer v Glasgow District Council (1974)**). The occupier of premises is not necessarily the owner of the premises. Premises could be any fixed or moveable structure and could include aircraft or ships.

b) Lynch Demolition Services is the occupier of the site as defined by the Occupiers' Liability (Scotland) Act 1960 because it controls access to the site. It is highly unlikely that Lynch could argue successfully that it took reasonable care to prevent the injuries or harm from occurring. Lynch should have realised that its precautions were totally inadequate to ensure the protection of young children and other vulnerable members of the public (see **Glasgow Corporation v Taylor (1922)**, **McGlone v British Railways Board (1966)** and **Titchener v British Railways Board (1984)**).

10 **a)** The most common defences that are used by the defender in an action of delict are:

- Contributory negligence (see **Hanlon v Cuthbertson (1981)**)
- *Volenti non fit injuria* (to one who is willing a wrongful act cannot be done) (see **ICI v Shatwell (1965)**)
- Prescription and limitation (see the Prescription and Limitation (Scotland) Act 1973)
- Compliance with statutory authority (see **Lord Advocate v North British Railways (1894)**)
- Necessity
- *Damnum fatale* (see **Caledonian Railway Co v Greenock Corporation (1917)**)
- Criminality (see **Ashton v Turner (1981)** and **Pitts v Hunt (1990)**)

b) No, Michael would not be advised to raise an action against the Zoo because it would probably fail. The Zoo would be able to rely on the defence of *volenti non fit injuria* (**see ICI v Shatwell (1965), McGlone v British Railways Board (1966)** and **Titchener v British Railways Board (1984)**). Michael knew that it was dangerous to enter the lions' enclosure, but he voluntarily assumed this risk in order to retrieve his phone. He has no one to blame but himself for his injuries.

11 a) **Donoghue v Stevenson (1932)** established the rule that a manufacturer owes a duty of care to anyone who may use his products or come into close contact with these products. Alternatively, however, a pursuer who has suffered harm as a result of a dangerous product can now make use of Part 1 of the Consumer Protection Act 1987. Unlike the test for negligence in **Donoghue v Stevenson (1932)**, the Consumer Protection Act 1987 imposes a burden of strict liability on the producer of the goods. Strict liability, it is important to remember, means that the pursuer does not have to prove fault. In other words, strict liability automatically presumes that the defect in the product must be the fault of the producer of the goods – there is no other reasonable explanation for the defect. The producer must come up with a credible explanation to show why he is not to blame for the injuries or loss that the pursuer has suffered. **Evans v Triplex Safety Glass Co Ltd (1936)** is often used to demonstrate why Part 1 of the Consumer Protection Act 1987 is an improvement on the legal principle which established a manufacturer's liability for dangerous products as laid down in **Donoghue v Stevenson (1932)**. In **Evans**, the pursuer's claim failed because he could not prove that the manufacturer was to blame for supplying a defective product. The windscreen might have been defective and dangerous, but the way in which the windscreen was installed may have made it a dangerous product. The pursuer could not prove with certainty which of these two possibilities was the more likely explanation.

b) The manufacturer would probably be able to rely on the development risks defence which allows the defender to escape liability because scientific or technical knowledge would not be able to pinpoint defects in the product at the time that it was supplied. In order to escape liability, the defender will have to show that no other producer of the goods could have discovered dangers lurking in the product. Manufacturers of mobile phones will no doubt be relieved to discover that they can rely on this defence if ten years from now scientists do manage to prove that these products cause cancer. The development risks defence is the only exception to the standard of strict liability in the Consumer Protection Act 1987. This defence is the statutory equivalent of Lord Denning's statement in **Roe v Ministry of Health (1954)** that 'we must not look at the 1947 accident with 1954 spectacles'.

12 a) *Res ipsa loquitur* means that the facts speak for themselves. There are situations where the only possible explanation for the harm suffered by the pursuer is that the defender's actions or failure to act caused it. There is no other credible explanation – the defender's negligent actions or omissions must have caused harm to the pursuer. The defender is then forced to bring evidence before the court to show why he is not liable to the pursuer. If the defender can show that there is a plausible explanation that demonstrates that he is not to blame, then the pursuer's claim will fail. However, the defender's explanation must be a plausible one and not one which is only theoretically possible. It should be remembered that the principle of the facts speaking for themselves does not remove the burden of proof from the pursuer to show that the defender was at fault. The pursuer must show that the facts are credible and that they do speak for themselves. The pursuer can only make use of this legal rule in the following circumstances:

1 The events which led to the pursuer suffering harm must have been controlled by the defender or his employees.

2 Loss or injury does not usually happen when reasonable care is taken by a responsible person.

3 The defender must not be able to provide an alternative and credible explanation for the harm suffered by the pursuer which effectively gets him off the hook.

Examples of the use of the maxim *res ipsa loquitur* from case law include: **Scott v London and St Katherine's Docks (1865)**, **Gee v Metropolitan Railway (1873)**, **Cassidy v Minister of Health (1951)** and **Radcliffe v Plymouth and Torbay Health Authority (1998)**.

b) Brian has a good claim against the supermarket and he would probably be successful in his claim for damages. Undoubtedly, Brian would be able to use the maxim *res ipsa loquitur* to win his case as outlined above in **10a)**.

13 a) In **Alcock and Others v Chief Constable of the Yorkshire Police (1992)** the House of Lords felt that although the secondary victims had suffered as a result of the incident at Hillsborough, stricter rules had to apply to their claims than was the case with the primary victims. The starting point of any secondary victim's claim for damages the psychiatric injuries must be reasonably foreseeable. This is only the first hurdle placed in the pursuer's way. There are a further three tests that the pursuer must satisfy:

- Do they belong to a group of individuals that the courts should recognise are capable of suffering psychiatric injury as a result of the defender's negligence?
- How close to the accident was the pursuer in terms of time and space?
- How was the psychiatric injury caused?

The pursuer will find the above tests very difficult to satisfy in order to succeed in his claim. Significantly, in Alcock all the pursuers (the secondary victims) failed to meet one of the three tests listed above and, therefore, none of the claims was successful. In **White and Others v Chief Constable of the South Yorkshire Police (1998)** the pursuers could not class themselves as primary victims. The pursuers in this case were police officers who had come to the rescue of many of the victims of the Hillsborough Disaster. The pursuers claimed that their employer, the South Yorkshire Police force, owed them a duty of care for the psychiatric injuries that they had suffered in the line of carrying out their duties and in their role as rescuers. The House of Lords disagreed stating that they were secondary victims. Therefore, the pursuers had to satisfy the tests laid down by the House of Lords in **Alcock**. The House of Lords stressed the fact that the pursuers lacked a close relationship with the primary victims (often expressed as the ties of love and affection). Their Lordships were at great pains to stress the fact that rescuers should not expect to receive preferential treatment when claiming compensation for psychiatric injuries that they had suffered.

b) The drivers and the passengers of the vehicles who are involved in the crash are, of course, primary victims and they will find it much easier to bring a claim for psychiatric injuries before the courts. In terms of the relatives of the primary victims, special care will have to be paid to the criteria laid down by the House of Lords in **Alcock and Others v Chief Constable of the Yorkshire Police (1992)**. It is, again, worth noting that all the claims of the relatives (who were secondary victims) in **Alcock** failed. The **Alcock** criteria is not easy to satisfy. Relatives of the primary victims may be able to rely on the previous decision of **McLoughlin v O'Brian (1983)** to establish a claim for psychiatric injury. The rescuers as a result of the decision in **White and Others v Chief Constable of the South Yorkshire Police (1998)** will be classed as secondary victims and, therefore, under the criteria outlined by the House of Lords in **Alcock (1992)**, it is unlikely that any of their claims for psychiatric injuries will succeed. In all probability, the rescuers will lack the necessary

ties of love and affection to sustain a successful claim.

c) Quite simply, it is unlikely that Tracy's claim for psychiatric injury would satisfy the tests laid down by **Alcock (1992)**. Furthermore, Tracy's situation is reminiscent of **Bourhill v Young (1942)** where a woman who had a nervous disposition went to the scene of an horrific accident to satisfy her own curiosity. The woman promptly suffered nervous shock when she witnessed the aftermath of the accident and claimed that this had caused her to miscarry her pregnancy. The court held that the driver of the motorcycle who caused the accident did not owe the woman a duty of care because she was not in his contemplation when he was driving negligently. She had come to the scene of the accident after it had occurred and had never been endangered by the driver's negligent actions.

14 a) Trespass is defined as a temporary intrusion upon land or property. A landowner's primary remedy will concern the right to have trespassers ejected from his land. However, the means used to effect the ejection of an individual from the property should be reasonable. A landowner would not be treated sympathetically by the courts if he was shown to have used force to eject a person from his property (see **Winans v Macrae (1885)**.

b) This would be said to occur if a landowner's use of his property causes harm or interference to a neighbour's property. Nuisance is not a one-off event but a series of ongoing occurrences. The neighbour would be entitled to apply to the courts for the purposes of an interdict. The landowner could even be liable in damages for the harm he has caused. It is important for us to remember that if the nuisance has been tolerated or consented to by a neighbour for over 20 years (the negative prescription period), he will have no remedy. In other words, his inaction or his consent means that he will have to live with the nuisance. For examples of nuisance see **Miller v Jackson (1977)**, **Webster v Lord Advocate (1984)**, RHM **Bakeries (Scotland) Ltd v Strathclyde Regional Council (1985)**. A defender will really only be able to justify a nuisance if he can prove that the nuisance occurred as a result of his compliance with statutory authority (see **Lord Advocate v North British Railways (1894)**).

c) Spiteful use of property rights may be actionable before the courts even if the act complained of is something the landowner is legally entitled to do (see **Campbell v Muir (1908)**). A neighbour must be able to prove in this situation that the landowner has used his legitimate rights purely for spite so as to prevent the neighbour making full use of his own property rights. The spiteful action need only occur once in order for the pursuer to prove malice on the part of the other landowner. The remedy of interdict is available and the issue of damages may also arise.

d) It has been (unsuccessfully) argued that an owner or an occupier of property could be strictly liable where something was poured or thrown out of a building (the *actio de effusis dejectis*) causing harm to the victim. Similarly, where something was placed on the building or attached to the building fell, causing harm to the victim, (the *actio de positis vel suspensis*) it has been argued (again unsuccessfully) that the owner or the occupier would be under strict liability. It has even been suggested that these delicts are not a proper part of Scots law. Bankton, one of the Institutional Writers, had argued, however, that Scots law had adopted these two actions from Roman law (*Institute* 1.4.31 and 32). Baron Hume, another Institutional Writer had discussed both actions in his *Lectures* Vol. 3, Chapter 16. Hume had, however, spoken about these actions in terms of negligence and fault as opposed to examples of strict liability. The position has now been clarified somewhat by the Court of Session's decision in **McDyer v Celtic Football and Athletic Company Ltd and Others (3 March 2000)**. The issue as the Court of Session saw it could be dealt with in terms of the Occupiers' Liability (Scotland) Act 1960. It will be remembered, of course, that the occupier has to demonstrate he has taken reasonable care to ensure that a person entering his premises will not suffer injury or damage by reason of any danger due to the state of the premises or of anything done or omitted to be done on them. The pursuer's claim based on the *actio de positis vel suspensis* implying strict liability was, therefore, largely irrelevant and unnecessary.

e) A landowner would not be entitled to divert the stream for irrigation and manufacturing purposes if this adversely affected the rights of other landowners whose property the river flowed through. Diverting the course of a stream is permissible as long as the water is returned to the stream before it enters the property of a lower proprietor. There are dangers attached to the diversion of streams and any landowner who carries out such an operation will owe very important responsibilities to his neighbours. Furthermore, under the Water Act 1989, it is an offence for an individual to pollute a river. At all times, landowners must have regard to the common interest of the owners in connection with the stream (see **Kerr v**

Earl of Orkney (1857) and **Caledonian Railway Co v Greenock Corporation (1917)**).

Chapter 4

1 a) Section 2 of the Sale of Goods Act 1979 defines a contract for the sale of goods as one where the seller transfers or agrees to transfer the property (ownership) of the goods for a money consideration called the price. The provisions of the Act only apply to transactions that operate by way of a sale of goods contract. The Act does not apply to arrangements which operate by way of a mortgage, pledge, charge or other security arrangement (Section 62(4)).

b) i) Section 2(4) of the Sale of Goods Act 1979 states that if the property in the goods is transferred from the seller to the buyer the contract is called a sale. So, upon the conclusion of a sale, ownership usually passes to the buyer immediately because the goods are identified and agreed upon.

ii) Section 2(5) of the Sale of Goods Act 1979 states that if the transfer of property in the goods is to take place at a future time or upon the fulfilment of some condition, the contract is called an agreement to sell. Therefore, in an agreement to sell, the passing of ownership is postponed until some time in the future, either by the mutual consent of the parties or after the fulfilment of some condition.

iii) Section 61(1): Sale of Goods Act 1979 describes specific goods as goods identified or agreed upon when the contract of sale is formed. Specific goods include an undivided share, specified as a fraction or a percentage of goods that have been identified and agreed upon by the seller and the buyer.

iv) The Sale of Goods Act does not define unascertained goods. These are goods which are not identified and agreed upon at the time when the contract was formed. Unascertained goods are goods that form part of a larger quantity held by the seller and the buyer cannot single out the goods that he will receive – the seller will have to do this and place the goods in a deliverable state. There are two types of unascertained goods those which form an unsevered (undivided) portion of a particular quantity of goods and those which are generic goods.

v) Future goods are goods that the seller must either manufacture or acquire from a third party. There can only be an agreement to sell and ownership of the goods will not pass to the buyer until the seller manufactures the goods or obtains them from a third party and the buyer is given notice of this fact.

c) i) Specific goods meaning that the parties have a sale.

ii) Unascertained goods meaning that the parties have an agreement to sell.

iii) Future goods meaning that the parties have an agreement to sell.

2 a) Generally speaking, where the seller is not the true owner of the goods or he has no authority to sell them, the buyer will not acquire property rights and the goods will have to be returned to their true owner (Section 12: Sale of Goods Act 1979). This is known as the *nemo dat quod non habet* rule which means that a seller can only pass such title to goods as he himself has. If the seller's title is defective in some way, this will also affect the buyer's title. The *nemo dat quod non habet* rule is only a general rule. Like most general rules in the law, however, there are a number of exceptions under both the common law and statute which might mean that someone who is not the true owner of the goods can pass good title to a third party. The practical effect of this is that the third party will often become the lawful owner of the goods despite the original owner's protests. The exceptions to the rule include:

- Personal bar (Section 21(1): Sale of Goods Act 1979)
- A sale under a voidable title (Section 23: Sale of Goods Act 1979)
- Mercantile agents
- Pawnbrokers
- The seller is still in possession of the goods (Section 24: Sale of Goods Act 1979)
- The buyer is (with the consent of the seller) in possession of the goods (Section 25: Sale of Goods Act 1979)

b) Unfortunately, Laura has dealt with a pawnbroker. Pawnbrokers are an exception to the *nemo dat quod non habet* rule outlined in Section 12 of the Sale of Goods Act 1979. If Laura has not retrieved the goods within the 30 days, the pawnbroker will be able to sell them to a third party in order to make good the debt that Laura owes to him.

3 a) According to Section 61(1), the Sale of Goods Act only applies to a particular class of goods – all corporeal, moveable property with the exception of money. Moveable goods are all goods which are by their very nature able to be physically transferred from seller to buyer in a contract of sale. Corporeal means that the goods are tangible (they have a

physical shape). Thus, corporeal moveable property covers all goods which are tangible and can be moved e.g. a chair, a table, a stereo system, a video cassette player, a DVD player, a pair of shoes, a necklace, a skirt and a television set – the list is endless.

b) The short answer is no – Derek and Marina will not be able to bring an action under the Sale of Goods Act 1979. The Act does not apply to heritable property i.e. land or buildings. The ornamental shrub is a fixture i.e. an item attached to or forming part of heritable property and some doubt exists as to whether it could be removed without causing damage. The rules surrounding the right to remove fixtures from heritable property should be consulted – not the Sale of Goods Act.

4 a) The Sale of Goods Act 1979 imposes certain duties upon a seller of goods with which he must comply. These duties or implied terms will form an important part of most contracts of sale. The implied terms cover the following issues:

- The seller's title or his right to sell the goods
- The way in which the goods are described
- The quality and the fitness of the goods
- Those situations where the goods are sold using a sample

These terms provide buyers with considerable protection and they are automatically part of the contract. The implied terms are contained in Sections 12 to 15 of the Sale of Goods Act.

b) i) Section 15(1): Sale of Goods Act 1979 states that a contract of sale is a contract of sale by sample where there is a term in the contract, express or implied, to that effect. The mere fact that the seller provides a sample to the buyer is not enough. There must be an express provision in the contract to that effect, or there must be evidence that the parties intended the sale to be by sample. Kevin has clearly entered a sale by sample which is governed by Section 15. There are three implied conditions in a sale by sample:

- That the bulk will correspond with the sample in quality (Section 15(2)(a))
- The buyer shall have a reasonable opportunity of comparing the bulk with the sample (Section 15(2)(b))
- That the goods will be free from any defect, making their quality unsatisfactory, which would not be apparent on reasonable examination of the sample (Section 15(2)(c))

The buyer will not have accepted the goods until he has had an opportunity to compare the bulk with the sample, and will be able, therefore, to reject the goods, even though they have been delivered, if the bulk does not correspond with the sample. The seller is entitled to assume that the buyer will examine the sample. This means that the buyer will lose any protection guaranteed by the implied condition of satisfactory quality if the defect could have been discovered by reasonable examination of the sample. This will be the case whether or not there has in fact been an examination of the sample. A reasonable examination for the purpose of a sale by sample is the type of examination which is usually carried out in the trade concerned (for cases involving sales by sample see **Ruben v Faire (1949)** and **Steels & Busks Ltd v Bleecker Bik & Co Ltd (1956)**).

ii) Section 14(2): Sale of Goods Act 1979 states that a seller selling goods in the course of business will be under a duty to ensure that the goods are of 'satisfactory quality'. Furthermore, Section 14(2A) states that goods are of satisfactory quality if they meet the standard that a reasonable person would regard as satisfactory, taking account of any description of the goods, the price (if relevant) and all the other relevant circumstances. Section 14(2B) provides a list containing five examples of quality that buyers can use to help them decide whether the goods are unsatisfactory:

- Fitness for all the purposes for which goods of the kind in question are commonly supplied
- Appearance and finish
- Freedom from minor defects
- Safety
- Durability

If a buyer felt that the seller had failed to provide goods which did not live up to just one of these aspects of quality, then the buyer would have a potential claim under Section 14(2). Buyers do not have to demonstrate that the seller has failed to meet all five aspects of quality in order to have a claim. Clearly, such a situation would only apply to the most dangerous, useless and unsatisfactory goods. The car that Tariq has purchased is not fit for its purpose and it is unsafe. Tariq should be able to reject the goods under Section 14 of the Sale of Goods Act and he should also be able to sue the seller for any loss or injury that he has suffered which was caused by the defective goods. The seller's insistence that this a problem for the manufacturer to deal with is wrong. Tariq's contract is with the seller who is strictly liable if the goods supplied do not meet the standard of satisfactory quality. The seller will have to sue the manufacturer, but this is not Tariq's problem.

The impact of the Sale and Supply of Goods to Consumers Regulations 2002 now has to be considered. The Regulations give the seller an opportunity to repair or replace goods which are considered to breach the standard of satisfactory quality. It more likely that a seller will wish to insist on his right to repair or replace the goods where minor breaches have occurred. In any case, the buyer in a sale of goods contract still retains the right to cancel the contract for breach of a material term in spite of what the Regulations say about any offers from the seller to repair or replace the goods. It is likely that Tariq will be able to insist on his right to have the contract with the seller cancelled (for cases dealing with satisfactory (merchantable) quality see **Jackson v Rotax Motor and Cycle Co (1910), Grant v Australian Knitting Mills Ltd (1936)** and **Millars of Falkirk v Turpie (1976)**).

iii) This is a breach of description in terms of Section 13 of the Sale of Goods Act 1979 (see **Moore & Co v Landauer & Co (1921)** and **Arcos Ltd v E A Ronaasen & Son (1932)**). However, since the introduction of the changes made by the Sale and Supply of Goods Act 1994, it is unlikely that the breach would be regarded as so serious to allow this buyer (Foundation Menswear) to reject the goods and treat the contract as rescinded because this is a sale involving two business parties. If the sale had involved a consumer buyer and a business seller, the right of rejection would be permitted regardless of whether the breach was minor.

5 a) An article will not be of satisfactory quality if it suffers from a manufacturing defect. In other words, a perfect article would have been completely acceptable to the buyer. It is the right article but it is faulty or defective. An article may not be fit for its purpose because of its design or its construction. It may not be defective but its construction or its design make it completely unsuitable and no amount of repair or adjustment can change this. It is a perfect article but the wrong article for the buyer's purpose e.g. a racing bicycle is not fit for the purpose of off-road racing – only a mountain bike would be adequate. If the seller supplied the buyer with a racing bicycle instead of a mountain bike, the item is not fit for its purpose (see **Baldry v Marshall (1925)**). In terms of the Sale of Goods Act 1979, Sections 14(2), 14(2A) and 14(2B) address the issue of satisfactory quality whereas Section 14(3) addresses the issue of fitness for purpose in relation to the goods.

b) There is nothing wrong or defective with the buses supplied which would cause a breach of the implied term relating to satisfactory quality (Sections

14(2), 14(2A) and 14(2B): Sale of Goods Act 1979). However, the buses are not fit for their purpose and this would be a breach of Section 14(3): Sale of Goods Act 1979. If Tartan Touring Services made clear to Cameron their requirements for the buses, then Cameron will be in breach of Section 14(3) (see also **Priest v Last (1903)** and **Griffiths v Peter Conway Ltd (1939)**).

6 **a)** The Sale and Supply of Goods to Consumers Regulations 2002 do contain a number of advantages for consumers. The introduction of new subsections 2D to 2F to Section 14 of the Sale of Goods Act 1979 which make a seller liable for public statements made in relation to the goods e.g. advertising and guarantees. The burden of proof would be placed firmly on the seller's shoulders to show that public statements had not influenced the buyer to enter the contract.

The Regulations also introduce new provisions to the Sale of Goods Act 1979 in the shape of Sections 48A to 48D. the aim of these new Sections is to give consumers more remedies in situations where the goods do not conform to the contract at the time when the buyer becomes the owner of the goods. Goods which do not conform to the contract of sale within six months of the date of delivery to the consumer will be presumed not to have been in conformity with the contract at the time of delivery.

In certain circumstances, the buyer may ask the seller to repair the goods or replace them. The seller will be under a duty to give effect to the buyer's wishes within a reasonable time. The seller must not cause significant inconvenience to the buyer and the seller has responsibility for paying any necessary costs which arise as a result of the buyer's choice of remedy (labour, material or postage). However, the buyer's rights are limited in the sense that it may be impossible for the seller to provide the buyer with his preferred remedy. Furthermore, the buyer's choice of remedy may either place the seller under a completely unreasonable burden or it may be simply more appropriate for the seller to give the buyer a reduction in the price of the goods or, as a last resort, cancellation of the contract (rescission) may be the only reasonable solution. Although the Regulations use the language of consumer choice, the seller will still have a great deal of say as to whether the goods are repaired or replaced.

If the seller fails to comply with the buyer's wishes within a reasonable time, the buyer will, in any case, be able to demand a reduction in price or rescission of the contract. The courts have power under the Regulations to award an appropriate remedy to a consumer – although it may not be the one originally requested. However, the remedy of rescission must still be exercised speedily in Scotland and the new Regulations most certainly do not give a consumer a six-month period in which to make up his mind whether to accept or reject the goods. The Regulations also establish a very peculiar legal position. The Regulations give the consumer a right of rescission in respect of the contract, but the seller may be able to side-step this by repairing or replacing the goods. However, many consumers may not realise that the Sale of Goods Act continues to give them a right of rescission which is completely independent of the new Regulations. Consumers who are aware of their legal rights will be able to push for rescission of the contract despite the Regulations.

Undoubtedly, the Regulations increase consumer protection, but they do contain a number of weaknesses. In terms of the buyer's right to insist upon a particular remedy, the Regulations may use the language of consumer choice. However, the seller will still have a great deal of say as to whether the goods are repaired or replaced. Furthermore, the two rights of rescission will only cause confusion to consumers and may even be exploited by unscrupulous traders. The positive aspects of the Regulations are the fact that guarantees are now directly enforceable against sellers of goods and the presumption that goods which develop defects within six months of purchase (assuming normal use by the consumer) must have been defective when purchased are certainly to be welcomed.

b) As explained above in **6a)**, the store is very much liable for the manufacturer's guarantee in terms of new subsections 2D to 2F to Section 14 of the Sale of Goods Act 1979 which make a seller liable for public statements made in relation to the goods e.g. advertising and guarantees. Under the Sale and Supply of Goods to Consumers Regulations 2002 outlined above, consumers have more remedies in situations where the goods do not conform to the contract at the time when the buyer becomes the owner of the goods. Ethsham could ask the seller to repair the goods or replace them. The seller, however, as discussed above can still determine the actual remedy. In many cases, cancellation of the contract (rescission) may be the only reasonable solution. Crucially, Ethsham still retains his right to have the contract cancelled under the Sale of Goods Act because the goods are clearly not of satisfactory quality. Section 15B of the Sale of Goods Act 1979 allows Ethsham to exercise his right of rejection of the goods. This remedy will only be available to the buyer if the seller has committed a material breach of contract e.g. a breach of one of the implied terms in sections 12, 13, 14 and 15. If the buyer chooses to reject the goods, he will be able to claim back part or all of the price that he may have paid. Additionally, he may also sue the seller for damages.

7 a) In theory, the seller could attempt to exclude various duties under the Sale of Goods Act 1979 (Section 55). The introduction of the Unfair Contract Terms Act 1977 and the Unfair Terms in Consumer Contracts Regulations 1999 has meant that a seller's ability to use such clauses has been considerably weakened. Section 20 of the Unfair Contract Terms Act states that the seller cannot attempt to exclude his liability for breaches of Section 12 in either a consumer or a non-consumer sale. Such an attempt by the seller would be automatically void. Breaches of Sections 13, 14 and 15 of the Sale of Goods Act will also be governed by Section 20 of the Unfair Contract Terms Act 1977. However, Section 17 of the Unfair Contract Terms Act classifies sales as either a consumer transaction or a non-consumer transaction. Any attempt by a seller to exclude or limit his liability in relation to Sections 13, 14 and 15 will be automatically void in terms of Section 20 of the Unfair Contract Terms Act. A seller in a non-consumer sale may be able to exclude or limit his liability in terms of Sections 13, 14 and 15 if he can show that this attempt is reasonable. Furthermore, Section 61(5A) of the Sale of Goods Act 1979 firmly places the burden of proof on the seller to show that the buyer is not acting as a consumer. The additional rights granted to consumers under the Sale and Supply of Goods to Consumers Regulations similarly cannot be excluded by the seller. The Unfair Contract Terms Act does not prevent a business seller from excluding or limiting his liability in a consumer transaction. The implied terms are sacred, of course, but the seller may be able to try his luck with some of the less important terms of the contract and this may be viewed as not an entirely unreasonable attempt. In terms of the test of reasonableness, useful guidelines are to be found in Section 24 and Schedule 2 of the Unfair Contract Terms Act.

As for the Unfair Terms in Consumer Contracts Regulations 1999, any standard term in consumer contract for the sale of goods (whether written or verbal) can be subjected to a test of fairness. Many, blatantly unfair terms will fall foul of the Regulations. Schedule 3 of the Regulations, it will be recalled, provides 17 examples of clauses that may be regarded as unfair.

b) This is clearly a non-consumer contract and the clause in question is an attempt to limit the seller's liability in terms of Sections 14(2), 14(2A) and 14(2B) of the Sale of Goods Act 1979. Section 55 of the 1979 Act does theoretically allow a seller to exclude or limit his liability under the Act, but this is subject to the seller being able to show that his actions are reasonable under the Unfair Contract Terms Act 1977. Following the cases of **Smith v Eric S Bush (1990)**, **Knight Machinery (Holdings) Ltd v Rennie (1995)** and **St Albans City and District Council v International Computers Ltd (1996)**, it is unlikely that the attempt by Specialist Software Solutions plc to limit its liability to Entertainment Services Ltd to just £10,000 would be viewed as a reasonable.

8 a) Risk refers to loss, damage or theft in respect of the goods and it is usually the owner (subject to the contractual terms) who will have to bear the risk in situations where the goods are lost, damaged or stolen (see **Philip Head & Sons v Showfronts Ltd (1970)**). The Sale and Supply of Goods to Consumers Regulations 2002 introduces a new rule which governs the operation of risk. It will now make a difference whether the transaction is classified as a consumer contract or a non-consumer (i.e. business) contract.

Where business contracts are concerned, Section 20 of the Sale of Goods Act 1979 states that, unless the parties agree differently, the owner of the goods will have to bear the risk of any loss or damage to the property. The general rule is that risk passes with ownership (but see **The Aliakmon (1986)** where risk had passed before the buyer became the owner of the goods). The seller will have to bear the risk to the goods until he transfers the ownership in them to the buyer. Transfer of ownership will usually (but not always) occur when a sale is formed between buyer and seller. Obviously, in an agreement to sell, ownership will not pass to the buyer until a later date or on the completion of some condition.

The new Regulations mean that Section 20 deals differently with consumer contracts. It will now be the case that risk will not pass to a consumer buyer until the goods are delivered by the seller to him. The seller could hand the goods to the buyer personally or to the buyer's agent. Once these conditions have been met, the buyer will be responsible for the goods.

b) i) This is a business contract (not a consumer contract) and Section 20 of the Sale of Goods Act 1979 would operate. Unfortunately, Smith Solicitors will have to bear the loss because ownership of the goods passed to them upon the conclusion of the sale. Smith Solicitors could always sue Luxury Leather in a delictual action if it became apparent that it had breached its duty to Smith Solicitors as custodians of the goods. However, in certain situations the rule in Section 20 could be made redundant. In a non-consumer contract (like the one here) if delivery of the goods was delayed and, as a result, they were damaged lost or stolen, the party responsible for the delay (the seller or the buyer) would have to bear responsibility for the loss. So, if the seller failed to deliver the goods on time to the buyer and after this the goods were damaged, lost or stolen, the seller would have to bear responsibility for this even if the buyer was now the owner and, therefore, potentially the one who has to bear the risk.

ii) Lynne and Euan have a consumer contract with Luxury Leather. The new Sale and Supply of Goods to Consumers Regulations 2002 mean that Section 20 of the Sale of Goods Act 1979 deals differently with consumer contracts. It will now be the case that risk will not pass to a consumer buyer until the goods are delivered by the seller to him. The seller could hand the goods to the buyer personally or to the buyer's agent. Once these conditions have been met, the buyer will be responsible for the goods.

9 All of the situations relate to Section 18 of the Sale of Goods Act 1979.

i) This situation involves a contract where there was an unconditional order for the sale of specific goods in a deliverable state. Property in the goods passed to Jasminder under Rule 1. She has become the owner of the goods and she is responsible for them and, therefore, she will have to bear the loss (see **Tarling v Baxter (1827)**).

ii) This situation involves a contract for the sale of specific goods and the seller is bound to do something to put them into a deliverable state. Property in the goods will not pass to Steve until the adjustments have been made to the car in terms of Rule 2. Until these adjustments are carried out, Reddie Motors remains the owner of the goods and, therefore, continues to have responsibility for the car (see **Underwood v Burgh Castle Brick & Cement Syndicate (1922)**).

iii) This situation involves a contract for the sale of goods in a deliverable state, but the seller is bound to weigh, measure or test, or do anything else to calculate the price. Property in the goods will not pass to FreshFields Supermarket in terms of Rule 3 until Farmer Giles weighs the potatoes in order to calculate the price (see **Nanka-Bruce v Commonwealth Trust Ltd (1926)**).

iv) This situation involves the goods being delivered to the buyer on approval or a sale or return basis. Property in the goods has passed to Norma in terms of Rule 4 when she did anything inconsistent with the seller's ownership by signifying her acceptance; or adopts the goods as her own (by using them); or retaining them without giving notice of rejection (see **Elphick v Barnes (1880)** and **Kirkham v Attenborough (1897)**).

v) This situation involves a contract for the sale of unascertained or future goods by description. Property in the goods passed to Bill from Sweeney's Slaughterhouse in terms of Rule 5 when goods, complying with the contractual description, were unconditionally appropriated to the contract in a deliverable state. Appropriation of the goods occurred when Andy and Jamal signed the delivery note and were allowed to take the goods away.

10 **a)** Section 19 of the Sale of Goods Act 1979 addresses the issue of retention of title to the goods. In certain situations, the seller may have delivered goods to the buyer, but a term in the contract will nonetheless allow the seller to retain ownership/title of the goods. The buyer may have possession of the goods, but he is not yet the owner of the property.

Usually, ownership of the goods will pass to the buyer when he complies with some condition laid down by the seller e.g. when all monies owed to the seller in connection with the sale have been paid. Conditions such as these might stipulate that the buyer must pay everything that he owes to the seller before ownership in the goods can be transferred. Very often, the seller will demand not just the price of the goods, but all debts owed to him whether connected with the sale or not. These types of contractual terms are known as Romalpa clauses and are named after a decision of the English Court of Appeal in 1976. These clauses are very useful because they allow the seller to reclaim goods or money owed on the event of the buyer's insolvency thus defeating the claims of other creditors (see **Aluminium Industrie Vaassen BV v Romalpa Aluminium Ltd (1976)** and **Armour and Another v Thyssen Edelstahlwerke AG (1990)**). However, these clauses do have their drawbacks. The usefulness of Romalpa clauses should not be overestimated. The seller will lose the protection of such a clause if the goods are sold by the buyer to third parties who then convert them into other products by making them undergo some form of manufacturing process (see **Borden (UK) Ltd v Scottish Timber Products Ltd (1981)**).

b) Most of the timber has been converted into other products and, following **Borden (UK) Ltd v Scottish Timber Products Ltd (1981)**, the courts will not allow Stuart to get back his timber which has been used to build the houses. However, he could attempt to repossess the small amount of timber that has not been used by Wylie. Critically, it does not appear that Wylie has sold any of the timber on to third parties and, therefore, it would seem that there would not be any money from the proceeds of sub-sales that Stuart could trace as in **Aluminium Industrie Vaassen BV v Romalpa Aluminium Ltd (1976)**. A Romalpa clause in this situation may not be particularly effective.

11 **a)** According to Section 61(1) delivery is defined as the voluntary transfer of possession from one person to another. Goods, therefore, are considered to be delivered if the seller delivers them physically to the buyer or his agent. In many situations, symbolic delivery of the goods will be enough, for example, where the seller hands over the only set of keys to the buyer granting him access to the warehouse where the goods are stored. Where bulk goods owned commonly are concerned (Sections 20A and 20B) delivery can occur when the goods are appropriated to the contract with the result that the ownership transfers from seller to buyer. It is worth emphasising that the delivery of the goods does not mean that the seller has necessarily transferred the ownership of the goods to the buyer.

b) i) Section 29. Where the contract stipulates that the seller must deliver the goods to the buyer but no time period for this has been agreed by the parties, delivery must take place within a reasonable time. Delivery must take place at a reasonable hour of the day.

ii) Section 30. Where a larger quantity of goods is delivered, the buyer may accept the amount and pay for the contract amount and reject the remainder. The buyer could accept all the goods if he so wishes, but he must pay for the extra goods. The buyer can only reject the whole of the goods if the surplus is a material breach of contract.

iii) Section 31. Unless the parties agree otherwise, the buyer should not have to accept delivery of the goods by instalments.

iv) Section 32, but a distinction is now made between a business buyer and a consumer buyer. If the contract states that the seller must deliver the goods to a business buyer, delivery to a carrier by the seller will discharge this duty. A seller must enter a contract of carriage on terms which are beneficial/reasonable to the buyer. In these

circumstances, the seller should have regard to the type of goods and all the circumstances when he enters a contract with the carrier. If the seller does not take reasonable care and the goods are damaged in carriage, the buyer may reject the goods and sue the seller for damages.

If the buyer is a consumer, delivery of the goods to a carrier by the seller is not to be regarded as delivery to the buyer. This will be the case where the seller is authorised or required to send the goods to the buyer. However, if the buyer arranges for the seller to deliver goods to a carrier who is acting as his agent, this will mean that the goods have been delivered to the buyer. After all, by appointing a carrier to act as his agent, the buyer is sending this person to uplift the goods on his behalf.

v) Section 34. The buyer must accept goods which are delivered and which conform to the contract. If the buyer has not yet had an opportunity to examine the goods which have been delivered, he is considered not to have accepted them until he has had a reasonable chance to examine them. The buyer, of course, will wish to examine the goods in order to ensure that they comply with the contract.

vi) Section 36. Unless the parties agree otherwise, if the buyer rightfully refuses to accept goods which have been delivered, he is not obliged to return them to the seller. All the buyer must do is inform the seller about his refusal to accept the goods.

vii) Section 37. If the buyer wrongfully neglects or refuses to take delivery of the goods, he will be liable for damages to the seller.

viii) Section 35A. The buyer may reject the goods owing to a breach of contract on the part of the seller which affects some or all of the goods. In this situation, the buyer will have the right of partial rejection. The buyer may even accept some of the goods i.e. those which are not affected by the breach and reject the remainder.

ix) Section 35. The buyer is considered to have accepted the goods:

- When he communicates his acceptance to the seller

- When he does anything in relation to the goods which is inconsistent with the seller still being the owner (e.g. by using them)

- When he has held on to the goods and he has not informed the seller that he intends to reject them. The buyer must inform the seller within a reasonable time that he intends to reject the goods. After the passage of a reasonable time, the buyer loses his right to cancel the contract

x) Section 33. Goods delivered to a distant place. If the seller agrees to deliver goods at his own risk, the risk of damage to or destruction of the goods remains with the seller until delivery is accomplished. This is regardless of whether ownership has passed to the buyer. Crucially, however, the buyer must accept any deterioration in the goods which normally occurs in the course of transit.

12 The Sale of Goods Act 1979 provides the buyer and the seller with a number of remedies should they find themselves victims of a breach of contract by the other party.

The buyer's remedies
- Specific implement (Section 52)
- Damages (Sections 15B, 51 and 53A)
- Rejection of the goods (Section 15B)

The seller's remedies
The remedies that a seller can take action under can be divided into two groups and are outlined in Section 38 of the Sale of Goods Act 1979:

- Personal remedies i.e. suing the buyer for the price of the goods and/or raising a claim for damages against the buyer

- Remedies against the goods i.e. lien, stoppage in transit and resale

The seller will wish to rely on these remedies usually when the buyer refuses to pay or cannot pay for the goods. Section 39 defines an unpaid seller.

Section 49 deals with an action for the price raised by the seller and Section 50 allows the seller to seek damages for non-acceptance of the goods by the buyer.

Sections 39 to 43 deal with the seller's right of lien and Section 44 outlines the right of the seller to stop the goods while they are in transit. Section 48 gives the seller the right to resell the goods in certain situations. Where the unpaid seller has used his right of lien or has exercised his right to stop the goods in transit, the right to resell the goods may be an attractive option. The right of resale can be used in situations where the goods are perishable (e.g. foodstuffs).

13 a) Section 2 of the Sale of Goods Act 1979 defines a contract for the sale of goods as one where the seller transfers or agrees to transfer the property (ownership) of the goods for a money consideration called the price.

The provisions of the Act only apply to transactions that operate by way of a sale of goods contract. The

Act does not apply to arrangements which operate by way of a mortgage, pledge, charge or other security arrangement (Section 62(4)). A security arrangement, for example, a mortgage arrangement is where a debtor grants security over an item of his property to a creditor in exchange for a loan. Under such an arrangement, the creditor hands over a sum of money to the debtor who, in turn, hands over his property. To the casual observer, this may look like a sale. However, the arrangement is merely a device whereby the creditor is protecting himself by insisting upon possession of the debtor's goods. Should the debtor fail to repay the loan, the creditor will refuse to hand over the goods and, in this way, he has managed to cut his losses to some extent. Sometimes, however, for reasons best known to the parties, it is not always simple to decide whether a transaction is a genuine sale and, therefore, covered by the 1979 Act, or some sort of security transaction which is outside the scope of the Act. This area of the law has often caused confusion for the Scottish courts (see **Aluminium Industrie Vaassen BV v Romalpa Aluminium Ltd (1976)** and **Armour and Another v Thyssen Edelstahlwerke AG (1990)**).

b) Sections 6 and 7 of the Sale of Goods Act address situations where the goods are said to have perished and, in this way, they are closely related to the issue of risk. These provisions relate to specific goods – not generic goods which are considered not to be capable of perishing or being destroyed. Section 6 states that where there is a contract for the sale of specific goods, and the goods have perished at the time that the contract was formed, such a contract will be declared void (see **Couturier v Hastie (1856)**). Section 7 applies to situations where the seller and the buyer have an agreement to sell specific goods and the goods subsequently perish before the risk passes to the buyer. In such situations, the contract would be regarded as voidable.

c) Sections 8 and 9 of the Sale of Goods Act deal with the important issue of the price that is to be paid by the buyer for the goods in question. After all, Section 2 makes it clear that a sale will only really be a sale if the buyer exchanges a money consideration called the price for the goods. According to Section 8, the parties can leave the price to be fixed by the contract or by reference to a method laid down by the contract. Alternatively, the parties may have had previous dealings that can be referred to in order to calculate the price. If the contract is silent on the issue of the price or there have been no previous dealings between the parties, the buyer must pay a reasonable price for the goods and what is reasonable will depend on the facts of each situation.

Section 9 does allow the parties to fix a price by appointing a third party to carry out a valuation of the goods. If such a valuation cannot or is not carried out, the contract is rendered voidable. If one of the parties to the contract of sale prevented the valuation from being carried out, the innocent party could bring an action for damages.

d) Capacity to enter into contracts is governed by Section 3 of the Sale of Goods Act which states that the parties must have contractual capacity. Capacity was extensively discussed in Chapter 2 and the 1979 Act does nothing to alter these rules.

e) Section 10 of the Sale of Goods Act makes it clear that, unless the parties agree differently, statements about time in relation to the sale of goods transaction are not to be regarded as a material term of the contract. In order to determine whether a contractual term about time is material, the content of the contract and the intentions of the parties will have to be examined. Late delivery of goods by the seller, for example, will not necessarily mean that the buyer has the right to treat the contract as cancelled. The most appropriate remedy for the seller's breach may be to lodge an action for damages. Additionally, Section 59 states that where references are made to a reasonable time, the question of what is a reasonable time is a question of fact (see **Shaw, Macfarlane & Co v Waddell & Sons (1890)**).

14 Morag will have to obtain a consumer credit licence (a standard licence as opposed to a group licence) from the Office of Fair Trading. One of the most distinctive features of the Consumer Credit Act 1974 is the fact that those businesses or individuals wishing to provide credit facilities to members of the public must be in possession of a licence. Failure to obtain a licence means the imposition of a number of civil and criminal penalties. Furthermore, licences are not just given to anyone. It is possible for a business to give credit to customers if this is regarded as an occasional transaction. Sometimes, businesses will give particularly good customers credit in order to pay for goods or services. As long as this does not happen very often, the business will not need a licence from the Office of Fair Trading. However, businesses will have to be particularly careful here because if giving credit to various customers became a common practice, they may very well be breaking the law if they failed to get a licence. The moral of the story is that if granting credit to customers becomes more frequent, it is better to

apply for a licence. Failure to obtain a licence has certain consequences:

1 It will be a criminal offence to provide credit without a licence (Section 39)

2 The unlicensed trader may be unable to enforce a regulated agreement against the debtor (Section 40)

3 An ancillary credit agreement will be unenforceable if the creditor has failed to obtain a licence when it was made (Section 148)

4 A regulated credit agreement will be unenforceable, if the credit broker who set it up did not possess a licence (Section 149)

However, a creditor who has broken the rules in relation to the licensing requirements of the Act can always apply to the Office of Fair Trading for what is known as a validating order. A validating order allows the creditor to enforce agreements which would otherwise fall foul of the licensing requirements in the Act.

Section 22 states that there are two types of licence which can be granted by the Office of Fair Trading:
• Standard
• Group

Standard licences are granted to individuals for a period of five years. The standard licence is personal and cannot be transferred by the licence holder to any other individual. This would mean that if the licence holder sold his credit business, the new owner would have to apply for a licence on his own merits and such an application may or may not be granted by the Office of Fair Trading. The Office of Fair Trading will only grant licences to those individuals who are considered to be fit and proper persons. Those persons who have previously broken the rules contained in the Consumer Credit Act 1974 need not apply for a licence.

If the applicant has breached equality laws such as the Sex Discrimination Act 1975, the Race Relations Act 1976 or the Disability Discrimination Act 1995, a licence will not be issued. It is worth pointing out that the scope of discrimination legislation has widened considerably since the Consumer Credit Act was first introduced. Criminal convictions for violence and dishonesty are likely to result in the applicant being refused a licence. If the applicant has been involved in any undesirable business practices, for example, he has been disqualified as a company director under the Company Directors (Disqualification) Act 1986, a licence will not be issued.

It is not merely the individuals who control credit businesses who are scrutinised, but also their employees, associates and agents who will have to meet the requirement that they be fit and proper persons.

However, merely because a licence has been issued is not the end of the story for the applicant. All licence holders must ensure that they conduct their businesses properly. Any undesirable conduct on their part could mean that the Office of Fair Trading may decide to suspend or, even more seriously, withdraw the licence.

15   Sheila and her husband can cancel the contract. As should be apparent from the study of contract law, it is usually the case that once a legally enforceable agreement has been formed both parties are now committed to it and for one of them to break the contract would give the other party the right to sue. Under the Consumer Credit Act 1974, however, it is possible for the debtor, in certain situations, to withdraw from the credit agreement without being sued by the creditor for breach of contract. The debtor's right to cancel an agreement was deliberately introduced in order to clamp down on the disreputable practice of door-to-door salesmen pressurising people to enter credit agreements which they did not want or could not afford.

Under Section 67, a debtor will have the right to cancel a credit agreement if two conditions are met:

- If you, the debtor, entered into face-to-face discussions with the creditor or the creditor's agents with the aim of entering a credit agreement

- The signing of the credit agreement by both parties did not take place on the creditor's business premises

If a debtor signed a credit agreement in his own home after discussions with the creditor's agent, then the debtor can take advantage of what is known as a 'cooling-off period'. This period gives the debtor time to decide whether he wishes to cancel the agreement or not. It does not matter whether the face-to-face discussions with the creditor took place at the creditor's place of business or in the debtor's home. In order to have the right to cancel, the debtor must not have signed the agreement on the creditor's business premises. This 'cooling-off period' runs for five days from when the debtor receives his second copy of the agreement.

If the agreement can be cancelled, there must be a notice next to the signature box on the form which tells the debtor that he has a right to cancel. The creditor must tell the debtor how and when he can cancel the contract.

16   Under Sections 137 to 140 of the Consumer Credit Act 1974, a court may examine the terms of a credit agreement in order to establish whether it operates fairly between the parties and to ensure that it is not an extortionate agreement. An agreement may be considered extortionate if the debtor is forced to make grossly exorbitant payments under the agreement to the creditor. The term grossly exorbitant means that the agreement would fall foul of the ordinary principles of fair dealing. In other words, a reasonable or fair-minded person would consider the agreement to be completely unbalanced in that it blatantly favoured the creditor's interests. Usually, a credit agreement will be examined in this way when the debtor makes an application to the court. How will the court make its decision? The court will look at the following factors:

- Current interest rates at the time when the bargain was made

- The personal circumstances of the debtor including his age, experience and health

- The level of financial pressure that the debtor was experiencing when he entered the agreement

- The level of risk that the creditor was accepting and his relationship with the debtor

- Any other material facts or circumstances

17   Yes, the bank should have taken more care when it used the advertisement. There are strict controls imposed on businesses which advertise credit facilities to members of the general public. Under Section 44 of the Consumer Credit Act 1974, the Secretary of State has the power to make Regulations in relation to credit advertising activities. Clearly, the ways in which credit are presented to members of the public could be a very influential reason for their decision to enter a credit agreement. It is, therefore, of vital importance that debtors are given the correct information by advertisers. Section 46 of the Act states that it is an offence for an advertisements to be false or misleading in a material respect. The duty imposed on creditors in Section 46 is fleshed out by the Consumer Credit (Advertising) Regulations 1989 (as amended). The 1989 Regulations cover advertising in any form and this would include print, radio, television, film, video, DVD, notices, goods, circular letters or price lists. Any attempt to advertise credit will fall within the reach of the Regulations. The Regulations provide strict guidelines as to how

an advertisement is to be presented (*its form*) and what sort of information will appear in it (*its content*). There are three types of regulated advertisement: simple, intermediate and full.

18 If the debtor defaults on the agreement, the creditor, in terms of Section 87 of the Consumer Credit Act 1974, must serve a default notice on the debtor. Without serving this default notice, the creditor is not entitled to use any of the following remedies for breach of contract:

1 To end the agreement

2 To demand earlier repayment of any money owed by the debtor under the agreement

3 To recover possession of any goods that the debtor holds

4 To behave as if any of the debtor's rights under the agreement have been suspended, limited or even terminated

5 To enforce any security

It should be noted that the terms of the credit agreement will often state what action the creditor will be able to take against the debtor if he defaults. Only some of the options listed in 1 to 5 may be available to the creditor. The agreement will, therefore, determine what the creditor can and cannot do. The important thing to remember is that any of the actions open to the creditor under the agreement will be useless if a default notice was not served on the debtor.

If the creditor wishes to sue for payments that the debtor has fallen behind with, he is entitled to so without having to serve a default notice. Furthermore, credit card companies often prevent debtors from using a card if the credit limit has been reached and default notices are not required for this type of action. Under Section 88, the default notice must contain certain important information.

Section 131 allows the creditor to apply to court for what is called a protection order. The creditor can also protect himself by including termination and accelerated payments clauses in the consumer credit agreement.

19 a) Running account credit is where the debtor can borrow money up to an agreed limit. This category would cover bank overdrafts, credit cards and store cards (Section 11: Consumer Credit Act).

b) Fixed-term credit is credit where the sum borrowed by the debtor is fixed at the beginning of the agreement. This category includes bank loans and hire purchase agreements (Section 11: Consumer Credit Act).

c) Restricted use credit is where the sum borrowed by the debtor is for an agreed purpose, for example, a car loan from a bank. This category includes bank loans and hire purchase.

d) Unrestricted use credit is where the debtor is completely free to spend the credit provided on whatever he wishes. This category would include credit cards, store cards and bank overdrafts.

e) Debtor-creditor agreements is where the debtor simply borrows money from the creditor. The creditor is not involved in any further transaction which the debtor may enter with a supplier of goods. The creditor lends the money to the debtor and this credit will be used to pay for the goods from the supplier. This is the traditional type of credit agreement and would cover such activities as bank loans.

f) Debtor-creditor-supplier agreements are where the creditor and the supplier of goods may be the same person or where the supplier has links to a creditor who will provide credit to the supplier's customers (the debtors). This is a very common arrangement where car dealerships are concerned in that customers will buy a car from the dealer and then be offered credit to pay for their purchase through a finance house or a bank associated with the dealer (Section 12: Consumer Credit Act 1974).

20 The Consumer Credit Act recognises a number of exempt agreements where, generally, the rules regulating consumer credit agreements do not apply. The following are exempt agreements:

1 Fixed sum debtor-creditor-supplier agreements where the credit borrowed must be repaid within one year and must not exceed four instalments.

2 Low cost debtor-creditor agreements where the cost of the credit does not exceed a predetermined rate of interest or a rate of interest that is one per cent above the highest of lenders' base rates in the 28 days leading up to the formation of the contract.

3 Debtor-creditor-supplier agreements where the purpose of the agreement is to enable the debtor to purchase land and the credit must be repaid in no more than four instalments.

4 Hire of a gas, electricity or water meter where the owner of the meter is a gas, electricity or water company and the meter is used to monitor the supply of gas, electricity or water under a relevant agreement for these types of services.

5 Credit to be used in relation to international trade transactions – the credit will be provided in

connection with an international trade contract i.e. where the parties to the contract are based in different states, for example, the UK and the US.

6 Running account debtor-creditor-supplier agreements where each periodical account (of the whole amount of the credit then outstanding) will be paid in a single payment.

7 House purchase or mortgage loans where these are provided by a local authority or a named bank, building society or insurance company.

Chapter 5

1 a) There are five ways in which an agency relationship can be created:

1 By express contract

2 Implied by the conduct of the parties or by law (see Section 5 of the Partnership Act 1890, Section 6 of the Limited Liability Partnership Act 2000 and **Hely-Hutchinson v Brayhead Ltd (1968)**)

3 By holding out (see **Hayman v American Cotton Oil Co (1907)**)

4 By ratification (see **Kelner v Baxter (1866)** and **Keighley Maxted & Co v Durant (1901)**)

5 By necessity (see **Couturier v Hastie (1856)**, **Great Northern Railway v Swaffield (1874)** and **Springer v Great Western Railway (1921)**)

b) i) Beverley is Katrina's agent and, therefore, Beverley negotiated a binding contract with Jocelyn on Katrina's behalf. Katrina has effectively appointed Beverley by holding her out as her agent. Katrina is personally barred from denying that Beverley is her agent (see **Hayman v American Cotton Oil Co (1907)**).

ii) This is an example of ratification. In order for the principal to be able to ratify an unauthorised transaction, a number of conditions must be satisfied:

- The agent must disclose all material facts surrounding the contract so that the principal is fully aware of all liabilities that he is taking on.

- The principal must ratify the contract within a reasonable time.

- The principal must have existed at the time the contract was entered into.

- The principal must have the power and capacity to ratify the act otherwise the contract will be void.

- The agent must act with an identifiable principal in mind and not contracting on his own with hope that he will find someone who will later ratify the contract. It is important that the third party knows that the agent *is* acting as an agent and does not believe the agent to be in business on his own account.

- The principal will not be in a position to ratify any contract that is illegal.

Jonathan has ratified or approved his agent's unauthorised actions and he is bound into a contract for the house *and* the adjoining piece of land (see **Kelner v Baxter (1866)** and **Keighley Maxted & Co v Durant (1901)**).

2 a) The relationship between an agent and his principal is known as a fiduciary relationship i.e. a relationship of trust. At all times, the agent is expected to act in the best interests of the principal. This means that the principal's interests must come first. The agent must ensure that there are no conflicts of interest. As with all contracts, the agent will enjoy the protection of certain rights, but the agreement also imposes certain duties which are owed to the principal.

The law imposes five key duties upon the Agent:

- To obey the instructions of the principal (see **Gilmour v Clark (1853)**)

- To exercise skill and care (see **Copland v Brogan (1916)** and **Chaudhry v Prabhakar (1989)**)

- To act in person (see **Black v Cornelius (1879)**)

- To keep proper accounts (see **Tyler v Logan (1904)**)

- To act in good faith (see **McPherson's Trustees v Watt (1877)**, **Liverpool Victoria Legal Friendly Society v Houston (1900)**, **Lothian v Jenolite Ltd (1969)**, **Islamic Republic of Iran Shipping Lines v Denby (1987)** and **Attorney-General for Hong Kong v Reid (1994)**).

The agent enjoys the following rights in relation to his principal under the agency agreement:

- Right to receive payment (see **Kennedy v Glass (1890)** and **Dudley v Barnet (1937)**)

- Right to be indemnified by the principal (see **Stevenson & Sons v Duncan (1842)** and **Drummond v Cairns (1852)**

- Right of lien over the principal's property (see **Sibbald v Gibson (1852)**)

b) Mitchell has entered into a contract with the prospective client on his principal's behalf. It does not matter if the principal does not wish to honour this contract with the tenant, Mitchell is still entitled to be paid for his services (see **Kennedy v Glass (1890)** and **Dudley v Barnet (1937)**). Furthermore, Mitchell is still entitled to be indemnified by the principal for any expenses that he has properly incurred in the course of his duties (see **Stevenson & Sons v Duncan (1842)** and **Drummond v Cairns (1852)**). If the tenant sued Mitchell for breach of the tenancy agreement in place of the principal, Mitchell would be entitled to be indemnified by the principal for this. Finally, Mitchell may be able to exercise his right of lien over any property of the principal that he rightfully possesses in order to make the principal come to his senses and pay for his services (see **Sibbald v Gibson (1852)**).

3 **a)** An agent can have two types of authority:
- Actual
- Ostensible

Actual authority is the true extent of the authority that the principal gives to an agent. The principal can give the agent this type of authority expressly or impliedly. Express, actual authority will be contained in either a written document or in verbal instructions that the principal issues to the agent (see **Ireland v Livingston (1872)**).

If a situation arises where the agent acts outwith his actual authority, but the principal does not discipline the agent for what would almost certainly be seen as a serious breach of the agency agreement, then any third parties dealing with the agent would be entitled to assume that the agent was acting within his actual authority. Where the principal appears to approve or endorse the actions of an agent acting outwith his actual authority, this is known as ratification.

Implied, actual authority will arise where the agent holds a particular position and it is implied by law or by the behaviour of the principal and the agent that this kind of agent would have actual authority to bind the principal into contracts with third parties (see Section 5 of the Partnership Act 1890, Section 6 of the Limited Liability Partnership Act 2000 and **Hely-Hutchinson v Brayhead Ltd (1968)**).

Ostensible authority is the authority that a third party believes that the agent possesses. Ostensible authority is not true authority, it is fictitious and exists only in the mind of the third party. The

principal, however, has encouraged the third party to believe that the agent has the necessary authority. The third party must show that the principal's statements or behaviour encouraged him to believe that the agent had the necessary authority (see **Watteau v Fenwick (1893), Barry, Ostlere & Shepherd Ltd v Edinburgh Cork Importing Co (1909), International Sponge Importers v Watt & Sons (1911)** and **Freeman & Lockyer v Buckhurst Park Properties (Mangal) Ltd (1964)**). A third party's claim that he believed that the agent had ostensible authority purely because the agent told him that he had been given authority by his principal will not be accepted by the courts. The false impression of authority must have been created by the principal's actions (see **Reckitt v Barnet & Company (1929)**).

The third party may have been encouraged by the principal to believe that the agent had authority to act in a particular way for the following reasons:

1 The agent's authority has been changed or limited in some way. Stupidly, however, the principal fails to tell third parties of this very important change and so third parties understandably continue to believe that the agent still has the same powers.

2 The agent did not have authority to act in a particular way when he entered a contract with the third party. The principal, however, decides to ratify or approve the contract and this leads the third party to assume that this type of contract is well within the agent's powers. Again, the principal will have failed to take steps to notify the third party of the true extent of the agent's authority.

3 The agent has had implied authority in the past, for example, he may be a partner in a firm or a director of a company. Third parties dealing with these types of agents would have been entitled to assume that they possessed certain powers or had authority to enter into contracts of a particular kind. However, these individuals may have had their authority limited or withdrawn by their principals, but this fact has not been publicised to third parties.

It is vitally important that the principal communicates any change in the agent's authority to third parties. If the principal does notify third parties about the true extent of the agent's authority then he will not be held accountable for any of the agent's unauthorised actions.

If there are circumstances which should have caused the third party to suspect that the agent was acting outwith his authority, but the third party still goes ahead with the contract then the principal will not be legally bound. The third party's remedy is to sue the agent for what is known as breach of warranty of authority.

b) In the case of **Reckitt v Barnet & Company (1929)** where an agent who had the authority to write cheques for the company, paid a private debt using money in his principal's account. *Held*: the principal was entitled to recover his money from the third party, as they should have suspected that the agent did not have the authority to write company cheques in order to pay a private debt. This is the type of transaction that the third party should have questioned because it should have been immediately obvious that the principal was unlikely to allow his bank account to be used by the agent in this way.

However, where Lindsey-Anne is concerned, she does not have authority to write cheques and we do not know if the store was aware of the limits on this particular partner's authority to bind the firm. In terms of Section 5 of the Partnership Act 1890, Lindsey-Anne as a partner does have authority implied by law to bind the firm into contract with third parties when acting in the normal course of the firm's business. See also **Hely-Hutchinson v Brayhead Ltd (1968)** for an example of an agent's implied authority. The question here would centre around whether or not the purchase of a computer should have excited the suspicions of the store. This seems like a perfectly normal type of transaction for a partner to enter on the firm's behalf. Furthermore, was the store even aware of the limits placed on Lindsey-Anne's authority? If it did have knowledge of this lack of authority on Lindsey-Anne's part, it would completely undermine its argument that she possessed ostensible authority to bind the firm. In the past have the other partners communicated the fact that Lindsey-Anne lacks authority to bind the firm to the store and other third parties?

If there are circumstances which should have caused the third party to suspect that the agent was acting outwith his authority, but the third party still goes ahead with the contract then the principal will not be legally bound. The third party's remedy is to sue the agent for what is known as breach of warranty of authority (see **Anderson v Croall (1903)**).

4 **a)** An agent expects to receive some sort of reward for performing services for the principal. In Scotland,

a person can act for someone very much like an agent, but this type of representative would not expect to receive a reward. Sometimes this type of relationship is referred to as gratuitous agency or unpaid agency. It is more properly called mandate and the person who acts in this way is known as a mandatary. Although acting on an unpaid basis, a mandatary will still owe a duty of care to the person for whom he is acting. This means that a mandatary will not be able to use the fact that he was acting unpaid as a defence to a claim of negligence.

b) Joe is acting on an unpaid basis as a mandatary (i.e. an unpaid agent) for Michelle. It would appear that Joe has been negligent when he was examining the car and this negligence has caused loss to Michelle. Following the cases of **Copland v Brogan (1916)** and **Chaudhry v Prabhakar (1989)**, it is likely that Joe will be liable to Michelle for the consequences of his negligence. It makes no difference that Joe was acting on an unpaid basis. A mandatary must take the same sort of care that would be expected of him in the management of his own affairs. Had Joe been looking for a car of his own, he would probably have taken much greater care than the level of care that he displayed when selecting a car for Michelle.

5 **a)** A fiduciary relationship is a relationship of confidence that imposes a special duty of care on one or both of the parties. Examples of such relationships include those of solicitor/client, principal/agent, doctor/patient, parent/child and the partners in a firm. If a party owes a fiduciary duty to someone else this means that he must disclose all material facts to the other person. The duty arising from these types of fiduciary relationships are different from the duties that arise under contracts *uberrimae fidei* i.e. of the utmost good faith. In contracts *uberrimae fidei*, it is the nature of the contract, for example, an insurance contract which requires disclosure in spite of the relationship between the parties. In the fiduciary situation it is the relationship of the parties and not the particular contract which gives rise to the need to disclose.

At all times, the agent is expected to act in the best interests of the principal. This means that the principal's interests must come first. The agent must ensure that there are no conflicts of interest. The agent must not divulge any confidential information in relation to the principal's business that he obtains in the course of his agency. It is often the case that a dishonest agent will be able to profit personally from the agency because of his position or because third parties may offer him a benefit or bribe if the agent introduces them to his principal. It is worth emphasising that an agent who sees the opportunity to make a fast buck or take advantage of some benefit which comes his way will not have the principal's best interests at heart. The agent may view these benefits as perks of the job, but such behaviour could result in disastrous consequences for the principal. The agent may not have properly scrutinised the deal proposed by the third party and this could cause the principal some serious losses in the future. There does not need to be an actual conflict between the agent's and the principal's interests. It is very often enough for there to be a potential conflict. If the agent sees an opportunity to make a profit, the principal should always be informed of this. It will then be completely up to the principal whether or not to allow the agent to receive the benefit. It is often forgotten that the only reason that the agent is in a position to receive a benefit is because the principal appointed him in the first place.

The extent of the agent's fiduciary duty is limited to how it affects the agency agreement. It is still entirely possible for an agent to promote his own interests when he is not acting for the principal. The agent may even act for a number of different principals. If a principal wished to prevent his agent from pursuing his own interests outside the agency agreement or from working on behalf of other principals, there would have to be an express term in the agency agreement to this end. Such a condition could never be implied into all agency agreements. However, such a restraint of trade might be declared illegal if it was in any way excessive or anti-competitive. For examples of the fiduciary nature of the agency relationship see the following cases **McPherson's Trustees v Watt (1877)**, **Liverpool Victoria Legal Friendly Society v Houston (1900)**, **Lothian v Jenolite Ltd (1969)**, **Islamic Republic of Iran Shipping Lines v Denby (1987)** and **Attorney-General for Hong Kong v Reid (1994)**.

b) Bob has breached his fiduciary duty to his principal by making secret profits. This is a very serious breach of the agency contract. There are a number of serious consequences which arise as a result of an agent making a secret profit:

1 The agent has committed a material breach of the agency agreement and the principal is, therefore entitled to terminate the contract with immediate effect.

2 The agent cannot claim payment for that particular transaction.

3 The agent can be sued by the principal with the intention of recovering the secret profit that the agent has made.

4 The third party may find that the principal refuses to honour the contract that the agent negotiated.

5 The third party himself may be sued by the principal if he bribed or encouraged the agent to breach his fiduciary duty to the principal.

6 If the third party refuses to pay the bribe or the commission to the agent, the agent cannot take legal action against the third party because their agreement is illegal and, therefore, unenforceable.

7 Bribery is a criminal offence in terms of the Prevention of Corruption Acts 1906 and 1916.

For examples of an agent making secret profits see **Islamic Republic of Iran Shipping Lines v Denby (1987)** and **Attorney-General for Hong Kong v Reid (1994)**.

6 In the event of an emergency, a person is deemed by law to have the authority to act as agent for another party. However, it must be impossible for the person acting as agent of necessity to contact the principal. Before the use of modern communications such as faxes, telephones, ship-to-shore radios and e-mail, this type of agency was extremely useful, but it is now highly unlikely that a principal would be unable to be contacted in an emergency situation. In saying that, however, this type of agency should not be written off completely and it may still undoubtedly have its uses. There will clearly be situations where an agent has to come to decision very rapidly in order to protect the principal's interests and he may not enjoy the luxury of attempting to communicate the principal in order to obtain further instructions. As long as the agent of necessity acts in good faith to protect the interests of the principal, he will not be held liable for any losses which his actions may have caused the principal (see **Couturier v Hastie (1856)**, **Great Northern Railway v Swaffield (1874)** and **Springer v Great Western Railway (1921)**).

7 a) Regulations 3 and 4 of the Commercial Agency Regulations 1993 describe the duties of an agent and his principal.

The agent's duties (Regulation 3)

- The agent must protect the principal's interests by acting dutifully and in good faith at all times.

- The agent must make proper efforts to negotiate and, where appropriate, conclude the transactions that he has responsibility for.

- The agent must provide the principal with all the information that he has at his disposal.

599

- The agent must obey all reasonable instructions given to him by the principal.

The principal's duties (Regulation 4)

- The principal must pay or remunerate the agent for carrying out his duties under the agency agreement.

- The principal must reimburse the agent for any expenses that the agent has incurred in the line of duty.

- The principal must provide the agent with the necessary documents and the necessary information relating to the goods in order for the agent to carry out his duties.

- The principal must tell the agent within a reasonable time whether he intends to honour or refuse to honour the contract that the agent has set up with a third party.

- The principal must inform the agent within a reasonable time of any breach of the contract with the third party that the principal is responsible for.

According to Regulation 5(1), the rights and duties contained in Regulations 3 and 4 are not negotiable and both parties are bound by them whether they like them or not.

b) i) The principal is legally obliged to give Lesley-Anne notice if he decides to terminate the agreement. Regulation 15 establishes compulsory minimum notice periods which the parties have to obey if they wish to end the agreement. The basic periods of notice are as follows:

- One month's notice during the first year of the agreement
- Two months' notice during the second year of the agreement
- Three months' notice during the third year or any subsequent year of the agreement

So, in total, Lesley-Anne would be entitled to seven months' notice since she has worked for the principal for seven years.

ii) The Agent's right to an indemnity or compensation is contained in Regulations 17 to 19. Indemnity and compensation are two different things as Lord MacFadyen in **Hardie Polymer Ltd v Polymerland Ltd (2001)** pointed out:

'Compensation and indemnity are distinct concepts. It is not surprising that there are elements of similarity between them, since they are alternative ways of making provision for the same situation, namely the termination of the agency contract.'

In **King v T Tunnock Ltd (2000)** the Court of Session made a distinction between compensation and indemnity:

'On any view indemnity and compensation, as set out by both Directive and Regulations, have different features … The agent is entitled to compensation for damage he suffers as a result of the termination of his relationship with the principal. The word "suffers" is in the present tense, which suggests that the point of time defining damage is the termination of the agency. Moreover, what is compensated is "the termination of his relations with his principal". The emphasis is not on his future loss but on the impact of the severance of his agency relationship with the principal. An agency generally has commercial value.'

According to Regulation 17, therefore, the agent will be entitled to be compensated by the principal where he has suffered loss as a result of the principal terminating the commercial agency agreement. Usually, according to Regulation 17(2), the agent shall be entitled to be compensated rather than indemnified, unless the commercial agency agreement specifies that she is entitled to receive an indemnity.

In the English High Court decision **Moore v Piretta PT Ltd (1998)** Deputy Judge John Mitting QC described the agent's claim to an indemnity in the following terms:

'The purpose of the indemnity seems to me to be to award a share of the goodwill built up by the efforts of the agent to him on the termination of the agency. Otherwise the whole benefit of that goodwill will remain with his former principal.'

An agent will be entitled to be compensated by the principal where he has suffered loss as a result of the principal terminating his agency agreement and he will be entitled to an indemnity where he has increased the number of the principal's customers or where he has dramatically increased the amount of the principal's business with existing customers.

It is likely that Lesley-Anne will be entitled to an indemnity to reflect her efforts in building up the principal's business. In terms of Regulation 17(4), the amount of the indemnity awarded to the agent shall not be greater than a figure equivalent to an indemnity for one year calculated from the commercial agent's average annual remuneration over the previous five years and, if the contract goes back less than five years, the indemnity shall be calculated on the average for the period in question (NB the question does not ask you to calculate the amount of an indemnity or compensation for that matter owed to Lesley-Anne).

It is important to note that the payment of an indemnity does not prevent the agent from seeking compensation or damages from the principal. Regulation 17(6) states that the agent shall be entitled to compensation for damages that he has suffered as a result of the principal ending the commercial agency agreement. Regulation 17(7) strongly suggests that the agent will have suffered loss or damage in one or both of the following situations:

- Loss of future commission by the agent

- The agent has been unable to recover any expenses which he properly incurred on the principal's behalf

The agent's claim for compensation should be lodged, however, within one year of the end of the agreement. If the agent's death has caused the agreement to end, then the agent's estate will not be prevented from pursuing the principal for any compensation or expenses owed.

For cases dealing with an agent's right to an indemnity or compensation see **Graham Page v Combined Shipping and Trading Co Ltd (1997)**, **Moore v Piretta PT Ltd (1998)**, **King v T. Tunnock Ltd (2000)**, **Duffen v FRABO *SpA* (2000)**, **Ingmar GB Ltd v Eaton Leonard Technologies Inc (2001)** and **Hardie Polymer Ltd v Polymerland Ltd (2001)**.

iii) Regulation 20 deals with restrictive covenants in commercial agency agreements. Firstly, in order for a restraint of trade clause to be valid, it must be in writing and it must cover the group of customers and goods to which the agent's work was connected. Secondly, the maximum amount of time that such clause can last for is two years after the end of the agency agreement. The clause in Lesley-Anne's agreements is, therefore, excessive and will be void.

iv) According to **Ingmar GB Ltd v Eaton Leonard Technologies Inc (2001)** the Regulations will apply even if the parties have attempted to exclude them by stating in their agreement that the agreement is governed by the law of a state which is not a member of the European Union.

8   a) General agents act for the principal in connection with all of his interests in a particular line of business. One example of a general agent is a solicitor. General agents can possess both actual and ostensible authority.

Special agents, on the other hand, have extremely limited authority. They usually act for the principal in one type of transaction only. An example of a special agent would be an estate agent. Special agents possess actual authority only.

See **Morrison v Statter (1885)** and **The Ocean Frost (1986)** for an illustration of general and special agents.

b) Where the third party is aware of the existence of the agent's principal, such a person is referred to as a disclosed principal. It does not matter whether the third party can name the principal personally (see **The Santa Carina (1977)**). It is important to determine whether the agent is acting for a disclosed or an undisclosed principal. Generally, an agent who acts for a disclosed principal plays no further part in proceedings when an agreement is eventually completed between the principal and the third party. Should a dispute arise in relation to the agreement, the agent – as long as he acted properly – will not be liable to the third party for the principal's failure to honour the agreement.

The position is more complicated where the agent has not revealed to the third party that he is acting for a principal. Should the principal fail to honour the agreement, the third party will, naturally enough, sue the agent. At this moment, the agent may then reveal the fact that he was acting as an a agent. It will be up to the third party whether he wishes to sue the principal or the agent for breach of contract. Once the third party makes this choice, such a decision will be final.

It is usually a sensible precaution on the agent's part to indicate to third parties that he is acting as an agent in order to avoid any potential liability in the future. It is widely understood that the initials pp at the end of a letter indicate that the signatory is acting as an agent and not acting in his personal capacity:

> Yours sincerely
> Alistair B Wylie
> pp The Business Law Consultancy

Therefore, Alistair B. Wylie is clearly indicating to anyone who receives this letter that he has signed the letter in his capacity as an agent of The Business Law Consultancy (see **Stewart v Shannessy (1900)**).

c) A *del credere* agent is an agent who introduces third parties to his principal and, critically, he promises to indemnify or compensate the principal if the contract does not go as planned and the principal suffers losses as a result (see **Couturier v Hastie (1856)**).

d) An agent can either be an employee or an independent contractor. An agent who is an employee will carry out services for the principal under a contract *of* service, whereas an independent contractor carries out services for the principal under a contract *for* services. It may be useful to think of a contract of service as an employment contract and, by way of a comparison, a contract for services involves a situation where the agent will hire out his services on an as required basis to the principal. A solicitor may serve as a useful example. If a solicitor works permanently for the legal services department of a local council, he will be an agent and an employee of the council. If, however, a solicitor is a partner in a private law firm and hires out his services to private clients as and when they require his advice and assistance, he will be acting as an agent, but he is an independent contractor and not an employee of his private clients.

Not all employees, of course, can call themselves agents of their employer. It should be remembered that the most important function of an agent is to bind his principal into contracts with third parties. Many employees will simply not have the power to do this. It is highly unlikely that someone who works on a factory production line and has absolutely no dealings with third parties would be in a position to describe himself as his employer's agent.

9 The agency relationship, like any contract, can be terminated in a number of different ways. This can be done by:
- Mutual agreement
- Principal withdrawing the agent's authority
- The agent withdrawing from the relationship
- Bankruptcy of the principal
- Death or insanity
- The expiry of a fixed term contract

In relation to a partnership, a former partner in order to escape liability will have to publicise his departure from the firm in the *Edinburgh Gazette* and this is regarded as giving proper notice to third parties of his changed role in relation to the business.

The termination of a commercial agency agreement is governed by the rules contained in Regulations 14 to 16 of the Commercial Agency Regulations 1993. As we have seen, Regulation 15 establishes compulsory minimum notice periods which the parties have to obey if they wish to end the agreement.

10 There are a number of different business organisations which exist under Scots Law:

- Sole Trader
- Partnerships (Partnership act 1890)
- Limited Partnerships (Limited Partnership Act 1907)
- Limited Liability Partnerships (Limited Liability Partnership Act 2000)
- Corporate Bodies (Companies Act 1985)

It is very important to be able to differentiate between types of business because they are all governed by different rules.

11 Section 24 of the Partnership Act 1890 will provide Cameron, Howard and Iain with many of the answers to the questions that they are asking. It should be stressed from the beginning, however, that the Partnership Act 1890 only provides guidelines which the partners are free to ignore if they so wish. In theory, the partners are largely left to run their business as they see fit. If the partners have chosen to depart from any of the rules contained in the Partnership Act 1890, the courts will have to respect this decision.

a) As regards the personal liability of each partner to the firm's creditors should the business run up debts or should it fail completely, all the partners are expected to contribute equally towards any losses that the firm may suffer. In other words, the three partners are jointly and severally liable for the firm's debts or losses. This means that the partners can be sued collectively (i.e. as a group) or individually by the firm's creditors. The firm's creditors are supposed to sue the firm first and it is only if the firm has no assets to meet its liabilities that the creditors should move against the partners. All partners can expect to share equally in the profits that a partnership makes.

b) Section 5 of the Partnership Act 1890 states that a partner in a firm is considered to be an agent of the firm and of his fellow partners. A partner will, therefore, have implied, actual authority to bind the firm and his fellow partners in respect of contracts negotiated and entered into with third parties in the usual course of the firm's business. Furthermore, according to Section 24 of the 1890 Act, all partners have the right to participate in the running of the partnership.

c) Section 24 states that All the partners must first agree before any new partner can join the partnership.

d) The relationship of the partners is characterised by its fiduciary nature and it is important that the partners disclose all material facts that could affect the partnership. Such material facts would include situations where some or all the partners are participating in other business ventures – especially rival business ventures. Generally speaking, the partners will not be allowed to participate in rival business ventures without first having obtained the consent of their fellow partners, which in many situations will not be forthcoming. If a partner goes ahead and participates in a rival business venture without informing his fellow partners, he may well be making secret profits with all the consequences that this entails. The Partnership Act 1890 spells out the fiduciary duties of a partner in the following ways:

1 Every partner must keep proper accounts when handling and receiving partnership funds on behalf of his fellow partners. A partner is also under a duty to inform his fellow partners about any matter which may affect the firm (Section 28).

2 Every partner must inform his fellow partners of any profit made or benefit received as a result of his position as a partner or as a result of using the firm's property or assets (Section 29).

3 Any partner who competes against the firm by running another business without having been given permission by his fellow partners will have to hand over all profits made in the course of the competing business to the firm (Section 30).

e) Sections 10, 11 and 12 of the Partnership Act impose the burden of vicarious liability on the firm for any delicts or negligent acts which are committed by the partners. This means that the firm will be liable to a third party if a partner injures the third party or if damage is caused to the third party's property while the partner is acting in the course of the firm's business,. It is important to stress that the firm will not be liable where one partner causes loss or injury to a fellow partner while acting in the course of the partnership business. In such a situation, the injured partner would have to sue the partner who had committed the wrongful act in his personal capacity.

f) The rules concerning termination of partnership are contained in Sections 32 to 35 of the Partnership Act 1890.

If a partnership was created for a fixed period of time, the business comes to an end when this period expires. The members of a firm may set up a business which is to operate for, say, five years (Section 32). Once this five-year period has passed, the business is at an end. However, there is nothing to stop the partners continuing in business together after the expiry of the five-year period if they are so minded.

If the firm was set up to achieve a particular goal, it will come to an end when this purpose is accomplished (Section 32).

The death of a partner dissolves the firm (Section 33), but Iain, Cameron and Howard have agreed that the partnership will not necessarily be dissolved due to the death of one of them.

The bankruptcy of a partner also dissolves the firm. The partnership agreement usually provides that the business shall continue to operate with the participation of the solvent partners. This means that the dissolution is, again, only a technical one, and the bankrupt partner's share is paid out to his trustee in bankruptcy. The partnership agreement must address the possibility of a member's bankruptcy occurring in the future so that the firm can continue to operate in these circumstances. It is no use agreeing to continue to keep the business running after the bankruptcy of one of the partners has occurred, if this eventuality is not covered by the partnership agreement (Section 33).

If a partner's share in the partnership comes under the control of a creditor to whom the partner owes a private debt, the remaining solvent partners of the firm can exercise an option to dissolve the business (Section 33). The Partnership Act 1890 does not indicate whether this can be done by a single partner, or by a majority of the partners or whether such a decision would have to be unanimous.

If the operation of the partnership becomes illegal, the business will be dissolved (Section 34).

A partner may apply to the courts so that an order for the dissolution of the partnership can be issued (Section 35) in the following circumstances: a partner suffers from some mental disorder or insanity; a partner suffers from some permanent incapacity; a partner conducts himself in a way that is harmful to the continued operation of the business; a partner persistently commits a breach of the partnership agreement or conducts himself in a way that it would be unreasonable to expect the other partners to continue working with him; where the business can only be carried on at a loss; or where the court thinks that it would be just and equitable that the partnership should be dissolved.

Under Section 17 of the Partnership Act, new partners joining the firm will not be responsible for any partnership debts or wrongful acts committed by the business that were run up or occurred before their involvement in the firm. Similarly, a partner who has left the firm will cease to have any responsibility for business liabilities after his departure. A former partner in order to escape liability will have to publicise his departure from the firm in the *Edinburgh Gazette* and this is regarded as giving proper notice to third parties of his changed role in relation to the business. It is worth pointing out that former partners continue to be liable for business debts or for wrongful acts committed by the partnership which occurred during their involvement with the firm.

g) Section 24 states that the partners can reach a decision by majority vote. However, any changes to the nature of the partnership agreement must be agreed by all of the partners. Section 25 prevents a majority of partners from expelling a fellow partner from the firm, unless this power is part of the contract of partnership. If such a power of expulsion exists, the partners who wish to make use of it must be seen to be acting in good faith.

12　A limited partnership allows the firm to have silent or limited partners who take no part in the day-to-day running of the firm's business and, furthermore, these individuals enjoy limited liability. This type of business is governed by the Limited Partnerships Act 1907. Unlike a traditional partnership, this type of business must be registered with the Registrar of Companies in Edinburgh. The following information must be supplied to the Registrar:

- The name of the limited partnership

- A brief description of the type of business that it carries on

- The location of its main office

- The full names of each of the partners

- A statement, if appropriate, of how long the partnership is to last and the date upon which the business began

- A statement that the partnership is limited and who the limited partners are

- The amount of each limited partner's contribution to the business

The Act allows at least one general partner and one limited partner to form a business. However, there must always be at least one general partner at any time. The limited partner is effectively a silent or a sleeping partner and plays no part in the day-to-day running of the business. In an ordinary partnership, all the partners operate under the burden of unlimited liability where they will all be responsible for the firm's debts. This is not the case in a limited partnership, where the limited partner will lose only the amount of money that he advanced to the firm. If the limited partner becomes involved in the daily management of the business, his liability for

business debts or delicts which were the responsibility of the business would become unlimited. Limited partners see their role as that of an investor wishing to make a profit. They do not want to be bogged down with the responsibilities of management. The 1907 Act makes it quite clear that a majority of the general partners will decide the aims and the policies of the business. A limited partner will not even be able to oppose the introduction of a new general partner if the existing general partners have made up their minds on this matter.

Even the death, lunacy or bankruptcy of a limited partner will not mean that the partnership has to be ended as with an ordinary firm. It will be the general partners who will decide when the business is to be ended. The major disadvantage of being a limited partner is that it will not be possible for such a person to withdraw his investment while the partnership is still trading. The general partners may allow a limited partner to transfer or assign his investment in the business to a third party, the public must be notified by the placing of an advertisement to this effect in the *Edinburgh Gazette.* These types of businesses tend to be encountered rarely because private limited companies are seen as a more popular means of investing money.

The relationship between the general partners is governed by the Partnership Act 1890 and the associated case law in mostly the same way as would be found in an ordinary firm.

13　The Limited Liability Partnership Act 2000 came into force on 6 April 2001. The Act introduces a new type of business vehicle in addition to companies, traditional partnerships, limited partnerships and sole traders. According to Section 1 of the Act, a limited liability partnership or LLP is a corporate body which has completely separate legal personality from that of its members. Section 1 also makes it very clear that the law of partnership does not apply to LLPs.

A business trading as a limited liability partnership will be immediately recognisable by the use of the initials LLP after its name.

It was originally thought that LLPs would be attractive business organisations for existing professional partnerships such as law firms, surveyors and accountants. In many situations, though they are exceptions, such businesses have faced difficulties in trying to run limited companies because of the rules laid down by their professional associations. The major advantage of setting an LLP for existing partnerships is that the members can limit their liability. In a traditional style partnership, it will be remembered that should the business fail and run up huge debts, the members will face the burden of unlimited liability. This effectively means that creditors of the partnership can and will pursue the members to their last penny. The partner's personal assets, for example, a home, savings, a car and other valuables will be eyed up by creditors. Existing limited companies, however, are prevented from re-registering as LLPs.

Section 2 of the Act contains the rules for establishing an LLP: it must have at least two members who have signed an incorporation document; the founding members of the LLP must register this incorporation document and other necessary documentation with the Registrar of Companies; and a fee of £95 is also payable by the proposed members of the LLP to the Registrar of Companies.

If an LLP operates with just one member for more than six months, the business loses the protection of limited liability and the remaining member will have complete responsibility for any business debts or liabilitites.

An LLP must be registered with the Registrar of Companies who will issue a certificate of incorporation signifying that the business has complied with all necessary legal requirements (Sections 2 and 3).

It is very important that those people who are involved in running an LLP should not be called partners. The proper term for these individuals is members. Section 4 states that the first members of the LLP are those individuals whose names appear on the incorporation document which is delivered to the Registrar. At least two members must be 'designated members' and their names must be given to the Registrar as such. Designated members have additional responsibilities in comparison to the general members of an LLP. The designated members will be responsible for administrative and filing duties which would normally be carried out by a director or a company secretary in a company.

Although there is no legal requirement for LLP members to commit anything to paper, Section 5 of the Act makes it clear that it would be a very sensible practice for the LLP members to draw up a detailed members' agreement (currently known as a partnership agreement). This agreement would deal with all the important issues that the business will face.

According to Section 6, the members of an LLP are to be regarded as the agents of the business. If an individual ceases to be an LLP member, this fact must be communicated to third parties dealing with the business and, additionally, there is a legal requirement to inform the Registrar of Companies. Failure to inform third parties dealing with the business that someone is no longer an LLP member means that the former member will continue to be regarded as being involved in the business.

Section 7 describes a number of situations where an individual will lose the right to be involved in the affairs of the LLP as a member.

An LLP is classed as a completely separate legal person from its members and the members enjoy limited liability, unlike partners in a traditional firm.

Any changes in the membership of an LLP must be notified to the Registrar of Companies within 14 days. When there is any change in the name or residential address of a member, notice of this fact must be given to the registrar within 28 days. The Registrar does not require notice where individuals either become or cease to be designated members of the LLP. Failure to comply with these notice requirements is a criminal offence (Section 9).

LLPs will have to publish financial accounts containing the same sorts of detail as a similarly sized limited company and these accounts and an annual return will have to be submitted to the Registrar of Companies (Sections 10 to 13).

14 Someone or a group of people will often be required to set up a company and comply with all the necessary registration procedures. Practical steps will have to be taken by such an individual or individuals such as buying or leasing property in order to have premises for a registered office, entering into contracts with third parties in order to buy or lease equipment that will be used by the new company or entering into contracts of employment with prospective employees of the new business. Clearly, it would not make good business sense to wait until all the legal requirements of the registration process had been complied with before attending to these important matters. The sooner everything is in place, the sooner the new business can begin to trade and, hopefully, begin to make profits for its members.

A person who takes care of these matters before the company is formed is referred to as a promoter. In **Twycross v Grant (1877)**, a promoter was defined as someone who undertakes to form a company with reference to a given project, and to set it going, and who takes the necessary steps to accomplish that purpose. A promoter of the company is not an agent of the company (see **Tinnevelly Sugar Refining Co v Mirrlees, Watson & Yaryan Co Ltd (1894)**). Section 36(4) of the Companies Act 1985 makes the legal position of promoters very clear. They are not to be regarded as agents of a non-existent company. As a promoter is not an agent of the new company, he has no right to be paid for his services. In reality, many promoters are likely to be directors or members of the new company and, therefore, they have an interest in setting the company up. In any case, the new board of directors may have powers in the Articles of Association to pay the promoter or reimburse him for his expenses.

The downside of being a promoter is that they are personally responsible for any contracts that they enter into with third parties. The company cannot sue or be sued in relation to contracts that were formed before it was registered. This is a dangerous situation for the promoter because it means that the company need not reimburse him for any expenses that he is out of pocket as a result of entering into contracts with third parties. A promoter is regarded as having a fiduciary relationship with the yet non-existent company. This means that the promoter cannot use his position to make a profit unless the directors or members of the new company are aware of this and are comfortable with this situation. This means that a promoter will have to account for everything that he has done in his role. It is not beyond the realms of possibility that the new board of directors or members might sue a promoter to regain any secret profit that he has made from his activities.

A promoter can always try to escape personal liability for contracts with third parties by insisting that third parties agree not to sue him in the event that the company fails to honour the contract once it has been registered. Alternatively, a promoter may insist that the contracts will only take effect when the new company is legally recognised and that such a contract will be between the new company and the third party.

15   All limited companies, whether private or public, must be registered under the Companies Act. This means that the company becomes an independent legal person in its own right, legally separate from its members and officers, a person recognised by the law, a person capable of having rights and taking on duties which the courts will recognise and enforce.

When a company with limited liability becomes a separate legal person this process is referred to as 'the veil of incorporation'.

It is worth remembering that separate corporate personality means that: the company can raise legal actions in its own right and be the subject of legal actions against it; the company has legal capacity and becomes a party to the contracts which it enters into; the company can exercise ownership over its property; the company continues to exist despite changes in its membership; and the company's members enjoy limited liability.

The concept of separate corporate personality was forcefully recognised by the House of Lords in the case of **Salomon v Salomon & Co Ltd (1897)**. A court will ignore the concept of separate corporate personality in the following circumstances:

1   In a public company, there must be at least two members. If, for a period of more than six months, the company operates with a single member this individual becomes personally responsible for all debts of the business.

2   If a company was set up so that the members can carry out an illegal activity, they will not be allowed to benefit from the Salomon rule.

3   In times of war, a company that is controlled by citizens of an enemy state will not be allowed to continue trading for the duration of hostilities. Normally, the law is not interested in the nationalities of individual members, but in times of war this becomes a very important issue.

4   Company officers, for example directors and company secretaries, will have to be especially careful when signing cheques in their personal capacity and where third parties will not be aware that they are doing so on behalf of the company. Additionally, the company officer can make an error when he writes the name of the company on a cheque that will be given to the third party. In both situations, the company officer will be personally responsible to the third party if the company does not meet the debt that the cheque represents.

When the concept of separate corporate personality is sometimes ignored by the courts, this is known as 'lifting the veil of incorporation'.

16   a)   According to Section 14 of the Companies Act 1985, the Memorandum of Association and the Articles of Association are together to be regarded as forming a binding contract between the members themselves and between the members and the company.

Section 14 has, therefore, a number of consequences for members of a company:

1   If a member feels that one of his membership rights that he enjoys under the Memorandum and the Articles has been ignored or abused by the company, he can raise a legal action against the company and force it to recognise these rights (see **Wood v Odessa Waterworks Co (1889)**).

2   The company can raise a legal action against members of the company who breach the rules regulating membership as laid out in the Memorandum and the Articles (see **Hickman v Kent or Romney Marsh Sheep Breeders' Association (1915)**).

3   The members can sue one another for breach of the Memorandum and the Articles (see **Rayfield v Hands (1960)**).

4   The rights given to members under the Memorandum and the Articles cannot be enforced by non-members or where the member is effectively acting as an outsider (see **Eley v Positive Life Assurance Co Ltd (1876)**).

b) i) Stephanie's position as a Director is under threat not her position as a shareholder which remains unaffected. Stephanie cannot rely upon Section 14 of the Companies Act 1985 to try and prevent her removal as a Director because this right does not relate to her role as a shareholder (see **Eley v Positive Life Assurance Co Ltd (1876)**).

ii) Emma must use the company's arbitration procedure and the company can raise a legal action against members of the company who breach the rules regulating membership as laid out in the Memorandum and the Articles by raising a legal action at the Court of Session (see **Hickman v Kent or Romney Marsh Sheep Breeders' Association (1915)**). Section 14 of the Companies Act 1985 means that the arbitration procedure forms part of a binding contract between Emma and her fellow shareholders and the company.

iii) Gillian's uncles must purchase her shares as they are bound to do so because the provisions in the company's Articles form a binding contract in terms of Section 14 of the Companies Act 1985 (see **Rayfield v Hands (1960)**).

iv) The shareholders will have to establish whether they are entitled to receive debentures in terms of the company's Articles of Association. If so, they can raise an action against the company in terms of Section 14 of the Companies Act 1985 to force the payment of dividends. However, if the payment of dividends is purely discretionary, the company may well have the right to issue debentures as an alternative (see **Wood v Odessa Waterworks Co (1889)**).

17 a) Clause 1: The name clause – Any name can be chosen for the business as long as the last word is 'limited', 'ltd' or 'plc'. A register of names is maintained by the Registrar of Companies at Companies House and names must comply with the Business Names Act 1985 (see **Exxon v Exxon Insurance Consultants (1982)**).

Clause 2: The registered office clause – Every company must have a registered office as soon as it commences trading or within 14 days of its incorporation, whichever is earlier. The memo must state whether the registered office is in Scotland or England.

Clause 3: The objects clause – This defines the purposes for which the company is incorporated. Prior to the Companies Act 1989, if a company was engaged in any activities or contracts not covered by the objects clause then these contracts were considered *ultra vires* i.e. outwith the powers of the company and could not be enforced by either the third party or the company.

Clause 4: The limitation of liability clause – This is a statement to confirm that the liability of the members is limited.

Clause 5: The capital clause – This states the amount of nominal or authorised share capital and its division into shares of a fixed amount.

Clause 6: The association clause – This states that the members wish to form a corporate body.

b) i) Ashbury is banking on the fact that its objects clause does not cover the construction of a ferry. The objects clause, of course, defines the purposes for which the company is incorporated. Prior to the Companies Act 1989, if a company was engaged in any activities or contracts not covered by the objects clause then these contracts were considered *ultra vires* i.e. outwith the powers of the company and could not be enforced by either the third party or the company. The *ultra vires* rule was originally established to protect potential and existing members of a company.

Companies were forced to list all of their business activities and they were not allowed to become involved in any business transaction which was not on the list. This meant that members could control the directors and prevent them from entering into contracts which might be regarded as risky in some way. More basically, all the members knew exactly what line of business the company was in and as long as the company confined itself to these activities everyone in theory was happy. Since the 1989 Act, companies are now allowed to state that its objects are to carry on a business as a 'general commercial company' meaning that it can be involved in any trade or business whatsoever. The effect of the changes introduced by the Companies Act 1989 is that Tartan Transport can enforce the contract against Ashbury which will not be allowed to rely upon the *ultra vires* rule.

ii) The consequences for Donna and her fellow directors is that directors and officers of the company may still be sued in their personal capacity by the company if they carry out any act or enter into any transaction which strictly speaking would be forbidden by the company's objects clause. Donna and her fellow directors have gone beyond the scope of their actual authority and their principal, the company, can sue them for breach of this authority.

18 Clearly, the members of a limited company and those of a public limited company enjoy the protection of limited liability in the event that either business organisation becomes insolvent. However, there are clear differences between these two business organisations.

The main characteristics of a private limited company are:

1 Company name must end in 'limited' or 'ltd'

2 The articles of association of a private limited company may provide for a right of pre-emption so that when a member wishes to sell or to transfer ownership of his shares he must first offer them to existing members

3 There is no minimum capital requirement

4 The shares in a private limited company cannot be traded or listed on the stock exchange

5 Only one director is required

6 In terms of the Companies (Single Member Private Limited Companies) Regulations 1992, a private company limited by shares or by guarantee need only have one member

7 There is no upper age limit for directors

8 Audited accounts must be produced within 10 months of the year end

9 Trading can start as soon as a Certificate of Incorporation is obtained

The main characteristics of a public limited company are:

1 The company name must end in 'public limited company' or 'plc'

2 Members must be free to transfer their shares as they please

3 A public company must have minimum issued share capital of at least £50,000

4 Shares can be listed on the stock exchange and can be traded

5 There must be at least two directors

6 There must be at least two members

7 Directors must retire when they reach the age of 70

8 Audited accounts must be produced within seven months of the year end

9 After incorporation, trading cannot begin until a trading certificate is issued by the Registrar of Companies upon satisfaction of the nominal value of share capital. This trading certificate is referred to as a section 117 certificate after the relevant section of the Companies Act 1985 which makes possession of such a document compulsory for public limited companies. Public companies cannot begin trading without having been issued with a section 117 certificate

Chapter 6

1 a) If you are an employee i.e. you have a contract of service, you are theoretically in a much better position than someone who has a contract for services i.e. an independent contractor. This is an absolutely critical distinction in UK employment law and one that we shall return to time and time again in this particular area. If you are an employee the law gives you greater protection and more benefits that you would not receive if you were merely an independent contractor for services. Some of the benefits/protections to which employees are entitled include: statutory protection against unfair dismissal; entitlement to compensation if they are made redundant; a statutory right to a minimum period of notice of termination of their employment contracts; rights to maternity pay and leave; rights to paid paternity leave; the right to time-off for public duties; the right to statutory sick pay; and access to important social security and welfare benefits.

It is worth emphasising that those individuals who work as independent contractors (under a contract for service) are highly unlikely to receive any of these benefits. So, it follows that if a particular contract comes to an end, an independent contractor, for example, will not be entitled to a redundancy payment. However, employers should be aware that other classes of people in the workforce, known by the catch-all term 'worker', have been given rights under a variety of statutes (see Sex Discrimination Act 1975, the Working Time Regulations 1998, the Part-time Workers Regulations 2000, the Employment Equality (Sexual Orientation) Regulations 2003 and the Employment Equality (Religion or Belief) Regulations 2003).

b) Over many years, British judges have developed a number of different tests in an attempt to determine whether someone works under a contract of service or a contract for services. However, the British courts have not always applied these tests in a way that makes sense to the lay person and even to lawyers. These tests include the: Control Test (see **Mersey Docks and Harbour Board v Coggins & Griffith (Liverpool) Ltd (1947)**); the Economic Reality Test (see **Ready Mixed Concrete (South East) Ltd v Minister of Pensions (1968)**); and the Organisation or Integration Test (see **Hall v Lorimer (1992)**).

These tests are different tools that a judge can use to determine whether a contract of service or a contract for services exists.

c) Following the decision of the House of Lords in **Carmichael v National Power PLC (2000)**, it is highly likely that Leigh, Lloyd and Laurence have a contract for services with the Metropolitan University of Aberdeen as guides in its Wilsonian Museum. In other words, the three individuals are not employees of the University. Therefore, none of them will be able to take the University to an Employment Tribunal alleging unfair dismissal.

One area of the law that causes particular difficulty for employers are contracts involving the use of casual and atypical workers. Casual and atypical are being increasingly used by employers and one of the main concerns here is whether these individuals should be given the benefit of employment rights. Usually, the employment status of such workers is resolved by asking a relatively simple question i.e. when the employer offers such an individual work is s/he bound to carry out the work for the employer? If the answer is in the positive, then the worker is likely to be an employee and not an independent contractor for services. In more recent times, the courts have also tended to stress the importance of a mutuality of obligation between an employer and employee. In other words, the employee is under a duty to

accept work when the employer requires his services. Leigh, Lloyd and Laurence are casual workers – they are not under an obligation to accept work that the University offers them.

2 **a)** It may now be said that true freedom of contract hardly exists at all as far as the employer is concerned. This doctrine is based on the idea that the parties are free to choose the terms and conditions which will be contained in the final version of the employment contract. The idea of freedom of contract also presupposes that genuine negotiations have taken place between the parties. It is debateable whether many employees ever really enjoyed the notion (let alone the practice) of freedom of contract. In any case, Parliament has intervened in so many ways that the employer has lost the right to dictate some of the most important terms of the contract.

Examples of parliamentary intervention include:

- The Employment Rights Act 1996
- Working Time Regulations 1998
- National Minimum Wage Act 1998
- The Employment Relations Act 1999
- The Maternity and Parental Leave etc. Regulations 1999
- The Maternity and Parental Leave (Amendment) Regulations 2001
- The Maternity and Parental Leave (Amendment) Regulations 2002
- The Employment Act 2002

Furthermore, many employment law provisions are the product of European Union rules which employers are not allowed to ignore: the Equal Treatment Directive and the Part-time Workers (Prevention of Less Favourable Treatment) Regulations 2000.

b) Helen's employer may argue that the parties to a contract are entitled to decide the terms of the employment contract. However, his proposals would include a breach of the Working Time Regulations 1998, a breach of the National Minimum Wage Act 1998 and a breach of the Maternity and Parental Leave etc Regulations 1999, the Maternity and Parental Leave (Amendment) Regulations 2001, the Maternity and Parental Leave (Amendment) Regulations 2002 and the Employment Act 2002.

3 **a)** Vicarious liability can arise where there is a contract of service meaning that the employer may be vicariously liable for the delicts or negligence of an employee. This means that the employee can be liable for harm that he did not directly cause. An employer can only be liable for the negligent acts of an employee not an independent contractor (see **Mersey Docks and Harbour Board v Coggins & Griffith (Liverpool) Ltd (1947)**). Vicarious liability of the employer is another area where it is very important to distinguish between an employee and an independent contractor.

For an employer to be vicariously liable, the harm must have been caused by the employee while within the scope of his employment. The courts will often look to see whether or not the employee was acting within the scope of his employment and this can be a difficult point to establish.

Generally, if the employee was acting for the purpose, protection or enhancement of the employer's business and was not using his employer's time for his own purposes then the employer would be held vicariously liable if the employee committed a delict.

Furthermore, an employer may be vicariously liable for the acts of an employee even if the employee:

- Did what he was employed to do but carrried out these functions in a negligent or unauthorised way

- Was negligent whilst doing something he was not authorised to do

- Committed the act outwith working hours

- Commits an assault in the course of the employment but only with a contract of service

See the following cases for examples of an employer's vicarious liability: **Century Insurance Co v Northern Ireland Transport Board (1942)**, **Conway v George Wimpey & Co (1951)**, **Williams v Hemphill (1966)** and **Rose v Plenty (1976)**.

Vicarious liability means that an employer and an employee are both jointly and severally liable for the negligent acts or omissions of the employee that result in harm being caused to third parties (see **Lister v Romford Ice and Cold Storage (1957)**).

b) Iain is an independent contractor brought in by the Council's education authority to carry out a job. The education authority is not responsible for Iain's actions (see **Mersey Docks and Harbour Board v Coggins & Griffith (Liverpool) Ltd (1947)**). Iain has been negligent and, therefore, the victims of his negligent acts or omissions should sue his employer – Sparks Ltd. Iain and Sparks Ltd are, of course, jointly and severally liable for any negligent acts or omissions which cause loss or injury.

Vicarious liability only becomes an issue when a contract of service exists. Generally speaking, individuals are not responsible for the negligent actions of an independent contractor (an individual acting under a contract for services).

4 a) A written statement of terms and conditions of employment should contain the following:

1 The employer's name

2 The employee's name

3 The date of commencement of employment and the period of any continuous employment

4 Wages/salary details

5 Details of working hours

6 Holiday entitlement/pay and entitlement to accrued holiday pay upon termination of the employment contract

7 Entitlement to sick pay

8 Pensionable service

9 Notice requirements

10 Job title or brief description of the job

11 Whether the job is permanent or for a fixed-term duration

12 The location(s) of the employee's place of work

13 Collective agreements and how they affect the employment contract

14 In situations where the employee may have to work outside the UK for more than a month, the length of such time, the currency in which wages are to be paid, details of any additional payments and benefits and terms about return to the UK

15 Details of the employer's disciplinary code should also be brought to the employee's attention in the written statement of particulars or should refer to a document containing the code to which the employee can readily access

A written statement covers a wide range of issues. To reiterate, such a statement must be provided to the employee within two months of the commencement of employment. The statement may be given to the employee by instalments, but a complete statement must be in the employee's possession within the two-month deadline.

If the employer and the employee decide to alter any terms and conditions of employment, a new written statement must be issued no later than one month after the changes have been introduced.

b) Under Section 1 of the Employment Rights Act 1996, employees must be issued with a written statement of the terms and particulars of their contract of employment. It should be noted that this statement is not the contract of employment. Merely, it provides general information about the nature of the relationship and the extent of the main provisions of the agreement. Such a statement must be issued to the employee within two months of the start of the employment contract. If the employer does not give the employee a copy of a written statement of terms and particulars, the employee can take him to an Employment Tribunal for the purpose of forcing him to issue such a statement. However, this is generally an unusual course of action on the part of the employee.

c) In terms of Section 1 of the Employment Rights Act 1996, Jennifer should have been issued with a written statement within two months of her commencing employment at the restaurant. Mark, her employer, has failed to do this. Furthermore, it is likely that Jennifer has been dismissed for continually requesting that she be issued with a written statement. Despite the fact that Jennifer has less than a year's continuous service with her employer, she can lodge a claim with the Office of Employment Tribunals alleging that she has been unfairly dismissed. She must lodge her Employment Tribunal claim within three months of the deadline for the employer to issue her with a written statement. In dismissal claims which involve the issuing of a written statement, the employee does not need to have a year's continuous service (Employment Rights Act 1996). Now, in terms of the Employment Act 2002, an employer who neglects to issue an employee with a written statement may be ordered by an Employment Tribunal to pay an employee four weeks' wages in respect of any failure to issue the statement.

5 a) The contract of employment can be influenced by the following sources – statute law, European law, the common law rights and duties of the parties, collective agreements, the written statement of terms and particulars of employment, handbooks, codes of practice and other documents issued by the employer.

b) Sometimes, employers will prefer to have a situation where terms and conditions of employment can be negotiated collectively with a large number of employees rather than by individual negotiations. Such arrangements are known as 'collective agreements'.

This arrangement allows groups of workers to be employed on identical or fairly similar terms and conditions of employment. Such agreements are usually found in workplaces where there is a recognised trade union which can negotiate with the employer.

It is important to realise that such agreements do not bind the employer and the trade union. It is important to stress that the trade union is not acting as an agent of the employees and, therefore, any agreement negotiated by the trade union with the employer are not legally enforceable against either the employer or the employees. If these agreements are to be enforceable, they must be made part of the employees' contracts of employment. This means that when changes are made to employees' contracts as a result of negotiations under the collective agreement, they will be automatically incorporated into the employees' contracts.

It is probably advisable for the employer to include an express provision in a contract of employment which mentions the collective agreement and the results of any negotiations concluded under such an agreement i.e. the fact that changes to contracts of employment automatically take effect upon the successful conclusion of negotiations between the employer and the trade union (see **City of Edinburgh Council v Brown (1999)** and **John Anderson v Pringle of Scotland (1998)**).

c) United Scottish Airlines has unilaterally departed from the provisions of the Collective Agreement which govern redundancy situations. This Agreement forms part of Shirley's contract of employment. Shirley could, therefore take action against her employer to have the provisions of the redundancy policy enforced (see **City of Edinburgh Council v Brown (1999)** and **John Anderson v Pringle of Scotland (1998)**). However, the employee in **John Anderson** forced his employer to abide by the terms of the Collective Agreement which governed redundancy, but ultimately this did not save his job. If Shirley was unfairly selected for redundancy, she always has the option of lodging a claim for unfair dismissal with the Office of Employment Tribunals in terms of the Employment Rights Act 1996.

6 a) The employer's duties under the contract of employment include – the payment of wages, providing work, indemnifying employees, treating employees with trust and respect and to take reasonable care for the safety of employees.

The common law duties of an employee are to provide personal service, to provide loyal service, to obey lawful and reasonable orders and to take reasonable care in the exercise of the employment.

NB All that this question asks is for an outline of the employer's and employee's duties only and not a full discussion of them.

b') I) Samir's employers have breached the duty of trust and confidence which they owe to their employees. An employer who breaches the duty of trust and confidence by running his business in a corrupt and dishonest manner and this conduct later destroys or seriously damages an employee's future career prospects may have to pay stigma damages to the employee (see **Malik v BCCI SA (1997)**). Generally, the employer owes a duty of care not to damage the employee's future career prospects (see also **Spring v Guardian Royal Assurance plc (1994)** and **Bartholomew v London Borough of Hackney (1999)**).

ii) William has a duty to pay his employees their wages, but he does not have a duty to provide them with work (see **Turner v Sawdon & Co (1901)** and **Collier v Sunday Referee Publishing Co Ltd (1940)**). An employer is also under a statutory duty not to make any unauthorised deductions from wages (see the Employment Rights Act 1996).

iii) Shona's employer is breaching its duty to take reasonable care for the safety of employees. An employer must take reasonable care to ensure that the work is properly and safely organised and an employer must take reasonable care to provide a safe working environment, but this does not mean that he has to ensure that employees are protected from all possible risks. For cases illustrating the employer's duty to take reasonable care for the safety of employees see **Latimer v AEC (1952)**, **Withers v Perry Chain (1961)** and **Walker v Northumberland County Council (1995)**. Furthermore, it is worth noting that the employer's common duties which aim to protect the health and safety of employees establishes a regime of civil liability. In other words, should the employer breach these duties, he will most likely face a civil action by the injured employee who will be attempting to recover compensation.

An employer may use two defences if a delictual claim is brought by an employee that he is in breach of one of his common law duties: contributory negligence and *volenti non fit injuria* (those who wish an injury cannot be injured).

The Health and Safety at Work Act 1974, on the other hand, makes an employer criminally liable if he fails to take reasonably practicable steps to protect the health and safety of his employees. An employer will, therefore, face criminal penalties in a criminal court for breaches of the Act. This means that an employer could face both a criminal action and a civil action for damages where he has neglected to obey the criminal law and the common law regulating the employees' health and safety.

iv) Norrie is being ordered to take part in an illegal activity and, therefore, Norrie's employer would not be able to argue that he has given this employee a lawful order. Norrie would be within his rights to refuse to obey this order (see **Ottoman Bank v Chakarian (1930)**, **Bouzourou v Ottoman Bank (1930)**, **Morrish v Henleys (Folkestone) Ltd (1973)** and **Macari v Celtic Football and Athletic Company Ltd (1999)**).

v) Gerry must not attempt to cheat his employer or to behave in a dishonest fashion towards his employer. This is clearly what he is doing by competing against his employer in order to make secret profits (see **Reading v Attorney-General (1951)**).

Furthermore, an employee is expected to serve his employer loyally which means that he must not do anything that would harm his employer's business by carrying out work for business rivals. Even work that the employee carries out in his own time may actually interfere with the employer's interests – especially if these activities could be viewed as harming the employer's business. The employee should not divulge any trade secrets or business secrets to his employer's rivals that he has acquired in the course of his employment (see **Forster & Sons Ltd v Suggett (1918)** and **Robb v Green (1895)**).

vi) David owes an implied duty of care to his employer and he committed an act of negligence by leaving the keys in the vehicles ignition. Breach of the duty of care may arise in situations where the employer is held liable to an innocent third party for the negligent actions of his employee. The employer (or more likely his insurance company) can always exercise the right to sue the employee for breach of his duty of care. Insurance companies appear to have an informal agreement that they will not pursue the employee for breach of his duty should they have to pay out to his employer under an insurance policy. This has meant in practice, that these types of cases tend to be few and far between, but not unheard of (see **Lister v**

Romford Ice and Cold Storage (1957) and Janata Bank v Ahmed (1981)).

7 a) The contract of employment can be terminated like any other contractual agreement, for example, material breach, mutual agreement, frustration, operation of law, completion of task and expiry of a fixed-term contract. However, it should be remembered that the Employment Rights Act 1996 lays down minimum periods of notice that the employer must adhere to when he wishes to terminate the contract.

b) Hannah's employer is treating the contract of employment as frustrated. Frustration occurs when the contract becomes impossible to perform or further performance becomes radically different from the agreement that was originally contemplated by the parties (**Lord Radcliffe: Davis Contractors Ltd v Fareham UDC (1956)**). The Employment Appeal Tribunal sitting in England has stated that frustration of contract in employment cases means that the employee loses his entitlement either to notice or to a payment in lieu of notice (**G F Sharp & Co Ltd v McMillan (1998)**) and, if this decision was followed in Scotland, Hannah would not be entitled to a period of notice or to a payment in lieu of notice.

8 a) Unfair dismissal should be seen as a dismissal which contravenes statute. If the employee qualifies for protection against unfair dismissal he can request that the employer provide a written reason for the dismissal. Failure by an employer to issue a written response would be highly suspect and an Employment Tribunal would be entitled to imply that the employer had not acted fairly when he dismissed the employee. Generally, an employee who has less than one year's continuous employment cannot lodge a claim for unfair dismissal with the Office of Employment Tribunals. There are, however, many exceptions to the rule that an employee cannot sue for unfair dismissal if the period of continuous service is less than one year (discrimination claims being the main exception). An employee who has been unfairly dismissed must lodge a claim.

Wrongful dismissal arises in situations where an employer dismisses the employee in breach of his contract. In order to claim that he has been wrongfully dismissed, the employee does not have to show that he has had continuous service with his employer for at least one year. Employees with over a year's continuous service can also claim wrongful dismissal. Claims for wrongful dismissal should be lodged with the Office of Employment Tribunals

within three months (less one day) of the date of the employee's dismissal.

b) Charlene would have a potential claim for wrongful dismissal i.e. a dismissal which is in breach of her contract of employment (see **Morran v Glasgow Council of Tenants (1998)**). We are not told about the precise reasons for Charlene's dismissal, but she may also have a claim for unfair dismissal in terms of the Employment Rights Act 1996. It would obviously be important to investigate Charlene's employment circumstances before talking about the possibility of an unfair dismissal claim.

9 a) The employee's right to claim constructive dismissal arises in situations where the employer's conduct is to be regarded as a material breach of the employment contract and the employee is left with no alternative but to resign. However, the employee's resignation is not treated as the act which terminates the contract, rather it is the employer's conduct. The employer's conduct must be so serious in order to justify the employee's decision to resign. When an employee claims that he has been constructively dismissed, he is claiming that he was unfairly dismissed. The right of constructive dismissal would arise in situations where the employer made unauthorised deductions from wages, where the employer refused to follow the proper disciplinary or grievance procedures or where the employee was ordered to use equipment that was clearly dangerous (see **Sharp v Western Excavating Ltd (1978)** and **Sinclair v Fritz Companies (1999)**).

b) Rose would have very strong grounds for resigning from her employment and claiming that she had been constructively dismissed. The employer has committed a material breach of contract by failing to investigate Rose's grievance and Rose has more than the year's continuous service required to take an unfair dismissal claim to an Employment Tribunal.

10 a) Penny has probably been dismissed from employment on the grounds of her trade union membership and activity. Such a dismissal would be unfair in terms of Section 152: Trade Union and Labour Relations (Consolidation) Act 1992 (see **O'Donovan v Central College of Commerce (2003)**).

b) An employee's misconduct could be used to justify dismissal in terms of Section 98(2) of the Employment Rights Act 1996. Although the act of misconduct committed by Colin took place outside his employment, his employer would be entitled to argue that it had a bearing on his continued employment with the Building Society. Customers of the Building Society would expect the manager to have a reputation for honesty and integrity. Colin now sadly lacks these qualities. It is likely that the Building Society could claim that Colin's dismissal for misconduct was justified in the circumstances (see **H B Raylor v McArdle EAT 573/84** and **McLean v McLane Ltd EAT 682/96**). The employer is under a duty, however, to carry out a reasonable investigation and he must have reasonably believed the employee to be guilty of misconduct in order for the dismissal to be fair (see **British Home Stores Ltd v Burchell (1980)**).

c) Section 139(1) of the Employment Rights Act 1996 states that dismissal on the grounds of redundancy will occur if:

1 The employer has ceased or intends to cease carrying on the business; or

2 The requirements for employees to carry out work of a particular kind or to carry it out at the place in which they are employed have ceased or diminished.

It is important to determine whether an employee has been dismissed on the grounds of redundancy or if the employee and the employer have both agreed to bring the contract to an end. Obviously, if both parties have agreed to a mutual termination of the contract of employment, no dismissal on the grounds of redundancy can be said to have taken place. It is vitally important to establish, therefore, who was responsible for bringing the employment to an end. If the employer was responsible, then potentially the employee has a claim for a redundancy payment and, if the procedures were not properly carried out, the employee may have a further claim for unfair dismissal (see **Caledonian Mining Ltd v Bassett & Steel (1987)** and **Murray v Foyle Meats Ltd (1999)**).

Dismissal on the grounds of redundancy will be automatically unfair if the employee was selected for redundancy in relation to any of the following:

1 Participation in trade union activities (Section 153: Trade Union and Labour Relations (Consolidation) Act 1992).

2 Pregnancy or for a reason connected with it (Section 99: Employment rights Act 1996).

3 Making a protected disclosure in terms of the Public Interest Disclosure Act 1998 (Section 103A: Employment Rights Act 1996).

4 Raising or taking action on the grounds of health and safety (Section 100: Employment Rights Act 1996).

5 Involvement in activities related to his role as a trustee of an occupational pension scheme (Section 102: Employment Rights Act 1996).

6 Assertion of the right not to be forced to work on a Sunday because was classified as a protected worker or a betting shop worker or because he has given an opting out notice to the employer (Section 101: Employment Rights Act 1996).

7 Assertion of certain statutory rights (Section 104: Employment Rights Act 1996).

8 Acting as an employee representative during consultations in relation to proposed redundancies or during the transfer of an undertaking (Section 103: Employment Rights Act 1996; and Regulations 10 and 11: Transfer of Undertakings (Protection of Employment) 1981).

d) Monica has been dismissed for making a public disclosure in terms of the Public Interest Disclosure Act 1998. This action by her employer constitutes an unfair dismissal in terms of Section 103A of the Employment Rights Act 1996 (see **Miklaszewicz v Stolt Offshore (2002)**).

In assessing how reasonably the person who made the disclosure has acted, an Employment Tribunal will wish to know to whom was the disclosure made, were serious concerns being raised by the disclosure, has the employer's conduct caused third parties to be exposed to danger, and has the disclosure breached a duty of confidence the employer owed a third party. If the disclosure was addressed to an employer or a prescribed regulator, the reasonableness of their response will be very important. Employment Tribunals will often examine an employer's internal whistle-blowing procedure (assuming, of course, that one exists) in order to assess if the employee's concerns or complaints were dealt with properly.

e) Reza is contractually bound to obtain the appropriate qualifications in order to secure his continued employment. He has failed to do this and his employer would be entitled to dismiss him on the grounds of his lack of qualifications in terms of Section 98(2) of the Employment Rights Act 1996 (see **Blackman v Post Office (1974)** and **Tayside Regional Council v McIntosh (1982)**). Reza's dismissal would, therefore, be fair.

f) Susan's dismissal is automatically unfair because her employer has decided to dismiss her for pregnancy-related reasons. This is a breach of Section 99 of the Employment Rights Act 1996 (see **O'Neill v Governors of St Thomas More (1996)**).

g) Arlene is being dismissed specifically on the grounds of her dreadful sickness record. Arlene's dismissal will be fair, in terms of Section 98(2) of the Employment Rights Act 1996, if the employer follows the guidelines laid down in **East Lindsey District Council v Daubney 1977** where the Employment Appeal Tribunal stated that before an employee decides to dismiss an employee on the grounds of ill-health proper consultation must have taken place. Proper consultation will consist of the following factors:

- The employer must hold discussions with the employee at the outset of the illness and these should continue throughout the course of the illness. The employee should be alerted when his dismissal is a serious option.

- There should be personal contact between the employer and the employee.

- The employee should be asked for his opinion regarding his medical condition by the employer.

- The employer should consider alternative employment for the employee within the organisation.

In **Taylorplan Catering (Scotland) Ltd v McInally (1980)** the Employment Appeal Tribunal again stressed the importance of the employer holding consultations with a sick employee. Such a consultation exercise means that the employer's need to have the employee present at work can be weighed against the employee's need to be given time to regain his health and fitness which makes his return to work possible.

This area is now more complicated as a result of the Disability Discrimination Act 1995. When dealing with an employee who is absent from work due to ill-health, a reasonable employer should take steps to establish whether the individual in question is suffering from a disability. A disability will affect not only the individual's ability to perform his job, but also his ability to perform normal day-to-day activities. If this is the case, the employer will have to make reasonable adjustments in terms of Section 6 of the Disability Discrimination Act 1995 to the employee's working conditions in order to aid his return to work.

h) Ellie has been dismissed for raising a health and safety complaint and probably for her role as a health and safety representative in the workplace. Her dismissal would be automatically unfair in terms of Section 100 of the Employment Rights Act 1996. Ellie does not need to have a year's continuous service with her employer in order to lodge a claim for unfair dismissal with the Office of Employment Tribunals (see **Hynes v D E Bliss (Builders) ET Case No. 12874/96** and **Harvest Press Ltd v McCaffrey (1999)**).

i) Sheelagh will have to dismiss Andrew in order not to contravene statute – specifically the Consumer Credit Act 1974. The dismissal will be fair in terms of Section 98(2) of the Employment Rights Act 1996 (see **Yarrow v QIS Ltd ET Case No. 1270/79** and **Appleyard v F M Smith (Hull) Ltd (1972)**). These kinds of dismissals are particularly common in relation to health and safety issues or where the employee holds a position as a driver and he has received a ban in terms of the road traffic legislation.

j) The employer's action in dismissing these three individuals is a breach of Section 16 and Schedule 5: Employment Relations Act 1999 because they are taking part in lawful, balloted industrial action. The employer is not allowed to dismiss employees who are taking part in lawful, balloted industrial action for the first eight weeks of such action. This protection is absolute as long as the employee does not commit a further unlawful act over and above his initial breach of contract (i.e. by going on strike). A dismissal, regardless of the employee's age or length of service, will be automatically unfair as long as it is connected to the industrial action. This statutory protection could be extended beyond the first eight weeks if the employer has not taken reasonable steps to end the dispute.

After the initial period of eight weeks has ended, the employer cannot be selective as to which employees he decides to dismiss. All those employees engaged in the industrial action must be dismissed no matter what their motives were for taking part might have been. If the employer decides to dismiss the employees who took part in industrial action, he cannot take back any of the dismissed employees for a period of at least three months.

If employees are taking part in unofficial industrial action, they will have no protection against dismissal. It is important to note that the employees who have been dismissed must be involved in unofficial action on the date of their dismissal. However, the employer cannot dismiss employees who have returned to work after taking part in an unofficial strike. A dismissal in those circumstances would not prevent these employees from lodging a claim for unfair dismissal with the Office of Employment Tribunals.

k) Kevin's employer has decided to dismiss him from his employment on the grounds of some other substantial reason. Section 98(1)(b) of the

615

Employment Rights Act 1996 gives an employer the opportunity to argue that an employee has been dismissed for some other substantial reason. This is a potentially a very broad category, but it should be viewed as dealing only with a very small number of situations that are not covered by the other four named categories in Section 98(2) of the 1996 Act

The employer must show that the substantial reason used to justify the employee's dismissal was potentially a fair one. Once this has been established, the employer must convince the Employment Tribunal that its actions leading to the dismissal of the employee have been reasonable. The substantial reason for dismissal must not be trivial or frivolous. The category of some other substantial reason has been used to justify dismissal where the employer tries to protect the employee from divulging business secrets to competitors or where the employee is attempting to establish a rival business of his own (see **Abey v R & E Holdings (Yorkshire) Ltd t/a Quick Pass School of Motoring ET Case No 14985/82**). In **Simmons v S D Graphics Ltd EAT 548/79** the Employment Appeal Tribunal pointed out that in situations where two employees with a close personal relationship both have access to confidential information, it is for the Tribunal to examine the facts in order to determine whether or not the decision of one of their employers to dismiss one of these individuals was for some other substantial reason.

11 Sections 111 to 132 of the Employment Rights Act 1996 contain much of the detail relating to remedies for unfair dismissal.

The two orders that an Employment Tribunal can issue requesting that the employee be re-employed are:
1 Reinstatement orders
2 Re-engagement orders

In most situations, an Employment Tribunal will award compensation to the dismissed employee. Compensation consists of two parts:
1 The basic award
2 The compensatory award

The basic award that the employee receives could be reduced for a number of reasons:

- Where the employee's conduct has contributed to the dismissal.

- Where the employer gave the employee a redundancy payment or ex-gratia payment.

- Where the employee has unreasonably refused an offer of reinstatement from the employer.

- Where the employee is aged 64, the award will be reduced by 1/12 for each whole month that has passed from his last birthday to the estimated retirement date (of 65).

The compensatory award for unfair dismissal from 1 February 2004 is subject to a limit of £55,000. The award will cover immediate loss of wages, future loss, loss of pension rights and loss of statutory protection. The maximum award may be much greater in health safety dismissals, whistle-blowing cases and cases involving discrimination.

Compensation for injury to feelings caused by the manner of the dismissal may now be awarded (see **Johnson v Unisys Ltd (2001)**: Lord Hoffman's *obiter* remark as against the much older rule established in **Norton Tool Co Ltd v Tewson (1972)** that compensation for dismissal only includes financial loss – not for injury to feelings). In February 2004, the English Court of Appeal in **Dunnachie v Kingston upon Hull City Council** stated that an award for unfair dismissal could also include injury to feelings. The English Court of Appeal overruled the Employment Appeal Tribunal's verdict in **Dunnachie** and is a major blow to the conventional wisdom that injury to feelings could not be included in an award for unfair dismissal as stated in **Norton**.

In several situations, the Employment Tribunal can issue an Interim Order which means that the dismissed employee's contract will continue to have legal force until the outcome of the case is decided. An Interim Order can also be used to prevent the employee from being dismissed until the Employment Tribunal has made its decision. The employee, therefore, will continue to enjoy the benefits of his employment contract while his claim for unfair dismissal is being heard and ultimately decided upon. An Interim Order will only be granted in trade union dismissals, health and safety dismissals and dismissals where the employee has made a protected disclosure.

Chapter 7

1 The types of discrimination in employment that United Kingdom legislation prohibits includes the following:

1 Gender or sex (the Equal Pay Act 1970, the Sex Discrimination Act 1975 (as amended), Equal Pay Directive 75/117/EEC, the Equal Treatment

Directive 76/207/EEC and the Sex Discrimination (Gender Reassignment) Regulations 1999).

2 Marital status (the Equal Pay Act 1970, the Sex Discrimination Act 1975 (as amended), Equal Pay Directive 75/117/EEC and the Equal Treatment Directive 76/207/EEC.

3 Colour, nationality, racial, ethnic or national origin (the Race Relations Act 1976 (as amended)).

4 Disability (the Disability Discrimination Act 1995).

5 Being a part-time worker (the Part-Time Workers (Prevention of Less Favourable Treatment) Regulations 2000).

6 Being a fixed-term worker (the Fixed-Term Employees (Prevention of Less Favourable Treatment) Regulations 2002).

7 Sexual orientation (the Employment Equality (Sexual Orientation) Regulations 2003).

8 Religious or philosophical beliefs (the Employment Equality (Religion or Belief) Regulations 2003).

2 An employee or a job applicant can experience discriminatory or less favourable treatment in the following situations:
- Lack of promotion and training opportunities
- Different pay scales and conditions of employment
- Unfairness in the recruitment process
- Dismissal from employment
- Failure to receive the same contractual benefits as fellow employees
- Different retirement ages
- Different dress codes
- Unilateral changes to an employee's contract of employment
- Age requirements in relation to certain posts
- Harassment and victimisation
- Selecting certain individuals for redundancy first
- Refusal to allow more flexible working patterns

Discrimination means that an individual or a group of individuals will suffer less favourable treatment by reason of gender or sex, transsexuality, colour, nationality, racial, ethnic or national origin, disability, sexual orientation, religious or philosophical beliefs or employment status and this difference in treatment cannot be objectively justified.

3 a) The concept of direct discrimination is found in Sections 1 (relating to women) and 2 (relating to men) of the Sex Discrimination Act and Section 1(1)(a) of the Race Relations Act centres around the concept that someone, for example, a woman or a member of an ethnic minority has suffered discrimination in relation to their employment if the employer treats them less favourably than he treats or would treat other persons. The reason for this less favourable treatment is related to the person's gender or their membership of a racial group. Very often, an employer will be accused of direct discrimination because he has consciously made a decision to discriminate against someone by reason of a person's gender or race (see **Greig v Community Industry (1979)**, **James v Eastleigh Borough Council (1990)**, **King v Great Britain-China Centre (1991)** and **Jones v Tower Boot (1997)**).

Indirect discrimination on the grounds of sex is unlawful in terms of Section 1(1)(b) and Section 2 of the Sex Discrimination Act 1975. Indirect discrimination on the grounds of colour or nationality is unlawful in terms of Section 1(1)(b) of the Race Relations Act 1976. The Race Regulations 2003 introduces a wider definition of indirect discrimination on the grounds of a person's racial, national or ethnic origin.

Indirect discrimination on the grounds of sex, colour or nationality, will occur when an employer:

- Applies to an individual a condition or requirement which the employer appears to apply equally to everyone; and

- The proportion of people from the affected person's group (based on sex, colour or nationality) that can comply is considerably smaller than the proportion of people not from that group who can comply with it; and

- The employer cannot justify the requirement or condition on gender neutral or non-racial grounds; and

- The requirement or condition is to the affected person's detriment, because he or she cannot comply with it.

At first glance, the condition or the requirement that the employer imposes on everyone looks completely harmless. However, upon a closer inspection, it becomes obvious that more men than women can comply *in practice* with the employer's condition or requirement or that more white people can comply with the requirement or condition than can people from an Afro-Caribbean background for example (see **Singh v Rowntree MacKintosh (1979)**, **J H Walker Ltd v Hussain & Ors (1996)** and **London Underground v Edwards (No 2) (1998)**).

The Race Regulations 2003 provide a wider definition of indirect discrimination than arguably is the case under the Sex Discrimination Act 1975 and as was the case in terms of the Race Relations Act prior to 19 July 2003. However, it is important to note that the new rules in the Regulations regarding indirect discrimination apply only to a person's race or ethnic or national origin. Discrimination on the basis of an individual's colour or nationality will still be covered by the previous definition of indirect discrimination as laid down in Section 1(1)(b) of the Race Relations Act 1976. This means that are now two types of indirect discrimination in race discrimination cases. According to Section 1A of the Race Relations Act, indirect discrimination will occur when an employer applies to another person:

- A provision, criterion or practice which the employer applies to everyone; and

- This provision, criterion or practice puts (or would put) people from the affected person's race or ethnic or national origin at a particular disadvantage; and

- The employer cannot show that the provision, criterion or practice is a proportionate means of achieving a legitimate aim.

The words 'provision, criterion, or practice' have a broader meaning than the words 'requirement or condition' which still apply to claims brought under the Race Relations Act in respect of a person's colour or nationality. The new wording will, therefore, apply to an employer's informal as well as formal practices. Informal practices might include advertising posts or promotion opportunities by word of mouth as opposed to advertising these positions formally. It is hoped that this will mean that many more people will be placed in a position where claims of indirect discrimination may be brought against their employers.

There is another important difference between the older definition of indirect discrimination and the more modern approach. Previously, individuals making a complaint often had to base their claim on complex statistical evidence in order to show that people belonging to their particular group were placed at more of a disadvantage in comparison to another group of people.

b) Advertisements used in the recruitment process or the use of particular job titles in employment will be unlawful if they give the impression that a person from a particular gender or racial group will be given preferential treatment. If a public house placed an advertisement in the local paper stating that it required a barman, it would give a strong impression that women need not apply for the

position as the employer obviously favours men over women. This would be an example of direct sex discrimination in terms of Section 1 of the Sex Discrimination Act 1975 (see **Greig v Community Industry (1979)** and **James v Eastleigh Borough Council (1990)**).

The advertisement is also an example of indirect sex discrimination and is, therefore, illegal in terms of Section 1(1)(b) and Section 2 of the Sex Discrimination Act 1975 for the following reasons:

In situations where an employer imposes 'desirable' and 'essential' criteria in a job advertisement, they may be examples of indirect discrimination (**Falkirk Council v Whyte (1997) IRLR 560**). In **Briggs v NE Education and Library Board (1990) IRLR 181** a requirement of the employer that the successful applicant for a job be able to work full-time was an example of indirect discrimination because fewer female applicants could comply in practice with this condition than their male counterparts. Furthermore, the statement that this position would suit a single person might mean that the employer is indirectly discriminating against job applicants who are married who might think that being single is a criterion for the job.

c) McTavish's recruitment procedures are clearly examples of indirect discrimination on the grounds of colour or nationality which would be unlawful in terms of Section 1(1)(b) of the Race Relations Act 1976 because the criteria for production line workers applies to an individual a condition or requirement which the employer appears to apply equally to everyone; and the proportion of people from the affected person's group (based on colour or nationality) that can comply is considerably smaller than the proportion of people not from that group who can comply with it; and the employer cannot justify the requirement or condition on non-racial grounds; and the requirement or condition is to the affected person's detriment, because he or she cannot comply with it. The criteria for production line workers may also be an example of indirect discrimination in terms of a person's race, ethnic or national origin. Section 1A of the Race Relations Act 1976 states that indirect discrimination by the employer will occur when he applies a provision, criterion or practice which is applied to everyone; and this provision, criterion or practice puts (or would put) people from the affected person's race or ethnic or national origin at a particular disadvantage; and the employer cannot show that the provision, criterion or practice is a proportionate means of achieving a legitimate aim. Fewer numbers of people from particular racial groups will possess a high degree of fluency in spoken and written English if compared with white applicants. This will also be true where the possession of educational qualifications from British schools and colleges is concerned because many members of racial groups may have been educated outside the UK. As for preference being given to residents of Dalry and its surrounding area, many of the inhabitants of this location will tend to be overwhelmingly white because racial minorities tend to congregate in larger towns and cities – again this requirement could be an example of indirect discrimination. The aptitude test could also be viewed as indirect discrimination because it will tend to favour those applicants coming from a white British cultural and educational background. As we have seen, in situations where an employer imposes 'desirable' and 'essential' criteria in a job advertisement, they may be examples of indirect discrimination (**Briggs v NE Education and Library Board (1990)** and **Falkirk Council v Whyte (1997)**).

Jutinder Singh, as a Sikh, is a member of racial group for the purposes of Section 3 of the Race Relations Act 1976. Section 3 of the Race Relations Act defines 'racial grounds' as meaning a person's colour, race, nationality or ethnic or national origins. The requirement that drivers have neat and tidy haircuts and be clean shaven is an example of indirect discrimination in terms of Section 1A of the Race Relations Act because fewer Sikhs in comparison with other racial groups can comply in practice with the employer's requirement. It is unlikely that McTavish would be successful if it tried to justify such a condition, although indirectly discriminating against Sikh employees or job applicants like Jutinder, on the grounds of hygiene in terms of Section 1(1)(b)(ii) of the Race Relations Act 1976 is permissible (see **Singh v Rowntree MacKintosh (1979)**).

4   a) To make offensive remarks of a sexually or racially motivated nature to a person will be regarded as direct sex or racial discrimination. Making discriminatory comments about a woman's body or racist comments in relation to a person's colour or race will amount to less favourable treatment. One sexually or racially motivated remark could amount to harassment. Employment Tribunals have been greatly assisted by the publication of a European Commission Code of Practice on Measures to Combat Sexual Harassment. In **Wadman v Carpenter Farrer Partnership (1993)** the Employment Appeal Tribunal stated that Tribunals should use the Code to decide when sexual harassment has taken place (see **also Porcelli v Strathclyde Regional Council (1986)**,

Institu Cleaning Co Ltd v Heads (1995) and **Jones v Tower Boot (1997)**).

In **Reed and Bull Information Systems v Stedman (1999) IRLR 299** the Employment Appeal Tribunal laid down some guidelines as to what constitutes unwanted conduct in cases of sexual harassment. The test for sexual harassment is a subjective one in that it great stress will be placed on the feelings of the person who was subjected to the remark or the behaviour in question. It is up to the recipient to decide what is welcome and what is offensive.

Obviously, racist remarks and racist behaviour should be treated completely differently in that they should not be tolerated at all. Racist remarks and behaviour will almost always be offensive in nature. The newly amended Race Relations Act now takes a much tougher approach to harassment. Section 3(A) states that harassment on the grounds of race or ethnic or national origin will be unlawful, if a person engages in unwanted conduct which has the purpose or effect of violating another person's dignity or creates an intimidating, hostile, offensive or disturbing environment. Section 3(A) makes it very clear that the perception or the opinion of the person claiming that they have suffered harassment will often be decisive in establishing that discrimination has occurred. Furthermore, Section 4 (2A) states that it is unlawful for an employer to subject any employee or a person who has applied for employment to harassment on the grounds of race or ethnic or national origin.

In terms of harassment in disability discrimination cases, Paragraph 6.22 of the Code of Practice states that the harassment of a disabled person will almost always amount to a detriment under the Disability Discrimination Act 1995. The disabled person must show that he has been subjected to harassment by his employer by reason of his disability (see **Verma v Herbie's Pizzas Ltd (2000) ET Case No 2701994/00**).

In terms of Regulation 4 of the Employment Equality (Sexual Orientation) Regulations 2003 and Regulation 4 of the Employment Equality (Religion or Belief) Regulations 2003, a person will be subjected to harassment on the grounds of their sexual orientation or religion or beliefs if they experience unwanted conduct that violates their dignity or creates an intimidating, hostile, degrading, humiliating or offensive environment.

b) Tony has undoubtedly committed various acts of sexual harassment against Sharon as outlined in question 4(b) itself.

5 **a)** Section 4 of the Sex Discrimination Act and Section 2 of the Race Relations Act provide an important range of safeguards and protection to individuals who have been involved in some way in sex and racial discrimination actions. Sometimes, the employer will subject an individual to less favourable treatment in the future because, at one time, they have had some involvement in a discrimination claim against the employer (see **Waters v Commissioner of Police for the Metropolis (2000)**). It will be unlawful for an employer to victimise or harass such individuals in the following situations:

1 Where a person has brought an Employment Tribunal or a court action against the employer under the Equal Pay Act 1970, Sex Discrimination Act 1975 or the Race Relations Act 1976.

2 Where a person has given evidence in support of someone who has taken an Employment Tribunal or a court action under the above legislation.

3 Where a person has taken a legitimate course of action, for example, making a complaint against the employer in relation to the above legislation.

4 Where a person has made allegations against the employer that discrimination has occurred which is unlawful in terms of the above legislation.

Section 55 of the Disability Discrimination Act 1995 deals with the concept of victimisation. It will be unlawful to victimise either a disabled or a non-disabled employee in circumstances that are very similar to those laid down in sex and race discrimination complaints. As we have seen, victimisation can continue after the employment relationship has ended, e.g., the employer's refusal to give a reference.

In terms of the Part-time Workers (Prevention of Less Favourable Treatment) Regulations 2000, any part-time worker who makes a complaint or proceeds with an action under the Regulations has the right not to be victimised by the employer. Victimisation could take the form of dismissal or some other detriment, for example, harassment. If the employer dismisses a part-time worker for enforcing her rights under the Regulations, such a dismissal will be automatically unfair (Regulation 7). This protection is also extended to any other worker who agrees to be a witness or give evidence in respect of any complaint made against an employer under the Regulations.

Regulation 6 of the Fixed-term Employees (Prevention of Less Favourable Treatment)

Regulations 2002 makes it very clear that employees who make complaints against the employer or who give evidence on behalf of a discriminated colleague have the right not to be victimised by the employer in respect of unfair dismissal or other detriments.

In terms of Regulation 5 of the Employment Equality (Sexual Orientation) Regulations and Regulation 5 of the Employment Equality (Religion or Belief) Regulations 2003, makes it illegal for an employer to behave in a way that amounts to victimisation of an employee i.e. treating people less favourably because of action they have taken under or in connection with both sets of Employment Equality Regulations, for example, made a formal complaint of discrimination or given evidence in an Employment Tribunal case.

Very significantly, the House of Lords decided that victimisation after a contract has ended is unlawful (see **Relaxion Group plc v Rhys-Harper (FC); D'Souza v London Borough of Lambeth; Jones v 3M Healthcare Limited and Others (2003) UKHL 33**).

b) Shamaila has undoubtedly suffered victimisation on racial grounds as a result of her ex-employer's refusal to give her a reference. The employer's refusal to give a reference to Shamaila is motivated by her decision to take out an Employment Tribunal claim alleging race discrimination. The employer's act of victimisation would be a breach of Section 2 of the Race Realtions Act 1976. The decision of the House of Lords in **Relaxion Group plc v Rhys-Harper (FC); D'Souza v London Borough of Lambeth; Jones v 3M Healthcare Limited and Others (2003)** means that people like Shamaila can now take action against their employers even after the employment has ended because acts of victimisation committed by employers can continue to take place.

6 **a)** This statement is highly accurate because until the introduction of the Employment Equality (Sexual Orientation) Regulations 2003, the House of Lords made it very clear that discrimination on the grounds of a person's sexual orientation was not covered by the Sex Discrimination Act 1975 (see **Macdonald v Advocate General for Scotland** and **Pearce v Governing Body of Mayfield School (2003)**).

As a result of the Human Rights Act 1998, a person will enjoy substantial protection in relation to his or her sexual orientation. Article 8 of the European Convention on Human Rights establishes the places a duty on a public authority to have respect for a person's private life. Furthermore, Article 14 of the

European Convention confers a right on individuals not to be subjected to discrimination. So, employers which are defined as a public authority will have to ensure that they do not discriminate against an employee on the grounds of sexual orientation.

From 1 December 2003 it is now unlawful to discriminate against someone by reason of that person's sexual orientation. The Employment Equality (Sexual Orientation) Regulations 2003 now provide protection to employees like Macdonald and Pearce who suffer discrimination in employment by reason of their sexual orientation. In the their judgement, the House of Lords drew attention to the new equality law, but stated that its introduction would be too late for both Macdonald and Pearce.

b) In terms of the Employment Equality (Sexual Orientation) Regulations 2003, Terry could attempt to argue that he has experienced an act of direct discrimination on the grounds of his sexual orientation (Regulation 3) when he was refused promotion. Terry will have the right to bring a discrimination claim on the grounds of his sexual orientation before the Employment Tribunal or the Sheriff Court.

7 **a)** An employer will be permitted to discriminate on the grounds of sex or race in certain, appropriate circumstances. An employer can, therefore, justify discriminatory treatment by claiming that a candidate for a job, promotion, training or other benefit must be of a particular gender or be a member of a particular racial group. Section 7 of the Sex Discrimination Act describes seven situations where the person's sex may be regarded as a genuine occupational qualification. The Sex Discrimination (Gender Reassignment) Regulations 1999 also introduce additional genuine occupational qualifications to the Sex Discrimination Act which apply to transsexuals only.

Where the issue of race is concerned, there is less scope for an employer to justify discriminatory treatment. Section 5 of the Race Relations Act lists three very limited situations where the person's colour, nationality, race, ethnic or national origins may be regarded as a genuine occupational qualification.

b) **i)** In terms of Section 7 of the Sex Discrimination Act 1975, Joanne would be able to claim that being female for the role of Juliet in Shakespeare's play is a genuine occupational qualification. It is necessary for physiological reasons (not physical strength or stamina) to cast a female actor. The employer requires a candidate to be a member of a particular sex.

ii) Kenny's decision not to employ Amanda as a labourer on the building site is an example of direct sex discrimination and, therefore breaches Section 1 of the Sex Discrimination Act 1975 (see **Greig v Community Industry (1979)**). Physical strength is not a genuine occupational qualification in terms of Section 7 of the Sex Discrimination Act 1975.

iii) Greenhill Men's Voluntary Association would probably be successful in justifying its decision to discriminate against Debbie by relying on the genuine occupational qualification laid down in Section 7 of the Sex Discrimination Act 1975. The holder of the job provides individuals with personal services aimed at promoting their welfare or educational services and where those services can be most effectively provided by a person of a particular sex – in this case a man.

iv) The Georgian Cultural Society would be able to rely on Section 5 of the Race Relations Act 1976. It will be a genuine occupational qualification where the holder of the job provides individuals with personal services aimed at promoting their welfare and where those services can be most effectively provided by a person of that particular racial group. Zura quite clearly meets the conditions laid down by this particular occupational qualification.

v) The restaurant owner's attempt to rely on Section 5 of the Race Relations Act 1976 by claiming that being Indian is a genuine occupational qualification for holding the post of chef would fail. The Race Relations Act does recognise situations where a person is required to serve food and drink to the public in a place where members of a particular racial group are required to promote authenticity. It does not matter whether this work is carried out on a paid basis or not. This genuine occupational requirement allows Indian and Chinese restaurants to employ Indian and Chinese waiting and bar staff in order to provide customers with an authentic experience. However, it does not cover situations where staff do not have contact with the public, for example, kitchen staff. Being ethnic Indian is not a genuine occupational requirement for working as a chef in the kitchen of an Indian restaurant. Angus has suffered direct race discrimination in terms of Section 1(1)(a) of the Race Relations Act 1976 (see **King v Great Britain-China Centre (1991)** and **Jones v Tower Boot (1997)**).

vi) The police service would be able to rely on the genuine occupational qualification contained in Section 5 of the Race Relations Act 1976 by claiming that an artist's or photographic model is required for the production of a work of art or visual image where members of particular racial groups are needed for reasons of authenticity.

8 Section 4A of the Race Relations Act 1976 allows an employer to impose a genuine occupational requirement in respect of job applicants. Theoretically, this is much wider than the limited genuine occupational qualifications allowed by Section 5 of the 1976 Act. It may be the case that certain jobs are best carried out by people belonging to particular race or who have particular ethnic or national origins. If this is indeed the case, an employer can legally discriminate in favour of certain races or people having certain ethnic backgrounds or national origins. However, an employer must show that imposing a genuine occupational requirement on the holder of a particular post is not disproportionate. Therefore, the employer must demonstrate that, having regard to the nature of the job or its context, it is best performed by a person who is a member of a particular race, ethnic or national group. Furthermore, by employing such a person the employer must be in a position to show that the benefits of discriminating in favour of particular applicants outweighs any disadvantages of such a policy.

Genuine occupational requirements do not apply to a job applicant's colour and nationality. An employer wishing to rely on a genuine occupational qualification in respect of an applicant's colour or nationality will have to continue to use the limited exceptions permitted by Section 5 of the Race Relations Act.

9 a) Section 1 of the Equal Pay Act ensures that each contract of employment contains an equality clause which means that it will be implied that men and women in the same employment should receive equal pay for equal work. The Equal Pay Act 1970 is not about establishing fair pay for everyone. Claims can only be brought under the Act if a person of a particular sex can show that she does not receive equal pay for equal work in comparison to a male colleague and the reason for this difference is related to her sex.

b) Pay has been defined as the ordinary basic or minimum wage or salary and any other consideration, whether in cash or in kind, which the worker receives, either directly or indirectly, in respect of his or her employment from his or her employer. The above definition does not just include a person's salary. It also applies to pensions, employers' contributions to pensions, concessionary travel, social security benefits, maternity pay, sick pay, paid leave, contractual and statutory

redundancy pay, paid leave, overtime pay and compensation for unfair dismissal.

c) i) Like work applies in situations where a woman is doing the same or broadly similar work to a man. There may indeed be differences between the work carried out by the man and the women, but these are so slight or have little practical importance (see **Capper Pass v Lawton (1977)**).

ii) Work rated as equivalent applies to situations where a job evaluation scheme is carried out. This category applies when a man and the woman are not be engaged in the same line of work. A woman who is employed as nursery nurse by a local council may be able to claim that she performs work rated as equivalent in comparison to a male clerical worker who receives a higher salary. Under the job evaluation scheme, both jobs must have an equal value in relation to the types of demands made upon a worker under such headings as effort, skill and decision-making. The jobs are broken down into their various functions and points will be awarded to each worker in relation to a function or heading. The scheme must be scrupulously fair in that it must be analytical and deploy objective (quantitative) criteria (**Eaton Ltd v Nuttall (1977)**). Furthermore, the study should have been carried out at the organisation where the employee and her comparator are employed. Should the female worker's job receive a different score from that of her male comparator, she will not be in a position to claim that her work should be rated as equivalent. Job evaluation schemes can always be challenged on the basis that the employer did not use objective criteria when comparing a woman's job with that of a male comparator (see **Ryder and 113 Others v Warwickshire County Council and Others ET Case No 1301481/97**).

iii) A woman may be able to claim that her work is equal value to that of a male comparator in situations where a job evaluation scheme has not been carried out. Again, the man and the woman are not engaged in like work, but this procedure allows the woman to compare herself to a man who is engaged in a completely different type of work. It is perfectly possible for the work carried out by a cleaning lady to be compared to that of a male solicitor who work for the same or associated employer. An Employment Tribunal can determine whether a woman is engaged in work of equal value in comparison to a male worker and the services of an independent expert are no longer required as used to be the case. When deciding whether a woman is employed in work of equal value, the Employment Tribunal will look at the demands made on the workers under such headings as effort, skill and decision-making (**Ms White and Others v Alstons (Colchester) Ltd (1987)**).

d) The Council may have a very good chance of defending the equal pay claim if it can rely on Section 1(3) of the Equal Pay Act 1970 which allows an employer to justify the difference in pay by claiming that it is related to a genuine material difference and is not based on the grounds of the person's sex (see **Glasgow City Council v Marshall (2000)**).

10 Yes, the employee's Employment Tribunal case will be helped by serving an equality questionnaire on the employer. By serving a questionnaire, it allows the employee to request important information from the employer which should help establish whether there is a potential claim for discrimination. The questionnaire and the responses can be used in evidence at an Employment Tribunal Hearing. It will be for the Employment Tribunal to decide whether discrimination has taken place. Employers are, therefore, encouraged to cooperate with such a questionnaire, but there may be some confidential information that they are entitled to withhold from the person bringing the complaint. If the employer fails or refuses to cooperate with the questionnaire procedure, this behaviour could be viewed very suspiciously by an Employment Tribunal in the where there is no justification on the employer's part.

11 **a)** Section 5 of the Disability Discrimination Act 1995 defines discrimination in relation to employment. Disability discrimination, according to Section 5, can occur in two ways:

1 An employer, for a reason related to a person's disability, may treat that person less favourably than he treats or would treat a person in relation to whom that reason does not apply and the employer cannot show that this treatment is justified.

2 An employer may discriminate against a disabled person in situations where he is under a duty to make reasonable adjustments (Section 6: Disability Discrimination Act 1995), but he fails to do this and can offer no justification for this failure.

The first type of discrimination has very close similarities to the concept of direct discrimination which is encountered in cases involving sex and race discrimination. There is one crucial difference, however, where disability is concerned because the employer's less favourable treatment of a disabled

employee can be justified. There is also a further type of discrimination which often arises in discrimination cases – victimisation (Section 55: Disability Discrimination Act 1995).

b) In terms of Section 6 of the Disability Discrimination Act 1995, an employee could experience discrimination where the employer either refuses or fails to make reasonable adjustments. Reasonable adjustments are measures which an employer will put in place in order to eliminate any physical features of the employer's premises or practices that would place a disabled person at a substantial (i.e. not trivial) disadvantage in comparison with a non-disabled person. When a disabled person brings a claim against an employer that he has failed to make reasonable adjustments, the Employment Tribunal must be satisfied that there is, in fact, a duty on the employer to make such adjustments. When such a duty has been established, the Employment Tribunal must then ask whether or not the employer has taken reasonable steps to put adjustments in place that will remove the substantial disadvantage in relation to the disabled person.

The Employment Tribunal can make use of Section 6(3) to decide whether the employer has failed to implement his duty. The following factors are reasonable adjustments that an employer might put in place:

1 Making adjustments to the employer's premises

2 Transferring some of his duties to another person

3 Giving him greater flexibility in his working hours

4 Transferring him to suitable, alternative employment

5 Changing his physical place of work

6 Permitting him to have time-off to attend medical treatment

7 Providing him with training opportunities

8 Modifying equipment for use by him

9 Modifying instructions and training or reference manuals

10 Modifying procedures for testing and assessment

11 Providing an interpreter or a scribe

12 Providing appropriate supervision

An employer may be able to argue that he is not under a duty to make reasonable adjustments if he either did not know or could not have been reasonably expected to know that an employee or a job applicant is disabled (Section 6(6)). However, this argument will fail if it can be implied that any of the employer's agents or employees had knowledge of the disability. From October 2004, the employer will have to take more active steps to discover whether any of his employees are, in fact, disabled and what reasonable adjustments can be put in place.

c) In order for an Employment Tribunal to be satisfied that Matthew has experienced less favourable treatment by reason of his disability, two issues must be addressed:

1 Whether the reason for the less favourable treatment is related to Matthew's disability.

2 Whether Matthew was treated less favourably in comparison with a person to whom this reason does not apply.

Clearly, the less favourable treatment is related to Matthew's disability and he was treated less favourably in comparison with a person to whom this reason did not apply.

It is totally wrong to assume that the appropriate comparison to be made in disability discrimination cases is for the disabled person to compare themselves to a person who is either not disabled or a person who does suffer from the disability that affects them in relation to the less favourable treatment complained of.

For illustrations of less favourable treatment on the grounds of a person's disability see **Portman v Bromley Hospitals NHS Trust (1996) EAT 1300/96** and **Clarke v Novacold Ltd (1999)**.

d) Simon's employers could argue that they are justified in dismissing him in terms of Section 5(3) of the Disability Discrimination Act 1995. Section 5(3) states that less favourable treatment of a disabled employee can only be justified if, but only if, the reason for the less favourable treatment is material to the circumstances of the particular case and substantial. It is for the employer to prove that the less favourable treatment was justified. When the employer relies on the justification defence, his reasons for doing so cannot be minor or trivial. The employer must demonstrate that he will face serious problems if he is not permitted to treat the employee less favourably on the grounds of disability.

Paragraph 6.21 of the Code of Practice gives a useful example of situations where the employer may be justified in treating a disabled employee less favourably. What if the employee, as a result of his disability, was prevented from performing the core duties of his contract and it was totally impracticable to transfer this individual to another post or it is simply not reasonable for the employer to make a transfer? In these situations, the employer may very well benefit from the defence that his treatment of the employee was justified (see **Mansoor v Guest & Chrimes Ltd (1997) ET Case No 2802060/97, A v London Borough of Hounslow (1998) EAT 1155** and **Callagan v Glasgow City Council (2001)**).

12 Kathy has suffered discrimination by reason of her status as a part-time worker. This is illegal in terms of the Part-time Workers (Prevention of Less Favourable Treatment) Regulations 2000. Regulation 5 is very explicit that it will be an act of discrimination to treat a part-time worker less favourably than a comparable full-time worker. Part-time workers have often experienced less favourable treatment at the hands of their employers in respect of being denied access to employment, promotion and training opportunities. There can also be significant differences (in a negative sense) between the terms and conditions that full-time workers enjoy and those of part-time workers.

As Kathy is an employee, she is quite clearly covered by the Part-time Workers Regulations 2000 (Regulation 1).

It is important that a part-time worker making an allegation of discrimination against her employer is able to compare herself to a full-time comparator. Regulation 2(3) lists various types of contracts which are considered to be very different in nature:

1 Employees employed under a contract that is not a contract of apprenticeship.

2 Employees employed under a contract of apprenticeship.

3 Workers who are not employees.

4 Any other description of worker that it is reasonable for the employer to treat differently from other workers on the ground that workers of that description have a different type of contract.

A part-time worker cannot compare herself to *any* full-time comparator. It would not be the correct legal approach for a part-time worker employed under an apprenticeship contract to compare her situation to full-time worker who is employed on a contract which is not an apprenticeship contract. A part-time apprentice alleging less favourable treatment must compare her situation with a worker employed under a full-time apprenticeship contract (see **Matthews and Others v Kent and Medway Towns Fire Authority and Others 2003**).

Generally speaking, part-time workers bringing a claim of less favourable treatment against their employer must meet the requirements laid down in Regulation 2(4) which makes it very clear that a part-time worker must demonstrate the following:

1 She and her comparator are employed by the same employer under the same type of contract; and

2 She and her comparator are engaged in the same or broadly similar work.

However, where Kathy is concerned the Regulations grant important rights to workers in two situations:

1 Those workers who have previously held a full-time position and who now wish to change to part-time work (Regulation 3).

2 Workers returning from a period of absence who previously held a full-time position but who now wish to change to a part-time work. This would cover workers returning from maternity leave (Regulation 4).

Workers in the above two situations may actually find that their part-time terms and conditions of employment are less favourable than their previous full-time employment. The Regulations come to these workers' assistance because they permit them to compare their current part-time contracts to their previous full-time contracts.

Kathy can ask the employer to explain the difference in treatment. The employer has 21 days from the employee requesting an explanation to issue a written statement laying down the reasons for the difference in treatment between part-time and full-time workers (Regulation 6). It is open to the employer to deny that any discrimination has taken place. The employer's statement can be used in Employment Tribunal proceedings at a later date. If the employer fails to provide a statement on request or issues reasons for the treatment that could be considered evasive, it is up to the Employment Tribunal to draw its own conclusions. If the employee still wishes to take matters further, she is entitled to lodge an Employment Tribunal application within three months (less one day) of the conduct complained of (Regulation 8).

An employer will be able to justify less favourable treatment on objective grounds. Objective reasons for discrimination may be that the part-time worker has inferior qualifications or less experience than her full-time colleague and this explains the difference in treatment (see **Glasgow City Council v Marshall (2000)** – an equal pay case where a material factor was held to be genuine and, therefore, objectively justified).

For cases involving allegations of part-time worker discrimination see **Clarke & Powell v Eley Kinoch Ltd (1982)**, **Bilka-Kaufhaus v Weber Von Hartz (1986)** and **R v Secretary of State for Employment ex parte Equal Opportunities Commission (1994)**.

13 Angela has experienced less favourable treatment as a result of her status as a fixed-term employee which is a breach of the Fixed-term Employees (Prevention of Less Favourable Treatment) Regulations 2002. For the purposes of the Regulations, a permanent employee is someone who is not on a fixed-term contract. Permanent employees will, therefore, enjoy contracts for an indefinite or an indeterminate period of time. A fixed-term employee is defined, in terms of the Regulations, as someone who is employed on a contract that will last for a specified period of time or whose employment will end when a specified task has been completed or when a specified event either occurs or does not occur (Regulation 1).

The fact that Angela's employer has refused to pay her sick pay is an example of less favourable treatment by reason of her fixed-term employee status in terms of Regulation 3. If a fixed-term employee decides to make an allegation of discrimination against the employer, it is important that they are able to compare themselves to a permanent employee (Regulation 2). The fixed-term employee cannot choose any permanent colleague with whom to compare himself. The comparator must be employed by the same employer and do the same or broadly similar work (the influence of the Equal Pay Act 1970 can undoubtedly be felt here). The employee must show that she has similar skills, qualifications and experience to her comparator. Like must be compared with like as much as possible. If the employee cannot point to a comparator in his workplace, he can always search for another permanent employee to make a comparison, as long as this individual is employed by the same employer the only difference being that he employed at a another workplace.

The employee has a right to ask the employer to respond to his allegation of discrimination. The employer should respond by issuing a written statement, within 21 days of the employee's original request, setting out the reasons for the treatment that the employee has experienced

(Regulation 5). The employer is perfectly at liberty to take issue with the employee's perception that he has somehow been discriminated against by reason of his status as a fixed-term employee. If the employee is still not satisfied with the employer's written response, she is entitled to lodge an Employment Tribunal application within three months (less one day) of the conduct complained of (Regulation 7).

An employer will only be able to justify less favourable treatment of a fixed-term employee on objective grounds (Regulation 4). An employer may be able to justify the less favourable treatment by bringing evidence which demonstrates that a permanent worker has better qualifications and/or more experience than the person bringing the complaint.

14 a) The Employment Equality (Religion or Belief) Regulations 2003 will for the first time, outlaw discrimination and harassment on grounds of religion or belief in large and small workplaces in England, Scotland and Wales, both in the private and public sectors. Admittedly, the Race Relations Act 1976 did, in very limited circumstances, prevent individuals suffering discrimination by reason of their religious beliefs (see **Mandla v Dowall Lee (1983); Seide v Gillette Industries Ltd (1980)** and **J H Walker Ltd v Hussain & Others (1996)**). However, the protection against religious discrimination which the Race Relations Act 1976 provided was patchy to say the least. The new Employment Equality Regulations will tackle the issue of religious discrimination in a much more systematic and satisfactory way.

According to the Regulations, a religion or belief is defined as being any religion, religious belief or similar philosophical belief. This does not include any philosophical or political belief unless it is similar to religious belief. Obviously, this definition would cover members of the Church of Scotland, the Roman Catholic Church, members of other Christian churches, Muslims, Jews, Hindus, Sikhs and Buddhists. It would not provide protection to someone with strong political beliefs, for example, a Marxist. Similarly, supporters of football clubs would not be protected by the Regulations.

b) The local authority may be able to justify its refusal to give Heather an interview for the post of Head Teacher by relying on Regulation 7 of the Employment Equality (Religion or Belief) Regulations 2003. Regulation 7 permits an employer to apply a genuine occupational requirement to particular employment. In certain situation, an employer will be able to insist that an

applicant or an employee must be of a particular religion or hold particular religious beliefs. Local authorities in Scotland will still be able to insist that being a practising Roman Catholic is a genuine occupational requirement for Head Teachers of Roman Catholic schools. When applying genuine occupational requirements, the Regulations state that the employer must either show that the individual to whom it is applied could not comply with the condition or the employer reasonably believed this to be the case.

15 a) i) As a result of the Sex Discrimination (Indirect Discrimination & Burden of Proof) Regulations 2001 implemented the EU Burden of Proof Directive (Council Directive 97/80/EC) into UK law, things have become much easier for an employee. In sex discrimination claims, it will be for the employee to show the facts that prove less favourable treatment and if the employer is unable to come up with a satisfactory explanation which would disprove the complaint, the Tribunal must now decide in favour of the employee. Previously, an Employment Tribunal could infer discrimination where the employee presented evidence that she had been discriminated against and where the employer failed to provide a satisfactory explanation for his treatment of the employee (**King v Great Britain-China Centre (1991)**). However, according to the House of Lords, the Employment Tribunal was not forced to reach this finding of less favourable treatment (**Zafar v Glasgow City Council (1998)**).

ii) In discrimination claims involving race, there are two standards to be applied. Where the employee is raising a discrimination claim on the grounds of his colour or nationality, the older standard of proof established in **King v Great Britain-China Centre (1991)** and **Zafar v Glasgow City Council (1998)** will apply. However, as a result of the Race Regulations 2003, discrimination claims involving a person's race or ethnic or national origin, the new burden of proof that is used in sex discrimination claims will apply. There is not much to separate the two burdens of proof for race claims and, in practice, once an employee has presented evidence which shows discrimination on the employer's part and the employer has failed to provide a satisfactory explanation of his behaviour, Employment Tribunals may, in any case, draw the appropriate conclusion.

iii) An equal pay claim – the burden of proof is on the Applicant to demonstrate that the employer has treated him or her less favourably in matters of pay and other contractual terms and conditions.

iv) How does a disabled employee prove that they have experienced less favourable treatment by reason of his disability at the hands of his employer? A decision of the Employment Tribunal – **Rowden v Dutton Gregory (2002)** – establishes a precedent that the rules governing the burden of proof in race discrimination claims (involving colour and nationality) should be used in disability claims. In **King**, it will be remembered that once an employee brought evidence to demonstrate discrimination on the employer's part and the employer failed to offer a satisfactory response in return, the Employment Tribunal was entitled to infer that discrimination had taken place. This now appears to be the case for employees taking disability claims to Tribunal.

v) + vi) In a part-time worker of fixed term-employee discrimination claim, an individual who claims that they have been discriminated against by an employer on the grounds of his or her employment status must bring evidence to support such a claim. Once evidence of discrimination has been established, it will be up to the employer to rebut this. If the employer is unable to do this, the Employment Tribunal is entitled to make a finding of less favourable treatment.

vii) + viii) In discrimination claims involving people's sexual orientation or religion or belief, Regulations 29 and 32 of the Employment Equality (Sexual Orientation) Regulations 2003 and Regulations 29 and 32 of the Employment Equality (Religion or Belief) Regulations 2003 state that the burden of proof will be placed on the person bringing the complaint to show that he has suffered an act of discrimination on the grounds of his sexual orientation or religion or beliefs if the claim is brought before either the Employment Tribunal or the Sheriff Court. Once the Employment Tribunal or the Sheriff Court is satisfied from the circumstances of the case that an act of discrimination has taken place, the complaint must be upheld if the employer is unable to provide a satisfactory explanation for his conduct. This favours the employee and goes further than **King v Great Britain-China Centre (1991)** and **Zafar v Glasgow City Council (1998)** where Employment Tribunals and courts were permitted to infer discrimination, but they were not forced to make this finding.

b) In all of the above discrimination claims, with the exception of an equal pay claim, an Applicant must lodge an application with the Office of Employment Tribunals within three months (less one day) of the discriminatory act complained of. So, if an employer committed an act of discrimination on 10 February, the Applicant should have lodged a claim by 9 May at the very latest. If the discrimination is one in a chain of events, the time limit begins to run from the last discriminatory act committed by the employer against the Applicant. In an equal pay claim, Section 2(4) of the Equal Pay Act 1970 states that a claim for equal pay must be lodged with the Office of Employment Tribunals either during a person's employment or within six months (less one day) of the termination of the employee's contract of employment.

ACKNOWLEDGEMENTS

This book would not have been completed without the support and assistance of a number of individuals.

We owe a great debt of gratitude to our colleagues in the Law Cognate Group at Central College of Commerce, in particular, Euan Millar, George Cran, Brian Welsh, Munro McCannell, John McInarlin, Valerie Robertson and Steven Murray - all of whom made helpful suggestions and alerted us to ongoing developments affecting the Scottish legal system.

Brian Allingham deserves special praise for agreeing to edit the text and for carrying out his editorial duties so conscientiously and professionally.

We would also like to thank Euan Millar, Legal Services Course Leader at Central College of Commerce, and Steven Leonard of Bell College who supported this project from the outset. Both Euan and Steven had the unenviable task of reading through the finished product and their very kind words and encouragement are greatly appreciated.

We also acknowledge the lasting influence of our law lecturers at the University of Strathclyde during our days as undergraduate students, especially Professor Kenneth Miller, Professor John A. K. Huntley, Professor Joseph Thomson, Mr William J. Stewart and Dr Alistair Clark.

We would like to thank John Mitchell, Katherine Bennett, Jim Donnelly and James Maroney at Hodder Gibson who encouraged throughout and who displayed a great deal of patience during the writing of this book.

We would like to acknowledge the support of our families and close friends who are no doubt as relieved as we are that this task is now at an end.

Finally, it should go without saying that any errors contained in this book are our responsibility alone.

Alistair B Wylie and Seán J Crossan

FURTHER READING

For those individuals who are interested in expanding their knowledge of the various topics covered in *Introductory Scots Law: Theory and Practice*, the following texts are particularly useful:

Craig, Victor and Miller, Kenneth, *Craig & Miller: Employment Law in Scotland*, Butterworths Law (Scotland), 2004

Huntley, John A. K., *Contract: Cases and Materials: Second Edition*, W. Green & Son, 2003

Marshall, Enid A., *General Principles of Scots Law: Seventh Edition*, W. Green & Son, 1999

Marshall, Enid A., *Scots Mercantile Law: Third Edition*, W. Green & Son, 1997

Marshall, Enid A., *Scottish Cases on Agency*, W. Green & Son, 1980

Marshall, Enid A., *Scottish Cases on Contract: Second Edition*, W. Green & Son, 1993

Stewart, William J., *A Casebook on Delict*, W. Green & Son, 1997

Stewart, William J., *Reparation: Liability for Delict*, W. Green & Son, 2003

Stewart, William J., *Delict: Third Edition*, W. Green & Son, 1998

Thomson, Joseph, *Delictual Liability Third Edition*, Butterworths Law (Scotland), 2004

Walker, David, *Principles of Scottish Private Law*, Clarendon Press, 1988

INDEX

(NB. Italic page numbers refer to summaries.)